Lecture Notes in Computer Science 655

Edited by G. Goos and J. Hartmanis

M. Bidoit C. Choppy (Eds.)

Recent Trends in Data Type Specification

8th Workshop on Specification of Abstract Data Types joint with the 3rd COMPASS Workshop
Dourdan, France, August 26-30, 1991
Selected Papers

Springer-Verlag
Berlin Heidelberg New York
London Paris Tokyo
Hong Kong Barcelona
Budapest

Series Editors

Gerhard Goos
Universität Karlsruhe
Postfach 69 80
Vincenz-Priessnitz-Straße 1
W-7500 Karlsruhe, FRG

Juris Hartmanis
Cornell University
Department of Computer Science
4130 Upson Hall
Ithaca, NY 14853, USA

Volume Editors

Michel Bidoit
LIENS, C.N.R.S. U.R.A. 1327 and Ecole Normale Supérieure
45, Rue d'Ulm, F-75230 Paris Cedex, France

Christine Choppy
L.R.I., C.N.R.S. U.R.A. 410 and University of Paris-Sud
Bat. 490, F-91405 Orsay Cedex, France

CR Subject Classification (1991): D.2.1-2, D.2.4, D.2.10-m, D.3.1-3, F.3.1-2

ISBN 3-540-56379-2 Springer-Verlag Berlin Heidelberg New York
ISBN 0-387-56379-2 Springer-Verlag New York Berlin Heidelberg

Printed in Germany

Typesetting: Camera ready by author/editor
45/3140-543210 - Printed on acid-free paper

Preface

The algebraic specification of abstract data types has been a flourishing research topic in computer science since 1974. The main goal of this work is to evolve theoretical foundations and a methodology to support the design and formal development of reliable software. The Eighth Workshop on Specification of Abstract Data Types was held jointly with the Third COMPASS Workshop, 26-30 August 1991, in the town of Dourdan, about 50 kilometers from Paris, and was organized by Michel Bidoit and Christine Choppy. The main topics covered by this joint workshop were:

- specification languages and program development
- algebraic specification of concurrency
- theorem proving
- object-oriented specifications
- order-sorted algebras
- abstract implementation and behavioural semantics.

The general feeling was that this joint workshop was extremely successful and that the contributions were of a high scientific level. Part of this success is due to E. Astesiano, H.-D. Ehrich, P.D. Mosses, and F. Orejas who accepted to prepare in depth surveys. The program committee (Michel Bidoit, Christine Choppy, Hartmut Ehrig, Bernd Krieg-Brückner, Fernando Orejas, Horst Reichel, and Don Sannella) selected a number of talks which represented the most interesting ideas and reflected the main trends in current research, and asked their presenters to contribute papers. The present volume contains the final version of the selected papers, together with the invited surveys. All of them underwent a careful refereeing process, and we are grateful to the following people who agreed to referee the papers:

E. Astesiano, J. Bergstra, G. Bernot, M. Bidoit, M. Broy, C. Choppy, I. Classen, M. Cerioli, H.-D. Ehrich, H. Ehrig, G. Ferrari, W. Fey, J.F. Fiadeiro, M.-C. Gaudel, M. Gogolla, J. Goguen, M. Grosse-Rhode, I. Guessarian, M. Kindler, M. Korff, H.-J. Kreowski, B. Krieg-Brückner, J. Loeckx, P.D. Mosses, F. Nickl, F. Orejas, P. Pepper, A. Poigné, G. Reggio, H. Reichel, D. Sannella, H. Schmidt, O. Schoett, G. Scollo, T. Stroup, A. Tarlecki, N. Van Diepen, U. Waldmann, E.G. Wagner, J. Zeyer.

Thanks to Evelyne Jorion and Hélène Outin for secretarial support, and to Gilles Bernot, Pierre Dauchy, Clément Roques, and Frédéric Voisin for helping with the workshop organization. The workshop was sponsored by the Université Paris-Sud, the Ecole Normale Supérieure and the C.N.R.S., and received financial support from the ESPRIT Basic Research Working Group COMPASS, the C.N.R.S., and the C.N.R.S. GDR de Programmation.

We would like to dedicate this volume to Stéphane Kaplan.

Orsay, August 1992 — Michel Bidoit and Christine Choppy

IN MEMORIAM

Stéphane Kaplan (1961–1991)

Stéphane Kaplan was a student of the Ecole Normale Supérieure in Mathematics; he became "agrégé" in Mathematics in 1981. He received his "Thèse de 3ème Cycle" diploma and his "Thèse d'Etat" diploma in 1982 and 1987 respectively, both in Computer Science from the University of Paris-Sud, Orsay, France.

He was appointed by the C.N.R.S. (Centre National de la Recherche Scientifique) since 1983 as a "Chargé de Recherches" (full-time researcher) at the L.R.I. (Laboratoire de Recherche en Informatique) at the University of Paris-Sud. He spent a year in 1985–1986 at the Weizmann Institute of Science, Rehovot, Israel, as a visiting scientist; he came back to Israel, on leave from C.N.R.S., from 1987 to 1990, while he taught as a senior lecturer in Computer Science at the University of Bar-Ilan (Ramat-Gan), and partly at the Hebrew University of Jerusalem.

He mainly contributed to advances in rewriting (in particular in conditional rewriting), and in the specification of concurrent systems (through the theory of "process specifications" that he developed).

He was bright, dynamic, open, intuitive and fast. In addition to his qualities as a research scientist, he was a very nice guy, with a good (and light) sense of humour, a love for music, and deep human insight.

Those of us who knew him will surely miss him a lot.

Table of Contents

Invited surveys

Contributed papers

Algebraic Specification of Concurrency*

Egidio Astesiano and Gianna Reggio

DISI
Dipartimento di Informatica e Scienze dell'Informazione
Università di Genova - Italy
{ astes , reggio } @ cisi.unige.it

Introduction

Let us first summarize what algebraic specification is about, following [66]. Algebraic specification methods provide techniques for data abstraction and the structured specification, validation and analysis of data structures.

Classically, a (concrete) data structure is modelled by a many-sorted algebra (possibly term-generated); various categories of many-sorted algebras can be considered, like total, partial, order-sorted, with predicates and so on. An isomorphism class of data structures is called an *abstract data type* (shortly *adt*) and an *algebraic specification* is a description of one or more abstract data types. There are various approaches for identifying classes of abstract data types associated with an algebraic specification, which constitute its semantics: initial, terminal, observational; a semantics is *loose* when it identifies a class (usually infinite) of adt's.

Since data structures can be very complex (a flight reservation system, e.g.), *structuring* and *parameterization* mechanisms are fundamental for building large specifications.

Together with a rigorous description of data structures, algebraic specifications support stepwise refinement from abstract specifications to more concrete descriptions (in the end, programs) of systems by means of the notion of *implementation* and techniques for proving *correctness* of implementations. In this respect formal *proof systems* associated with algebraic specifications play a fundamental role. Finally *specification languages* provide a linguistic support to algebraic specifications.

The purpose of the algebraic specification of concurrent systems is to specify structures where some data represent processes or states of processes, i.e. objects about which it is possible to speak of dynamic evolution and interaction with other processes; more generally we can consider as the subject of algebraic specification of concurrency those structures able to describe entities which may be active participants of events. Such data structures will be called simply "concurrent systems", where "concurrent" conveys different meanings, from "occurring together" to "compete for the same resources" and to "cooperate for achieving the same aim".

The aim of this paper is twofold: to analyse the aims and the nature of the algebraic specifications of concurrency and to give, as examples, a short overview of some (not all) relevant work.

* This work has been supported by COMPASS-Esprit-BRA-W.G. the project MURST 40% "Metodi e specifiche per la concorrenza" and by "Progetto Finalizzato Sistemi Informatici e Calcolo Parallelo" of C.N.R. (Italy).

In Sect. 1 we introduce some basic concepts and terminology about processes: the various models around which the specification models are built and the fundamental issues of (observational) semantics, formal description and specification; moreover we give some illustrative examples of specification problems to be used later for making more concrete some general considerations and for assessing different methods.

In Sect. 2 we try to qualify the field: indicating three different fundamental motivations/viewpoints (and distinguishing between methods and instances); then outlining the issues to deal with; finally illustrating by two significant examples/approaches how this field stimulates innovations and improvements beyond the classical theory of adt's.

In Sect. 3 we outline some relevant approaches; the presentation is related to the issues discussed in Sect. 2 and the specification examples presented in Sect. 1. However, being impossible to report on all methods, we have mainly used some approaches to illustrate, as examples, concrete ways of tackling the issues of the field..

1 Processes and Concurrent Systems

Informally a process is an entity with the capability of performing an activity within which it may interact with other entities and/or with the environment. The interaction may consist in communicating, synchronizing, cooperating, acting in parallel, competing for resources with other processes and/or with the environment.

By a concurrent system we informally mean a process consisting of component processes that are operating concurrently.

We are of course interested in those aspects of processes that support the design and implementation of software systems. Thus we are looking for a formal support to the specification, programming, implementation and verification phases. For this it is crucial to have good models for processes.

Now, the usual formal model of a sequential software system (program) as input/output, or state to state, function is no longer adequate for processes. Moreover, to date no single model seems to capture all the relevant formal aspects of a process. Hence in the following we will briefly introduce the most significant formal models which have been used in connection with the algebraic specification of processes. In the meantime we introduce some terminology typical of concurrency, which will be useful in the sequel.

Warning. We are presenting basic models and not formalisms; for example, labelled transition systems (and variations) are the common basic model for different formalisms like CCS, CSP, MEIJE, Π-calculus, etc. Moreover some formalisms, notably the many variations of Petri nets, allow to represent different aspects of systems and provide a variety of basic models. However our aim here is only to give the non-expert in concurrency some very basic information, in order to understand the following presentation of specification formalisms. It is not at all an overview of existing formalisms in concurrency.

1.1 Basic Models

Labelled Transition Systems. The use of labelled transition systems for modelling processes has been advocated mainly by Milner and Plotkin (see [50, 55]).

A *labelled transition system* (shortly *lts*) is a triple $(STATE, LABEL, \rightarrow)$, where $STATE$ and $LABEL$ are two sets and $\rightarrow \subseteq STATE \times LABEL \times STATE$. A triple $(s, l, s') \in \rightarrow$, also written $s \xrightarrow{l} s'$, means that the process modelled by the lts has the capability of passing from the state s into the state s' under an interaction with the external environment represented by the label l. In the simplest case, when the transition is purely internal to the system and there is no relationship with the environment, the label can be dropped or better represented by a special element, which is usually written τ (as in CCS) and called "silent move" or "internal action".

For example, the capabilities associated with a process executing an action of receiving a message, briefly denoted by $Rec(x, ch)$, assigned as value to a variable x on a channel ch could be represented by a set of labelled transitions of the form $s \xrightarrow{Rec(v,ch)} s'(v)$ (one for each v in the set of values that can be received). That means that the process can pass from the state s (corresponding to the situation immediately before the execution of $Rec(x, ch)$) into a state $s'(v)$ (which records that the value v has been received and assigned to the variable x) performing an action of receiving v from the outside along the channel ch.

The capabilities associated with a process executing the action of sending the message e on the channel ch, briefly denoted by $Send(e, ch)$, could be represented by the labelled transition $s \xrightarrow{Send(v_0,ch)} s'$. That means that the process can pass from the state s (corresponding to the situation immediately before the execution of $Send(e, ch)$) to the state s' performing the action of sending the value of the expression e in s (v_0) along the channel ch. Notice that an lts may have several different transitions starting from the same state and that allows us to represent the nondeterministic behaviour of processes.

We need also to model groups of interacting processes; in these cases we can use particular classes of lts's built from some component lts's. The states of the overall system have as subparts states of the component systems and its transitions are determined by the transitions of the component systems. For example the parallel composition p of two processes p_1 and p_2 (which interact by exchanging messages through channels) could be represented by a state $cs = \{s_1, s_2\}$, where s_1 and s_2 represent the initial states of the two processes p_1 and p_2. Assuming the transitions of the components $s_1 \xrightarrow{Rec(v_0,ch)} s'_1$ and $s_2 \xrightarrow{Send(v_0,ch)} s'_2$, the following transition of cs corresponds to the synchronized exchange of the value v_0 between p_1 and p_2: $cs \xrightarrow{\tau} \{s'_1, s'_2\}$ (the transition is labelled by τ since there is no need of further interaction with the world outside p).

Nondeterminism can also come from parallelism, for example when a process can perform some action with at least two other processes. Consider the process p_1 above in parallel with p_2 and with a process p_3 in a state s_3 having the capability $s_3 \xrightarrow{Send(v_0,ch)} s'_3$; clearly there are at least two exclusive possible transitions of the system consisting of the three processes in parallel. Specifically:

$\{s_1, s_2, s_3\} \xrightarrow{\tau} \{s'_1, s'_2, s_3\}$ and $\{s_1, s_2, s_3\} \xrightarrow{\tau} \{s'_1, s_2, s'_3\}$.

Lts's are very suitable for composing processes in a modular way; however they require a further procedure of abstraction for eliminating details and representing causality relationships between events. Indeed lts's are usually a too detailed description of processes, so that equivalent processes may be described by two different values (labelled trees with states) in an lts. Thus it is necessary to define semantics via equivalence classes and there is an extensive literature on the subject (see e.g. [37]). This issue is discussed in some more detail in Sect. 1.2 and, from a very general algebraic viewpoint, encompassing lts's in Sect. 2.3.

Event Structures. We may model processes by considering a set of notable facts which can happen during their activity called *events* (e.g., sending/receiving a value, changing/testing the content of a local storage) and then by describing the relevant relationships among them, as *causality* and *mutual exclusion*. In this way we can give a view of the processes more abstract than using lts's.

Formally a process is modelled by an *event structure* (see [65]), i.e. a triple $(E, \geq, \#)$, where E is a set (the events), $\geq$ is a partial order on E (causality relation) and $\#$ is binary relation on E (mutual exclusion relation).

It is important to note that using event structures we can describe in a simple way processes where two events are truly concurrent (i.e., where there is no causal/temporal relationship between them).

Consider, for example, the event structure *ES* graphically represented in Fig. 1; there the events e_1 and e_2 are truly concurrent: i.e. there is no relationship between the happening of e_1 with the happening of e_2 and vice versa; while e_3 may happen only after that e_1 and e_2 have happened; and e_2 and e_4 cannot happen simultaneously.

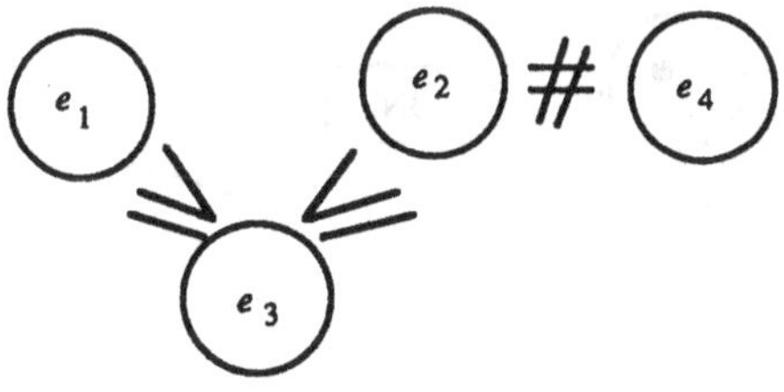

Fig. 1. An event structure *ES*

Unfortunately it is not easy to give a simple way for composing the event structures modelling the component processes of a complex concurrent system to get the structure modelling the whole system (see e.g. [64] which requires non-trivial categorical techniques).

Petri Nets. Petri nets are probably the oldest and best-known model of processes (see e.g. [59]). Starting from the original definition, nowadays many variations of Petri nets have been developed with different basic models. Here we briefly outline some typical features of this kind of models by considering a very basic one, which is now called Petri net (i.e. directed bipartite graph).

A *Petri net* is a directed graph $PN = (N, A)$, where the set of the nodes N is split into ***places*** and ***transitions***, $N = P \cup T$, and the arcs connect only places to transitions and transitions to places. Given a transition t, the ***premise*** and the ***consequence*** of t are the following sets of places: $\{p \mid \text{there exists an arc from } p \text{ to } t\}$ and $\{p \mid \text{there exists an arc from } t \text{ to } p\}$ (notice that in general the two sets are not disjoint).

To describe the dynamic behaviour of Petri nets we consider marked nets, i.e. nets where each place is marked by a number of tokens. In a marked net a transition is enabled when all places in its premise have at least a token. An enabled transition may *fire* changing the marking of the net as follows: a token is eliminated by all the places in its premise and a token is added to all places in its consequence. Then the dynamic activity of a marked net is given by the firing of its enabled transitions; notice that in general more than one transition is enabled, so that a net can be used to model also nondeterministic processes. A marked net models a process in a particular situation, while the firing of the transitions describes its possible activities.

Petri nets are very popular since they allow to give nice graphical representations of the activity of the processes; however also in this case it is not very simple and natural to compose the nets describing the component processes of a complex system to get the net describing the whole system; to this end particular kinds of nets have been developed (see e.g. the superposed automata of [15]). For a survey on modular approaches to Petri nets see [16].

In Fig. 2 we report a simple example of a marked Petri net with three transitions and five places which describes a system transferring the tokens from the places IN1 and IN2 into the place OUT.

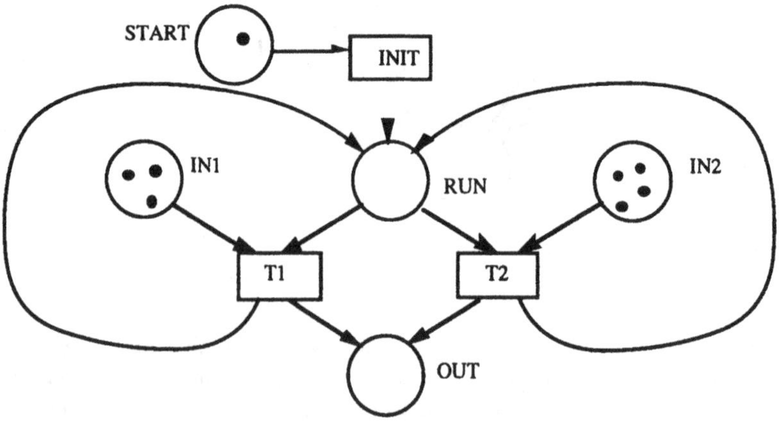

Fig. 2. A Petri net

Dataflows. The dataflow approach (see e.g. [41]) provides a completely different, but more specialized, model. The basic idea is to see a process as a box able to receive in an asynchronous way values along some input lines (or channels) and then to return other values along some output lines always in an asynchronous way. Here asynchronous means that values are received also if the process is performing some calculation on other values received previously and the output values are returned also if the receiver is not immediately ready to get them.

Thus a dataflow may be modelled by a function from tuples of (also infinite) sequences of values (those received on the input channels) into tuples of (also infinite) sequences of values (those returned on the output channels).

In this framework it is easy to compose several dataflows together: it is just as to compose functions.

This model is particularly apt to describe processes which interact in the above asynchronous way, while it is not very convenient for describing processes interacting synchronously.

In Fig. 3 we report a simple example of a dataflow network which describes a system receiving in input integer numbers on channel i and returning those which are positive, zero and negative respectively on channels p, z and n; the two component dataflows SEL_POS and SEL_NEG select respectively the positive and negative numbers.

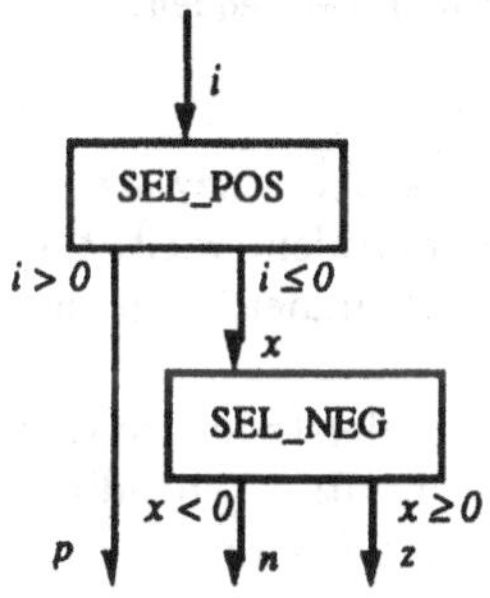

Fig. 3. A dataflow network

1.2 Semantics

Whatever kind of model we choose, when describing processes we have still the problem of defining the right semantic equivalence, i.e. in general it is not true that two processes are semantically equivalent iff they have associated the same model. In this section we consider this problem only for the lts's, but the situation is analogous for the other models, for which other notions of semantic equivalence have been developed.

Given an lts we can associate with each process the so called transition tree. A transition tree is a labelled tree whose nodes are decorated by states, whose arcs are decorated by labels, where the order of the branches is not considered and two identically decorated subtrees with the same root are considered as a unique one, and finally there is an arc decorated by l between two nodes decorated respectively by s and s' iff $s \xrightarrow{l} s'$.

By associating with a process p the transition tree having as root the initial state of p we give an operational semantics: two processes are operationally equivalent whenever the associated transition trees are the same, see [51]. But usually such semantics is too fine, since it takes into account all details of the process activity. It may happen that two processes which we consider semantically equivalent have associated different trees. A simple case is when we consider the trees associated with two sequential processes (i.e., performing only sequential commands), represented by two states p and p', thus they perform only internal activities (i.e., no interactions with the external environment); the associated transition trees (reported in Fig. 4) are unary trees, with all the arcs labelled by the symbol of internal action τ. If we

$$p \xrightarrow{\tau} p_1 \xrightarrow{\tau} \cdots \xrightarrow{\tau} p_n \xrightarrow{\tau} p_F$$

$$p' \xrightarrow{\tau} p'_1 \cdots \xrightarrow{\tau} p'_m \xrightarrow{\tau} p'_F$$

Fig. 4. Transition trees associated with two sequential processes

consider an input-output semantics, then they are equivalent iff p, p' are equivalent w.r.t. the input and p_F, p'_F are equivalent w.r.t. the output; the differences about other aspects (intermediate states, number of the intermediate transitions, etc.) are not considered.

From this simple example, we understand also that we can get various interesting semantics on processes modelled by lts's depending on what we observe of them. For instance, consider the well-known strong bisimulation of Park ([53]) and the trace semantics ([38]). In the first case, two processes are equivalent iff they have associated the same transition trees after forgetting the states. In the second case, two processes are equivalent iff the corresponding sets of traces (streams of labels obtained travelling along all paths starting from the roots of the associated transition trees) are the same. In general, the semantics of processes depends on what we are interested to observe: i.e., the semantics of processes is observational.

In Fig. 5 we report the transition trees associated with two processes p_1 and p_2 which are equivalent w.r.t. the trace semantics but not w.r.t. the strong bisimulation.

One of the most interesting techniques for defining observational semantics for (finite and infinite) processes is the Park's bisimulation semantics (see [53, 51]). Assume that we have an lts $(STATE, LABEL, \rightarrow)$; then a binary relation R on $STATE$ is a *(strong) bisimulation relation* iff for all $(s_1, s_2) \in STATE$ s.t. $s_1 \, R \, s_2$

1. if $s_1 \xrightarrow{l} s'_1$, then there exists s'_2 s.t. $s_2 \xrightarrow{l} s'_2$ and $s'_1 \, R \, s'_2$
2. if $s_2 \xrightarrow{l} s'_2$, then there exists s'_1 s.t. $s_1 \xrightarrow{l} s'_1$ and $s'_1 \, R \, s'_2$.

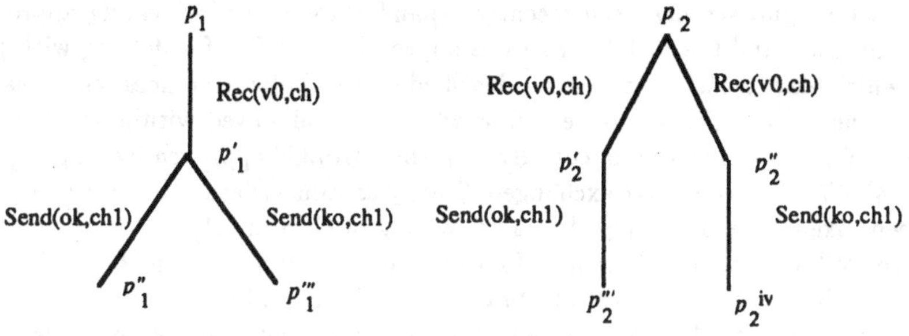

Fig. 5. Transition trees associated with the processes p_1 and p_2

It can be shown that there exists a maximum bisimulation relation $\sim$ characterized by $\sim = \cup\{R \mid R$ is a bisimulation relation $\}$. What we get in this case is just the strong (bisimulation) equivalence; but there are many possible and interesting variations (see e.g. [51, 2]).

1.3 Formal Description and Specification

After choosing a particular kind of models for processes, there are two main approaches to formally describing (specifying) a process:

- *(model-oriented)* a process corresponds to a class of semantically equivalent models given by exhibiting a particular element of the class;
- *(property-oriented)* a process is specified by giving a set of properties, which determines a class of models (those having the required properties).

In general the above approaches have associated an appropriate syntactic support, respectively:

- a language s.t. each of its expressions corresponds to one model; then the language expressions may be used to define the processes via an appropriate semantic equivalence;
- a logical (specification) language s.t. its formulae express properties of the models together with a validity relation saying when a model has the property expressed by a formula; then a process is specified by giving a set of such formulae, which determine a class of models (those satisfying the formulae).

Algebraic specification of concurrency falls under the second (property-oriented) paradigm for which several logical languages have been proposed, based on modal / temporal logics in the case of lts's, event structures and Petri nets (see e.g. [56, 45]) and on first-order logic for characterizing dataflows.

In the literature several languages for supporting the first (model-oriented) approach have been proposed; among them we can recall CCS (Calculus of Communicating Processes) for lts's with strong bisimulation (see [50, 51]), CSP for lts's with trace semantics (see [38]), the various process algebras of the Amsterdam school (see e.g. [18, 14]) and so on.

The CCS approach has been recently expanded to a very interesting approach, the Π-calculus (and the mobile processes approach, see [52]), for dealing with processes which may exchange processes (identified indirectly by references) as messages. Notably the same problem has been first addressed and solved within an approach to the algebraic specification of concurrency, the SMoLCS approach (see e.g. [7] and Sect. 3.4) where processes are exchanged directly as values/data. This last viewpoint has been taken up and developed as an updating of CCS in [61].

In the following we briefly report, for example and further use, the full definitions of finite CCS and of the process algebra PA (see [14] Sect. 3).

CCS and process algebras represent the two prominent description styles based on the model of lts's. Milner defines inductively the transitions by SOS rules and then apart a semantics; while the Amsterdam group defines axiomatically the derived semantic equivalence (as initial semantics).

Finite CCS. Assume that $\mathcal{A}$ is a given set of basic action names and let $\overline{\mathcal{A}}$, $\mathcal{L}$ denote respectively the set of the complementary actions $\{\overline{a} \mid a \in \mathcal{A}\}$ and of the labels $\mathcal{A} \cup \overline{\mathcal{A}} \cup \{\tau\}$.

The set of CCS expressions $\mathcal{E}$ is inductively defined as follows.

- $nil \in \mathcal{E}$ (the process unable to perform any action)
- $\alpha.e \in \mathcal{E}$ for all $e \in \mathcal{E}$ and $\alpha \in \mathcal{L}$ (action prefixing)
- $e_1 + e_2 \in \mathcal{E}$ for all $e_1, e_2 \in \mathcal{E}$ (nondeterministic choice)
- $e_1 \parallel e_2 \in \mathcal{E}$ for all $e_1, e_2 \in \mathcal{E}$ (parallel composition)
- $e\backslash a \in \mathcal{E}$ for all $e \in \mathcal{E}$ and $a \in \mathcal{A}$ (restriction)

The lts associated with CCS is $(\mathcal{E}, \mathcal{L}, \rightarrow)$, where $\rightarrow$ is inductively defined by the following rules.

$$\frac{}{\alpha.e \xrightarrow{\alpha} e} \qquad \frac{e_1 \xrightarrow{\alpha} e_1'}{e_1 + e_2 \xrightarrow{\alpha} e_1'} \qquad \frac{e_2 \xrightarrow{\alpha} e_2'}{e_1 + e_2 \xrightarrow{\alpha} e_2'}$$

$$\frac{e_1 \xrightarrow{\alpha} e_1'}{e_1 \parallel e_2 \xrightarrow{\alpha} e_1' \parallel e_2} \qquad \frac{e_2 \xrightarrow{\alpha} e_2'}{e_1 \parallel e_2 \xrightarrow{\alpha} e_1 \parallel e_2'}$$

$$\frac{e_1 \xrightarrow{\alpha_1} e_1' \quad e_2 \xrightarrow{\alpha_2} e_2'}{e_1 \parallel e_2 \xrightarrow{\tau} e_1' \parallel e_2'} \; \alpha_1 = \overline{\alpha_2} \text{ or } \alpha_2 = \overline{\alpha_1} \qquad \frac{e \xrightarrow{\alpha} e'}{e\backslash a \xrightarrow{\alpha} e'\backslash a} \; \alpha \neq a, \overline{a}$$

Two CCS expression are considered semantically equivalent iff they are strongly bisimilar (see Sect. 1.2). An equivalent alternative of Milner's CCS is the MEIJE Calculus of Boudol and Austry [13] with the related elegant foundational work of De Simone [31].

The process algebra PA. Let A be a given set of *atomic actions*; the set of the PA expressions E is inductively defined as follows.

- $\mathsf{A} \subseteq \mathsf{E}$ (processes performing just one atomic action)
- $x.y \in \mathsf{E}$ for all $x, y \in \mathsf{E}$ (sequential composition)
- $x + y \in \mathsf{E}$ for all $x, y \in \mathsf{E}$ (nondeterministic choice)
- $x \parallel y \in \mathsf{E}$ for all $x, y \in \mathsf{E}$ (parallel composition)
- $x \lfloor\!\lfloor y \in \mathsf{E}$ for all $x, y \in \mathsf{E}$ (left merge)

Differently from the CCS case, here we do not associate an lts to the language (and then consider as semantically equivalent the expressions strongly bisimilar); we give instead directly a list of axioms identifying the expressions strongly bisimilar in the sense that equalities between terms in the initial model correspond to strong bisimulation equivalence. Notice that in order to do that we need to introduce an auxiliary operator ($\lfloor$).

$x + y = y + x \qquad (x + y) + z = x + (y + z) \qquad x + x = x$

$(x + y).z = (x.z) + (y.z) \qquad (x.y).z = x.(y.z)$

$x \parallel y = (x \lfloor y) + (y \lfloor x)$

$a \lfloor x = a.x \qquad (a.x) \lfloor y = a.(x \parallel y) \qquad (x + y) \lfloor z = (x \lfloor z) + (y \lfloor z)$

1.4 Illustrative Examples of Specification Problems

In order to give the flavor of what "specification of concurrent systems" means, we present some illustrative examples, which will be used in the sequel as reference for making more concrete some general considerations and for assessing different specification methods. Some very interesting specification problems (ten in all) have been proposed and discussed in a Cambridge Workshop, 1983, whose proceedings [32] may be of interest for the readers.

First we consider the problem of specifying a parameterized family of concurrent architectures: for each fixed set of parameters we get the specification of a family of essentially equivalent architectures. Then we briefly consider a more abstract level of specification, where we are concerned with looser requirements about architectures. The distinction here between the two cases looks rather fuzzy; however it has a great impact on the specification techniques. Later on when speaking of algebraic specifications we will see that this distinction will be similar to the one between non-loose and loose (or ultra-loose) algebraic specifications. In order to avoid confusion, in this paper we will call *abstract specifications* (AS) the first and *very abstract specifications* (VAS) the second ones; in the following section we will propose a more rigorous qualification of the two.

Specification of a Family of Concurrent Systems. The problem here is to specify a family of concurrent architectures (each one briefly called *CA*).

The structure of a *CA* is informally described below and graphically represented in Fig. 6, where the ovals represent the active components, the squares the passive ones and the straight lines the interactions among the components. A *CA* consists of a variable number of processes and a buffer shared among the processes; "variable" means that processes may terminate and new processes may be created. Processes can communicate among them by exchanging messages in a synchronous mode throughout channels (handshaking communication) and either reading or writing messages on the buffer; moreover the processes could also communicate with the outside world (consisting of other similar architectures) sending and receiving messages in a broadcasting mode; messages are simply values.

Each process has a local memory (private) and its activity is defined by a sequence of commands defined by the following pattern rules.

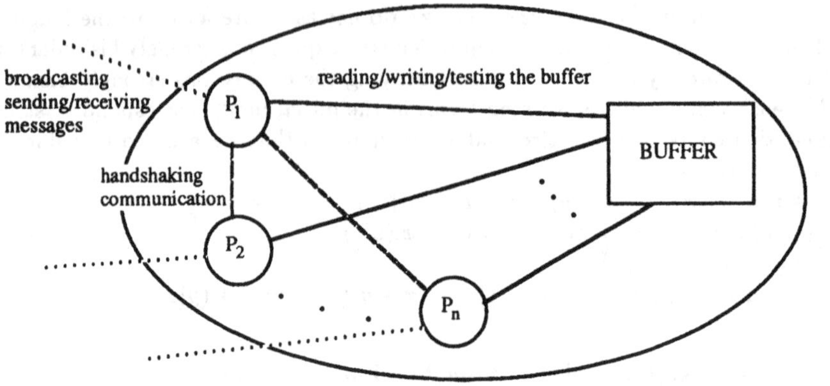

Fig. 6. A *CA* architecture

$$
\begin{array}{llr}
c & ::= Write(x) \mid Read(x) \mid Test(x) & (1)\\
 & \quad Send(x, ch) \mid Rec(x, ch) \mid BSend(x) \mid BRec(x) \mid & (2)\\
 & \quad Start(c) \mid Stop \mid & (3)\\
 & \quad c_1 ; c_2 \mid c_1 + c_2 \mid & (4)\\
 & \quad \c{S}kip \mid seq\text{-}c & (5)
\end{array}
$$

where x, ch, seq-c are respectively the nonterminals for variables, channel identifiers and sequential commands. A *CA* process may:

- write the value of a variable on the buffer, read a value from the buffer and assign it to a variable and test if the buffer is empty (the result of the test is assigned to a boolean variable) (1);
- exchange messages along the channels in a handshaking way and with the environment outside *CA* in a broadcasting way (2);
- create a new process with a given command part (and initial empty local memory) and terminate its execution (3);
- perform the sequential composition of two commands and nondeterministically choose between two commands (4);
- execute sequential commands not further specified (i.e. commands which do not require an interaction with other processes, nor with the buffer, nor with the environment outside *CA*) (5).

We are interested in specifying all instances of *CA*, where each instance is determined by an initial state, i.e., a set of processes and a buffer in some initial states.

To test the modularity and the possibility of giving specifications with "reusable" parts of the various methods we consider several versions of *CA* differing either for the kind of the data used by the processes, or the buffer organization, or the mode in which the process components perform their activity in parallel; each version of the architecture is denoted by $CA(D_i, B_h, A_j, P_k)$, where D_i, B_h, A_j, P_k represent respectively the assumptions on the data, the buffer organization, the buffer access and the kind of parallelism.

The data handled by *CA* processes may be: D_1) integer numbers, booleans and Pascal-like arrays of data; D_2) as D_1 but also the *CA* processes are data; D_3) as D_2 but also functions having as argument and result processes are data.

The buffer may be organized as: B_1) unbounded queue; B_2) unbounded stack; B_3) cell, which can contain at most one element.

The requirements on multiple simultaneous accesses to the buffer may be: A_1) several simultaneous accesses (i.e., writing, reading, testing) are not allowed; A_2) only several simultaneous testings are allowed; A_3) only several simultaneous testings and writings are allowed and the simultaneous writings of the values $v_1, \ldots, v_n$ could nondeterministically result into writing $v_1, \ldots, v_n$ in any order.

The requirements on the way the *CA* processes act in parallel may be: P_1) except for the synchronous interactions required by handshaking communications, the processes perform their activity in an interleaving mode; P_2) except for the synchronous interactions required by handshaking communications and the requirements on simultaneous buffer accesses, the processes perform their activity in a completely free parallel mode; P_3) as P_1 but reading takes precedence over writing.

The architecture *CA_NET* consists of several instances of *CA* in parallel, which interact by exchanging messages in a broadcasting mode (see Fig. 7). In this case the various components of the network perform their activity in a maximal parallel mode (i.e., no component can stay idle).

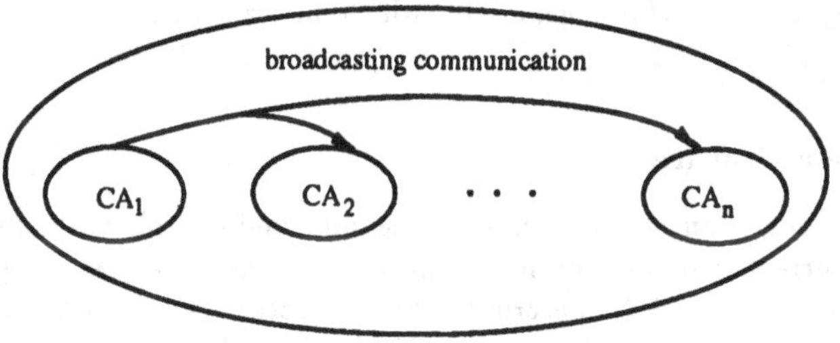

Fig. 7. *CA_NET* architecture

Abstract Requirements of a Computer Network. Here we want to express formally the abstract requirements for a computer network, without fully describing it. We need to express both requirements about the structure of the network (static properties) and about its activity (dynamic properties), as exemplified in the following

Static properties: the network must have between 10 and 20 computer components and must be able to store k bytes of information.

Dynamic properties: they may be further distinguished in:

safety properties: requirements about what should not happen during the system activity (e.g., no deadlock situation may arise [i.e., the network can stop its activity only when all computer components have terminated their activities], the percentage of the used storage will never be more than 95%);

liveness properties: requirements about what must happen during the system activity (e.g., if a command "run a certain correct C program" is given to one of the computers, then eventually the program result will appear on the computer screen; if a computer sends a message to another computer of the network, then eventually either the network breaks down or the message is received).

Note that we do not want to make any other assumption; thus we do not impose conditions about:

- the way the components are connected,
- the presence of auxiliary passive components (e.g., storage devices),
- the way the components interact among them and so on.

Thus to give the required specification means to formally identify the class of all networks satisfying the listed properties; this class includes, e.g., a network consisting of 10 Sun3 computers, five auxiliary disks connected by an Ethernet cable backbone; but also a network consisting of 15 PCIBM XT connected by a token ring.

2 Issues in Algebraic Specification of Concurrency

First we briefly review the aims of algebraic specifications of concurrency; then we try to identify the items/dimensions by which we can assess and relate different approaches.

2.1 Aims and Nature

Three Motivations/Viewpoints. While the meaning and the role of the formal specification of concurrent systems is clear, it is natural to ask why algebraic specifications, which have been invented for describing data structures and apparently deal with static data, should be adopted for describing intrinsically dynamic structures (and of course whether this approach is sensible and viable). There seem to be *three main motivations* for that, corresponding to *three views* of the relationship between data types and concurrent systems.

V1 Handling static adt's Concurrent systems use various data structures, whose abstract formal specification is most appropriately expressed by an algebraic specification.

V2 Abstract concurrent structure The abstract structure of a concurrent system (either globally or at a certain stage of its evolution) is conveniently described as an abstract data type.

V3 Abstract dynamic data types Concurrent systems themselves can be seen as data manipulated by other systems and functions, as any other data.

We will see those three motivations/views quite clearly reflected in various approaches, at a different level of integration.

We can now illustrate the different views by means of the examples of the *CA* architectures of Sect. 1.4.

V1 Under the assumption on the data handled by the processes D_1, for specifying a *CA* architecture we need to formally define a complex data structure (there are data of type integer, boolean and array with different dimensions). For giving an abstract specification of such architecture, we have to abstractly specify the above data structure and that could be conveniently done by an algebraic specification.

V2 Each *CA* architecture consists of an unordered group of processes plus a buffer shared among them, where the buffer organization depends on the assumption B_i. This structure may be abstractly defined by saying that an architecture is a couple consisting of a multiset of processes (since there may be two identical processes) and of a buffer, which is, depending on B_i, either a queue, or a stack, or a single value. Then it may be specified by giving first appropriate combinators for describing the buffer structure and for putting processes and buffer together, and later qualifying such operators by means of axioms. Thus the structure of a *CA* could be abstractly specified by an algebraic specification.

V3 We need a formalism fully supporting the third viewpoint whenever we want to specify the *CA* architectures following the assumptions on data D_2 (also *CA* processes are data) and D_3 (also functions from processes into processes are data) [2].

Methods and Instances. Whatever the motivation and the technical approach, a key distinction has to be made between "methods for" and "instances of" algebraic specification of concurrent systems; this is just the distinction between methods for specifying abstract data types and particular specifications of some data types. This remark is particularly relevant in concurrency, where algebraic techniques have found important applications in the description of abstract concurrent systems (viewpoint **V2**). For example, considering processes as data qualified by a set of axioms, we may obtain a theory of processes which is the analogous of a theory of rings or groups or, as a more familiar example to computer scientists, a theory of stacks or queues. Though this is a very important and fruitful viewpoint, we cannot consider these theories among the methods of algebraic specification of concurrency, which should instead provide techniques and guidelines for defining (classes of) abstract concurrent systems, as much as the classical algebraic specification formal methods for specifying (classes of) abstract data types. In particular it seems natural to require that methods of algebraic specification of concurrency reduce to some methods for the specification of abstract data types, i.e., that the viewpoint **V1** is always incorporated. For particular algebraic process theories, which are not methods, see, for example, the very elegant and informative book by M. Hennessy [37], where the axiomatizations of several simple concurrent languages are given.

A simple example of algebraic process theory, PA, has been given in Sect. 1.3. Here below we show how to turn the inductive definition of CCS given in the same section into an algebraic specification, which is an instance of the algebraic specification method based on conditional specifications (see [25] and Sect. 3.4).

[2] *CA* architectures following assumption D_3 are not unrealistic products of theoreticians but can be found in real systems: some Unix commands are modelled as functions from processes into processes and the denotation of an Ada task type is a function returning a process.

spec $CCS =$
sorts exp, act, lab
opns
$a_1, a_2, a_3, \ldots : \to act$
$-: act \to lab$
$\overline{-}: act \to lab$
$\tau: \to lab$
$nil: \to exp$
$-.-: lab \times exp \to exp$
$- + -: exp \times exp \to exp$
$- \parallel -: exp \times exp \to exp$
$-\backslash -: exp \times act \to exp$
preds
$- \xrightarrow{-} -: exp \times lab \times exp$
axioms

$$\alpha.e \xrightarrow{\alpha} e$$
$$e_1 \xrightarrow{\alpha} e_1' \supset e_1 + e_2 \xrightarrow{\alpha} e_1' \qquad e_2 \xrightarrow{\alpha} e_2' \supset e_1 + e_2 \xrightarrow{\alpha} e_2'$$
$$e_1 \xrightarrow{\alpha} e_1' \supset e_1 \parallel e_2 \xrightarrow{\alpha} e_1' \parallel e_2 \qquad e_2 \xrightarrow{\alpha} e_2' \supset e_1 \parallel e_2 \xrightarrow{\alpha} e_1 \parallel e_2'$$
$$e_1 \xrightarrow{t} e_1' \wedge e_2 \xrightarrow{t'} e_2' \supset e_1 \parallel e_2 \xrightarrow{\tau} e_1' \parallel e_2' \quad \text{for all } t, t' \text{ s.t. } t' = \bar{t} \text{ or } t = \overline{t'}$$
$$e \xrightarrow{t} e' \supset e\backslash a \xrightarrow{t} e'\backslash a \qquad \text{for all } t \neq a, \bar{a}$$

The initial model I_{CCS} of CCS determines an abstract lts, whose sets of states and labels are respectively $(I_{CCS})_{exp}$, $(I_{CCS})_{lab}$ and whose transition relation is $\to^{I_{CCS}}$; then the elements of $(I_{CCS})_{exp}$ are further identified by bisimulation semantics. Notice that, assuming as primitive the sorts *act* and *lab*, the final semantics of *CCS* as a hierarchical specification coincides with the initial semantics.

2.2 Items for Taxonomy

Guided by the discussion about the aims of Sect. 2.1, we try to define some items for locating various approaches and obtaining a reasonable taxonomy. We will refer implicitly to those items in the following when discussing some approaches. We do not pretend all the items to be completely independent, and this is why we do not call these items just dimensions; anyway their relationship should be clear from our presentation.

Specification Formalism. Even when it is not explicitly stated and whenever possible, we try to identify a *basic specification formalism* more or less under the institution paradigm, in the sense of Burstall and Goguen [26].

A *basic specification* consists of a set of sentences over a signature; its models are those structures on the signature satisfying the sentences. Sometimes (basic) specifications denote classes of structures satisfying some properties; we will stick to the syntactic view of a specification as a presentation, so that it makes sense to speak of semantics of specifications.

It is important here to distinguish the models of a specification from what we call *basic concurrent models*; i.e., the structures that represent semantically processes/concurrent systems (see Sect. 1.1).

Also, as we anticipated in Sect. 2, we would normally expect that an algebraic specification formalism for concurrency reduces to an associated *algebraic specification formalism for abstract data types*, whenever one does not consider processes, but just static data types.

Starting with a *basic specification formalism*, we may build more complex specifications by suitable operations over basic specifications. A linguistic support to such operations constitutes a *specification language*.

Support for Concurrency. There are two aspects by which concurrency is dealt with in a method for the formal specification of concurrency: the *basic concurrent models* for processes and the *primitives for concurrency*.

Typical *basic concurrent models* are labelled transition systems with the associated, possibly infinite, labelled transition trees, Petri nets of various kinds, stream processing functions (dataflows), which have been briefly illustrated in Sect. 1.1. There are also approaches, like process algebra, apparently qualifying processes just by axioms without any reference to an underlying structure. But inevitably any such axiomatization is driven by a hidden structure and any method which does not explicitly refer to a model, either provides a manner of descriptions of basic concurrent models or leaves the burden of identifying and describing such a model to the user.

By *primitives for concurrency* we refer to higher-level aspects of concurrent systems concerning operations for structuring processes, and the mode of the interactions of processes and of their evolutions. Typical primitives are: operations for composing processes in parallel or hierarchically; communication mechanisms like synchronous and asynchronous message passing and shared variables; global evolution modes, like interleaving, free and maximal parallelism.

For specifying the *CA* architectures of Sect. 1.4, for example, we need to consider processes interacting by synchronously exchanging messages and by accessing a shared buffer; while the nodes of the network *CA_NET* interact by broadcasting communication; moreover such processes may evolve in parallel either in an interleaving or free mode (P_1 and P_2) or in an interleaving mode where the conflicts on the buffer access are solved by giving precedence to reading w.r.t. writing (P_3).

Semantics and Level of Abstraction. As for classical adt specifications, here specifications may determine one or more abstract concurrent systems, where by abstract concurrent systems we mean an isomorphism class of concurrent systems; those abstract concurrent systems are the *semantics* of the specification.

In the first case it is intended that a specification determines just one isomorphism class. In the second case the semantics (sometimes we just say the specification) is *loose*; in the classical sense a loose semantics determines a class of non-isomorphic structures on Σ; we may also speak of *ultra-loose* specifications in various senses, for example when we consider structures also over signatures with some relation with Σ. Since there is not a general agreement on the meaning of loose and especially of ultra-loose, in the present context we prefer to speak of *very abstract specifications (VAS)*, qualifying instead as *abstract specifications (AS)* those identifying one abstract concurrent system.

Semantics is one of the most delicate and interesting topics in concurrency; we will see that essentially three approaches are followed:

- adopting a given semantics for processes, just connecting it to a semantics for usual adt's; this is possible whenever there is a clear separation between processes and the data they manipulate;
- defining, by adding suitable axioms, a classical semantics, e.g., initial or final, in a way that captures the wanted semantics for processes;
- providing new semantic paradigms for adt's, which are able to accommodate semantics sensible for data which are processes, thus extending the classical semantic theory for adt's.

We will discuss in some more detail the issue of semantics in the following section.

It turns out that VAS of concurrent systems need specification formalisms (say institutions) and semantics which go beyond those in use for classical static adt's in two respects. Notions of ultra-loose semantics have to be developed in order to abstract from the particular structure of an architecture; these abstractions cannot be captured simply by means of the classical notion of satisfaction. Moreover we have to go beyond equational and conditional logic, since, in order to express requirements on events and their relationship (sometimes distinguished in safety and liveness properties) we need the power of first-order logic, possibly with infinitary conjunctions, and of various forms of temporal logic. This necessity of encompassing classical adt specification for VAS explains why most algebraic methods are mainly concerned with AS. Thus we will have to deal mainly with AS and only briefly we will discuss the VAS issue.

Integration. By integration we refer to the two following distinct aspects:

- the level of integration of abstract data types and concurrent features;
- the extent to which a specification of a concurrent system is truly an algebraic specification and can exploit classical concepts and results of general algebraic specifications.

For classifying the integration of adt's and concurrent features we may refer to the three viewpoints illustrated in Sect. 2 and related to three motivations for making specification of concurrency algebraic: *inclusion of static data types* (**V1**) in a fixed concurrent structure, *algebraic specification* also *for the concurrent structure* (**V2**) a finally considering processes as data themselves, what we call *dynamic data types* (**V3**). As long as a method always subsumes as a special case a general method for specifying classical adt's, we may consider the three above viewpoints arranged in an order of increasing integration. Clearly the dynamic data type viewpoint corresponds also to an overall algebraic framework, but different possibilities arise, as we shall see, especially following the first viewpoint, which leaves separate the specification of the static adt's and of the concurrent structure, but may result in a completely algebraic specification.

Applications. It seems that we are still at an infancy stage for speaking in general of applications to real industrial cases. However it makes sense to look at applications in a broader sense: use of a method in proposal for standard tools, in research projects, in prototyping, in industrial case-studies. To some extent we may also guess at potential applications, looking at the varieties of example applications a method has shown.

Tools. It is a widely accepted dogma that there is no hope of real use of algebraic specifications without a convenient toolset for editing, verifying and animating specifications. Specification of concurrency adds a new challenge in many senses: concurrent rewriting systems are typically non-confluent and non-terminating; even when applicable, some general tools for algebraic specifications are inefficient to master the complexity of the dynamic behaviour of processes; finally the verification procedures, in order to deal with various observational semantics for processes, need specific techniques, far beyond the case of equational or conditional deduction.

Pragmatics. Note that the point here is not just feasibility or expressive power, but also convenience. As M. Broy points out in [22]

> "most important properties of specification methods are not only the underlying theoretical concepts but more pragmatic issues such as readability, tractability, support for structuring, possibilities of visual aids and machine support".

2.3 Beyond Classical Algebraic Specifications

The algebraic approach to specification applied to concurrency poses some new problems, whose solution is of general interest to the theory of algebraic specifications. A typical issue which has stimulated new techniques, beyond the classical ones, is semantics. We present briefly two recent theories, which are representative of the two main approaches to the algebraic semantics of processes. The first, "projection specifications", is an interesting variation of the initial approach taken in the process algebra school; in this approach the axioms embed a particular semantics and processes are limit points in a complete metric space, which is also a continuous initial algebra.

The second, "observational specifications", takes the bisimulation approach (typical of CCS) extending it to general algebraic specifications; it encompasses, as specializations, most presently known sensible semantics for processes together with all classical semantics for adt's.

Projection Specifications When specifying processes frequently we need to consider "infinite elements"; for example, when processes are modelled by means of (possibly) infinite trees, when the result or the observation of a process is a (possibly) infinite stream of values and so on. The projection specifications developed by the Ehrig's group in Berlin, and especially by M. Grosse-Rhode in his Diplom thesis (see [35, 36]) allows us to specify algebraically infinite objects.

The key ideas of projection specifications are the following:

- infinite objects are seen as limit points in complete metrics spaces, called projection spaces, since the metric is defined in terms of projections; moreover the continuity of operations ensures that the models are continuous algebras;
- the algebraic specifications of infinite objects include the specification of projections and thus embody the metric; the associated continuous model is obtained by a standard construction.

This approach is much related to the metric approach developed by the de Bakker's school in Amsterdam (see [30]) as a development of a pioneering paper by Arnold and Nivat [1]. The key difference here is the explicit specification of projections.

Projection specifications are almost as usual total equational algebraic specifications, but with an explicit projection operation for each sort $p\text{-}s: nat \times s \rightarrow s$; some constraints are added thus obtaining the constrained projection specifications to ensure conservative extensions of the naturals, if used in the projections, and compatibility of operations with projections.

Projection algebras are models of constrained projection specifications; they are characterized by the fact that every carrier is a projection space and the operations are projection compatible. By defining suitable projection morphisms, for every projection specification PS, the projection algebras which are PS models become a category $Cat(PS)$, which admits (free and) initial algebra T_{PS}.

By a standard construction procedure on projections, with every projection algebra a continuous algebra is associated which is complete (i.e., every carrier is a complete projection space) and separated (i.e., equality of projections implies equality of the limits). Thus the semantics of a projection specification PS is the initial complete separated algebra CT_{PS} which is associated with the initial algebra T_{PS} and is initial in the category of complete separated projection algebras.

Moreover projection specifications have nice properties like existence of free construction and the amalgamation and extension properties, so that the modularization and parameterization techniques and the results for classical equational specifications may be fully extended to projection specifications.

The theory of projection spaces and specifications provides a way of specifying processes as infinite objects of some kind, defining their projections, The nice aspect is that whenever processes are specified in this way, there is a full integration of data and processes, because processes are data themselves (viewpoint **V3**: dynamic data types). Moreover this theory, not being bound to a particular model of processes, nor languages, nor method, can be incorporated in other methods (for example, it seems possible to use it within the SMoLCS approach, see Sect. 3.4, for associating semantics in a pure algebraic way as in [6]).

Here we report the projection specification of the process algebra PA already considered in Sect. 1.3, but in this case we have the initial complete separated algebra which considers also infinite processes, while in 1.3 only the finite ones are considered.

spec $PA\text{-}Pr$ =
  enrich $PNAT$ **by**
  sorts exp
  opns
    $a_1, a_2, a_3, \ldots : \rightarrow exp$
    $\_.\_: exp \times exp \rightarrow exp$
    $\_ + \_: exp \times exp \rightarrow exp$
    $\_ \parallel \_: exp \times exp \rightarrow exp$
    $\_\lfloor\_: exp \times exp \rightarrow exp$
    $p\text{-}exp: nat \times exp \rightarrow exp$
  axioms
    $x + y = y + x \qquad (x + y) + z = x + (y + z) \qquad x + x = x$

$(x + y).z = (x.z) + (y.z) \qquad (x.y).z = x.(y.z)$
$x \parallel y = (x \lfloor y) + (y \lfloor x)$
$a \lfloor x = a.x \qquad (a.x) \lfloor y = a.(x \parallel y) \qquad (x + y) \lfloor z = (x \lfloor z) + (y \lfloor z)$
for all $i \geq 1$
$\quad p\text{-}exp(n, a_i) = a_i$
$\quad p\text{-}exp(0, a_i.x) = a_i$
$\quad p\text{-}exp(Succ(n), a_i.x) = a_i.p\text{-}exp(n, x)$
$p\text{-}exp(n, x + y) = p\text{-}exp(n, x) + p\text{-}exp(n, y)$

Here *PNAT* is the projection specification of natural numbers with the usual operations 0 and *Succ*.

Observational Structures and Specifications The usual semantics for basic algebraic specifications in general are not adequate for specifications of processes. Consider, for example, the algebraic specification *CCS* of finite CCS given in Sect. 2.1. Initial and final semantics of *CCS*, which coincide, do not represent the right semantics for CCS (for example, *nil* and *nil* + *nil* are not identified, since there are no axioms requiring the identification of terms of sort *exp*).

Also the common form of observational semantics for algebraic specification (sometime called behavioural semantics as in [66]) allows only to express particular bisimulation semantics: those which may be characterized by primitive observations (see [10] for a general treatment and [6] for the particular case of weak bisimulation; while in [12] a lattice of simulation relations is defined, whose greatest element can be seen as a possible correspondent of bisimulation in an algebraic framework). However behavioural semantics cannot be used for general bisimulation semantics, for example in the case of higher-order processes (i.e., when processes are communicated among processes).

The semantics of CCS is given usually by means of several variations of bisimulation. However various problems are encountered when extending bisimulation semantics to algebraic specifications. Consider the higher-order extension of the finite CCS (algebraically specified in Sect. 2.1) which is formally defined below.

spec *HCCS* =
  enrich *CCS* **by**
  opns
    Pcom: *exp* → *act*
  – also communicating a process is a basic action

In this case a bisimulation semantics must determine an algebra; thus instead of bisimulation relations we have to consider families of relations on the carriers of the initial model indexed on the sorts of the specification $R = \{R_s\}_{s \in \{exp, act, lab\}}$; so if the maximum bisimulation is a congruence, then the resulting semantics will be the quotient algebra I_{HCCS}/R.

Then we have to give conditions for R being a bisimulation, which must differ from those of 2.3, otherwise *Pcom*(*nil*).*nil* and *Pcom*(*nil* + *nil*).*nil* will be distinguished by the maximum strong bisimulation (while each reasonable extension of strong bisimulation should identify them, since both communicate strongly bisimilar processes); more generally the condition for R_{exp} being a bisimulation of 1.2 can be rephrased as follows. For all e_1, e_2 s.t. $e_1 \; R_{exp} \; e_2$

- if e_1 passes an experiment $EXP_1 = x \xrightarrow{l_1} e'_1$ (i.e. the formula $x \xrightarrow{l_1} e'_1$ holds on e_1), then e_2 passes another experiment $EXP_2 = x \xrightarrow{l_2} e'_2$ R-similar to EXP_1;
- analogous condition for e_2;

where $x \xrightarrow{l_1} e'_1$ R-similar to $x \xrightarrow{l_2} e'_2$ means $l_1 = l_2$ and $e'_1 \, R_{exp} \, e'_2$.

For coping with higher-order CCS we have just to modify the notion of R-similar experiment; now $x \xrightarrow{l_1} e'_1$ R-similar to $x \xrightarrow{l_2} e'_2$ iff $e_1 \, R_{exp} \, e_2$ and either $(l_1 = l_2)$ or $(l_1 = Pcom(e'), l_2 = Pcom(e'')$ and $e' \, R_{exp} \, e'')$ or $(l_1 = \overline{Pcom(e')}, l_2 = \overline{Pcom(e'')}$ and $e' \, R_{exp} \, e'')$.

What about R_{act} and R_{lab}? We have to extend the identifications on processes to the elements of other sorts, since they may have process components.

R_{act} : For all a_1, a_2, $a_1 \, R_{act} \, a_2$ implies
either $(a_1 = a_2)$ or $(a_1 = Pcom(e'), a_2 = Pcom(e'')$ and $e' \, R_{exp} \, e'')$.
R_{lab} : For all l_1, l_2, $l_1 \, R_{act} \, l_2$ implies
either $(l_1 = a_1, l_2 = a_2)$ or $(l_1 = \overline{a_1}, l_2 = \overline{a_2})$ with $a_1 \, R_{act} \, a_2$.

The above problems (and many others) are tackled within the theory of observational structures and specifications, which we sketch below (see [2] for a full treatment). The result is a new theory of adt semantics on its own, encompassing the classical treatment.

An *observational structure* essentially consists of a first-order structure (or algebra with predicates) equipped with

- *experiments*: (possibly infinitary) first-order contexts for observable elements;
- a *similarity law* for experiments: a function which, given a (similarity) relation on the elements of the algebra, generates a similarity relation on experiments;
- a *propagation law* for relations: a function which propagates a (similarity) relation on the observable elements to a (similarity) relation on elements of the other sorts.

With each observational structure a family of *observational relations* is associated, with a maximum that we call *observational equivalence*. This equivalence, as expected, is not always a congruence; thus it is shown how to derive canonically an approximating congruence and also how to define observational equivalences which are congruences. Whenever this equivalence is a congruence we get an observational semantics by the usual quotient operation.

The construction is a much abstract version of Park's construction of maximum bisimulation (see Sect. 1.2). Indeed, observational structures capture the essential ingredients for defining over algebraic structures those semantics which share with the original notion of bisimulation semantics the feature of being maximum fixpoints of suitable transformations. Hence the associated proof technique is effective: in order to show that two elements are semantically equivalent, just find an observational relation to which they belong. As a desired consequence many known bisimulation semantics for processes (presently, all known to us) are special cases of this construction. But *observational structures are not at all confined to a generalization of bisimulation semantics for processes.* Indeed because of their abstract nature and of the flexibility in the choice of the similarity laws for experiments and of the propagation laws for relations, they can be applied to give a wide range of semantics for abstract data types. It can be shown indeed that the full class of well-known semantics, like initial, final and various behavioural semantics, are special cases of this paradigm.

An *observational specification* is a particular case of observational structure in which we make explicit use of an algebraic specification *SPEC*; moreover the algebra component of the structure is the initial model of *SPEC* and the propagation and similarity laws are derived by the axioms of the specification as follows.

- The *free axiomatic propagation law* provides the minimal propagation of the identifications on the observed elements to the whole structure (i.e., to all nonobserved sorts and all predicates) which preserves the algebraic structure and the validity of the specification axioms about non observed elements and predicates.
- The *free axiomatic similarity law* considers equivalent two experiments if and only if they at most differ for subcomponents which are related by the above free axiomatic propagation law.

3 Outline of Some Approaches

We have selected a number of relevant approaches, which are briefly presented with an implicit reference to the items of Sect. 2; moreover for each one we comment its application to the example specification problems (the *CA* architectures) presented in Sect. 1.4.

3.1 The Process Specification Formalism for Process Algebras (PSF)

PSF (see [46]) is the process specification formalism developed by Mauw and Veltink as a base for a set of tools to support process algebra of Bergstra, Klop et al' (see e.g., [18, 14]). The main goal in the design of PSF was to provide a specification language with a formal syntax similar to the process algebra ACP (see [14] Sect. 4) but also with a notion of data type; to this end ASF (the Algebraic Specification Formalism of [17], which is based on the formal theory of abstract data types) has been incorporated.

The basic specification formalism is equational logic with total algebras. The theory and language of ASF is adopted for handling modular and parameterized specifications.

A PSF specification consists of a series of modules, distinguished in data modules and process modules.

Data modules are algebraic specifications of adt's with initial semantics.

Process modules are algebraic specifications of processes. Formally a process module has the following form.

process module NAME
  begin
    atoms – atomic action symbols declaration
    $A: s_1 \times \ldots \times s_n$

...

processes – process symbols declaration

$P: s_1 \times \ldots \times s_n$

...

set of atoms – set of atoms used with the hiding and encapsulation operation declaration

$H = \ldots$ – using set comprehension

...

communications – explicit definition of synchronous actions and of the resulting label

$a_1 \mid a_2 = a_3$

...

definitions

$P(x_1, \ldots, x_n) =$ ACP-expression

end NAME

Processes are particular data structures obtained from operators like "+", "||", ";", "**hide**" and "**encaps**", elementary processes called atomic actions and recursive definitions; the given (equational) axiomatization determines a particular semantics over these structures embodying ideas of concurrency. This is best understood looking at the hidden basic concurrent model behind process algebra which are lts's as in CCS and many other approaches; then the axioms provides semantics like strong, trace or bisimulation semantics and others. The hidden model is made evident in some presentations of PSF, where ACP processes are described by means of SOS-like rules (see [54]) describing transitions. Anyway, since ACP provides essentially a language schema for processes, it is irrelevant, except for building the tools, how its semantics is given, either by equations or by transitions plus semantic equivalences.

It is instead important to notice that in PSF:

- the synchronization of actions can be defined explicitly in the communication part, i.e. the synchronization mechanism is not fixed and is parameterized;
- the execution mode is interleaving.

The interface between processes and adt's is as follows:

- the atomic actions may have as components values of the specified adt's;
- it is possible to define recursively families of processes indexed on the elements of some sort;
- an infinitary non-deterministic choice indexed on the elements of some sort is available.

Note that there is no notion of global data and the communication mechanism is by message passing.

The semantics of the data part is a classical algebraic semantics by initiality; the semantics of processes is in general a bisimulation semantics which gives a congruence on the term algebra. Thus the semantics identifies an isomorphism class of structures, i.e., an adt.

The data part is strictly distinguished from the process part, i.e., the first viewpoint of including the specification of static adt's into a formalism for concurrency is followed; but also the concurrent structure is here specified algebraically though with a fixed set of primitives parameterized on the actions and on synchronization structure. The result is a completely algebraic specification to which all the techniques and results of ASF can be applied nicely.

Particularly powerful are the modularization mechanisms in PSF, which are borrowed from ASF but are truly dealing with integration of adt's and processes: the module concept supports importing and exporting also of processes and actions.

There is a vast literature on the use of process algebra with a detailed treatment of classical examples and correctness proof for implementation. However these examples should not be confused with applications of a specification method like PSF, which has been introduced indeed for supporting industrial applications. Clearly PSF is practically applicable to a wide range of significant cases, but we see a limitation in its strict policy of message passing and no provision for data sharing; in many cases some amount of coding is required which is not in the spirit of abstract specifications. The same remark applies to execution modes other than interleaving, which have to be simulated by appropriate use of synchronization and restriction mechanisms.

PSF has been devised as a basis for the development of a toolset (see e.g. [46]). This toolset is currently in an advanced phase of development ([47]); in particular a simulator, a term rewriting and a proof assistant has been implemented. From the design of the toolset, it seems that this would be a most interesting feature of PSF.

Some of the *CA* architectures may reasonable specified using PSF; clearly the buffer has to be realized by means of a particular process (all buffer organizations may be handled).

The following variations of *CA* cannot be specified in PSF: D_2 and D_3 (PSF does not support the viewpoint **V3**) and also P_2 and P_3 since PSF allows only interleaving execution mode for processes and does not offer a way to solve conflicts; for the same reason also *CA_NET* cannot be specified in PSF.

3.2 LOTOS

LOTOS has been probably the first internationally known (since 1984) algebraic specification formalism for concurrency (see [27, 40]); most importantly it is an official ISO language specification for open distributed systems, a qualification which alone would rank it high in an ideal value scale of possible important applications. However LOTOS is interesting also because it represents an early paradigm of which PSF can be considered an improvement. Because of this, we do not go into a detailed discussion of LOTOS; it is enough to compare it to PSF for understanding its structure.

LOTOS adds classical adt specifications into a language for concurrency as PSF; but it uses ACT ONE ([34]) instead of ASF and a process description based on an extension of CCS with several derived combinators (e.g. input/output of strucutured values, sequential composition with possible value passing, enabling/disabling operators) instead of the process algebra ACP.

The basic specification formalism (equational logic with total algebras) is the same and also bisimulation semantics for processes.

PSF is an improvement over LOTOS (see a discussion in [47]), since it allows more freedom in the definition of synchronization mechanisms and supports import/export of action/processes thus being more flexibile for stepwise development.

Along all these years LOTOS has been used in several practical applications and moreover nowadays a toolset for helping to write down LOTOS specifications has been developed (see e.g. the ESPRIT project LOTOSHERE [62]).

3.3 ACP with Shared Data

This approach is due to S. Kaplan and has been presented in [42, 43]. The situation is very similar to the one in PSF: strict hierarchical separation between data and processes and processes specified by a schematic language. The difference is that now the actions operate on the data and thus what is parametric is now the specification of the effect of actions on data.

The basic specification formalism is equational logic with total algebras. Any specification language that supports this basic formalism can be used to provide methods for modularization and parameterization; PLUSS (see [21]) is explicitly quoted as such a possible language.

A process specification is in two layers:

- the data part, which is a classical algebraic specification of some basic data structures; data represent the concurrent states of the (global) environment which is manipulated by processes;
- the *process* part, specifying the agents that act concurrently on the data. Processes are built out of basic entities called *actions*, by means of the operators (those typical of process algebra) ";", "||", "+".

The interactions of processes with data is modelled by an application operator $- :: - : process \times data \rightarrow data$. For example we can build a process stack by means of operations like $PUSH\colon item \rightarrow process$; then we can specify its effect with an axiom like: $PUSH(i) :: d = Push(i, d)$.

The states of a concurrent system have always the form "*process* :: *data*" and they are of type data; for example

$$(PUSH(i_1) \mid\mid PUSH(i_2) \mid\mid PUSH(i_3) \mid\mid POP) :: Push(i, Empty).$$

For making easier the specification, it is possible to declare composed actions, i.e., processes built from atomic actions by ";", "+" and "||", also in a parameterized way. The general form of a process specification is as follows:

process specification: *SPEC*
  data specification: *DATA*
  atomic actions: *A*
  composite actions: *C*
  equations for atomic actions: EQ_A
  equations for composite actions: EQ_C
end process specification: *SPEC*

The communication mechanism is by shared data and indeed the actions are used for manipulating the global data, while there is no provision for message passing.

The basic concurrent model is the process algebra ACP: i.e., no explicit model is given since processes are treated as static data, but the hidden models are lts's. The axioms for processes axiomatize the execution mode by interleaving of atomic actions and trace semantics. Note that trace semantics refers to the basic model for concurrency and not to the overall semantics for processes (see below).

Semantics is done by purely algebraic methods, i.e. it is hierarchical on data specification with an overall observational semantics, given by a congruence corresponding to a final algebra. Indeed the semantics of a process specification *SPEC* is given by translating *SPEC* into a classical algebraic specification *SEM(SPEC)*. The specification *SEM(SPEC)* has a standard part consisting in equations for defining the operators on processes (those of ACP) and the semantics of the application operators of processes to data.

The overall semantics of *SEM(SPEC)* is observational in an algebraic sense, i.e. it gives an observational congruence corresponding to a final algebra; this semantics formalizes an input-output semantics for processes with respect to data, as it is sensible for a concurrent system which represents non-deterministic transitions from a data configuration to another one (recall that the overall state of the system is of sort data).

Infinite processes are possible by means of fixpoint operator "$\mu\, p.E[p]$", whose semantics is axiomatically given by the unfolding equation as usual; dynamic processes, which may modify their structure depending on the environment, are obtained by a conditional operator.

Being fully algebraic, the approach can use various operators for composing specifications and of course parameterization and notions of implementation (and indeed the approach was developed in the same environment of PLUSS and ASSPEGIQUE). But it also provides a special composition operator for process specifications "$|||$" showing that under certain conditions one can convert a specification $SPEC_1 \mathbin{|||} \ldots \mathbin{|||} SPEC_n$ into a basic specification. This operation is viewed as a first step towards multilevel structuring, which is not exploited.

There is no mention in the literature of significant applications; however it can be easily understood that the method is viable whenever and only when we have to model concurrent architectures where the communications is by shared data. Converting models with message passing would imply some coding, which inevitably affects the level of abstraction.

No special tools. If the processes are finite then it is understandable that the usual tools for algebraic specification work.

Some of the *CA* architectures may be specified using this approach; however the handshaking communication between processes has to be simulated using particular shared structures and so, as said before, what we get is more an implementation of the architecture that an abstract specification. Clearly all kinds of buffer organization (variations B_1, B_2 and B_3) may be specified. Moreover, since also this formalism is based on the ACP, it has has the same restrictions of PSF: so we cannot specify neither the *CA* architectures corresponding to variations D_2, D_3, P_2, P_3 nor the network *CA_NET*.

3.4 Dynamic Specifications and SMoLCS

The core of the SMoLCS approach has been developed, mainly by E. Astesiano and G. Reggio at the University of Genova, with a significant contribution by M. Wirsing of the University of Passau, since 1983, first within the Italian national project CNET (Campus Net, the prototype design of a local area network). While the core of the method has been unchanged, significant improvements and additions have been made since, especially for what concern semantics, tools and specifications at higher-level of abstraction. Curiously enough its theoretical development has been always accompanied and partly driven by applications; indeed at the time of its appearance in the international literature [3, 4] a full SMoLCS specification of the prototype CNET communication architecture had been already completed [4]; the first tools have been developed for application to the draft formal specification of full Ada; the most recent development for very abstract specifications have been required for applications to two industrial case studies.

As a most distinctive feature, SMoLCS supports, within one specification formalism, different ways of specifying concurrent systems, adapting the description to the level of abstraction of the specified system. In its current version it even supports explicitly various forms of very abstract specification, which will be discussed among others in a later section; here we present just abstract specifications.

Any institution which support conditional specifications with predicates can be used as algebraic specification formalism; a privileged one is $\mathcal{CONDYN}$, the institution of conditional dynamic specifications with partial (total) [order-sorted] algebras with predicates. Though most examples have been given in an ASL-like metalanguage [11], SMoLCS is not bound to any particular specification language, as long as it supports at least conditional specifications with predicates, parameterization and modularization mechanisms.

SMoLCS is centered around the following ideas.

- Processes are specified algebraically as lts's and are themselves data as any other; thus can be manipulated by functions and processes (viewpoint **V3**: dynamic data types); in particular higher-order concurrent systems and calculi are supported (actually they have been first introduced and developed within the SMoLCS approach, see [7]).
- It supports the user-defined specification of any kind of concurrent structure, communication mechanism (from message passing to shared data) and execution modes (from interleaving to priorities).
- This support is provided by modularization, hierarchization and parameterization mechanisms for defining and combining parts of a system, with possibly reusable components of any kind (data, actions, communication and execution mode schemas).
- Semantics also is user defined, following a schema for defining observations of the system depending on a viewpoint.

A process is specified by giving a dynamic specification (an algebraic transition system, as it was called until '89), which is as follows.

- A *dynamic signature* $D\Sigma$ is a couple (Σ, DS) where:
  * $\Sigma = (S, OP, PR)$ is a predicate signature,
  * $DS \subseteq S$ (the elements in DS are the *dynamic sorts*, i.e. the sorts corresponding to states of lts's),
  * for all $st \in DS$ there exist a sort $l\text{-}st \in S - DS$ (the sort of the labels) and a predicate $- \xrightarrow{-} - : st \times l\text{-}st \times st \in PR$ (the transition predicate).
- A *dynamic algebra* on $D\Sigma$ (shortly $D\Sigma$-algebra) is just a Σ-algebra.
- An *absract dynamic data type* (shortly *addt*) is an isomorphism class of dynamic algebras on a signature.
- A couple $(D\Sigma, Ax)$, where $D\Sigma$ is a dynamic signature and Ax a set of first-order formulae on $D\Sigma$ is called a *dynamic specification*.

The axioms may refer both to static aspects (e.g., values, states of a system) and to the dynamic aspects, i.e. concerning the transitions predicates.

By algebra we mean usually a many-sorted algebra with predicates; though we generally prefer, for reasons of convenience in applications, to use partial algebras, there are no problem to use, for example, total or order-sorted algebras.

There are various institutions of dynamic specifications depending on the form of the axioms. For the purpose of abstract specifications the most interesting is $\mathcal{CONDYN}$, the institution of conditional dynamic specifications, with axioms of the form

$$\wedge_{i=1,\dots,n}\alpha_i \supset \alpha,$$

where α_i and α are atoms, i.e., formulae of the form $t = t'$ or $Pr(t_1, \dots, t_n)$ with Pr predicate symbol (in the case of partial algebras the equality in the formulae is interpreted as existential equality).

$\mathcal{CONDYN}$ has some nice features; indeed a conditional dynamic specification has always an initial model which defines an associated lts; moreover it is possible to make a clear distinction between static and dynamic axioms, the last ones being those where α has the form $s \xrightarrow{l} s'$.

Depending on the degree of separation between static and dynamic aspects in the axioms, various simple inductive ways of defining the associated lts's are possible.

- A dynamic specification determines an addt, according to a semantics that can be user defined following a schema for defining observational semantics. There are essentially two ways in SMoLCS for associating a semantics: by adding axioms defining observations and thus getting semantics as a terminal semantics (a terminal congruence, see especially [6]), or by defining over the specification an observational structure, as specified in [2] (see also Sect. 2.3) and getting an observational equivalence, which has to be proven to be a congruence; sufficient conditions are given to ensure this.

  Observational equivalence includes as a special case all presently known sensible semantics for concurrency like trace and bisimulation (strong, weak, branching, distributed), etc. Since observational semantics is obtained as a maximum fixed point of a suitable monotonic transformation, the same proof technique of bisimulation can be applied.

- A support to modular specification of concurrent systems is then given accordingly to the following schema, where we outline the methodological aspects, leaving apart the algebraic formalism, which can be found in the quoted papers.

  A *concurrent system* is specified as follows: the states $(p_1 \mid \dots \mid p_n \mid i)$ are a multiset of states of the process components and a value i representing the global information.

  The transitions are specified splitting the specification in several steps, where at each step some partial moves are defined using the partial moves defined at the previous step; at the first step the partial moves are defined starting from the transitions of process components.

The rules defining the transitions at the first step have form

$$\frac{p_i \xRightarrow{pl_i} p'_i \qquad i = 1, \ldots, n}{p_1 \mid \ldots \mid p_n \mid mp \mid i \xrightarrow{l} p'_1 \mid \ldots \mid p'_n \mid mp \mid i'} \quad cond$$

where $\Rightarrow$ denotes the transition relation of the process components, mp, i, i', the pl_1's, l and *cond* are metaexpressions and the p_i's and p'_i's are metavariables not appearing in *cond*; while the rules defining the transitions of the next steps have form

$$\frac{mp_j \mid i \overset{l_j}{\rightsquigarrow} mp'_j \mid i'_j \qquad j = 1, \ldots, n}{mp_1 \mid \ldots \mid mp_n \mid mp \mid i \xrightarrow{l} mp'_1 \mid \ldots \mid mp'_n \mid mp \mid i'} \quad cond$$

where $\rightsquigarrow$ denotes either the transition relation corresponding to the partial moves of the previous steps or $\rightarrow$, mp, i, i', the l_j's, i'_j, l and *cond* are metaexpressions and the mp_j's and mp'_j's are metavariables not appearing in *cond*.
It is shown that any specification of a concurrent system may be reduced to a canonical form consisting of the composition of three particular steps, respectively for synchronization, parallelism and monitoring, which are characterized by rules of the the form respectively:

Synchronization

$$\frac{p_j \xRightarrow{l_j} p'_j \qquad j = 1, \ldots, n}{p_1 \mid \ldots \mid p_n \mid i \xrightarrow{sl} p'_1 \mid \ldots \mid p'_n \mid i'} \quad cond$$

Parallelism

$$\frac{mp \mid i \xrightarrow{sl} mp' \mid i'}{mp \mid i \overset{sl}{\rightsquigarrow} mp' \mid i'}$$

$$\frac{mp_j \mid i \overset{pl_j}{\rightsquigarrow} mp'_j \mid i'_j \qquad j = 1, 2}{mp_1 \mid mp_2 \mid i \overset{pl_1//pl_2}{\rightsquigarrow} mp'_1 \mid mp'_2 \mid i'} \quad cond$$

Monitoring

$$\frac{mp \mid i \overset{pl}{\rightsquigarrow} mp' \mid i'}{mp \mid mp_1 \mid i \xrightarrow{extl} mp' \mid mp_1 \mid i'} \quad cond$$

Appropriate algebraic parameterized schemas are given for expressing the three steps; ultimately the specification of a system can be formally viewed as an adt specification which is an instantiation of a parameterized specification, say $SMoLCS(\ldots)$, where the parameters refer to various user defined aspects concerning dynamics and data. It is clearly possible then to reuse parts of specifications and also to structure hierarchically systems, corresponding to nested calling on different parameters, say $SMoLCS(\ldots, SMoLCS(\ldots), \ldots)$.

SMoLCS has been applied to significant case-studies, the most important being the specification of the underlying concurrent model in the formal definition of full

Ada (EEC-Map project The Draft Formal Definition of ANSI/STD 1815A see [5]). Among other applications, the description of a local area architecture in [4] and two-cases studies proposed by ENEL (Italian National Electricity Board) are concerning an hydro-electric central and a high-tension station for distribution of electric power.

For industrial applications it still lacks standardization and a complete toolset. A simulator, the SMoLCS rapid prototyping system based on RAP ([39]), has been in use since 1987, consisting of a tree-builder and a tree-walker. Currently a specification metalanguage for the SMoLCS specifications of concurrent systems and a related toolset is under development. The toolset includes a syntax-directed editor and a much more efficient redoing of the simulator equipped with a graphical interface for showing the results.

Following the SMoLCS approach it is possible to specify all *CA* architectures and the network *CA_NET* without implementing/simulating their concurrent features; such features may be abstractly specified by giving appropriate axioms for the various steps (the full specifications can be found in [8]). In this case it is important to note that the various assumptions on the data, on the buffer access and organization and on the parallelism are formalized by appropriate parameters of the parameterized adt *SMoLCS*; thus if we have the specification of the *CA* corresponding to a particular choice of such assumptions, say $CA(D_3, B_1, A_1, P_2)$, to get the specification for another choice, say $CA(D_3, B_3, A_1, P_2)$, it is sufficient to change the parameter corresponding to the buffer access (rules for the parallelism step).

3.5 Conditional Rewriting Logic

In [49] and, as application to object systems in [48], Meseguer advocates a formalism called "Conditional Rewriting Logic" as a unifying model of concurrency.

Meseguer work resembles much the SMoLCS approach (of which he was not aware when writing [49, 48]) but it differs in one fundamental point, as we will see. For example, the specifications of object systems in the second paper use for state configurations multisets of objects (processes) and information as in SMoLCS. Indeed it will be rather easy to understand that approach by comparing it to SMoLCS.

Seen from the specification viewpoint the proposed method can be viewed as a specialization of dynamic specifications in which:

- the transitions are seen as rewriting steps;
- a set of labelled conditional rewriting rules ($g: t \to t'$) is given, which constitute the proper axioms of the specification;
- a fixed set of conditional axioms is given defining the propagation of the rewriting steps by reflexivity, congruence, replacement and transitivity (in Meseguer's view a concurrent rewriting is characterized by the use of the replacement rule).

This work contains some very interesting ideas for theoretical foundations of concurrency, in particular the notion of semantics as a congruence over terms representing proofs; moreover it gives some very elegant insight into a categorical semantics. However for the moment those definitions are not able to embody significant observational semantics, which (personal communication) will constitute the subject of some future work.

The propagation axioms are the characterizing feature of Conditional Rewriting Logic; and indeed they justify the name of the approach (rewriting and logic). However, while being useful and elegant in some cases (for example in some application to Petri nets, which were the inspiring case), these axioms make this approach not convenient, in our view, for application to significant concurrent systems. The propagation rules imply that the actions corresponding to rewritings are not capabilities, but effective actions (silent moves in CCS). This implies that one cannot simulate labelled transitions (which are not explicitly supported) for representing capabilities. Hence what is a basic support for modular composition of open process modules (i.e., processes with capabilities toward the external world) is lacking. In most significant examples that we have encountered this makes specifications less modular than they should be.

Using the Conditional Rewriting Logic we can specify all *CA* variations and the network *CA_NET*; but the variations D_2 and D_3 are very hard to realize. The problem is that these specifications are very little modular due to the propagation axioms. We cannot first describe the rewritings of the processes and then those of the architectures, since if a process p can perform some rewriting only in some particular context, we have to specify only the architecture rewritings. So we cannot give a specification of the processes and then use it for all variations of *CA*; moreover we cannot use the specification of *CA* for specifying *CA_NET*. For the same reason the specification of *CA* choosing variations D_2 and D_3 are possible but very complicated, since we can only describe the rewritings of the architectures, otherwise the processes can perform some activity while they are communicated or stored in the buffer.

We should wait for more examples and applications, also remembering that probably the aims of that work are different from the classical specification of concurrent systems. Indeed the main application is currently related to the design, semantics and implementation of a specification language for concurrent modules. Quite interestingly, the semantics is driving the implementation down to the realization of the hardware architecture, which gives the project, in our view, a particular value as for the application of formal techniques to software engineering.

A somewhat related approach has been pursued in [28].

3.6 Stream Processing Functions

In various papers [22, 23, 24] and in projects M. Broy has developed since 1983 an approach to the formal specification of concurrent systems which is a combination of algebraic specifications, streams, predicate logic and functional programming.

The approach is denotational in nature: it provides a language and its semantics; thus it does not qualify as a typical algebraic formalism. However we briefly present it for matter of comparison; it may indeed use classic formalisms for the specification of abstract data types and it may apply first-order and temporal logic for describing properties of the agents.

The basic models are dataflow architectures and the structuring primitives are those typical for dataflows (which can be elegantly obtained as derived operators, because of the specification formalism and its semantics). Any other kind of concurrent architectures and of communication mechanisms have to be simulated.

There is a clear distinction between processes (agents) and data which may be defined as adt with some semantics; thus viewpoint **V1** is followed, since the concurrent architecture is not defined algebraically.

The overall specification is not algebraic and thus we cannot speak of adt specification. However the specifications which use first-order and temporal logic formulae identify classes of concurrent systems, thus VAS is supported.

Let us to see the approach in some more detail.

Broy's approach is built around a dataflow view of concurrent systems; consequently his basic semantic models are sets of continuous functions mapping tuples of streams to tuple of streams, see Sect. 1.1. Thus a process, called agent, has n input lines and m output lines. On every input line a finite or infinite sequence of data is transmitted to the agent and on every output line a finite sequence of data is generated by the agent. The input lines and output lines have internal (local) names that are used in a predicate for expressing the relationships between input and output.

A typical example is the following:

agent *store* = **input stream data** *d*, **stream bool** *b*, **output stream data** *r*
first *b* ⇒ *r* = *store*(**rest** *d*,**rest** *b*)
¬**first** *b* ⇒ *r* = **first** *d* & *store*(*d*,**rest***b*)

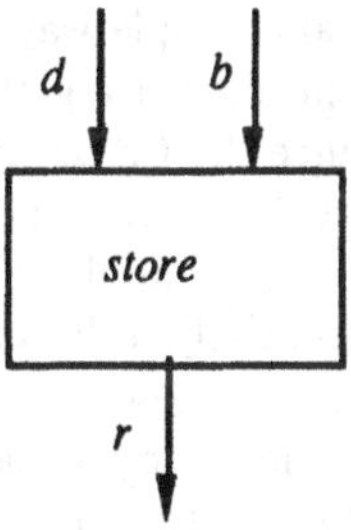

Here *d*, *b*, *r* are used both as variables and as internal names.

Also nondeterministic agents are admitted, as in

agent *infinite* = **output stream bool** *r*
r = **true** & *r* ∨ *r* = **false** & *r*;

thus there are two possible output streams:

r = **true** & **true** & ... and *r* = **false** & **false** & ....

From the examples we see that formulae are used for defining the streams of data, using of course primitive functions on streams like **first** and **rest**. Formulae may be first-order and also temporal logic formulas with operator like next, eventually and necessarily.

Sets of agents and recursive agents may be defined.

A semantics of a specification is given in the usual denotational way using basic domains and environments; the basic domains are data and agents:

$$D =_{def} DATA_{\perp} \cup STREAM(DATA)$$

$$AGENT =_{def} \{f \in [D^m \to D^n] \mid n, m \in \mathbb{N}\}$$

where *DATA* is a set of atomic data objects, but it may also be given by an abstract data type specification; $DATA_\perp$ is the flat cpo associated with *DATA*. The semantics of a family of agent definitions is the set of all agent environments that fulfill the specification. For very technical reasons with any agent identifier a set of agents (functions) is associated instead of functions from tuples of streams into sets of tuples of streams.

An interesting feature of the formalism is that basic structuring operators like parallel composition "||", sequential composition "." and feedback "C_j^i" may be obtained as derived operators. If a_1 and a_2 are defined by

agent a_1 = **input stream** x_1 **output stream** y_1 H_1 **end**
agent a_2 = **input stream** x_2 **output stream** y_2 H_2 **end**

then $a_3 = a_1 \parallel a_2$ is defined as

agent a_3 = **input stream** x_1, x_2 **output stream** y_1, y_2 $H_1 \wedge H_2$ **end**

Of course in this formalism algorithms may be described and thus so-called algorithmic agents can be defined.

Much importance is given to correctness, relative to safety (partial correctness) and liveness (robust correctness) properties, and to correctness of implementations, which are defined in a very elegant and simple way.

The *CA* architectures may be specified using this formalism, but the resulting specifications are not very natural since the *CA* architectures are based on communicating processes and so we have to realize their concurrent features using dataflows.

Broy's approach finds its most elegant applications in the specification of concurrent architectures which have essentially a dataflow structure. Indeed some nice examples of applications have been given, showing the potential applicability, at least for those architectures which are amenable to a dataflow structure. The method has also been applied in an EEC-MAP project (n. 785) in conjunction with industries, for giving a formal basis to the MASCOT method.

3.7 Algebraic Petri Nets

In the literature there are several papers presenting specification formalisms integrating Petri nets and algebraic specifications of adt's (in general not the elementary Petri nets introduced in Sect. 1.1 but e.g. predicate/transition or coloured nets); most of them follow the viewpoint **V1** but some one uses the algebraic techniques and results for handling, for example, nets composition or describing the firing rules. Here we briefly list some of the approaches known by the authors, but we do not claim that they are the only one. For a survey paper on this topic following viewpoint **V1** see e.g. [60]; where it is also shown that results about invariants could be obtained by classical algebraic results.

The Milan group has worked out a formalism "OBJSA Nets" combining Superposed Automata Nets (SA) with the possibility of defining the tokens and the transitions by means of parameterized algebraic OBJ specifications (see e.g. [15]).

OBJSA can be summarized as follows. The net structure is given as usual in superposed automata nets; the individuals flowing in the net consist of a name part, which models instances individuality and is not modified by transition firing, and a data part, which represents the data structure and can be modified by transition firing; the overall net system can be obtained through composition of the net models of its components (viewpoint **V1**).

Vautherin in [63] presents an algebraic version of coloured Petri nets, where the tokens of different colour are represented by elements of different sorts in the initial model of a specification of an adt and the structure of the net is given as usual (viewpoint **V1**), while Dimitrovici and Hummert in [33] show how to compose such nets by using categorical techniques.

In the following we report a simple example of these algebraic coloured Petri nets specifying a bounded buffer, containing natural numbers, organized as a queue. The tokens used in the net are defined by the initial model of a specification of the queues of natural numbers with the usual operations (Nil, InQueue, DeQueue, First and Length), which we do not report here. The schema of the net is graphically reported in Fig. 8; the arcs connecting places and transitions are labelled by open terms representing tokens; while the transitions are labelled by equations involving the variables appearing in such terms ($TKVar$); a transition may fire when for some evaluation V of the variables $TKVar$ satisfying its equation in the premise there are the tokens obtained by evaluating with V the relative terms.

Transition GET takes an element x from place $P1$ and puts within the queue q in place P, when the buffer is not full, i.e. when the equation $(\mathit{Length}(q) \leq n-1) = \mathit{True}$ holds. Transition $RETURN$ takes the first element out of the queue $\mathit{First}(q)$ and put it in the place $P2$, when the queue is not empty, i.e. when the equation $(\mathit{Length}(q) > 0) = \mathit{True}$ holds.

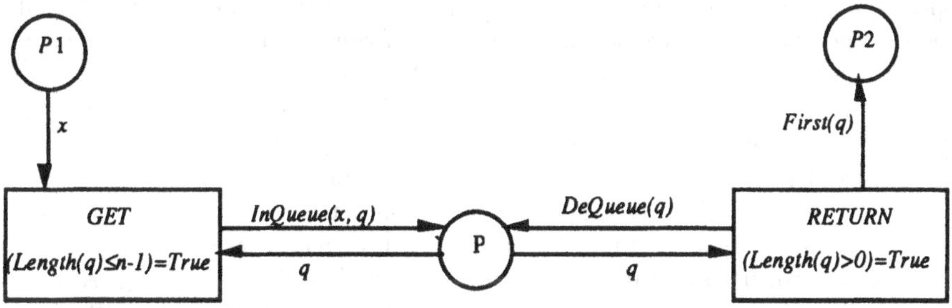

Fig. 8. An algebraic coloured net.

Bettaz in [19] and in [20] presents the so called "Algebraic Term Nets" and shows how such nets and their firing activity may be described by means of an algebraic specification of an adt (viewpoint **V2**).

Algebraic Petri nets has been also used as a basis for a specification metalanguage for distributed systems with real-time features [44].

4 Very Abstract Specifications of Concurrent Systems

In Sect. 2 we have already introduced the distinction between abstract and very abstract specifications of concurrent systems (shortly AS and VAS). An AS abstractly determines a concurrent system, i.e. it describes in an abstract way the system concurrent structure (which are its component processes and how they are arranged in the system) and activity; while a VAS abstractly determines a class of concurrent systems by giving only the relevant properties about their structure and activity.

Here we briefly list the algebraic approaches to specification of concurrency reported in Sect. 3 which can be extended to handle VAS's.

The Broy's approach, see Sect. 3.6, allows to express very abstract properties about the dynamic activity of classes of dataflow networks by using either first-order logics or various forms of temporal logics [22]; the last ones permit to formalize in a simple way liveness properties. However, this formalism does not allow to express requirements about the distributed structure of the networks. The dynamic requirements about a computer net given in Sect. 1.4 can be formalized using this approach, while the static ones cannot be considered. More importantly in this case we have also a notion of implementation between specifications of different abstraction levels; and in the literature there are examples of complete proofs of the correctness of some implementation (e.g. [24]).

Also in the framework of dynamic specifications, see Sect. 3.4, it is possible to give specifications of concurrent systems VAS both w.r.t. static and dynamic properties. Dynamic specifications are extended with the possibility of expressing very abstract properties about the dynamic activity of concurrent systems just by replacing conditional logic with more powerful ones. Initially first-order (infinitary) logic was considered, but it does not allow to express liveness properties; logics which integrates the combinators of temporal logic in the algebraic framework have been proposed in [29] and, more recently, in [58] whose "event logic" permits the formalization of the abstract properties of the activity of concurrent systems in terms of causal/temporal relationships among non-instantaneous events.

For what concerns the static (structure) properties, [57, 9] propose a subclass of the dynamic algebras, called "entity algebras", equipped with particular sorts, operations and predicates for describing the concurrent structure of the dynamic elements. Moreover, whichever logic for dynamic properties mentioned before (conditional, temporal, event, ...) may be extended with special predicates for formalizing abstract properties about the structure of dynamic elements ([57, 9]). Also for the dynamic VAS introduced above there is a notion of implementation extending that for specifications of static adt's of [66] (see [29, 57]); in these cases it is possible also to define particular kinds of implementations which e.g. preserve/refine the concurrent structure of a system, the atomicity grain of the activity of a system and so on. All the requirements about a computer net given in Sect. 1.4 can be simply formalized using dynamic VAS.

Acknowledgements. We thank H.Ehrig and F.De Cindio for various helpful comments.

References

1. A. Arnold and M. Nivat. Metric interpretations of infinite trees and semantics of non deterministic recursive programs. *TCS*, 11:181–205, 1980.
2. E. Astesiano, A. Giovini, and G. Reggio. Observational structures and their logic. *TCS*, 96, 1992..
3. E. Astesiano, G.F. Mascari, G. Reggio, and M. Wirsing. On the parameterized algebraic specification of concurrent systems. In H. Ehrig, C. Floyd, M. Nivat, and J. Thatcher, editors, *Proc. TAPSOFT'85, Vol. 1*, number 185 in Lecture Notes in Computer Science, pages 342–358, Berlin, 1985. Springer Verlag.
4. E. Astesiano, F. Mazzanti, G. Reggio, and E. Zucca. Formal specification of a concurrent architecture in a real project. In *A Broad Perspective of Current Developments, Proc. ICS'85 (ACM International Computing Symposium)*, pages 185–195, Amsterdam, 1985. North-Holland.
5. E. Astesiano, C. Bendix Nielsen, N. Botta, A. Fantechi, A. Giovini, P. Inverardi, E. Karlsen, F. Mazzanti, J. Storbank Pedersen, G. Reggio, and E. Zucca. The draft formal definition of Ada. Deliverable, CEC MAP project: The Draft Formal Definition of ANSI/STD 1815A Ada, 1986.
6. E. Astesiano and G. Reggio. An outline of the SMoLCS approach. In M. Venturini Zilli, editor, *Mathematical Models for the Semantics of Parallelism, Proc. Advanced School on Mathematical Models of Parallelism, Roma, 1986*, number 280 in Lecture Notes in Computer Science, pages 81–113, Berlin, 1987. Springer Verlag.
7. E. Astesiano and G. Reggio. SMoLCS-driven concurrent calculi. In H. Ehrig, R. Kowalski, G. Levi, and U. Montanari, editors, *Proc. TAPSOFT'87, Vol. 1*, number 249 in Lecture Notes in Computer Science, pages 169–201, Berlin, 1987. Springer Verlag.
8. E. Astesiano and G. Reggio. A structural approach to the formal modelization and specification of concurrent systems. Technical Report 0, Formal Methods Group, Dipartimento di Matematica, Università di Genova, Italy, 1991.
9. E. Astesiano and G. Reggio. Entity institutions: Frameworks for dynamic systems. in preparation, 1992.
10. E. Astesiano, G. Reggio, and M. Wirsing. Relational specification and observational semantics. In *Proc. MFCS'86*, number 233 in Lecture Notes in Computer Science, pages 209–217, Berlin, 1986. Springer Verlag.
11. E. Astesiano and M. Wirising. An introduction to ASL. In L.G.L.T. Meertens, editor, *Program Specification and Transformation*, pages 343–365. North-Holland, 1987.
12. E. Astesiano and M. Wirising. Bisimulation in algebraic specifications. In M. Nivat and H. Ait-Kaci, editors, *Proc. of the Colloquium on Resolution of Equations in Algebraic Structures*, San Diego, 1989. Academic Press.
13. D. Austry and G. Boudol. Algebre de processus et synchronisation. *TCS*, 30:91–31, 1984.
14. J.C.M. Baeten and W.P. Weijland. *Process Algebra*. Cambridge University Press, Cambridge, 1990.
15. E. Battiston, F. De Cindio, and G. Mauri. OBJSA nets: a class of high-level nets having objects as domains. In G. Rozemberg, editor, *Advances in Petri Nets*, number 340 in Lecture Notes in Computer Science, pages 20–43, Berlin, 1988. Springer Verlag.
16. L. Berardinello and F. De Cindio. A survey of basic net models and modular net classes. In G. Rozemberg, editor, *Advances in Petri Nets*, Lecture Notes in Computer Science, Berlin, 1992. Springer Verlag. To appear.

17. J.A. Bergstra, J. Heering, and P. Klint. ASF - an Algebraic Specification Formalism. Technical Report CS-R8705, Centre for Mathematics and Computer Science, Amsterdam, 1987.
18. J.A. Bergstra and J.W. Klop. Process algebra for synchronous communication. *Information & Control*, 60(1/3):109–137, 1984.
19. M. Bettaz. An association of algebraic term nets and abstract data types for specifying real communication protocols. In H. Ehrig, K.P. Jantke, F. Orejas, and H. Reichel, editors, *Recent Trends in Data Type Specification*, number 534 in Lecture Notes in Computer Science, pages 11–30, Berlin, 1991. Springer Verlag.
20. M. Bettaz. How to specify nondeterminism and true concurrency with algebraic term nets. Draft, 1992.
21. M. Bidoit. *PLUSS, un langage pour le developpment de specifications algebriques modulaires.* These d'Etat, Universite de Paris-Sud, 1989.
22. M. Broy. Specification and top down design of distributed systems. In H. Ehrig, C. Floyd, M. Nivat, and J. Thatcher, editors, *Proc. TAPSOFT'85, Vol. 1*, number 185 in Lecture Notes in Computer Science, pages 4–28, Berlin, 1985. Springer Verlag.
23. M. Broy. Predicative specifications for functional programs describing communicating networks. *Information Processing Letters*, 25:2, 1987.
24. M. Broy. An example for the design of distributed systems in a formal setting: The lift problem. Techinical Report MIP P 8802, University of Passau, 1988.
25. M. Broy and M. Wirsing. Partial abstract types. *Acta Informatica*, 18:47–64, 1982.
26. R.M. Burstall and J.A. Goguen. Introducing institutions. In E. Clarke and D. Kozen, editors, *Logics of Programming Workshop*, number 164 in Lecture Notes in Computer Science, pages 221–255, Berlin, 1984. Springer Verlag.
27. V. Carchiolo, A. Faro, F. Minassale, and G. Scollo. Some topics in the design of the specification language LOTOS. In M. Paul and B. Robinet, editors, *Proc. 4th Int. Symp. on Programming*, number 167 in Lecture Notes in Computer Science, Berlin, 1984. Springer Verlag.
28. A. Corradini, G.L. Ferrari, and U. Montanari. Transition systems with algebraic structure as models of computation. In I. Guessarian, editor, *Proc. of 18-eme Ecole de Printemps en Informatique Theorique, Semantique du Parallelism*, number 469 in Lecture Notes in Computer Science, pages 185–222, Berlin, 1990. Springer Verlag.
29. G. Costa and G. Reggio. Abstract dynamic data types: a temporal logic approach. In A. Tarlecki, editor, *Proc. MFCS'91*, number 520 in Lecture Notes in Computer Science, pages 103–112, Berlin, 1991. Springer Verlag.
30. J.W. de Bakker and J.I. Zucker. Processes and the denotational semantics of concurrency. *Information & Control*, 54:70–120, 1982.
31. R. de Simone. Higher-level synchronising devices in Meije - SCCS. *TCS*, 37:245–267, 1985.
32. B.T. Denvir, W.T. Hardwood, M.J. Jackson, and M.J. Wray, editors. *The Analysis of Concurrent Systems.* Number 207 in Lecture Notes in Computer Science. Springer Verlag, Berlin, 1985.
33. C. Dimitrovici and U. Hummert. Composition of algebraic high-level nets. In H. Ehrig, K.P. Jantke, F. Orejas, and H. Reichel, editors, *Recent Trends in Data Type Specification*, number 534 in Lecture Notes in Computer Science, pages 52–73, Berlin, 1991. Springer Verlag.
34. H. Ehrig, W. Fey, and H. Hansen. ACT ONE: An algebraic specification language with two levels of semantics. Technical Report 83-01, TUB, Berlin, 1983.
35. H. Ehrig, F. Parisi Presicce, P. Boehm, C. Rieckhoff, C. Dimitrovici, and M. Grosse-Rhode. Algebraic data type and process specifications based on projection spaces. In

D.Sannella and A. Tarlecki, editors, *Recent Trends in Data Type Specification*, number 332 in Lecture Notes in Computer Science, pages 23–43, Berlin, 1988. Springer Verlag.

36. M. Grosse-Rhode and H. Ehrig. Transformation of combined data type and process specifications using projection algebras. In *Stepwise refinenment of distributed systems*, number 430 in Lecture Notes in Computer Science, pages 301–339, Berlin, 1990. Springer Verlag.
37. M. Hennessy. *Algebraic theory of processes.* The MIT Press, Cambridge, Massachusetts, 1988.
38. C.A.R. Hoare. *Communicating Sequential Processes.* Prentice Hall, London, 1985.
39. H. Hussmann. Rapid prototyping for algebraic specifications: RAP system user's manual. Technical Report MIP P 8504, University of Passau, 1985.
40. I.S.O. LOTOS – A formal description technique based on the temporal ordering of observational behaviour. IS 8807, International Organization for Standardization, 1989.
41. G. Kahn. The semantics of a simple language for parallel programming. In J.L. Rosenfeld, editor, *Information Processing 77*, pages 471–475, Amsterdam, 1974. North-Holland.
42. S. Kaplan. Algebraic specification of concurrent systems. *TCS*, 9:90–115, 1989.
43. S. Kaplan and A. Pnueli. Specification and implementation of concurrently accessed data. In *Proc. STACS '87 (Symposium on Theoretical Aspects of Computer Science)*, number 247 in Lecture Notes in Computer Science, Berlin, 1987. Springer Verlag.
44. B. Kraemer. *Concepts, Syntax and Semantics of SEGRAS – A specification Language for Distributed Systems.* Oldenbourg verlag, Munchen, Wien, 1989.
45. K. Lodaya and P. S. Thiagarajan. A modal logic for a subclass of event structures. In T. Ottmann, editor, *Proceeding of ICALP'87*, number 267 in Lecture Notes in Computer Science, pages 290–303, Berlin, 1987. Springer Verlag.
46. S. Mauw and G.J. Veltink. An introduction to PSF_d. In J. Diaz and F. Orejas, editors, *Proc. TAPSOFT'89, Vol. 2*, number 352 in Lecture Notes in Computer Science, pages 272 – 285, Berlin, 1989. Springer Verlag.
47. S. Mauw and G.J. Veltink. A proof assistant for PSF. In K. Larsen and A. Skou, editors, *Proc. Third Workshop on Computer Aided Verification, Vol. 1*, pages 200 – 211, Aalborg, Denmark, 1991. The University of Aalborg.
48. J. Meseguer. A logical theory of concurrent objects. In *ECOOP-OOPSLA'90 Conference on Object-Oriented Programming, Ottawa Canada, October 1990*, pages 101–115. ACM, 1990.
49. J. Meseguer. Rewriting as a unified model of concurrency. *TCS*, 96, 1992.
50. R. Milner. *A Calculus of Communicating Systems.* Number 92 in Lecture Notes in Computer Science. Springer Verlag, Berlin, 1980.
51. R. Milner. *Communication and concurrency.* Prentice Hall, London, 1989.
52. R. Milner, J. Parrow, and D. Walker. A calculus of mobile processes - Part I. *Information and Computation*, 1992. To appear.
53. D. Park. Concurrency and automata on infinite sequences. In *Proc. 5th GI Conference*, number 104 in Lecture Notes in Computer Science, Berlin, 1981. Springer Verlag.
54. G. Plotkin. A structural approach to operational semantics. Lecture notes, Aarhus University, 1981.
55. G. Plotkin. An operational semantics for CSP. In D. Bjorner, editor, *Proc. IFIP TC 2-Working conference: Formal description of programming concepts*, pages 199–223, Amsterdam, 1983. North-Holland.
56. A. Pnueli. Applications of temporal logic to the specification and verification of reactive systems: a survey of current trends. In *Current Trends in Concurrency*, number 224 in Lecture Notes in Computer Science, pages 510–584, Berlin, 1986. Springer Verlag.

57. G. Reggio. Entities: an istitution for dynamic systems. In H. Ehrig, K.P. Jantke, F. Orejas, and H. Reichel, editors, *Recent Trends in Data Type Specification*, number 534 in Lecture Notes in Computer Science, pages 244–265, Berlin, 1991. Springer Verlag.
58. G. Reggio. Event logic for specifying abstract dynamic data types. In the same volume, 1992.
59. W. Reisig. *Petri nets: an introduction*. Number 4 in EATCS Monographs on Theoretical Computer Science. Springer Verlag, Berlin, 1985.
60. W. Reisig. Petri nets and algebraic specifications. *TCS*, 80:1–34, 1991.
61. B. Thomsen. A calculus of higher-order communicating systems. In *Proceeding of POPL Conference*, pages 143–154, 1989.
62. P. van Eijk. Tools for LOTOS, a Lotosfere overview. Memoranda Informatica 91-25, Universiteit Twente - Faculteit der Informatica, Enscede, 1991.
63. J. Vautherin. Parallel system specifications with coloured Petri nets and algebraic data types. In G. Rozemberg, editor, *Advances in Petri Nets*, number 266 in Lecture Notes in Computer Science, Berlin, 1987. Springer Verlag.
64. G. Winskel. Event structure semantics for CCS and related languages. In M. Nielsen and E.M. Schmidt, editors, *Proc. 9th ICALP*, number 140 in Lecture Notes in Computer Science, pages 561–576, Berlin, 1982. Springer Verlag.
65. G. Winskel. An introduction to event structures. In J.W. de Bakker, W.-P. de Roever, and G. Rozemberg, editors, *Linear Time, Branching Time and Partial Order in Logics and Models for Concurrency*, number 354 in Lecture Notes in Computer Science, pages 364–397, Berlin, 1989. Springer Verlag.
66. M. Wirsing. Algebraic specifications. In van Leeuwen Jan, editor, *Handbook of Theoret. Comput. Sci.*, volume B, pages 675–788. Elsevier, 1990.

Objects and Their Specification *

Hans-Dieter Ehrich
Martin Gogolla
Abteilung Datenbanken, Technische Universität, Postfach 3329
W-3300 Braunschweig, GERMANY

Amilcar Sernadas
Computer Science Group, INESC, Apartado 10105
1017 Lisbon Codex, PORTUGAL

Abstract

Object-oriented concepts and constructions are explained in an informal and language-independent way. Various algebraic approaches for dealing with objects and their specification are examined, ADT-based ones as well as process-based ones. The conclusion is that the process view of objects seems to be more appropriate than the data type view.

1 Introduction

There is a peculiar confusion around the notions of object and abstract data type in practice: while the latter has been made mathematically precise as an isomorphism class of algebras, practitioners tend to view an abstract data type as an encapsulated module exporting a set of procedures through which its data can be accessed and manipulated. The bridge to the theory is to look at the module's set of internal states as a carrier, and its procedures as operations of an algebra.

The problem with this view is that it blurs the distinction between data and objects.

The integers constitute a basic example of a data type. Another popular example is a stack. Pragmatically, however, integers and stacks are quite different. The integer data type provides a supply of values which can be used, say, as actual parameters in procedure calls. A stack, on the other hand, is a unit of structure and behavior: its states are not meant to be used as actual parameters in procedure calls. Rather, the stack *as a whole* is subject to operations. An integer is added to another integer to give a result which is a third integer. A stack entry, however, is pushed onto a stack, and we still look at the latter as being the same stack, although its state has changed.

*This work was partly supported by the EC under ESPRIT BRA WG 3264 COMPASS, under ESPRIT BRA WG 3023 IS-CORE and by JNICT under PMCT/C/TIT/178/90 FAC3 contract.

That is, a stack is an *object*, not a data type: it has an *identity* which persists through change. It seems that, for the most part, the practical success of abstract data types is one of object–orientation.

There are many languages, systems, methods and approaches in computing which call themselves "object–oriented" by now, among them object–oriented programming languages like SmallTalk [GR83], C++ [St86] and Eiffel [Me88], object–oriented database systems like GemStone [BOS91], O_2 [De91], IRIS [Fi87] and ORION [Ki88], and object–oriented system development methods like GOOD [SS86], MOOD [Ke88] and HOOD [Hei88].

High–level system specification languages and design methodologies are evolving which are based on object–oriented concepts and techniques. [Ve91] gives an overview of recent work in this area. We are cooperating in the ESPRIT BRA Working Group IS-CORE where a graphical language [SGCS91, SRGS91, SSGRG91, SGGSR91] and a textual counterpart [JSS90, JHSS91, JSS91, JSHS91, SJ91] for designing, specifying and implementing object communities are being developed.

But what precisely is an object? As we have seen, it has an internal state and a certain behavior reflected by its operations: it is a *unit of structure and behavior* — and it has an *identity* which persists through change. Moreover, dynamic objects somehow *communicate* with each other, they are classified by object *types*, collected into object *classes*, related by various forms of *inheritance*, and composed to form *complex* objects.

This rich world of concepts and constructions seems to be very fertile: An enormous amount of work is being invested in developing object–oriented techniques for software engineering. Evidently, there is much hope that software production and maintenance can be made more effective, more productive, more adequate, and more reliable this way. Indeed, object–oriented languages and systems as well as design and implementation methods are invading all disciplines of software engineering.

With all these practical developments, it is amazing that theoretical foundations for object–oriented concepts and constructions do not have found so wide attention yet. Matters are changing slowly: there are formal approaches to object–oriented programming language semantics [CP89], database concepts [Be91, GKS91], and specification languages [GW90]. Besides this, also language– and system–independent discussions of fundamental object–oriented issues are evolving [Cu91, HC89, LP90].

In the IS-CORE working group, the first and third authors have been cooperating in the latter direction. Recent contributions to semantic fundamentals are [ESS90, ES90, EGS91, CS91, CSS91, SE90, SEC90, SFSE89], emphasizing the process view of objects. In cooperation, logic fundamentals of object specification have been developed [FM91a, FM91b, FS91, FSMS90]. A first result harmonizing logics and semantics of object specification can be found in [FCSM91].

A systematic formalization of basic object–oriented concepts and constructions in terms of this theory has been published in [ES91] and, together with features of an object–oriented specification language and methodology, in [SJE91].

In the second section of this paper, we give an informal account of these ideas. In the third section, we examine various approaches for dealing with objects and their specification, ADT–based ones as well as process–based ones. The conclusion is that the process view of objects seems to be more appropriate than the data type view.

2 Object–Oriented Concepts and Constructions

In this section, we give an informal account of our view of object–oriented concepts and constructions. The purpose is to establish requirements for formalization of object–orientation, not a formalization itself: we declare the intuitive basis on which to evaluate formal approaches. First steps towards formalization are discussed in section 3.

We feel that it is necessary to discuss the intuitive background at some length, because of the confusion and disagreement on fundamental terms in this area. We took some pain to make the definitions precise enough to serve their purpose, but they are not meant to be a formalization yet.

In order to be short and concise, we present one particular view rather than giving a review of alternative opinions and philosophies. Whenever appropriate, however, we drop a hint at other viewpoints.

2.1 Templates

In natural language, we refer to objects by substantives, but we use the same substantive in two different ways: with the definite article **the** (or words like **this** or **that**) for referring to specific individual objects, and with the indefinite article **a** for referring to generic terms.

The distinction between individual objects and generic terms is somewhat sloppy in natural language. Consider, for example, the sentence

- *This computer is a SUN workstation; it works quite well.*

Does the speaker want to say that the specific SUN workstation referred to by *this* works quite well, or does she want to say that SUN workstations *in general* work quite well? The first meaning is probably more obvious, but you can hear people talk like this with the second meaning in mind.

In computing, we have to be very specific about this distinction. For generic terms, the word *type* is often used, but this word is overloaded with too many connotations. We avoid it and prefer to speak of *object templates* if we mean generic objects without individual identity. The notion of an *object class* is easily confused with this, but it means something else, namely a time–varying collection of objects! We will be back to this.

An object template represents the common structure and behavior pattern of some kind of object.

The basic ingredients of structure and behavior are *observations* and *actions*. For instance, for a queue object with integer entries, we might have

- observations `front=7 , rear=2 , size=3 , ...`

- actions `create , enter(7) , leave , ...`

with obvious meanings. It is essential that we are general enough to allow for *concurrency*. In a nonempty queue, for instance, `enter`(4) and `leave` may occur simultaneously, and this simultaneous occurrence can be considered as *one* composite action `enter`(4)||`leave`. Moreover, also actions and observations can occur at the same time, giving rise to expressions like `enter`(4)||`front`=7 or `size`=3||`rear`=2|| `leave`.

But what do the latter expressions mean? They are neither pure actions nor pure observations. In order to make sense of this, we introduce the concept of *event* as a generalization of actions and observations:

- *an event is anything which can occur in one instant of time.*

Let E be a given set of events including atomic actions, atomic observations, and simultaneous combinations of finitely many of these. Obviously, we have a binary operation $\|$ on E which should be associative, commutative and idempotent, and it should satisfy the cancellation law. Adding, for completeness and convenience, a neutral element 1 standing for *nothing happens* (or, rather, nothing *visible* happens, i.e., it might represent a *hidden* event), we obtain an

- *event monoid* $\bar{E} = (E, \|, 1)$

with the above properties as the basic event structure to work with.

An object template has an event monoid associated with it, representing the events which can possibly happen to this kind of object. But, of course, it is not sufficient to know *which* events can happen, we need to know *how* they can happen in sequence or concurrently.

A *process* is a well known concept modelling precisely this. There are many process models and languages in the literature, including CSP, CCS, ACP, Petri nets, labelled transition systems, various trace models, etc. We cannot go into process theory here, and fortunately we need not: we are ready to accept any sufficiently powerful process model for modelling object template behavior.

In order to help the reader's intuition, however, she might envisage labelled transition systems (lts) as an example process model: an object template has states, and it can move (non-deterministically) from state to state by transitions labelled by events (only actions will actually change state, observations will leave it fixed). A mathematical elaboration of this model can be found in [CSS91], and a more abstract denotational model is outlined in [ES91]. Other appropriate process categories are currently being investigated, denotational and operational ones [CS91, CSS91], and also logic-based ones [FM91a, FSMS90]. An interesting unifying approach can be found in [Me91].

Templates in isolation, however, are not enough for capturing the relevant object-oriented concepts: for studying inheritance and interaction, we have to deal with suitable *relationships between* templates. In this respect, process theory offers only rudimentary help. We found it necessary to develop a general and powerful notion of *process morphism* as some kind of "behavior preserving map" between processes [ES91, ESS90, ES90, SE90, SFSE89, SSE87]. Amazingly, one single concept turned out to be sufficient for dealing with inheritance as well as interaction!

Templates and template morphisms constitute a well known mathematical structure called a *category*. We have been able to find instances of process categories where not only the morphisms are appropriate for modelling inheritance and interaction, but where also fundamental process operations are reflected by basic categorial constructions: parallel composition by limits, and internal choice by colimits [ES91, CS91].

In what follows, we will need one special case of template morphism in particular, namely *projection*: a template is projected to a part or an aspect of itself by mapping all "global" states to their "local" part or aspect, and correspondingly for transitions. The events relevant for the part or aspect are maintained, while the remaining events are "hidden" by mapping them to 1. Please note that nondeterminism might be introduced this way.

For example, let **twoqueue** be the template for objects consisting of two queues working in parallel, without any interaction between them. The states of **twoqueue** are all pairs (q_1, q_2) of states of the two component queues, whereas the events (labels) are given by the product of the two event monoids, i.e., all events of the form $e_1 \parallel e_2$ where e_1 is an event of the first queue and e_2 is one of the second. Let **queue** be the template for just one such queue. Then we have two obvious projections p_i : **twoqueue** $\rightarrow$ **queue**, $i = 1, 2$, where p_i leaves the i–th queue fixed and "forgets" the other one by mapping all actions and all observations to 1.

For another example, let **queue** be as above, and let **deque** (double–ended queue) be like a queue, but with actions to enter and to leave at both ends: there is an obvious "abstraction" a : **deque** $\rightarrow$ **queue** leaving the states fixed but "forgetting" the additional actions.

These examples demonstrate the twofold use of template morphisms: for restricting to a constituent part and for abstracting an aspect.

2.2 Objects

What is an object ? Its behavior is a process, but an object is more than its behavior: there may be many objects with the same behavior, but they are different as objects. That is, an object has an *identity* while a process has not. Only if we can distinguish clearly between individual objects is it possible to treat object concepts like inheritance and interaction in a clean and satisfactory way: interaction is a relationship between *different* objects, while inheritance relates aspects of the *same* object.

Object identities are atomic items whose principle purpose is to characterize objects uniquely. Thus, the most important properties of identities are the following: we should know which of them are equal and which are not, and we should have enough of them around to give all objects of interest a separate identity. Identities are associated with templates to represent individual objects — or, rather, *aspects* of objects, as we will see.

Given templates and identities, we may combine them to pairs $b.t$ (to be read "*b as t*"), expressing that object b has behavior pattern t. But there are objects with several behavior patterns! For instance, a given person may be looked at as an employee, a patient, a car driver, a person as such, or a combination of all these aspects. Indeed, this is at the heart of inheritance: *b.t denotes just one aspect of an object* – there may be others with the same identity!

Definition 2.1 : An *object aspect* – or *aspect* for short – is a pair $b.t$ where b is an identity and t is a template.

Definition 2.2 : Let $b.t$ and $c.u$ be two aspects, and let $h : t \to u$ be a template morphism. Then we call $h : b.t \to c.u$ an *aspect morphism.*

Aspect morphisms are nothing else but template morphisms with identities attached. The identities, however, are not just decoration: they give us the possibility to make a fundamental distinction between the following two kinds of aspect morphisms.

Definition 2.3 : An aspect morphism $h : b.t \to c.u$ is called an *inheritance morphisms* iff $b = c$. Otherwise, it is called an *interaction morphism.*

The following example illustrates the notions introduced so far.

Example 2.4 : Let `el_dvice` be a behavior template for electronic devices, and let `computer` be a template for computers. Assuming that each computer IS An electronic device, there is a template morphism h : `computer` → `el_dvice` (roughly speaking, the `el_dvice` part in `computer` is left fixed, while the rest of `computer` is projected to 1).

If `SUN` denotes a particular computer, it has the aspects

`SUN.computer`	(`SUN` as a computer)	and
`SUN.el_dvice`	(`SUN` as an electronic device),	

related by the inheritance morphism h : `SUN.computer` ⟶ `SUN.el_dvice` .

Let `powsply` and `cpu` be templates for power supplies and central processing units, respectively. Assuming that each electronic device HAS A power supply and each computer HAS A cpu, we have *template* morphisms f : `el_dvice` → `powsply` and g : `computer` → `cpu`, respectively. If `PXX` denotes a specific power supply and `CYY` denotes a specific cpu, we might have *interaction* morphisms f' : `SUN.el_dvice` → `PXX.powsply` and, say, g' : `SUN.computer` → `CYY.cpu`. f' expresses that the `SUN` computer – as an electronic device – HAS THE `PXX` power supply, and g' expresses that the `SUN` computer HAS THE cpu `CYY`.

These examples show special forms of interaction, namely between objects (aspects) and their *parts.* More general forms of interaction are established via *shared parts.* For example, if the interaction between `SUN`'s power supply and cpu is some specific cable `CBZ`, we can naively view the cable as an object `CBZ.cable` which is part of both `PXX.powsply` and `CYY.cpu`. This is expressed by a *sharing diagram*

`CYY.cpu` ⟶ `CBZ.cable` ⟵ `PXX.powsply`

A more realistic way of modeling this would consider the cable as a separate object not contained in the cpu and not in the power supply either. Rather, the cable would share contacts with both. ∘

This shows that objects may appear in different aspects, all with the same identity but with different behavior templates, related by inheritance morphisms. The information which aspects are related by inheritance morphisms is usually given by *template* morphisms *prescribing* inheritance. For example, we specify h : `computer` → `el_dvice` in order to express that each computer IS An electronic device, imposing that whenever we have an instance computer, say `SUN.computer`, then it necessarily IS THE electronic device `SUN.el_dvice` inherited by h as an aspect morphisms, h : `SUN.computer` → `SUN.el_dvice` .

Definition 2.5 : Template morphisms intended to prescribe inheritance are called *inheritance schema morphisms*. An *inheritance schema* is a collection of templates related by inheritance schema morphisms.

Example 2.6 : In the following inheritance schema, arrowheads are omitted: the morphisms go upward.

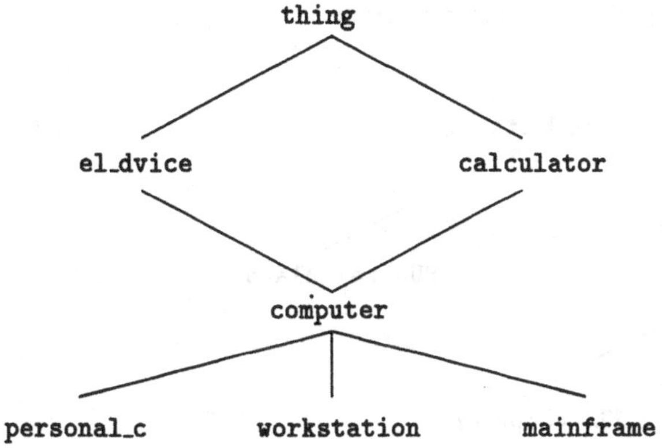

○

Practically speaking, we create an object by providing an identity b and a template t. Then this object $b.t$ has *all* aspects obtained by relating the same identity b to all "derived" aspects t' for which there is an inheritance schema morphisms $t \to t'$ in the schema.

Thus, an object is an aspect together with all its derived aspects. All aspects of one object have the same identity – and *no other* aspect should have this identity!

But the latter statement is not meaningful unless we say which aspects are there, i.e., we can only talk about objects *within a given collection of aspects.* Of course, the collection will also contain aspect morphisms expressing how its members interact, we will be back to this. And if an aspect is given, all its derived aspects with respect to a given inheritance schema should also be in the collection.

Definition 2.7 : An *aspect community* is a collection of aspects and interaction morphisms. It is said to be *closed* with respect to a given inheritance schema iff, whenever an aspect $a.t$ is in the community and an inheritance morphism $t \to t'$ is in the schema, then we also have $a.t'$ in the community.

Definition 2.8 : An *object community* – or *community* for short – consists of an inheritance schema and an aspect community which is closed with respect to it.

Definition 2.9 : Let an object community be given, and let a be an object identity. The *aspect graph* of a in that community is the graph consisting of all aspects in the community with the identity a as nodes, and all inheritance morphisms lifted from the schema as edges.

By lifting we mean that whenever $a.t$ and $a.t'$ are in the aspect graph of object a and $t \to t'$ is in the schema, then also $a.t \to a.t'$ is in the aspect graph.

One could argue that the object with identity a is the aspect graph of a. Intuitively, an object with identity a is a collection of consistent aspects. But, as we will see, we take a simpler and more practical approach.

Example 2.10 : Consider an object community containing the inheritance schema in Example 2.6, a particular workstation named `SUN`, and a particular calculator named `UPN`. By inheritance, `SUN` automatically is a computer, an electronic device, a calculator, and a thing. Since `UPN` is a calculator, it is also a thing, etc. So we have the following object diagrams:

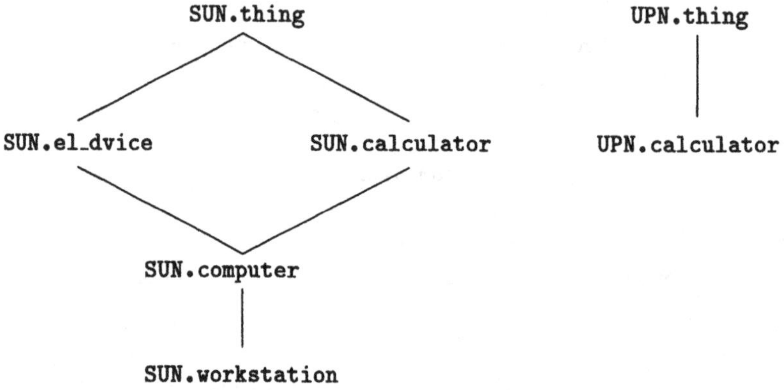

o

In a given community, an object is usually constructed by picking a specific identity a and associating it with a specific template t, yielding a *core* aspect $a.t$ for this object. Then the object diagram of a is determined by all aspects $a.t'$ where t' is related to t by an inheritance schema morphism $t \rightarrow t'$. Consequently, object diagrams have an inheritance morphism from the core aspect to any other aspect.

Definition 2.11 : An object community is called *regular* iff each aspect graph of an object in it has a core aspect.

While the notion of object should probably be taken as that of its aspect graph in general, we can make things easier and closer to popular use in a regular community: here it is safe to identify objects with their core aspects.

Definition 2.12 : In a regular community, an *object* b is the core aspect of its aspect graph.

Clearly, from the core aspect and the inheritance schema we can recover the entire aspect graph.

Since, according to this definition, objects are special aspects, we immediately have a notion of object morphism: it is an aspect morphism between objects.

2.3 Classes

Objects rarely occur in isolation, they usually appear as members of *classes*. A warning is in order: the notion of class is subject to considerable confusion! Essentially, there seem to be two different schools. The first one says that a class is a sort of abstraction of patterns, i.e., an intensional description of an invariant set of potential members. The other one says that a class is an extensional collection of objects which may vary from state to state. Both notions are needed. We capture the first one by *templates*, and we use the word class in the second sense.

That is, a class is a time–varying collection of objects as members – and this means that a class is a particular kind of object itself!

Or should we say *aspects* rather than objects? With the distinction between objects and aspects made above, we have to be careful with what can be a member of a given class, and whether a class is an aspect or an object. Let us first look at the member problem.

Example 2.13 : Referring to the inheritance schema in Example 2.6, let `CEQ` – the computer equipment – be a class of computers of some company `Z`. Let `MAC` be a specific personal computer in `Z`, and let `SUN` be a specific workstation in `Z`. The question is: are the objects `MAC.personal_c` and `SUN.workstation` members of `CEQ`, or rather their aspects `MAC.computer` and`SUN. computer`? ○

It is easier to work with *homogeneous* classes where all members have the same template, so we formally adopt the second alternative: each class has a fixed member template. We call this member template the *type* of the class. But, since each aspect of an object carries its identity and thus determines the object uniquely, there is no objection to considering, for example, the `MAC.personal_c` a member of the class `CEQ`.

Therefore, while classes are formally homogeneous, they have a heterogeneous – or polymorphic – flavor when working with inheritance: each object with an appropriate aspect whose template is the type of the class can be a member of that class!

Classes can be specialized by inheritance. For example, if we define a club as a class of persons, we might subsequently define special classes like a football club, a motor club, and a chess club.

Therefore, we consider classes as aspects. The class events are actions like inserting and deleting members, and observations are attribute-value pairs with attributes like the current number of members and the current set of (identities of) members. In most object–oriented systems, standard class events are provided implicitly, they need not be specified by the user.

Definition 2.14 : Let t be a template. An *object class* – or *class* for short – of type t is an aspect $C = a_C.t_C$ where a_C is the *class name* and $t_C = (E_C, P_C)$ is the *class template*. If `ID` is a given set of identities, the *class events* E_C contain

- actions `insert(ID)` , `delete(ID)`
- observations `population=set(ID)` , `#population=nat` .

The *class process* P_C describes the proper dynamic behavior in terms of the class events. ○

In practice, we would probably have the information in the environment which member identities can go with which class, i.e., some typing of identities. In this case, the argument `ID` in the above definition should be replaced by `ID`(C), the set of member identities which can be used in class C, and the notion of class type should comprise `ID`(C) along with the member template t.

Definition 2.15 : Let $C = a_C{\cdot}t_C$ be a class of type t. An *aspect* $a{\cdot}t$ is called a *member* of C iff a is an element of the population of C. An *object* $b{\cdot}u$ is called a *member* of C iff it has an aspect $b{\cdot}t$ which is a member of C.

This definition justifies our calling a class an *object* class, not an *aspect* class: the members may be considered to be the objects having the relevant aspects, emphasizing the polymorphic viewpoint.

Since classes are objects or aspects of objects, there is no difficulty in constructing meta–classes, i.e., classes of classes of ...

Definition 2.16 : A class C is called a *meta–class* iff its type is a class template.

Since class templates tend to be homogeneous even if their types are not, a meta–class may have classes of different types as members. For example, we could define the class of all clubs in a given city without generalizing the club member templates so as to provide an abstract and uniform one for all clubs.

Sometimes, we might want to restrict the members of a meta–class to contain sub–populations of a given class. For example, we may devise classes `CEQ(D)` for the computer equipment of each department `D` of company `Z`, given the class `CEQ` of computers in the company (cf. Example 2.13).

Definition 2.17 : Let C_1 and C_2 be classes. C_1 is called a *meta–class of* C_2 iff (1) the type of C_1 is the template of C_2, and (2) each member of C_1 is a class whose population is a subset of that of C_2.

Since classes are aspects, we immediately have a notion of *class morphism*: it is just an aspect morphism between classes.

Please note that the dynamic evolution of a class is completely separated from the dynamic behavior of its members. Typically, a class changes its state by inserting and deleting members, i.e., by changing its population. If the population does not change, then the state of the class does not change, even if some of its members change their state! Formally, this is achieved by having only the member *identities* in the class.

2.4 Inheritance

When we build an object–oriented system, we must provide an *inheritance schema* (cf. Definition 2.5). Without it, the very notion of object does not make sense. In this section, we investigate how to construct such an inheritance schema: which are the inheritance morphisms of interest, and how are they used to grow the schema step by step?

The inheritance morphisms of interest seem to be special indeed: in all cases we found meaningful so far, the underlying event maps were *surjective*. Since they are total anyway, this means that *all* events of both partners are involved in an inheritance relationship. And this makes sense: if we take a template and add features, we have to define how the inherited features are affected; and if we take a template and hide features, we have to take into account how the hidden features affect those inherited.

For any reasonable process model, the template morphisms with surjective event maps will be the *epimorphisms*, i.e., those morphisms r having the property that whenever $r;p = r;q$, then $p = q$. We found a special case of epimorphism useful which reflects an especially well–behaved inheritance relationship where the smaller aspect is "protected" in a certain sense: retractions. A *retraction* is a morphism $r : t \to u$ for which there is a reverse morphism $q : u \to t$ such that $q; r = id_u$. Retractions are always epimorphisms.

Intuitively speaking, the target of a retraction, i.e., the smaller aspect, is not affected by events outside its scope, it is *encapsulated*. As a consequence, retractions maintain the degree of nondeterminism: if the bigger aspect is deterministic, so is the smaller one.

Example 2.18 : Referring to Example 2.6, consider the inheritance schema morphism h : `computer` → `el_dvice` expressing that each computer is an electronic device. Let `el_dvice` have the following events:

- actions `switch_on` , `switch_off`
- observations `is_on` , `is_off`

By inheritance, `computer` has corresponding events `switch_on_c`, `switch_off_c`, etc. h sends `switch_on_c` to `switch_on` expressing that the `switch_on_c` of the computer is the `switch_on` inherited from `el_dvice`, and similarly for the other events. But what about the other events of `computer`, i.e., the ones not inherited? For example, there might be

- actions `press_key` , `click_mouse` , ...
- observations `screen=dark` , ...

Well, all these events are mapped to 1 indicating that they are *hidden* when viewing a computer as an electronic device.

Concerning the processes of the templates, we would expect that a `computer`'s behavior "contains" that of an `el_dvice`: also a computer is bound to the protocol of switching on before being able to switch off, etc.

Naturally, the template morphism h : `computer` → `el_dvice` is a retraction: there is also an embedding g : `el_dvice` → `computer` such that $g; f$ is the identity on `el_dvice`. Intuitively, this means that the `el_dvice` aspect of a computer is protected in the sense that it cannot be influenced by `computer` events which are not also `el_dvice` events: a `computer` can only be switched off by its `el_dvice` switch.

This would not be so if we had a strange computer which, say, can be switched off by other means, not using the `el_dvice` switch (perhaps by a software option...). In this case, we would have *side effects* of the computer on its `el_dvice` aspect: the latter would change its state from `is_on` to `is_off`, but would not be able to observe the reason for it locally: its `switch_off` was not used. In this case, the morphism h would still be an epimorphism, but not a retraction. Please note how nondeterminism is introduced for the local `el_dvice` aspect. ∘

Let an inheritance schema be given. If we have a surjective inheritance morphism $h : t \to u$ not (yet) in the schema, we can use it in two ways to enlarge the schema:

- if t is already in the schema, we create u and connect it to the schema via $h : t \to u$,
- if u is already in the schema, we create t and connect it to the schema via $h : t \to u$.

The first construction step corresponds to *specialization*, the second one to *abstraction*.

The most popular object–oriented construction is *specialization*, constructing the inheritance schema in a top–down fashion, adding more and more details. For example, the inheritance schema in Example 2.6 was constructed this way, moving from **thing** to **el_dvice** and **calculator**, etc. By "inheritance", many people mean just specialization.

The reverse construction, however, makes sense, too: *abstraction* means to grow the inheritance schema upward, hiding details (but not forgetting them: beware of side effects!). Taking our example inheritance schema, if we find out later on that computers – among others – belong to the sensitive items in a company which require special safety measures, we might consider introducing a template **sensitive** as an abstraction of **computer**.

Both specialization and abstraction may occur in *multiple* versions: we have *several* templates, say $u_1, \ldots, u_n$, already in the schema and construct a new one, say t, by relating it to $u_1, \ldots, u_n$ simultaneously. In the case of specialization, i.e., $h_i : t \rightarrow u_i$ for $i = 1, \ldots, n$, it is common to speak of "multiple inheritance". In the case of abstraction, i.e., $h_i : u_i \rightarrow t$ for $i = 1, \ldots, n$, we may speak of *generalization*.

Example 2.19 : Referring to Example 2.6 and assuming top–down construction, the template for **computer** is constructed by multiple specialization (multiple inheritance) from **el_dvice** and **calculator**. ∘

Example 2.20 : If we would have constructed the schema in Definition 2.6 in a bottom–up way, we would have obtained **thing** as a generalization of **el_dvice** and **calculator**.

A less contrived example of generalization, however, is the following: if we have templates **person** and **company** in our schema, we might encounter the need to generalize both to **contract_partner**. ∘

We note in passing that, with respect to objects, we have two kinds of generalization. For a computer c, its c**.thing** aspect is a proper generalization of its c**.el_dvice** and c**.calculator** aspects. We would not expect to have an object, however, which is both a person and a company. Thus, the proper generalization **contract_partner** of **person** and **company** in the schema would only appear as single object abstractions p**.person** $\rightarrow$ p**.contract_partner** or c**.company** $\rightarrow$ c**.contract_partner** on the instance level, but not as a proper object generalization.

2.5 Interaction

When we build an object–oriented system, we must provide an *object community* (cf. Definition 2.8). Without it, the very notion of object does not make sense. In what follows, we investigate how to construct such an object community: which are the interaction morphisms of interest, and how are they used to grow the community step by step?

The basic mechanism of interaction in our approach is *sharing parts*, as illustrated in example 2.4. In the simplest case, the shared part may be a single action, modeling a "global" action which is seen by all objects sharing it. In this case, the "part" plays the role of a communication *port*, and the shared ports can be seen as a communication *channel*, allowing for symmetric and synchronous communication.

Other forms of communication (asymmetric, asynchronous,...) can be modeled and explained on these grounds, but we cannot go into detail here. Please note that shared parts playing the role of communication channels are objects themselves! Thus, they may have static structure (observable attributes) as well as dynamic behavior (the communication protocol).

As with inheritance morphisms, we found that interaction morphisms are *epimorphisms* in all meaningful cases. And this makes sense, too. An interaction morphism $h : a{\bullet}t \rightarrow b{\bullet}u$ tells that the aspect $a{\bullet}t$ has the part $b{\bullet}u$, and how this part is affected by its embedding into the whole: this has to be specified for *all* items in the part!

As with inheritance morphisms, we found that *retractions* model an especially meaningful case of part–of relationship, namely *encapsulated* parts which are not affected by events outside their scope.

Example 2.21 : Referring to Example 2.4, the interaction morphisms

$$\texttt{CYY.cpu} \longrightarrow \texttt{CBZ.cable} \longleftarrow \texttt{PXX.powsply}$$

express that the cable CBZ is a shared part of the cpu CYY and the power supply PXX.

Suppose the events relevant for cables are voltage level observation and switch–on/switch–off actions. The sharing expresses that, if the power supply is switched on, the cable and the cpu are switched on at the same time, etc. If the cable's voltage level depends only on the shared switch actions, the cable is an encapsulated part of both cpu and power supply, and the interaction morphisms are retractions. If, however, events from outside can influence the voltage level (say, by magnetic induction), then the sharing morphisms are just epimorphisms, no retractions. ∘

Let an object community be given. If we have a surjective interaction morphism $h : a{\bullet}t \rightarrow b{\bullet}u$ not (yet) in the community, we can use h in two ways to enlarge it:

- if $a{\bullet}t$ is already in the community, we create $b{\bullet}u$ and connect it to the community via $h : a{\bullet}t \rightarrow b{\bullet}u$,
- if $b{\bullet}u$ is already in the community, we create $a{\bullet}t$ and connect it to the community via $h : a{\bullet}t \rightarrow b{\bullet}u$.

After connecting the new morphism to the community, we have to close it with respect to the schema (cf. Definition 2.7), i.e., add all aspects derived from the new one by inheritance.

By *incorporation* we mean the construction step of taking a part and enlarging it by adding new items. Most often the *multiple* version of this is used, taking several parts and aggregating them. We will be back to this.

The reverse construction is also quite often used in the single version, we call it *interfacing*. Interfacing is like abstraction, but it creates an object with a new identity.

Example 2.22 Consider the construction of a database view on top of a database: this is interfacing. Please note that it is quite common to have non–encapsulated interaction: a non–updateable view would display many changes which cannot be explained from local actions! That is, the interaction morphism from the database to its view is not a retraction. ∘

Both incorporation and interfacing may occur in *multiple* versions: we have several objects, say $b_1{\bullet}u_1, \ldots, b_n{\bullet}u_n$, already in the community and construct a new one, say $a.t$, by relating it to $b_1.u_1, \ldots, b_n.u_n$ simultaneously. In the case of incorporation, i.e., $h_i : a.t \rightarrow b_i.u_i$ for $i = 1, \ldots, n$, we have *aggregation* as mentioned above. In the case of interfacing, i.e., $h_i : b_i.u_i \rightarrow a.t$ for $i = 1, \ldots, n$, we have *synchronization* by sharing.

The latter was illustrated above in Example 2.18 (cf. also Example 2.4). An example for aggregation is the following.

Example 2.23 : Referring again to Example 2.4, suppose that `PXX.powsply` and `CYY.cpu` have been constructed and we want to assemble them (and other parts which we ignore here) to form our `SUN.computer`. Then we have to aggregate the parts and provide the epimorphisms (retractions in this case?) f: `SUN.computer` $\rightarrow$ `PXX.powsply` and g: `SUN.computer` $\rightarrow$ `CYY.cpu` showing the relationships to the parts. Please note that f sends the cpu items within the `SUN` to 1, while it sends the power supply items to themselves (modulo renaming). The same holds for g, with cpu taking the place of power supply. ○

It is remarkable how much symmetry the inheritance and interaction constructions display. Their mathematical core is the same, namely epimorphisms between aspects. Taking the constructions in either direction and considering single and multiple versions, we arrive at the following table:

Object Constructs	*inheritance*	*interaction*
small-to-big/single	specialization	incorporation
small-to-big/multiple	mult. specialization	aggregation
big-to-small/single	abstraction	interfacing
big-to-small/multiple	generalization	synchronization

For each of these cases, we also have the encapsulated variant where the epimorphisms are retractions.

3 Object–Oriented Specification Approaches

3.1 FOOPS

FOOPS [GM87, GW90] (Functional Object-Oriented Programming System) is an object–oriented programming system with a declarative functional style. It is designed to preserve the essence of both functional and object–oriented programming: functional programming provides abstract data types for object attribute values, while object–oriented programming limits access to an object's state via methods associated with the specific object. In FOOPS, data elements are unchanging entities, while objects are persistent but changing entities.

Among many other concepts, FOOPS knows *functional* and *object* modules. Very roughly speaking, *functional modules* correspond to definitions of abstract data types in OBJ3 [GW88]. The underlying logic employs conditional equations and a form of sort inheritance via subsorting. The semantics is constructed by initial algebras. *Object modules* allow to define specific methods and attributes by means of conditional equations. Objects modules with a distinguished object sort correspond to classes. The state of an object – the attribues (or more generally the observable properties) – may change when certain methods are performed on it. Special methods, *new* and *remove* for object creation and deletion, are provided with any object module. Object modules are allowed to have sub–modules, thus providing a form of class inheritance. Three different kinds of semantics have been proposed for the object level:

- A *reflective semantics* representing the FOOPS database and all object manipulating methods as a functional module, i.e., as an abstract data type.
- A *direct algebraic semantics* employing hidden sorts to model states.
- A *sheaf semantics* modelling objects as sheaves and systems as collections of sheaves and sheaf morphisms.

As an example we consider a FOOPS specification describing integer cells in an object–oriented fashion. An attribute `get` and a method `set` are defined as follows

```
omod CELL                               \* object module     *\
  cl Cell                               \* class             *\
  pr INT                                \* protecting        *\
  at get : Cell -> Int                  \* attribute         *\
  me set : Cell Int -> Cell             \* method            *\
  eq get(set(C,N)) = N                  \* equation          *\
endo                                    \* end object module *\
```

FOOPS has a sophisticated user–defined syntax and therefore it is possible to denote this specification in the more readable form given below. Additionally, an operation `declare_: Integer` for the declaration of variables is introduced. The definition of this operation employs the method `new` provided automatically with each class.

```
omod CELL                                  \* object module     *\
  cl Cell                                  \* class             *\
  pr INT                                   \* protecting        *\
  at _ : Cell -> Int                       \* attribute         *\
  me _:=_ : Cell Int -> Cell               \* method            *\
  eq C := N = N                            \* equation          *\
  op (declare_: Integer) : Id -> Cell      \* operation         *\
  eq declare I : Integer = new(I)          \* equation          *\
endo                                       \* end object module *\
```

Using this definition of CELL, one can create new cell objects and apply methods to them in a convenient way. For example, FOOPS can evaluate the following lines.

```
declare x : Integer ;
declare y : Integer ;
x := 5 ;
y := x .
```

Generally speaking, object modules like those given above denote *theories* which specify "templates" as introduced in section 2. The power of specifying object dynamics, i.e. processes, is not quite clear, but there seem to be limitations, especially concerning the capability to specify infinite (non-terminating) behavior and full concurrency.

In the hidden-sorted algebra approach to semantics (cf. [Go91], object identities are associated with particular models of theories where each such model is a particular algebra of possible process states. The permissible algebras are given by observational equivalence.

Inheritance relationships are modeled at the syntactic level, by theory morphisms. The corresponding semantic relationship between aspects of the same object is not discussed in the FOOPS literature, but it seems that "cryptomorphisms" as introduced in [TBG89] (or, rather, their opposites) can do the job [Go92].

Using cryptomorphisms, it is also possible to model interaction along the lines outlined in section 2 [Go92]. So far, this point has not been emphasized in the FOOPS literature.

In conclusion, barring details which still have to be worked out, FOOPS has the potential of expressing all object-oriented concepts and constructions as outlined in section 2.

3.2 Entity Algebras

Entity algebras [Re91] provide models for data types, processes, and objects. They are special partial algebras with predicates [BW82] including the following features:

- The elements of certain sorts represent *dynamic elements*, called entities. Their dynamics is realized by allowing to perform labelled transitions.
- Entities may have *subcomponents*. The structure of these subcomponent entities is not fixed but can be defined by appropriate operations and axioms.
- Entities are given *identities* so that subcomponents can be retrieved and sharing of subcomponents can be described.

The entity algebra approach is based on previous work by the Genova and Passau Abstract Data Type groups (see for instance [AR87a, AR87b, AGRZ89, BZ89]). Another feature is that the approach distinguishes between *specifications-in-the-small* corresponding to usual specifications of dynamic systems as abstract data types and *specifications-in-the-large* suitable for expressing abstract properties of classes of dynamic systems.

Entity specifications distinguish between static sorts (like `int` or `bool`) and dynamic sorts (like `queue-with-state`). For each dynamic sort `s` providing the values of sort `s`, there are additionally sorts `ident(s)` and `ent(s)`. The elements in `ident(s)` are the identities for sort `s` and `ent(s)` represents the entities of sort `s`. Consequently, there is an operation

$$\_:\_ : \mathtt{ident(s)} \times \mathtt{s} \rightarrow \mathtt{ent(s)}$$

for the construction of entities. Dynamics is realized by providing a sort `lab(s)` where the possible transitions (or labels) for entities are collected (e.g., labels like `remove` or `put` for entity sort `queue-with-state`). The concrete behavior of entities is specified by axioms for predicates of the form

$$\_ \texttt{---\_--->} \_ : \texttt{ent(s)} \times \texttt{lab(s)} \times \texttt{ent(s)}$$

Thus, the process model in this approach is labelled transition systems. Please note that the entities (or objects) are constructed by giving an identity and a current value for the object state. Therefore, elements in dynamic sorts are object states rather than (abstract) objects. The same holds for the object-oriented algebraic specification language OS introduced by Ruth Breu [Bre91].

The following specification defines an object-oriented version of data type queue. The entities of sort `ent(queue)` represent the objects of the class queue, the elements in `ident(queue)` are the identifiers for queues.

```
enrich INT by
  dsorts queue
  opns
    Empty : -> queue                                      total
    Get : queue -> ident(int)
    Remove : ent(queue) -> ent(queue)
    Put : ent(int) x queue -> queue
    A, B, ..., ABC, ... -> ident(queue)
    _.Empty : ident(queue) -> lab(queue)                  total
    _=_.Get : ident(int) x ident(queue) -> lab(queue)     total
    _.Remove : ident(queue) -> lab(queue)                 total
    _.Put(_) : ident(queue) x ent(int) -> lab(queue)      total
  preds
    _Diff_ : ident(queue) x ident(queue)
    Unused : ident(int) x queue
  axioms
    A Diff B ... A Diff ABC ...
    Get(Put(id:i,Empty)) = id
    DEF(Get(q)) => Get(Put(ei,q)) = Get(q)
    Remove(id:Put(ei,Empty)) = id:Empty
    Remove(id:q)=eq => Remove(id,Put(ei,q))=eq
    Unused(id,Empty)
    id Diff id' & Unused(id,q) => Unused(id,Put(id':i,q))
    Unused(id,q) => DEF(Put(id:i,q))
    id:q ---id.Empty---> id:Empty
    DEF(Put(ei,q)) => ( id:q ---id.Put(ei)---> id:Put(ei,q) )
    DEF(Remove(q)) => ( id:q ---id.Remove---> id:Remove(q) )
    ...
end enrich
```

Operations which have the sorts queue or `ent(queue)` as argument or result sorts – in this case `Empty`, `Put`, `Remove`, and `Get` – define the methods of class queue. The application of methods is specified by giving axioms for the transition predicate. Transitions are labelled by sending appropriate messages. If we now have the queue object `MYQUEUE:Put(INT_ENT1,Put(INT_ENT2,Empty))` (provided `int` objects `INT_ENT1` and `INT_ENT2 are given)`, the application of the methods `MYQUEUE.Remove` and `MYQUEUE.Empty` yield `MYQUEUE:Put(INT_ENT1,Empty)` and `MYQUEUE:Empty`, respectively.

Based on the algebraic semantics of processes as developed in [AR87a, AR87b], the semantics can be given by various observational equivalences, for example (generalized) bisimulation.

The literature on entity algebras does not address inheritance and interaction explicitly. A concept which compares with template (aspect) morphisms as described in section 2 is missing, but inheritance and interaction can probably be handled by different means and on different levels of abstraction. However, it would be interesting to see whether the entity algebra approach can be extended to include inheritance and interaction on the abstraction level of section 2.

Entity algebras do have a concept for subcomponents which can be shared, providing a means of symmetric and synchronous interaction as described in section 2. Together with the algebraic approach to concurrency invented in [AR87a], powerful means for expressing interaction of processes are available, with different kinds of parallelism and even with higher-order processes.

3.3 OBLOG

The languages OBLOG [CSS89] (OBject LOGic) and its successor TROLL [JHSS91] (Textual Representation of an Object Logic Language) were developed hand in hand with the conceptual framework outlined in section 2. Information systems are described as communities of interacting objects. Object templates specify processes and observations on these processes.

The languages employ features of *equational logic* for the specification of data, events, and identities and they use elements of *temporal*, *dynamic*, and *deontic logic* for system behavior and abstract system properties. Object templates introduce the objects' attributes characterising the objects' state and define the actions (called "events" in the language) modifying these attributes. The effect of performing actions is described by valuation rules. Additionally, safety and liveness properties can be specified.

As a specification example for the TROLL language, we consider a bank account. After importing the data types used, the attribute section determines the observable properties of accounts. The events (i.e., actions) specify the possible state transitions. Both, attribute values and state transitions have to satisfy the conditions given in the constraints part. The valuation section defines the effect of events, and the behavior part states permissions and obligations for events to occur, employing a deontic logic.

```
TEMPLATE account
  DATA TYPES |BankCustomer|, money, bool, UpdateType
  ATTRIBUTES
    CONSTANT Holder:|BankCustomer|
```

```
    CONSTANT Type:{checking,saving}
    Balance:money
    CreditLimit:money
    DERIVED MaxWithdrawal:money
  EVENTS
    BIRTH open(Holder:|BankCustomer|, Type:{checking,saving})
    DEATH close
    new_credit_limit(Amount:money)
    accept_update(Type:UpdateType, Amount:money)
    update_failed
    withdrawal(Amount:money)
    deposit(Amount:money)
  CONSTRAINTS
    INITIAL CreditLimit = 0
  DERIVATION
    MaxWithdrawal = Balance + CreditLimit
  VALUATION
    VARIABLES m:money
    [new_credit_limit(m)] CreditLimit = m
    [withdrawal(m)] Balance = Balance - m
    [deposit(m)] Balance = Balance + m
    ...
  BEHAVIOR
    PERMISSIONS
      VARIABLES t,t1:UpdateType; m,m1,m2:money
      { Balance = 0 } close
      { NOT SOMETIME(AFTER(accept_update(t1,m1)))
          SINCE LAST(AFTER(update_failed) OR
                     AFTER(deposit(m2)) OR
                     AFTER(withdrawal(m2))) } accept_update(t,m)
      ...
     OBLIGATIONS ...
END TEMPLATE account
```

The semantics of such specifications is not fully worked out yet, but there are semantic models available which have been designed for this purpose, meeting all requirements described in section 2.

Essentially, these models provide categorial process models which can be used for formalizing these conceps: processes formalizing templates, and process morphisms formalizing template morphisms. This way, there is a heavy emphasis on object *dynamics*.

In what follows, we briefly outline one particular such model (cf. [ES91] for more detail).

The basic event structure is an *event monoid* $\bar{E} = (E, \|, 1)$ which is associative, commutative, idempotent, and satisfies the cancellation law. Intuitively, $\|$ denotes simultaneous occurrence of events, and 1 denotes the empty event.

Event monoids $\bar{E}_i = (E_i, \|_i, 1_i)$, $i = 1, 2$, can be related by *event monoid mor-*

phisms $h : \bar{E}_1 \to \bar{E}_2$ which are structure preserving maps $h : E_1 \to E_2$ satisfying the properties $h(1_1) = 1_2$ and $h(e_1 \parallel_1 e_2) = h(e_1) \parallel_2 h(e_2)$. Henceforth, we will omit the indexes from $\parallel$ and 1 as long as there is no danger of confusion.

Let $\bar{E} = (E, \parallel, 1)$ be an event monoid. A subset $M \subseteq E$ is called a *menu*: it might appear on a screen as a selection of events (actions and observations) which may occur next. For a collection α of menues, $\bigcup \alpha$ denotes the union of these menues, i.e., $\bigcup \alpha = \{e \mid \exists M \epsilon \alpha : e \epsilon M\}$.

A *process* over an alphabet $\bar{E}$ is a map $\mu : E^* \to 2^{2^E}$ satisfying the following conditions for each $\tau \epsilon E^*$:

1. $\bigcup \mu(\tau) \epsilon \mu(\tau)$
2. $\forall X, Y \subseteq E \ : \ X \subseteq Y \subseteq \bigcup \mu(\tau) \ \wedge \ X \epsilon \mu(\tau) \ \Rightarrow \ Y \epsilon \mu(\tau)$

The intuition might help that each $M \epsilon \mu(\tau)$ corresponds to a state of knowledge about what might possibly occur next after the history τ of the system.

Let $\mu_i : E_i^* \to 2^{2^{E_i}}$, $i = 1, 2$, be processes over alphabets $\bar{E}_1$ and $\bar{E}_2$, respectively. Let $h : \bar{E}_1 \to \bar{E}_2$ be a monoid morphism. h is called a *process morphism* iff the following condition holds:

$$h(\mu_1(\tau)) \subseteq \mu_2(h(\tau)) \text{ for each } \tau \epsilon E_1^* .$$

In this notation, h is extended to traces as well as sets and families of sets by elementwise application. For example, $h(ef) = h(e)h(f)$ and $h(\{\{a\}, \{a, b\}\}) = \{\{h(a)\}, \{h(a), h(b)\}\}$.

It is not hard to prove that processes and process morphisms as defined above form a category. We call this category *NDM*, the *N*on-*D*eterministic *M*enu model.

We cannot develop the mathematics of *NDM* in this paper. We claim, however, that

- *NDM* is complete, and limits reflect parallel composition,
- *NDM* is cocomplete, and colimits reflect internal choice.

Therefore, this model is especially well suited to model the object–oriented concepts explained in section 2. The reader is referred to [ES91] for further details.

3.4 Processes as Abstract Data Types

There are various approaches for the specification of processes by algebraic methods, by Bergstra and Klop [BK86], by the Berlin Abstract Data Type group [EPPB+90], by Kaplan [Kap89], and others. The main idea behind these approaches is to introduce sorts for actions and processes explicitly and to provide operations like prefixing, parallel composition, choice, etc., for the combination of processes. The logic employs (conditional) equations. On the semantic side, the approaches use continuous algebras, projection spaces, or some form of observational or behavioral semantics.

It is perhaps not fair to evaluate these approaches on the basis of how well they meet requirements of object–orientation, since most of them do not claim to do so.

But there are quite a few allusions – more or less vague – that these approaches might be useful for the theory of objects, so a few remarks are in order.

The general idea is to give an object–oriented flavor by adding identification to processes. For instance, Große–Rhode [GR91] considers the following concepts: *objects as states* (the state of the system is the aggregation of all local object states); *objects for local behavior* (local process specifications define the dynamic behavior of objects); *class definitions* (Berlin module specifications serve as class definitions which are similar to object templates in the sense of section 2); *class combinators* (class combinators are the usual Berlin module operations building large modules from smaller ones); *(strict) inheritance:* (inheritance corresponds to union, import actualization or extension of modules). Objects are defined only on the syntactic level, they are enrichments of the specification representing the state of the system. The semantics of state changes of processes consists of the syntactic modification of the underlying specification.

Berlin module specifications are also used by Parisi-Presicce and Pierantonio [PP91] in order to explain inheritance mechanisms in object–oriented programming.

Another effort following these lines is CMSL (Conceptual Model Specification Language) proposed by Wieringa [Wie91].

Although some object–oriented concepts can be expressed in these approaches, there are some problems with this approach. *Inheritance* is no problem, at least not on the theory (or template) level: like in the FOOPS approach, specification or theory morphisms do the job. On the instance level, however, an obvious concept for modeling inheritance or interaction is missing.

The main problem is with *identification.* The problems with inheritance and interaction are consequences of identification problems. The relevant question here is: *what is the unit identified?*

One obvious unit of identification is a specification (or theory) specifying some kind of object (aspect), i.e., a template. However, object identification is a little more demanding than just giving names to templates. Rather, what is needed is a *dynamic* mechanism for generating, maintaining, and destroying objects (aspects) as named units *"at runtime"*. Object classes are time–varying collections of objects (aspects) with *different* names but with the *same* template. This is an essential feature of object–orientation, it is one of the reasons why, for example, MODULA2 is not considered object–oriented.

In most of the algebraic approaches mentioned above, the way of handling this is to introduce a sort `ID` of identities and introduce `ID` as a parameter sort for the create operation(s). For example, instead of `create:→stack`, we have `create:ID→stack`. This way, however, we obtain what we might call *a set of named process states* instead of a set of process states within a named object. That is, the named unit is an *object state* rather than an object. Moreover, all states of all objects are grouped together in one structure (carrier of an algebra).

As a consequence, algebra morphisms preserving this structure do not appropriately reflect inheritance and interaction at the instance level. For example, it is not possible to express formally that a user interacts with one specific stack, not with all the others around, using algebra morphisms that have the carrier set of all states of all stacks as source or target, respectively.

4 Conclusions

Let us first summarize the object-oriented concepts and constructions of section 2. Templates are generic objects without individual identity. Identities are associated with templates to represent aspects of individual objects. Interaction is a relationship between different objects, while inheritance relates aspects of the same object. Objects and aspects appear as members of classes. A class is again an aspect with a time-varying set of aspects as members. Since classes are objects or aspects of objects, there is no difficulty in constructing meta-classes having classes of different types as members.

By means of an object-oriented approach, systems can be elegantly described as communities of interacting objects. As has been pointed out, the notion of an object only makes sense within an object community. Please remember that an object community must be closed with respect to inheritance and must provide unique identifiers for objects, among others.

The algebraic approaches to object specification and semantics investigated in this paper suggests that an appropriate theory of objects should be based on processes rather than data types. This is obvious in the approaches investigated in sections 3.2 and 3.3. At first sight, the FOOPS approach described in section 3.1 seems to contradict this conclusion, but a closer look reveals that it does not: by employing hidden sorts and observational equivalence, this approach is based on an algebraic state machine model of processes rather than abstract data types.

It should be mentioned that not everything relevant to object specification – i.e., specification of object communities – is addressed in this paper. A full-fledged language and system for specification and design must provide means for specifying data types, (types of) identities, inheritance schemata (e.g., for specialization and generalization), interaction schemata (e.g., for aggregation and synchronization patterns), generic modules and actualization, classes and instances, etc.

The important issue of object reification (or implementation or refinement) has not been addressed in this paper. A satisfactory treatment is still missing, but there are promising approaches borrowing ideas from abstract data type implementation and from process refinement.

Acknowledgements

Thanks to all colleagues who contributed to the development of ideas presented here. Special thanks are due to our COMPASS collegues Egidio Astesiano, Hartmut Ehrig, Martin Große-Rhode, and Gianna Reggio for stimulating discussions on algebraic process theory, and to the ISCORE partners who took part in developing object theory and specification language features. In particular, Cristina Sernadas participated in discussing the basic ideas of objects and object descriptions. She, Ralf Jungclaus, Thorsten Hartmann, and Gunter Saake were involved in defining the TROLL language. Thanks to Ralf Jungclaus and Thorsten Hartmann for providing the TROLL example. Felix Costa's contributions to object semantics are greatfully acknowledged.

Special thanks are due to Joseph Goguen and Egidio Astesiano for correcting errors and misconceptions in an earlier draft of this paper. Of course, the authors are fully responsible for all errors that are still there.

References

[AR87a] Astesiano,A.;Reggio,G.: An outline of the SMoLCS approach. Proc. Advanced School on Mathematical Models for Parallelism (M.Venturini Zilli, ed.), LNCS 280, Springer–Verlag, Berlin 1987, 81–113

[AR87b] Astesiano,A.;Reggio,G.: SMoLCS–driven concurrent calculi. Proc. TAPSOFT'87 Vol.1, (H.Ehrig et al, eds.), LNCS 249, Springer–Verlag, Berlin 1987, 169–201

[AGRZ89] Astesiano,E.;Giovini,A.;Reggio,G.;Zucca,E.: An integrated algebraic approach to the specification of data types, processes, and objects. Proc. Algebraic Methods - Tools and Applications, LNCS 394, 1989, 91–116

[Be91] Beeri,C.: Theoretical Foundations for OODB's – a Personal Perspective. Database Engineering, to appear

[BK86] Bergstra,J.A.;Klop,J.W.: Algebra of communicating processes. CWI Monographs Series, Proc. of the CWI Symposium Mathmatics and Computer Science, North–Holland, Amsterdam 1986, 89–138

[BOS91] Butterworth,P.;Otis,A.;Stein,J.: The GemStone Object Database Management System. Comm. ACM 34 (1991), 64–77

[Bre91] Breu,R.: Algebraic specification techniques in object–oriented programming environments. Ph.D. Thesis, Passau University; also: LNCS, Springer 1991.

[BW82] Broy,M.;Wirsing,M.: Partial abstract types. Acta Informatica 18, 1982, 47–64

[BZ89] Breu,R.;Zucca,E.: An algebraic compositional semantics of an object–oriented notation with concurrency. Proc 9th Conf. on Foundations of Software Technology and Theoretical Computer Science, LNCS 405, 1989, 131–142

[CP89] Cook,W.;Palsberg,J.: A Denotational Semantics of Inheritance and its Correctness. Proc. OOPSLA'89, ACM Press, 433–443

[CS91] Costa,J.-F.;Sernadas,A.: Process Models within a Categorial Framework. INESC Research Report, Lisbon 1991, submitted for publication

[CSS89] Costa,J.-F.;Sernadas,A.;Sernadas,C.: OBL–89 User's Manual – Version 2.3. Internal Report, INESC Lisbon 1989.

[CSS91] Costa,J.-F.;Sernadas,A.;Sernadas,C.: Objects as Non–Sequential Machines. Information Systems – Correctness and Reusability, Proc. ISCORE Workshop'91 (G.Saake, A.Sernadas, eds.), Informatik–Berichte 91–03, Tech. Univ. Braunschweig 1991, 25–60

[Cu91] Cusack,E.: Refinement, Conformance and Inheritance. Formal Aspects of Computing 3 (1991), 129–141

[De91] Deux,O. et al: The O_2 System. Comm. ACM 34 (1991), 35–48

[DMN67] Dahl,O.-J.;Myrhaug,B.;Nygaard,K.: SIMULA 67, Common Base Language. Norwegian Computer Center, Oslo 1967

[EBO91] Ehrig,H.;Baldamus,M.;Orejas,F.: New concepts for amalgamation and extension in the framework of specification logics. Technical Report No. 91/05, Computer Science Department, TU Berlin 1991.

[EGS91] Ehrich,H.-D.;Goguen,J.A.;Sernadas,A.: A Categorial Theory of Objects as Observed Processes. Proc. REX/FOOL School/Workshop, deBakker,J.W. et. al. (eds.), LNCS 489, Springer–Verlag, Berlin 1991, 203–228

[EPPB+90] Ehrig,H.; Parisi-Presicce,F.; Boehm,P.; Rieckhoff,C.; Dimitrovici,Ch.; Große-Rhode,M.: Combining data type specifications and recursive process specifications using projection algebras. Theoretical Computer Science 71 1990, 347–380

[ESS90] Ehrich,H.-D.;Sernadas,A.;Sernadas,C.: From Data Types to Object Types. Journal of Information Processing and Cybernetics EIK 26 (1990) 1/2, 33–48

[ES90] Ehrich,H.-D.;Sernadas,A.: Algebraic Implementation of Objects over Objects. Proc. REX Workshop on Stepwise Refinement of Distributed Systems: Models, Formalism, Correctness. deBakkerJ.W.;deRoever,W.-P.; Rozenberg,G. (eds.), LNCS 430, Springer–Verlag, Berlin 1990, 239–266

[ES91] Ehrich,H.-D.;Sernadas,A.: Fundamental Object Concepts and Constructions. Information Systems – Correctness and Reusability, Proc. ISCORE Workshop'91 (G.Saake, A.Sernadas, eds.), Informatik–Berichte 91–03, Tech. Univ. Braunschweig 1991, 1–24

[FCSM91] Fiadeiro,J.;Costa,J.-F.;Sernadas,A.;Maibaum,T.: (Terminal) Process Semantics of Temporal Logic Specification. Unpublished draft, Dept. of Computing, Imperial College, London 1991

[Fi87] Fishman,D. et al: IRIS: An Object–Oriented Database Management System. ACM Trans. Off. Inf. Sys. 5 (1987)

[FM91a] Fiadeiro,J.;Maibaum,T.: Describing, Structuring and Implementing Objects. Proc. REX/FOOL School/Workshop, deBakker,J.W. et. al. (eds.), LNCS 489, Springer–Verlag, Berlin 1991

[FM91b] Fiadeiro,J.;Maibaum,T.: Temporal Theories as Modularisation Units for Concurrent System Specification, to appear in Formal Aspects of Computing

[FS91] Fiadeiro,J.;Sernadas,A.: Logics of Modal Terms for System Specification. Journal of Logic and Computation 1 (1991), 357–395

[FSMS90] Fiadeiro,J.;Sernadas,C.;Maibaum,T.;Saake,G.: Proof–Theoretic Semantics of Object–Oriented Specification Constructs. Proc. IFIP 2.6 Working Conference DS-4, Meersman,R.;Kent,W. (eds.), North–Holland, Amsterdam 1991

[GKS91] Gottlob,G.;Kappel,G.;Schrefl,M.: Semantics of Object–Oriented Data Models — The Evolving Algebra Approach. Proc. Int. Workshop on Information Systems for the 90's, Schmidt,J.W. (ed.), Springer LNCS 1991

[GM87] Goguen,J.A.;Meseguer,J.: Unifying functional, object–oriented and relational programming with logical semantics. Research Direction in Object-Oriented Programming, B.Shriver,P.Wegner (eds.), MIT Press 1987, 417–477

[Go73] Goguen,J.: Categorical Foundations for General Systems Theory. Advances in Cybernetics and Systems Research, Transcripta Books, 1973, 121–130

[Go75] Goguen,J.: Objects. International Journal of General Systems, 1 (1975), 237–243

[Go89] Goguen,J.: A Categorical Manifesto. Technical Report PRG-72, Programming Research Group, Oxford University, March 1989. To appear in Mathematical Structures in Computer Science.

[Go90] Goguen,J.: Sheaf Semantics of Concurrent Interacting Objects, 1990. To appear in Mathematical Structures in Computer Science.

[Go91] Goguen,J.: Types as Theories. Proc. Conf. on Topology and Category Theory in Computer Science, Oxford University Press 1991, 357–390

[Go92] Goguen,J.: personal communication

[GR83] Goldberg,A.;Robson,D.: Smalltalk 80: The Language and its Implementation. Addison–Wesley, New York 1983

[GR91] Große–Rhode,M.: Towards object–oriented algebraic specifications. Proc. 7th Workshop on Specification of Abstract Data Types, Wusterhausen (Dosse), H. Ehrig, K.P. Jantke, F. Orejas, H. Reichel (Eds.), LNCS 534, 1991

[GW88] Goguen,J.A.;Winkler,T.: Introducing OBJ3. SRI International, Technical Report SRI-CSL-88-9, 1988.

[GW90] Goguen,J.;Wolfram,D.: On Types and FOOPS. Proc. IFIP 2.6 Working Conference DS-4, Meersman,R.;Kent,W. (eds.), North–Holland, Amsterdam 1991

[HC89] Hayes,F.;Coleman,D.: Objects and Inheritance: An Algebraic View. Technical Memo, HP Labs, Information Management Lab, Bristol 1989

[Hei88] Heitz,M.: HOOD: A Hierarchical Object–Oriented Design Method. Proc. 3rd German Ada Users Congress, Munich 1988, 12-1 - 12-9

[JHSS91] Jungclaus,R.;Hartmann,T.;Saake,G.;Sernadas,C.: Introduction to TROLL — A Language for Object–Oriented Specification of Information Systems. Information Systems - Correctness and Reusability, Proc. ISCORE Workshop'91 (G.Saake, A.Sernadas, eds.), Informatik–Berichte 91–03, Tech. Univ. Braunschweig 1991, 97–128

[JSH91] Jungclaus, R.; Saake, G.; Hartmann, T.:Language Features for Object-Oriented Conceptual Modeling. In:Proc. 10th Int. Conf. on the ER-approach (T.J. Teorey,ed.), San Mateo, E/R Institute 1991, 309–324.

[JSHS91] Jungclaus,R.;Saake,G.;Hartmann,T.;Sernadas,C.: Object–Oriented Specification of Information Systems: The TROLL Language. Informatik–Bericht, TU Braunschweig 1991. To appear

[JSS90] Jungclaus,R.;Saake,G.;Sernadas,C.: Using Active Objects for Query Processing. Proc. IFIP 2.6 Working Conference DS-4, Meersman,R.;Kent,W. (eds.), North–Holland, Amsterdam 1991

[JSS91] Jungclaus,R.;Saake,G.;Sernadas,C.: Formal Specification of Object Systems. Proc. TAPSOFT'91, Abramsky,S.;Maibaum,T.S.E. (eds.), Brighton (UK) 1991

[Kap89] Kaplan,S.: Algebraic specification of concurrent systems. Theoretical Computer Science, 1989.

[Ke88] Kerth,N,: MOOD: A Methodology for Structured Object–Oriented Design. Tutorial presented at OOPSLA'88, San Diego 1988

[Ki88] Kim,W. et al: Features of the ORION Object–Oriented DBMS. In Object–Oriented Concepts, Databases, and Applications, Kim,W. and Lochovsky,E.H. (eds.), Addison–Wesley 1988

[Ki90] Kim,W.: Object–Oriented Databases: Definition and Research Directions. IEEE Transactions on Knowledge and Data Engineering 2 (1990), 327–341

[LP90] Lin,H.;Pong,M.: Modelling Multiple Inheritance with Colimits. Formal Aspects of Computing 2 (1990), 301–311

[Me88] Meyer,B.: Object–Oriented Software Construction. Prentice–Hall, Englewood Cliffs 1988

[Me91] Meseguer,J.: Conditional Rewriting Logic as a Unified Model of Concurrency. Technical Report SRI–CSL–91–05, Computer Science Laboratory, SRI International, Menlo Park 1991

[PP91] Parisi-Presicce,F.;Pierantonio,A.: Towards the algebraic specification of classes in object–oriented programming. Bulletin of the EATCS, Vol. 45,1991, 86-97

[Re91] Reggio,G.: Entities: Institutions for dynamic systems. Proc. 7th Workshop on Specification of Abstract Data Types, Wusterhausen (Dosse), H. Ehrig, K.P. Jantke, F. Orejas, H. Reichel (Eds.), LNCS 534, 1991

[SE90] Sernadas,A.;Ehrich,H.-D.: What is an object, after all ? Proc. IFIP 2.6 Working Conference DS-4, Meersman,R.;Kent,W. (eds.), North-Holland, Amsterdam 1991

[SEC90] Sernadas,A.;Ehrich,H.-D.;Costa,J.-F.: From Processes to Objects. The INESC Journal of Research and Development 1 (1990), 7–27

[SGGSR91] Sernadas, C.; Gouveia, P.; Gouveia, J.; Sernadas, A.; Resende, P.: The Reification Dimension in Object-oriented Database Design. Proc. Int. Workshop on Specification of Database Systems, Glasgow 1991, Springer-Verlag, to appear

[SFSE89] Sernadas,A.;Fiadeiro,J.;Sernadas,C.;Ehrich,H.-D.: The Basic Building Blocks of Information Systems. Proc. IFIP 8.1 Working Conference, Falkenberg,E.; Lindgreen,P. (eds.), North-Holland, Amsterdam 1989, 225–246

[SGCS91] Sernadas,C.;Gouveia,P.;Costa,J.-F.;Sernadas,A.: Graph-theoretic Semantics of Oblog - Diagrammatic Language for Object-oriented Specifications. Information Systems - Correctness and Reusability, Proc. ISCORE Workshop'91 (G.Saake, A.Sernadas, eds.), Informatik-Berichte 91–03, Tech. Univ. Braunschweig 1991, 61–96

[SJ91] Saake,G.;Jungclaus,R.: Specification of Database Applications in the TROLL Language. Proc. Int. Workshop on Specification of Database Systems, Glasgow 1991 , Springer-Verlag, to appear

[SJE91] Saake,G.;Jungclaus,R.;Ehrich,H.-D.: Object-Oriented Specification and Stepwise Refinement. Proc. IFIP TC6 Int'l Workshop on Open Distributed Processing, Berlin 1991, to be published by North-Holland

[SRGS91] Sernadas, C.; Resende, P.; Gouveia, P.; Sernadas, A.: In-the-large Object-oriented Design of Information Systems. Proc IFIP 8.1 Working Conference on the Object-oriented Approach in Information Systems, van Assche, F.; Moulin, B.; Rolland, C. (eds.), Quebec City (Canada) 1991, North Holland, to appear

[SS86] Seidewitz,E.;Stark,M.: General Object-Oriented Software Development. Document No. SEL-86-002, NASA Goddard Space Flight Center, Greenbelt, Maryland 1986

[SSE87] Sernadas,A.;Sernadas,C.;Ehrich,H.-D.: Object-Oriented Specification of Databases: An Algebraic Approach. Proc. 13th VLDB, Stocker,P.M.; Kent,W. (eds.), Morgan-Kaufmann Publ. Inc., Los Altos 1987, 107–116

[SSGRG91] Sernadas,A.;Sernadas,C.;Gouveia,P.;Resende,P.;Gouveia,J.: Oblog - An Informal Introduction, INESC Lisbon, 1991.

[St86] Stroustrup,B.: The C++ Programming Language. Addison Wesley, Reading, Mass. 1986

[TBG89] Tarlecki,A.; Burstall,R.; Goguen,J.: Indexed Categories as a Tool for the Semantics of Computation. Technical Monograph PRG-77, August 1989, Oxford University Computing Laboratory.

[Ve91] Verharen, E.M.: Object-oriented System Development: An Overview. Information Systems - Correctness and Reusability, Proc. ISCORE Workshop'91 (G.Saake, A.Sernadas, eds.), Informatik-Berichte 91–03, Tech. Univ. Braunschweig 1991, 202–234

[We89] Wegner,P.: Learning the Language. Byte 14 (1989), 245–253

[Wie91] Wieringa,R.: A formalization of objects using equational dynamic logic. Proc. 2nd Int. Conf. on Deductive and Object-Oriented Databases, Munich 1991

The Use of Sorts in Algebraic Specifications

Peter D. Mosses *

Computer Science Department, Aarhus University,
Ny Munkegade, Bldg. 540, DK-8000 Aarhus C, Denmark

Abstract. Algebraic specification frameworks exploit a variety of sort disciplines. The treatment of sorts has a considerable influence on the ease with which such features as partiality and polymorphism can be specified. This survey gives an accessible overview of various frameworks, focusing on their sort disciplines and assessing their strengths and weaknesses for practical applications. Familiarity with the basic notions of algebraic specification is assumed.

1 Introduction

We are going to survey the variety of ways in which *sorts* are used in algebraic specifications. Let's agree first on some basic terminology. It is assumed that you are already familiar with the main concepts of algebraic specifications—otherwise see an expository text such as [12] or the Handbook chapter on algebraic specification [52].

An *algebra* consists essentially of a *universe*, or *carrier*, of *values*, together with some distinguished *operations* on values (operations of no arguments being called *constants*). The *signature* of an algebra provides *symbols* for distinguishing the operations. *Terms* are constructed from symbols and *variables*. In a particular algebra, an *assignment* of values to variables determines the values of terms.

An *algebraic specification* determines a signature, and restricts the class of all algebras with that signature using *axioms*: each algebra in the specified class has to *satisfy* all the axioms. An axiom is often just an equation between terms, universally quantified over all the variables that occur in it. A specification may also impose *constraints*, for instance to narrow the specified class to *initial* algebras, or to *reachable* ones. We call an algebra in the specified class a *model* for the specification. The class of specified algebras is generally called an *abstract data type*.[1]

The basic notions of signature, algebra, axiom, and satisfaction can be embellished in various ways, without departing from the fundamental idea of algebraic specification. This flexibility is captured formally by the notion of an *institution* [21, 22]. Roughly, an institution consists of particular kinds of signatures, structures, and axioms together with a satisfaction relation (between structures and axioms) that is invariant under signature translation. The structures may be algebras or they may be more general, e.g., first-order structures that have relations as well as operations; the definitions are formulated abstractly, using category theory. Some

* Internet: pdmosses@daimi.aau.dk

[1] Some authors prefer to reserve *abstract data type* for when the specified algebras form an isomorphism class.

interesting results can be obtained independently of the details of particular institutions, for instance a general framework for modules has been provided [45]. Similarly for the notion of a *specification logic* [13], which is even more general than that of an institution.

The following variations on the theme of algebraic specification—separately or together—correspond to particular institutions or specification logics.

- Operations may be *total* or *partial*.
- Values may be classified by *sorts*, and operations *restricted* to specified sorts of arguments.
- Carriers may be *structured*, e.g., as posets or lattices.
- *Relations* may be allowed, as well as operations.
- Operations may be *nondeterministic*.
- Operations may be *higher-order*, being considered as values themselves.
- Axioms may be restricted to special kinds of formulae, such as equations, conditional equations, Horn clauses, or first-order predicate sentences.
- Constraints may be allowed, e.g., to reachable, initial, or final algebras.
- Observationally or behaviourally equivalent algebras may be included in the class of specified algebras even though they do not satisfy all the specified axioms.

Most of the above variations have been developed with the aim of improving the pragmatic aspects of algebraic specification of abstract data types, to make them better suited for *realistic* applications. Here, we are to focus on the use of *sorts* in algebraic specifications. This is quite a rich topic, particularly relevant to pragmatics. Subsidiary issues include the treatment of partiality and errors, subtypes, polymorphism, and type-checking. We restrict our attention to *first-order* frameworks, deferring a study of higher-order algebraic specifications to a future paper.

2 Sorts

The essence of a *sort* is that it *classifies* a collection of *individual* values, according to some common properties. Thus a sort has an *extension*: the set of individuals that it classifies. But two sorts with the same extension may have different *intension*, and thus remain distinct. For instance, the sort of all integers greater than zero has the same extension as the sort of all natural numbers with a well-defined reciprocal, but these sorts may still be regarded as different; the difference is in their intension. When the *symbol* used to identify a sort is regarded as part of the sort's intension, different sort symbols always identify distinct sorts.

In everyday parlance, we tend to make little distinction between the nouns 'sort', 'type', and 'kind'. The conventional usage of these words in the computer science literature has, however, given them different connotations: *sorts* are rather mundane, subsidiary entities used for 'tidy housekeeping' in logic and algebraic specifications; *types* are generally much more exciting, as they have whole theories built around them, and they are related in interesting ways to logic; *kinds* are merely for classifying types. For simplicity, let's keep to the word 'sort' in this survey, even when we look at unorthodox algebraic specification frameworks where the usage of sorts is quite reminiscent of that of types and kinds. Similarly, we'll use 'individual' rather than 'object' or 'element'.

Now that we have some idea of *what* a sort is, let's consider *why* we should bother at all to specify sorts in algebraic specifications. Why is it useful to classify a collection of individuals?

First of all, classification according to common properties is a fundamental *abstraction* principle, allowing us to perceive (or at least, to express our perception of) order amongst chaos. Simply by classifying a particular set of individuals together, we draw attention to the existence of *some* relationship between them.

Another important use of sorts is to allow us to specify the *functionalities* of operations, i.e., what sort of result each operation returns when applied to arguments of appropriate sorts. Some frameworks only allow one functionality to be specified for each operation, thus preventing so-called *overloading*, but this seems unfortunate: when exploited judiciously, overloading can be very useful. For instance, we might want to specify a print operation for all sorts of values. Or we might want an if-then-else operation, where the sort of the second and third arguments could be arbitrary. Functionality specifications can be regarded as particular kinds of axioms—although for technical reasons, they are more commonly treated as part of signatures, and usually at least one functionality for each operation must be specified.

When the extensions of sorts can overlap, we expect so-called *subsort polymorphism*. E.g., positive integers of sort pos may also be classified in the sort nat of all natural numbers. Then a product operation on natural numbers not only has functionality nat,nat→nat but also pos,pos→pos; similarly for sorts classifying just even (or just odd) numbers, and for the singleton sorts classifying just zero and one! However, many restrictions of the sorts of arguments lead to uninteresting sorts of returned values, and it is pointless to specify these as functionalities.

In axioms, sorts are generally used for *restricting* assignments to *variables*. Axioms are often (implicitly or explicitly) universally quantified over all variables that occur in them; the use of sorts can restrict this quantification, and thereby the application of the axiom, to particular subsets of the universe. For instance, the product operation may be commutative on numbers but not on matrices; the commutativity axiom for product must then be restricted to numbers. In the absence of overloaded operations, sort restrictions on variables are implicit, being determined by the functionalities of the operations applied to them.

Now let's consider what is perhaps the most common use of sorts: the attempt to avoid *partial* operations, by restricting each of them to a corresponding total operation on the domain of definition. This is desirable, because the logic and technical details of algebraic specifications are somewhat simpler when partial operations are avoided. On the other hand, we shall see that it isn't so easy to avoid partial operations completely.

When specifying mathematical structures such as groups and rings, the carrier of a specified algebra is *homogeneous*, and each operation can be applied to any individuals, usually returning a well-defined individual value. (Fields and categories involve partial operations, though.) But almost all interesting abstract data types for use in computer science—and a few in mathematics, such as vector spaces—involve *heterogeneous* carriers. In general, all operations on heterogeneous carriers are inherently partial, when considered as functions on the entire collection of individuals. For instance, an abstract data type of lists of numbers obviously involves numbers as well as lists; but there is no point in applying list operations (head, tail, etc.) to numbers, and although it can be useful to extend some numerical operations (product, for instance) to lists, this is by no means essential.

The use of sorts to classify the individuals of a heterogeneous collection, together with the specification of operation functionalities, allows us to forbid terms where operations are applied to unintended argument values. Thus we may regard operations as being restricted to values in the argument sorts specified in their functionalities. With values including both numbers and lists, for instance, product can be restricted to numbers, and head and tail to (nonempty) lists; the application of product to a list, or of head and tail to numbers, is simply forbidden, syntactically.

Often, it is easy to check for forbidden terms, using the functionalities of operations. This is important in connection with systems that implement algebraic specifications: the user can be warned about a simple mistake before a time-consuming and futile evaluation is started. But it isn't always so easy: for instance, it can be undecidable whether, in an application of the list operation head, the value of argument term is the empty list or not. If the application is forbidden, we get the anomalous situation where forbidden terms can be obtained from allowed ones, using the axioms as rewrite rules; if it is allowed, we are forced to take partial operations seriously.

An alternative technique for skirting around partial operations is to introduce special *error* values, to represent the undefined results of operations when they are applied to unintended arguments. Then all operations are total, but of course they now have to be specified on the error values, as well as on the 'okay' values. This can be tedious, although certain assumptions, such as *strictness* on error values, allow most of the extra axioms to be left implicit.

Instead of trying to avoid partiality, one could simply accept it as a somewhat awkward fact of life, and consider *partial algebras* where operations are partial functions in the usual, mathematical sense. But one has to be careful about the precise interpretation of equality—strong or existential—and about the logic used for deduction. The notion of homomorphism between algebras is less obvious, too. In practice, because of such technical irritations, most popular approaches for algebraic specifications keep to total algebras, simulating partiality as best they can. In any case, there are other uses for sorts than trying to avoid partiality, and frameworks for partial algebras exploit sorts just as much as those for total algebras do. Hence we pay only scant attention to partial algebras in this paper.

To conclude this motivation for sorts, let us note a few uses of them that are perhaps somewhat less obvious than those explained above:

- *Term rewriting* is used to implement algebraic specifications. It generally involves large-scale searching of axioms (oriented as rewrite rules) to find a match with a part of a term to be evaluated. By keeping track of sorts (and subsorts), the search space can be dramatically reduced. Similarly for automatic theorem-proving.
- Sorts can be used to represent *nondeterministic* choices between individuals. The individuals classified by a sort are then regarded as alternatives.
- Finally, sorts have major technical significance for the definition of so-called *initial* (or data) *constraints*. This is because the ordinary reduct functor forgets about operations, and about entire sorts of values; when there are no sorts, it doesn't forget any values at all!

So much for *what* sorts are, and *why* it is useful to specify them. But by focussing on sorts so much, we have been neglecting the individual values somewhat. It is important to bear in mind that we don't specify sorts for their own sake: it is the individual values, and the operations upon these, that are the aim of an algebraic specification, and the sorts are only there to *facilitate* the specification.

In the remaining sections we consider *how* sorts are specified in the major frameworks that have been developed over the past 15 years or more. The appendices illustrate the use of most of these frameworks to specify a simple abstract data type of lists.

3 Many-Sorted Algebras

Let us start with a brief look at the basic framework known as *many-sorted algebras* (MSA) in the formulation proposed by the ADJ group [24]. From a theoretical point of view, this framework is perhaps the most tractable of all those presented here; but it is also the one most beset by pragmatic deficiencies.

A signature of a many-sorted algebra consists of a set of sort symbols S together with a set of operation symbols and their functionalities. Overloading is (usually) allowed, so each operation symbol may have several functionalities. Axioms of MSA specifications are often restricted to sorted equations, or positive conditional equations; variables are restricted to specified sorts. Such specifications always have initial models.

The universe of a many-sorted algebra A consists of a family A_s of sets of values, one for each sort symbol $s \in S$. For each functionality $s_1, \ldots, s_n \rightarrow s$ of each operation symbol f in the signature, A provides a total function $f_A : A_{s_1} \times \cdots \times A_{s_n} \rightarrow A_s$. Note that the A_s may overlap, or even coincide.

The main pragmatic problem with ordinary MSA is how to accommodate *error* values. For instance, consider a specification of rational numbers: if there is only one sort of rational number, it ought to contain zero, but then division by zero cannot be forbidden by the functionality. Because all operations are required to be total, this results in a nonstandard rational value, i.e., an error value. (To specify the value of division by zero to be some particular standard rational value, e.g., zero, would amount to ignoring the existence of this error.) Similarly for a specification of possibly-empty lists: taking the head of the empty list gives an error value. Such error values are especially awkward in parameterized specifications, which are supposed to leave parameter sorts undisturbed.

The solution originally proposed [24] is quite costly. For each sort $s \in S$, one introduces an error value e_s, a truth-valued operation ok_s (specified to be true except on e_s), an if-then-else operation ife_s, and a plethora of derived operations. These operations can then be used to specify appropriate equations for error propagation. But 'the resulting total specification ... is unbelievably complicated' [24]. See Sect. 9.1 for an example. The problems with this explicit treatment of errors led to the development of various frameworks where the treatment of errors can be specified more concisely; we consider the major ones in the next section.

Another pragmatic problem with MSA is the difficulty of specifying sort inclusions, i.e., *subsorts*. Suppose, for instance, that we want to have the sort nat for all natural numbers, and pos for positive ones. With MSA, we cannot specify that for each model A the carrier set A_{pos} *has* to be *included* in A_{nat} (or more precisely, that the difference between these carrier sets is just the value of the zero constant). Thus the relation of such {nat, pos}-sorted models to the standard mathematical algebra of natural numbers is obscure. Moreover, we have to specify each numerical operation twice: once on nat, and again on pos.

Order-sorted algebras address these problems directly; we shall consider them in Sect. 6. A less direct solution, available when conditional equations are allowed, is to introduce an auxiliary operation i:pos→nat and specify that it is injective, i.e., one-one. From a theoretical point of view, there is not much difference between an injective operation and a set inclusion. But in practice, specifications using such auxiliary operations explicitly would be rather tedious to write.

It is debatable whether *overloading* should be allowed in MSA or not. Theoretically, overloading is dispensable: any class of algebras that can be specified with overloaded operation symbols can—up to a signature translation—also be specified without overloading. Pragmatically, however, overloading can be quite convenient, and it is often exploited in mathematical notation.

Some care is needed when overloading is allowed. For suppose that we have an overloaded constant c of two different sorts s_1, s_2, as well as an overloaded operation f with the functionalities $f : s_1 \to s$ and $f : s_2 \to s$. The term $f(c)$ is simply ambiguous! Its value could differ, according to whether the argument is regarded as being of sort s_1 or s_2. The sort of value required by the context should be the same in each case, namely s, so that doesn't help with disambiguation. Perhaps mathematicians don't worry too much about notational ambiguities arising from overloaded constants in their formulae, because they usually know which value is intended from a wider context. However, that hardly justifies allowing overloaded constants in algebraic specifications, where one generally aims for reusable modules that can be understood by themselves, independently of context.

Even when overloaded constants are forbidden in MSA, there is still a problem with ambiguity, although at a different level. Suppose two carrier sets A_{s_1} and A_{s_2} overlap, and let $x \in A_{s_1} \cap A_{s_2}$. When $f : s_1 \to s'_1$ and $f : s_2 \to s'_2$ is an overloaded operation, $f_A(x)$ is not, in general, well-defined: its value depends on whether x is regarded as an element of A_{s_1} or of A_{s_2}. Perhaps one should consider restricting models of MSA specifications to those where each overloaded operation always gives the same result when applied to the same values, regardless of the sorts of the values? We shall return to this point when considering order-sorted algebras, where some attention has been paid to it.

Despite the problems concerning error values and overloading, much has been achieved within the MSA framework, and it provided the basis for the development and popularization of the entire topic of algebraic specification. Some users still prefer this straightforward framework to the more complicated ones considered in the rest of this survey.

4 Partiality

Having seen the complications that can arise in total algebraic specifications due to error values, we might be tempted to let operations be ordinary partial functions and represent errors by undefinedness, following Broy and Wirsing [8] and Reichel

[44], see also [2, 9]. As ordinary partial functions are *strict* on undefinedness, error propagation is implicit; moreover, variables in axioms are only assigned defined values. Thus the auxiliary ok and ife operations introduced in the preceding section are unnecessary here.

But there are some drawbacks. For instance, there is the dilemma of whether to interpret equations *existentially*, to hold only when the values of both the equated terms are defined, or *strongly*, to hold also when both the values are undefined. Similarly, homomorphisms could be total or partial functions, and each choice has certain merits.

Some care is needed to exclude models where operations are more partial than intended. As well as equations, one may specify definedness axioms $\mathsf{D}(t)$ to this end. See Sect. 9.2 for an example. In the framework of *hierarchical* specifications [8], definedness is often implied by the presence of selector operations.

Kreowski [27] proposes that partial algebras can be simply obtained from *based* total algebras. The idea is to give first a base specification, whose initial algebra provides all the values of interest, for example, the usual natural numbers. Then one extends it to a specification with operations that may give errors, such as applying predecessor to zero or dividing by zero. The ordinary total initial algebra of the extended specification can then be made into a partial algebra by restricting operations to being defined when they return values of the base algebra, ignoring all the extra error values.

The basic framework of (first-order) partial algebras doesn't cater for non-strict operations, such as if-then-else. Astesiano and Cerioli [3] propose a framework of so-called *don't care algebras* that allows non-strict (monotonic) operations, and they make a revealing study of the relationship between total and partial algebras. However, most operations of ordinary abstract data types *are* strict, and when strictness is no longer implicit, it has to be specified explicitly by axioms, which might be tedious in practice. The relationship between total and partial algebras is further investigated in an abstract setting in [4].

Poigné [40] defines a framework that can be seen as a generalization of the standard partial algebra framework. He distinguishes between sorts and types: sorts are essentially syntactic, used in signatures for restricting the allowed terms; types are semantic, with the classification of individual values into types being specified by axioms. The whole framework is based on Scott's logic of partiality. See also the description of Poigné's Typed Horn Logic in Sect. 7.5.

Now let us leave partial algebras, and look at some total algebra frameworks that deal with errors more efficiently than the original many-sorted algebra framework does.

5 Errors and Exceptions

Several proposals have been made for extending the basic framework of total many-sorted algebras to accommodate error values, aiming at better pragmatics. As well as the proposals considered in this section, also the order-sorted algebras considered in Sect. 6 cater for errors.

5.1 Error Algebras

The signatures of Goguen's *error algebras* [18] distinguish between *okay* and *error* operations. For each sort $s \in S$ the carrier set A_s is partitioned into okay values and error values. All operations are required to return an error value whenever any argument is an error value; error operations always return error values. Axioms are divided into okay equations and error equations. An okay equation $t_1 = t_2$ holds for all variable assignments such that both t_1 and t_2 have okay values; an error equation $t_1 = t_2$ holds whenever either t_1 or t_2 evaluates to an error.

However, this framework has the serious defect that when any operation in a specification has a *zero*, the strict treatment of errors conflicts with the zero axiom, causing all values (of the sort concerned, at least) to become error values! For instance, if err is an error value of sort nat, we have 0 = prod(0,err) = err ... See Sect. 9.3 for an example of an error algebra specification where this problem doesn't arise.

5.2 Algebras with Okay Predicates

An alternative to dividing signatures into okay and error operations is to divide them into okay and *unsafe* operations as proposed by Gogolla, Drosten, Lipeck, and Ehrich [17], see also [15, 16]. Carriers are still divided into okay and error values, i.e., equipped with *okay predicates*. An okay operation always returns an okay value when all its arguments are okay values; an unsafe operation may or may not return an error value. Now all operations may return okay values, even when their arguments are error values, thus general error recovery and exception handling are possible—and inconsistency between zeros and error propagation can be avoided.

Variables for use in axioms are each declared to be okay or unsafe, and only okay values may be assigned to okay variables. As there is no implicit error propagation, one has to specify rather a lot of tedious axioms, unless one can accept the presence of a large number of distinct error values of each sort. See Sect. 9.4 for an example.

Another problem is that when the specified values are bounded, and exceeding the bounds is to give an error, the constructor operations are unsafe, and then the okay values of the initial model do not include the expected ones. (In fact one can use auxiliary sorts and operations to get around this problem, but the required specifications are too tedious for practical use.)

Essentially, it seems that this approach corresponds fairly closely to the way errors are treated using ordinary many-sorted algebras, but by keeping the okay predicates implicit and using two kinds of variables, the number of axioms required is kept down to an acceptable level. It can also be seen as a particular discipline in order-sorted algebraic specifications, called *stratification* [49].

5.3 Exception Algebras

The *E,R algebras* of Bidoit [7] provide not only implicit error propagation, but also specification of recovery cases, i.e., exception handling, which override propagation. But the interest of this framework is reduced by the fact that E,R algebraic specifications do not in general have initial models.

The *exception algebras* proposed by Bernot, Bidoit, and Choppy [5] develop the main ideas of E,R algebras, now providing a framework where specifications do have initial models. The aim is to cater not only for errors but also for general exception-handling.

An exception signature consists of an ordinary many-sorted signature, together with a set of exception *labels*, which correspond to a secondary classification of values, orthogonal to the sorts. An exception algebra has a family of sets of values, indexed by the exception labels together with a special label for okay values. Specifications have to declare the so-called okay *forms*, which are used to determine the okay terms. This is more flexible than a mere division of operations into okay and error (or unsafe) operations; for instance, terms that evaluate to okay values of bounded structures can now be classified as okay.

The axioms are divided into okay axioms, labelling axioms, and generalized axioms. The okay axioms are positive conditional equations, to be satisfied only for assignments of okay *terms* to variables. An okay term may have the same value as a non-okay term, so in contrast to the exception labels, the okay label is attached to terms, rather than to values. For instance, when specifying bounded integers, max-int is an okay term but succ(max-int) is not, even though one specifies the equality of the values of these terms among the axioms.

The labelling axioms classify values using labels; a labelling may be conditional upon other labellings, and on equations. These labels are not automatically propagated by operations. The generalized axioms are equations (possibly conditional on labellings and equations) which specify exception-handling and error recovery.

The resulting framework seems extremely powerful, but specifications look somewhat intricate. See Sect. 9.5 for an example. Moreover, the axioms required to specify okay forms for bounded structures seem to require terms whose size is proportional to the bound!

5.4 Label Algebras

Bernot and Le Gall [6] further explore the idea of attaching labels to terms. They propose *label algebras*, where no distinction need be made between okay and exception labels: all labels are attached to terms rather than values, and used to restrict assignments to variables in axioms. They show examples where this extra generality is useful, in connection with exception-handling and with observability. Moreover, it is easy to specify that particular labels are determined by the values of the terms to which they are attached, whereupon they can be regarded as unary predicates on values, classifying them rather like conventional sorts do.

Label algebras are considered to be too low-level for direct use, in general, so we don't illustrate their specification here. Higher-level frameworks that correspond to particular disciplines of labelling can be defined by translation into label algebras. For instance, Bernot and Le Gall define a generalization (and simplification) of the exception algebras mentioned above in this way. However, the notion of satisfaction of axioms by label algebras involves consideration of term algebras freely generated by sets of values, which may seem a bit complicated. Label algebras do not provide an institution, at least not straightforwardly, it seems.

6 Sort Inclusions

Suppose that we have a collection of individual values, to be classified into sorts. There is no reason why each individual should necessarily be classified uniquely! For instance, the number one could be classified not only as a natural number, but also as a positive number, an integer, a rational number, etc. Moreover, some sorts are naturally seen as being *subsorts* of other sorts: we expect the natural numbers to be included in the integers, etc.

Technically, many-sorted algebras already allow the sort-indexed carrier sets to overlap, so that an individual value may in fact be classified as of more than one sort. But it is not possible to *specify* that such properties must hold, since an equation always relates individuals of the same sort (and no assumptions can be made about any relationship between the values returned by overloaded operation symbols). Any many-sorted algebraic specification may thus have models where carriers overlap, and models where they don't. Multiple classification of an individual here is merely accidental. However, there are technical and pragmatic reasons for allowing it: so that a single model value may *implement* several unrelated abstract data, for instance.

Now, the extensions of sorts are sets, and sets are partially-ordered by inclusion, so it is natural to allow the specification of a partial order $\leq$ on the set of sorts S. (A pre-order might correspond better to the intensional nature of sorts. In practice, it doesn't usually matter whether mutually-included sorts are regarded as equal or not.) Signatures with partially-ordered sorts are called *order-sorted*, as are algebras with such signatures. Order-sorted algebras should not to be confused with *partially-ordered algebras* [33] where for each s in an ordinary *set* of sorts, the carrier set A_s is equipped with a partial order.

Order-sorted algebras support *subsort polymorphism* : when an operation is available both on some sort and on a subsort, both versions of it necessarily give the same result when applied to a value of the subsort. The partial order on sorts also supports an economical treatment of errors and exception-handling, allowing error supersorts as well as restrictions of partial operations to subsorts on which they are total.

For instance, with rational numbers of sort rat we may introduce extra values to represent errors such as trying to divide by zero, including them in a supersort, say errata, of rat. Then we may *extend* all the numerical operations from rat to errata, specifying that they give error values when applied to error values. The simplest way to do this is perhaps to treat erroneous applications of operations themselves as error values, not specifying any equations for them at all.

Alternatively, we may *restrict* division to applications where the second argument is in the subsort of nonzero rationals, forbidding the user to write terms that involve division by zero when evaluated. Here, however, there is the problem that it is usually not *syntactically* apparent whether an argument term might evaluate to zero or not, just from the functionalities of the operations in it: addition maps a positive and a negative integer to an arbitrary integer, possibly zero, for example. We shall return to this problem shortly.

There are two main approaches to order-sorted algebras, one of them due to Goguen together with Meseguer, the other developed by Gogolla, Poigné, and Smolka. The two approaches differ in what at first might appear to be a trifling technical detail, but which on closer scrutiny turns out to be a major conceptual disagreement about the nature of subsorts, as explained below.

6.1 Overloaded Order-Sorted Algebras

Goguen [19] was the first to propose a framework for order-sorted algebras (OSA). Subsequently, together with Meseguer, he developed the framework in a series of papers, culminating so far in the first part of a definitive presentation [23]. This development was closely linked to that of the OBJ system [25], which implements OSA specifications.

The formal details of OSA signatures and algebras are a bit more burdensome than in the original many-sorted algebraic framework. The sorts of an order-sorted signature are equipped with a partial order $\leq$, and the functionalities of operations must be *monotonic*: when $f : s_1, \ldots s_n \rightarrow s$, $f : s'_1, \ldots, s'_n \rightarrow s'$, and all $s_i \leq s'_i$ then $s \leq s'$. For simplicity, signatures are sometimes required to be *regular*, a condition which guarantees that every term has a least sort; a weaker condition that guarantees this is *preregularity* [23, Section 5.1].

An order-sorted algebra A is here a many-sorted algebra such that $s \leq s'$ implies $A_s \leq A_{s'}$ and moreover:

(*) when $f : s_1, \ldots s_n \rightarrow s$, $f : s'_1, \ldots, s'_n \rightarrow s'$, and all $s_i \leq s'_i$ (hence also $s \leq s'$) then the restriction of $f_A : A_{s'_1} \times \cdots \times A_{s'_n} \rightarrow A_{s'}$ to $A_{s_1} \times \cdots \times A_{s_n}$ is the same function as $f_A : A_{s_1} \times \cdots \times A_{s_n} \rightarrow A_s$.

It is important to realize that when the sorts s_i and s'_i are *not* related by inclusion, the two functions denoted by f need not be related at all, and may return different results when applied to the same argument values! Goguen and Meseguer [23] argue for keeping this feature, which is known as *overloading*, or *ad hoc* polymorphism, for they want MSA to be a special case of OSA, obtainable merely by letting the inclusion order $\leq$ be the identity relation. But this seems to conflict with a basic intuition underlying the subsort relation: that sorts represent classification of a single collection of individuals. We shall return to this discussion in the next subsection, when we look at an alternative approach to OSA.

Axioms of OSA specifications are similar to those of MSA specifications, except that the (least) sorts of terms in equations need not be the same—although they have to be *connected* by inclusions. *Sort constraints* are allowed, for use in specifying bounded structures; these correspond to conditional functionalities, but are axioms, rather than being part of signatures.

Not all terms that ought to denote values are allowed. For example, consider the standard specification of the sort nat of natural numbers with successor operation succ : nat $\rightarrow$ pos and a partial predecessor operation pred : pos $\rightarrow$ nat, where pos $\leq$ nat is the subsort of positive integers: the term pred(pred(succ(succ(0)))) is not allowed! But with pred(succ(n)) = n as an obvious axiom for n:nat, we expect succ(0) = pred(succ(succ(0))), hence 0 = pred(succ(0)) = pred(pred(succ(succ(0)))). Thus allowed terms can be demonstrably equal to forbidden ones, which seems somewhat anomalous. This is essentially the same problem that arises with trying to forbid terms involving division by zero: the functionalities of operations are not sufficiently precise. Here we should have not only succ : nat $\rightarrow$ pos but also succ : pos $\rightarrow$ pos2, where pos2 is the sort of all integers from 2 upwards, and so on *ad infinitum*.

Goguen and Meseguer [23, Section 3.3] propose inserting *retracts* in forbidden terms to give them 'the benefit of the doubt at parse time'. Here a retract maps a sort to a subsort, being identity on the values already in the subsort. For instance the insertion of the retract r : nat → pos allows pred(r(pred(succ(succ(0))))) to be well-formed. The trouble is that although such retracts have a simple *operational* semantics in this framework, they are essentially *partial* operations. A term such as r(0) should surely not have a value of sort pos! Nevertheless, the insertion of retracts doesn't interfere with equality: it provides a so-called conservative extension—although only with respect to direct consequence, not the inductive consequences that hold in the initial model.

To give an *algebraic* interpretation of retracts, Goguen and Meseguer consider the specifications obtained by adding all possible retract operations, together with their defining equations, to order-sorted specifications. The initial algebras of the original specifications get homomorphically injected into those of the extended specifications. But now the *semantics* of each order-sorted specification has been changed, and the notion of such a specification being *correct* with respect to some intended model should presumably be redefined.

Despite the mentioned anomalies, the overloaded OSA framework succeeds in eliminating many of the pragmatic deficiencies of the MSA framework. See Sect. 9.6 for an example specification. Let us leave it at that, and turn to an alternative approach to order-sorted algebras.

6.2 Universal Order-Sorted Algebras

Rather than insisting that OSA be a true generalization of the traditional framework of MSA, one can take the view that the really essential notion is that of a *universe* of individuals, with each operation symbol identifying a *single* (partial) operation on that universe, and with sorts corresponding to subsets of the universe.

This approach to OSA was developed by Gogolla [14], Poigné [39], and Smolka [47], see also [49]. Essentially, the difference from the overloaded OSA framework described in the previous section is that now the carrier sets are united into a single universe, and condition (*) is replaced by the stronger:

(**) when $f : s_1, \dots s_n \to s$ and $f : s'_1, \dots, s'_n \to s'$, then the restrictions of the functions $f_A : A_{s_1} \times \dots \times A_{s_n} \to A_s$ and $f_A : A_{s'_1} \times \dots \times A_{s'_n} \to A_{s'}$ to the intersections $(A_{s_1} \cap A_{s'_1}) \times \dots \times (A_{s_n} \cap A_{s'_n})$ are the same.

Notice that this condition is entirely independent of the sort inclusion relation. It can be understood as a condition for *sort-independent semantics*: a legal term should always have the same value, regardless of what sorts are ascribed to its subterms. Let us refer to this variant as *universal* order-sorted algebras. (Waldmann [51] calls them 'non-overloaded' algebras, since each operation symbol is interpreted as a single function; but that conflicts somewhat with the conventional understanding of what overloading is.)

Goguen and Meseguer [23, Section 5.2] mount an attack on universal OSA, claiming that it has 'serious drawbacks'; but their arguments do not seem terribly convincing. For instance, they want to allow 'an algebra in which 0 and 1 are both Booleans and naturals, and in which + is both addition and exclusive or of Booleans'. It seems that 0 and 1 here refer to the standard natural numbers, as the argument does not necessarily involve overloaded constants (which prevent regularity). Both the overloaded and universal OSA frameworks allow such values to occur in the carrier sets of *unrelated* sorts. The only disagreement here is about whether the symbol + can be overloaded so that $x+x$ returns 0 when x denotes 1 of sort Boolean, but 2 when x denotes 1 of sort natural; overloaded OSA allows this model, whereas universal OSA doesn't. The statement that order-sorted logic *must* be 'in principle a refinement of many-sorted logic' [23, Section 5.2] seems to be somewhat dogmatic.

Despite the conceptual and technical differences between the treatment of subsorts in overloaded OSA and universal OSA, for most purposes they can be used interchangeably. For instance, the example in Sect. 9.6 serves just as well for universal OSA as for overloaded OSA. However, universal and overloaded OSA do *not* provide the same notion of satisfaction. For example, suppose we have constants a:A, b:B where A and B are subsorts of C, and let us specify a = b. If we have an overloaded operation f with f : A → D and f : B → D, universal OSA models always satisfy f(a) = f(b), but overloaded OSA ones don't!

For an analysis of numerous technical points concerning overloaded and universal OSA, see the forthcoming paper by Waldmann [51]. Goguen [20] proposes a *hidden-sorted* version of OSA where the values with hidden sorts represent internal states of *objects*. He also shows there how to define an institution for *behavioural* satisfaction.

6.3 Generalized Order-Sorted Algebras

Poigné [42] proposes a generalized framework for OSA, which includes universal OSA as a special case. The main idea is to use a *set* of partial orders on sorts, rather than just a single one. Sorts that occur in different partial orders are treated as in overloaded OSA, whereas those that occur in the same partial order are treated as in universal OSA.

The proposed framework does *not* fully include overloaded OSA as a special case: there are pathological examples of overloaded OSA models that are not generalized OSA models, for instance with a supersort for two otherwise unrelated sorts that have some nonexpressible value in common. However, this framework does successfully generalize both MSA and universal OSA.

6.4 Inclusions and Subtypes

Martí-Oliet and Meseguer [30] make a useful analysis of the difference between the notions of subtype as *inclusion* (as in OSA) and subtype as *coercion*. They conclude that as well as the inclusion partial order $\leq$ on sorts, one should as well consider a *generalized subtype* relation $\leq:$ containing $\leq$ as a subrelation, where $s \leq: s'$ holds when there is an implicit coercion from s to s'. They only require $\leq:$ to be a preorder. For instance, with Cartesian and polar coordinates, we might have coercions both ways.

Qian [43] has also developed an interesting framework catering for coercions, which are more general than subsort inclusions.

6.5 Generator Induction

Owe and Dahl [38] propose some restrictions on order-sorted algebras, so as to cater for generator inductive function definitions. They prohibit (incidental) overloading, and insist that minimal sorts denote *disjoint* sets of values; this allows signatures to be completed with all unions and intersections, and similarly for functionalities.

The emphasis of this work is on a particular style of functional programming, and the authors argue *against* the specification of general algebraic axioms.

7 Classified and Unified Algebras

The following approaches treat sorts *semantically*, using axioms to specify classification.

7.1 Classified Algebras

Perhaps the most *logical* way of classifying individuals into sorts is to let a sort be a unary predicate on the universe, i.e., a subset of it. This technique is well-known from first-order logic, under the name *relativization*. It was first proposed for use in algebraic specifications by Wadge [50] who defined a framework called *classified algebras*—not to be confused with the framework of the same name later proposed by Poigné [40].

Essentially, a signature of a classified algebra is a pair (F, S) where F is a ranked[2] alphabet of operation symbols and S is an alphabet of sort symbols, including the distinguished symbol anything. Axioms are equations $t_1 = t_2$, and so-called declarations written $t : s$, where t is a term and $s \in S$. Variables in terms are written with sort symbols $s \in S$ as subscripts, and assignments to them are restricted to values that are classified as being of the specified sorts.

A classified algebra A has a nonempty universe, a *total* function on the universe for each $f \in F$, and a subset of the universe for each $s \in S$; the subset for anything is the entire universe. A declaration $t : s$ holds in a particular algebra if the value of the term t is an element of the set denoted by s, for all assignments to the variables in t of values from the sets denoted by their sorts. The satisfaction of equations by algebras is as usual, bearing in mind the same restrictions on assignments as for declarations.

It is easy to see that classified algebras can be regarded as a special case of unsorted Horn clause (with equality) specifications: sort symbols correspond to unary predicate symbols, declarations are just formulae that apply the predicates. Sort restrictions on variables X_s correspond to hypotheses $X : s$ with unsorted variables. Thus we should expect classified algebra specifications to have initial models, as they do indeed.

Classified algebras combine technical simplicity with high expressiveness. For instance, partiality and errors can represented by operations returning values that are not classified by any sort—although one can also classify error values, if desired. There are usually lots of these error values, but they don't get in the way, because

[2] Wadge left alphabets unranked, for no apparent reason!

variables are automatically restricted to non-error values of particular sorts. Functionalities can be expressed concisely as declarations, i.e., axioms; so can sort inclusions. Overloading and subsort polymorphism are natural, since each operation symbol stands for a single operation on the entire classified universe. See Sect. 9.7 for an example.

Of course, there is a price to pay for such simplicity: sort checking is undecidable! This is because classification is essentially *semantic*, in contrast to the *syntactic* notion of sort in the frameworks we considered earlier. Whether $t : s$ holds (for a ground term t) depends in general not only on declarations concerning the symbols in t, but also on equations that relate t to other terms. Anyway, one could easily define restrictions on classified specifications to make sort checking decidable. Alternatively, it might be acceptable to use interactive theorem proving for sort checking in general classified specifications (by analogy with the Nuprl system [11]).

Wadge sketches some ideas for generalizing classified algebras, to allow user-specified operations on sorts, and classifications of sorts. But this seems to be getting into the realm of higher-order logic, and it is unclear whether initial models of such specifications would always exist. Wadge's paper makes refreshing reading, and it influenced several other approaches.

7.2 Galactic Algebras

The framework of *galactic algebras*, or *G-algebras*, proposed by Mégrelis [31, 32] is essentially a partial algebra variant of the classified algebras discussed in the preceding section. A signature consists of a set of sort symbols S and a ranked alphabet of operation symbols F. The special sort symbol '***' corresponds to 'anything' in classified algebras. Axioms are equations $t_1 = t_2$, membership formulae $t : s$ where $s \in S$, and domain (definedness) formulae $\$t$. Moreover, each variable x is globally restricted to a particular sort by a confinement axiom $x :: s$.

A G-algebra A is like a classified algebra, having a nonempty universe and a subset of it for each sort symbol. Each operation symbol is here interpreted as a *partial* function on the universe of A, as are all terms (relative to a fixed ordering of the variables). Equations and membership formulae are interpreted *existentially*, for example $t : s$ can only hold when t denotes a *total* function on the subsets of the universe of A indicated by the sorts of variables occurring in t.

Functionalities and subsort inclusions are provided as axioms, abbreviating particular sets of formulae. See Sect. 9.8 for an example of a G-algebra specification exploiting such axioms (written with a less Spartan notation than that used by Mégrelis).

C. and H. Kirchner [26] find that the framework of G-algebras is particularly useful for order-sorted term rewriting. The basic idea is to compute sorts of terms and deduce equalities simultaneously, decorating terms with their currently-proved sorts. This allows the relaxation of some rather severe conditions that have to be imposed in OSA frameworks to obtain completeness of rewriting with respect to deduction. See also [10, 51].

7.3 Polymorphically Order-Sorted Types

Smolka has developed a framework for logic programming over *polymorphically order-sorted types* [48]. It is not directly relevant to algebraic specifications, because value operations are always free constructors, and cannot be related by equations. Thus natural numbers with zero and successor can be specified, but not together with the usual predecessor operation. Nevertheless, the treatment of sorts is particularly interesting, so let us look at it briefly.

The essential idea is to define *sort* constants and operations by equations. (Then relations on values are defined by declarations of the sorts of their arguments together with some definite clauses.) For example, the sort constant nat is equated to the union of the sorts zero and pos. The value constant 0 constructs the only value of sort zero. The value operation succ constructs values of sort pos from values of sort nat. Of course, when a sort is equated to a union of two other sorts, the latter are thereby subsorts of the former.

This framework provides support for parametric polymorphism in a way that is arguably superior to that of order-sorted algebras. The idea is to define sort operations in the same way as sort constants, using equations and sort union, with sort variables that range over all the specified sorts. For instance, one may specify a sort operation list(T), thus providing list(pos) as a subsort of list(nat), as well as particular sorts of nested lists such as list(list(nat)). Sort operations are always monotonic with respect to sort inclusion. See Sect. 9.9 for the full specification of lists (which is possible only because no value equations are required). Notice that the treatment of parametric polymorphism is achieved within the ordinary specification logic, rather than by using some meta-logic of module instantiation.

7.4 Equational Type Logic

Manca, Salibra, and Scollo [28, 29] propose *Equational Type Logic* (ETL), which is another framework where sorts are treated semantically. Like conventional frameworks, it caters for ordinary (conditional) equational algebraic specifications of individuals and operations upon them. It resembles classified algebras in the way that individuals can be classified into sorts, but now (as in Smolka's approach in the preceding section) sorts are values, not predicates, and operations on sorts can be specified. The result is a rather simple, elegant, and expressive framework, coping well with partiality and polymorphism. Let's look at the formal details.

Algebras in ETL are called *type algebras*. The signature of a type algebra is an unsorted, ranked alphabet of operation symbols. Thus there are no restrictions on term formation. A type algebra A is simply a conventional (total) unsorted algebra together with an arbitrary binary 'typing' relation $:_A$ on its carrier.

Axioms in specifications are simply Horn clauses involving equations $t_1 = t_2$ and/or sort assignments $t_1 : t_2$. Variables in axioms are unsorted, ranging over the entire universe of a type algebra. But the effect of sorted variables can easily be obtained, using conditions of the form $x : t$, which only hold when the value of x is an individual of sort t (an arbitrary term, not merely a constant symbol). Specifications always have initial models.

Values that are not in the typing relation (on either side) are *underdefined*, and may be viewed as error values. Such an implicit specification of errors is usually very concise, but errors are *not* automatically propagated by operations, in general—except in initial models, under the assumption that all variables are restricted by sort assignments in conditions. Moreover, with implicit error specification, checking whether an arbitrary (ground) term denotes an error or not is undecidable. Alternatively, one can explicitly classify error values, if desired, as in classified algebras. Automatic restriction of variables to non-error values is not available, however; such restrictions are to be specified explicitly by sort assignments in conditions.

Although sort inclusion is not provided as a relation, it can be represented straightforwardly by specifying a general sort union operation ∪ and using $x \cup y = y$ to express that x is a subsort of y. But sorts that happen to have the same extension are not necessarily equal, so some care is needed. (An alternative representation of sort inclusion directly as an operation is given in [46].) In contrast to Smolka's approach above, and to unified algebras below, sort operations are not necessarily monotonic with respect to sort inclusion, so if one wants list(pos) to be a subsort of list(nat), this has to be specified explicitly. Thus subsort polymorphism is possible, but not guaranteed.

The functionality of an ordinary operation f that is total on individuals of sorts $s_1, \ldots, s_n$ can be expressed by a clause $x_1 : s_1, \ldots, x_n : s_n \Rightarrow f(x_1, \ldots, x_n) : s$, and overloading is obviously allowed. But note that such functionality clauses are not required at all! Parametric polymorphism can be specified, much as in Smolka's approach. See Sect. 9.10 for an example.

Finally, notice that the typing relation can be used not only to classify individuals into sorts, but also sorts into meta-sorts, i.e., kinds. However, it doesn't seem that this feature is needed much in the practical examples of ETL specifications seen so far.

7.5 Typed Horn Logic

Poigné [41] proposes a further framework involving Horn clauses and typing relations. Here the primitive formulae are: $x : t$, asserting that x exists and is of type t; $t :: k$, asserting that t exists and is of 'order' (i.e., *kind*) k; and $k\,!$, asserting merely that k is an existing order. No syntactic distinction is made between operations on individuals, types, and orders. Equality is treated existentially, as a partial equivalence relation. Models are based on Scott's theory of partiality. Specifications resemble those in ETL above; see Sect. 9.11 for an example.

7.6 Term Declaration Logic

Aczel's *Term Declaration Logic* (TDL) [1] appears to be related to ETL and Typed Horn Logic. Here, a *pre-signature* consists of pairwise disjoints sets of sort symbols, operation symbols and variables. A signature consists of a presignature together with restrictions of its variables to particular sorts and *declarations*. A *formation* declaration is written $\tau \downarrow$, and a *sorting* declaration is written $\tau : s$, where τ is a *sort* term and s is a sort symbol. A subsort inclusion is declared using $s' : s$, and a functionality is written $f(s_1, \ldots, s_n) : s$. A pre-term t constructed from variables and operation symbols is deemed to be a *term* when $\sigma t \downarrow$ can be proved using some simple inference rules, where σt is the sort term obtained by replacing variables in t by the sorts to which they are restricted. Similarly, t is of sort s if $t : s$ can be proved.

A specification consists of a signature together with a set of equations between terms. A *pre-algebra* provides a universe of individuals, a subset of it for each sort symbol, and a partial function on it for each operation symbol. An *algebra* is (roughly) a pre-algebra where the domain of definition of each partial function corresponds to the argument sorts in some provable functionality for the function. See Sect. 9.12 for the usual example.

7.7 Unified Algebras

Let us conclude our survey of first-order frameworks for algebraic specification with so-called *unified algebras* [36, 34, 35]. I developed this framework for use in specifying data for action semantic descriptions of programming languages [37], but it might have more general applicability. The starting point was order-sorted algebras; the foregoing work of Wadge on classified algebras provided much inspiration, as did Smolka's work on the semantics of order-sorted Horn logic [47]. Unified algebras has much in common with ETL (above), although the initial developments of the two approaches were independent.

The signature of a unified algebra is just a ranked alphabet. The universe of a unified algebra A is a (distributive) lattice with a bottom value, together with a distinguished subset I_A of *individuals*. The operations of a unified algebra are required to be monotone (total) functions on the lattice; they are *not* required to be strict or additive, nor to preserve the property of individuality.

All the values of a unified algebra may be thought of as sorts, with the individuals corresponding to singleton sorts. However, the individuals do *not* have to be the atoms of the lattice, just above the bottom: for instance, the meet of two individuals is below both of them, but need not be identified with the bottom value. The partial order of the lattice $\leq$ represents sort inclusion; join $x \mid y$ is sort union and meet $x \,\&\, y$ is sort intersection. Those values that do not include any individuals at all, such as the bottom value denoted by the constant 'nothing', are vacuous sorts, representing the lack of a result from applying an operation to unintended arguments. A special case of a unified algebra is a *power algebra*, whose universe is a power set, with the singletons as individuals [35].

The axioms of unified algebraic specifications are Horn clauses involving equations $t_1 = t_2$, inclusions $t_1 \leq t_2$, and *individual* inclusions $t_1 : t_2$. An equation holds in a unified algebra A when the terms have identical values, whether or not these values are individuals, proper sorts, or vacuous; an inclusion holds when the values of the terms are in the partial order of the sort lattice; and an individual inclusion $t_1 : t_2$ holds when the value of t_1 is not only included in that of t_2, but also in the distinguished subset of individuals I_A. See Sect. 9.13 for an example specification. Note that the example exploits some natural abbreviations for axioms that correspond to functionalities of (total, partial, or unrestricted) operations; the expansions of these formal abbreviations are defined in [37].

Unified algebraic specifications always have initial models, because they are essentially just unsorted Horn clause logic (with equality) specifications: the lattice structure and monotonicity of operations can all be captured by Horn clauses. One reason for not restricting attention to the power algebras mentioned above is that even very simple specifications fail to have initial models. A similar point is made by Smolka [48].

Although it can be shown that unified algebras provide a *liberal* institution, with the usual notion of reduct functor, it is problematic to define useful constraints in such an unsorted framework, because the ordinary reduct functor only forgets operations—never values. However, by using a *more forgetful* reduct functor (treating all ground terms as if they were sorts) one can simulate the way that many-sorted and order-sorted forgetful functors deal with values, thereby providing constraints that have the expected meaning.

The main virtues of unified algebras are, in my own view, as follows:

- It is easy to express conventional (universal) OSA specifications: functionalities and subsort inclusions in order-sorted signatures are simply expressed as axioms in unified algebraic specifications.
- Partial operations are represented semantically by total operations that may return vacuous sorts. The undefinedness of a value can be specified by equating it to the constant denoting the bottom value. The bottom value is included in every sort, and allows error *individuals* to be avoided.
- The monotonic extension of operations from individuals to proper sorts is useful for specifying sort equations, such as nat = 0 | succ(nat). There is no distinction between an individual such as 0 and the sort that includes just that individual (which is possible because sorts of sorts are not needed).
- Parametric polymorphism and generic data types can be easily specified, using sort restriction operations. For instance, consider a binary operation L[of D] which restricts the sort of lists L to those lists whose components are of data sort D. Notice that monotonicity gives list[of 0] $\leq$ list[of nat] $\leq$ list[of int], assuming nat $\leq$ int.
- Dependent sorts can be specified too, for instance using an operation that maps each individual natural number to the sort of lists with length at most that number. The fact that individuals are a special case of sorts avoids some pedantic details.
- Instantiation of generic specifications can be achieved by specifying sort equations as axioms, instead of having to use translation.

Perhaps there are some drawbacks too? Well, sorts are nonextensional, so unspecified values do not automatically get equated with the bottom value: a careless specification may give rise to a large number of distinct vacuous sorts, all representing errors. Although these don't get in the way at all, they are there. Sort checking is obviously undecidable in general—as for most systems that allow dependent sorts. Variables that range over all sorts, or over all subsorts of a specified sort, easily give rise to inconsistency between obvious-looking axioms: proper sorts correspond to nondeterministic choices between individuals, and it is well-known that extra care is needed with specifying nondeterministic operations. The assumption of monotonicity (useful for defining constraints) prevents a straightforward extension to higher-order unified algebras with function space construction as an ordinary operation. Finally, when a many-sorted or order-sorted specification is translated straightforwardly into a unified algebraic specification, the loose semantics of the specifications are quite different, although their initial algebras are closely related.

8 Conclusion

A tentative conclusion might be that frameworks which cater for sort inclusions have superseded those that don't. In particular, it seems that error algebras and algebras with okay predicates can be regarded as particular disciplines of order-sorted algebras. Label algebras provide a rather different way of generalizing many-sorted algebras.

The tendency is perhaps also to move from a syntactic notion of sort to a semantic one, abandoning decidability of sort checking in favour of allowing an expressive algebra of sorts. Perhaps order-sorted algebras themselves are best regarded as particular, efficiently-implementable disciplines of the essentially unsorted frameworks of ETL [29] or unified algebras [35]? Further comparison of both the theoretical and pragmatic aspects of these frameworks is required before any definite conclusions can be drawn.

But however interesting sorts in algebraic specifications have become, remember: they are only there to help specifying individuals and their operations!

Acknowledgments: Many of the participants at the 8th WADT meeting in Dourdan contributed to this survey by pointing out inaccuracies in the preliminary version, and telling me about serious omissions that I had made. Răzvan Diaconescu kindly let me see a draft of his analysis of the relationship between various frameworks that support subsorts. Joseph Goguen patiently explained numerous technical and conceptual points that I had misunderstood concerning OSA. Axel Poigné gave me some useful comments, especially concerning the relationship between total and partial algebras. Thanks to Christine Choppy and Michel Bidoit for encouraging me to write this survey, and for inviting me to present it at the 8th WADT.

9 Examples

The examples given below illustrate most of the approaches that we have discussed above. For simplicity, the specified abstract data type in each case is merely *generic lists of data*.[3] It is supposed to be erroneous to attempt to take the head or tail of an empty-list. We don't bother to specify module parameterization.

To ease the comparison of the examples, we use a uniform style of notation throughout. This often differs in appearance from that advocated and used by the authors of the illustrated approaches.

Some of the examples assume that the Boolean truth-values and operations are already specified appropriately.

[3] To make at least a notational change from stacks!

9.1 Many-Sorted Algebras

sorts: data, list.

ops: nil : $\rightarrow$ list,
cons : data, list $\rightarrow$ list,
head : list $\rightarrow$ data,
tail : list $\rightarrow$ list,
e_{data} : $\rightarrow$ data,
e_{list} : $\rightarrow$ list,
ifok : data, list, data $\rightarrow$ data,
ifok : data, list, list $\rightarrow$ list,
ok : data $\rightarrow$ boole,
ok : list $\rightarrow$ boole.

vars: d,d':data, l,l':list.

axioms:

(1) ifok(d, l, head(cons(d,l))) = d.
(2) ifok(d, l, tail(cons(d,l))) = l.
(3) head(nil) = e_{data}.
(4) tail(nil) = e_{list}.
(5) ok(e_{data}) = false.
(6) ok(e_{list}) = false.
(7) ok(nil) = true.
(8) ok(cons(d,l)) = ok(d) $\wedge$ ok(l).
(9) cons(e_{data},l) = e_{list}.
(10) cons(d,e_{list}) = e_{list}.
(11) head(e_{list}) = e_{data}.
(12) tail(e_{list}) = e_{list}.
(13) ifok(d,l,d') =
ife(ok(d) $\wedge$ ok(l), d', e_{data}).
(14) ifok(d,l,l') =
ife(ok(d) $\wedge$ ok(l), l', e_{list}).

9.2 Partial Algebras

sorts: data, list.

ops: nil : $\rightarrow$ list,
cons : data, list $\rightarrow$ list,
head : list $\rightarrow$ data,
tail : list $\rightarrow$ list.

vars: d:data, l:list.

axioms:

(1) head(cons(d,l)) = d.
(2) tail(cons(d,l)) = l.
(3) D(nil).

9.3 Error Algebras

sorts: data, list.

ops: nil : $\rightarrow$ list,
cons : data, list $\rightarrow$ list,
head : list $\rightarrow$ data,
tail : list $\rightarrow$ list.

err-ops: e_{data} : $\rightarrow$ data,
e_{list} : $\rightarrow$ list.

vars: d:data, l:list.

ok-axioms:

(1) head(cons(d,l)) = d.
(2) tail(cons(d,l)) = l.

err-axioms:

(3) head(nil) = e_{data}.
(4) tail(nil) = e_{list}.

9.4 Algebras with Okay Predicates

sorts: data, list.

ops: nil : $\rightarrow$ list,
cons : data, list $\rightarrow$ list,
head : list $\rightarrow$ data (*unsafe*),
tail : list $\rightarrow$ list (*unsafe*),
e_{data} : $\rightarrow$ data (*unsafe*),
e_{list} : $\rightarrow$ list (*unsafe*).

vars: d:data, l:list.
d':data, l':list (*unsafe*).

axioms:

(1) head(cons(d,l)) = d.
(2) tail(cons(d,l)) = l.
(3) head(nil) = e_{data}.
(4) tail(nil) = e_{list}.
(5) cons(e_{data},l') = e_{list}.
(6) cons(d',e_{list}) = e_{list}.
(7) head(e_{list}) = e_{data}.
(8) tail(e_{list}) = e_{list}.

9.5 Exception Algebras

sorts: data, list.

ops: nil : $\rightarrow$ list,
cons : data, list $\rightarrow$ list,
head : list $\rightarrow$ data,
tail : list $\rightarrow$ list.

labels: e_{data}, e_{list}.

ok-forms:

(1) nil $\in$ Ok-Frm.

(2) $d \in$ Ok-Frm $\wedge$ $l \in$ Ok-Frm $\Rightarrow$ cons(d,l) $\in$ Ok-Frm.

ok-axioms:

(3) head(cons(d,l)) $= d$.

(4) tail(cons(d,l)) $= l$.

label-axioms:

(5) head(nil) $\in e_{data}$.

(6) tail(nil) $\in e_{list}$.

(7) $d \in e_{data}$ $\Rightarrow$ cons(d,l) $\in e_{list}$.

(8) $l \in e_{list}$ $\Rightarrow$ cons(d,l) $\in e_{list}$.

(9) $l \in e_{list}$ $\Rightarrow$ head(l) $\in e_{data}$.

(10) $l \in e_{list}$ $\Rightarrow$ tail(l) $\in e_{list}$.

general-axioms: *none.*

9.6 Order-Sorted Algebras

sorts: data, list, nelist.

subsorts: nelist $\leq$ list.

ops: nil : $\rightarrow$ list,
cons : data, list $\rightarrow$ nelist,
head : nelist $\rightarrow$ data,
tail : nelist $\rightarrow$ list.

vars: d:data, l:list.

axioms:

(1) head(cons(d,l)) $= d$.

(2) tail(cons(d,l)) $= l$.

Using supersorts instead of subsorts:

sorts: data, list, err-data, err-list.

subsorts: data $\leq$ err-data,
list $\leq$ err-list.

ops: nil : $\rightarrow$ list,
cons : data, list $\rightarrow$ list,
head : list $\rightarrow$ err-data,
tail : list $\rightarrow$ err-list.

vars: d:data, l:list.

axioms:

(1) head(cons(d,l)) $= d$.

(2) tail(cons(d,l)) $= l$.

9.7 Classified Algebras

sorts: data, list.

ops: nil, cons, head, tail.

axioms:

(1) nil : list.

(2) cons(d_{data},l_{list}) : list.

(3) head(cons(d_{data},l_{list})) $= d_{data}$.

(4) tail(cons(d_{data},l_{list})) $= l_{list}$.

Optionally, one may add:

sorts: nelist.

axioms:

(5) cons(d_{data},l_{list}) : nelist.

(6) head(l_{nelist}) : data.

(7) tail(l_{nelist}) : list.

9.8 G-Algebras

sorts: data, list, nelist.

ops: nil, cons(_,_), head(_), tail(_).

vars: d, l.

axioms:

(1) d :: data. l :: list.

(2) nil : list.

(3) cons(_,_) : data, list $\rightarrow$ nelist.

(4) head(_): nelist $\rightarrow$ data.

(5) tail(_): nelist $\rightarrow$ list.

(6) head(cons(d, l)) $= d$.

(7) tail(cons(d, l)) $= l$.

9.9 Polymorphically Order-Sorted Types

(1) $\mathsf{list}(T) := \mathsf{elist} \sqcup \mathsf{nelist}(T)$.

(2) $\mathsf{elist} := \mathsf{elist} \sqcup \mathsf{nelist}$.

(3) $\mathsf{elist} := \mathsf{nil}{:}[\,]$.

(4) $\mathsf{nelist}(T) := \mathsf{cons}{:}T \times \mathsf{list}(T)$.

9.10 Equational Type Logic

(1) nil : list.

(2) d : data, l : list $\Rightarrow$ cons(d,l) : list.

(3) d : data, l : list $\Rightarrow$
head(cons(d,l)) = d.

(4) d : data, l : list $\Rightarrow$
tail(cons(d,l)) = l.

9.11 Typed Horn Logic

orders: type.
types: list(_), list+(_), type.
ops: nil, cons(_,_), head(_), tail(_).
decl:

(1) $\vdash$ type ! .

(2) t :: type $\vdash$ list(t) : type.

(3) t :: type $\vdash$ list+(t) : type.

(4) t :: type $\vdash$ nil : list(t).

(5) t :: type, l : list(t), d : t $\vdash$
cons(d,l) : list+(t).

(6) t :: type, l : list+(t) $\vdash$ head(l) : list(t).

(7) t :: type, l : list+(t) $\vdash$ tail(l) : list(t).

axioms:

(8) t :: type, l : list(t), d : t $\vdash$
head(cons(d,l)) = d.

(9) t :: type, l : list(t), d : t $\vdash$
tail(cons(d,l)) = l.

9.12 Term Declaration Logic

sorts: data, list.
declarations:

(1) elist : list.

(2) cons(data,list) : list.

(3) head(cons(data,list)) : data.

(4) tail(cons(data,list)) : list.

variables: d : data, l : list.
equations:

(5) head(cons(d,l)) = d.

(6) tail(cons(d,l)) = l.

In fact the last two declarations can be obtained as consequences of the equations.

9.13 Unified Algebras

ops: data, list, nil, cons(_,_), head_ , tail_ .
axioms:

(1) nil : list.

(2) cons(_,_) :: data, list → list (*total*).

(3) head_ :: list → data (*partial*).

(4) tail_ :: list → list (*partial*).

(5) head cons(d:data,l:list) = d.

(6) tail cons(d:data,l:list) = l.

Optional extras:

op: _[of _] .
axioms:

(7) list = nil | cons(data,list).

(8) _[of _] :: list, data → list.

(9) list[of data] = list.

(10) list[of nothing] = nil.

(11) $D \leq$ data $\Rightarrow$

  (1) cons(_,_) ::
  D, list[of D] → list[of D];

  (2) head_ :: list[of D] → D;

  (3) tail_ :: list[of D] → list[of D];

  (4) nil[of D] = nil;

  (5) cons(d:data,l:list)[of D] =
  cons(d & D, l[of D]);

  (6) nothing[of D] = nothing;

  (7) ((L_1≤list) | (L_2≤list))[of D] =
  L_1[of D] | L_2[of D].

References

1. P. Aczel. Term declaration logic and generalized composita. In *LICS'91, Proc. 6th Ann. Symp. on Logic in Computer Science*, pages 22–30. IEEE, 1991.
2. H. Andréka, P. Burmeister, and I. Németi. Quasi-varieties of partial algebras – a unifying approach towards a two-valued model theory for partial algebras. Preprint 557, FB Mathematik und Informatik, TH Darmstadt, 1980.
3. E. Astesiano and M. Cerioli. Non-strict don't care algebras and specifications. In *Proc. TAPSOFT'91, Brighton*, number 493 in Lecture Notes in Computer Science, pages 121–142. Springer-Verlag, 1991.
4. E. Astesiano and M. Cerioli. Relationships between logical frameworks. This volume, 1992.
5. G. Bernot, M. Bidoit, and C. Choppy. Abstract data types with exception handling: an initial approach based on a distinction between exceptions and errors. *Theoretical Comput. Sci.*, 46:13–46, 1986.
6. G. Bernot and P. Le Gall. Label algebras. This volume, 1992.
7. M. Bidoit. Algebraic specification of exception handling and error recovery by means of declarations and equations. In *ICALP'84, Proc. Int. Coll. on Automata, Languages, and Programming, Antwerp*, number 172 in Lecture Notes in Computer Science, pages 95–108. Springer-Verlag, 1984.
8. M. Broy and M. Wirsing. Partial abstract types. *Acta Inf.*, 18:47–64, 1982.
9. P. Burmeister. *A Model-Theoretic Oriented Approach to Partial Algebras*. Akademie-Verlag, Berlin, 1986.
10. H. Comon. Completion of rewrite systems with membership constraints. Technical report, SUNY at Stony Brook, 1991.
11. R. L. Constable et al. *Implementing Mathematics with the Nuprl Proof Development System*. Prentice-Hall, 1986.
12. H. Ehrig and B. Mahr. *Fundamentals of Algebraic Specification 1: Equations and Initial Semantics*. Number 6 in EATCS Monographs on Theoretical Computer Science. Springer-Verlag, 1985.
13. H. Ehrig, P. Pepper, and F. Orejas. On recent trends in algebraic specification. In *ICALP'89, Proc. Int. Coll. on Automata, Languages, and Programming, Torino*, number 372 in Lecture Notes in Computer Science, pages 263–288. Springer-Verlag, 1989.
14. M. Gogolla. Partially ordered sorts in algebraic specifications. In *Proc. 1984 Colloq. on Trees in Algebra and Programming, Bordeaux*, pages 139–153. Cambridge University Press, 1984.
15. M. Gogolla. A final algebra semantics for errors and exceptions. In *Recent Trends in Data Type Specification*, number 116 in Series IFB, pages 89–103. Springer-Verlag, 1985.
16. M. Gogolla. On parametric algebraic specifications with clean error handling. In *TAPSOFT'87, Proc. Int. Joint Conf. on Theory and Practice of Software Development, Pisa, Volume 1*, number 249 in Lecture Notes in Computer Science, pages 81–95. Springer-Verlag, 1987.
17. M. Gogolla, K. Drosten, U. Lipeck, and H.-D. Ehrich. Algebraic and operational semantics of specifications allowing exceptions and errors. *Theoretical Comput. Sci.*, 34:289–313, 1984.
18. J. A. Goguen. Abstract errors for abstract data types. In *Proc. IFIP Working Conference on the Formal Description of Programming Concepts, St. Andrews, New Brunswick, 1977*. North-Holland, 1978.
19. J. A. Goguen. Order sorted algebra. Semantics and Theory of Computation Report 14, UCLA Computer Science Dept., 1978.

20. J. A. Goguen. Types as theories. In *Proc. Symposium on General Topology and Applications*. Oxford University Press, 1990.
21. J. A. Goguen and R. M. Burstall. Introducing institutions. In *Proc. Logics of Programming Workshop*, number 164 in Lecture Notes in Computer Science, pages 221–256. Springer-Verlag, 1984.
22. J. A. Goguen and R. M. Burstall. A study in the foundations of programming methodology: specifications, institutions, charters and parchments. In *Proc. Workshop on Category Theory and Computer Programming, Guildford*, number 240 in Lecture Notes in Computer Science, pages 313–333. Springer-Verlag, 1986.
23. J. A. Goguen and J. Meseguer. Order-sorted algebra I: Equational deduction for multiple inheritance, overloading, exceptions and partial operations. Technical Report SRI-CSL-89-10, Computer Science Lab., SRI International, July 1989.
24. J. A. Goguen, J. W. Thatcher, and E. G. Wagner. An initial algebra approach to the specification, correctness, and implementation of abstract data types. In R. T. Yeh, editor, *Current Trends in Programming Methodology*, volume IV. Prentice-Hall, 1978.
25. J. A. Goguen and T. Winkler. Introducing OBJ3. Technical Report SRI-CSL-88-9, Computer Science Lab., SRI International, 1988.
26. C. Kirchner and H. Kirchner. Order-sorted computations in G-algebra. Draft, INRIA-Lorraine & CRIN, Nancy, December 1991.
27. H.-J. Kreowski. Partial algebras flow from algebraic specifications. In *ICALP'87, Proc. Int. Coll. on Automata, Languages, and Programming, Karlsruhe*, number 267 in Lecture Notes in Computer Science, pages 521–530. Springer-Verlag, 1987.
28. V. Manca, A. Salibra, and G. Scollo. Equational type logic. *Theoretical Comput. Sci.*, 77:131–159, 1990.
29. V. Manca, A. Salibra, and G. Scollo. On the expressiveness of equational type logic. In *The Unified Computation Laboratory*. Oxford University Press, 1992. To appear.
30. N. Martí-Oliet and J. Mesguer. Inclusions and subtypes. Technical Report SRI-CSL-90-16, Computer Science Lab., SRI International, 1990.
31. A. Mégrelis. *Algèbre Galactique*. PhD thesis, Univ. de Nancy, 1990.
32. A. Mégrelis. Partial algebra + order-sorted algebra = galactic algebra. Tech. Report CRIN 90-R-108, Centre de Recherche en Informatique de Nancy, 1990.
33. B. Möller. On the algebraic specification of infinite objects – ordered and continuous models of algebraic types. *Acta Inf.*, 22:537–578, 1985.
34. P. D. Mosses. Unified algebras and action semantics. In *STACS'89, Proc. Symp. on Theoretical Aspects of Computer Science, Paderborn*, number 349 in Lecture Notes in Computer Science, pages 17–35. Springer-Verlag, 1989.
35. P. D. Mosses. Unified algebras and institutions. In *LICS'89, Proc. 4th Ann. Symp. on Logic in Computer Science*, pages 304–312. IEEE, 1989.
36. P. D. Mosses. Unified algebras and modules. In *POPL'89, Proc. 16th Ann. ACM Symp. on Principles of Programming Languages*, pages 329–343. ACM, 1989.
37. P. D. Mosses. *Action Semantics*. Tracts in Theoretical Computer Science. Cambridge University Press, 1992.
38. O. Owe and O.-J. Dahl. Generator induction in order-sorted algebras. *Formal Aspects of Computing*, 3:2–20, 1991.
39. A. Poigné. Another look at parameterization using algebraic specifications with subsorts. In *MFCS'84, Proc. Symp. on Math. Foundations of Computer Science*, number 176 in Lecture Notes in Computer Science. Springer-Verlag, 1984.
40. A. Poigné. Partial algebras, subsorting and dependent types. In D. Sannella and A. Tarlecki, editors, *Recent Trends in Data Type Specification*, number 332 in Lecture Notes in Computer Science, pages 208–234. Springer-Verlag, 1988.

41. A. Poigné. Typed Horn logic. In *MFCS'90, Proc. Symp. on Math. Foundations of Computer Science*, number 452 in Lecture Notes in Computer Science, pages 470–477. Springer-Verlag, 1990.
42. A. Poigné. Once more on order-sorted algebra. In *MFCS'91, Proc. Symp. on Math. Foundations of Computer Science*, number 520 in Lecture Notes in Computer Science, pages 397–405. Springer-Verlag, 1991.
43. Z. Qian. Relation-sorted algebraic specifications with built-in coercers: parameterization and parameter passing. In *Proc. Workshop on Categorical Methods in Computer Science with Aspects from Topology*, number 393 in Lecture Notes in Computer Science, pages 244–260. Springer-Verlag, 1989.
44. H. Reichel. *Initial Computability, Algebraic Specifications, and Partial Algebras*. Number 2 in The International Series of Monographs on Computer Science. Oxford University Press, 1987.
45. D. Sannella and A. Tarlecki. Specifications in an arbitrary institution. *Information and Computation*, 76:165–210, 1988.
46. G. Scollo. On the use of equational type logic for software engineering and protocol design. In Numidio, editor, *Proc. 1st Maghrebin Conf. on Artificial Intelligence and Software Engineering, Constantine, Algeria, 1989*, pages 460–485, 1991. Also available as Memoranda Informatica 89-52, Univ. Twente.
47. G. Smolka. Order-sorted Horn logic: Semantics and deduction. SEKI Report SR–86–17, FB Informatik, Universität Kaiserslautern, 1986.
48. G. Smolka. *Logic Programming over Polymorphically Order-Sorted Types*. PhD thesis, Universität Kaiserslautern, 1989.
49. G. Smolka, W. Nutt, J. A. Goguen, and J. Meseguer. Order-sorted equational computation. In *Proc. Colloq. on Resolution of Equations in Algebraic Structures, Austin*. Academic Press, 1989.
50. W. W. Wadge. Classified algebras. Theory of Computation Report 46, University of Warwick, 1982.
51. U. Waldmann. Semantics of order-sorted specifications. To appear in *Theoretical Comput. Sci.*, 1992.
52. M. Wirsing. Algebraic specification. In J. van Leeuwen, A. Meyer, M. Nivat, M. Paterson, and D. Perrin, editors, *Handbook of Theoretical Computer Science*, volume B, chapter 13. Elsevier Science Publishers, Amsterdam; and MIT Press, 1990.

Implementation and Behavioural Equivalence: A Survey

Fernando Orejas

Dept. Leng. Sist. Inf., Univ. Polit. Cataluña
Barcelona, SPAIN

Marisa Navarro, Ana Sánchez

Dept. Leng. Sist. Inf., Univ. del Pais Vasco
San Sebastian, SPAIN

Abstract In this paper we try to shed some light over the similarities and differences among the different approaches to define implementations and behavioural equivalence. For obvious reasons, we do not discuss all existing approaches individually. However a formal framework is used to discuss the most important ones. Additionally, some issues concerning implementations that in our opinion are often misunderstood, especially transitivity of implementation correctness and its rôle in the software development process, are discussed in detail.

1. Introduction

In 1972 Hoare [Hoa 72] presented the first notion of data type implementation in the literature. This was the beginning of a long series of papers dealing with the same concept (without trying to be exhaustive we may cite [GTW 76, GHM 78, EKP 78, EL 80, Ore 81, Ehr 82, EKMP 82, GM 82, SW 82, EK 83, Gan 83, SW 83, KA 84, Poi 84, Ore 85, BBC 86, BMPW 86, Sch 87, ST 87, ST 88, Hen 89, Ber 89, Ehg 89, EA 91]). Why such a number of different approaches? The reasons are several: sometimes the framework is different ("loose" vs "initial" specifications, parameterized vs non-parameterized specifications, partial vs total data types, etc.); sometimes the aim is different (some approaches would stress only "semantic" aspects of implementations while others would focus on "syntactic" or "proof-theoretic" aspects); even sometimes (as we will see) the intuition underlying the various approaches is different.

In this paper we will try to shed some light over the similarities and differences of all these approaches, although for obvious reasons we will not discuss each of them individually. A large part of this discussion has been based in [ST 88] which was already highly clarifying.

The concept of behavioural equivalence is very related to the notion of implementation, since one of the original motivations to study behavioural issues was to provide a new framework for a powerful and simple notion of implementation. For several reasons a certain number of different approaches have also been introduced in the literature (again without trying to be exhaustive we may cite [Rei 81, GM 82, SW 83, MG 85, ST 87, Sch 87, Hen 88, NO 88,

ONE 89, BB 91]. In the same spirit, in the second part of the paper, we have tried to clarify all these approaches.

The rest of the paper is structured in four sections. The last one deals with behavioural equivalence, while the first three of them study several issues concerning implementations. In particular, in section 2 we discuss the different intuitions for the notion of implementation. In section 3 we concentrate on the so-called "simulations" providing a framework (based on [ST 88]) useful to analyze the various approaches. Finally, section 4 discusses some common misunderstandings around the different implementation concepts.

Acknowledgements This paper would not have been written without the kind invitation from Michel Bidoit and Christine Choppy. Also, it is the result of the work of many people (which are mentioned in the paper and can be found in the references) and of several discussions that F. Orejas had in the last 10 (?) years especially with Hartmut Ehrig, Joseph Goguen, José Meseguer, Don Sannella and Martin Wirsing. More precisely, some discussions with H. Ehrig during his last stay in Barcelona were very valuable for the concrete writing of the paper. The authors would also like to thank the referees for their comments that have contributed to improve this final version. This work has been partially supported by the Esprit Basic Working Group COMPASS (ref. 3264).

2. What is an Implementation?

In the framework of software development programs may be seen as the result of a process starting from a "high-level specification" SP0 and ending at a "low level program" P. In between, different "lower-level specifications" SP1, ..., SPn are produced. This process is called "implementation" and P is said to be an implementation of SP0 (and of SP1, ..., SPn). In our context, we will also consider SPi to be an implementation of SPj (whenever $i > j$).

If we analyze this implementation process in detail we may recognize three different kinds of steps (often intertwined). These kinds of steps can themselves be called implementations and have provided intuition for different kinds of implementation concepts. They can be described as follows:

(1) Translation

SP' is a *translation* of SP if SP' describes the "same" objects as SP but in a "more concrete" language (or logic). For instance, suppose that SP is the specification of the gcd using first order logic as follows:

$$gcd(x,y) \mid x \ \wedge \ gcd(x,y) \mid y \ \wedge \ \forall z\,(z \mid x \ \wedge \ z \mid y \ \Rightarrow \ z \leq gcd(x,y))$$

then a recursive definition, as follows, could be considered as an implementation by translation of SP:

```
gcd(x,y) = if          x< y   then gcd(x, y - x)
           else if     x > y  then gcd(x - y, y)
           else x
```

Some specific kinds of translation implementations have been studied in [Ore 85, BW 88, KS 88]. The general problem of relating specifications written in terms of different logics has been treated in the framework of institutions by the definition of different kinds of *institution morphisms* (see for instance [GB 84, Mes 89, ST 88] and especially [AC 90]).

(2) Refinement

SP' is a *refinement* of SP if the class of objects described by SP' is included in the class of objects described by SP. The intuition behind this kind of implementation steps is the following: SP is a "loose" specification of a system in the sense that several different realizations are possible; then SP' includes some new design decisions that rule out some of these possible realizations (hopefully not all of them). For instance, suppose that SP is the specification of a choice operation over a sequence of integers as follows:

choice: seq_of_int → integer

not(empty(s)) ⇒ choice (s) is_in s

i.e. the models of SP are all the possible *choice* functions over sequences, then the following specification could be considered as a refinement implementation of SP:

choice: seq_of_int → integer

choice (append(s,n)) = n

i.e. this new specification restricts the models of SP to only one, where choice coincides with the head operation.

Refinement implementations were at some point advocated to be the "right" notion of implementation for loose specifications [SW 83, ST 87a]. Also this kind of refinement steps have been studied in the framework of specification design (see for instance [CO 88, OSC 89]).

(3) Simulation

SP' simulates SP if the models of SP' *behave* like all the models of SP. This is the most classical notion of implementation [Hoa 72] and is related to previous notions in automata theory. Classical examples of this kind of "simulation" are the implementation of sets by sequences or the implementation of stacks by means of arrays and pointers. Most of the implementation approaches in the literature fall into this category [GTW 76, GHM 76, EKP 78, Ore 81, Ehr 82, EKMP 82, GM 82, EK 83, Gan 83, KA 84, Ore 85, BBC 86, BMPW 86, Poi 84, Ber 89]). However some others (e.g. [SW 82, ST 88, Sch 87, Hen 89]) prefer to mix the two notions of *refinement* and *simulation* : SP' implements SP if the models of SP' *behave* like (some) models of SP. Mixing these two concepts into one definition seems reasonable if specifications are loose since the definition becomes in a sense simpler (see remark 3.5.3), but if specifications are monomorphic (e.g. initial specifications) then this mixture makes no sense: if a specification SP' implements SP either the model of SP' simulates the model of SP or else SP' would be inconsistent. In some different specification frameworks (like VDM, see e.g. [BJ 82]) simulation implementations are called *data reification*.

In the rest of the paper we will mainly discuss simulation implementations. However, sometimes other kinds of implementations in combination with simulation will be considered.

3. Implementations: Syntax and Semantics

Implementations may be studied from two different points of view. On the one hand, given specifications SP1 = (Σ1,E1) and SP2 = (Σ2,E2), where E1 and E2 are sets of formulae over any suitable logic (i.e. not necessarily equations), we may consider that implementing the data type specified by SP1 by the data type specified by SP2 consists in defining the operations (and the data sorts) in Σ1 in terms of the operations (and data sorts) from Σ2, in such a way that the enriched SP2-models "behave" like the SP1-models ([GTW 76, GHM 76, EKP 78, Ore 81, EL 80, Ehr 82, EKMP 82, GM 82, SW 82, EK 83, Gan 83, KA 84, Ore 85, Poi 85, BBC 86, ST 88, Ber 89]). In this sense, syntactically, an implementation would be an enrichment together with a mapping (technically, a signature morphism) relating the sorts and operations from Σ1 with the sorts and operations from the enriched Σ2 signature and, semantically, it would be a *construction* (associated to the enrichment) together with some kind of abstraction that relates the models of SP1 with the enriched SP2-models.

A simpler point of view [SW 83, ST 87, BMPW 86, Sch 87, Hen 89]) consists in, first, assuming that the enrichment has already taken place (i.e. the operations and data types in Σ1 are present in some sense in SP2) and, second, considering that an implementation is just the relation between SP1 and SP2. In this sense, syntactically, an implementation would just be a signature morphism relating sorts and operations in Σ1 to those in Σ2 and, semantically, it would be the abstraction relating SP1 to SP2-models.

In what follows we will consider that implementations include the enrichment step. The reasons are several: the most important one is that in our context it seems to be the most adequate for discussing the different approaches. Furthermore, the fact of identifying at the syntactic level implementations with (some) enrichments provides a clearer picture of the modular structure of the system being designed.

3.1 Definition (Syntax of Implementations)

Given two specifications SP1 and SP2, the syntax of an implementation I of SP1 by SP2 consists of:

1) An enrichment (Σ, E) of SP2

and 2) A signature morphism $h: \Sigma 1 \rightarrow \Sigma 2+\Sigma$

Now, in order to define the semantics of implementations we will first define the concepts of constructors and abstractors. Constructors are intended to give semantics to the enrichment associated to the implementation while abstractors define which is the class of algebras that "simulate" a given model.

3.2 Definition (Constructors)

Given two specifications SP1 and SP2, with SP1 $\subseteq$ SP2, a constructor is a mapping from Mod(SP1) to $2^{Mod(SP2)}$, i.e. a constructor associates SP2 model classes to SP1 models.

3.3 Definition (Abstractors)

Given a specification SP = (Σ, E), an abstractor α on Σ is a mapping from Mod(SP) to $2^{Mod(\Sigma)}$ satisfying:

a) *Reflexivity* $\forall A \in Mod(SP)\ A \in \alpha(A)$

b) *Transitivity* $\forall A1 \in Mod(\Sigma)\ \forall A2,A3 \in Mod(SP)$ if $A1 \in \alpha(A2)$ and $A2 \in \alpha(A3)$ then $A1 \in \alpha(A3)$.

3.4 Definition (Semantics and Correctness of Implementations)

Semantically, an implementation I of SP1 by SP2, whose syntax is ((Σ, E), h), is a pair ($U_h \cdot \kappa_I$, α_I), where κ_I is a constructor from SP2-models to SP2+(Σ,E)-model classes, κ_I: Mod(SP2) $\rightarrow 2^{Mod(SP2+(\Sigma,E))}$, α_I is an abstractor over $\Sigma 1$, α_I: Mod(SP1) $\rightarrow 2^{Mod(\Sigma 1)}$, and U_h is the forgetful functor associated to h, U_h: Mod($\Sigma 2+\Sigma$) $\rightarrow$ Mod($\Sigma 1$).

I is correct iff $\forall A1' \in U_h \cdot \kappa_I(Mod(SP2))$ there exists $A1 \in Mod(SP1)$ such that $A1' \in \alpha_I(A1)$ and vice versa, i.e., $\forall A1 \in Mod(SP1)\ \exists A1' \in U_h \cdot \kappa_I(Mod(SP2))$ such that $A1' \in \alpha_I(A1)$.

3.5 Remarks

1. The above definition (especially with respect to the notion of constructor) takes into account the possibility of defining "loose implementations", i.e. implementations in which the enrichment defining the implementation is loose. This can be the case, for instance, when defining the implementation of sets (including a choice operation) in terms of sequences: in that case we may like to define choice over sequences in a "loose" manner (i.e. as in the example in section 2). If we are working in a "monomorphic" framework (for instance initial semantics) we would probably define constructors as some kind of functors (for instance free functors, if this is possible).

2. Although the previous definitions are inspired by those of [ST 88] there are a number of differences. In their paper, Sannella and Tarlecki define two general notions of implementation: *constructor* and *abstractor* implementations. The former notion is defined just in terms of a constructor, while the latter is defined in terms of both a constructor and an abstractor. However, constructors ans abstractors are not exactly the same thing in our both approaches. First, [ST 88] only consider "monomorphic constructors" (i.e. functions mapping SP1-models into SP2-models) though they work in a loose framework. The second difference concerns the underlying intuition of what "is" the constructor and what "is" the abstractor of a given implementation approach: for instance, we consider the "reachability" step of [EKMP 82] as part of the abstractor (see case study 3.6.5) while they consider it included in the constructor. The third difference is a consequence of the previous one: their notion of abstractor satisfies the following symmetry condition, since abstractors are assumed to be defined in terms of a behavioural equivalence relation (see 3.6.7 and 5):

$$A1 \in \alpha(A2) \text{ implies } A2 \in \alpha(A1)$$

We have not asked for this condition because a number of implementation approaches in the literature (e.g. [Hoa 72, EKMP 82]) would not fit into our framework. Note that this would not be the case for [ST 88] since they would handle these approaches without using any abstractor, i.e. these are constructor implementations.

3. If in the previous definition we would have defined implementation correctness suppressing the "and vice versa" (i.e. I is correct iff $\forall A1' \in U_h \cdot \kappa_I(Mod(SP2))$ there exists $A1 \in Mod(SP1)$ such that $A1' \in \alpha_I(A1)$) then the implementation notion defined would have mixed "simulation" with "refinement" as described in the previous section. Note that in this case if SP2 is inconsistent I would trivially be considered a correct implementation. However it must also be noted that, SP2 would be considered an incorrect specification.

4. In some approaches other additional correctness conditions have been considered: for instance OP-completeness [EKMP 82] or persistency of the enrichment defining the implementation [EK 83]. The reasons for these additional conditions may be different. For example, persistency in [EK 83] is a consequence of the framework involved (persistent parameterized specifications). On the other hand, OP-completeness in [EKMP 82] is a consequence of trying to avoid the possibility of having implementations that would be "technically" correct but that would not correspond to any "real" implementation.

5. Note that the above definitions could cover reasonable notions of *bounded implementations* [KA 84, Bre 91], i.e. implementations where the implementing data type has some kind of size restrictions with respect to the implemented data type (for instance this happens when defining the implementation of an unbounded stack by a bounded array). In particular it would be enough to consider that $\alpha_I(A)$ includes all *bounded simulations* of A. On the other hand, our framework can not cover reasonable notions of *approximation implementations*, i.e. implementations where the values of the implementing data types describe incompletely, in some not fully precise way, the values of the implemented data type (for instance, when implementing the reals by some floating point representation). The reason is that the correctness of such implementations may be related to some precision factor that may be not preserved by the transitivity condition of abstractors.

3.6 Case Studies of Implementation Concepts

In what follows we will discuss some of the "main" implementation approaches in the literature using the framework introduced above .

3.6.1 Hoare 1972

The essential ideas about simulation implementations were presented in [Hoa 72]. He defined implementations by means of a partial "abstraction function", F_A: Concrete_type $\rightarrow$ Abstract_type, mapping concrete values into the abstract object they represent. F_A was assumed to be a many-one function because an abstract value can be represented by many concrete ones and it was assumed to be partial because not every concrete value represents an abstract one. The domain of the abstraction function was considered to be defined by an invariant condition. Additionally, though not explicitly stated in that way, F_A was assumed to be a (partial) homomorphism since it was assumed to commute (when defined) with the operations. A typical example underlying this intuition is the implementation of a stack by an array and an integer (the height of the stack). Not every array-integer pair represents a stack: for instance this happens when the integer is negative. Additionally, many array-integer pairs may represent the same stack: <A,i > and <A',i > represent the same stack if for every

$j \leq i$, A[j] = A'[j]. [Hoa 72] invented the terms ***representation domain*** to denote the domain of definition of the abstraction function, and ***representation equivalence*** to denote the equivalence relation induced by the abstraction function.

[Hoa 72] assumes that the enrichment defining the implementation has already been done and that the signature morphism relating the concrete and abstract signatures is just an inclusion (perhaps, together with a sort renaming). Therefore to describe this approach in our framework it is enough to define the abstraction relation. Obviously, $A2 \in \alpha_I(A1)$ iff there exists any abstraction function (i.e. partial homomorphism) F such that A1 = F(A2).

3.6.2 Goguen, Thatcher, Wagner 1976

[GTW 76] presented the first notion of implementation within the algebraic framework, more precisely within the initial algebra framework. However their approach was quite limited. According to them, implementations were defined by ***derivors***. Essentially, this is equivalent to considering that to implement SP by SP' we have to enrich SP' with the operations from Σ (after identifying in some way the sorts in Σ and in Σ'), adding for every σ in Σ an equation of the kind:

$$\sigma(X1,...,Xn) = t$$

with $t \in T_{\Sigma'}(X)$. That is, syntactically, an implementation according to [GTW 76] is such a limited kind of enrichment together with an inclusion morphism (up to sort renaming). Semantically, the constructor associated to this enrichment is just the standard free functor and the abstractor used for defining implementation correctness is defined as follows:

$$A2 \in \alpha(A1) \text{ iff } A2/\equiv\, \supseteq A1$$

where $\equiv$ is some congruence on A2 (actually $\equiv$ would play the role of the representation equivalence). [Ore 81] and [Ore 85] generalized this framework by allowing the derivors to be *infinite* or *recursive*, that is, in the equations defining the enrichment, as above, t is allowed to be infinite or to involve operations from Σ. The constructor associated to this enrichment is defined by means of least fixpoints. Additionally, [Ore 81] introduced a notion of "partial representation" allowing to cope with bounded implementations (see 3.5.5).

3.6.3 Ehrich 1982

[Ehr 82] eliminated all kind of restrictions concerning the enrichments for defining implementations. According to him an implementation of SP1 by SP2 is a triple I = (SP2', f, t) with specification morphisms f: SP2 $\rightarrow$ SP2' and t: SP1 $\rightarrow$ SP2'. Therefore, in our framework, the syntax of the implementation would be the enrichment associated to SP2 and SP2' defined by f, and the specification morphism t (seen as signature morphism). The semantics associated to the enrichment is just the free construction and the abstractor is defined essentially as in [GTW 76]. [Ehr 82] was in a sense a formalization of [GHM 78], which was the first approach to handle implementations just at the specification level. Unfortunately, [GHM 78] lacked formality.

3.6.4 Ehrig, Kreowski, Mahr, Padawitz 1982

[EKMP 82] was a crucial paper. They analyzed thoroughly implementations providing a new approach, proving that some previous definitions were semantically inadequate and showing the main difficulties concerning all these concepts. Essentially, their approach can be explained as follows. Syntactically an implementation of SP1 by SP2 is an enrichment over SP2 (they imposed certain limitations on the kind of enrichment to be used but not for technical reasons, just because they thought that this was more appropriate according to intuition). Semantically, an implementation is a functor that is defined by the composition of three other functors: SYNTHESIS, which is the meaning of the enrichment defining the implementation (the free functor); RESTRICT is the composition of two other functors, the forgetful functor that forgets the sorts and operations from the enriched SP2 not in SP1, and REACH that eliminates the *junk* elements defined by the implementation, i.e. all concrete values not representing any abstract value; finally IDENTIFICATION that identifies all concrete values that represent the same abstract value: in fact IDENTIFICATION is just obtained by making a quotient with the equations from SP1.

Let us see now an example. Suppose that we want to implement sets of integers by sequences of integers. That is the implemented (abstract) specification is:

```
SP1 = INTEGER +  BOOLEAN
                 sorts        set
                 operations
                     Ø:          → set
                     add:        set x int → set
                     _ is-in _ : int x set → bool
                 equations
                     add(add(S,n),n) = add(S,n)
                     add(add(S,n),n') = add(add(S,n'),n)
                     n is-in Ø = false
                     n is-in add(S,n') = (n eq n') or (n is-in S)
```

and the implementing (concrete) specification is:

```
SP2 = INTEGER +  sorts     seq
                 operations
                     e-s:   → seq
                     app:   seq x int → seq
```

Now, according to [EKMP 82] a possible implementation would be the following enrichment over SP2:

```
I =  sorts set
     operations
          c: seq → set
          Ø:      → set
          add: set x int → set
          _ is-in _ : int x set → bool
     equations
          Ø = c(e-s)
          n is-in Ø = false
          n is-in c(app(S,n')) = (n eq n') or (n is-in c(S))
          add(c(S),n) = c(S) if n is-in c(S) = true
          add(c(S),n) = c(app(S,n))  if n is-in c(S) = false
```

In this example c is an *operation implementing sorts*, i.e. an operation that describes how values of abstract sorts are defined in terms of values of concrete sorts. In this case we have that the values of sort set are a copy of the values of sort seq. However not every sequence represents a "valid" set in this implementation: only "copies" of sequences without repetitions can be generated using the set operations. This means that the representation domain in this example would be the sequences without repetitions. Moreover, one given set may be represented by more than one sequence: in particular any set is represented by any sequence including exactly the elements of the set.

The semantics of this implementation is defined as follows:

a) Given the initial algebra T_{SP2} defining the sequences of integers, SYNT(T_{SP2}) defines an algebra with an additional sort set, whose carrier contains a copy of the sequence carrier. Moreover the set operations in this algebra work as specified by the equations.

b) RESTRICTION forgets the sequence sort, all sequence operations and the copy operation. Additionally it "eliminates" from the set carrier all copies of sequences including a repeated element.

c) Finally IDENTIFICATION performs a quotient with respect to the set equations identifying (the copies of) all permutations of a given sequence.

This implementation is said to be RI-correct because ID·REST·SYNT(T_{SP2}) $\equiv T_{SP1}$. Additionally [EKMP 82] defined another correctness condition called OP-completeness (see remark 3.5.4) which is also satisfied by the example above. This condition essentially says that the implementation describes the operations from SP1 in terms of the operations in SP2 (and of the operations implementing sorts).

Therefore in our framework we can consider that the constructor associated to this kind of implementations is the free constructor associated to the given enrichment and the corresponding abstractor is defined as follows:

$$A2 \in \alpha(A1) \text{ iff } ID \cdot REACH\,(A2) \equiv A1$$

As said above [EKMP 82] did more than just providing a new concept of implementation. They noted that if, instead of defining the semantics of implementations as the composition ID·REST·SYNT (RI-semantics), they would have defined it as the composition REST·ID·SYNT (IR-semantics) then the associated correctness condition REST·ID·SYNT (T_{SP2}) $\equiv T_{SP1}$ (IR-correctness) would essentially coincide with the one defined in [GTW 76, Ehr 82]. But then they also noted that IR-correctness was strictly more restrictive than RI-correctness. The following example shows the problem. Suppose that we want to implement the data type specified as follows:

SP1 = **sorts** twonat
operations
0: → twonat
s: twonat → twonat
equations
s(s(x)) = s(x)

using as concrete type the integers specified as follows:

SP2 = **sorts** int
operations zero: $\rightarrow$ int
succ: int $\rightarrow$ int
pred: int $\rightarrow$ int
equations
pred(succ(n)) = n
succ(pred(n)) = n

Now, suppose that we define the following implementation:

I = **sorts** twonat
operations c: int $\rightarrow$ twonat
0: $\rightarrow$ twonat
s: twonat $\rightarrow$ twonat
equations
0 = c(zero)
s(c(n)) = c(succ(n))

This implementation is RI-correct: given T_{SP2}, SYNT defines an algebra with an additional sort twonat, whose carrier is a copy of the integers, and two additional operations 0 and s which "work" as the zero and the successor on the copy of the integers; REST forgets the integer sort and the integer operations, and eliminates from the twonat carrier the copies of all the negative integers; finally ID identifies (the copies of) all positive integers strictly greater than zero yielding an algebra with exactly two values (0 and 1) which is isomorphic to the initial SP1-algebra. However the implementation is not IR-correct: applying ID after synthesis collapses the twonat carrier into a single element since:

c(x) = c(succ(pred(x))) = s(c(pred(x))) = s(s(c(pred(x)))) = s(c(succ(pred(x)))) = s(c(x))

therefore after applying REST we obtain an algebra with a single value which is not isomorphic to T_{SP1}.

As a consequence, it can be concluded that the implementation concepts defined in [GTW 76, Ehr 82] were not fully adequate. Actually, in [EL 80] an RI-version of the approach in [Ehr 82] was given. On the other hand, [EKMP 82] also noted that IR-correctness was easier to prove than RI-correctness: IR-correctness is equivalent to a hierarchy-consistency condition, but there is no similar proof-theoretical characterization of RI-correctness (cf. 4.3)

Finally [EKMP 82] showed what it seemed to be a very unpleasant result: implementations are not transitive, i.e. if I1 is an implementation of SP1 in terms of SP2 and I2 is an implementation of SP2 in terms of SP3 then putting together I1 and I2 does not necessarily provide a correct implementation of SP1 in terms of SP3. This may be seen using the following counter-example:

Let SP1 be a specification of the booleans:

SP1 = **sorts** bool
operations true: $\rightarrow$ bool
false: $\rightarrow$ bool

SP2 is a specification of the natural numbers:

SP2 = **sorts** nat
operations 0: → nat
s: nat → nat

and SP3 is a specification of the integers as the one above. Now an implementation of SP1 in terms of SP2 is the following one:

I1 = **sorts** bool
operations
c1: nat → bool
true: → bool
false: → bool
equations
true = c1(0)
false = c1(s(n))

that is, according to this implementation, 0 represents the value true and false is represented by any natural greater than 0. SP1 is implemented by SP2 in the most obvious way, i.e. the non-negative integers represent the naturals:

I2 = **sorts** nat
operations
c2: int → nat
0: → nat
s: nat → nat
equations
0 = c2(zero)
s(c2(n)) = c2(succ(n))

The two implementations are obviously RI-correct and even IR-correct (the reader may easily check this), however if we put them together we obtain the following I12:

I12 = **sorts** bool, nat
operations
c1: nat → bool
true: → bool
false: → bool
c2: int → nat
0: → nat
s: nat → nat
equations
true = c1(0)
false = c1(s(n))
0 = c2(zero)
s(c2(n)) = c2(succ(n))

which is not correct (neither RI nor IR) since SYNT(T_{SP3}) satisfies true=false:

true = c1(0) = c1(c2(zero)) = c1(c2(succ(pred(zero)))) = c1(s(c2(pred(zero)))) = false

Transitivity of implementations within the [EKMP 82] approach was studied in detail in [Ore 83, Ore 84]. More discussion on the issue can be found in [Ore 86, ST 88] and in sections 4.1 and 4.2 of this paper.

An approach obviously related to [EKMP 82] is [EK 83] defining implementations in the framework of parameterized specifications. However, due to technical reasons, it was only possible to define them in terms of IR-semantics instead of the more powerful RI one. More recently, the approach in [EK 83] was extended in [Ehg 89, EA 91] to the RI-case studying the horizontal-vertical compatibility problem (see section 4.2) in a general setting.

3.6.5 Variations on [EKMP 82]

The problems in the approach of [EKMP 82] concerning transitivity of implementations and the difficulty of proving RI-correctness are mainly due to the problem of junk elimination, i.e. if we were able to ensure the non-existence of values outside the representation domain, these and other related problems would be solved or, at least, easier to solve. In this spirit [Poi 84], [BBC 86], [Ber 89] and very recently [San 91] have tried to avoid the generation of junk by the operations implementing sorts. [Poi 84] uses order sorted algebra (the junk is left in a supersort that can be forgotten afterwards) but this provides some additional technical complication (due to the order sorted framework) and there is a kind of sort proliferation that make specifications less manageable. [BBC 84, Ber 89] use a technique of "sort replication" that also allows to avoid junk generation, but the main problem, as in the former case, is sort proliferation. Finally, [San 91] works with partial algebra (sort-implementing operations are partial). This does not complicate the framework much and sort proliferation is avoided. Additionally, in [San 91] the definition of the associated abstractor uses behavioural equivalence (see 7. below) instead of identification.

3.6.6 Implementations for the Loose Approach

[BMPW 86] and [SW 82] provided an approach similar (in the sense that the abstractor used is essentially the same) to [EKMP 82] but in the framework of loose semantics. This means that constructors here are loose and that, with respect to implementation correctness, they use the mixture of simulation and refinement already mentioned (see remark 3.5.3). [BMPW 86] dealt with the non parameterized case and [SW 82] with the parameterized one.

3.6.7 Behaviour Implementations

Abstractors based on REACH - IDENTIFICATION are in a sense restrictive. In particular we have seen how to implement sets by sequences but in [EKMP 82] and similar frameworks it would be impossible to implement sequences by sets. Let us see an example in which such kind of implementation makes sense. Let sequences be specified as follows:

SP1 = INTEGER + BOOLEAN +

sorts seq

operations

e-s: → seq

app: seq x int → seq

_ is-in _ : int x seq → bool

equations

n is-in e-s = false

n is-in app(S,n') = (n eq n') or (n is-in S)

and suppose that in the system we are designing we do not plan to have any additional operation on sequences (like head or tail). Then, in that case, sequences have the same *observable behaviour* as sets (see section 5) and as a consequence sets could be considered a correct implementation of these sequences. The issue is that we can have a situation in which not only many concrete values may represent an abstract value but also many abstract values (observationally equivalent) may be represented by a single concrete value. Based on this intuition a number of approaches [GM 82, ST 87, Sch 87, ST 88, Niv 87, Hen 89, San 91] defined implementations using behavioural equivalence instead of identification. That means defining the abstractor as follows:

$$A1 \in \alpha(A2) \text{ iff } REACH(A1) \equiv_{Beh} A2$$

if eliminating junk is necessary and:

$$A1 \in \alpha(A2) \text{ iff } A1 \equiv_{Beh} A2$$

otherwise.

It must be noted that there is a quite important difference between *identification* and *behaviour* implementations. In the identification case, when defining an implementation of SP1 by SP2 we may assume for simplicity that all sorts and operations in SP1 are being implemented in terms of sorts and operations in SP2. However this is not possible for behaviour implementations. In this kind of approaches the behavioural semantics of the implemented specification SP1 is usually defined in terms of the sorts and operations from SP1 have the "same interpretation" in SP2 (i.e. that are "not implemented"). For instance, in the example above we would consider that the sorts *int* and *bool* are not implemented: this allows defining the right behavioural semantics to the *Sequence* specification. As a consequence, if I is an implementation of SP1 by SP2 and I' is another implementation of SP1 by SP3 then, α_I and $\alpha_{I'}$ will always be equal when dealing with identification implementations; however, when dealing with behaviour implementations, α_I and $\alpha_{I'}$ may be different if the sorts and operations from SP1 which are implemented by I and I', respectively, are different.

4. Three Common Misunderstandings about Implementations

In this section we will discuss some aspects concerning implementations that have been misunderstood by many people. They concern, on the one hand, transitivity of implementations and, on the other, the greater or smaller difficulty on proving implementations correct. In both cases there is a widespread feeling that the situation in the loose case is better. We will see that this is not really true.

4.1 Transitivity of Implementations (Part one)

As we have seen above (case study 3.6.4) [EKMP 82] proved that in their approach implementations are not transitive. Since then almost always, when presenting a new approach, it has become a kind of tradition to show that the new approach is better than [EKMP 82] because of satisfying transitivity implementations. Moreover, since many of these approaches are in the loose framework, this has given many people the feeling that the lack of transitivity is a problem of the initial approach. In what follows we will see that this is not quite true. We will show that the lack of transitivity is a consequence of many factors but it is not especially a consequence of working in the initial framework. To prove this last statement in a simple way it is enough to note that the loose framework is more general than the initial one, in the sense that if SP is an "initial" specification there must be a "loose" specification SP' such that Mod(SP') = $\{A / A \cong T_{SP}\}$, otherwise that loose framework would not be powerful enough for specification. Now suppose that we have a transitive implementation concept for our loose framework, then this very implementation concept would also satisfy transitivity for the initial one.

Let us now see what are the real causes of the lack of transitivity. Suppose that $I = ((\Sigma,E),$ $h: SP1 \rightarrow SP2 + (\Sigma,E))$ is a correct implementation of SP1 by SP2 and $I' = ((\Sigma',E'),$ $h': SP2 \rightarrow SP3 + (\Sigma',E'))$ is a correct implementation of SP2 by SP3, with $(U_h \cdot \kappa, \alpha_I)$ and $(U_{h'} \cdot \kappa', \alpha_{I'})$ being the semantics of I and I' respectively. Implementations are transitive if the composition of I and I' is a correct implementation of SP1 by SP3. But, what is the "composition" of I and I'? There are three possible answers:

1) The simplest answer corresponds to the approaches in where it is considered that the enrichment defining that implementation has been done a priori, i.e. syntactically I and I' consist only of the specification morphisms $h: SP1 \rightarrow SP2$ and $h': SP2 \rightarrow SP3$ and semantically they can be identified with forgetting functors U_h and $U_{h'}$ and the abstractors α_I and $\alpha_{I'}$. Then transitivity is defined by the following fact:

4.1.1 Fact (Transitivity of Implementations 1)

If $I = (\emptyset, h: SP1 \rightarrow SP2)$ is a correct implementation of SP1 by SP2 and $I' = (\emptyset,$ $h': SP2 \rightarrow SP3))$ is a correct implementation of SP2 by SP3, with (U_h, α_I) and $(U_{h'}, \alpha_{I'})$ being the semantics of I and I' respectively then the composition $I \cdot I' = (\emptyset,$ $h' \cdot h: SP1 \rightarrow SP3)$, with semantics $(U_{h' \cdot h}, \alpha_{I.I'})$ is correct iff $\forall A3 \in Mod(SP3)$ $\exists A1 \in Mod(SP1)$ such that $U_h(U_{h'}(A3)) \in \alpha_{I.I'}(A1)$ and $\forall A1 \in Mod(SP1)$ $\exists A3 \in Mod(SP3)$ such that $U_h(U_{h'}(A3)) \in \alpha_{I.I'}(A1)$.

Remark $\alpha_{I.I'}$ is the abstractor associated to the composition of I and I'. In general, it will depend on the signatures of the abstract and concrete specifications, $\Sigma 1$ and $\Sigma 3$, and of $h' \cdot h$. Its definition depends on the given implementation approach. For instance, in implementation frameworks based REACH-ID or just ID, $\alpha_{I.I'}$ would coincide with α_I. However, in behaviour implementation frameworks $\alpha_{I.I'}(A)$ would consist of the class of $\Sigma 1$-models which are behaviorally equivalent to A with respect to the set of sorts $\{s \in Obs1 / h(s) \in Obs2\}$, where Obs1 and Obs2 are the set of sorts which are considered observable in implementations I and I', respectively.

To prove transitivity, we may use the following proposition:

4.1.2 Proposition

The composition $I \cdot I' = (\emptyset, h' \cdot h: SP1 \rightarrow SP3)$, with semantics $(U_{h' \cdot h}, \alpha_{I.I'})$ is correct if the following condition *C1* holds:

C1) $\forall A2 \in Mod(\Sigma 2)$ such that there exists an $A2' \in Mod(SP2)$ with $A2 \in \alpha_{I'}(A2')$, it holds that if $U_h(A2') \in \alpha_I(A1)$ for $A1 \in Mod(SP1)$, then $U_h(A2) \in \alpha_{I.I'}(A1)$.

Proof

Suppose A3 is in Mod(SP3), then since I' is correct $\exists A2 \in Mod(SP2)$ such that $U_{h'}(A3) \in \alpha_{I'}(A2)$. Now, since I is correct $\exists A1 \in Mod(SP1)$ such that $U_h(A2) \in \alpha_I(A1)$. But *C1* implies that $U_h(U_{h'}(A3)) \in \alpha_{I.I'}(A1)$. Conversely, if $A1 \in Mod(SP1)$ then since I is correct $\exists A2 \in Mod(SP2)$ such that $U_h(A2) \in \alpha_I(A1)$, and since I' is correct $\exists A3 \in Mod(SP3)$ such that $U_{h'}(A3) \in \alpha_{I'}(A2)$. But *C1* implies again that $U_h(U_{h'}(A3)) \in \alpha_{I.I'}(A1)$. ♦

Now the above condition is satisfied by the abstractors considered so far. Therefore all these implementation approaches are transitive.

We include the proof for only two different abstractors:

1.1) Abstractors defined by reachability and identification (see case study 3.6.4) in the initial semantics framework: the condition to prove is provided by the following proposition:

4.1.3 Proposition (Transitivity of REACH-ID Implementations)

$\forall A2 \in Mod(\Sigma2)$ if $ID' \cdot REACH'(A2) \cong T_{SP2}$ and $ID \cdot REACH\ (U_h(T_{SP2})) \cong T_{SP1}$ then $ID \cdot REACH\ (U_h(A_2)) \cong T_{SP1}$

Proof

If $ID' \cdot REACH'(A2) \cong T_{SP2}$ then a homomorphism from REACH'(A2) to T_{SP2} exists and therefore also from $REACH(U_h(REACH'(A2)))$ to $REACH(U_h(T_{SP2}))$, but $REACH(U_h(REACH'(A2)) = REACH(U_h(A2))$ and then, we can ensure the existence of a homomorphism from $ID \cdot REACH(U_h(A_2))$ to $ID \cdot REACH(U_h(T_{SP2}))$, that is, to T_{SP1} and we have $ID \cdot REACH\ (U_h(A_2)) \cong T_{SP1}$ since $ID \cdot REACH(U_h(A2))$ is finitely generated. ♦

1.2) Abstractors defined by reachability and behaviour within the loose framework: in this case the condition to prove is:

4.1.4 Proposition (Transitivity of Behaviour Implementations)

$\forall A2 \in Mod(\Sigma2)$ such that there exists an $A2' \in Mod(SP2)$ and $A1 \in Mod(SP1)$ with $REACH'(A2) \equiv_{Beh} A2'$ and $REACH\ (U_h(A2')) \equiv_{Beh} A1$ then $REACH\ (U_h(A_2)) \equiv_{Beh} A1$

Proof

If $REACH'(A_2) \equiv_{I'\text{-}Beh} A2'$ then $REACH(U_h(REACH'(A2))) \equiv_{I.I'\text{-}Beh} REACH(U_h(A2'))$, but $REACH(U_h(REACH'(A2)) = REACH(U_h(A2))$ and $REACH(U_h(A2')) \equiv_{I.I'\text{-}Beh} A1$ and we have $REACH(U_h(A2)) \equiv_{I.I'\text{-}Beh} A1$. ♦

2) The second answer corresponds to what we may call "semantic" transitivity: we consider composition only at the semantic level, i.e. the composition of I and I' is an implementation $I'' = (U_h \cdot \kappa \cdot U_{h'} \cdot \kappa', \alpha_{I.I'})$ which may not be expressible at the syntactic level.

However there is a technical problem in the definition of the composition $U_h \cdot \kappa \cdot U_{h'} \cdot \kappa'$. This problem is that κ is defined from Mod(SP2) into $\Sigma 1$-models, but if A3 is in Mod(SP3) then we can only be sure that $U_{h'} \cdot \kappa'(A)$ is a $\Sigma 2$-model. A possible solution could be to consider that constructors are actually defined on all Σ-models, but then the semantics of the constructor may differ slightly even when applied to an SP-model. This may be the case if constructors are free constructions: in particular, if κ and κ' are the free constructions from

SP2 into SP1 and from $\Sigma 2$ into SP1, respectively, then in general $\kappa(A) \neq \kappa'(A)$. Anyhow, if we suppose this composition correctly defined then correctness of I" is equivalent to:

$\forall A3 \in U_h \cdot \kappa \cdot U_{h'} \cdot \kappa'(Mod(SP3))\ \exists A1 \in Mod(SP1)$ such that $A3 \in \alpha_{I.I'}(A1)$ and $\forall A1 \in Mod(SP1)\ \exists A3 \in U_h \cdot \kappa \cdot U_{h''} \cdot \kappa'(Mod(SP3))$ such that $A3 \in \alpha_{I.I'}(A1)$.

Now this holds if we can prove:

C2) $\forall A2 \in Mod(\Sigma 2)$ such that there exists an $A2' \in Mod(SP2)$ with $A2 \in \alpha_{I'}(A2')$, it holds that if $U_h \cdot \kappa(A2') \in \alpha_I(A1)$ then $U_h \cdot \kappa(A2) \in \alpha_{I.I'}(A1)$.

Unfortunately condition *C2* does not hold for a number of approaches, with [EKMP 82] being one of them. In particular if the abstractors "include" REACH then most likely the condition will not hold. Conversely, if the abstractors do not include REACH (because we have been able to avoid junk generation) then for the usual abstractors that condition holds. This happens for instance in [BBC 86, Ber 89, San 91].

It must be remarked that, according to [ST 88], [EKMP 82] and other similar approaches would indeed satisfy the property of semantic transitivity. This would be a consequence of the different intuition underlying their notions of constructor and abstractor (see remark 3.5.2). In particular, according to [ST 88], an [EKMP 82] implementation I of SP1 by SP2 is a constructor implementation, i.e. I denotes a constructor κ from Mod(SP2) into Mod(SP1), moreover κ is defined as the composition of SYNT, U_h, REACH and ID. In this sense, if I and I' denote the constructors κ: Mod(SP2) $\rightarrow$ Mod(SP1) and κ': Mod(SP3) $\rightarrow$ Mod(SP2), respectively, then $\kappa \cdot \kappa'$ would be a constructor from Mod(SP3) to Mod(SP1).

We do not share this view. On the one hand, we consider that the fact that, for a given A2, ID(REACH(A2)) is isomorphic to A1 is just a special case of $A2 \equiv_{Beh} A1$ (for a suitable notion of behavioural equivalence). As a consequence, we think that [EKMP 82] is better described by means of an abstractor implementation, where the corresponding abstractor is defined in terms of ID and REACH. Nevertheless, even if we consider [EKMP 82] as a constructor implementation, this would not ensure the semantic transitivity of any kind of (reasonable) implementation approach. In particular, abstractor implementations could still be a problem. On the other hand, we consider that constructors should correspond to specification units that (letting apart computability issues) can be ***translated*** into programming language constructs (for more details, see 4.2 below). In this sense, we cannot think of REACH as a reasonable constructor. From our point of view, this latter question is critical because what is really important is what happens at the end of the software design process (i.e. whether we can infere the correctness of the ***final*** system from the correctness of each development step) and this may be independent of the transitivity (or non-transitivity) of implementation correctness, but has more to do with the some properties of the ***final programming language*** (see 4.2). In particular, assuming that [EKMP 82] satisfies semantic transitivity will not guarantee the final correctness of a system that has been developed using their notion of implementation correctness. In particular, this would be the case if we consider the counter-example for transitivity shown in 3.6.4, together with the assumption that the ***final*** programming language is OBJ or other equational programming language. Conversely, even if we do not assume that [EKMP 82] satisfies semantic transitivity we may discover that this causes no trouble with respect to the final correctness of a system if the programming language we are using is adequate (satisfies the properties stated in 4.2) with respect to the notion of implementation we are using.

3) The third possibility is to consider "syntactic" composition, i.e. I" is the implementation $((\Sigma,E)+(\Sigma',E'), h'\cdot h: SP1 \rightarrow SP3 + (\Sigma,E) + (\Sigma',E'))$. The first problem we may have is that I" may violate some "a priori" condition. For instance in some implementation approaches for parameterized specifications like [GM 82, EK 83] the enrichment defining the implementation must be persistent with respect to the formal parameter specification. In these approaches it may be the case that the given I" is not persistent even if I and I' are so.

The second problem concerns the semantics of I": in principle we do not know anything about it for it depends on the framework we are working in, i.e. transitivity would fully depend on how the constructors are actually defined.

To conclude we have seen that transitivity depends on many aspects: on considering the enrichment as part of the implementations or not, on the concrete implementation concept (whether it includes REACH or not), etc. but not especially on the fact of working in a loose or monomorphic approach.

4.2 Transitivity of Implementations (Part two)

We have seen above that some definitions of implementation are not transitive. This seems to be quite terrible, since transitivity appears to be one of the bases of stepwise software development. However, lack of transitivity is not necessarily a problem as is explained in [Ore 86]. Below we will see why.

In [GB 80] software design was explained in terms of a bidimensional refinement process: vertical refinements would be implementations and horizontal refinements would be enrichments (SP1 is a horizontal refinement of SP2 if SP2 is an enrichment of SP1). For instance, the description of "words" in terms of "letters" would be a horizontal refinement. In this framework it was established that the following composition properties had to hold:

1. *Vertical composition*, i.e. transitivity of implementations and

2. *Horizontal composition*: If SP2(SP1) is a parameterized specification, SP3 is an actual parameter, I1 is an implementation of SP2(SP1) by SP2'(SP1) and I2 is an implementation of SP3 by SP3', then the composition of I1 and I2 should be an implementation of SP2(SP3) by SP2'(SP3')

Similarly to the case of transitivity of implementations, a number of approaches (for the same reasons) do not satisfy the horizontal composition property either. Now, in our opinion, to better understand this problem we must add a third dimension to the software design process: translation (see section 2.).

Suppose that we are specifying a problem whose final implementation will be, for instance, in Modula. Suppose that at some point we define the implementation I1 of a specification SP1 (for instance sets of integers) in terms of a specification SP2 (for instance binary trees) and later we define the implementation I2 of SP2 in terms of SP3 (arrays). Suppose further that we are using a specification logic (for instance equational logic) and an implementation concept embedded in this logic that does not satisfy transitivity. This means that we cannot be sure that I1 composed with I2 is a correct implementation of SP1 by SP3. But why do we need to put together the equational specifications of I1 and I2?. If we write the modules in Modula meeting the specifications of I1 and I2 we can be sure that this composition will work well (at least that should happen in any reasonable programming language). That is, to guarantee the correctness of stepwise software design the two composition properties stated above must be satisfied at the lowest level of translation (i.e. the programming language level), but not necessarily before.

To discuss the problem in detail we have to go into an *institutional* framework [GB 84]. We assume that we have two institutions L and L' corresponding to a programming and a specification language, respectively. For instance L may be equational logic and L' may be Modula. Additionally, for the sake of simplicity, we assume that L and L' have the same categories of signatures and models (a more careful analysis would have needed to relate the two institutions by means of some kind of institution morphism [GB 84, Mes 89, ST 88, AC 90]). Moreover, we suppose that in both institutions certain specification morphisms denote a simple form of *modules* or *enrichments* (obviously, we could have considered a more powerful form of modules, as in [EM 89, ST 89], but this one is enough for our purposes), in particular, if h: SP1 → SP2 is a module we consider that its meaning is given by an associated constructor κ_h: Mod(SP1) → $2^{Mod(SP2)}$. In order to "put together" modules we consider only the operation of *module composition* defined at the specification level as morphism composition and at the model level as the composition of the associated constructors, i.e. given h_1: SP1 → SP2 and h_2: SP2 → SP3 the composition $h_2 \cdot h_1$: SP1 → SP3 is a module whose semantics is given by the constructor $\kappa_{h_2 \cdot h_1}$ defined for every A in Mod(SP1), $\kappa_{h_2 \cdot h_1}(A) = \{\kappa_{h_2}(A') / A' \in \kappa_{h_1}(A)\}$. For the sake of simplicity we do not consider other module operations, such as union [EM 89], because often they can be "simulated" by using just composition.

Now, in the case of L', we will assume some additional things (which are most often true for programming languages). First we assume that L' is a specification logic that has pushouts, amalgamations and extensions [EBCO 91]. Also, we consider that if h: SP1 → SP2 is a module then SP1 includes no axioms, i.e this is equivalent to assuming that κ_h is defined from Mod(Σ1) to $2^{Mod(SP2)}$, where Σ1 is the signature of SP1. Additionally, we assume that κ_h is always strongly persistent, i.e. for every $A2 \in \kappa_h(A1)$ $U_h(A2) = A1$. Moreover, in L' we consider a more general form of module composition than the one defined for L. In particular, if h_1: SP1 → SP2 and h_2: SP3 → SP4 are two modules in L' and f: Σ3 → Σ2 is a signature morphism then we define the composition $h_2 \bullet_f h_1$ (or just $h_2 \bullet h_1$ when f may be inferred from the context) at the specification level as $h_2' \cdot h_1$, where h2' is defined by the following pushout diagram:

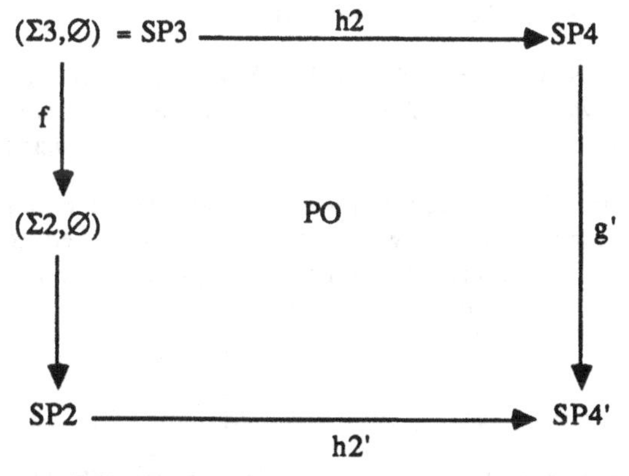

At the model level, the constructor associated to $h_2 \bullet_f h_1$ is defined by $\kappa_{h_2}' \cdot \kappa_{h_1}$, where κ_{h_2}' is the extension of κ_{h_2} with respect to the above pushout diagram. Finally, according to intuition about programming languages, we can assume that specifications in L' are monomorphic, i.e. for every SP in L', Mod(SP) consists of only one model up to isomorphism. Similarly, if h: SP1 → SP2 is a module in L' then, for every A in Mod(Σ1), $\kappa_h(A)$ consists only of one model up to isomorphism.

4.2.1 Definition (Translation)

Given two specifications SP and SP' in L and L', respectively, we say that SP' is a translation of SP, denoted SP'∈τ(SP) iff Sig(SP) = Sig(SP') and Mod(SP) = Mod(SP'). Similarly, given two modules h: SP1 → SP2 and h': SP1' → SP2' in L and L', respectively, such that the signatures of SP1 and SP1' coincide, we say that h' is a translation of h, denoted h'∈τ(h) iff for every A in Mod(SP1) $\kappa_h(A) = \kappa_{h'}(A)$.

It must be noted that not every specification in L has a translation in L'. In particular, at most monomorphic specifications in L have a translation in L'. Then, to characterize the situation where a program "implements" a specification we introduce the notion of *realization*. This notion depends obviously on the kind of abstractors associated to the implementation concept used.

4.2.2 Definition (Realization)

Given two specifications SP and SP' in L and L', respectively, such that there is a signature morphism f: Σ' → Σ, we say that SP' is a realization of SP, denoted SP'∈ρ(SP) iff ∀A'∈Mod(SP') ∃A∈Mod(SP) such that $U_f(A') \in \alpha(A)$. Similarly, given two modules h: SP1 → SP2 and h': SP1' → SP2' in L and L', respectively, such that Σ1 = Σ1' and there is a morphism signature f: Σ2' → Σ2, we say that h' is a realization of h, denoted h'∈ρ(h) iff ∀A1∈Mod(SP1) ∀A2'∈$\kappa_{h'}(A1)$ ∃A2∈$\kappa_h(A1)$ such that $U_f(A2') \in \alpha(A2)$.

Then, the correctness problem of software design consists in showing that the final system (or program) obtained as the result of a series of refinement steps from a given specification SP is a realization of SP. Moreover the correctness of the final outcome must be a consequence of the correctness of each of the steps. However, before continuing further, we have to extend the notion of implementation to the case of modules:

4.2.3 Definition (Module Implementation)

Given two modules h: SP1 → SP2 and h': SP1 → SP2' we say that h is implemented by h' in terms of I = (m,f), where m is a module m: SP2' → SP3 and f is a signature morphism f: Σ2 → Σ3 iff ∀A1∈Mod(SP1) ∀A3∈$\kappa_{m \cdot h'}(A1)$ ∃A2∈$\kappa_h(A1)$ such that $U_f(A3) \in \alpha(A2)$.

Note that in the above definition we are allowing *refinement* in the sense of sect. 1. Now, the process of modular stepwise software design can be described as follows. Given a specification SP consisting of a set of modules, i.e. SP = $h_n \cdot \ldots \cdot h_1$ [†], then at every step we perform one of the following actions:

---

† Better would have been to write SP = $h_n \cdot \ldots \cdot h_1(SP_0)$ for a given basic specification SP_0, however for the sake of simplicity we can consider that SP_0 is the *empty* specification.

- either we implement (within the institution L) one of the modules h_i in terms of another module h_i' and an implementation I = (h,j), where h_i' and h may themselves be composed of a number of modules i.e. $h_i' = h_{mi}' \cdot \ldots \cdot h_{1i}'$ and $h = h_p'' \cdot \ldots \cdot h_1''$, which can later be implemented separately.

- or else we translate a module h in L into another module $h' \in \tau(h)$ in L'.

Therefore we may describe the software design process by means of a tree whose root is labeled by the given specification SP, its sons are labeled by $h_1,\ldots,h_n$ and if a node of the tree is labeled by the module h in L and at some step:

- h is implemented by $h_n' \cdot \ldots \cdot h_1'$ in terms of $I = (m_k \cdot \ldots \cdot m_1, f)$ then the sons of h are labeled by $h_1',\ldots, h_n', m_1,\ldots,m_k$.

- h is translated into $h' \in \tau(h)$ in L' then the only son of h is labeled by h'.

In this context the correctness problem consists in showing that if $m_1,\ldots,m_j$ are the leaves of the design tree then $m_j \bullet \ldots \bullet m_1$ is a realization of h. In what follows we will see that to prove this it is enough to satisfy the following horizontal and vertical composition properties at the program level:

P1) Vertical Composition in L'

Given modules h: SP1 → SP2, h': SP1 → SP2' and h": SP1 → SP2" and given implementations I = (m,f) and I' = (m';f') of h by h' and of h' by h", respectively, then I" = ($m \bullet_{f'} m'$, $f' \bullet_m f$) is an implementation of h by h" (see diagram below)

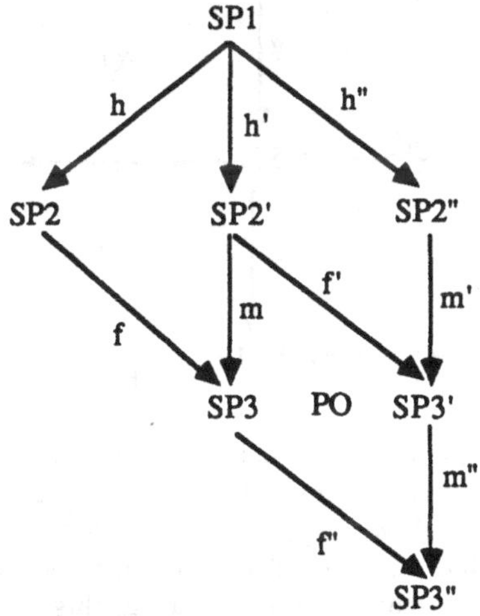

i.e. $\forall A1 \in Mod(SP1)\ \forall A3 \in \kappa_{m \bullet m' \cdot h''}(A1)\ \exists A2 \in \kappa_h(A1)$ such that $U_{f' \bullet f}(A3) \in \alpha(A2)$.

P2) Horizontal Composition I

Given modules h1: SP0 → SP1, h2: SP0 → SP2 and h3: SP0' → SP3, given an implementation I = (m1,f1) of h1 by h2 and given a morphism g: SP0 → SP3 then I' =

(m1', f1'), where m1' and f1' are defined in the following diagram, where all square subdiagrams except the one at the top are pushouts:

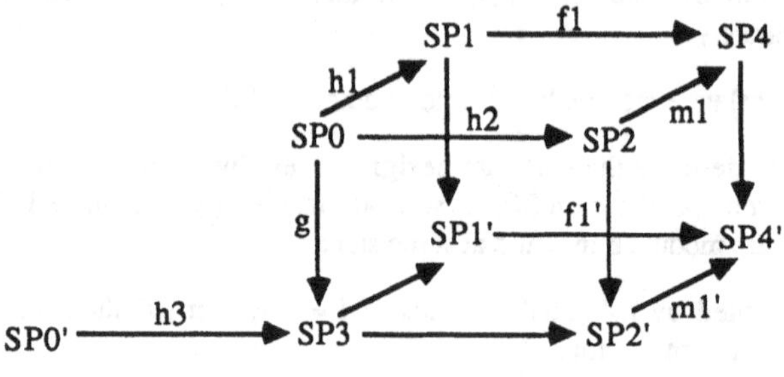

is an implementation of h1 $\bullet_g$ h3 by h2 $\bullet_g$ h3, i.e. $\forall A0' \in Mod(SP0')$ $\forall A4' \in \kappa_{m \bullet (h2 \bullet h3)}(A0')$ $\exists A2 \in \kappa_{h1 \bullet h3}(A0')$ such that $U_{f'}(A4') \in \alpha(A2)$.

P3) Horizontal Composition II

Given modules h1: SP0 → SP1, h2: SP0' → SP2 and h3: SP0' → SP3, given an implementation I = (m,f) of h2 by h3 and given a morphism g: SP0 → SP2 then $\forall A0' \in Mod(SP0')$ $\forall A4' \in \kappa_{h1 \bullet (f \cdot g)(m \cdot h3)}(A0')$ $\exists A2' \in \kappa_{h1 \bullet h2}(A0')$ such that $U_{f'}(A4') \in \alpha(A2')$, where f' is defined in the following pushout diagram:

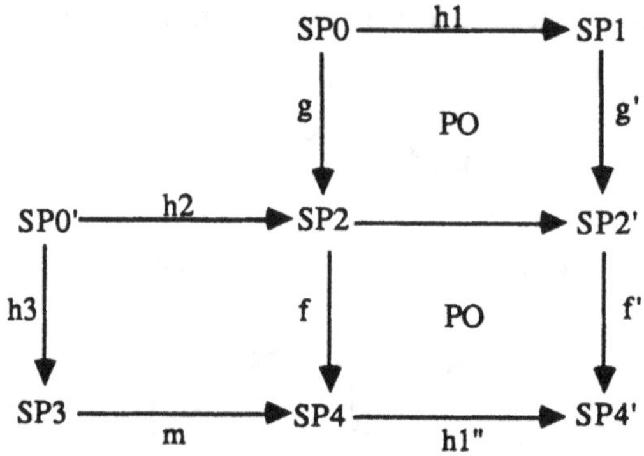

Intuitively, property P2) states that if h2 is an implementation of h1, then if we "apply" both over h3 then h2(h3) is an implementation of h1(h3). Conversely, P3) states that if h3 is an implementation of h2 then if we "apply" h1 over both we get that h1(h3) is an implementation of h1(h2). It can be noted that the property called *stability* [Sch 87, ST 89] can be seen just as a special case of P3. In particular, stability coincides with P3) if m is the identity and α is defined in terms of behavioural equivalence.

Now to prove the main result we will use the following lemmas which are a consequence of properties P1, P2 and P3.

4.2.4 Lemma

Given modules h1 and h2 in L and h3 and h4 in L' such that h3 is a realization of h1 and h4 is a realization of h2, then h4 • h3 is a realization of h2·h1.

4.2.5 Lemma

Given modules h1 and h2 in L and h3 and h4 in L' such that I = (m,f) is an implementation of h1 by h2, h3 is a realization of h1 and h4 is a realization of m, then h4 • h3 is a realization of h1.

4.2.6 Theorem (Correctness of Stepwise Software Design)

Assuming that the institution L' satisfies the properties P1, P2 and P3 then if T is a software design tree whose root is a specification SP in L and whose leaves are the modules $m_1,...,m_j$ then $m_j \bullet ... \bullet m_1$ is a realization of SP.

Proof

1. If T consists just of the root labeled by the module h and the leave labeled by $h' \in \tau(h)$ then trivially the theorem holds since h' is a realization of h.

h is implemented by $h_n' \cdot ... \cdot h_1'$ in terms of $I = (m_k \cdot ... \cdot m_1, f)$ then the sons of h are labeled by $h_1',..., h_n', m_1,...,m_k$

2. If T consists of a root labeled by h which is implemented by $h_n \cdot ... \cdot h_1$ in terms of $I = (m_k \cdot ... \cdot m_1, f)$, then by induction we may assume that, for every j, if the leaves of the subtree having as root h_j (resp. m_j) are the modules $h_{j1}',..., h_{ji}'$ (resp. $m_{j1}',...,m_{ji}'$), then $h_{ji}' \bullet ... \bullet h_{j1}'$ (resp. $m_{ji}' \bullet ... \bullet m_{j1}'$) is a realization of h_j (resp. m_j). But, as a consequence of lemma 4.2.4, this means that $h_{ki}' \bullet ... \bullet h_{11}'$ (resp. $m_{ki}' \bullet ... \bullet m_{j1}'$) is a realization of $h_n \cdot ... \cdot h_1$ (resp. $m_k \cdot ... \cdot m_1$), and by lemma 4.2.5, $m_{ki}' \bullet ... \bullet m_{j1}' \bullet h_{ki}' \bullet ... \bullet h_{11}'$ is a realization of h.

The case where the root is labeled by SP and its sons are labeled with $h_1,..., h_n$, with $SP = h_n \cdot ... \cdot h_1$, is just a special case of 2. ♦

The consequence of all this is that if a given concept of implementation lacks transitivity then it is not really too important as far as we are dealing with specifications (and not with programs) and as far as the programming language satisfies the adequate properties.

4.3 Proving Implementations Correct

Although there have been so many approaches for defining different notions of implementation there has been considerably less effort on studying how to prove them correct. To our knowledge only the Berlin group [EKMP 82, Pad 83] and recently [Hen 91, Far 89] have dealt with this subject. Now, in some papers within the loose approach (e.g. [SW 83]) implementation correctness is stated to be equivalent to logical entailment and, in this sense, this has given many people the feeling that proving implementation correctness in the loose approach is much simpler than in monomorphic (e.g. initial) approaches. Again this is not so. In what follows we will see why: first we will present the main ideas for proving RI and IR-correctness in [EKMP 82]; then we will deal with the general case; finally we will see what happens in [SW 83].

As seen in case study 3.6.4, [EKMP 82] defined two notions of implementation correctness, RI and IR-correctness as follows:

Given SP1 and SP2, an implementation $I = (\Sigma,E)$ of SP1 by SP2 is

RI-correct iff $ID \cdot REST \cdot SYNT(T_{SP2}) \cong T_{SP1}$

IR-correct iff $REST \cdot ID \cdot SYNT(T_{SP2}) \cong T_{SP1}$

Moreover they proved that IR-correctness is equivalent to a hierarchical consistency condition as follows:

Theorem 4.3.1 ([EKMP 82])

An implementation I = (Σ,E) of SP1 by SP2 is IR-correct iff SP2+(Σ,E)+E1 is hierarchy consistent with respect to SP1, i.e. $\forall t1, t2 \in T_{\Sigma 1}$ E2+E+E1 |- t1=t2 iff E1|- t1=t2.

Now proof techniques for this kind of conditions have been thoroughly studied in connection with the proof of correctness of modules and parameterized specifications [Pad 83, Pad 85] and in relation with inductionless induction theorem proving [Mus 80, Gog 80, JK 86].

No similar nice result was obtained for RI-correctness. Therefore the most reasonable way of checking RI-correctness consists in using the previous result as a sufficient condition. However if we are able to avoid the REACH step included in RESTRICTION (as it is done in [BBC 86, Ber 89, San 91], see 3.6.5) then RI-correctness and IR-correctness may coincide and as a consequence the previous result would also apply to RI-correctness.

If we look at the general case, implementation correctness is defined as follows:

Given an implementation I = ((Σ, E), h) of SP1 by SP2, with semantics $(U_h \cdot \kappa_I, \alpha_I)$, I is correct iff $\forall A2 \in U_h \cdot \kappa_I(Mod(SP2))\ \exists A1 \in Mod(SP1)$ such that $A2 \in \alpha_I(A1)$ and $\forall A1 \in Mod(SP1)\ \exists A2 \in U_h \cdot \kappa_I(Mod(SP2))$ such that $A2 \in \alpha_I(A1)$.

Now being more concrete, if we can avoid REACH, we may consider that $A2 \in \alpha(A1)$ iff $A1 \equiv_{Beh} A2$, for a reasonable notion of behavioural equivalence (see 3.6.7 and section 5). This means that in this case implementation correctness is equivalent to:

$\forall A2 \in U_h \cdot \kappa_I(Mod(SP2))\ \exists A1 \in Mod(SP1)$ such that $A2 \equiv_{Beh} A1$ and $\forall A1 \in Mod(SP1)$ $\exists A2 \in U_h \cdot \kappa_I(Mod(SP2))$ such that $A2 \equiv_{Beh} A1$.

More precisely, if we consider κ(Mod(SP2)) as Mod(SP2+ (Σ, E)) then proving implementation correctness is equivalent to showing that SP2+ (Σ, E) is a behaviour conservative extension of SP1, i.e. SP2+ (Σ, E) is behaviourally hierarchy consistent and sufficiently complete with respect to SP1. These concepts have been studied in [Niv 87, NO 88]. Additionally, a technique for proving properties of behaviour specifications called *context induction* has been recently developed by Hennicker [Hen 91].

Now, as said above, in some papers (like [SW 83]) it is stated that *SP1 is implemented by SP2 iff SP1 |= SP2* (note that this definition is based on refinement, according to section 1, otherwise the associated correctness condition would have been: SP1 |= SP2 and SP2 |= SP1), which seems quite more easy to prove than checking that something is a behavioural conservative extension. The problem is that this definition so simple "makes sense" because the underlying specification language, ASL, is powerful enough to express "simulation" using the very language. That is, if we want to define in ASL the implementation of sets by strings (as the one in 3.6.4) we could define:

SP3 = **enrich** SP2 **by** I
SP4 = **derive** SP3 **by** h
SP5 = **restrict** SP4 **wrt** Σ1
SP6 = **quotient** SP5 **by** E1

where SP1 is the set specification, SP2 is the sequence specification, I is the implementation I=(Σ,E) and h is the signature morphism from Σ1 to Σ2+Σ. Then the effect would be similar to saying:

Mod(SP6) = ID·REST·SYNT(Mod(SP2))

The consequence of all this is that having a theorem prover for the logic underlying ASL it would be very simple to prove any kind of implementation correct [Far 89]. But otherwise, proving "more complex" implementations written in a "more modest" language would most probably be simpler than proving general theorems in ASL.

5. Behavioural Equivalence and Behavioural Semantics

The intuition behind behaviour specifications may be explained by means of the following example. Suppose that we have the specification below:

```
SP = INTEGER + BOOLEAN
          sorts s
          operations
               e-s:  → s
               add:  s x int → s
               _ is-in _ : int x s → bool
          equations
               add(add(s,n),n') = add(add(s,n'),n)
               n is-in e-s = false
               n is-in app(S,n') = (n eq n') or (n is-in S)
```

The meaning of SP in the initial framework would be the algebra of finite multisets of integers. If we take final semantics [Wan 79] then SP would denote finite sets of integers. If we consider loose semantics then we would probably have among the models both sets and multisets and also other algebras satisfying the specification. However from the standpoint of software design by data abstraction all of these semantics are considered unsatisfactory.

Usually in software engineering it is considered that the models of a specification must be all "software systems" or "program modules" that may satisfy our needs expressed by the specification. Let us see that all the "standard" semantics exclude some "interesting" model for the example above. First, we know that a program module whose semantics is the type of finite multisets of integers would obviously satisfy the needs expressed by the specification, therefore final semantics is inadequate because it rules out an interesting model. If the semantics of the module is the type of finite sets of integers then this module would also satisfy our needs, because if we consider type s to be "abstract" we do not care about what the elements of s actually are, we would only care about getting the "right" answers to our operations: in particular, according to the operations in the signature, we want that if we have added a 6 to an element of type s and we ask if 6 is in that element, then the answer must be true. But we do not care about how many times 6 has been added to that element. Therefore initial semantics is inadequate because it rules out another interesting model. It could seem that loose semantics is the right approach, but we may see that it suffers from similar problems. In particular, if we have a module whose semantics is the type of sequences of integers then this module will also satisfy our needs for the same reasons that we considered sets satisfactory. However the algebra of sequences does not satisfy the specification (it does not satisfy the first axiom) and as a consequence it is ruled out of loose semantics.

Behaviour semantics has its roots in final semantics and was first introduced in [GGM 76] and later by Reichel [Rei 81] and Goguen and Meseguer [GM 82], since then quite a number of approaches can be found in the literature [SW 83, MG 85, ST 87, Sch 87, Hen 88, NO 88, ONE 89, BB 91]. There are especially three intuitions underlying behavioural semantics:

1. Some "aspects" of software systems can be *observed* and some others can not. For instance in the example above we could consider that elements of sort s are not observable while boolean answers are. These observations are part of behavioural specifications, i.e.:

5.1 Definition

A *behavioral specification* BSP is a pair (SP,Obs), where SP is a standard specification and Obs describes what is observable in SP.

2. The "classical" notion of satisfaction is not adequate, since "interesting" models may not satisfy in the usual sense some axioms (as happened in the example above). Instead a notion of *behavioural satisfaction* is needed. One possible definition is as follows:

5.2 Definition (Behavioural Satisfaction I)

An algebra A *behaviourally satisfies* an axiom with respect to the given set of observations iff it satisfies (in the classical sense) all its "observable consequences".

3. The idea of abstraction "up to isomorphism" is not adequate (at least with respect to the standard concept of isomorphism). Abstraction "up to behavioural equivalence" is needed instead. Two models are behaviourally equivalent if all observations provide the same "results" in the two models. For instance, in the example above, sets and sequences can be considered behaviourally equivalent, for if we consider that the observations are exactly the terms in T_Σ of boolean sort, then these terms would evaluate exactly the same in the two models.

Therefore the main characteristics defining any approach to behavioural semantics are the following:

1. What is "observed" in the approach
2. The behavioural satisfaction relation associated to these kind of observations, and
3. The behavioural equivalence relation defined in the approach.

Concerning the first question, the following aspects have been considered to be observations in the literature:

1. Sorts: this is the most used approach [Rei 81, GM 82, MG 85, Sch 87, NO 88, ONE 89]. The idea is that certain sorts (or types) are observable and some others are not. Implicitly it is considered that not all "computations" are interesting: only computations having observable input and result must be relevant. That is, in this approach, Obs is just a finite set of sorts.

2. Values: although "sort observation" may be considered in accordance with actual "practice" in programming (where types are considered either observable or private), that approach may be thought insufficient for some purposes, especially with respect to implementation definition. In previous sections we have seen how behavioural equivalence could be used for defining the abstractors associated to implementations, however if a REACH step is needed in these implementations then we may try to embed it within the behavioural equivalence. This can be done by considering that the values that would be "deleted" by REACH are non observable. Therefore we would consider that in every sort of every model some values are observable and some others are not. This is the approach taken by Hennicker [Hen 88, 89, 91]. The concrete way he defines the observable values is by means of the specification of an "observation predicate". That is, in his framework, a specification consists of two kinds of axioms: standard axioms and axioms for defining the observable elements of every model. For instance, if when defining the integers we would want to state that only positive integers are observable we could write the following axiom:

$$n > 0 \Rightarrow Obs(n)$$

3. Computations: sort observations, as said above, implicitly divide all computations (i.e. terms in $T_\Sigma(X)$, where the variables in the term denote the "parameters" or the "input" of the computation) into two classes: non-observable and observable computations, i.e. computations with observable input and output sorts. Now for similar reasons as in the previous case, this may be thought too rigid. Instead [SW 83] consider that, given a behaviour specification BSP = (SP,Obs), Obs may be any arbitrary set of computations i.e. Obs $\subseteq T_\Sigma(X)$. This approach may be seen also as implicitly defining that some values are observable and some others are not. In particular, we may think that all ground observable computations define observable values and, additionally, if v1, ..., vn are observable values and t1 is an observable computation with n parameters of the right sorts then the "result" of t(v1,...,vn) is an observable value.

As a special case of this approach we may also cite [BB 91] where Obs is defined to be a set of operations i.e. Obs $\subseteq\Sigma$.

4. Formula: The goal of [ST 87] was to study behavioural specifications in an institution independent framework. As a consequence they were unable to use sorts, values or computations as observations, since all these concepts are institution dependent. Therefore they chose as observations set of formulae. In this sense their approach can be considered the most general one: formulae of the kind t=t (if equality is allowed in the given institution) allow to "simulate" computations observation .

The behavioural satisfaction relation may be defined in two different ways which are usually equivalent (if both exist). The first one can be found above (def. 5.2), the second one is in terms of behavioural equivalence:

5.3 Definition (Behavioural Satisfaction II)

An algebra A *behaviourally satisfies* a specification BSP = (SP,Obs) iff there is a model of SP behaviourally equivalent to A.

In our opinion the first definition is preferable since it allows to speak about single axiom satisfaction. However it may pose problems depending on the kind of axioms considered. In particular only the case of equational specifications (and a restricted case of conditional specifications) has been considered. Being specific, the way observable consequences are defined in these frameworks is as follows:

5.4 Definition

Given a behavioural specification BSP = (SP,Obs), a *context* of sort s is a term $c \in T_\Sigma(\{x\})$ such that the variable x is of sort s. Given a term t, c[t] denotes the term obtained by substituting in c the variable x by the term t. Given an equation e: $\forall X.t1 = t2$, the *observable consequences* of e in an algebra A are all the equations $c[\sigma(t1)] = c[\sigma(t2)]$, for all contexts c and substitutions $\sigma: X \to T_\Sigma$, such that $c[\sigma(t1)]$ and $c[\sigma(t2)]$ denote observable values in A.

5.5 Remarks

1. The above definition depends on the concept of *observable value*, which depends on the approach taken to define observations. In particular, if sorts are observed then we may consider that the observable values are all values of observable sort. If computations are observed then we may consider that a) the values of ground observable computations are observable values and b) if $t \in T_\Sigma(\{x_1,...,x_n\})$ is an observable computation and $v_1, ..., v_n$ are observable values then the value of the term $t[x_1/v_1,...,x_n/v_n]$ is an observable value.

2. It must be noted that not all definitions of observable consequence are exactly like the one above. In particular in some approaches (e.g. [Rei 81]) observable consequences, with respect to sorts observation, are defined as follows:

Given an equation e: $\forall X.t1 = t2$, the *observable consequences* of e are all the equations $c[t1] = c[t2]$, for all contexts c of observable sort.

This definition is more restrictive than 5.4 in the sense that algebras that would behaviourally satisfy a given specification using definition 5.4 may not be behavioural models of the specification in the case of [Rei 81]. The problem is that junk elements of non-observable sorts may hamper behavioural satisfaction (!). This may be seen with the following example:

```
SP = BOOL+ sorts s
           Obs  bool
           operations
                 a,b:  → s
                 p : s → bool
           equations
                 p(x) =true
```

Now suppose that A is an algebra with three elements of sort s, i.e. $A_s = \{0,1,2\}$, with $a_A = 0$ and $b_A = 1$ (i.e. 2 is a junk element). Suppose further that p is defined on A as follows:

$p_A(0) = true$
$p_A(1) = true$
$p_A(2) = false$

Now, A does not satisfy SP with respect to Reichel's notion, since the equation p(x) =true is not satisfied for x=2 . However A would be a behavioural model of SP with respect to definition 5.4 since the observable consequences of p(x) =true would be the equations p(a) =true and p(b)=true, i.e. the non-observable junk value 2 does not hamper satisfaction in this case. [BB91] defines a behavioural satisfaction relation with the same problems.

3. The definition of behavioural satisfaction based on the concept of observable consequence (def. 5.2) makes sense only for equations or for conditional equations with observable conditions. Trying to generalize this definition to other kind of formula may yield awkward results as the following example shows:

Let SP be the following specification

SP = BOOL + **sorts** s
Obs bool
operations
a,b: $\rightarrow$ s
equations
$a = b \Rightarrow true = false$

and suppose that we have extended behavioural satisfaction to ground conditional equations in the most obvious way (we do not consider equations with variables because it is not needed in the example):

$A|=_{Beh}\ t_1=t_1' \ \& \dots \&\ t_n = t_n' \Rightarrow t = t'$ iff if $A|=_{Beh}\ t_i=t_i'$ for every i in (0..n) then $A|=_{Beh}\ t=t'$

Then the algebra A defined as follows:

$A_s = \{0, 1\}$, $A_{bool} = \{t, f\}$, $a_A = 0$, $b_A = 1$, $true_A = t$, $false_A = f$

satisfies SP in the standard sense but it does not satisfy SP behaviourally, since a and b are observably equal in A but true and false are observably different.

The definition of behavioural equivalence has similar difficulties: not being aware of certain subtleties may have the effect of providing a too restrictive equivalence. The "adequate" (in the sense of less restrictive) definition is the following one [MG 85]:

Definition 5.6

Given a behaviour specification BSP = (SP,Obs) and two Σ-algebras A1 and A2 we say that A1 is behaviourally equivalent to A2 with respect to Obs, denoted $A1 \equiv_{Obs} A2$, iff the observable values of A1 and A2 coincide and for every observable computation $t \in T_\Sigma(\{x1,\dots, xn\})$ and observable values v1,...,vn we have that:

$$t^{A1}(v1,\dots,vn) = t^{A2}(v1,\dots,vn)$$

Actually the definition in [MG 85] is slightly more general, since it allows the existence of a bijection among the observable values of A1 and A2 (see also [SW 83, ST 87a, NO 88, ONE 89]) instead of asking for strict equality. Also, as said above this definition can be made more restrictive: in particular, in [Rei 81, BB91] non observable junk may be the cause that two algebras are not considered behaviourally equivalent, although they would have been so according to definition 5.6.

In most of the approaches behavioural semantics has been just a way of approaching implementation concepts. In this sense, after providing the basic definitions and some results, these approaches do not continue further. However this is not the case for Reichel's [Rei 81, 85] and the Barcelona [Niv 87, NO 88, ONE 89, ON 91, EBCO 91] approaches and, to a lesser extent, of [GM 82]. In these approaches behavioural specifications are studied in the same detail as other specification formalisms: analyzing the existence or not of the different constructions that are used in the semantics of structuring operations. In general, almost all constructions extend nicely, although in some cases with some restrictions. However these extensions are not always easy due to some specific subtleties taking place in the behavioural framework. To give a simple example of these "subtleties" we may consider the fact that the behavioural framework is not an institution [GB 84] in an obvious way (for details, see [EBCO 91]).

BIBLIOGRAPHY

[AC 90] E. Astesiano, M. Cerioli: Commuting between institutions via simulation. Res. Report 2, University of Genoa (1990).

[Ber 89] G. Bernot: Correctness Proofs for Abstract Implementations. *Information and Computation* 80, 121-151 (1989).

[BB 91] G. Bernot, M.Bidoit: Proving the correctness of Algebraically Specified Software: Modularity and Observability Issues. Report LIENS-91-8, Dept. de Mathematiques et Informatique, Ecole Normale Superieur, Paris (1991).

[BBC 86] G. Bernot, M.Bidoit, C. Choppy: Abstract implementations and correctness proofs. *Proc. 3rd. Symp. on Theoretical Aspects of Computer Science.* Springer LNCS 210, 236-251 (1986).

[BJ 82] D. Bjørner, C. Jones: *Formal Specification and Software Development*, Prentice Hall Int. (1982).

[Bre 91] M. Breu: Bounded implementations of algebraic specifications. 8th Workshop on Specification of Abstract Data Types, Dourdan, France (1991).

[BMPW 86] M. Broy, B. Möller, P. Pepper, M. Wirsing: Algebraic implementations preserve program correctness. *Science of Computer Programming* 7, 35-53 (1986).

[BW 88] F.L. Bauer, M. Wirsing: Crypt-Equivalent Algebraic specifications. *Acta Informatica* 25 (2), 11-153 (1988).

[CO 88] S. Clérici, F. Orejas: GSBL: an algebraic specification language based on inheritance. *Proc. 1988 European Conf. on Object Oriented Programming*, Oslo. Springer LNCS 322, 78-92 (1988).

[EL 80] H.-D. Ehrich, U. Lipeck: Proving implementation correct -two alternative approaches. *Information Processing 80*, 83-88 (1980).

[Ehr 82] H.-D. Ehrich: On the theory of specification, implementation and parameterization of abstract data types. *Journal of the Assoc. for Computing Machinery* 29, 206-207 (1982).

[Ehg 89] H. Ehrig: Concepts and compatibility requirements for implementations and transformation of specifications, Algebraic Specification Column Part 6, *EATCS Bulletin 38*, April 1989.

[EA 91] H. Ehrig, H. Adametz: New compatibility results for implementations within the initial algebraic approach, Algebraic Specification Column Part 11, *EATCS Bulletin 43*, February 1991.

[EBCO 91] H. Ehrig, M. Baldamus, F. Cornelius, F. Orejas: Theory of algebraic module specifications including behavioural semantics and constraints, Proc. AMAST 91, to appear in Springer LNCS (1991).

[EK 83] H. Ehrig, H.-J. Kreowski: Compatibility of parameter passing and implementation of parameterized data types. *Theoretical Computer Science* 27(3), 255-286 (1983).

[EKMP 82] H. Ehrig, H.-J. Kreowski, B. Mahr, P. Padawitz: Algebraic implementation of abstract data types. *Theoretical Computer Science* 20, 209-263 (1982).

[EKP 78] H. Ehrig, H.-J. Kreowski, P. Padawitz: Stepwise specification and implementation of abstract data types. *Proc. 5th. Intl. Colloq. on Automata, Languages and Programming*, Udine. Springer LNCS 62, 205-226 (1978).

[EM 85] H. Ehrig, B. Mahr: *Fundamentals of Algebraic Specifications 1*, Springer 1985.

[EM 89] H. Ehrig, B. Mahr: *Fundamentals of Algebraic Specifications 2*, Springer 1989.

[Far 89] J. Farrés-Casals: Proving Correctness of Constructor Implementations. *Proc. MFCS 89*, Springer LNCS 379, 225-235 (1989).

[Gan 83] H. Ganzinger: Parameterized specifications: parameter passing and implementation with respect to observability. *ACM Trans. on Programming Languages and Systems* 5 (3), 318-354 (1983).

[GB 80] J.A. Goguen, R.M. Burstall: CAT, a system for the structured elaboration of correct programs from structured specifications. Technical report CSL-118, Computer Science Laboratory, SRI International (1980).

[GB 84] J.A. Goguen, R.M. Burstall: Introducing institutions. *Proc. Logics of Programming Workshop*, Carnegie-Mellon. Springer LNCS 164, 221-256 (1984).

[GGM 76] V. Giarratana, F. Gimona, U. Montanari: Observability concepts in abstract data type specification, *Proc. MFCS'76*, Springer LNCS 45 (1976) 576-587.

[GHM 78] J.V. Guttag, E. Horowitz, D.R. Musser: Abstract data types and software validation. Research Report ISI/RR-76-48, University of Southern California (1976). Also in: *Communications of the ACM*, Vol 21, 12, 1048-1063 (1978).

[GM 82] J.A. Goguen, J. Meseguer: Universal realization, persistent interconnection and implementation of abstract modules. *Proc. 9th Intl. Colloq. on Automata, Languages and Programming*, Aarhus. Springer LNCS 140, 265-281 (1982).

[GTW 76] J.A. Goguen, J.W. Thatcher, E.G. Wagner: An initial algebra approach to the specification, correctness and implementation of abstract data types. IBM Report RC-6487, IBM T.J. Watson Research Center, Yorktown Heights (1976). Also in: *Current Trends in Programming Methodology, Vol. 4: Data Structuring* (R.T. Yeh, ed.) Prentice-hall, 80-149 (1978).

[Hen 88] R. Hennicker: Beobachtungsorientierte Spezifikationen. Ph.D. thesis, Universität Passau (1988).

[Hen 89] R. Hennicker: Observational implementations. *Proc. 6th Symp. on Theoretical Aspects of Computer Science*, Paderborn. Springer LNCS 349 (1989).

[Hen 91] R. Hennicker: Observational implementation of algebraic specifications. *Acta Informatica* 28, 187-230 (1991).

[Hoa 72] C.A.R. Hoare: Proofs of correctness of data representations, *Acta Informatica* 1, 271-281 (1972).

[JK 86] J.P. Jouannaud, E. Kounalis: Proof by induction in equational theories without constructors. *Proc. IEEE Symp. on Logic in Computer Science*, Boston, 358-366 (1986).

[KA 84] S. Kamin, M. Archer: Partial Implementations of Abstract Data Types: A Dissenting View on Errors. *Proc. Int. Symposium on Semantics of Data Types*, Sophia-Antipolis. Springer LNCS 173, 317-336 (1984).

[KS 88] D. Kapur, M. Srivas: Computability and implementability issues in abstract data types. *Science of Computer Programming* 10, 33-63 (1988).

[Mes 89] J. Meseguer: General logics. *Proc. Logic Colloquium '87*, Granada. North Holland (1989).

[MG 85] J. Meseguer, J.A. Goguen: Initiality, induction and computability. In: *Algebraic Methods in Semantics* (M. Nivat and J. Reynolds, eds.). Cambridge Univ. Press, 459-540 (1985).

[Niv 87] P. Nivela: Semántica de comportamiento para especificaciones algebraicas. Ph.D. Thesis, Universitat Politècnica de Catalunya, Barcelona (1987).

[NO 88] P. Nivela, F. Orejas: Initial behavioural semantics for algebraic specifications. *Recent Trends in Data Type Specification, Selected Papers from the 5th Workshop on Specification of Abstract Data Types*, Gullane, Scotland. Springer LNCS 332, 184-207 (1988).

[Ore 81] F. Orejas: On the representation of data types. *Proc. Intl. Coll. on Formalization of programming concepts*. Springer LNCS 107, 419-431 (1981).

[Ore 83] F. Orejas: Characterizing composability of abstract implementations. *Proc. 1983 Intl. Conf. on Foundations of Computation Theory*, Borgholm, Sweden. Springer LNCS 158 (1983).

[Ore 84] F. Orejas: A proof system for checking composability of implementations of abstract data types. *Proc. of the Intl. Symp. on Semantics of Data Types*, Sophia-Antipolis. Springer LNCS 173 (1984).

[Ore 85] F. Orejas: On implementability and computability in abstract data types. In: *Algebra, Logics and Combinatorics in Computer Science*. North-Holland (1985).

[Ore 86] F. Orejas: The role of abstraction in program development (response). *Proc. IFIP Congress 1986*, Dublin. North-Holland, 143-146 (1986).

[ON 91] F. Orejas, P. Nivela: Constraints for behavioural specifications. *Recent Trends in Data Type Specification, Selected Papers from the 7h Workshop on Specification of Abstract Data Types*, Wusterhausen/Dosse, Germany. Springer LNCS 534, 220-245 (1991).

[ONE 89] F. Orejas, P. Nivela, H. Ehrig: Semantical constructions for categories of behavioural specifications. *Proc. Workshop on Categorical Methods in Computer Science with Aspects from Topology*. Springer LNCS 393, 220-241 (1989).

[OSC 89] F. Orejas, V. Sacristan, S. Clérici: Development of algebraic specifications with constraints. *Proc. Workshop on Categorical Methods in Computer Science with Aspects from Topology*. Springer LNCS 393, 102-123 (1989).

[Pad 83] P. Padawitz: Correctness, completeness and consistency of equational data type specifications, PhD thesis, T.U. Berlin (1983).

[Pad 85] P. Padawitz: Parameter preserving data type specifications *Proc.1985 Intl. Conf. on Theory and Practice if Software Development*. Springer LNCS 186, 323-341 (1989)

[Poi 84] A. Poigné: Another look at parameterization using subsorts, Proc. MFCS 84, Springer LNCS 176 (1984).

[Rei 81] H. Reichel: Behavioural equivalence - a unifying concept for initial and final specification methods. *Proc. 3rd. Hungarian Comp. Sci. Conference*, 27-39 (1981).

[San 91] A. Sánchez: PhD Thesis (forthcoming).

[Sch 87] O. Schoett: Data Abstraction and the Correctness of Modular Programming. Ph.D. thesis; Report CST-42-87, Dept. of Computer Science, Univ. of Edinburgh (1987).

[ST 87] D.T. Sannella, A. Tarlecki: On observational equivalence and algebraic specification. *Journal of Computer and System Sciences* 34, 150-178 (1987).

[ST 88] D.T. Sannella, A. Tarlecki: Toward formal development of programs from algebraic specifications: implementations revisited. Extend abstract in : *Proc. Joint Conf. on Theory and Practice of Software Development*, Pisa, Springer LNCS 249, 96-110 (1987); full version in Acta Informatica 25, 233-281 (1988).

[ST 89] D.T. Sannella, A. Tarlecki: Toward formal development of ML programs: foundations and methodology. LFCS Report Series Department of Computer Science, University of Edinburgh ECS-LFCS-89-71(1989). Actualizar.

[SW 82] D.T. Sannella, M. Wirsing: Implementation of parameterized specifications. *Proc. 9th Intl. Colloq. on Automata, Languages and Programming*, Aarhus. Springer LNCS 140, 473-488 (1982).

[SW 83] D.T. Sannella, M. Wirsing: A kernel language for algebraic specification and implementation. *Proc. 1983 Intl. Conf. on Foundations of Computation Theory*, Borgholm, Sweden. Springer LNCS 158, 413-427 (1983).

[Wan 79] M. Wand, Final algebra semantics and data type extensions, JCSS 19 (1979).

Relationships between Logical Frameworks*

Egidio Astesiano and Maura Cerioli[1]

DISI–Dipartimento di Informatica e Scienze dell'Informazione,
Università di Genova, Viale Benedetto XV, 16132 Genova, Italy,
e-mail: {astes,cerioli}@cisi.unige.it

Abstract. Adopting the concept of institution to represent logical frames, we have introduced in a previous paper the concept of simulation of an institution by another. Here we first show how simulations can be used to investigate the relationships between frames, distinguishing three levels, corresponding to different kinds of simulations: "set-theoretic", where the individual models of different frames are related disregarding their categorical and logical interconnection, "categorical", where the relation is between the categories of models, and "logical", where the relation is between specifications. Then we propose a concept of translation of inference systems along simulations such that soundness and completeness are preserved.

1 Introduction

Starting from the point of view that results should depend only on the very nature of the problems and not on the frame used to formalize them, in [2] we have introduced the concept of simulation of a logical formalism, viewed as an institution [8, 9], by another one and investigated the modularity properties of simulations w.r.t. specification languages and their relationship with the implementation relation.

The basic idea of simulation is encoding the syntax, i.e. signatures and sentences, of a new frame by that of an already known formalism in a way consistent with the semantics, in order to transfer results and tools. To formalize the consistency of the translation of the syntax w.r.t. the semantics, we require that every model of the new frame is represented by (at least) one of the old frame that satisfies the same sentences (under translation). Thus a simulation consists of three components: the two maps translating new signatures and sentences into old ones, and a partial surjective map which translates old models into new ones.

In this paper we use the concept of simulation mainly to analyse the different levels of relationship between frames and to translate inference systems from one institution to another, preserving soundness and completeness.

In the literature it is often claimed that a frame is *equivalent* to another one, usually in the sense that both solve the same kind of problems, or that in both the results are equivalently (un)satisfactory. But the meaning of equivalence is usually not formally defined and quite often used to denote different levels of relationship. Indeed we can distinguish (and formalize by means of simulations) three different

* This work has been partially supported by Esprit-BRA W.G. n.3264 Compass, Progetto Finalizzato Sistemi Informatici e Calcolo Parallelo of C.N.R. (Italy), MURST-40% Modelli e Specifiche di Sistemi Concorrenti

levels, depending on whether the correspondence is between models, or categories of models, or specifications (theories). At the *set-theoretic* level, for every model in the new frame a model in the old frame can be found that represents the given one, in the sense that it satisfies the same formulas, or, more precisely, that it satisfies corresponding formulas. This is formalized by requiring that there exists a simulation from the new into the old frame (s.t. the domains of the model component corresponds to a, possibly non-full, subcategory of the old models). At this level most properties are missing, in particular no structured way of defining models is guaranteed to be preserved, because it usually involves categorical constructions. To have a *categorical* correspondence between two frames, at least the domain of the simulation has to be a full subcategory of the old models; moreover some more properties have to be required depending on the categorical structures that are intended to be preserved. Here we are focusing on the initial structures and give minimal conditions to preserve initiality; the analysis of the properties needed to deal with other categorical structures are still in progress. Even if there is a categorical simulation, the power of the specification languages in the two frames can be quite different; in particular it is possible that in the new frame some categories are definable by sets of sentences that are not so in the old one (and vice versa). To guarantee that the relationship is at the *logical level*, i.e. for every specification (i.e. the class of models which satisfy a set of sentences) in the new frame there exists a specification in the old frame equivalent to the given one in the categorical sense, we have to require not only that the domain of the model component is a full subcategory of the category of old models, but also that it is described by a set of old sentences.

The second point discussed in this paper is the translation of inference systems along simulations. Since every simulation can be seen as a coding of a new formalism into a known one, we are mostly interested in mapping inference systems from the old into the new institution. The basic idea for translating an inference system $\vdash'$ in the old institution $\mathcal{I}'$ along a simulation μ of $\mathcal{I}$ by $\mathcal{I}'$ is that an $\mathcal{I}$-formula ϕ is deducible from a set Φ of $\mathcal{I}$-formulas iff $\mu(\Phi) \vdash' \mu(\phi)$. In this way we build an inference system for $\mathcal{I}$ which consists of a preprocessing (the coding of both the premises and the consequence in terms of $\mathcal{I}'$-sentences), the running of the system $\vdash'$ and possibly a post-processing (the decoding of the answer). Since the validity of sentences is preserved by simulation and every $\mathcal{I}$-model is represented by at least one $\mathcal{I}'$-model, the soundness of $\vdash'$ w.r.t. $\mathcal{I}'$ guarantees the soundness w.r.t. $\mathcal{I}$ of its translation. Moreover, since every $\mathcal{I}$-model is simulated by some $\mathcal{I}'$-model, if $\vdash'$ is complete w.r.t. a class Φ of $\mathcal{I}'$-sentences and the domain of the simulation, then $\vdash'$ is complete w.r.t. every class of $\mathcal{I}$-sentences whose image along the simulation is contained in Φ and the $\mathcal{I}$-models. Thus simulations reflect sound and complete inference systems. As an application and an illustration of the above results we show that a sound and equationally complete inference system for the partial conditional higher-order frame can be obtained starting from every sound and equationally complete inference system for the partial conditional first-order frame.

The paper is organized as follows. In section 2 the basic definitions of institution and simulation are presented with the help of a simple example; then simulations are used to formally define three different levels of relationship between institutions and illustrated by the hierarchy of encoding partiality in the total frame. Section 3 is devoted to the translation of inference systems along simulation, to the proof that soundness and completeness are preserved and to the instantiation of these results to two basic examples. Finally, in section 4 some related work is mentioned and compared to ours.

2 Simulations and Relationships between Logical Frames

In this section we illustrate by a case study the different levels of relationship between logical frames and how this difference is captured by the notion of simulation.

2.1 Basic Simulations

To introduce the concept of simulation (see e.g. [2]) and the correspondent notation from an intuitive point of view, we begin with an informal example, which is the reduction of many-sorted equational Horn-clause logic, from now on $\mathcal{MS}$, to one-sorted Horn-clause logic, from now on $\mathcal{L}$, making explicit the typing of the variables (see e.g. [18]). In this example, as in the following ones, the notation for many-sorted open formulas has been slightly changed w.r.t. the usual algebraic notation, according to [9]. Indeed in order to make the translation of formulas along signature morphisms easier, a partial function $V: X \rightarrow S$, the *typing of variables*, is prefixed to any conditional formula on the signature (S, F) and variables $\{X_s\}_{s \in S}$, where $X_s = V^{-1}(s)$ are the s-typed variables. From now on we will assume that the domain of V is finitary for every formula $V.\phi$ in order to our translation work; to allow infinitary quantification in the many-sorted case, infinitary conjunctions in the premises are needed in the one-sorted case. In the following a simulation is denoted by μ, possibly decorated.

Example 2.1 Let us fix a many-sorted signature Σ with sorts S and function symbols F. We define the translation of Σ into a one-sorted signature $\mu_{Sign}(\Sigma)$, by setting $\mu_{Sign}(\Sigma) = (Op', P')$, where Op'_n is the disjoint union of $F_{s_1 \ldots s_n, s}$, i.e. of the n-ary function symbol sets, disregarding type of arguments and results (so that any Σ-term is an (Op', P')-term, too), and P' contains only the typing predicates, i.e. $P'_1 = \{\_ : s \mid s \in S\}$, where the symbol $\_$ denotes the place of the argument in a postfix notation, and $P'_k = \emptyset \quad \forall k \neq 1$.

With the help of the typing predicates, any many-sorted conditional equation over Σ can be translated into a one-sorted equivalent one over $\mu_{Sign}(\Sigma)$; indeed let us consider a many-sorted formula $\xi = (V.t_1 = t'_1 \wedge \ldots \wedge t_n = t'_n \supset t = t')$ over Σ and the variables x_i, where $V(x_i) = s_i$ for $i = 1 \ldots k$, and define

$$\mu_{Sen_\Sigma}(\xi) = (x_1 : s_1 \wedge \ldots \wedge x_k : s_k \wedge t_1 = t'_1 \wedge \ldots \wedge t_n = t'_n \supset t = t').$$

Then in $\mu_{Sen_\Sigma}(\xi)$, the translation of ξ over μ_{Sign}, the information about the typing of the variables is carried by the predicates $x_i : s_i$ in the premises.

To illustrate in which sense $\mu_{Sen_\Sigma}(\xi)$ is equivalent to ξ, a class $dom(\mu)_\Sigma$ of one-sorted algebras is chosen, which soundly represents the many-sorted algebras and s.t. a one-sorted algebra satisfies $\mu_{Sen_\Sigma}(\xi)$ iff the many-sorted algebra represented by it satisfies ξ. Again the typing predicates are used to simulate the different carriers of a many-sorted algebra: a one-sorted algebra $\mathtt{A}'$ is a sound representation of a many-sorted algebra A, we write $\mathsf{A} = \mu_{Mod_\Sigma}(\mathtt{A}')$, iff whenever the arguments of a function are appropriately typed also the result is appropriately typed, i.e. $a_i : s_i^{A'}$ for $i = 1 \dots n$ implies $f^{A'}(a_1, \dots, a_n) : s^{A'}$ for any $f \in F_{s_1 \dots s_n, s}$. If A' satisfies this condition, then A is the many-sorted algebra $(\{s^A\}_{s \in S}, \{f^A\}_{f \in F})$, where $s^A = \{a \mid a : s^{A'}\}$ and f^A is the restriction of $f^{A'}$ to $s_1^A \times \dots \times s_n^A$; the above condition guarantees that the interpretation of the function symbols in A yields total functions. It is easy to check that A' satisfies $\mu_{Sen_\Sigma}(\xi)$ iff A satisfies ξ. Note that one-sorted algebras differing only on elements which do not satisfy any typing predicate represent the same many-sorted algebra.

Thus for every many-sorted signature Σ, a homogeneous signature $\mu_{Sign}(\Sigma)$ and two functions are defined: μ_{Sen_Σ}, which translates many sorted equational conditional sentences on Σ into homogeneous conditional sentences on $\mu_{Sign}(\Sigma)$ built on typing predicates and equalities, and μ_{Mod_Σ}, which partially translates homogeneous first-order structures on $\mu_{Sign}(\Sigma)$ into many-sorted algebras on Σ and is surjective, as it is immediate to check.

Since the change of notation, via signature morphisms, has a great relevance in the algebraic approach, being used for example to bind the actual to the formal parameters in parameterized specifications and to "put theories together to make specifications", we have to investigate the compatibility between the coding functions μ_{Sen_Σ} and μ_{Mod_Σ} defined for any signature Σ and the changes of notation.

Let $\bar{\sigma}: \Sigma_1 \to \Sigma_2$ be a morphism of many-sorted signatures, i.e. a pair of functions $\sigma: S_1 \to S_2$, renaming the sorts, and $\phi: F_1 \to F_2$ translating function symbols in a consistent way w.r.t. the sort renaming (i.e. if $f: s_1 \times \dots \times s_n \to s$, then $\phi(f): \sigma(s_1) \times \dots \times \sigma(s_n) \to \sigma(s)$). Then $\bar{\sigma}$ naturally induces a homogeneous signature morphism $\mu_{Sign}(\bar{\sigma}) = (\psi', \pi')$ from $\mu_{Sign}(\Sigma_1)$ into $\mu_{Sign}(\Sigma_2)$, defined by $\psi'(f) = \phi(f)$ for any $f \in F$ and $\pi'(\_ : s) = \_ : \sigma(s)$ for any $s \in S$. It is easy to check that the translation of sentences is compatible with signature morphisms, i.e. that $\mu_{Sen_{\Sigma_2}}(\bar{\sigma}(\xi)) = \mu_{Sign}(\bar{\sigma})(\mu_{Sen_{\Sigma_1}}(\xi))$, where the application of a signature morphism to a sentence is the usual renaming of function (and predicate) symbols, plus the obvious translation of variable typing in ξ. Instead the partiality of the translation of algebras makes the compatibility between the algebra translations and signature morphisms delicate. Indeed it is intuitive to expect that the translation along a signature morphism of a one-sorted algebra simulating a many-sorted algebra simulates the translation of that many-sorted algebra; more formally, recalling that algebras are translated along signature morphisms in a countervariant direction into their *reduct*, we have that if $A' \in dom(\mu)_{\Sigma_2}$, then $A'_{|\mu_{Sign}(\bar{\sigma})} \in dom(\mu)_{\Sigma_1}$ and $(\mu_{Mod_{\Sigma_2}}(A'))_{|\bar{\sigma}} = \mu_{Mod_{\Sigma_1}}(A'_{|\mu_{Sign}(\bar{\sigma})})$. But the converse of the first implication does not hold, i.e. $A'_{|\mu_{Sign}(\bar{\sigma})} \in dom(\mu)_{\Sigma_1}$ does not imply $A' \in dom(\mu)_{\Sigma_2}$, as illustrated by the following example.

Let Σ_2 be the many-sorted signature $(\{nat\}, (\{0: \to nat, inc, dec: nat \to nat\})$, Σ_1 be its subsignature $(\{nat\}, (\{0: \to nat, inc: nat \to nat\})$, and $\bar{\sigma}$ be the embedding of Σ_1 into Σ_2. Consider now the one sorted algebra A' on $\mu_{Sign}(\Sigma_2)$, defined by

$$|A'| = \mathbb{Z} \qquad\qquad a : nat^{A'} \iff a \in \mathbb{N}$$
$$0^{A'} = 0 \qquad inc^{A'}(x) = x + 1 \qquad dec^{A'}(x) = x - 1$$

Then $A' \notin dom(\mu)_{\Sigma_2}$, because $0 : nat$ holds, but $dec^{A'}(0) : nat$ does not and hence $dec^{A'}$ on appropriately typed input yields an untyped output. However $A'_{|\bar{\sigma}}$ is the same as $\mathbf{A}'$ but *dec* has been dropped, hence it obviously belongs to $dom(\mu)_{\Sigma_1}$.

Therefore we have a weaker condition (called *partial naturality*) for algebras than the one for sentences: if $\mathbf{A}' \in dom(\mu)_{\Sigma_2}$, then $\mathbf{A}'_{|\mu_{Sign}(\bar{\sigma})} \in dom(\mu)_{\Sigma_1}$ and $(\mu_{Mod\,\Sigma_2}(\mathbf{A}'))_{|\bar{\sigma}} = \mu_{Mod\,\Sigma_1}(\mathbf{A}'_{|\mu_{Sign}(\bar{\sigma})})$. □

Let us abstract from the above construction the general aspects of the coding of a *new* (many-sorted) into an *old* (one-sorted) formalism:

- to each *new* signature an *old* signature corresponds;
- to each *new* sentence an *old* sentence corresponds;
- not any *old* algebra represents a *new* one, but to each *new* algebra at least one *old* corresponds, so that *old* algebras are (partially) translated by a surjective mapping.

This scheme generalizes to the frame of institutions by lifting maps to the proper categorical objects, taking care of the delicate points due to the partiality of model translation, and requiring that the only non-categorical structure, i.e. the validity relation, is preserved by them.

Def. 2.2 [[8] def.14] An *institution* $\mathcal{I}$ consists of

- a category **Sign** of *signatures*;
- a functor Sen: **Sign** $\rightarrow$ **Set** giving the set of *sentences* over a given signature;
- a functor Mod: $\mathbf{Sign}^{op} \rightarrow \mathbf{Cat}^2$ giving the category of *models* of a given signature;
- a satisfaction relation $\models \subseteq |Mod(\Sigma)| \times Sen(\Sigma)^3$ for each Σ in **Sign**, sometimes denoted $\models_\Sigma$, such that for each morphism $\phi: \Sigma_1 \rightarrow \Sigma_2$ in **Sign**, the *Satisfaction Condition*

$$M' \models Sen(\phi)(\xi) \iff Mod(\phi)(M') \models \xi$$

holds for each M' in $|Mod(\Sigma_2)|$ and each ξ in $Sen(\Sigma_1)$. □

Since models are partially mapped, the usual notion of natural transformation is insufficient to describe the translation of the (*old*) model functor and we have to explicitly deal with the *partiality* of each component of this "partially"-natural transformation.

Def. 2.3 Let $\mathcal{I} = (\mathbf{Sign}, Sen, Mod, \models)$ and $\mathcal{I}' = (\mathbf{Sign}', Sen', Mod', \models')$ be institutions. Then a *simulation* $\mu: \mathcal{I} \rightarrow \mathcal{I}'$ consists of

- a functor μ_{Sign}: **Sign** $\rightarrow$ **Sign**$'$;
- a natural transformation $\mu_{Sen}: Sen \rightarrow Sen' \cdot \mu_{Sign}$, i.e. a natural family of functions $\mu_{Sen\,\Sigma}: Sen(\Sigma) \rightarrow Sen'(\mu_{Sign}(\Sigma))$, and

[2] Usually **Cat** denotes the category of small categories; but in most significant examples from computer science non-small categories are needed as models and hence we use **Cat** to denote the category of all the categories whose objects belong to a suitable universe, that we never mention, as usual. In this way we avoid the well known foundational problems arising whenever one speaks of the *category of all the categories*. For a similar remark see also [9, 13, 22]

[3] for any category **C** we denote by |**C**| the class of the objects of **C**.

- a surjective *partially-natural* transformation $\mu_{Mod}: Mod' \cdot \mu_{Sign} \rightarrow Mod$, that is a family of functors $\mu_{Mod_\Sigma}: dom(\mu)_\Sigma \rightarrow Mod(\Sigma)$, where $dom(\mu)_\Sigma$ is a (non-necessarily full) subcategory of $Mod'(\mu_{Sign}(\Sigma))$ s.t.
  - μ_{Mod_Σ} is surjective on $|Mod(\Sigma)|$;
  - the family is partially-natural, i.e. for any signature morphism $\sigma \in \mathbf{Sign}(\Sigma_1, \Sigma_2)$

$$Mod(\sigma) \cdot \mu_{Mod_{\Sigma_2}} = [\mu_{Mod_{\Sigma_1}} \cdot Mod'(\mu_{Sign}(\sigma))]_{|dom(\mu)_{\Sigma_2}}$$

s.t. the following *satisfaction condition* holds:

$$A \models \mu_{Sen_\Sigma}(\xi) \iff \mu_{Mod_\Sigma}(A) \models \xi$$

for all $\Sigma \in |\mathbf{Sign}|$, all $A \in |dom(\mu)_\Sigma|$ and all $\xi \in Sen(\Sigma)$. □

Note that the partial-naturalitycondition implies the following condition

$$Mod'(\mu_{Sign}(\sigma))(dom(\mu)_{\Sigma_2}) \subseteq dom(\mu)_{\Sigma_1}.$$

In the sequel, for any simulation μ, we will use μ also to denote its components, if the context makes clear the nature of the component.

It is easy to check that $\mu: \mathcal{MS} \rightarrow \mathcal{L}$, whose components were informally sketched in Example 2.1, is a simulation, from now on denoted μ^M (the superscript M stands for *Many-sorted*) in order to reserve the symbol μ to denote a generic simulation.

2.2 A Paradigmatic Example: Partial versus Total Specifications

Here we illustrate the use of the notion of simulation, with its various specializations, as a tool for understanding the relationship between two formalisms with respect to the solution of a problem. We have chosen as a paradigmatic example the specification of (strict) partial functions in a partial and a total frame. The following analysis, though not pretending to be exhaustive especially on the pragmatic side, will highlight the subtleties of the relationship between the two frames and possibly reveal some misbeliefs.

Semantic Level. First we analyse the relationship between partial and total frames from a semantic point of view, i.e. disregarding their logics. Formally this means that we are working on institutions *without sentences*. Let us recall the basic ingredients of the partial frame (see [6, 7, 20]).

Def. 2.4 A *partial algebra* A on a signature $\Sigma = (S, F)$ consists of a family $\{s^A\}_{s \in S}$ of sets and of a family $\{f^A\}_{f \in F_{w,s}}$ of partial functions s.t. if $w = \emptyset$, then either f^A is undefined or $f^A \in s^A$, else $w = s_1 \ldots s_n$ and $f^A: s_1^A \times \ldots \times s_n^A \rightarrow_p s^A$. A *homomorphism* from A into B is a family $h = \{h_s: s^A \rightarrow s^B\}_{s \in S}$ of total functions, s.t. for any $f \in F_{s_1 \ldots s_n,s}$ and any $a_i \in s_i^A$, for $i = 1 \ldots n$, $f^A(a_1, \ldots, a_n) \in s^A$ implies $h_s(f^A(a_1, \ldots, a_n)) = f^B(h_{s_1}(a_1), \ldots, h_{s_n}(a_n))$.

Let us denote by $\mathcal{PAR}_0$ the institution of partial algebras without sentences and by $\mathcal{MS}_0$ the institution of total many-sorted algebras without sentences. □

In the algebraic community there is a widespread belief that partiality can also be handled without explicit partial functions, in the usual total frame, simply by introducing a distinguished constant $\bot$ (one for each sort) to represent the undefined computations; in this way to any partial algebra A its trivial totalization corresponds. Following this intuition it is possible to define a *simulation* $\mu_0^\bot$ of partial by total algebras, where every partial algebra is simulated by its trivial totalization; but some homomorphisms between the trivial totalizations of partial algebras cannot be translated into homomorphisms of partial algebras, because the image of some *defined* element (i.e. of elements different from $\bot$) may be *undefined* (i.e. equal to $\bot$), while the homomorphisms of partial algebras are *total* functions. Therefore the domain of the simulation is not a full subcategory of the models and hence most categorical properties are missing. Let us formalize this in terms of simulation.

Def. 2.5 The simulation $\mu_0^\bot: \mathcal{PAR}_0 \to \mathcal{MS}_0$ consists of:

- $\mu_0^\bot: \mathbf{Sign}_{\mathcal{PAR}} \to \mathbf{Sign}_{\mathcal{MS}}$ is defined by $\mu_0^\bot((S,F)) = (S,F')$, where if $w \neq \emptyset$, then $F'_{w,s} = F_{w,s}$ else $F'_{\emptyset,s} = F_{\emptyset,s} \cup \{\bot_s\}$, and by $\mu_0^\bot((\sigma,\phi)) = (\sigma,\phi')$,where $\phi'(f) = \phi(f)$ for any $f \in F_{w.s}$ and $\phi(\bot_s) = \bot_{\sigma(s)}$.
- $\mu_0^\bot: \emptyset \to \emptyset$ is the empty natural transformation;
- $\mu_0^\bot: Mod_{\mathcal{MS}} \cdot \mu_0^\bot \to Mod_{\mathcal{PAR}}$ is defined by:
  - $dom(\mu_0^\bot)_\Sigma$ is the subcategory of $Mod_{\mathcal{MS}}(\mu_0^\bot(\Sigma))$ whose objects are the total algebras A' s.t. $f^{\mathsf{A}'}(a_1,\ldots,a_n) \neq \bot_s$ implies $a_i \neq \bot^{\mathsf{A}'_{s_i}}$ for all $i = 1\ldots n$ for any $f \in F_{s_1\ldots s_n,s}$ (*strictness*) and whose arrows are the homomorphisms $\mathsf{h}' \in Mod_{\mathcal{MS}}(\mu_0^\bot(\Sigma))(\mathsf{A}',\mathsf{B}')$ s.t. $a \neq \bot_s^{\mathsf{A}'}$ implies $\mathsf{h}'_s(a) \neq \bot_s^{\mathsf{A}'}$ for any $s \in S$.
  - for any $\mathsf{A}' \in dom(\mu_0^\bot)_\Sigma$ the partial algebra $A = \mu_0^\bot{}_\Sigma(\mathsf{A}')$ consists of $s^A = s^{\mathsf{A}'} - \{\bot_s^{\mathsf{A}'}\}$ for any $s \in S$ and for any $f \in F_{s_1\ldots s_n,s}$ and every $(a_1,\ldots,a_n)$, with $a_i \in s_i^A$ for $i = 1\ldots n$, if $f^{\mathsf{A}'}(a_1,\ldots,a_n) \neq \bot_s^{\mathsf{A}'}$, then $f^A(a_1,\ldots,a_n) = f^{\mathsf{A}'}(a_1,\ldots,a_n)$, else $f^{\mathsf{A}'}(a_1,\ldots,a_n)$ is undefined;
  - $\mu_0^\bot{}_\Sigma(\mathsf{h}')$ is the restriction of h' to $s^{\mu_0^\bot{}_\Sigma(\mathsf{A}')}$. □

Note that formally strictness is not needed, because there are no sentences whose validity has to be preserved; however we prefer to require the strictness condition, because it is more intuitive specifying strict partial algebras and it will be needed in the sequel, to deal with logics.

Although obviously A' and $\mu_0^\bot{}_\Sigma(\mathsf{A}')$ are strictly related from a set theoretic point of view, the correspondence, due to the domain of $\mu_0^\bot$ being a non-full subcategory, is not adequate for categorical purposes, in particular the initial model is not preserved by $\mu_0^\bot$. Indeed in both frames the initial model is characterized by the well known *no junk* and *no confusion* conditions of [14], which mean that every element is denoted by some term and that two ground terms are equal in the initial object iff they are equal in every algebra of the class (in the partial frame the existential equality is considered, holding if both sides denote the same element of the carrier, so that also the *minimal definedness* holds). Thus the minimal equality (no-confusion) of the initial model in the total frame implies, in particular, the minimal equality with $\bot$ and hence the *maximal* definedness of its translation; therefore in most cases the translation of the initial model is not initial.

Categorical Level. We are now looking for simulations preserving properties like initiality. For this note that another way of coding partiality in terms of total algebras is to split every carrier by a typing predicate in typed (i.e. defined) and untyped elements and to represent every partial function by a total one which results in an untyped element over every input outside its domain (for similar approaches see e.g. [11], where one-sorted total algebras are used, [16] and [17]). Moreover, in order to handle logical formulas, in the following we also introduce a binary predicate, which plays the role of the existential equality, and holds on a' and b' iff a' and b' are equal and appropriately typed. The corresponding simulation is as follows.

Def. 2.6 Let us denote by $\mathcal{TL}_0$ the institution of typed first-order structures (total many-sorted algebras with predicates) without sentences.

The simulation ${\mu^P}_0: \mathcal{PAR}_0 \to \mathcal{TL}_0$ consists of:

- ${\mu^P}_0$: $\mathbf{Sign}_{\mathcal{PAR}} \to \mathbf{Sign}_{\mathcal{TL}}$ consists of ${\mu^P}_0((S,F)) = (S',F',P')$, where $S' = S$, $F' = F$ and if $w = ss$, then $P'_{ss} = \{eq_s\}$, if $w = s$, then $P'_s = \{D_s\}$, otherwise $P'_w = \emptyset$, and ${\mu^P}_0((\sigma,\phi)) = (\sigma',\phi',\pi')$,where $\sigma' = \sigma$, $\phi' = \phi$, $\pi'(D_s) = D_{\sigma(s)}$ and $\pi'(eq_s) = eq_{\sigma(s)}$.
- ${\mu^P}_0$ is the empty natural transformation;
- ${\mu^P}_0$: $Mod_{\mathcal{TL}} \cdot {\mu^P}_0 \to Mod_{\mathcal{PAR}}$ is defined by:
  - $dom({\mu^P}_0)_\Sigma$ is the full subcategory of $Mod_{\mathcal{TL}}(\mu^P(\Sigma))$ whose objects are the total algebras A' s.t. for any $f \in F_{s_1 \ldots s_n,s}$ if ${D_s}^{\mathsf{A}'}(f^{\mathsf{A}'}(a_1,\ldots,a_n))$ holds, then ${D_{s_i}}^{\mathsf{A}'}(a_i)$ holds, too, for all $i = 1 \ldots n$ (*strictness*) and $eq_s^{\mathsf{A}'}(a,b)$ iff $a = b$ and ${D_s}^{\mathsf{A}'}(a)$, ${D_s}^{\mathsf{A}'}(b)$.
  - for every $\mathsf{A}' \in dom(\mu^P)_\Sigma$ the partial algebra $A = {\mu^P}_{0\Sigma}(\mathsf{A}')$ consists of $s^A = {D_s}^{\mathsf{A}'}$ for any $s \in S$ and for any $f \in F$ and every $a_i \in s_i^A$ if ${D_s}^{\mathsf{A}'}(f^{\mathsf{A}'}(a_1,\ldots,a_n))$ holds, then $f^A(a_1,\ldots,a_n) = f^{\mathsf{A}'}(a_1,\ldots,a_n)$, else $f^A(a_1,\ldots,a_n)$ is undefined.
  - for any $h \in dom({\mu^P}_0)_\Sigma(\mathsf{A}',\mathsf{B}')$ the arrow ${\mu^P}_\Sigma(\mathsf{h}')$ is $\mathsf{h}'_{|{\mu^P}_\Sigma(\mathsf{A}')}$. □

Now initial models are translated along ${\mu^P}_0$ to initial models; the proof follows a pattern common to most algebraic frames. First it is shown that the translation I of an initial object is *weakly* initial (i.e. that there exists at least one arrow from I into any object), so that the *no-confusion* condition holds; the weak initiality comes from $dom({\mu^P}_0)_\Sigma$ being a full subcategory of the total models and ${\mu^P}_0$ being surjective on the objects. Then I is shown to be term-generated, so that the *no-junk* condition holds, too, because the total initial object is term-generated and term-generatedness is preserved by ${\mu^P}_0$.

Abstracting from the two main points of the above proof technique, we can define the *categorical* simulations, which preserve "term-generatedness" and whose domains are full subcategories. and show that categorical simulations preserve initiality.

Def. 2.7 Let $\mathbf{C}$ be a category and c be an object of $\mathbf{C}$; then c is called *inductive* iff $\mathbf{C}(c,c')$ has at most one element for every $c' \in \mathbf{C}$. For every subcategory $\mathbf{C}'$ of $\mathbf{C}$, c is called *weakly initial* in $\mathbf{C}'$ iff $\mathbf{C}'(c,c')$ has at least one element for every $c' \in \mathbf{C}'$.

Let $\mathcal{I}$ and $\mathcal{I}'$ be institutions and μ be a simulation from $\mathcal{I}$ into $\mathcal{I}'$. Then μ is called *categorical* iff every $dom(\mu)_\Sigma$ is a full sub-category of $Mod'(\Sigma)$ and μ_Σ preserves the inductive objects of $Mod'(\mu(\Sigma))$ belonging to $dom(\mu)_\Sigma$. □

Note that the property of being categorical only involves the model components of simulations (and, implicitly, the translation of signatures); thus if two simulations coincide on signatures and models and the first is categorical, then also the second one is so, independently of the formulas that are chosen as sentences of the institutions and their translation.

In most algebraic frames the interesting classes of models are closed w.r.t. subalgebras and this guarantees that their initial models, if any, are term-generated; this can be generalized to every categorical frame, noting that the notion of subalgebra generalizes to the categorical concept of *regular subobject*. Let us first recall the definition of regular sub-object.

Def. 2.8 Let $\mathbf{C}$ be a category and $f, g \in \mathbf{C}(A, B)$ be a pair of parallel arrows. Then an arrow $e \in \mathbf{C}(E, A)$ is an *equalizer* of f and g iff it satisfies the following conditions

- $f \cdot e = g \cdot e$ (*e equalizes f* and g);
- for any $k \in \mathbf{C}(K, A)$ s.t. $f \cdot k = g \cdot k$ there exists a unique $\pi \in \mathbf{C}(K, E)$ s.t. $e \cdot \pi = k$ (*k factorizes trough e*).

If $e \in \mathbf{C}(E, A)$ is an equalizer of some f and g, E is a *regular subobject* of A. □

Lemma 2.9 Let $\mathbf{C}$ be a category having equalizers and $\mathbf{C}'$ be a subcategory of $\mathbf{C}$ closed under equalizers and regular subobjects. Then I is initial in $\mathbf{C}'$ only if I is inductive in $\mathbf{C}$. □

It is worth to note that both the institutions of partial as well as total many-sorted algebras, with or without predicates, have equalizers, and that the model classes of positive Horn-clauses are closed w.r.t. regular subobjects (in general they are not closed w.r.t. generic subobjects); thus the following proposition applies in most cases.

Prop. 2.10 Let $\mathcal{I} = (\mathbf{Sign}, Sen, Mod, \models)$ and $\mathcal{I}' = (\mathbf{Sign}', Sen', Mod', \models')$ be institutions s.t. for any $\Sigma' \in |\mathbf{Sign}'|$ the category $Mod'(\Sigma')$ has equalizers and μ be a categorical simulation from $\mathcal{I}$ into $\mathcal{I}'$. If I' is initial in a full subcategory $\mathbf{C}'$ of $dom(\mu)_\Sigma$ closed w.r.t. regular subobjects (performed in $Mod'(\mu(\Sigma))$), then $\mu_\Sigma(I')$ is initial in $\mu_\Sigma(\mathbf{C}')$. □

Cor. 2.11 Let $\mathbf{C}'$ be a full subcategory of $dom({\mu^P}_0)_\Sigma$ closed w.r.t. subalgebras and I' be the initial object in $\mathbf{C}'$. Then ${\mu^P}_0(\mathsf{I}')$ is initial in ${\mu^P}_0(\mathbf{C}')$. □

Logical Level. Let us consider now the logical aspect of partial and total frames and investigate the equivalences of their expressive power. In the total [partial] frame we consider, as usual, the institution $\mathcal{TL}$ [$\mathcal{EPAR}$] of positive Horn-clauses [built on existential equality] and its subinstitution $\mathcal{GTL}$ [$\mathcal{GEPAR}$] where the sentences are without variables.

Let us consider first the trivial simulation $\mu_0^\perp$. Let A' be in $dom(\mu_0^\perp)_\Sigma$ and consider a ground existential equality $t = t'$; then $A = \mu_0^\perp{}_\Sigma(\mathsf{A}')$ satisfies $t = t'$ iff t^A and t'^A denote the same element of $s^A = s^{\mathsf{A}'} - \{\perp_s\}$, i.e. iff $t^{\mathsf{A}'} = t'^{\mathsf{A}'} \neq \perp_s$; thus to generalize $\mu_0^\perp$ to a simulation from $\mathcal{GEPAR}$, a stronger (and unusual) logic than the positive Horn-clauses is needed in the total frame. Therefore the trivial totalization fails in both the categorical and the logical aspects, in the sense that, although it is true that any partial algebra is equivalent from a set theoretic point of view to its trivial totalization, the equivalence becomes false if algebra morphisms are considered; moreover it relates Horn-Clauses to a more powerful first-order fragment.

Let us consider now the simulation ${\mu^P}_0$. Every ground Horn-clause is naturally translated into the total frame, just by replacing every existential equality symbol with the corresponding predicate *eq*. However if variables appear in the formula, this translation from the partial to the total frame does not preserve the validity of sentences. Indeed, consider for example $D_s(x)$; then obviously any partial algebra satisfies it (undefined elements do not exist), while some total algebras in the domain of ${\mu^P}_0$ do not, because valuations of variables in the total frame range also over the elements which do not satisfy the definedness predicates (and hence are dropped by the simulation). More generally the valuations for the total frame which range over undefined elements must not be taken in account, in order to establish the validity of translations of partial sentences. To overcome this problem it is sufficient to add to the premises of every sentence the definedness assertions for each of its variables, so that every valuation s.t. $V(x) = a$ and $\neg D(a)$ satisfies the sentence, because one of the premises is false; thus the validity only depends on "defined" valuations also in the total case. Note that in this way equations with variables in the partial frame are translated into conditional axioms of the total formalism. This, together with the fact that the simulation ${\mu^P}_0$ (properly generalized to deal with sentences) is categorical, illustrates the deep reason for the model classes of partial equational specifications being quasi-varieties (see [24]), like the model classes of total conditional specifications, and not varieties, as the model classes of total equational specifications are (see [14]).

Def. 2.12 The categorical simulation $\mu^P: \mathcal{EPAR} \to \mathcal{TL}$ coincides with ${\mu^P}_0$ on signatures and models, and on sentences is defined by

$${\mu^P}_\Sigma(\xi) = D_{s_1}(x_1) \wedge \ldots \wedge D_{s_k}(x_k) \wedge eq_{s'_1}(t_1, t'_1) \wedge \ldots \wedge eq_{s'_n}(t_n, t'_n) \supset eq_s(t, t')$$

where $\xi = (t_1 = t'_1 \wedge \ldots \wedge t_n = t'_n \supset t = t')$ and $x_1, \ldots, x_k$ are the variables of ξ. □

Since the domain of μ^P is the model class of the following axioms $th(\mu^P)$:

$$D_s(f(x_1, \ldots, x_n)) \supset D_{s_i}(x_i) \text{ for } i = 1 \ldots n \ (\textit{strictness}) \text{ and}$$

$$D_s(x) \wedge D_s(y) \wedge x = y \Leftrightarrow eq_s(x, y), \text{ i.e.}$$

$D_s(x) \wedge D_s(y) \wedge x = y \supset eq_s(x, y)$, $eq_s(x, y) \supset D_s(x)$, $eq_s(x, y) \supset D_s(y)$ and $eq_s(x, y) \supset x = y$, every model class of a partial *presentation* (Σ, Ax) is simulated by the model class of the total presentation $(\mu^P(\Sigma), {\mu^P}_\Sigma(Ax) \cup th(\mu^P))$. We call *logical* this kind of simulation, i.e. simulations translating presentations into presentations.

Def. 2.13 Let $\mathcal{I} = (\mathbf{Sign}, Sen, Mod, \models)$ and $\mathcal{I}' = (\mathbf{Sign}', Sen', Mod', \models')$ be institutions and μ be a simulation from $\mathcal{I}$ into $\mathcal{I}'$. Then μ is called *logical* iff it is categorical and $dom(\mu)_\Sigma$ is the model class of a set $th(\mu)_\Sigma \subseteq Sen'(\mu(\Sigma))$ of sentences for every $\Sigma \in |\mathbf{Sign}|$. □

Although in general the family $\{th(\mu)_\Sigma\}_{\Sigma\in|\mathbf{Sign}|}$ is not functorial, i.e. it is not possible to define a sub-functor F of Sen s.t. $F(\Sigma) = th(\mu)_\Sigma$, if we consider the family of the closures under logical consequences $\{th(\mu)^\bullet_\Sigma\}_{\Sigma\in|\mathbf{Sign}|}$, where $th(\mu)^\bullet_\Sigma = \{\alpha \mid A' \models' \alpha \quad \forall A' \in dom(\mu)_\Sigma\}$, then the partial-naturality condition on $\{dom(\mu)_\Sigma\}_{\Sigma\in|\mathbf{Sign}|}$ guarantees the functoriality of $\{th(\mu)^\bullet_\Sigma\}_{\Sigma\in|\mathbf{Sign}|}$ and hence every logical simulation is a map of institutions, too (see [13]). On the converse any surjective map of institutions is a logical simulation. In the next section logical simulations are also used to tailor inference systems to the domain of simulations.

Since the translations via μ^P of ground partial Horn Clauses are ground Horn Clauses, μ^P can be specialized to a simulation between the institutions $\mathcal{GEPAR}$ and $\mathcal{GTL}$. It is still categorical, but is not logical anymore; indeed axioms with variables are needed to define the domain, as the following example shows.

Example 2.14 For any signature $\Sigma = (S, F) \in |\mathbf{Sign}_{\mathcal{EPAR}}|$ with at least one function symbol there does not exist a set $th' \subseteq Sen'(\mu^P(\Sigma))$ of ground sentences s.t. $dom(\mu^P)_\Sigma$ is the class of models of th'. Indeed there exists an algebra A' which belongs to the model class of any set of ground Horn-clauses but does not to $dom(\mu^P)_\Sigma$. Let A' be defined by $s^{\mathsf{A}'} = \{1_s, 2_s\}$ for all $s \in S$, $f^{\mathsf{A}'}(x_1, \ldots, x_n) = 1_s$ for all $f \in F_{s_1\ldots s_n,s}$, $eq_s^{\mathsf{A}'} = \{(1_s, 1_s)\}$ and $D_s{}^{\mathsf{A}'} = \{1_s\}$. Then for any ground term $t \in T_{\Sigma,s}$, its evaluation in A' is 1_s and hence A' satisfies any ground formula. But A' does not belong to $dom(\mu^P)_\Sigma$, because functions are not strict; indeed $D_s{}^{\mathsf{A}'}(f^{\mathsf{A}'}(2_{s1}, \ldots, 2_{sn}))$ but $\neg D_{s_i}{}^{\mathsf{A}'}(2_{s_i})$. □

3 Inference System Translation

In this section we show how to translate inference systems via simulation in such a way that soundness and completeness of inference systems are preserved, and then apply this technique to a few specific examples and show that the results of [18] and of [4, 5] are instances of more general properties. Some more applications may be found in [11], where translations of partial, of Horn-clauses and of Order-sorted logics in terms of equational type logic are presented in order to use the ET-inference system and the connected rewrite tools; although these translations are not formalized as simulations, they can be so and the results obtained by their applications are an instance of the ones presented in the next subsection.

3.1 General Results

According to the intuition that a simulation codes a new institution in terms of an old one, inference systems are translated via simulation; so that, starting from an inference system for $\mathcal{I}'$ and using a simulation $\mu: \mathcal{I} \to \mathcal{I}'$, a new system for $\mathcal{I}$ is built, which consists of: the preprocessing μ of the sentences of $\mathcal{I}$, coding them as sentences of $\mathcal{I}'$, followed by the application of the given system for $\mathcal{I}'$, and possibly by the postprocessing μ^{-1} to decode the results.

Def. 3.1 Let $\mathcal{I} = (\mathbf{Sign}, Sen, Mod, \models)$ be an institution and $\vdash$ be an inference system for $Sen(\Sigma)$, i.e. any relation $\vdash \subseteq \wp(Sen(\Sigma)) \times Sen(\Sigma)$. Then $\vdash$ is *sound* for

$C \subseteq |Mod(\Sigma)|$ iff for any $\phi \in Sen(\Sigma)$ and any $\Gamma \subseteq Sen(\Sigma)$, $\Gamma \vdash \phi$ implies that for all $A \in C$ if $A \models_\Sigma \gamma$ for all $\gamma \in \Gamma$, then $A \models_\Sigma \phi$. If C is $|Mod(\Sigma)|$, then $\vdash$ is shortly said sound.

For any $\Psi \subseteq Sen(\Sigma)$ and any $C \subseteq |Mod(\Sigma)|$, the system $\vdash$ is *complete* w.r.t. Ψ and C iff for any $\psi \in \Psi$ and any $\Gamma \subseteq Sen(\Sigma)$

$$A \models_\Sigma \gamma \text{ for all } \gamma \in \Gamma \text{ implies } A \models_\Sigma \psi \quad \text{for any } A \in C$$

implies $\Gamma \vdash \psi$. If C is $|Mod(\Sigma)|$, then $\vdash$ is shortly said complete w.r.t. Ψ.

For any simulation $\mu: \mathcal{I} \rightarrow \mathcal{I}'$ and any inference system $\vdash'$ for $Sen'(\mu(\Sigma))$, the inference system $\vdash'^{\mu}$ for $Sen(\Sigma)$ is defined by: $\Gamma \vdash'^{\mu} \phi$ iff $\mu(\Gamma) \vdash' \mu(\phi)$. □

The definition of completeness as it stands is a generalization of the notion of completeness in algebraic frames; indeed, for examples, in the frame of (both partial and total) conditional specifications the *equational completeness* of a system $\vdash$ means that if an equation $t = t'$ holds in the model class of a set of conditional axioms Γ, then $\Gamma \vdash t = t'$. Thus the premises Γ are any set of sentences, while the consequence has to be an equation, i.e. a sentence in the selected subclass.

Note that if reflexivity, monotonicity and transitivity are required by the definition of inference system, as for the *entailment systems* of [13], then simulations preserve these properties, so that the translation of an entailment system is an entailment system, too.

Prop. 3.2 Let $\mathcal{I} = (\mathbf{Sign}, Sen, Mod, \models)$ and $\mathcal{I}' = (\mathbf{Sign}', Sen', Mod', \models')$ be institutions, $\mu: \mathcal{I} \rightarrow \mathcal{I}'$ be a simulation and $\vdash'$ be an inference system for $Sen'(\mu(\Sigma))$.

1. if $\vdash'$ is *reflexive*, i.e. $\{\phi'\} \vdash' \phi'$, then $\vdash'^{\mu}$ is reflexive, too;
2. if $\vdash'$ is *monotonic*, i.e. $\Gamma'_1 \vdash' \phi'$ and $\Gamma'_1 \subseteq \Gamma'_2$ imply $\Gamma'_2 \vdash' \phi'$, then $\vdash'^{\mu}$ is monotonic;
3. if $\vdash'$ is *transitive*, i.e. $\Gamma' \vdash' \phi'_i$ for all $i \in I$ and $\{\phi'_i \mid i \in I\} \vdash' \phi'$ imply $\Gamma \vdash' \phi'$, then $\vdash'^{\mu}$ is transitive, too.
4. if $\vdash$ is *compact*, i.e. $\Gamma' \vdash' \phi'$ implies that there exists a finite $\Gamma'_1 \subseteq \Gamma'$ s.t. $\Gamma'_1 \vdash' \phi$, then $\vdash'^{\mu}$ is compact, too. □

Cor. 3.3 Let $\mathcal{I}' = (\mathbf{Sign}', Sen', Mod', \models')$ be an institution and $\vdash' = \{\vdash'_{\Sigma'} \mid \Sigma' \in |\mathbf{Sign}'|\}$ be an *entailment system* for $\mathcal{I}'$ (see definition 1 of [13]), i.e. a family of reflexive, monotonic and transitive relations $\vdash'_{\Sigma'} \subseteq \wp(Sen'(\Sigma')) \times Sen'(\Sigma')$ satisfying the following condition

* if $\Gamma' \vdash'_{\Sigma'_1} \phi'$, then for every $\sigma' \in \mathbf{Sign}'(\Sigma'_1, \Sigma'_2)$, $Sen'(\sigma')(\Gamma') \vdash_{\Sigma'_2} Sen'(\sigma')(\phi')$.

Then for any institution $\mathcal{I} = (\mathbf{Sign}, Sen, Mod, \models)$ and any simulation $\mu: \mathcal{I} \rightarrow \mathcal{I}'$ the family $\vdash'^{\mu} = \{\vdash'^{\mu}_{\Sigma} = \vdash'^{\mu}_{\mu(\Sigma)} \mid \Sigma \in |\mathbf{Sign}|\}$ is an entailment system for $\mathcal{I}$. □

The properties of simulations guarantee that if a system $\vdash'$ in the old institution $\mathcal{I}'$ is sound and complete w.r.t. the domain of the simulation μ, then the obtained system $\vdash'^{\mu}$ is sound and complete for $\mathcal{I}$, too, as the following theorem shows.

Theorem 3.4 Let $\mathcal{I}$ and $\mathcal{I}'$ be institutions, $\mu: \mathcal{I} \rightarrow \mathcal{I}'$ be a simulation and $\vdash'$ be an inference system for $Sen'(\mu(\Sigma))$:

1. if $\vdash'$ is sound for $|dom(\mu)_\Sigma|$, then $\vdash'^{\mu}$ is sound, too;

2. if $\vdash'$ is complete for $C' \subseteq |dom(\mu)_\Sigma|$ and $\Psi' \subseteq Sen'(\mu(\Sigma))$, then $\vdash'^{\mu}$ is complete for $\mu_\Sigma(C')$ and $\mu^{-1}(\Psi')$. □

Note that if a system $\vdash'$ is sound for $Mod'(\mu(\Sigma))$, then it is sound for any of its subcategories and hence any general system for $\mathcal{I}'$ is sufficient, if only soundness matters; but if completeness is considered too, then the system $\vdash'$ is required to be complete for the domain of the simulation, which is a subclass of the whole model class, and hence in general needs not be even sound for the whole model class. Thus in general $\vdash'$ is not a general system for the new institution, but it is tailored to the simulation, contrary to the intuition that simulations translate general results from one formalism to another. However, if the domain of μ coincides with the model class of some set th' of sentences, and hence in particular if μ is logical, then starting from any sound and complete inference system w.r.t. the whole class of models, we can apply the above theorem to the system $\vdash'_{th'}$, defined by $\Phi \vdash'_{th'} \phi$ iff $\Phi \cup th \vdash' \phi$, thus recovering the desired level of generality.

Cor. 3.5 Let $\mathcal{I}$ and $\mathcal{I}'$ be institutions, $\mu: \mathcal{I} \rightarrow \mathcal{I}'$ be a simulation s.t. $dom(\mu)_\Sigma = \{A' \mid A' \models'_{\mu(\Sigma)} \alpha', \alpha' \in th'\}$ for some $th' \subseteq Sen'(\mu(\Sigma))$ and $\vdash'$ be an inference system for $Sen'(\mu(\Sigma))$, which is sound and complete w.r.t. $\Psi' \subseteq Sen'(\mu(\Sigma))$. Then $\vdash'^{\mu}_{th'}$ is sound and complete w.r.t. $\mu^{-1}(\Psi')$, where $\vdash_{th'}$ denotes the system defined by $\Phi' \vdash_{th'} \phi'$ iff $\Phi' \cup th' \vdash \phi'$. □

So far the main interest was on the translation of inference systems from the old into the new frame; however, note that soundness and completeness are preserved in the opposite direction, too.

3.2 Applications

Many-sorted and Untyped Logic. As it was first pointed out in [14], the Birkhoff calculus for equational logic trivially generalized to the many-sorted case is not sound, if empty carriers are allowed. To solve this problem there are two main approaches: changing the notion of validity so that the Birkhoff calculus is sound also for the many-sorted case (see e.g. section 1 of [18] and of [10]), and using more sophisticated inference systems (see e.g. [14]). Since there exists the simulation $\mu^M: \mathcal{MS} \rightarrow \mathcal{L}$ of many-sorted by classical logic, applying the above Corollary 3.5, any sound and complete inference system for the classical logic may be translated into a sound and equationally complete system for the many-sorted calculus. Consider for example the homogeneous Birkhoff system, which consists of axioms for the equality to be a congruence and for substitution, enriched by the modus ponens rule.

Prop. 3.6 The Birkhoff system is sound and complete w.r.t. the set GEq of the ground equations $\{t = t' \mid t, t' \in T_\Sigma\}$, i.e. for any set Γ of conditional sentences and any ground equation $t = t'$

$$\Gamma \vdash t = t' \iff (\mathtt{A} \models_{\mathcal{L}} t = t' \quad \forall \mathtt{A} \quad s.t.\ \mathtt{A} \models_{\mathcal{L}} \gamma \quad \forall \gamma \in \Gamma). \ \square$$

Cor. 3.7 The translation $\vdash'^{\mu^M}_{th(\mu^M)}$ of the Birkhoff system along μ^M is sound and equationally complete, i.e. for any many-sorted ground equation $t = t'$ and any set Ax of many-sorted conditional equations $Ax \vdash'^{\mu^M}_{th(\mu^M)} \emptyset.t = t'$ iff ($\mathsf{A} \models_{\mathcal{MS}} \alpha$ for all $\alpha \in Ax$ implies $\mathsf{A} \models_{\mathcal{MS}} \emptyset.t = t'$) for every many-sorted algebra A, where $\emptyset$ denotes the empty type assignment to the empty set of variables. □

Thus, because of the above corollary we have an equational calculus for every set Ax of conditional formulas in the many sorted frame, that consists of

Preprocessing $x_1 : s_1 \wedge \ldots \wedge x_k : s_k \wedge t_1 = t'_1 \wedge \ldots \wedge t_n = t'_n \supset t = t'$ for all $\alpha = (V.t_1 = t'_1 \wedge \ldots \wedge t_n = t'_n \supset t = t') \in Ax$ on variables $\{x_1, \ldots, x_n\}$ of type $V(x_i) = s_i$.

Apply the Birkhoff system (with default *well formedness* axioms for every $op \in F_{s_1 \ldots s_k, s}$) $\quad x_1 : s_1 \wedge \ldots \wedge x_k : s_k \supset op(x_1, \ldots, x_k) : s$

Postprocessing Output $\emptyset.t = t'$ for all deduced $t = t'$.

Note that, since the image along μ^M of an open equality is a conditional axiom, to show that the above calculus is complete w.r.t. *non-ground* equalities, we should first prove that the Birkhoff system is complete w.r.t. sentences of the form $x_1 : s_1 \wedge \ldots \wedge x_n : s_n \supset t = t'$, while the equational completeness is not sufficient.

In sections 2 and 3 of [18] it is shown, implicitly using the simulation μ^M and proving a subset of the results of the first subsection for this particular case, that the [14] equational calculus is an optimized version of a classical first-order inference system, so that soundness and completeness may be derived from the results of homogeneous first-order logic. Although the direct proofs of soundness and completeness of the Meseguer-Goguen system are not difficult, we think that the existence of a simulation, μ^M, which relates this system to (one version of) the classical Birkhoff system, enlightens the value of the Meseguer-Goguen results, showing that their system is not just a technical trick to overcome the empty carrier problem, but is also an elegant application of general results known from the homogeneous case.

Partial Higher-order into First-order Types. Recently higher-order specifications have become a standard tool in algebraic specifications, with a particular interest in the specification of partial higher-order functions. Higher-order functional spaces can be handled using the usual first-order algebraic specifications (see e.g. [15]), by restricting the signatures (S, F) to the ones where S is a subset of a set of functional sorts (i.e. $S \subseteq B^{\rightarrow}$, where $B^{\rightarrow}$ is inductively defined by $B \subseteq B^{\rightarrow}$ and $s_1 \ldots s_{n+1} \in B^{\rightarrow}$ implies $s_1 \times \ldots \times s_n \rightarrow s_{n+1} \in B^{\rightarrow}$) s.t. for every $(s_1 \times \ldots \times s_n \rightarrow s_{n+1}) \in S$ an explicit application operator belongs to the signature; moreover the models are required to be extensional, i.e. two elements of a functional sort yielding the same result on every input have to be equal. From a logical point of view, in the total case (see [12, 19]) an equationally complete system for the higher-order models may be obtained by enriching any (first-order) equationally complete system by the rule

$$* \frac{f(x_1, \ldots, x_n) = g(x_1, \ldots, x_n)}{f = g}$$ f, g terms of sort $(s_1 \times \ldots \times s_n \rightarrow s_{n+1})$; x_i variable of sort s_i not appearing in f and g.

Instead in the partial case the above rule $*$ is insufficient to achieve a complete system; for a detailed discussion of this point see [4, 5]. However there is a logical simulation based on a skolemization procedure of higher-order by strongly conditional partial algebras (i.e. partial algebras with Horn-clauses based on both existential and *strong* equalities, where a strong equality holds iff either the existential equality holds or both sides are undefined), so that Corollary 3.5 applies and hence an equationally complete system for the higher-order models may be simulated by any equationally complete system for strongly conditional partial models. The intuition of this construction is that for each couple f, g of distinct functional elements a *witness* of their difference, i.e. an input (tuple) a s.t. $f(a) \neq g(a)$, exists; thus it is sufficient to introduce function symbols to denote the witnesses.

Def. 3.8 Let $\mathcal{PAR}$ be the institution of partial algebras with strongly conditional formulas as sentences (for references see [1, 3]) and $\mathcal{PHO}$ be the institution of extensional partial algebras on higher-order signatures with strongly conditional formulas as sentences, too (for references see [5]). Let $\mu^E: \mathcal{PHO} \to \mathcal{PAR}$ be the simulation consisting of:

- μ^E: $\mathbf{Sign}_{\mathcal{PHO}} \to \mathbf{Sign}_{\mathcal{PAR}}$ is defined by $\mu^E((S, F)) = (S', F')$, where $S = S'$ and $F' = F \cup_{s=(s_1 \times \ldots \times s_n \to s_{n+1}) \in S} \{x_{s,i}: s \times s \to s_i \mid i = 1, \ldots, n\}$ and $\mu^E((\sigma, \phi)) = (\sigma, \phi')$, where $\phi'(f) = \phi(f)$ for all $f \in F$ and $\phi(x_{s,i}) = x_{\sigma(s),i}$.
- μ^E: $Sen_{\mathcal{PHO}} \to Sen_{\mathcal{PAR}} \cdot \mu^E$ is the embedding natural transformation.
- μ^E: $Mod_{\mathcal{PAR}} \cdot \mu^E \to Mod_{\mathcal{PHO}}$ is defined by
  - $dom(\mu^E)_\Sigma$ is the full subcategory of $Mod_{\mathcal{PAR}}(\mu^E((\sigma, \phi)))$ whose objects are the partial algebras A which satisfy the set $th(\mu^E)$ of axioms $\forall f, g : s. f(x_{s,1}(f,g), \ldots, x_{s,n}(f,g)) = g(x_{s,1}(f,g), \ldots, x_{s,n}(f,g)) \supset f = g$ for all $(s_1 \times \ldots \times s_n \to s_{n+1}) \in S$
  - Let $\iota: \Sigma \to \mu^E(\Sigma)$ be the signature embedding; then $\mu^E(A') = Mod_{\mathcal{PHO}}(\iota)(A')$ and $\mu^E(h') = Mod_{\mathcal{PHO}}(\iota)(h')$. In the following we denote $Mod_{\mathcal{PHO}}(\iota)(A')$ by $A'_{|\Sigma}$ and $Mod_{\mathcal{PHO}}(\iota)(h')$ by $h'_{|\Sigma}$

Since μ^E is the identity and μ^E is a family of forgetful functors, it is quite easy to check that μ^E is a simulation: the only non-trivial step is to check that μ^E is surjective on the objects, i.e. that for any extensional algebra A there exists an expansion A' of A (i.e. an algebra A' s.t. $A'_{|\Sigma} = \mathsf{A}$) s.t. $A' \in |dom(\mu^E)_\Sigma|$. Hence we only have to define $x_{s,i}^{A'}$ on A in such a way that A' satisfies the axioms

$$\forall f, g : s. f(x_{s,1}(f,g), \ldots, x_{s,n}(f,g)) = g(x_{s,1}(f,g), \ldots, x_{s,n}(f,g)) \supset f = g$$

Since A is extensional, for all $s = s_1 \times \ldots \times s_n \to s_{n+1}$ and all $\phi, \psi \in s^{\mathsf{A}}$ either $\phi = \psi$ or there exist $a_i \in s_i^{\mathsf{A}}$ for $i = 1 \ldots n$ s.t. $\phi(a_1, \ldots, a_n) \neq \psi(a_1, \ldots, a_n)$; in the first case let $x_{s,i}^{A'}(\phi, \psi)$ be undefined for $i = 1 \ldots n$, in the second one let $x_{s,i}^{A'}(\phi, \psi)$ be such an a_i for $i = 1 \ldots n$. Then it is easy to check that $A' \in dom(\mu^E)_\Sigma$. □

Prop. 3.9 Let CL be the inference system for the partial strongly conditional logic, defined in [3]. The translation $\vdash'^{\mu^E}_{th(\mu^E)}$ of the CL system along μ^E is sound and equationally complete, i.e. for any either strong or existential equality ϵ on variables X and any set Ax of conditional formulas $Ax \vdash'^{\mu^E}_{th(\mu^E)} D(X) \supset \epsilon$ iff for every higher-order partial algebra A

$$\mathsf{A} \models_{\mathcal{PHO}} \alpha \text{ for all } \alpha \in Ax \text{ implies } \mathsf{A} \models_{\mathcal{PHO}} D(X) \supset \epsilon. \ \square$$

4 Related Work

Similar concepts. Due to the relevance of the interaction of different formal systems, several attempts to "put together institutions" have been developed and are still under development; let us summarize some related works. In the sequel we use, as a convention, "new" to denote the elements of the source of any arrow between institutions (independently from the direction of its components) and "old" to denote the element of the target. The first notion of arrow between institutions is that of *institution morphism*, introduced in [8]. Institution morphisms capture the idea of enriching an institution by new features and are mainly used to define *duplex* institutions, where sentences from an institution and constraints from another one are both available. Technically, morphisms differ from simulations, because they translate signatures and models covariantly, and sentences in the opposite direction. A closer (to simulations) notion of institution arrow is the *coding*, presented in the draft [25] to investigate on the expressive power of LF (Edinburgh Logical Framework). Indeed the direction of the components of coding is the same as the one of simulation and the philosophy is that the old model class can be partitioned in subclasses, each one representing some new model, in the sense that a class satisfies (the translation of) the same formulas which are satisfied by the represented model. Thus, from a technical point of view, there are three main differences: the model component is total, it is non-necessarily surjective, and the satisfaction preserving condition is between a new model and the whole class of its old representations. The main issue of [24] is "putting together" representation of logics in the common frame of the LF-institution. A quite close notion is that of *map* of [8] by Meseguer (see [13]), which follows the same intuition as logical simulations: maps relate new specifications to old ones and models are consistently translated from the old into the new frame; however the two notions are not exactly the same. Indeed maps of institutions are not required to be surjective (but if they are, then are also logical simulations); on the converse logical simulations are map. Although the two notions are strictly related, they are used for different purposes; indeed in [13] the focus is on the logical side, so that tools are introduced to deal with entailment systems, proofs and proof calculi, and then applied to propose semantics for logic programming, while the semantic side is quite neglected. It is still under development (see [21]) a new tool, called *transformation*, to relate pre-institutions (which are institutions where the satisfaction condition and the categorical structure of models have been dropped) and hence, in particular, institutions. Transformations translate every new sentence into a set of old sentences and every new model into a set of old models, requiring that a sentence is satisfied by a model iff its translation is satisfied by the class of models which is the translation of the model. In [21] the different levels of pre-institutions and transformations between them are analysed and some results are presented that are strictly connected to classical logic, like compactness theorems.

From institution independence to simulation independence The modularity principle applied to algebraic specifications requires that large specifications may be built starting from smaller ones, using specification languages, like ASL and *Clear*. The first attempt to generalize specification languages abstracting away from the frame chosen to define basic specifications, is the concept of *institution independent* language, proposed and illustrated on a significant example by Sannella and

Tarlecki in [22], where, to build specifications in a uniform way w.r.t. the adopted frame, operations are defined using only the elements common to every institution, like signatures, models and sentences, and mathematical constructions on them. In [2], adding to the work in [22], ***simulation-independent*** languages are introduced, which are institution independent languages s.t. any simulation behaves as a homomorphism w.r.t. them; thus for any simulation-independent language the input specifications can be defined in different frames and then translated into a common frame, where the specification building operation is performed, and the result is independent from the chosen "super"frame, in the sense that the translation via simulation of the result into any other frame is equal to the result of the operation in the other frame on the translation of the inputs.

Third dimension of implementation Implementation, or, better, refinement (see [23]), has two directions of composition: vertical (refinement of refinement is refinement, too) and horizontal (if a parameterized specification sp_1 is a refinement of sp_2 and an actual parameter p_1 is a refinement of p_2, then the application $sp_1(p_1)$ is a refinement of $sp_2(p_2)$). Using simulations, a third direction is added (see [2]); indeed specifications defined in the old institution are implementations of their translations in the new and the three compositions are compatible.

Acknowledgements. We would like to thank J. Goguen, J. Meseguer, D. Sannella, P. Scollo and A. Tarlecki for the fruitful discussions on the subject and the referees for pointing out some delicate points.

References

1. E. Astesiano and M. Cerioli. On the existence of initial models for partial (higher-order) conditional specifications. In *TAPSOFT'89*, number 351 in Lecture Notes in Computer Science, pages 74–88, Berlin, 1989. Springer Verlag.
2. E. Astesiano and M. Cerioli. Commuting between institutions via simulation. Technical report, University of Genova, 1990.
3. E. Astesiano and M. Cerioli. Free objects and equational deduction for partial conditional specifications. Technical report, University of Genova, 1990.
4. E. Astesiano and M. Cerioli. Partial higher-order specifications. In *Math. Found. of Comp. Sci. '91*, number 520 in Lecture Notes in Computer Science, pages 74–84, Berlin, 1991. Springer Verlag.
5. E. Astesiano and M. Cerioli. Partial higher-order specifications. *Fundamenta Informaticae*, 16(2), 1992. To appear.
6. M. Broy and M. Wirsing. Partial abstract types. *Acta Informatica*, (18):47–64, 1982.
7. P. Burmeister. Partial algebras - survey of an unifying approach towards a two-valued model theory for partial algebras. *Algebra Universalis*, 15, 1982.
8. R. Burstall and J. Goguen. Introducing institutions. In E. Clarke and D. Kozen, editors, *Logics of Programming Workshop*, number 164 in Lecture Notes in Computer Science, pages 221–255, Berlin, 1984. Springer Verlag.
9. R. Burstall and J. Goguen. Institutions: Abstract model theory for specification and programming. Technical report, Computer Science Lab., SRI International, 1990.
10. V. Manca and A. Salibra. Equational calculi for many-sorted algebras with empty carriers. In *Math. Found. of Comp. Sci. '90*, number 452 in Lecture Notes in Computer Science, 1990.

11. V. Manca, A. Salibra, and G. Scollo. On the expressiveness of equational type logic. In C. Rattray and R. Clark, editors, *The Unified Computation Laboratory*. Oxford University Press, 1992.
12. K. Meinke. Universal algebra in higher types. *Theoretical Computer Science*, 1992.
13. J. Meseguer. General logics. In *Logic Colloquium '87*. North Holland, 1989.
14. J. Meseguer and J. Goguen. *Initiality, Induction and Computability*, pages 459–540. Cambridge University Press, Cambridge, 1985.
15. B. Möller. Algebraic specifications with higher-order operations. In *IFIP TC 2 Working Conference on Program Specification and Transformation*. North Holland, 1987.
16. P. Mosses. Unified algebras and modules. Technical Report DAIMI PB-266, CS Dept., Aarhus University, 1988.
17. M. Navarro, P. Nivela, F. Orejas, and A. Sanchez. On translating partial to total specifications with applications to theorem proving for partial specifications. Technical Report LSI-89-21, Universitat Politecnica de Catalunya, 1990.
18. P. Padawitz and M. Wirsing. Completeness of many-sorted equational logic revisited. *Bulletin EATCS*, (24), 1984.
19. Z. Qian. Higher-order order-sorted algebras. In *2nd International Conference on Algebraic and Logic Programming*, Lecture Notes in Computer Science, Berlin, 1990.
20. H. Reichel. *Initial Computability, Algebraic Specifications, and Partial Algebras*. Oxford University Press, 1987.
21. A. Salibra and G. Scollo. A soft stairway to institutions. In this volume, August 1991.
22. D. Sannella and A. Tarlecki. Specifications in an arbitrary institution. *Information and Computation*, (76):165–210, 1988.
23. D. Sannella and M. Wirsing. Implementations of parameterized specifications. In *9th Colloquium on Automata, Languages and Programming*, number 140 in Lecture Notes in Computer Science, Berlin, 1982. Springer Verlag.
24. A. Tarlecki. Quasi-varieties in abstract algebraic institutions. *Journal of Computer and System Science*, (33):333–360, 1986.
25. A. Tarlecki. Institution representation. draft note, November 1987.

Label algebras: a systematic use of terms

Gilles Bernot
LIENS, CNRS URA 1327,
45 rue d'Ulm,
75230 PARIS Cedex 05 FRANCE.
bernot@dmi.ens.fr

Pascale Le Gall
LRI, CNRS URA 410,
Bat. 490, Université Paris-Sud
91405 Orsay, FRANCE.
legall@lri.lri.fr

Abstract:

We give the main definitions and results of a new framework for algebraic specifications: the framework of *label algebras*. The main idea underlying our approach is that the semantics of algebraic specifications can be deeply improved when the satisfaction relation is defined via assignments with range in *terms* instead of values. Surprisingly, there are several cases where even if two terms have the same value, it is possible that one of them is a suitable instance of a variable in a formula while the other one is not. It is for instance the case for algebraic specifications with exception handling or with observability features. We show that our approach is a useful tool for solving this problem.

Keywords: algebraic specifications, exception handling, initial semantics, observability, subsorting, structured specifications.

1 Introduction

This paper is an overview of a new framework for algebraic specifications: the framework of *label algebras*. Many applications of abstract data types require specialized semantics (e.g. observability issues, exception handling, partial functions, etc). For such applications, it has been shown that the simple semantics pioneeringly proposed by the ADJ group [GTW78] cannot be applied directly, they often lead to inconsistencies, or unreadable specifications. The reason why simple semantics are not suitable is often that the scope of an axiom is too wide. When variables are universally quantified over a sort, several instances of an axiom can lead to inconsistencies. For example, for exception handling, the scope of certain axioms must be restricted to non-exceptional assignments only; for observability purposes, only observable consequences of an axiom must be taken into account (usually via observable contexts); for partial functions, only assignments belonging to some definition domains must be considered; etc. Several powerful general frameworks, such as order-sorted algebras [Gog78] or unified algebras [Mos89] can be used to restrict the scope of the axioms, allowing a more elaborated definition of the acceptable assignments. These frameworks usually consider assignments which substitute values for variables. Our claim in this paper is that, for some cases, assignments which range in terms are more suitable. Surprisingly, it turns out that even if two terms have the same value, it is possible that one of them is a suitable instance of a variable while the other one is not. For instance, in [BB91] it is shown that observability may sometimes require to characterize a set of observable terms while sets of observable values would not be powerful enough. In the same way, [BBC86] pointed out that exception handling with bounded data structures requires to characterize a set of "Ok-terms" and that considering only sets of "Ok-values" leads to inconsistencies (see Section 2). Label algebras will allow us to "type" terms instead of values: two terms which have the same value can be labelled with distinct *labels*, while a classical "type" (even in order-sorted algebras) must be shared by all the terms having the same value. Thus, label algebras can be considered as a tool to avoid inconsistencies where the "types" of terms (i.e. *labels*) play a role similar to sorts and subsorts in [Gog78]. As described in Section 5.2, we have already used label algebras to define exception algebras (an algebraic framework for exception handling) but the application domain of label algebras seems to be much more general than exception handling.

The paper is organized as follows. In Section 2, from an example with exception handling, we will point out the importance of terms in the field of first-order algebraic specifications and we will show the advantage of "labelling" terms in order to specify exceptions. In Section 3, we will define the framework of label algebras. The main results (e.g. initiality results) will be established in Section 4. In Section 5, we will first sketch out how far this framework can be applied to several classical subjects in abstract data types, such as partial functions, observability features, etc; and then, we will rapidly explain how a new formalism of exception algebras is defined, related to the one of label algebras. Recapitulation and perspectives can be found in Section 6.

We assume that the reader is familiar with algebraic specifications ([GTW78], [EM85], [GB84]) and with the elementary definitions of category theory [McL71].

2 The importance of terms within algebraic specifications

We have claimed that several approaches to algebraic specification require to take care of terms. In this section, we mention two applications whose semantics closely depend on terms. Anyway, it is clear that label algebras, defined in Section 3, are interesting in any case.

First, let us consider algebraic specifications with observability features. A crucial aspect of observational specifications is that "what is observable" must be carefully specified. It is often very difficult to prove that two values are observationally equal (while it is sufficient to exhibit two observations which distinguish them to prove that they are observationnally distinct). In [Hen89], R. Hennicker uses a predicate *Obs* to characterize the observable values. This powerful framework leads to legible specifications and it provides some theorem-proving methods. Nevertheless, it has been shown in [BB91] that there are some specifications which are inconsistent when observability is carried by values and that these inconsistencies can be avoided when observability is expressed with respect to a subset ΣObs of the signature Σ. The use of a subset of the signature leads consequently to consider a subset of terms instead of values (see also Section 5.1).

Now, we will go in more details with an example containing exception handling features. Since the work of [GTW78], a lot of algebraic approaches have been proposed to treat many exception handling features such as declaration of exceptions, recovery, etc. For instance, [Gog78], [FGJM85], [GM89], [GDLE84], [Gog87] give solutions to the algebraic treatment of "intrinsic errors" (such as *pred*(0) or *pop*(*empty*)), with implicit error propagation and possible recoveries, but they are not able to treat other kinds of errors, especially those arising with bounded data structures (see [Bre91] for the crucial importance of bounded data structures). The most difficult point is to simultaneously handle bounded data structures and certain recoveries of exceptional values:

Example 1 In order to specify bounded natural numbers it is indeed not too difficult to specify that all the values belonging to $[0 \ldots maxint]$ are Ok-values [BBC86]; let us assume that this is done. We also have to specify that the operation *succ* raises an exception when applied to *maxint*, e.g. *TooLarge*; let us assume that this is done too. When specifying the operation *pred*, we must have the following axiom:

$$pred(succ(x)) = x \tag{1}$$

which is a "normal property" and, as such, should be understood with certain implicit preconditions such as "*if* x *and* $succ(x)$ *are Ok-values*" for example. Let us assume now that we want to recover all *TooLarge* values on *maxint*. We will then necessarily have $succ(maxint) = maxint$.

Since the values of these two terms are equal, we will have to choose: either both of them are erroneous values, or both of them are Ok-values. The first case is not acceptable because it does not cope with our intuition of "recovery." (Moreover, when considering the value $m = maxint - 1$ we clearly need that $pred(maxint) = m$, as a particular case of our "normal property" about *pred*. Thus $succ(m) = maxint$ must be considered as a normal value.) Unfortunately, since $succ(maxint)$ has then a normal value, $x = maxint$ is an acceptable assignment for (1) and we get the following inconsistency: $m = pred(maxint) = pred(succ(maxint)) = maxint$ which propagates in the same way, and all values are equal to 0. Let us point out that subsorting [Gog78] cannot be used to specify such bounded data structures with recoveries. The axiom (1) necessarily gives rise to a similar inconsistency because sorts are attached to values. Two terms having the same value must share the same subsorts; consequently *maxint* and $succ(maxint)$ cannot be distinguished.

Remark 1 Not all readers will accept this idea of recovery from exceptions within specifications. However, one sould not forget that such semantics of exception handling are usual and well founded in programming languages (e.g. CLU [LG86]). Thus, it would be a pity if specification languages had semantics with a weaker expressive power.

Indeed, it is precisely the difference between "exception handling" and "error handling." The term $succ(maxint)$ is not erroneous but it is exceptional while the term *maxint* is not exceptional; the semantics must take this fact into account. This leads to the following idea: the term *maxint* is an acceptable substitute for the variable x in the equation (1) while $succ(maxint)$ is not, even though *maxint* and $succ(maxint)$ have the same value. Thus, exception handling requires to take care of terms inside the algebras, and good functional semantics for exception handling should allow such distinctions. This idea has been formalized in [BBC86], where "Ok-terms" are declared: the term $succ^{maxint}(0)$ is "labelled" by *Ok* while the term $succ^{maxint+1}(0)$ is not;[1] and the acceptable instantiations of a normal property (called "Ok-axiom") are implicitly restricted to Ok-terms only. This solves the inconsistencies due to the recovery $succ(maxint) = maxint$ with the axiom (1).

These considerations have been our main motivation to develop the framework of *label algebras*.

Usually, algebras have (heterogeneous) sets of values as carriers [GTW78], [EM85]. Let us remember that a many-sorted signature is usually a couple $< S, \Sigma >$ where S is a finite set of sorts (or type names) and Σ is a finite set of operation names with arity in $S^* \times S$; the objects (algebras) of the category $Alg(\Sigma)$ are heterogeneous sets, A, partitioned as $A = \{A_s\}_{s \in S}$, and with, for each operation name "$f : s_1 \ldots s_n \rightarrow s$" in Σ $(0 \leq n)$, a total function $f_A : A_{s_1} \times \ldots \times A_{s_n} \rightarrow A_s$; the morphisms of $Alg(\Sigma)$ (Σ-morphisms) being obviously the sort-preserving, operation-preserving applications.

As a consequence of our remarks, labelled terms will also be considered as "first-class citizen objects." Given an algebra A, the satisfaction of a normal property will be defined using terms (the usual definition only involves values). A simple idea could be to consider both A and T_Σ (the ground term algebra over Σ). Unfortunately, finitely generated algebras (i.e. such that the initial Σ-morphism from T_Σ to A is surjective) are not powerful enough to cope with enrichment, parameterization or abstract implementation. How is one to deal with both terms and non-reachable values ? This question is solved by working with the free Σ-term algebra $T_\Sigma(A)$. Let us remember its definition.

Notation 1 *Given a heterogeneous set of "variables" $V = \{V_s\}_{s \in S}$, the* free Σ-term algebra with variables in V *is the least Σ-algebra $T_\Sigma(V)$ (with respect to the preorder induced by the Σ-morphisms) such that $V \subseteq T_\Sigma(V)$.*
Since V is not necessarily enumerable, we can consider $T_\Sigma(A)$ for every algebra A. An element of $T_\Sigma(A)$ is a Σ-term such that each leaf is either a constant symbol of Σ, or a value of A.

For example, if $\mathbf{Z} = \{\ldots, -2, -1, 0, 1, 2, \ldots\}$ is the algebra of all integers over the signature $\{zero, succ\_, pred\_\}$, then $succ(succ(zero))$, $succ(succ(0))$, $succ(1)$, etc. are *distinct* elements of $T_\Sigma(\mathbf{Z})$, even though they have the same value when evaluated in $\mathbf{Z}$.

The main technical point underlying our framework is to systematically use $T_\Sigma(A)$ directly inside the *label algebras*. This allows us to have a very precise definition of the satisfaction relation, using assignments with range in $T_\Sigma(A)$ instead of A. Intuitively, a term in $T_\Sigma(A)$ reflects the "history" of a value; it is a "computation tree" which results in a value. Of course, several histories can provide the same value. This is the reason why labelling is more powerful than typing: it allows us to "diagnose" the history in order to apply a specific treatment or not. Nevertheless, we must be able to map each term to its final value. The canonical evaluation morphism $eval_A : T_\Sigma(A) \longrightarrow A$, deduced from the Σ-algebra structure of A, sends

[1] $succ^i(0)$ is an abbreviation for $succ(succ(\ldots(0)))$ where $succ$ occurs i times.

each term to its final value. Of course, *in the end*, the satisfaction of an equality must be checked on values; thus, $eval_A$ is a crucial tool for defining the satisfaction relation on equational atoms. However, the applicable assignments can be precisely restricted to certain kinds of terms/histories *before* checking equalities on values, and this is the reason why the inconsistencies mentioned above can be solved with label algebras.

Notation 2 *We write* $\overline{A} = T_\Sigma(A)$ *and for every* Σ*-morphism* $\mu : A \to B$, $\overline{\mu} : \overline{A} \to \overline{B}$ *denotes the canonical* Σ*-morphism which extends* μ *to the corresponding free algebras.*

3 Label algebras

3.1 Basic definitions

Definition 1 *A* label signature *is a triple* $\Sigma L = < S, \Sigma, L >$ *where* $< S, \Sigma >$ *is a usual many-sorted signature and* L *is a finite set of* labels.

A ΣL-algebra *is a pair* $\mathcal{A} = (A, \{l_A\}_{l \in L})$ *where* A *is a* Σ*-algebra, and* $\{l_A\}_{l \in L}$ *is a* L*-indexed family such that, for each* l *in* L, l_A *is a subset of* $\overline{A}$.

There are no conditions about the subsets l_A: they can intersect several sorts, they can be empty, they are not necessarily disjoint and their union $(\bigcup_{l \in L} l_A)$ does not necessarily cover $\overline{A}$.

Definition 2 *Let* $\mathcal{A} = (A, \{l_A\}_{l \in L})$ *and* $\mathcal{B} = (B, \{l_B\}_{l \in L})$ *be two* ΣL*-algebras. A* ΣL*-morphism* $h : \mathcal{A} \to \mathcal{B}$ *is a* Σ*-morphism from* A *to* B *such that* $\forall l \in L$, $\overline{h}(l_A) \subseteq l_B$.

We denote $\leq$ *the preorder defined by:* $\mathcal{A} \leq \mathcal{B}$ *if and only if there exists a* ΣL*-morphism from* $\mathcal{A}$ *to* $\mathcal{B}$.

When there is no ambiguity about the signature under consideration, ΣL-algebras and ΣL-morphisms will be called *label algebras* and *label morphisms*, or even algebras and morphisms respectively.

Definition 3 *The category of all* ΣL*-algebras and* ΣL*-morphisms is denoted by* $Alg_{Lbl}(\Sigma L)$.

$\mathcal{T}_{\Sigma L}$ *is the* ΣL*-algebra such that the underlying* Σ*-algebra of* $\mathcal{T}_{\Sigma L}$ *is the ground term algebra* T_Σ *and for each* l *in* L, $l_{T_{\Sigma L}}$ *is empty.*

Triv (or $Triv_{\Sigma L}$ *if there is an ambiguity on the signature) is the* ΣL*-algebra such that the underlying* Σ*-algebra of Triv is the trivial algebra Triv which contains only one element in* $Triv_s$ *for each* s *in* S*, and for each* l *in* L, $l_{Triv} = \overline{Triv}$.

The ΣL-algebra $\mathcal{T}_{\Sigma L}$ (resp. *Triv*) is clearly initial (resp. terminal) in $Alg_{Lbl}(\Sigma L)$. As usual, a ΣL-algebra $\mathcal{A}$ is called *finitely generated* iff the initial ΣL-morphism from $\mathcal{T}_{\Sigma L}$ to $\mathcal{A}$ is an epimorphism. Thus, $\mathcal{A}$ is finitely generated iff the underlying morphism from T_Σ to A is surjective.

Definition 4 *The full subcategory of* $Alg_{Lbl}(\Sigma L)$ *containing the finitely generated algebras is denoted by* $Gen_{Lbl}(\Sigma L)$*. Moreover, the signature* ΣL *is* sensible *iff Triv belongs to* $Gen_{Lbl}(\Sigma L)$.

The category $Gen_{Lbl}(\Sigma L)$ has the same initial object as $Alg_{Lbl}(\Sigma L)$, and if ΣL is sensible (i.e. if there exists at least one ground term of each sort) then it has the same terminal object too.[2]

Not surprisingly, a "label specification" will be defined by a (label) signature and a set of well-formed formulae (axioms):

Definition 5 *Given a label signature ΣL, a ΣL-*axiom *is a well formed formula built on:*

- atoms*: these are either equalities $(u = v)$ such that u and v are Σ-terms with variables, u and v being of the same sort, or labelling atoms $(w \epsilon l)$ such that w is a Σ-term with variables and l is a label belonging to L,*
- connectives*: these are the propositional connectives, belonging to $\{\neg, \wedge, \vee, \Rightarrow\}$.*

Every variable is implicitly universally quantified.

A ΣL-axiom is called positive conditional *if and only if it is of the form $a_1 \wedge \ldots \wedge a_n \Rightarrow a$ where the a_i and a are (positive) atoms (if $n = 0$ then the axiom is reduced to a).*

The predicate " ϵ " should be read "*is labelled by*".

Definition 6 *A* label specification *is a couple $SP =< \Sigma L, Ax >$ where ΣL is a label signature and Ax is a set of ΣL-axioms. SP is called* positive conditional *iff all its axioms are positive conditional.*

The *satisfaction relation* is indeed the crucial definition of this section. It is of prime importance to remark that we consider assignments with range in $\overline{A} = T_{\Sigma}(A)$ (terms) instead of A (values):

Definition 7 *Let $\mathcal{A} = (A, \{l_{\mathcal{A}}\}_{l \in L})$ be a ΣL-algebra.*

- *$\mathcal{A}$ satisfies $(u = v)$, where u and v are two terms of the same sort in $\overline{A}$, means that, in A, $eval_{\mathcal{A}}(u) = eval_{\mathcal{A}}(v)$ [the symbol "$=$" denoting set-theoretic equality in the carrier of A].*
- *$\mathcal{A}$ satisfies $(w \epsilon l)$, where $w \in \overline{A}$ and $l \in L$, means that $w \in l_{\mathcal{A}}$ [the symbol "$\in$" denoting set-theoretic membership].*
- *Given a ΣL-axiom φ, $\mathcal{A}$* satisfies *φ, denoted by $\mathcal{A} \models \varphi$, means that for all assignments $\sigma : V \to \overline{A}$ (V covering all the variables of φ), $\mathcal{A}$ satisfies $\sigma(\varphi)$ according to the "ground atomic satisfaction" defined above and the truth tables of the propositional connectives.*

$\mathcal{A}$ satisfies a label specification SP iff $\mathcal{A}$ satisfies all its axioms. $Alg_{Lbl}(SP)$ is the full subcategory of $Alg_{Lbl}(\Sigma L)$ containing the algebras which satisfy SP. A similar notation applies to Gen_{Lbl}.

Notice that $Alg_{Lbl}(SP)$ or $Gen_{Lbl}(SP)$ can be empty categories (for example when SP contains φ and $\neg\varphi$). Provided the axioms of SP never contain the connective "$\neg$",

[2]If the signature is not sensible, we have to be careful with equational reasonning, even for formulas where labels are not involved [MS87]

$Alg_{Lbl}(SP)$ has the same terminal object as $Alg_{Lbl}(\Sigma L)$: *Triv*. However, as usual, initiality results can be generally obtained only for positive conditional specifications [WB80]. These results are presented in Section 4.

3.2 The partial evaluation constraint

Certain applications of label algebras require that if a term $t \in \overline{A}$ is labelled by l then every *partial evaluation* of t is still labelled by l. For instance, let us return to observability. The predicate *Obs* used by [Hen89] to characterise the observable values can be reflected by a label: $t \epsilon Obs$ will now mean that the term t is observable. Let us consider the algebra A on $\mathbf{Z}$ with boolean relatives and let us assume that A is observed via some boolean terms of $\overline{A}$. If the term $[pred(pred(0)) \leq succ(succ(0))]$ is labelled by *Obs*, then we clearly would like $[pred(-1) \leq succ(1)]$ to also be observable (i.e. labelled by *Obs*), as well as $[-2 \leq succ(1)]$, $[-2 \leq 2]$, or *true* itself. Similarly, when exception handling is involved, if the term $((3+4)-5)$ is an *Ok*-term (i.e. labelled by *Ok*), then we probably would like for $(7-5)$, or 2, to be also labelled by *Ok*. More generally, the terms labelled by *Ok* are computation trees which contain only "normal treatments." This means that an exceptional treatment cannot appear at any stage of the evaluation of such terms. Thus, any partial evaluation of any term labelled by *Ok* can also be labelled by *Ok*. Intuitively, since a term of $\overline{A}$ reflects the history of a value, if this history does not raise exceptional cases then it can be entirely or partially forgotten (via partial evaluations); but it cannot be forgotten if the term is exceptional because exceptional treatments are specified with respect to this history. Thus, this partial evaluation constraint should not be required for labels which are intended as exception names (For more details, see Section 5.2.) Summing up, some labels of a label signature should meet the so-called partial evaluation constraint, while others should not.

Definition 8 *A* constrained label signature *is a triple $\widehat{\Sigma L} = < S, \Sigma, \hat{L} >$ where $< S, \Sigma >$ is a usual signature and $\hat{L}$ is a pair (L, C) such that L and C are disjoint sets of labels. The labels of L are called "unconstrained;" those of C are called "constrained." We shall note $\tilde{L} = L \cup C$ the set of all labels, and $\Sigma\tilde{L} = < S, \Sigma, \tilde{L} >$ the corresponding (unconstrained) label signature.*

A constrained label signature can be seen as a label signature (with respect to $\tilde{L}$) such that a subset of constrained labels (C) is distinguished.

Definition 9 *Let A be a Σ-algebra and let t be a term in $\overline{A} = T_{\Sigma}(A)$.*

Let u be (an occurrence of) a subterm of t and let v be any term in $\overline{A}$ of the same sort as u. The term $t[u \leftarrow v]$ is the term of $\overline{A}$ obtained by replacing (the considered occurrence of) u by v in t.

When v is the value $eval_A(u)$ of A (remember that the carrier of A is included in the carrier of $\overline{A} = T_{\Sigma}(A)$),[3] the term $t[u \leftarrow eval_A(u)]$ is a partial evaluation *of t. More generally, a term t' is a partial evaluation of t if it can be obtained from t by a finite sequence of such partial evaluations.*

For example, $(7-5)$ is a partial evaluation of $(3+4)-5$ while $6-4$ is not.

[3]but A is not a subalgebra of $\overline{A}$

Definition 10 *Given a constrained label signature $\widehat{\Sigma L}$. A $\widehat{\Sigma L}$-algebra is a label algebra over the signature $\Sigma\widetilde{L}$ which satisfies the following* partial evaluation constraint*: for every label l in C and for every term t in $\overline{A}$, if t belongs to l_A then all partial evaluations of t belong to l_A as well.*

$Alg_{Lbl}(\widehat{\Sigma L})$ is the full subcategory of $Alg_{Lbl}(\Sigma\widetilde{L})$ which contains all the $\widehat{\Sigma L}$-algebras. A similar notation applies to Gen_{Lbl}.

Intuitively, the stability of labelling by constrained labels with respect to partial evaluation means that, as soon as a term has been labelled, one can forget its "old history" without modifying its constrained labels. Equivalently, since a term represents a computation of tree, it means that constrained labelling does not depend on the particular computational strategy. The only point which matters is that there exists at least one strategy which yields the constrained label.

Remark 2 $T_{\Sigma\widetilde{L}}$ and *Triv* are constrained label algebras, whatever C is.

If t' is a partial evaluation of t then $eval_A(t') = eval_A(t)$ (the converse property is obviously false). Moreover, for every constrained label algebra $\mathcal{A}$, as the (constant) term $eval_A(t)$ is a partial evaluation of t, constrained labels are compatible with $eval_A$ in the sense that $\forall l \in C, eval_A(l_A) \subseteq l_A$.

The partial evaluation constraint cannot be specified using label axioms.

Definition 11 *Given a constrained signature $\widehat{\Sigma L}$, a $\widehat{\Sigma L}$*-axiom *is simply a $\Sigma\widetilde{L}$-axiom. A* constrained label specification *is a pair $\widehat{SP} = < \widehat{\Sigma L}, Ax >$ where $\widehat{\Sigma L}$ is a constrained label signature and Ax is a set of $\widehat{\Sigma L}$-axioms.*

The category $Alg_{Lbl}(\widehat{SP})$ is the full subcategory of $Alg_{Lbl}(\widehat{\Sigma L})$ containing the algebras satisfying Ax (according to the satisfaction relation defined in Definition 7). An object of $Alg_{Lbl}(\widehat{SP})$ is called a $\widehat{SP}$-algebra. (Similar definitions hold for $Gen_{Lbl}(\widehat{SP})$)

A signature name (or specification name, etc.) surrounded by a hat means now "constrained."

4 Initiality results

This section deals with initiality results. We show that the classical results of [GTW78] can be extended to the framework of label algebras. They are given for constrained label specifications. Of course, they remain valid for unconstrained label specifications, since an unconstrained specification *SP* is a constrained specification $\widehat{SP}$ such that $C = \emptyset$. For lack of space, the results are not proved or their proofs are only sketched. Complete proofs can be found in [BL91].

Theorem 1 *Let $\widehat{SP}$ be a positive conditional $\widehat{\Sigma L}$-specification. Let $\mathcal{X}$ be a $\Sigma\widetilde{L}$-algebra. Let R be a binary relation over X compatible with the sorts of the signature (i.e. R is a subset of $\bigcup_{s \in S} X_s \times X_s$). There is a least $\widehat{SP}$-algebra $\mathcal{Y}$ (with respect to the preorder of Definition 2) such that there exists a label morphism $h_Y : \mathcal{X} \to \mathcal{Y}$ and such that $(\mathcal{Y}, h_Y)$ is compatible with R (i.e. $\forall x, y \in X,\ x\ R\ y \implies h_Y(x) = h_Y(y)$).*

Sketch of proof: Let F be the family of all pairs $(\mathcal{Z}, h_{\mathcal{Z}} : \mathcal{X} \to \mathcal{Z})$ compatible with R. Let us consider the $\Sigma\widetilde{L}$-algebra $\mathcal{Y} = (Y, \{l_Y\}_{l \in \widetilde{L}})$ as the quotient algebra of $\mathcal{X}$ (h_Y is the quotient $\Sigma\widetilde{L}$-morphism) defined by:

- $\forall x, y \in X,\ (\ h_Y(x) = h_Y(y) \Leftrightarrow (\forall (\mathcal{Z}, h_{\mathcal{Z}}) \in F,\ h_{\mathcal{Z}}(x) = h_{\mathcal{Z}}(y))\ )$
- $\forall l \in \widetilde{L},\ \forall x \in \overline{X},\ (\ \overline{h_Y}(x) \in l_Y \Leftrightarrow (\forall (\mathcal{Z}, h_{\mathcal{Z}}) \in F,\ \overline{h_{\mathcal{Z}}}(x) \in l_{\mathcal{Z}})\ )$

For every $(\mathcal{Z}, h_{\mathcal{Z}})$ in F, there exists a $\Sigma\widetilde{L}$-morphism $\mu_{\mathcal{Z}} : \mathcal{Y} \to \mathcal{Z}$ defined by $\forall x \in X, \mu_{\mathcal{Z}}(h_Y(x)) = h_{\mathcal{Z}}(x)$. Consequently, if $(\mathcal{Y}, h_Y)$ belongs to F then it is its smallest element. It is then not too difficult to prove that $(\mathcal{Y}, h_Y)$ is compatible with R and that $\mathcal{Y}$ satisfies $\widehat{SP}$. This concludes the proof of the theorem. ∎

Theorem 2 *Let $\widehat{SP}$ be a positive conditional label specification. $Alg_{Lbl}(\widehat{SP})$ and $Gen_{Lbl}(\widehat{SP})$ have an initial object $\mathcal{T}_{\widehat{SP}}$. Triv is final in $Alg_{Lbl}(\widehat{SP})$ (and in $Gen_{Lbl}(\widehat{SP})$ if $\widehat{\Sigma L}$ is sensible).*

Sketch of proof: by using Theorem 1 with $R = \emptyset$, $\mathcal{X} = \mathcal{T}_{\Sigma\widetilde{L}}$, we get $\mathcal{Y} = \mathcal{T}_{\widehat{SP}}$. ∎

In general, the initial algebra is not isomorphic to the trivial algebra. Several examples can be found in [Ber92] [LeG92].

The purpose of the remainder of this section is to give some basic tools for manipulating structured positive conditional label specifications. We first define the *forgetful functor* U associated with a structured presentation, then the *synthesis functor* F, and we prove that F is left adjoint to U.

Definition 12 *Let $\mu : \widehat{\Sigma L_1} \to \widehat{\Sigma L_2}$ be a signature morphism.*[4] *The forgetful functor $U_\mu : Alg_{Lbl}(\widehat{\Sigma L_2}) \to Alg_{Lbl}(\widehat{\Sigma L_1})$ is defined as follows:*

- *for each $\widehat{\Sigma L_2}$-algebra $\mathcal{A}$, $U_\mu(\mathcal{A})$ is the $\widehat{\Sigma L_1}$-algebra $\mathcal{B}$ defined by:*
  $\forall s \in S_1,\ B_s = A_{\mu(s)}$; $\forall l \in \widetilde{L_1},\ l_B = \mu(l)_{\mathcal{A}} \cap \overline{B}$; *and* $\forall f \in \Sigma_1,\ f_B = \mu(f)_{\mathcal{A}}$;
- *for each $\widehat{\Sigma L_2}$-morphism $\eta : \mathcal{A} \to \mathcal{A}'$, $U_\mu(\eta) : U_\mu(\mathcal{A}) \to U_\mu(\mathcal{A}')$ is the $\widehat{\Sigma L_1}$-morphism $U_\mu(\eta)$ defined by all the restrictions of η of the form:*
  $$U_\mu(\eta)_s : B_s = A_{\mu(s)} \to B'_s = A'_{\mu(s)}$$

Remark 3 $\mathcal{B} = U_\mu(\mathcal{A})$ satisfies the partial evaluation constraint with respect to $\widehat{L_1}$ and $\overline{U_\mu(\eta)}$ clearly preserves the labels of $\widetilde{L_1}$.

Theorem 3 *Let $\mu : \widehat{\Sigma L_1} \to \widehat{\Sigma L_2}$ be a signature morphism. Let $\widehat{SP_1}$ and $\widehat{SP_2}$ be two label specifications, over the signatures $\widehat{\Sigma L_1}$ and $\widehat{\Sigma L_2}$ respectively, such that $\mu(Ax_1) \subseteq Ax_2$. Let U_μ be the forgetful functor from $Alg_{Lbl}(\widehat{\Sigma L_2})$ to $Alg_{Lbl}(\widehat{\Sigma L_1})$. The restriction of U_μ to $Alg_{Lbl}(\widehat{SP_2})$ can be co-restricted to $Alg_{Lbl}(\widehat{SP_1})$. More generally, for all $\widehat{\Sigma L_2}$-algebras $\mathcal{A}$ and for all $\widehat{\Sigma L_1}$-axioms φ we have:*
$$\mathcal{A} \models \mu(\varphi) \implies U_\mu(\mathcal{A}) \models \varphi$$

Remark 4 Theorem 3 does not require the axiom φ to be positive conditional.

[4] Signature morphisms are defined in an obvious way: $S_1 \to S_2$, $\Sigma_1 \to \Sigma_2$, $L_1 \to L_2$ and $C_1 \to C_2$

The reverse implication is not valid in general, as shown by the following example. Consequently, the so-called "satisfaction condition" does not hold for label algebras; the framework of label algebras is not an institution [GB84]. However, it forms a pre-institution with the rps property [SS91].

Example 2 Let ΣL_1 be the label signature defined by $S_1 = \{ \textit{thesort} \}$, $\Sigma_1 = \{ \textit{cst1} : \rightarrow \textit{thesort} \}$ and $L_1 = \{ \textit{thelabel} \}$ (it does no matter if *thelabel* is constrained or not in this example). Let ΣL_2 be the label signature defined by $S_2 = S_1$, $\Sigma_2 = \{ \textit{cst1} : \rightarrow \textit{thesort} \ , \ \textit{cst2} : \rightarrow \textit{thesort} \}$ and $L_2 = L_1$. We clearly have $\Sigma L_1 \subset \Sigma L_2$. Let $\mathcal{A}$ be the ΣL_2-algebra defined by: $A = \{a = \textit{cst1}_A = \textit{cst2}_A\}$ (A is a singleton) and by: $\textit{thelabel}_{\mathcal{A}} = \{ a \ , \ \textit{cst1} \}$ (let us remind that $T_{\Sigma_2}(A) = \{ a \ , \ \textit{cst1} \ , \ \textit{cst2} \}$). The ΣL_1-algebra $U(\mathcal{A})$ is then characterised by $U(A) = \{a = \textit{cst1}_{U(A)}\}$ and $\textit{thelabel}_{U(\mathcal{A})} = \{ a \ , \ \textit{cst1} \}$.

Thus, $\textit{thelabel}_{U(\mathcal{A})} = T_{\Sigma_1}(U(A))$. Consequently, $U(\mathcal{A})$ satisfies the ΣL_1-axiom "$x \in \textit{thelabel}$" while $\mathcal{A}$ does not (as *cst2* does not belong to $\textit{thelabel}_{\mathcal{A}}$).

Theorem 4 *Let $\widehat{SP}_1$ and $\widehat{SP}_2$ be two positive conditional label specifications such that $\widehat{SP}_1 \subseteq \widehat{SP}_2$. There exists a synthesis functor $F : Alg_{Lbl}(\widehat{SP}_1) \rightarrow Alg_{Lbl}(\widehat{SP}_2)$ which is a left adjoint to U.*

Sketch of proof: For every $\widehat{SP}_1$-algebra $\mathcal{A}$, $F(\mathcal{A})$ is a quotient of $T_{\Sigma_2}(\mathcal{A})$ (with a careful definition of the labelling for $\widehat{L_1}$ deduced from the one of $\mathcal{A}$). This quotient is defined using Theorem 1. The adjunction can be proved with the Yoneda lemma [McL71]. ∎

As usual, the adjunction $I_{\mathcal{A}} : \mathcal{A} \rightarrow U(F(\mathcal{A}))$ can be used to define *hierarchical consistency* ("no-collapse" property) and *sufficient completeness* ("no-junk" property) for structured specifications.

Remark 5 We have shown in this subsection that the framework of label algebras does not form an institution [GB84], even if restricted to positive conditional axioms, because Example 2 shows that we do not have the reverse implication of the satisfaction condition given in the Theorem 3. Indeed, we have proved that the framework of positive conditional label algebras form a specification logic which has free constructions ([EBO91], [EBCO91]). Let us point out that the specification logic of label algebras *does not* have amalgamations (as defined in [EBCO91]). The reason *a priori* is that we show in Section 5.1 that observational semantics can be reflected within label algebras, and [EBCO91] has proved that observational semantics do not have amalgamations in general. It is the same for extensions (at least if we do not restrict the definition of morphisms).

5 Some applications of label algebras

We have mentioned so far that labels can be used within frameworks devoted to observability or exception handling. Indeed, labels provide a great tool to express several other features already developed in the field of (first-order) algebraic specifications.

5.1 Some possible applications

We have mentioned in the introduction that the framework of label algebras can be shown as an extension of more standard algebraic approaches based on "multityping." More precisely, we can *specify multityping* by means of label specifications. Indeed the difference between a label and a type is that labels are carried by terms (in $\overline{A}$) while type names are carried by values (in A). Thus a label l can easily play the role of a type name: it is sufficient to saturate each fiber of $eval_A : \overline{A} \rightarrow A$ which contains a term labelled by l. This is easily specified by a ΣL-axiom of the form:

$$x \epsilon l \wedge x = y \Longrightarrow y \epsilon l$$

where x and y are variables. For every model A satisfying such axioms for l belonging to L, two terms u and v of $\overline{A}$ having equal values in A are necessarily labelled by the same labels, thus labels can play the role of types. Notice that we should write one axiom of this form for each sort belonging to S because the variables x and y are typed in S in our framework. Nevertheless, insofar as we intend to simulate types by labels, S should be a singleton. Thus, the "typing" of terms, as well as variables, becomes explicit in the precondition of each axiom. Therefore, this approach leads to consider typing as "membership constraints." For finitely generated algebras, such a specification style facilitates theorem-proving, as demonstrated in [Smo86], [Com90].

An advantage of such an approach is that additional properties about types, according to the needs of the considered application, can be easily specified within the same framework. For example, let us consider a property such as $s \leq s'$ between two sorts in the framework of *order-sorted algebras* [FGJM85]. It can be specified within the framework of label specifications by $x \epsilon s \Rightarrow x \epsilon s'$ where s and s' are labels which simulate the corresponding (sub)sorts.

In the same way, it is possible to specify *dependent types* such as binary search tree (the specifications of natural numbers and booleans are supposed already written):

$S = \{All\}$
$\Sigma = \{empty :\rightarrow All; node : All\ All\ All \rightarrow All; root, max, min : All \rightarrow All\}$
$L = \{Bool, Nat, Notdefined, Bst, Sta, Gta\}$[5]

with the following axioms, under initial semantics:

$empty \ \epsilon\ Bst$
$max(empty) \ \epsilon\ Sta$
$min(empty) \ \epsilon\ Gta$
$x \ \epsilon\ Sta \wedge n \ \epsilon\ Nat \Longrightarrow x \leq n = true$
$x \ \epsilon\ Gta \wedge n \ \epsilon\ Nat \Longrightarrow n \leq x = true$
$a \ \epsilon\ Bst \wedge b \ \epsilon\ Bst \wedge n \ \epsilon\ Nat \wedge max(a) \leq n = true \wedge n \leq min(b) = true \Longrightarrow$
$node\ a\ n\ b \ \epsilon\ Bst$
$root(empty) \ \epsilon\ Notdefined$
$node\ a\ n\ b \ \epsilon\ Bst \Longrightarrow root\ (node\ a\ n\ b) = n$

[5] *Bst* for Binary Search Tree; *Sta* for *Smaller-Than-All* and *Gta* for *Greater-Than-All*

Some other extensions of subsorting are: unified algebras ([Mos89]), typed algebras ([MSS90]) or G-algebras ([Meg90]). The two first approaches allow to treat sorts exactly as ordinary terms because one can consider operations taking sorts as arguments. Moreover, these three formalisms allow to use sorts within formulas. Label algebras do not allow for operations to take sorts or labels as arguments and only the labels can explicitly appear in formulas. In return, these three formalisms do not offer the main advantage of label algebras: two terms that share the same value can be distinguished by labelling them. In other words, we propose a proper algebraic treatment where the rule of replacement of equal by equal is not a prerequisite. Thus, label algebras provides the specifier with an extension of subsorting of very different nature than [Mos89] [MSS90] [Meg90]. It would certainly be fruitful in future works to incorporate their better homogeneity between sorts and terms into our approach.

Algebraic specifications with *partial functions* can also be reflected via label specifications. They often rely on an additional predicate D which is used to specify the definition domain of each operation of the signature ([BW82] and others). Thus, atoms are either equalities, or of the form $D(t)$, where t is a term with variables. It is of course not difficult to translate $D(t)$ to ($t \in IsDefined$); we simply have to specify the propagation of the definition domains with respect to any operation f of the signature:

$$f(x_1,\ldots,x_n) \in IsDefined \Longrightarrow x_1 \in IsDefined \wedge \ldots \wedge x_n \in IsDefined$$

Then, the label *IsDefined* can be used in the preconditions of the axioms defining the partial operations in such a way that every label algebra $\mathcal{A}$ satisfying the resulting label specification has the property that $eval_{\mathcal{A}}(IsDefined_{\mathcal{A}})$ is a subset of A that, together with the operations of $\mathcal{A}$ restricted to it, behaves like a partial algebra satisfying the original specification (see also [AC91]).

In the same way, labels can be used to give a refined semantics of the predefined *predicates of specification languages*. For example in *Pluss* [Bid89], an expression of the form "t **is defined when** *something*" can be reflected by the following label axiom: $something \Rightarrow t \in IsDefined$

More generally, labels are indeed unary predicates on terms; thus, they can be at least used as *predicates* on values (using the label axiom already mentioned for multityping). The advantage of such predicates is that their semantics is not defined via a hidden boolean sort: using booleans to define predicates is often unsatisfactory because it assumes that the specification is consistent with respect to boolean values. In this way, labels can advantageously be used in a specification to provide additional information about the specified data types. For instance, we can write:

$$0 \in Even$$
$$n \in Even \Longrightarrow succ(n) \in Odd$$
$$n \in Odd \Longrightarrow succ(n) \in Even$$
$$exp(n,0) = succ(0)$$
$$succ(m) \in Odd \Longrightarrow exp(n, succ(m)) = exp(n,m) \times n$$
$$m \in Even \Longrightarrow exp(n,m) = exp(n \times n\ ,\ m\ div\ succ(succ(0)))$$

Let us return to the application of label algebras to observability (see Section 2). Clearly, the predicate *Obs* used by [Hen89] can be reflected by a label. More generally, labels can be used to characterise observable *terms*. By distinguishing a subset ΣObs of Σ, the framework of [BB91] introduces two distinct notions that reflect a hierarchy in the definition of observability. The terms that only contain operations belonging to ΣObs are said to "allow observability" (the other ones can never be observed). Then, a term "allowing observability" really becomes "observable" only if it belongs to an observable sort. It is not difficult to reflect the observational hierarchy defined in [BB91] by using two distinct labels denoted *AllowsObs* and *Obs*. For each operation f allowing observability (i.e. belonging to the considered subset ΣObs of the signature), it is sufficient to consider the following label axiom:

$$x_1 \in AllowsObs \wedge \ldots \wedge x_n \in AllowsObs \iff f(x_1, \ldots, x_n) \in AllowsObs$$

The fact that a term allowing observability becomes observable if and only if it belongs to an observable sort s can easily be specified by the label axiom (one axiom for each observable sort): $x \in AllowsObs \Leftrightarrow x \in Obs$ where x is a variable of sort s. As shown in [BB91], this label *Obs* is carried by terms, not by values, contrarily to the predicate *Obs* used in [Hen89]. Hopefully, the advantages of the Hennicker's approach should be preserved, since they mainly rely on the explicit specification of the predicate *Obs*.

5.2 Application to exception handling

Let us define the framework of exception algebras as a specialization of the one of label algebras, where the labels are used for exception handling purposes. The particular label *Ok* will be distinguished to characterize the normal cases; exception names and error messages will be reflected by all the other labels. This allows us to take exception names into account in the axioms. Intuitively, in an exception algebra $\mathcal{A}$, $t \in l_{\mathcal{A}}$ with $l \neq Ok$ will mean that the computation defined by t leads to the exception name l; and $t \in Ok_{\mathcal{A}}$ will mean that the computation defined by t is a "normal" computation (i.e. it does not need an exceptional treatment and the computation is successful). An exception signature is then by definition a label signature $\widehat{\Sigma L}$ with $\widehat{L} = (L, \{Ok\})$ where L is the set of exception names. In order to reflect the specific behaviours of data with exception handling, we add a few implicit label axioms.

An important implicit aspect is the "common future" property. Let us consider $\mathcal{A}$ reflecting the natural numbers bounded by *maxint*, the terms $succ^i(0)$ with $i \leq maxint$ being labelled by *Ok*. Let us assume that $succ^{maxint+1}(0)$ is recovered on $succ^{maxint}(0)$. Once this recovering is done, we want everything to happen as if the exception $succ^{maxint+1}(0)$ were never raised; we view this as the meaning of the word recovery. The same non-empty succession of operations applied to $succ^{maxint}(0)$ or to $succ^{maxint+1}(0)$ should return the same value and raise the same exception names. If $succ^{maxint+1}(0)$ is labelled by *TooLarge*, then the term $t = succ^{maxint+2}(0)$ should also be labelled by *TooLarge*, since $succ^{maxint+1}(0) = t[succ^{maxint+1}(0) \leftarrow succ^{maxint}(0)]$. Let us point out that, since $pred(succ^{maxint}(0))$ does not raise any exception names, there is no reason for $pred(succ^{maxint+1}(0))$ to be labelled by *TooLarge*. The common future property is *not* a bottom-up propagation rule for exception names.

In a label algebra $\mathcal{A}$, $eval_{\mathcal{A}}(u) = eval_{\mathcal{A}}(v)$ implies for every term t containing u as proper subterm, that t and $t[u \leftarrow v]$ have the same value, but it does not imply that they have the same labels. On the contrary, such a property will be required for exception names in exception algebras. An exception algebra is then by definition a $\widehat{\Sigma L}$-algebra which satisfies the common future property.

As usual, when specifying a data structure with exception handling features, the specifier first declares the desired *Ok*-part. Let us assume that all the terms $succ^i(0)$ with $i \leq maxint$ are labelled by *Ok* and that the specification contains also the following "normal axiom:" $pred(succ(n)) = n$. Then, for instance, the term $pred(succ(0))$ should also belong to the *Ok*-domain because its computation does not require any exceptional treatment and leads to the *Ok*-term 0 via the previous normal axiom. By a terseness principle, labelling by *Ok* must be *implicitly* propagated through the axioms kept for normal cases. Since label algebras have no implicit aspects, the semantics of exception specifications must implicitly add label axioms reflecting these properties.

As *Ok*-axioms require special semantics, it is necessary to separate the axioms concerning exceptional cases (given by *GenAx*) from the *Ok*-axioms which concern normal cases. Thus an exception specification *SPEC* is defined as a triple $< \widehat{\Sigma L}, GenAx, OkAx >$ where *GenAx* is a set of generalized axioms (which are positive conditional $\widehat{\Sigma L}$-axioms) and where *OkAx* is a set of *Ok*-axioms (which are positive conditional $\widehat{\Sigma L}$-axioms with a conclusion of the form $u = v$).

- *GenAx* is mainly devoted to exception handling. Its first purpose concerns labelling of terms. The axioms with a conclusion of the form $t \epsilon Ok$ (resp. $t \epsilon l$ with $l \in L$) mean that t is a normal term (resp. the outermost operation of the term t raises the exception name l). The second purpose of *GenAx* is to handle the exceptional cases, in particular to specify recoveries, according to the previous labelling of terms. The corresponding axioms will have a conclusion of the form $u = v$. As the axioms of *GenAx* concern all terms, exceptional or not, the satisfaction of such axioms will simply be the same as for label axioms.

- *OkAx* is entirely devoted to the normal cases, and will only concern terms labelled by *Ok*. The semantics of *OkAx* must be carefully restricted to *Ok*-assignments, in order to avoid inconsistencies (see Section 2). It will both treat equalities between *Ok*-terms and carefully propagate labelling by *Ok* through these equalities.

(For an example of exception specification, see Example 3 below)

Definition 13 *Let $\widehat{\Sigma L}$ be an exception signature. An exception algebra $\mathcal{A}$ satisfies an Ok-axiom of the form $P \Rightarrow v = w$, where P is the precondition,*[6] *if and only if for all assignments σ with range in $\overline{A}$ (covering all the variables of the axiom) which satisfy the precondition (i.e. $\mathcal{A}$ as $\widehat{\Sigma L}$-algebra satisfies the "ground" label axiom $\sigma(P)$), the two following properties hold:*

[6] P is a conjunction of atoms or may be empty.

Ok-propagation: *if at least one of the terms* $\sigma(v)$ *or* $\sigma(w)$ *belongs to* Ok_A *and the other one is of the form* $f(t_1,\ldots,t_p)$ *with all the* t_i *belonging to* Ok_A[7], *then both* $\sigma(v)$ *and* $\sigma(w)$ *belong to* Ok_A.

Ok-equality: *if* $\sigma(v)$ *and* $\sigma(w)$ *belong to* Ok_A *then* $eval_A(\sigma(v)) = eval_A(\sigma(w))$.

The first property of the definition reflects a careful propagation of the label *Ok* (which starts from the *Ok*-terms declared in *GenAx*). Intuitively, such an innermost evaluation reflects an implicit propagation of exceptions because a term can be required to be labelled by *Ok* through an *Ok*-axiom only if all the arguments of its outermost operation are already labelled by *Ok*. The second property specifies the equalities that must hold for the normal cases. Two terms can be required to get the same evaluation through an *Ok*-axiom only if they are both labelled by *Ok*.

We denote by $Alg_{Exc}(SPEC)$ the full subcategory of $Alg_{Lbl}(\widehat{\Sigma L})$ containing the exception algebras satisfying *SPEC* (i.e. which satisfy every axiom of *SPEC*).

Theorem 5 *Let* $SPEC = < \widehat{\Sigma L}, GenAx, OkAx >$ *be an exception specification. There exists a positive conditional label specification* $Tr(SPEC)$, *over the same label signature* $\widehat{\Sigma L}$ *such that* $Alg_{Exc}(SPEC) = Alg_{Lbl}(Tr(SPEC))$.

Sketch of proof: It is sufficient to add well-chosen label axioms which reflect the common future property and to add for each *Ok*-axiom of *SPEC* a finite set of label axioms reflecting Definition 13. ∎

$Tr(SPEC)$ only contains positive conditional axioms. Thus, from Section 4 we have:

Corollary 1 *Let SPEC be an exception specification.* $Alg_{Exc}(SPEC)$ *has an initial object* T_{SPEC}.

Moreover, given two exception specifications $SPEC_1$ *and* $SPEC_2$ *such that* $SPEC_1 \subseteq SPEC_2$, *the forgetful functor* $U : Alg_{Exc}(SPEC_2) \rightarrow Alg_{Exc}(SPEC_1)$ *exists and has a left adjoint functor F.*

Example 3 Let $BoundedNat = < \{Nat\}, \{0 :\rightarrow Nat; succ, pred : Nat \rightarrow Nat\}, (\{TooLarge, Negative\}, \{Ok\}) >$ be an exception signature. An example of exception specification over this signature is given by:

$$\begin{array}{lll} GenAx & : & succ^{maxint}(0) \in Ok \\ & & succ(n) \in Ok \Rightarrow n \in Ok \\ & & succ^{maxint+1}(0) \in TooLarge \\ & & pred(0) \in Negative \\ & & succ(n) \in TooLarge \Longrightarrow succ(n) = n \\ OkAx & : & pred(succ(n)) = n \\ & Where : & n : Nat \end{array}$$

The two first axioms specify the *Ok* domain of *Nat*. It is not necessary to declare *all* the *Ok*-terms (the label *Ok* will be automatically be propagated to terms such as *pred(succ(0))* via the *Ok*-axiom). Even if it is generally easier to recursively specify the *Ok* domain, it is not mandatory; it is only desirable to specify at least one term for each intended *Ok*-value. The third and fourth axioms declare exception

[7] *p* may be equal to 0

names. Their meaning is that the operation *succ* (resp. *pred*) raises the exception *TooLarge* (resp. *Negative*) when applied to *maxint* (resp. 0). Finally, the last axiom of *GenAx* recovers the terms labelled by *TooLarge* by expressing the following exceptional treatment: *"if the operation succ raises the exception TooLarge, then do not perform it."*.

When compared to the formalism of [BBC86], our formalism is much simpler because its semantics can be translated into that of label algebras, which is more easily understandable. Moreover, we argued in Section 2 the great advantage of labelling terms instead of values with respect to the label *Ok*. But, it is also crucial to label terms (and not values) by the exception names. In [BBC86], exception names are carried by values instead of terms (while the label *Ok* is aptly carried by terms). If we consider the last axiom of *GenAx* in Example 3, this would lead to inconsistencies. The term *succ*(*maxint*) being equal to the term *maxint*, both of them are labelled by *TooLarge*. Let $m = maxint - 1$; since *maxint* is labelled by *TooLarge*, we get the following inconsistency: $maxint = succ(m) = m$. This inconsistency propagates in the same way, and all values are equal to 0. Thus, our formalism of exception algebras as an application of label algebras, is not only simpler than [BBC86] but it is also better than [BBC86] on pragmatic grounds because it allows Example 3 as a correct, consistent specification.

The same argument applies for all existing formalisms because they all reflect exception names (or definition domains) by sorts or predicates on values. It even applies if we extend the boolean domain as suggested in [Poi88] following the Scott-Fourman theory of partiality [Sco77].

As already mentioned (see Section 3.2), it would not be interesting to consider a partial evaluation constraint with respect to $\widehat{L} = (\emptyset, L \cup \{Ok\})$. In Example 3, the partial evaluation constraint for the label *TooLarge* would lead to label the constant *maxint* with *TooLarge* since *maxint* is a partial evaluation of *succ*(*maxint*). Thus, an *Ok*-value would be labelled by an exception name, just because an exceptionnal term labelled by this exception name is recovered on it. This would be againts our intuition that *maxint* first of all represents a normal case.

Summing up, as for the application to exception handling, all the possible applications mentioned in Section 5.1 require some generic label axioms which must be *implicit*. These axioms should be considered as modifiers of the semantics. Thus, the framework of label algebras provides us with "low level" algebraic specifications. When an algebraic specification *SPEC* is written according to some special semantics (e.g. observational specifications or exception algebras), it has to be "compiled" (translated) to a label specification $Tr(SPEC)$.

6 Conclusion

We have shown that observational approaches or exception handling are usefully served by a refined notion of the satisfaction relation for algebraic specifications. The scope of an axiom must be restricted to carefully chosen patterns, because a satisfaction relation based on assignments with range in values often raises inconsistencies. A more elaborated notion of assignment has been considered: assignment with range in terms. This allows us to restrict the scope of an axiom to certain suitable patterns, and solves the inconsistencies raised by exception handling. We use *labels* to characterise these suitable patterns. In order to avoid inconsistencies, labels must not go through equational atoms; thus, two terms having the same value do not necessarily carry the same labels. We have first defined the framework of *label algebras*, that provides labels with suitable semantics. The scope of the label axioms is carefully delimited by labels which serve as special marks on terms.

We have applied with success the formalism of label algebras in order to avoid the inconsistencies raised by exception handling. This approach is powerful enough to cope with all usual exception handling features such as implicit propagation of exceptions, possible recoveries, declaration of exception names, bounded data structures, etc.

The application domain of label algebras seems to be much more general than exception handling. Indeed, labels provide a great tool to express several other features developed in the field of (first-order) algebraic specifications. We have outlined in Section 5.1 how label algebras can generalise more standard algebraic approaches such as order-sorted algebras [Gog78], partial functions [BW82] or observability features ([Hen89], [BB91]). However, as for the application to exception handling, all the specific applications of label algebras require certain *implicit* label axioms or constraints. Thus, the framework of label algebras provides us with "low-level" algebraic specifications: in a generic way, the specific semantical aspects of a given approach (e.g. subsorting or exception handling) can be specified by a well-chosen set of label axioms.

We have shown in Section 4 that the framework of label algebras restricted to positive conditional axioms, and consequently the one of exception algebras, form a specification logic which has free constructions ([EBO91], [EBCO91]).[8] These results provide us with a first basis to study modularity for label specifications. However, modularity and parameterisation should be studied according to the specific application under consideration (behavioural specifications, exception specifications, etc). Indeed, it can be shown that the existing frameworks for modularity do not cope with exception handling because structured exception specification must allow erroneous "junk" (see [BBC86]).

Several other extensions of the framework of label algebras will probably give promising results. Intuitively, labels are unary predicates on terms, possibly built on values. In order to facilitate certain applications of label algebras, we plan to generalise labels to "labels of strictly positive arity." Theorem-proving methods according to the semantics of label algebras should be studied in future works. Higher order label specifications may also be dealt with in future works. Last, but not least, let us mention that bounded data structures play a crucial role in the theory of *testing* because test data sets should contain many elementary tests near the bounds. One aim of our current research is to extend the theory of test data selection from algebraic specifications as described in [BGM91] to exception specifications.

Acknowledgements: We would like to thank Pippo Scollo for a careful reading of the draft version of this paper. Several discussions with Marie-Claude Gaudel and

[8] but it does not form a liberal institution [GB84].

Michel Bidoit have been helpful. This work has been partially supported by CNRS GRECO de Programmation and EEC Working Group COMPASS.

References

[AC91] Astesiano E., Cerioli M. *Non-strict don't care algebras and specifications.* TAPSOFT CAAP, Brighton U.K., April 1991, Springer-Verlag LNCS 493, p.121-142.

[BB91] Bernot G., Bidoit M. *Proving the correctness of algebraically specified software: Modularity and Observability issues.* Proc. of AMAST-2, Second Conference of Algebraic Methodology and Software Technology, Iowa City, Iowa, USA, May 1991.

[BBC86] Bernot G., Bidoit M., Choppy C. *Abstract data types with exception handling : an initial approach based on a distinction between exceptions and errors.* Theoretical Computer Science, Vol.46, n.1, pp.13-45, Elsevier Science Pub. B.V. (North-Holland), November 1986. (Also LRI Report 251, Orsay, Dec. 1985.)

[BGM91] Bernot G., Gaudel M.C., Marre B. *Software testing based on formal specifications: a theory and a tool.* to appear in Software Engineering Journal, December 1991.

[Ber92] Bernot G. *Diplôme d'Habilitation à diriger des Recherches en Sciences,* Université de Paris XI, Orsay, 1992.

[BL91] Bernot G., Le Gall P. *Label algebras and exception handling.* To appear in LRI Research Report, Université de Paris XI, Orsay, 1991.

[Bid89] Bidoit M. *Pluss, un langage pour le développement de spécifications algébriques modulaires.* Thèse d'état, University of Orsay Paris XI, 1989.

[Bre91] Breu M. *Bounded Implementation of Algebraic Specifications.* 8th Workshop on Specification od Abstract DataTypes, Dourdan, 1991.

[BW82] Broy M., Wirsing M. *Partial abstract data types.* Acta Informatica, Vol.18-1, Nov. 1982.

[Com90] Comon H. *Equational formulas in order-sorted algebras.* Proc. ICALP, Warwick, Springer-Verlag, July 1990.

[EBCO91] Ehrig H., Baldamus M., Cornelius F., Orejas F. *Theory of algebraic module specification including behavioural semantics, constraints and aspects of generalized morphisms.* Proc. of AMAST-2, Second Conference of Algebraic Methodology and Software Technology, Iowa City, Iowa, USA, May 1991.

[EBO91] Ehrig H., Baldamus M., Orejas F. *New concepts for amalgamation and extension in the framework of specification logics.* Research report Bericht-No 91/05, Technische Universitat Berlin, May 1991.

[EM85] Ehrig H., Mahr B. *Fundamentals of Algebraic Specification 1. Equations and initial semantics.* EATCS Monographs on Theoretical Computer Science, Vol.6, Springer-Verlag, 1985.

[FGJM85] Futatsugi K., Goguen J., Jouannaud J-P., Meseguer J. *Principles of OBJ2.* Proc. 12th ACM Symp. on Principle of Programming Languages, New Orleans, january 1985.

[GB84] Goguen J.A., Burstall R.M. *Introducing institutions.* Proc. of the Workshop on Logics of Programming, Springer-Verlag LNCS 164, pp.221-256, 1984.

[GDLE84] Gogolla M., Drosten K., Lipeck U., Ehrich H.D. *Algebraic and operational semantics of specifications allowing exceptions and errors.* Theoretical Computer Science 34, North Holland, 1984, pp.289-313.

[GM89] Goguen J.A., Meseguer J. *Order-sorted algebra I: equational deduction for multiple inheritance, overloading, exceptions and partial operations.* Technical Report SRI-CSL-89-10, SRI, July 1989.

[Gog78] Goguen J.A. *Order sorted algebras: exceptions and error sorts, coercion and overloading operators.* Univ. California Los Angeles, Semantics Theory of Computation Report n.14, Dec. 1978.

[Gog83] Gogolla M. *Algebraic specification with partially ordered sorts and declarations.* Research report Forschungsbericht No 169, University of Dormund, 1983.

[Gog87] Gogolla M. *On parametric algebraic specifications with clean error handling.* Proc. Joint Conf. on Theory and Practice of Software Development, Pisa (1987), Springer-Verlag LNCS 249, pp.81-95.

[GTW78] Goguen J.A., Thatcher J.W., Wagner E.G. *An Initial Algebra Approach to the Specification, Correctness, and Implementation of Abstract Data Types.* Current Trends in Programming Methodology, ed. R.T. Yeh, Printice-Hall, Vol.IV, pp.80-149, 1978. (Also IBM Report RC 6487, October 1976.)

[Hen89] Hennicker R. *Implementation of Parameterized Observational Specifications.* TapSoft, Barcelona, LNCS 351, vol.1, pp.290-305, 1989.

[LeG92] Le Gall P. *Algèbres étiquetées, traitement d'exception et test de logiciel* Draft version of Thèse de Doctorat, Université de Paris XI, Orsay, 1992.

[LG86] Liskov B., Guttag J. *Abstraction and specification in program development.* The MIT Press and McGraw-Hill Book Company, 1986.

[Meg90] Mégrelis A. *Algèbre galactique - Un procédé de calcul formel, relatif aux semi-fonctions, à l'inclusion et à l'égalité* Thèse de doctorat, Université Nancy I, september 1990.

[Mos89] Mosses P. *Unified algebras and Institutions*. Proc. of IEEE LICS'89, Fourth Annual Symposium on Logic in Computer Science, June 1989, Asilomar, California.

[MS87] Manca V., Salibra A. *Soundness and completeness of the Birkhoff equational calculus for many-sorted algebras with possibly empty carrier sets* Draft University of Pisa, September 1987, to appear in TCS 1992.

[MSS90] Manca V., Salibra A., Scollo G. *Equational Type Logic*. Conference on Algebraic Methodology and Software Technology, Iowa City, IA, May 1989, TCS 77, p 131-159

[McL71] Mac Lane S. *Categories for the working mathematician*. Graduate texts in mathematics, 5, Springer-Verlag, 1971

[Poi88] Poigne A. *Partial algebras, Subsorting, and dependent types*. 5th Workshop on Specification of Abstract Data Types, Gullane, September 1987, LNCS 332, p. 208-234.

[Sco77] Scott D.S. *Identity and Existence in Intutionistic Logic*. In: Applications of Sheaves, Proc. Durham, Lectures Notes in Mathematics 753.

[Smo86] Smolka G. *Order-sorted horn logic: semantics and deduction*. Research report SR-86-17, Univ. Kaiserslautern, Oct. 1986.

[SS91] Salibra A., Scollo G. *A soft stairway to institutions* 8th Workshop on Specification od Abstract DataTypes, Dourdan, 1991.

[WB80] Wirsing M., Broy M. *Abstract data types as lattices of finitely generated models*. Proc. of the 9th Int. Symposium on Mathematical Foundations of Computer Science (MFCS), Rydzyna, Poland, Sept. 1980.

How to Specify Non Determinism and True Concurrency with Algebraic Term Nets

Mohamed Bettaz, Mourad Maouche

Institut d'Informatique - Université de Constantine
Constantine 25 000 - Algeria

Abstract. The objective of this paper is twofold. First we modify and extend the definition of Algebraic Term Nets [2] in order to make them concurrent objects. Then we give them an interpretation in terms of **rewrite logic**. The proposed logic acts as an axiomatisation allowing us to study the behavior of Algebraic Term Nets by deduction in such a logic. Moreover we present and discuss a general approach allowing us to write the axioms in such a way that our nets are executed **coherently** and with a maximum of true concurrency.

Keywords and phrases. Abstract data types, high-level Petri nets, true concurrency, rewrite logic.

1 Introduction

Algebraic Term Nets (ATNets) are a form of high-level net/(abstract) data model motivated by the need of practical applications [2, 4]. They combine the strength of abstract data types with that of Petri nets. Abstract data types are used for their *data abstraction* power and solid mathematical foundation, while Petri nets are used for their foundation in concurrency and dynamics. Moreover both formalisms are able to be processed by machine. Similar models are the many-sorted high-level nets [8], the algebraic high-level nets [11], the Petri nets and algebraic specifications [13] and many others. Billington's work is perhaps closest to ours, since his work was motivated by a backgroud in protocols and Numerical Petri Nets [6, 15]. However our work may be considered as generalizing the work in [8], since we are using abstract data types *with axioms*, while this is not the case in [8]. Moreover it seems that the interpretation of our nets into rewrite logic may lead to handle in an easy way the concept of *generalized inhibitor arc* [8], and the concept of *global variables* [15].

The objective of this paper is twofold. First we redefine ATNets in order to make them *truly* concurrent objects. Then we give them an interpretation in terms of rewrite logic [12]. The proposed logic acts as an axiomatisation allowing us to study the behavior of ATNets by deduction in such a logic. Moreover we present and discuss a general approach enabling us to write the axioms in such a way that ATNets are executed *coherently* and with a maximum of true concurrency. This approach realizes a form of *global control* (on the activity of the ATNet) similar to that realized by the *monitoring step* defined in [1] w.r.t. the maximal parallelism execution mode.

According to [12], what makes a system concurrent is precisely the existence of an *additional algebraic structure*. For the particular case of ATNets we make use of two such structures. The first one is used to redefine ATNets at the syntactic level, i.e., to give the syntactic definitions of arcs inscriptions, markings, etc... This structure allows us to consider ATNets as *schemas* in the sense of [11] and [14]. The advantage of such schemas is that they can be used to specify classes of systems. The second structure is used at a semantic level in the sense that it allows ATNets to become *interpretable* in terms of rewrite logic. This structure allows us to consider our schemas as abstract ones, in the sense that the elements of the algebraic structure are interpreted modulo a set of equations. Our objective is to free the net behavior from syntactic constraints. ATNets redefined in this way will be called CATNets (an acronym for Concurrent Algebraic Term Nets). The main difference between ATNets and CATNets is that the first ones were lacking suitable additional structures and were exhibiting nondeterministic behavior rather than concurrent one.

The paper is organized in the following way. In section 2 we give the definition of CATNets. In section 3 we explain the dynamic behavior of CATNets thru their interpretation in terms of rewrite logic. The rewrite logic consists of a set of axioms and a set of deduction rules. The axioms are *rewrite rules* describing transitions effects as elementary types of changes. The deduction rules allow us to draw valid conclusions about the evolution of the CATNet from these changes. The choice of rewrite rules rather than equations is motivated by the fact that the intended rewrite logic is a logic of *becoming* or change, rather than a logic of equality in a static sense [12]. In section 4 we present and discuss our approach of writing down the set of axioms. In section 5 we give two simple examples. The first one describes a *wrong behavior* of the *ticket machine*, and is intended just to illustrate the use of CATNets and their interpretation in terms of the rewrite logic. The second example describes the behavior of a simplified fault tolerant system, and is intended to illustrate the expressiveness of CATNets w.r.t. situations presenting a maximum of true concurrency. In section 6 we outline some semantic issues. In section 7 we conclude by situating our contribution among present and future works.

2 CATNets

Let us start this section by recalling some *standard* notions and notations from the field of algebraic specifications. The reader interested in more detail may consult for instance [10]. A signature SIG = (S, OP) consists of a set S, the set of sorts and a set OP, the set of operation symbols together with their *declaration* which specifies the names of the domain and co-domain of each of the operation symbols. As in [8] we use the term *Boolean signature* to mean a signature where one of the sorts is Boolean (bool). Similarly, the term *Natural signature* is used when one of the sorts corresponds to the Naturals (nat). A SIG-algebra A is a pair $A = (S_A, OP_A)$ where $S_A = (A_s)_{s \in S}$ is the set of carriers and $OP_A = (\sigma_A)_{\sigma \in OP}$ the set of corresponding functions. When there is no ambiguity the name of an algebra will be used to denote the algebra itself as well as its set of carriers. We denote by $T_{SIG}(X)$ the SIG-algebra of SIG-terms with variables in an S-sorted set X. Similarly, given a set E of SIG(X)-equations, $T_{SIG,E}(X)$ denotes the SIG-algebra of equivalence classes of SIG-terms with variables in X modulo the equations E. We let $[x]_E$ or just [x] denote the E-equivalence class of x. $MT_{SIG,E}(X)$ denotes the *many-sorted* free commutative monoid over $T_{SIG,E}(X)$ with $\oplus$ the usual internal operation, and $\emptyset_M$ the identity element.

- $MT_{SIG,E}(X) = \{\underline{m}:T_{SIG,E}(X) \dashrightarrow T_{SIG,E}(X)_{nat} \;/\; \underline{m} \text{ has a finite support}\}$
- $\emptyset_M$ is the function with value 0
- $(\underline{m} \oplus \underline{n})([t]) = [add(\underline{m}([t]),\underline{n}([t]))] \in T_{SIG,E}(X)_{nat} \quad \forall\, [t] \in T_{SIG,E}(X)$

The elements of $MT_{SIG,E}(X)$ can be considered as linear combinations

$$\underline{m} = \bigoplus_{i=1}^{n} [\mu i][ti]; \quad [ti] \in T_{SIG,E}(X); \quad [\mu i] = \underline{m}([ti]) \in T_{SIG,E}(X)_{nat}$$

Hence elements of $MT_{SIG,E}(X)$ can be considered as multisets over $T_{SIG,E}(X)$. CATNets are defined on an algebraic structure which will be called data structure. From a methodological point of view our definition of CATNets is inspired from [8] and [11].

2.1 Definition (CATNet data structure)

Let CATdas(E,X) denote the structure of equivalence classes of multisets of $MT_{SIG,E}(X)$ modulo the associative, commutative and identity (ACI) axioms of $\oplus$. This structure will be called CATNet data structure, and $[x]_\oplus$ will denote the equivalence class of $\underline{x}$, w.r.t. to the ACI axioms for $\oplus$.

2.2 Definition (CATNet)

Let SIG = (S, OP) be a Natural and Boolean signature, X an S-sorted set of variables and E a set of SIG(X)-equations.
A CATNet is a structure (P,T,s,IC,DT,CT,C,TC) where

- P is a set of places;
- T is a set of transitions such that $P \cap T = \emptyset$;
- s: P ---> S is a function that associates a sort with each place;
- IC: (P x T) ---> CATdas(E,X) is a partial function such that for every (p,t) $\in$ domain(IC), IC(p,t) $\in$ $CATdas(E,X)_{s(p)}$;
- DT: (P x T) ---> CATdas(E,X) is a function such that for every (p,t) $\in$ (P x T), DT(p,t) $\in$ $CATdas(E,X)_{s(p)}$;
- CT: (P x T) ---> CATdas(E,X) is a function such that for every (p,t) $\in$ (P x T), CT(p,t) $\in$ $CATdas(E,X)_{s(p)}$;
- C: P ---> CATdas(E,$\emptyset$) is a function such that for every p $\in$ P C(p) $\in$ $CATdas(E,\emptyset)_{s(p)}$;
- TC: T ---> $CATdas(E,X)_{bool}$ is a function such that for every t $\in$ T TC(t) $\in$ $CATdas(X(t))_{bool}$, where X(t) is the set of variables occurring in IC(p,t) (when defined), DT(p,t) and CT(p,t) for every p $\in$ P. X(t) will be called the transition context.

2.3 Definition (marked CATNet)

A marked CATNet is a CATNet with a function M: P ---> CATdas(E,$\emptyset$) such that for every p $\in$ P M(p) $\in$ $CATdas(E,\emptyset)_{s(p)}$ and $M(p) \subseteq C(p)$

Comments:

- Roughly speaking, the IC (Input Condition) and CT (Created Tokens) functions play *similar* roles to those played, respectively, by the *Pre* and *Post* functions in usual Petri nets. A difference between the two kinds of nets is that the *destroyed tokens* defined implicitly by the Pre function are defined explicitly by the function called DT (Destroyed Tokens).

• CATNets will be represented by graphs as it is usually the case for other types of Petri nets. Our representation is borrowed from that used in [6]. IC is inscribed to the left of a transition input arc, as seen by an observer at the transition. DT is inscribed to the right of each input arc, as seen by our observer. CT is inscribed next to each output arc of a transition. TC is delimited by square brackets, and written next to or inside the associated transition. All this is summarized by the generic CATNet in Fig. 1. When an arc is valuated by CT(p,t) = $\emptyset_M$ or by DT(p,t) = $\emptyset_M$ and in the same time IC(p,t) is undefined, this arc is not reported. However an arc valuated by IC(p,t) = $\emptyset_M$ is always reported. This notation will be explained when giving the CATNet semantics.

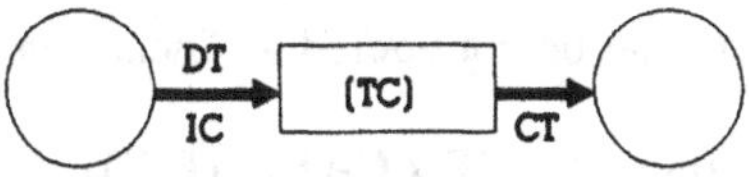

Fig. 1. A Generic CATNet

3 Dynamic Behavior of CATNets

Hybrid net/abstract data models are usually given semantics in one of the following two ways: by defining proper firing rules as in [7], or by interpreting them as other objects with a predefined semantics. This is the case of [14], where a Petri net-like schema (the Σ-schema concept) is given an interpretation in terms of coloured Petri nets; or the case of [8] defining the similar concept of Abstract P-Graph and giving it an interpretation in terms of P-net [7]. For the case of CATNets it is worthwhile to mention that it is not easy to explain their behavior merely by giving the equivalent of a firing-like rule. This is because of their higher level of abstraction as well as their concurrent behavior. We may however informally comment this behavior in the following way. A transition t is enabled when various conditions are simultaneously true. The first condition is that every IC(p,t) for each input place p is *contained* in M(p). The second condition is that TC(t) is true. Finally the addition of CT(p,t) to each output place p must not result in p exceeding its capacity. When t is fired DT(p,t) is removed from the input place p and simultaneously CT(p,t) is added to the output place p. When the context of a transition is not empty, it is supposed that the necessary instantiations are taking place in a *consistent* way. Moreover if one or more transitions are enabled without being in conflict, it(they) may be fired concurrently. Up to concurrency and data structure, the behavior of CATNets may be compared to the behavior exhibited by Numerical Petri Nets [6]. However the precise semantics of CATNets follows from their interpretation in terms of rewrite logic. In this section we will precise this logic. In the next section we introduce our approach of writing down the axioms. In order to achieve this, we first have to define our second additional algebraic structure. Let $BT_{SIG,E}(X)$ be the many-sorted free commutative monoid over the cartesian product (P x CATdas(E,X)) with ⊗ the usual internal operation and $Ø_B$ the identity element.

- $BT_{SIG,E}(X)$ = {$\underline{b}$: (P x CATdas(E,X)) ---> $T_{SIG,E}(X)_{nat}$ / $\underline{b}$ has a finite support}

- $Ø_B$ is the function with value 0

- ($\underline{b}$ ⊗ $\underline{c}$) (p,$[m]_⊕$) = [add($\underline{b}$(p,$[m]_⊕$),$\underline{c}$(p,$[m]_⊕$))] ∀ p ∈ P;
∀ $[m]_⊕$ ∈ CATdas(E,X)

The elements of $BT_{SIG,E}(X)$ can be considered as linear combinations

$$\underline{b} = \bigotimes_{j=1}^{n} [\nu j](pj,[mj]_\oplus); \quad (pj,[mj]_\oplus) \in (P \times CATdas(E,X));$$

and $[\nu j]$ = $\underline{b}$(pj,$[mj]_⊕$) ∈ $T_{SIG,E}(X)_{nat}$;

Hence elements of $BT_{SIG,E}(X)$ can be considered as multisets over (P x CATdas(E,X)).

3.1 Definition (CATNet semantic structure)

Let P be the set of places of a given CATNet and CATdas(E,X) its data structure. The **CATNet semantic structure**, denoted CATses(E,X), is the structure of equivalence classes of multisets of $BT_{SIG,E}(X)$ modulo the ACI axioms of ⊗.

Notation:

$[x]_⊗$ denotes the equivalence class of $\underline{x}$, w.r.t. the ACI axioms for ⊗

$|[x]_⊕|$ denotes that $[x]_⊕$ has to be interpreted modulo E ∪ $ACI_⊕$

$|[x]_⊗|$ denotes that $[x]_⊗$ has to be interpreted modulo E ∪ $ACI_⊕$ ∪$ACI_⊗$

3.2 Definition (CATNet state)

Let P = {p1,...,ps} be the set of places of a given CATNet and CATses(E,X) its semantic structure. A CATNet state is an element of CATses(E,Ø) of the form

$$\underline{s} = |[\bigotimes_{j=1}^{s} [\nu j](pj,[mj]_\oplus)]_\otimes|$$

$\underline{s}$ may be written in the form $| [\bigotimes_{j=1}^{s} (pj, [\nu j][mj] \oplus)]\otimes |$

which may also be written as $|[\bigotimes_{j=1}^{s} (pj,[nj]\oplus)]\otimes |$

or also as $|[\bigotimes_{j=1}^{s} (pj,M(pj)] \otimes |$

3.3 Definition (CATNet rewrite theory)

Let T be the set of transitions of a given CATNet, CATdas(E,X) its data structure, and CATses(E,X) its semantic structure. A **CATNet rewrite theory** is a set of triples $R \subset T \times (CATses(E,X))^2 \times CATdas(E,X)_{bool}$. The elements of R are called rewrite rules. A rewrite rule, in its general form, is a labelled *sequent*

$$(t, (|[\bigotimes_{k=1}^{x}(p_{\alpha k}, [l_k]\oplus)]\otimes|, |[\bigotimes_{k=1}^{y}(p'_{\beta k}, [l'_k]\oplus)]\otimes|),boolexp)$$

$l_k \in CATdas(E,X)_{s(p\alpha k)}$, $l'_k \in CATdas(E,X)_{s(p'\beta k)}$
$t \in T$ boolexp is a boolean expression

$x \leq |P|; y \leq |P|; p_{\alpha k} \in P^t_{inp}$; $p'_{\beta k} \in P^t_{inp} \cup P^t_{out}$, where $P^t_{inp} = \{p \in P | (p,t) \in dom(IC)\}$ and $P^t_{out} = \{p \in P/ CT(p,t) \neq \emptyset_M\}$.
A rewrite rule will be denoted by

$$t : |[\bigotimes_{k=1}^{x}(p_{\alpha k}, [l_k]\oplus)]\otimes| \dashrightarrow |[\bigotimes_{k=1}^{y}(p'_{\beta k}, [l'_k]\oplus)]\otimes \qquad \textbf{if } boolexp,$$

Given a rewrite theory R, we say that R entails a sequent $\underline{s} \dashrightarrow \underline{s}'$, where $(\underline{s}, \underline{s}') \in (CATses(E,\emptyset))^2$ is a pair of states, **iff** $\underline{s} \dashrightarrow \underline{s}'$ can be obtained by finite (and concurrent) applications of the following rules of deduction.

(1) Reflexivity

$$\forall\ |[b]_\otimes| \quad \frac{}{|[b]_\otimes| \dashrightarrow |[b]_\otimes|}$$

(2) Congruence

$$\frac{\forall\ |[b1]_\otimes|,\ |[b'1]_\otimes|,\ |[b2]_\otimes|,\ |[b'2]_\otimes| \qquad |[b1]_\otimes| \dashrightarrow |[b'1]_\otimes| \qquad |[b2]_\otimes| \dashrightarrow |[b'2]_\otimes|}{|[b1]_\otimes \otimes [b2]_\otimes| \dashrightarrow |[b'1]_\otimes \otimes [b'2]_\otimes|}$$

(3) Replacement

For each rewrite rule $t{:}\,|[b(x1,\ldots,xn)]_\otimes| \dashrightarrow |[b'(x1,\ldots,xn)_\otimes|$ in R

$$\frac{[t1] = [t'1] \qquad [tn] = [t'n]}{|[b(\bar{t}/\bar{x})]_\otimes| \dashrightarrow |[b'(\bar{t}'/\bar{x})]_\otimes|}$$

where $\bar{t}/\bar{x}$ is an abbreviation for t1/x1,...,tn/xn, and $\bar{t}'/\bar{x}$ is an abbreviation for t'1/x1,...,t'n/xn.

$\bar{t}/\bar{x}$ and $\bar{t}'/\bar{x}$ denote *substitutions* of $\bar{t}$ for $\bar{x}$, respectively of $\bar{t}'$ for $\bar{x}$.

(4) Splitting and recombination

$\forall\ p \in P$, $\forall\ [n]_\oplus \in CATdas(E,X)_{s(p)}$, and $\forall\ [mi]_\oplus \in CATdas(E,X)_{s(p)}$; $i=1,\ldots,np$

$$\frac{|[n]_\oplus| = |[\bigoplus_{i=1}^{np} mi]_\oplus|}{|[(p,[n]_\oplus)]_\otimes| = |[\bigotimes_{i=1}^{np}(p,[mi]_\oplus)]_\otimes|}$$

$$\frac{\forall\ p \in P;\ \forall\ [n]_\oplus, [n']_\oplus \in CATdas(E,X)_{s(p)}}{|[(p,[n]_\oplus)]_\otimes| \otimes |[(p,[n']_\oplus)]_\otimes| = |[(p, [n]_\oplus \oplus [n']_\oplus)]_\otimes|}$$

(5) Identity

$$\forall\ p \in P \quad \frac{}{(p, \emptyset_M) = \emptyset_B}$$

Comments:

Informally speaking, the rewrite logic, i.e., the rewrite theory and the deduction rules, mean that the behavior of CATNets is given by a deduction-like system which, given a state $\underline{s}$, seeks for all possible basic changes (the axioms) and tries to compose them (the deduction rules) in such a way to reach the next state $\underline{s}'$ corresponding to the intended concurrent computation of the net. The rules of deduction indicate that concurrent rewriting is performed modulo the axioms E given by the user in his (her) specification, but also modulo the ACI axioms for $\oplus$, and for $\otimes$. This allows to free rewriting from syntactic constraints of a term representation (rewriting modulo E) and to deal with the concurrent behavior of the CATNets (rewriting modulo ACI).

The replacement rule is used when the context of a transition is not empty. In this case the rewrite rule(s) associated with the transition acts as a procedure where the variables play the role of formal parameters and the replacement the role of parameter instantiation or passing.

The deduction rules (4) allow us, by *judiciously* splitting and recombining different multisets of E-equivalence classes of terms to detect CATNet computations exhibiting a maximum of parallelism.

4 Rewrite Rules

The objective of this section is to present and motivate our approach of writing the rewrite rules associated to a concrete CATNet. As stated before this approach has to allow for detecting the maximum of true concurrency exhibited by the CATNet behavior. For lack of space we will consider, without loss of generality, the case when the Transition Conditions are always true, and all the capacities are infinite.

A transition effect is represented by a rewrite rule, the general form of which is given by definition 3.3. The *enabling aspect* of the transition may be represented either within the boolexp part of the rewrite rule or within the left-hand side of this rule. We will rather adopt the second way, since it seems to solve our problem in a uniform way without requiring conditional rules. The *firing aspect* of the transition will be represented by a proof allowing us to deduce a CATNet state from a previous one, by using our rewrite rule as an axiom and anyone of the deduction rules stated in section 3. A concurrent firing is thus represented by *concurrent proofs*. These proofs have to be composed in such a way to capture *correctly* the intended CATNet behavior. In the remaining part of this section we will explain in an *incremental* way our approach of writing the axioms. In order to enhance the readability, we will start by treating the simplest case, i.e., a net consisting of one transition, one input place, one output place, and with arcs inscribed by closed multisets. Our investigations lead us to consider three different kinds of situations depending on the relation between IC(p,t) and DT(p,t).

case1 $|[IC(p,t)]_{\oplus}| = |[DT(p,t)]_{\oplus}|$

This situation corresponds to the case of usual Petri nets, in which a firing consists in IC(p,t) being transformed in CT(p,t). Thus the form of the axiom is a rewrite rule capturing just this kind of transformation. This rule corresponds to a particular instantiation of the general formulae given in definition 3.3 with just one input place p_α and one output place p'_β:

$$t: |[(p_\alpha, IC(p_\alpha, t))]_{\otimes}| \dashrightarrow |[(p'_\beta, CT(p'_\beta, t))]_{\otimes}|$$

case2 $|[IC(p,t)]_{\oplus}| \cap |[DT(p,t)]_{\oplus}| = \emptyset_M$

This situation corresponds to the case, in which the firing corresponds to (DT(p,t) ∩ M(p)) being transformed in CT(p,t). However this transformation requires the verification of the Input Condition, i.e., the inclusion of IC(p,t) in the current CATNet state. We suggest for this situation to use a rule transforming IC(p,t) into itself. The axiom is then a rule consisting from the composition of the two previous transformations. The instantiation of the general formulae in this case takes the following form.

$$t: |[(p_\alpha, IC(p_\alpha, t))]_{\otimes} \otimes [(p_\alpha, DT(p_\alpha, t) \cap M(p_\alpha))]_{\otimes}| \dashrightarrow |[(p_\alpha, IC(p_\alpha, t))]_{\otimes} \otimes [(p'_\beta, CT(p'_\beta, t))]_{\otimes}|$$

Case3 $|[IC(p,t)]_{\oplus}| \cap |[DT(p,t)]_{\oplus}| \neq \emptyset_M$

This situation is similar to the previous one; however the proposed rule may be seen as an incorrect interpretation of the intented CATNet behavior because of the redundancy due to the overlapping between IC(p,t) and DT(p,t). Moreover this rule may mask some of the potential occurrences of true concurrency.

This case may however be solved in an elegant way by remarking that it could be brought to the two already treated cases. This is achieved by replacing the transition falling in this case by two transitions which, when fired concurrently, give the same global effect as our transition. This replacement is illustrated by Fig. 2.

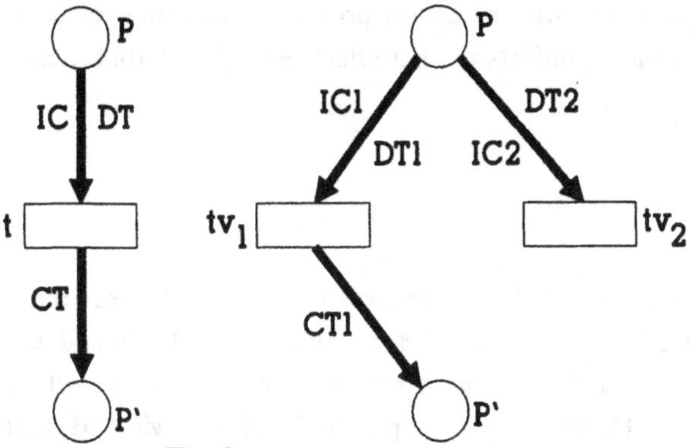

Fig. 2. Transition Decomposition

$$tv_2:\ IC2 = |[IC(p,t) - (M(p) \cap DT(p,t))]_{\oplus}|$$

$$DT2 = |[(M(p) \cap DT(p,t)) - IC(p,t)]_{\oplus}|$$

$$tv_1:\ IC1 = DT1 = |[IC(p,t) \cap DT(p,t)]_{\oplus}|$$

$$CT1 = |[CT(p',t)]_{\oplus}|$$

The transition tv_1 corresponds to case1 while the transition tv_2 corresponds to case2.

The form of an axiom corresponding to a transition with one input place and more than one output place is obtained from that of the previous ones by replacing in the right-hand side of the axiom the element $[(p'_\beta,CT(p'_\beta,t))]_{\otimes}$ by the following one:

$$[\bigotimes_{k=1}^{y}(p'_{\beta k},CT(p'_{\beta k},t))]_{\otimes} \quad \text{with} \quad p'_{\beta k} \in P^t_{out} \text{ and } y = |P^t_{out}|;$$

We let call this kind of transition a *basic* one. Then the situation where a transition has more than one input place may be considered as a composition-like of different basic ones.

Finally when the context X(t) of a transition is not empty, a variable occurring in more than one arc inscription, w.r.t. this transition, has to be instantiated in a consistent way in the sense that this variable has to be assigned the same value. It is worthwhile to mention that the choice of the appropriate rule in this case is strongly depending on this value.

We hope that it is clear from our explanation how the presented approach of writing the axioms together with the splitting and recombination deduction rules allow for executions of CATNets with a maximum of true concurrency; and how it allows to deal in a coherent way with situations presenting structural conflicts, i.e. to allow executions when these conflicts are not effective and to forbid them in the opposite case.

5 Examples

For lack of space we will limit ourselves to two simple examples. The first one describes a *wrong behavior* of the *ticket machine* [12], and is intended just to illustrate the use of CATNets and their interpretation in terms of the rewrite logic defined in sections 4 and 5. However, from a practical point of view, describing abnormal behaviors may be advantageously exploited for diagnosis purposes. The second example describes the behavior of an environment offering multiple services in a fault tolerant way by setting a redundancy mechanism. It is intended to illustrate the expressiveness of CATNets w.r.t. situations presenting a maximum of true concurrency.

5.1 Example (Ticket machine)

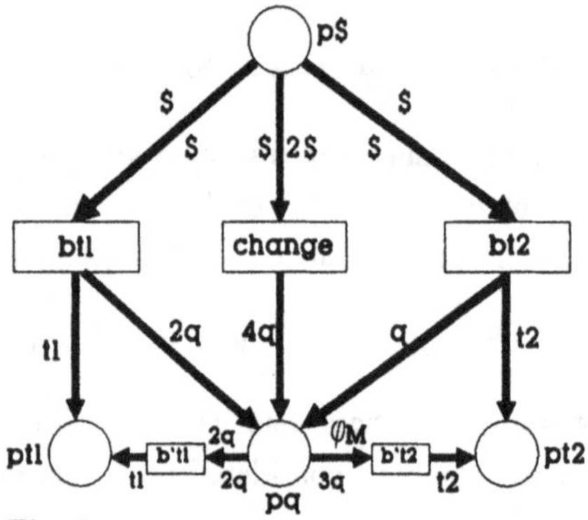

Fig. 3. Ticket Machine With Wrong Behavior

The CATNet given in Fig. 3. represents a machine to buy subway tickets. With a dollar we can buy a ticket t1 by pushing the button bt1 and get two quarters back. If we push bt2 instead, we get a longer distance ticket t2 and one quarter back. Similar buttons allow purchasing the tickets with quarters. Finally, with one dollar we can get four quarters by pushing *change*. However, in this last case, we can observe a wrong behavior in the sense that the machine takes two dollars (i.e. one dollar more than expected) for four quarters. Moreover when pushing b't2, we can observe that we get a ticket t2 and our three quarters back (i.e. the ticket is issued for nothing).

Rewrite rules

bt1: $(p_\$, \$) \dashrightarrow (p_{t1} , t1) \otimes (p_q , 2q)$

bt2: $(p_\$, \$) \dashrightarrow (p_{t2} , t2) \otimes (p_q , q)$

b't1: $(p_q , 2q) \dashrightarrow (p_{t1} , t1)$

b't2: $(p_q , 3q) \dashrightarrow (p_{t2} , t2) \otimes (p_q , 3q)$

change: $(p_\$, \$) \otimes (p_\$, \$) \dashrightarrow (p_q , 4q)$

Suppose, for example, that we begin in a state with two dollars and three quarters. Then, by pushing the buttons change and b't2 concurrently we end up with one ticket t2 and seven quarters. This result may be obtained by deductions in our logic. These deductions are omitted because of their triviality.

5.2 Example (fault tolerant multiserver)

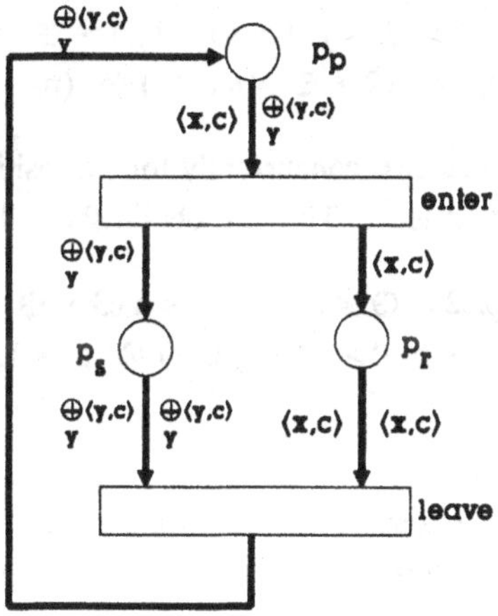

Fig. 4. A Simplified Model of a Fault Tolerant System

The CATNet represented in Fig. 4. modelizes the behavior of an environment where a given service may be offered by a class of *identical* servers (in p_p). Taking a class of servers rather than one has to allow for augmenting the degree of availability of this service in crash situations. A concurrent firing of the transition *enter* corresponds to a satisfaction of concurrent requests to different classes of servers. When a server is selected (deposited in p_r), all the servers of the same class are no longer available (deposited in p_s) A concurrent firing of *leave* corresponds to ending a set of concurrent services. This means that the corresponding servers are available again.

We omit to consider the transition *crash* (expressing the simultaneous loss of concurrent servers), together with the transition *repair* (expressing the repair of crashed servers), because of their irrelevance to our purpose.

Notations:

$\langle x,c \rangle$ denotes the server x of the class c

$\bigoplus_{y} \langle y,c \rangle$ denotes the multiset of the servers of the class c

p_p denotes the place with free-servers

p_r denotes the place with working-servers

p_s denotes the place with disabled-servers

A possible scenario:

Suppose, for example, that we begin in the following state:

$\underline{s} = |[(p_p, \langle h,c0 \rangle \oplus \langle i,c1 \rangle \oplus \langle j,c1 \rangle \oplus \langle k,c1 \rangle \oplus \langle l,c0 \rangle) \otimes (p_s, \langle o,c2 \rangle \oplus \langle p,c2 \rangle \oplus \langle m,c3 \rangle \oplus \langle q,c2 \rangle \oplus \langle n,c3 \rangle) \otimes (p_r, \langle q,c2 \rangle \oplus \langle n,c3 \rangle)]_{\otimes}|$

From this initial state we can fire concurrently four transitions: twice the transition enter and twice the transition leave. Thus we obtain the following final state.

$\underline{s}' = |[(p_p, \langle o,c2 \rangle \oplus \langle p,c2 \rangle \oplus \langle q,c2 \rangle \oplus \langle n,c3 \rangle \oplus \langle m,c3 \rangle) \otimes (p_s, \langle i,c1 \rangle \oplus \langle j,c1 \rangle \oplus \langle k,c1 \rangle \oplus \langle h,c0 \rangle \oplus \langle l,c0 \rangle) \otimes (p_r, \langle h,c0 \rangle \oplus \langle i,c1 \rangle)]_{\otimes}|$

The axioms :

The axiom corresponding to enter is given according to case3 : $IC(p_p, enter) \cap DT(p_p, enter) = \langle x,c \rangle \neq \emptyset_M$; Thus this transition will be replaced by two transitions called enter1 and enter2.

enter1: $|[(p_p, \langle x,c \rangle)]_{\otimes}| \dashrightarrow |[(p_s, \bigoplus_{y} \langle y,c \rangle) \otimes (p_r, \langle x,c \rangle)]_{\otimes}|$

enter2: $|[(p_p, \emptyset_M) \otimes (p_p, \bigoplus_{y \neq x} \langle y,c \rangle)]_{\otimes}| \dashrightarrow |[(p_p, \emptyset_M)]_{\otimes}|$

The axiom corresponding to leave is given according to case1.

leave: $|[(p_s, \bigoplus_{y} \langle y,c \rangle) \otimes (p_r, \langle x,c \rangle)]_{\otimes}| \dashrightarrow |[(p_p, \bigoplus_{y} \langle y,c \rangle)]_{\otimes}|$

6 Semantic Issues

According to [12], the model of a rewrite logic is a category, since it seems to capture nicely the intuitive idea of a "rewrite system". In the particular case of CATNets the concept of category seems to capture nicely the intuitive idea of the concurrent *token game* visualizing the dynamics of the CATNets. In other terms the model of our logic is a category whose objects are ($E \cup ACI_{\oplus} \cup ACI_{\otimes}$)-equivalence classes of states and whose morphisms are concurrent proofs.

7 Conclusion

In this paper we set a formal definition for the concept of CATNets and gave it an interpretation in terms of rewrite logic. Thanks to this interpretation it becomes possible to study the behavior of CATNets by formal methods. Moreover the proposed logic allows us to *execute* CATNets with a maximum of true concurrency. This result is achieved thanks to the "splitting and recombination" deduction rule but mainly to the strategy adopted for writing the axioms. It is worthwhile to mention that the difference, at this level, between our work and the work by [12] is that the *equivalent* of such a strategy is lacking in his work, perhaps because of his considering only a simple case of Petri net. On another hand our work may be considered as generalizing the work in [8], since we are using abstract data types *with axioms*, while this is not the case in [8]. Moreover it seems that the interpretation of CATNets into rewrite logic may lead to handle in an easy way the concept of *generalized inhibitor arc* [5], and the concept of global variables [15]. A work on this subject is nearing completion.

For lack of space we limited ourselves to two simple examples, dealing just with nonconditional rewrite rules. The practical significance of the CATNet concept will be shown in future works thru the specification of more concrete problems such us the router problem [3], or similar problems mainly from the field of communication software [5], hardware diagnosis, and software testing. These works are actually under preparation. In the meantime we are actualizing our graphical editor-simulator for ATNets [9], in order to make it *usable* for CATNets.

It is worthwhile to mention that the current work was primarily devoted to the descriptive aspects of the proposed formalism rather than to its proof ones (i.e. theorems and automatic analysis methods). Let us however remark that at the present time these problems are partially investigated.

Acknowledgements

This work is supported by a grant from the Algerian Ministry of Higher Education under research-contract number B2501/01/02/91. The authors are grateful to H. Reichel, E. Astesiano, G. Reggio and two anonymous referees for many suggestions on the subject of this paper.

References

1. E. Astesiano, G. Reggio: A structural approach to the formal modelization and specification of concurrent systems. Dipartimento di Matematica, Universita di Genova 1990
2. M. Bettaz: An Association of Algebraic Term Nets and Abstract Data Types for Specifying Real Communication Protocols. In: H. Ehrig, K.P. Jantke, F. Orejas, H. Reichel (eds.): Recent Trends in Data Type Specification. Lecture Notes in Computer Science 534. Springer-Verlag 1991, pp. 11-30
3. M. Bettaz: On the Expressiveness of Algebraic Term Nets. 6th International Workshop on Software Specification and Design. Concurrency and Distribution Track. Como 10/1991
4. M. Bettaz, A. Choutri: Algebraic Term Nets, a Formalism for Specifying Communication Software in the OSI Framework. In: CMI Rattray, RG Clark (eds.): The Unified Computation Laboratory. Oxford University Press 1992 , pp. 293-305
5. M. Bettaz, M. Maouche, M. Soualmi, M. Boukebeche: Using ECATNets for Specifying Communication Software in the OSI Framework. ICCI Conference 5/92, Torento, IEEE
6. J. Billington et al.: PROTEAN, A High-Level Petri Net Tool for the Specification and Verification of Communication Protocols. IEEE Transactions on Software Engineering. Vol.14, 3, 3/1988
7. J. Billington: Extensions to Coloured Petri Nets. In Proceedings of the Third International Workshop on Petri Nets and Performance Models. Kyoto 12/1989
8. J. Billington: Many-Sorted High-Level Nets. In Proceedings of the Third International Workshop on Petri Nets and Performance Models. Kyoto 12/1989
9. O. Bounouioua, M. Bettaz: A Graphical Editor-Simulator for Algebraic Term Nets. In Proceedings of the Second Maghrebin Conference on SE and AI. Tunis 4/1992

10. H. Ehrig, B. Mahr: Fundamentals of Algebraic Specifications 1. Springer EATCS Monographs on Theoretical Computer Science, 1985

11. H. Ehrig, M. Grose-Rhode, A. Heise: Specification Techniques for Concurrent and Distributed Systems. In Proceedings of the Second Maghrebin Conference on SE and AI. Tunis 4/1992

12. J. Meseguer: A Logical Theory of Concurrent Objects. In Proceedings ECOOP/OOPSLA '90. Ottawa 10/1990, ACM.

13. W. Reizig: Petri Nets and Algebraic Specifications. TCS 80, 1-34, 1991

14. J. Vautherin: Parallel System Specification with Colored Petri Nets and Algebraic Abstract Data Types. 7th European Workshop on Application and Theory of Petri Nets. Oxford 1986

15. M. Wilbur-Ham: Numerical Petri Nets a Guide, version 2. Telecom Australia, Research Laboratory 1987

Bounded Implementation of Algebraic Specifications

Michael Breu

European Methodology and Systems Center, SNI AG*

AP 432, Otto-Hahn-Ring 6, D-8000 München 83

Email: Michael.Breu@sniap.mchp.sni.de

Abstract

A specification and implementation method is proposed which tackles the problem of transition from infinite abstract data types to the finite structures of a physical machine. This is achieved by specifying the idealized properties of a data type and its bounds separately. An implementation has to realize the structure of the data type inside the specified bounds only.

1. Introduction

Algebraic specifications are often ascribed attributes like abstractness, clarity, precision, problem orientation and implementation' independence. Indeed a variety of algebraic specification techniques have been developed to describe module interfaces abstractly, i.e. hiding internal structures, like ACT-TWO [Ehrig, Mahr 90], Obscure [Loeckx 90], PLUSS [Bidoit et al. 89]. Another advantage of algebraic specifications is their executability with term rewriting tools, allowing rapid prototyping in an early stage [Hußmann 85/87].

All these advantages diminish or even disappear, if one takes the finite nature of physical machines with overflow conditions into account and tries to describe these finite structures with algebraic specifications. The first discovery is that in general conditional equations are necessary to describe bounded structures. This would be no big problem, because the theory of conditional equations is already well established. But specifications turn out to become rather complex and also clumsy. They suffer from decreasing readability, abstractness and implementation independence. Term rewriting becomes at least less efficient.

---

* This work is based on my PhD-thesis, carried out at the Universität Passau and the Technische Universität München

Specification techniques like partial abstract types ([Broy, Wirsing 82]) or order-sortedness ([Smolka et al. 87]) allow the modelling of partial functions but are not suited for modelling boundedness. Other approaches to handle error situations and exceptions like overflow conditions are error algebras [Goguen 77], exception algebras [Bernot et al. 86] and their refinement to label algebras [Le Gall, Bernot 91]. They are designed to give a precise abstract semantics of bounded abstract machines. But they are not suited to give a smooth (i.e. easy to write and easy to understand) specification of bounded abstract data types that is implementation independent.

Other approaches try to solve the problem of boundedness by adapting the implementation relation. A *robust implementation*, as proposed in [Nipkow 87] and [Breu 90], introduces additional error handling. The converse, called *partial implementation*, was investigated by [Kamin, Archer 84] and refined by [Nipkow 87] and [Schoett 87]. Partial implementations allow the transition from unbounded to bounded data structures. But in the extreme case such an implementation relation also allows one to implement any data type by the empty data type that does not contain any useful data elements. Thus the view of an abstract interface specification as a contract between the user of an implementation and the designer of that implementation (cf. [Bauer 81]) is rendered void.

This paper proposes a specification and implementation method that preserves the clarity, abstractness and implementation independence also for specification with bounds and the view of fulfilling a contract by the development of an implementation. The key idea is the separation of a specification into an idealistic part that specifies the general behaviour of the data structure and an additional part that describes the bounds of the developed implementation in terms of the idealistic specification.

Such a separation has several advantages. In general it is easier to write a specification without including any bounds. This specification already allows first investigations of its properties with verification or rapid prototyping tools. The specification of bounds may be added in a separate step. Since the bounds often only become clear when the design of the implementation is finished, the abstract specification of bounds may be added later. Also there may be several implementations for the same idealistic specification with different bounds.

The paper is organized as follows. This section finishes with the introduction of basic notations of terms, formulae and algebras. The next section gives a formalization of specifications and discusses the methodological impact of separating idealistic specification and specification of bounds. Section 3 defines bounded implementations illustrated by a small example. This is followed by a short study of properties preserved under bounded implementations.

Basic Definitions

To make this paper self contained, we include here basic notations for algebraic specifications. They are based on the approach of many sorted, partial, strict algebras in [Broy, Wirsing 82], extended by predicates. We assume that every carrier set of an algebra contains the special element $\perp$, standing for the undefined element. In formulas quantified variables range only over defined elements. Keeping these essentials in mind, the experienced reader can skip the following definition.

Definition

A *signature* Σ is a triple (S, F, P) of a set of sort identifiers S, a set of function identifiers F and a set of predicate identifiers P. Function and and predicate identifiers are associated with their arities in S^+ or S^* resp., denoted by $f: s_1, \ldots, s_n \to s \in F$ and $p: s_1, \ldots, s_n \in P$. Let $\Sigma = (S, F, P)$ and $\Sigma' = (S', F', P')$ be two signatures. A *signature morphism* $\alpha: \Sigma \to \Sigma'$ is a triple $(\alpha_S: S \to S', \alpha_F: F \to F', \alpha_P: P \to P')$ of mappings that fulfil the following consistency condition:

$$\text{for all } f: s_1,\ldots,s_n \to s \in F\text{: } \alpha_F(f)\text{: } \alpha_S(s_1),\ldots,\alpha_S(s_n) \to \alpha_S(s) \in F'$$
$$\text{and for all } p: s_1,\ldots,s_n \in P\text{ : } \alpha_P(p)\text{: } \alpha_S(s_1),\ldots,\alpha_S(s_n) \in P'.$$

If $S \subseteq S'$, $F \subseteq F'$, $P \subseteq P'$ then Σ is a *subsignature* of Σ', denoted by $\Sigma \subseteq \Sigma'$.

An S-indexed set $X = (X_s)_{s \in S}$ of variable identifiers is called a *variable set*.

The S-indexed set $W(\Sigma, X) = (W_s(\Sigma, X))_{s \in S}$ of *terms* over the signature $\Sigma = (S, F, P)$ and the variable set X is defined as the smallest set fulfilling the following condition:

$X_s \subseteq W_s(\Sigma, X)$, $\perp \in W_s(\Sigma, X)$ for all $s \in S$,

and if $f: s_1,\ldots,s_n \to s \in F$, $t_i \in W_{s_i}(\Sigma, X)$ for $i = 1,\ldots,n$, then also $f(t_1,\ldots,t_n) \in W_s(\Sigma, X)$.

$W(\Sigma, \emptyset)$ is abbreviated by $W(\Sigma)$. Its elements are called *ground terms*. The set $\mathfrak{F}(\Sigma, X)$ of all *Σ-formulas* is the smallest set fulfilling the following condition:

if $p: s_1, \ldots, s_n \in P$, $t_i \in W_{s_i}(\Sigma, X)$ for $i = 1,\ldots,n$, then $p\ t_1 \ldots t_n \in \mathfrak{F}(\Sigma, X)$,

if $t, t' \in W_s(\Sigma, X)$ then $t \equiv t' \in \mathfrak{F}(\Sigma, X)$ and $\mathbf{D}\ t \in \mathfrak{F}(\Sigma, X)$ for all $s \in S$.

if $\Phi, \Phi' \in \mathfrak{F}(\Sigma, X)$ and $x \in X_s$, then also $(\Phi \wedge \Phi')$, $(\Phi \vee \Phi')$, $(\Phi \Rightarrow \Phi')$, $(\Phi \Leftrightarrow \Phi')$, $(\neg\Phi)$, ***true***, ***false***, (***for all*** x: s Φ), (***exist*** x: s Φ) $\in \mathfrak{F}(\Sigma, X)$.

Let $\Sigma = (S, F, P)$ be a signature. A *Σ-algebra* is a triple $((s^{\perp A})_{s \in S}, (f^A)_{f \in F}, (p^A)_{p \in P})$, of a family of carrier sets $s^{\perp A}$ for all $s \in S$, a family of partial (but via the element $\perp$ totalized) functions $f^A: s_1^{\perp A} \times \ldots \times s_n^{\perp A} \to s^{\perp A}$ for every $f: s_1,\ldots,s_n \to s \in F$ and a family of predicates $p^A \subseteq s_1^{\perp A} \times \ldots \times s_n^{\perp A}$ for every $p: s_1, \ldots, s_n \in P$. Every carrier set $s^{\perp A}$ contains the undefined element $\perp$. All f^A are strict, i.e. $f^A(a_1, \ldots, a_n) = \perp$ if $a_i = \perp$ for any $i \in \{1, \ldots, n\}$. $s^{\perp A} \setminus \{\perp\}$ is denoted by s^A.

Let X be a variable set. A *valuation* $\eta: X \to A$ is an S-indexed family of mappings $\eta_s: X_s \to s^{\perp A}$. A valuation is extended to a *term interpretation* $(\eta^*: W_s(\Sigma, X) \to s^{\perp A})_{s \in S}$ as usual and to a *formula interpretation* $\eta^*: \mathfrak{F}(\Sigma, X) \to \{tt, ff\}$ in the following way:

$\eta^*(p\ t_1 \ldots t_n)$, $\eta^*(\neg\Phi)$, $\eta^*(\Phi \wedge \Phi')$, …, $\eta^*(\mathit{true})$, $\eta^*(\mathit{false})$ are defined as usual,

$\eta^*(t \equiv t') = \text{tt}$ iff $\eta^*(t) = \eta^*(t')$, $\eta^*(\mathbf{D}t) = \text{tt}$ iff $\eta^*(t) \neq \perp$,

$\eta^*($***for all*** $x{:}s\ \Phi) = tt$, iff $\eta'^*(\Phi) = tt$ for all valuations η' with $\eta'(x) \neq \perp$ which coincide with η on $X \setminus \{x\}$, otherwise $\eta^*($***for all*** $x{:}s\ \Phi) = ff$.

$\eta^*(\textbf{\textit{exist}}\ x{:}s\ \Phi) = tt$, iff $\eta'^*(\Phi) = tt$ for some valuation η' with $\eta'(x)\neq\perp$ which coincides with η on $X\setminus\{x\}$, otherwise $\eta^*(\textbf{\textit{exist}}\ x{:}s\ \Phi) = ff$.

Validity of a formula Φ under a valuation η, i.e. $\eta^*(\Phi)=tt$, is denoted by $A \models_\eta \Phi$, validity under all valuations by $A \models \Phi$, validity of a set E of formulas by $A \models E$ and validity in a class M of Σ-algebras by $M \models E$.

Let A be a Σ-algebra. A Σ-algebra B is a *subalgebra* of A, iff $s^{\perp B} \subseteq s^{\perp A}$ for all $s \in S$ and the functions and predicates of B coincide with those of A restricted to the carrier sets of B.

Let $\Sigma = (S, F, P)$ and $\Sigma' = (S', F', P')$ be two signatures, $\alpha: \Sigma \to \Sigma'$ a signature morphism and A a Σ'-algebra. The Σ-algebra B is the *α-reduct* of A (denoted by $A|_\alpha$), iff $s^{\perp B}=\alpha(s)^{\perp A}$ for all $s \in S$, $f^B=\alpha(f)^A$ for all $f \in F$, $p^B = \alpha(p)^A$ for all $p \in P$. If α is an injection, i.e. especially $\Sigma \subseteq \Sigma'$, then $A|_\Sigma$ stands for $A|_\alpha$.

Let $\Sigma \subseteq \Sigma'$ and A be a Σ'-algebra. Then A is *term generated by* Σ iff there exists no proper subalgebra of $A|_\Sigma$.

□

2. Idealistic specifications and the specification of bounds

As motivated in the introduction a specification is separated into the design of the idealistic properties of a data type and into the documentation of the restrictions of its implementation. We employ the technique of loose specifications to get a uniform specification framework for both. Idealistic specifications are simply specifications with loosely specified bounds. The bounds are refined in an additional step.

We enlarge the specification method of partial abstract types by predicates that describe bounds. There are two alternatives to specify bounds: a representation oriented approach or a computation oriented approach.

At first glance it seems reasonable to introduce predicates on sorts which define for each element, whether it is represented in the implementation or not. In this case an implementation must preserve all function applications yielding a result which is representable. The observability concept of Hennicker ([Hennicker 88]) could be employed for such a solution.

But a computation may fail, although its result is representable. A simple example is the definition of the binomial coefficient

$$\binom{n}{k} =_{\text{def}} \frac{n!}{(n-k)!\,k!} \quad \text{for } n, k \in \mathbb{N}, k \leq n, \text{ (where .! denotes the factorial function).}$$

If the definition above is used as an algorithm working on machine numbers, bounded for example to the interval $[-2^{15}, 2^{15}-1]$, an overflow condition for the computation of $\binom{10}{2} = 45$ occurs, because $10! > 2^{15}$.

While binomial coefficients could be computed by a more efficient algorithm, it is in general not evident how to avoid e.g. stack overflow conditions on a finite stack, although the result of a computation may be representable.

The second alternative addresses this effect by introducing for each function a predicate on the domain of this function. These predicates identify those arguments for which the corresponding function application must return correct results. If we analyse for example the computational structure of the expression $\frac{n!}{(n-k)!\,k!}$, we see that the overflow is caused by the evaluation of $n!$ (assuming $0 \le k \le n$). The arguments for which the computation of the function $\binom{\cdot}{\cdot}: \mathbb{N} \times \mathbb{N} \to \mathbb{N}$ on machine numbers in the interval $[-2^{15}, 2^{15}-1]$ is successful may be described by the set $\{(n, k) \in \mathbb{N} \times \mathbb{N};\ k \le n \le 2^{15}-1 \wedge n! \le 2^{15}-1\}$.

This is formalized in the following definition. It also includes the notion of auxiliary functions that may be introduced to compute the size or any other complexity measure of an object. The set of function identifiers is therefore divided into the subset F to denote functions to be implemented and a subset AF of identifiers for auxiliary functions that do not contribute to term generation and need not be implemented.

Definition

A *bound signature* is a signature $(S, F \cup AF, P)$, where $F \cap AF = \emptyset$ and the set of predicates P contains exactly the identifiers

$correct\_f: s_1, \ldots, s_n$ for each $f: s_1, \ldots, s_n \to s \in F$.

A bound signature is denoted by $\langle S, F, AF \rangle$.

A *specification* SP is a pair (Σ, E) of a bound signature Σ and a set of closed Σ-formulas E.

A Σ-algebra A is a *model* of (Σ, E) if $A \models E$ and A is term generated wrt. $\langle S, F, \emptyset \rangle$, where $\Sigma = \langle S, F, AF \rangle$.

The class of models of a specification SP is denoted by *Mod*(SP).

□

We illustrate this definition by the following simple example. More challenging examples, like a compiler from a simple applicative language with conditionals to a stack machine with a variety of bounds, can be found in [Breu 91]. In the sequel we use some syntactic sugaring similarly to the RAP language ([Hußmann 85/87]) that should for the most part be self explaining.

Example (idealistic specification of finite sets)

The following specification of finite sets is straight forward and may be found in several variants in the literature. It is based on the primitive specifications BOOL and NAT of booleans and natural numbers which are included in the appendix. The operators + and **enrich** are just abbreviations for the syntactic union of the signatures and axioms. Comments are included in curly brackets. In order to increase the readability of formulas, the special comment {display: ...} introduces an alternative mixfix notation for functions. The formula $b = \mathit{true}$, where b is a term of sort **Bool** is sometimes abbreviated by the term b itself.

```
type FINSET
  enrich NAT + BOOL
  sort Fset
  func eset:     () Fset,                     { display: ∅ }
       ins:      (Nat, Fset) Fset,
       is_elem:  (Nat, Fset) Bool,            { display: .∈. }
       card:     (Fset) Nat                   { display: |.| }
  axioms for all s: Fset, n, m: Nat
  n ∈ ∅ = false,
  m ∈ ins(n, s) = or(equal_Nat(n, m), m ∈ s),
  ins(m, ins(n, s)) = ins(n, ins(m, s)),
  ins(n, ins(n, s)) = ins(n, s),
  |∅| = 0,
  (n ∈ s) ⇒ |ins(n, s)| = |s|,
  (n ∈ s) = false ⇒ |ins(n, s)| = |s| +1
endoftype
```

The declaration of a function *f* with **func** *f*: ..., automatically includes the declaration of the correctness predicate *correct_f* .... Nevertheless the above specification contains no information about the bounds of an implementation, i.e. the correctness predicates are totally loose. □

After having specified the idealistic properties of a data type there are two possible strategies to proceed. Following a top-down strategy, the idealistic specification would be enriched by a specification of bounds. The user of the implementation to be realized may pose certain bounds onto the idealistic specification that make it suitable for his application. But in general bounds are mainly influenced by the physical target machine. It is difficult not to require too wide bounds in advance that cannot be fulfilled (at least not efficiently) by a certain type of machine.

This is a reason to follow a bottom-up strategy. The bounds of the idealistic specification are fixed after finishing the bounded implementation. Such a strategy is typical if we want to impement a software library and want to document its bounds for its users after choosing a specific implementation.

Of course often a mixed strategy is advisable by sketching a suitable implementation first, fixing the bounds, and carrying out the details of the implementations afterwards.

Example (FINSET continued)

We will give the bounds for the specification FINSET first and present an implementation later. But it should not be concealed that we have already a certain implementation by sequences in mind. Therefore we choose a bound on the cardinality of sets. The specification FINSET is enriched by an auxiliary constant *maxcard*. Insertion of an element *n* into a set *s* works if *n* is already contained in *s*, or if the cardinality of *s* is smaller than *maxcard*. Again the specifications BOOLB and NATB of the bounds of BOOL and NAT, resp., can be found in the appendix.

```
type FINSETB
  enrich FINSET + NATB + BOOLB
auxfunc maxcard: () Nat

axioms for all s:Fset, n: Nat
  maxcard = 100,        { or any other reasonable constant }
  correct_eset,
  correct_ins n s ⇔ or(n ∈ s, |s| +1 ≤ maxcard),
  correct_is_elem n s,
  correct_card s
endoftype
```

An alternative implementation by finite bitarrays, resembling the representation of the PASCAL type `set` in many compilers, can be expressed by restricting to the subsets of the interval [0..*maxelem*]. This is expressed by the following specification.

```
type FINSETB2
  enrich FINSET + NATB + BOOLB
auxfunc maxelem: () Nat

axioms for all s:Fset, n: Nat
  maxelem = 63,        { compiler dependent ! }
  correct_eset,
  correct_ins n s ⇔ n ≤ maxelem,
  correct_is_elem n s,
  correct_card s
endoftype
```

Insertion is only correct if the element inserted is smaller than *maxelem*.

□

Remark: These specifications are still loose, because the correctness predicates are not fixed for undefined arguments (recall that the bounded variables *n* and *s* only range over defined elements). It is not very useful to specify that an implementation should guarantee the correct function application for undefined arguments. In order to embed the restrict-forget-identify implementation relation of [Ehrig et al. 82] and [Sannella, Wirsing 82] in this approach, we use the fact that for every model of the specification another model of the specification can be constructed in which all correctness predicates are false for undefined arguments. We will make this more precise in a remark at the end of section 3.

The separation of idealistic specifications and additional specifications of bounds is only a methodological view. Both have a uniform logical framework. An idealistic specification should not contain information about bounds. In contrast, the enrichment to the bounds specification is limited to the description of bounds. Especially it should not introduce any new non-auxiliary functions.

3. Bounded Implementations

In this section a correctness relation between an implementation and its specification is established. In order to distinguish between the different levels, we shall use the attribute *concrete* for the implementation level and the attribute *abstract* for the specification level, like e.g. concrete model standing for the implementing algebra and abstract model standing for the specified algebra. How is an implementation given? Since we want to make a gradual development over several levels, we assume that every level is described by a specification with bounds. If the bottom specification gives exactly the behaviour of a finite physically realizable machine, the correctness predicates of the models should be chosen as total, i.e. everything is finally correctly implemented. But often in an intermediate step idealistic unbounded data structures are involved that may be implemented with bounds in a later stage.

To relate the concrete and the abstract level a simulation concept is proposed which is based on classical homomorphisms. Simulation concepts, defined with the dual notion of congruences and quotients, are the implementation relations in [ADJ 78], [Ehrig et al. 82] and [Sannella, Wirsing 82]. They can be understood as refinements of the inspiring ideas of Hoare ([Hoare 72]). He introduced so-called abstraction functions that map concrete objects to the abstract objects they represent. Interestingly enough Hoare already addressed the problem of bounded implementations, which was forgotten (or ignored?) till it was taken up again by Kamin and Archer.

Here we use partial abstraction functions, since certain concrete objects may not represent any abstract object. The homomorphism property of the abstraction functions ensures that concrete functions simulate abstract ones. I.e. the application of a concrete function to concrete arguments must return a representation of the application of the abstract function to the represented arguments. For bounded implementations we restrict such a simulation to function application of correct arguments. This means that the commutativity in the following diagram is constrained by the correctness of the argument $\varphi(a)$.

$$correct\_f^A\,\varphi(a) \Rightarrow$$

$$
\begin{array}{ccc}
\varphi(a) & \xleftarrow{\;\varphi\;} & a \\
\downarrow{\scriptstyle f^A} & & \downarrow{\scriptstyle f^{AI}} \\
f^A(\varphi(a)) & \xleftarrow{\;\varphi\;} & f^{AI}(a) \\
= \varphi(f^{AI}(a)) & &
\end{array}
$$

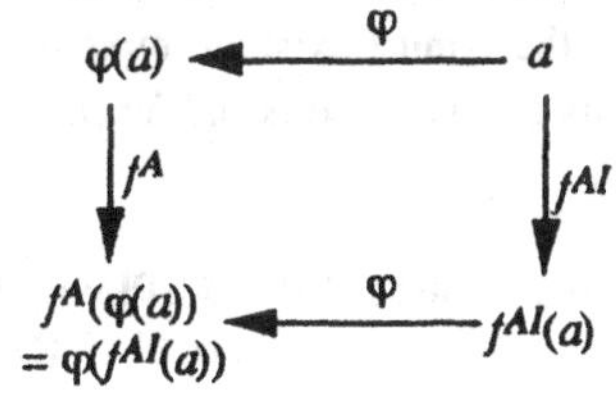

Thus we get the notion of a bounds preserving homomorphism.

Definition

Let $\Sigma = \langle S, F, \emptyset \rangle$ be a bound signature and A, AI two Σ-algebras.

A *bounds preserving homomorphism* $\varphi: AI \to A$ is a family of partial abstraction functions $(\varphi_s : s^{\perp AI} \to s^{\perp A})_{s \in S}$ such that for all $f: s_1, \ldots, s_n \to s \in F$ and all $a_1 \in s_1^{\perp AI}, \ldots, a_n \in s_n^{\perp AI}$

$$correct\_f^A\,\varphi_{s_1}(a_1)\ldots\varphi_{s_n}(a_n) \Rightarrow \varphi_s(f^{AI}(a_1,\ldots,a_n)) = f^A(\varphi_{s_1}(a_1),\ldots,\varphi_{s_n}(a_n)) \quad (1)$$

and $correct\_f^A\,\varphi_{s_1}(a_1)\ldots\varphi_{s_n}(a_n) \Rightarrow correct\_f^{AI}\,a_1 \ldots a_n.$ $\qquad (2)$

We say that AI is a *bounded implementation* of A via φ, denoted by $A \xrightarrow{\;\varphi\;}_B AI$.

$\square$

Remarks: Condition (1) states the conditional simulation property. Condition (2) guarantees that the bounds of an implementation are not smaller than the abstract ones, as illustrated in the following figure. This is necessary for the composition of successive implementation steps.

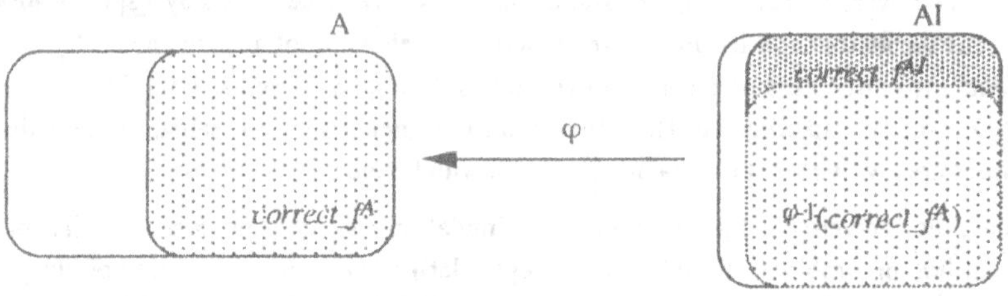

The definition of a bounds preserving homomorphism seems very close to the definition of a *partial* homomorphism in [Kamin, Archer 84], which can (slightly simplified and adapted to our notational framework) be defined by the two conditions

$$correct\_f^{AI}\ a_1 \ldots a_n \Rightarrow \varphi_s(f^{AI}(a_1,\ldots,a_n)) = f^A(\varphi_{s1}(a_1),\ldots,\varphi_{sn}(a_n)) \qquad (1')$$

and $$correct\_f^{AI}\ a_1 \ldots a_n \Rightarrow correct\_f^A\ \varphi_{s1}(a_1) \ldots \varphi_{sn}(a_n). \qquad (2')$$

Kamin and Archer intended to document the correctly implemented part of the abstract model in the implementation itself. Therefore these conditions (1') and (2') are quite the reverse of (1) and (2). This means that the bounds of the *implementation* decides about the validity of the simulation property. Both conditions are still fulfilled, if the correctness predicates of *A* are enlarged. In this respect the contract view is lost.

The definition above ignores auxiliary functions, because they need not to be implemented. The next definition extends the implementation relation to specifications. The implementation relation on algebras is combined with model class refinement. For every model *AI* of the concrete specification there must exist an implemented model of the abstract specification. Additionally, the facility to rename sorts and functions is included.

Definition

Let be given two specifications SP and SPI with bound signatures $\langle S, F, HF \rangle$ and $\langle SI, FI, HFI \rangle$ resp., and a signature morphism $\alpha: \langle S, F, \emptyset \rangle \rightarrow \langle SI, FI, HFI \rangle$ with

$$correct\_\alpha(f) = \alpha(correct\_f) \quad \text{for all } f \in F.$$

Then SPI is a *bounded implementation* of SP via α (denoted by SP $\overset{\alpha}{\leadsto}_B$ SPI) iff

for all $AI \in$ Mod(SPI)

there exists a model $A \in Mod$(SP) and

a bounds preserving homomorphism $\varphi: AI|_\alpha \rightarrow A|_{\langle S,F,\emptyset \rangle}$.

□

The following lemma shows that bounded implementations may be developed step by step. The composition of two implementation steps yields again a bounded implementation. To formulate this lemma we assume that .°. denotes the componentwise functional composition of morphisms. The proof is straight forward.

Lemma (Transitivity of bounded implementations)

Let A_1, A_2 and A_3 be $\langle S, F, \emptyset\rangle$-algebras and $\varphi_1: A_1 \to A_2$ and $\varphi_2: A_2 \to A_3$ bounds preserving homomorphisms. Then

$$A_2 \overset{\varphi_1}{\rightsquigarrow}_B A_1 \text{ and } A_3 \overset{\varphi_2}{\rightsquigarrow}_B A_2 \text{ implies } A_3 \overset{\varphi_1 \circ \varphi_2}{\rightsquigarrow}_B A_1.$$

Let SP_1, SP_2 and SP_3 be specifications and α_1 and α_2 signature morphisms such that

$$SP_2 \overset{\alpha_1}{\rightsquigarrow}_B SP_1 \text{ and } SP_3 \overset{\alpha_2}{\rightsquigarrow}_B SP_2 \text{. Then } SP_3 \overset{\alpha_1 \circ \alpha_2}{\rightsquigarrow}_B SP_1.$$

□

To demonstrate a bounded implementation we proceed with the FINSET example.

Example

We give an implementation based on the following type of sequences bounded to a maximal length of 100 elements. Again the specification is divided into an idealistic specification and its bounds which are chosen as total because we assume this finite data type can be implemented completely on a physical machine.

```
type BOUNDED_SEQ
  enrich NAT + BOOL
sort Seq
func eseq:        () Seq,
     app:         (Nat, Seq) Seq,
     rest:        (Seq) Seq,
     first, length: (Seq) Nat,
     isempty:     (Seq) Bool,
     maxlength:  () Nat
axioms for all s: Seq, n: Nat
  maxlength = 100,
  length(eseq) = 0,
  length(s)+1 ≤ maxlength ⇒ length(app(n, s)) = length(s)+1,
  not(length(s) +1 ≤ maxlength) ⇒ ¬D app(n, s),
  isempty(eseq),
  length(s) +1 ≤ maxlength ⇒ isempty(app(n, s)) = false,
  ¬D rest(eseq),
  length(s) +1 ≤ maxlength ⇒ rest(app(n, s)) = s,
  first(eseq) = 0,
  length(s) +1 ≤ maxlength ⇒ first(app(n, s)) = n
endoftype

type BOUNDED_SEQB
  enrich BOUNDED_SEQ + NATB + BOOLB
axioms for all s: Seq, n: Nat
  correct_eseq,
  correct_app s n,
  correct_rest s,
  correct_first s,
  correct_length s,
  correct_isempty s,
  correct_maxlength
endoftype
```

The following specification implements sets on bounded sequences by avoiding to append the same element twice.

```
type IMPL_FINSET
  enrich BOUNDED_SEQ
func ins:      (Nat, Seq) Seq,
     card:     (Seq) Nat,
     is_elem:  (Nat, Seq) Bool
axioms for all n, m: Nat, s: Seq
  is_elem(n, eseq) = false,
  is_elem(n, app(m, s)) = or(equal_Nat(n, m), is_elem(n, s)),

  is_elem(n, s) = true => ins(n, s) = s,
  is_elem(n, s) = false => ins(n, s) = app(n, s),

  card(eseq) = 0,
  is_elem(n, s) = true  => card(app(n, s)) = card(s),
  is_elem(n, s) = false => card(app(n, s)) = card(s) +1
endoftype
```

For this specification we are free to fix the bounds. But since we are still working on finite sequences, we can also assume total correctness predicates.

```
type IMPL_FINSETB
  enrich IMPL_FINSET + BOUNDED_SEQB
axioms for all s: Seq, n: Nat
  correct_ins n s,
  correct_is_elem n s,
  correct_card s
endoftype
```

The signature morphism α connecting FINSETB and IMPL_FINSETB is the identity except α(**FSet**) = **Seq**, α(*eset*) = *eseq*, α(*correct_eset*) = *correct_eseq*.

It can be shown that

$$\text{FINSETB} \overset{\alpha}{\rightsquigarrow}_{B} \text{IMPL\_FINSETB}$$

holds.

Proof sketch

For every model *AI* of IMPL_FINSETB we have to construct a model *A* of FINSETB. For the signature $\Sigma_{NATB+BOOLB}$ of NATB and BOOLB we can simply take the same reduct, i.e.

$$A|_{\Sigma_{NATB+BOOLB}} =_{def} AI|_{\Sigma_{NATB+BOOLB}},$$

For the carrier set $\mathbf{Fset}^A$ we take $\wp_{fin}(\mathbf{Nat}^{AI})$, i.e. the set of all finite subsets of $\mathbf{Nat}^{AI}$. The other functions and predicates in *A* are chosen as usual so that *A* is a model of FINSETB.

It remains to construct a bounds perserving homomorphism φ from *AI* to *A* (to be precise from and to the appropriate reducts of *A* and *AI*). For $\varphi_{\mathbf{Nat}}$ and $\varphi_{\mathbf{Bool}}$ we choose the identity. For $\varphi_{\mathbf{Fset}}$ we choose

$$\varphi_{\mathbf{Fset}}(eseq^A) =_{def} \emptyset; \quad \varphi_{\mathbf{Fset}}(\perp) =_{def} \perp$$

$$\varphi_{\mathbf{Fset}}(app^{AI}(n, s)) =_{\mathrm{def}} \begin{cases} \varphi_{\mathbf{Fset}}(s) \cup \{n\} & \text{if } app^{AI}(n, s) \neq \bot \text{ and } n \text{ does not occur in the sequence } s \\ \bot & \text{otherwise} \end{cases}$$

for all $s \in \mathbf{Seq}^{\bot A}$ and $n \in \mathbf{Nat}^{\bot A}$.

It is an easy exercise to prove that φ is a bounds preserving homomorphism.

In all models of the implementation IMPL_FINSETB the evaluation of the term

iselem(0, ins(2, ins(0, Ø)))

returns a result as specified in FINSETB, but the evaluation of the term

iselem(0, ins(100, ins(99, ... ins(0, Ø)...)))

causes an overflow condition not specified in FINSETB.

□

In the rest of this section we want to discuss, under which condition the forget-restrict-identify implementation method used in [Ehrig et al. 82] and [Sannella, Wirsing 82] can be embedded in a bounded implementation. The FRI-strategy uses three steps to reconstruct the abstract model A from a concrete implementing model AI. The forget-step corresponds to the renaming α and is neglected in the following discussion. So let A and AI have the same signature $\Sigma = (S, F, \emptyset)$, but A and AI are not necessarily term generated. The restrict step restricts AI to its term generated part R, i.e. the smallest subalgebra of AI. Finally the identify step requires the existence of a congruence ▪ on R, such that the quotient of R via ▪ is isomorphic to A.

This congruence ▪ can be described equivalently by a *classical homomorphism* $\varphi: R \to A = (\varphi_s: s^{\bot R} \to s^{\bot A})_{s \in S}$ such that for all $f: s_1, \ldots, s_n \to s \in F$ and all $a_1 \in s_1{}^{\bot R}, \ldots, a_n \in s_n{}^{\bot R}$

$$\varphi_s(f^R(a_1,\ldots,a_n)) = f^A(\varphi_{s_1}(a_1),\ldots,\varphi_{s_n}(a_n)).$$

The FRI-strategy is only developed for idealized implementations. But we can extend A and AI to algebras $\underline{A}$ and $\underline{AI}$ with signature $\langle S, F, \emptyset \rangle$ by adding correctness predicates, such that $\underline{AI}$ is a bounded implementation of $\underline{A}$.

The homomorphism $\varphi: R \to A$ can be extended to a bounds preserving homomorphism $\varphi_B: \underline{AI} \to \underline{A}$ in the following way.

$$\varphi_{B_s}(a) = \begin{cases} \varphi_s(a) & \text{if } a \text{ is contained in } s^{\bot R} \\ \bot & \text{otherwise} \end{cases}.$$

For $\underline{A}$ and $\underline{AI}$ we choose correctness predicates that hold for all arguments except for undefined ones, i.e. for all $f: s_1, \ldots, s_n \to s$

for all $a_1 \in s_1{}^{\bot A}, \ldots, a_n \in s_n{}^{\bot A}$ $\quad$ $correct\_f^{\underline{A}}\ a_1 \ldots a_n$ holds iff $a_i \neq \bot$ for all i

and for all $b_1 \in s_1{}^{\bot AI}, \ldots, b_n \in s_n{}^{\bot AI}$ $\quad$ $correct\_f^{\underline{AI}}\ b_1 \ldots b_n$ holds iff $b_i \neq \bot$ for all i.

It is easy to proof that $\underline{AI}$ is a bounded implementation of $\underline{A}$ via φ_B.

Note that the correctness predicates of $\underline{A}$ are nearly total. As already mentioned it is in general not useful to require correct function applications for undefined arguments. In other words a specification of nearly total bounds as e.g. in BOUNDED_SEQB guarantees in some sense an idealized implementation.

4. Properties

In this section we will have a closer look on the properties which are preserved under bounded implementation. Given a model of an abstract specification, two questions are important: Which computations are preserved under all bounded implementation? — and — Which abstract elements have a representation in all bounded implementation?

Computations here mean the evaluation of terms. It is important, that we can characterize when a computation in an implementation (under a certain valuation) returns a representation of the corresponding computation in the abstract model (under the corresponding valuation). We call terms t with this property *interpreted correctly in all implementations*, and denote it by **C** t. The valuation of free variables in t are interpreted as representations of some abstract elements. I.e. these valuations are translated by abstraction functions to the corresponding abstract valuations.

The correct interpretation **C** t is a semantic condition ranging over the class of implementing models. To reason about **C** t only in the theory of the abstract level, we want a syntactic criterion for **C** that can be decided independently of investigating all implementations. A simple criterion is given by a translation *COR* of a term t into a Σ-formula, that represents the correct application of each function occuring in t.

Definition

Let $\Sigma = \langle S, F, \emptyset \rangle$ be a bound signature, X a variable set and A a Σ-algebra. Then for any term $t \in W(\Sigma, X)$ we define

$A \models \mathbf{C}\, t$ iff for all bounded implementations $A \overset{\varphi}{\rightsquigarrow}_B AI$ and all valuations $\eta: X \rightarrow AI$

$$\varphi(\eta^*(t)) = (\varphi \circ \eta)^*(t)$$

The translation COR: $W(\Sigma, X) \rightarrow \Im(\Sigma, X)$ is defined as

$COR(x) = \textbf{\textit{true}}$, $COR(\bot) = \textbf{\textit{true}}$,

$COR(f(t_1, \ldots, t_n)) = correct\_f\; t_1 \ldots t_n \wedge COR(t_1) \wedge \ldots \wedge COR(t_n)$

□

Remark: The notation $A \models \mathbf{C}\, t$ is a slight abuse of the double turnstyle, because $\mathbf{C}\, t$ is not a Σ-formula, especially **C** depends on the structure of t, not only on its interpretation.

The following lemma shows that *COR* is a sufficient criterion for **C**. It is also a necessary criterion for terms with defined interpretation.

Lemma

Let $\Sigma = \langle S, F, \emptyset \rangle$ be a bound signature with variable set X and A a Σ-algebra generated by Σ. Then for every term $t \in W(\Sigma, X)$

(1) $A \models COR(t)$ implies $A \models \mathbf{C}\, t$

(2) $A \models \mathbf{C}\, t$ and $A \models \mathbf{D}\, t$ implies $A \models COR(t)$

□

Remarks on the proof: The proof of (1) is a simple induction over the structure of t, whereas (2) is (as all kinds of completeness proofs) a rather complex construction of an implementing term model. The exact proof can be found in [Breu 91].

Example

Let F be any model of the specification FINSETB. For a term $t = iselem(ins(tn, ts), tn)$, where tn and ts stand for subterms, with $F \models \mathbf{D}\, t$, we can ask whether t returns correct results in any implementation of F. With the lemma above and the axioms of FINSETB we can conclude

$$F \models \mathbf{C}\ iselem(ins(tn, ts), tn)$$

iff $\quad F \models correct\_iselem\ ins(tn, ts)\ tn \ \wedge\ correct\_ins(tn, ts) \wedge COR(tn) \wedge COR(ts)$

iff $\quad F \models or(is\_elem(tn, ts), card(ts) + 1 \leq maxcard) \wedge COR(tn) \wedge COR(ts)$

I.e. $iselem(ins(tn, ts), tn)$ is correctly interpreted in all implementations, iff ts and tn are correctly interpreted and tn is contained in ts or the cardinality of ts is smaller than $maxcard$. □

The following specification is a counterexample for the more liberal proposition

(2') $\quad A \models \mathbf{C}\, t$ implies $A \models COR(t)$.

Counterexample

The specification UNDEF describes natural numbers and a function *undef*, that is undefined for all arguments:

```
type UNDEF
  sort N
  func z: () N,        s, p, undef: (N) N
axioms for all n: N
  D z, ¬D p(z), p(s(n)) ≡ n,
  ¬D undef(n),
  correct_z,           correct_s n,
  ¬correct_p z,        correct_p s(n),
  correct_undef n,     correct_undef ⊥
endoftype
```

The function *undef* is totally unbounded, i.e. it must return correct results for all elements in N including ⊥. The constant z is not in the bounds of p. Let A be any model of UNDEF and $A \overset{\varphi}{\rightsquigarrow}_B AI$ be a bounded implementation. Then for the term $t = undef(p(z))$ the following holds.

$$t^A = \bot = \varphi(t^{AI}), \quad \text{because } \varphi(undef^{AI}(n)) = undef^A(\varphi(n)) = \bot \text{ for all } n \in N^{\bot AI},$$

i.e. $A \models \mathbf{C}\, t$, but $A \not\models COR(t)$, because $A \not\models correct\_undef\ p(z) \wedge correct\_p\ z \wedge correct\_z$. □

In [Breu 91] a sufficient and necessary characterization of $\mathbf{C}\, t$ by a Σ-formula is given. It is based on a monotonicity analysis of t. But such a criterion is very complex and, as we see from part (2) of the lemma above, only interesting for terms with undefined interpretation.

The second question is strongly connected to the representation oriented approach sketched at the beginning of the second section. In that approach all those elements are explicitely characterized that have a representation in every bounded implementation. For the computation oriented approach we model such an characterization with the *COR*-formula.

Lemma

Let $\Sigma=\langle S, F, \emptyset\rangle$ be a bound signature and A a Σ-algebra that is term generated by Σ. Let a be an arbitrary element of $s^{\perp A}$ for any $s \in S$. Then the following two propositions are equivalent.

(1) for all bounded implementations $A \overset{\varphi}{\rightsquigarrow}_B AI$ there exists an element $a' \in s^{\perp AI}$ with

$$\varphi(a') = a$$

(2) there exists a term $t \in W(\Sigma)$ with $t^A = a$ and $A \models COR(t)$.

□

Again (2) ⇒ (1) can be proved by a simple induction on the structure of t. The other way round is a construction of an implementing term algebra. See [Breu 91] for details.

The direction (1) ⇒ (2) of the previous lemma shows that every element that cannot be constructed by a term t with $A \models COR(t)$ does not have a representation in some bounded implementation.

Example

For the interpretation of the term *ins(1, ∅)* in a model of specification FINSETB there exists a representation in all implementations, because

$$correct\_ins\ 1\ \emptyset \quad \wedge \quad correct_{\perp}eset \wedge COR(1)$$

holds in all models of FINSETB.

But there exist implementations that contain no representation of the interpretation of the term

$$t =_{def} ins(100, ins(99, \ldots ins(0, \emptyset)\ldots))$$

because $card(t) = 101$ in all models, and thus $\neg COR(t)$.

□

The two previous lemmata show that we can answer both questions by reasoning completely in a calculus at the abstract level.

5. Conclusion

The purpose of this paper was to give an outline how bounds can be dealt with in an algebraic framework. A semantically sound foundation for the transition from idealistic specifications to finite physical machines was given. But formalization is not the captivating advantage of this approach. Rather its accordance with an intuitive way of proceeding makes it practical. Enriching an idealistic specification by its bounds is easy to handle and to apply. The idealistic specification preserves all its nice properties and makes it easy to apply rapid prototyping tools at the abstract level.

It must be mentioned that certain kinds of implementations that may be relevant in practice are still excluded. An example is the implementation of sets by bounded sequences that allow multiple insertion of the same elements into a sequence. In this case reasonable bounds for FINSET cannot be given, because insertion into a representation of any nonempty set may cause an overflow. This effect always occurs if redundant storage is not reclaimed. To model this, a slightly more complex approach allowing a more detailed look into the structure of objects must be used.

What was also not worked out here is the issue of modularity. In general there is a strong correlation between the bounds of a basic part of a specification and that part which is built upon it. Referring to the examples, suppose an intermediate step in which we would have based the specification IMPL_FINSET onto a specification SEQ of arbitrary long sequences. To implement SEQ finally by BOUNDED_SEQ we would have introduced appropiate bounds SEQB on SEQ. These bounds would have influenced the bounds of IMPL_FINSET. The dependencies of the bounds of hierarchically structured specifications must be clarified.

In the introduction it was claimed that algebraic specifications allow an implementation independent description of modules. This applies for idealistic specifications. It turns out that bounds specifications in general reveal much of the internal structure of an implementation. But this is no problem as far as the description of the bounds is expressed in terms of the abstract specification. The user is not forced to go through the code of the implementation to see its limitations. So finally it can be stated that the attributes abstractness, clarity, preciseness, problem orientation and implementation independence still apply to the sum of idealistic specifications and bounds specification.

Acknowledgements

I am very grateful to my wife. She has improved the quality of the paper significantly by proof reading it and by providing a pleasant environment for this work.

References

[ADJ 78] J. A. Goguen, J. W. Thatcher, E. G. Wagner, *An initial algebra approach to the specification, correctness and implementation of abstract data types*, in: R. T. Yeh (ed.): Current trends in programming methodology, Vol. 4, Data structuring, pp. 80-149 (Prentice-Hall, Englewood Cliffs, 1978)

[Bauer 81] F. L. Bauer: *Programming as fulfilment of a contract*, in: P. Henderson (ed.): System design, Infotech: State of the Art Report 9:6, pp. 165-174 (Pergamon Infotech Ltd., Maidenhead, 1981)

[Breu 90] M. Breu: *Development of implementations*, in: PROgram Development by SPECification and TRAnsformation, Volume I, PROSPECTRA - Esprit Project Number 390, Report M2.2.S4 - R - 11.0, 1990 (to appear in LNCS)

[Breu 91] M. Breu: *Endliche Implementierung algebraischer Spezifikationen*, Ph.D. Thesis (in German), technical report TUM I9111, Institut für Informatik, TU München, (1991)

[Broy, Wirsing 82] M. Broy, M. Wirsing: *Partial abstract types*, Acta Informatica 18, pp. 47-64 (1982)

[Bernot et al. 86] G. Bernot, M. Bidoit, C. Choppy: *Abstract data types with exception handling: An initial approach based on a distinction between exceptions and errors*, Theoretical Computer Science 46, p. 13-45 (1986)

[Bidoit et al. 89] M. Bidoit, M.-C. Gaudel, A. Mauboussin: *How to make algebraic specifications more understandable?*, in: M. Wirsing, J.A. Bergstra (eds.): Algebraic methods: Theory, Tools and Applications, LNCS 394 (Springer, Berlin, 1989)

[Ehrig et al. 82] H. Ehrig, H.-J. Kreowski, B. Mahr, P. Padawitz: *Algebraic implementation of abstract data types*, Theoretical Computer Science 20, pp. 209-263 (1982)

[Ehrig, Mahr 90] H. Ehrig, B. Mahr: *Fundamentals of Algebraic Specification 2*, EATCS Monographs on Theoretical Computer Science 21 (Springer, Berlin, 1990)

[Goguen 77] J. A. Goguen: *Abstract errors for abstract data types*, In: E. Neuhold (ed.): Formal description of programming concepts (North Holland, Amsterdam, 1977)

[Hennicker 88] R. Hennicker, *Beobachtungsorientierte Spezifikationen*, Dissertation, Universität Passau (1988) (shortened version in: R. Hennicker: *Observational Implementations*, in: B. Monien, R. Cori (eds.): Proc. STACS 89, LNCS 349, 1989, pp. 59-71)

[Hoare 72] C. A. R. Hoare: *Proofs of correctness of data representations*, Acta Informatica 1, 1972, pp. 271-281 (1972)

[Hußmann 85/87] H. Hußmann: *Rapid prototyping for algebraic specifications - RAP system user's manual*, technischer Report MIP-8504 (Universität Passau, Passau, 1985, 2. second extended edition 1987)

[Kamin, Archer 84] S. Kamin, M. Archer, *Partial implementation of abstract data types: a dissenting view on errors*, In: L G. Kuhn, D.B. MacQueen, G. Plotkin (eds.): Semantics of data types, International Symposium ... 1984, LNCS 173, pp. 317-336 (Springer , Berlin, 1984)

[Le Gall, Bernot 91] P. le Gall, G. Bernot: *Label algebras and exception handling*, 8th Workshop on Specification of Abstract Data Types, Dourdan (1991)

[Loeckx 90] J. Loeckx: *The specification system OBSCURE*, Bull. EATCS 40, pp. 169-171 (1990)

[Nipkow 87] T. Nipkow: *Observing nondeterministic data types*, in: D.T. Sannella, A. Tarlecki (eds.): Recent Trends in Data Type Specifications, LNCS 332 (Springer, Bln, 1989)

[Sannella, Wirsing 82] D. T. Sannella, M. Wirsing: *Implementation of parameterised specifications*, Internal Report CSR-103-82, Department of Computer Science, University of Edinburgh (1982) (Extended Abstract in: Proc. ICALP 82, 9th Int. coll. on automata, languages and programming, Aarhus, Denmark, LNCS 140, S. 473-488 (1982))

[Schoett 87] O. Schoett, *Data abstraction and the correctness of modular programming*, Ph. D. Thesis, University of Edinburgh (1987)

[Smolka et al. 87] G. Smolka, W. Nutt, J. A. Goguen, J. Meseguer: *Order-Sorted Equational Computation*. SEKI-Report SR-87-14, Universität Kaiserslautern, Fachbereich Informatik, 1987

Appendix

The basic specifications BOOL and NAT and their bounds are as follows.

```
type BOOL
  sort Bool
  func true, false: () Bool,
       not:          (Bool) Bool,
       or, and:      (Bool, Bool) Bool
  axioms for all x:Bool
    ¬(true = false) ,
    not(false) = true,
    not(true) = false,
    and(false, x) = false,
    and(x, false) = false,
    and(true, x) = x,
    and(x, true) = x,
    or(true, x) = true,
    or(x, true) = true,
    or(false, x) = x,
    or(x, false) = x,
endoftype
```

```
type BOOLB
  enrich BOOL
axioms for all x, y: Bool
  correct_true,
  correct_false,
  correct_not x,
  correct_and x y,
  correct_or x y
endoftype
```

```
type NAT
  enrich BOOL
  sort Nat
  func zero: () Nat, { display: 0 }
       succ: (Nat) Nat, { display: . +1 }
       pred: (Nat) Nat, { display: . -1 }
       iszero: (Nat) Bool,
       le:   (Nat, Nat) Bool,
                        { display: . ≤ . }
       equal_Nat: (Nat, Nat) Bool
  axioms for all n, m: Nat
  ¬D pred(0),
  pred(succ(n)) = n,
  iszero(0) = true,
  iszero(succ(n)) = false,
  0 ≤ n,
  succ(n) ≤ 0 = false,
  succ(n) ≤ succ(m) = n ≤ m,

  equal_Nat(n, m) = and( n ≤ m, m ≤ n )
endoftype
```

```
type NATB
  enrich NAT, BOOLB
auxfunc maxnat: () Nat
axioms for all n, m: Nat
  maxnat = …,    { some reasonable constant }
  correct_zero,
  correct_succ n  ⇔ succ(n) ≤ maxnat,
  correct_iszero n,
  correct_pred n ⇔ ¬iszero(n),
  correct_le n m,
  correct_equal_Nat n m
endoftype
```

New Concepts of Amalgamation and Extension for a General Theory of Specifications

Hartmut Ehrig, Michael Baldamus
Technical University Berlin
(Germany)
Fernando Orejas
Universidad Politecchnica Catalunya
(Spain)

April 1992

ABSTRACT

The concepts of amalgamation and extension are of fundamental importance for various kinds of equational and behavioural algebraic specifications. They are studied in the unifying framework of a specification logic and in the corresponding category of generalized morphisms. This leads to interesting characterizations via pushouts and to the concepts of generalized amalgamation and generalized extension which are new even in the special case of equational algebraic specifications. These results are promising for a general theory of parameterized and module specifications where strong persistency of functors can be relaxed by weaker properties.

CONTENTS

1. INTRODUCTION

The concepts of amalgamation and extension play a fundamental role in the theory of parameterized algebraic specifications (see [TWW 78/82], [EM 85]) and in the theory of algebraic module specifications (see [EM 90]). In addition to equational algebraic specifications which are used in [EM 85] and [EM 90] they have been applied to various kinds of behavioural specifications (see [ONE 89]). In fact, main parts of the theory of parameterized specifications and algebraic module specifications can be formulated using pushouts, free constructions, amalgamation and extension within the framework of a specification logic. In [EBCO 91/92] we show that the framework of specification logics is more suitable for such a theory than that of institutions introduced by Burstall and Goguen (see [GB 84], [ST 84]).

In the appendix of [EBCO 91] we have mentioned already that amalgamation can be considered as a special pushout in the category of generalized morphisms GMSL associated with a specification logic SL and that general pushouts in GMSL can be interpreted as generalized amalgamation. The main purpose of this paper is to study the concepts of amalgamation and extension in the framework of a specification logic SL and the associated category GMSL, and to introduce the notions of generalized amalgamation and generalized extension. This seems to be promising for a theory of parameterized and module specification where strong persistency of functors can be relaxed by weaker properties. A special case of generalized amalgamation and generalized extension is amalgamation and extension up to isomorphism, called ISO-amalgamation and ISO-extension, which allows to use persistent functors instead of strongly persistent functors in the case of extension.

This discussion in the appendix of [EBCO 91], published in the preliminary version of the AMAST'91-proceedings, is only mentioned in the conclusion of [EBCO 92], published in the final version of the AMAST'91-proceedings, because our impression is that its topic deserves a more detailed examination in the framework of the present paper.

The present paper is only a first step to introduce the notions of generalized amalgamation and generalized extension and to extend some results from the standard to the generalized case. The development of a theory of compositionality for data types without persistency remains open as an interesting research topic. For a more detailed motivation of our new concepts, a discussion of the corresponding results and the relationship to similar approaches in the literature we refer to our conclusion in section 5.

A short version of the first three sections of this paper has appeared as an announcement in the algebraic specification column of the EATCS Bulletin. In this paper we only give short remarks concerning the proofs. Detailed proofs for the results of this paper are given in our Technical Report [EBO 91].

Acknowledgements

We are grateful to John Gray and Andrej Tarlecki pointing out to us the relevance of indexed categories and fibred categories in connection with our notion of a specification logic. Although the original aims of the both approaches are quite different it seems worthwhile to study this relationship in more detail. Moreover we are greateful to the referees of this paper for some of their comments.

In first discussions for this paper in early 1991 we were joined by Martin Große-Rhode and Felix Cornelius and this topic will continue to be a joint research topic between the algebraic specification groups in Berlin and Barcelona. Last but not least thanks again to Helga Barnewitz for excellent typing.

2. AMALGAMATION AND EXTENSION IN A SPECIFICATION LOGIC

The notions of amalgamation and extension were introduced in [BP 85] and [EM 85] as fundamental constructions for algebras and functors based on pushout diagrams for equational algebraic specifications. They play a fundamental role for correctness and compositionality of parameterized specifications in [EM 85] and module specifications in [EM 90]. In fact these constructions can be formulated independent of the underlying specification logic or institution in the sense of [GB 84] and [ST 84]. The notion of a specification logic was introduced in a restricted sense in [Ma 89] in order to

classify different kinds of first order logical specifications. The general version of a specification logic as used in this paper was introduced in our recent trends paper for ICALP'89 [EPO 89]. From a categorical point of view the notion of a specification logic is equivalent to the notions of indexed categories (see [JP 78], [BGT 89]) and fibred categories (see [Gro 63], [Gra 65], [Ben 85]).
In this section we review the notion of a specification logic introduced in [EPO 89] and formulate the concepts of free constructions, pushouts, amalgamation and extension in this framework. In contrast to some previous versions (see [EPO 89], [Ehr 89], [EBCO 91]) these concepts are formulated as local and global properties.

2.1 DEFINITION (Specification Logic)

A specification logic SL is a pair (**ASPEC**, Catmod) where **ASPEC** is a category of abstract specifications and Catmod:**ASPEC**^{op} → **CATCAT** is a functor, that associates to every specification ASPEC in **ASPEC** its category of models **Catmod(ASPEC)** which is an object in the "quasi-category" **CATCAT** of all categories.

Remarks

1. The functor Catmod assigns to each abstract specification ASPEC a category **Catmod(ASPEC)** which usually consist of all models satisfying ASPEC, together with their associated morphisms. Actually there is a close relationship to institutions in the sense of [GB 84] and [ST 84]. This is discussed in more detail in the example 2.2.2. Note that there is no explicit satisfaction relation contained in the notion of a specification logic and thus certain syntactical and semantical properties have to be required. These are defined in 2.3 - 2.6 below.
2. If f:ASPEC1 → ASPEC2 is a morphism in **ASPEC** then Catmod(f):**Catmod(ASPEC2)** → **Catmod(ASPEC1)** is usually called the forgetful functor associated to f and it is usually denoted by V_f. Note that the functor Catmod is contravariant in **ASPEC** (denoted by **ASPEC**^{op}) such that all arrows are reversed.

2.2 EXAMPLES (Specification Logics)

1. The equational specification logic EQSL = (**SPEC**, Catmod) consists of the category **SPEC** of equational algebraic specifications and the functor Catmod assigns to each specification SPEC in **SPEC** the category **Alg(SPEC)**, i.e. **Catmod(SPEC)** = **Alg(SPEC)**. Replacing equations by conditional equations we obtain the conditional equational specification logic CEQSL.
2. For each institution INST = (**SIGN**, Sen, Mod, ⊨) the corresponding specification logic SL(INST) = (**ASPEC**, Catmod) is defined in the following way: We take **ASPEC** to be the category of all presentations (SIG, E), where SIG is an object in **SIGN** and E a subset of all sentences Sen(SIG), and all presentation morphisms. Catmod(SIG, E) is defined to be the full subcategory of Mod(SIG) having as objects exactly those which satisfy E. Actually, we only need one direction of the satisfaction condition of institutions to ensure that the functor Mod can be restricted to Catmod, such that also weak institutions satisfying only A ⊨ Sen(f) (e) ⇒ V_f(A) ⊨ e for all signature morphisms f:SIG1 → SIG2, all SIG2-models A and all SIG1-sentences e define a corresponding specification logic.
3. The behavioral equational specification logic BEQSL = (**BSPEC**, BCatmod) consists of the category **BSPEC** of behavioral specifications and the functor BCatmod assigning to each behavioral

specification BSPEC the category **Beh(BSPEC)** (see [NO 88], [ONE 89]). BEQSL cannot be generated by an institution in a non trivial way but only by a weak institution (see example 2). Hence it is an important example of a specification formalism which can be studied in the framework of specification logics but not in the framework of institutions. More details are given in [EBCO 91].

4. In [EBCO 91] we show how to enrich an arbitrary specification logic SL by constraints leading to a new specification logic SLC which inherits some of the properties of SL. In this way we obtain from examples 1-3 the corresponding specification EQSLC, CEQSLC, and BEQSLC with constraints.

5. The projection specification logic PROSL = (**PROSPEC**, PCatmod) consists of the category **PROSPEC** of projection specifications and the functor PCatmod which assigns to each projection specification PROSPEC the category $Cat_{compl,sep}$(PROSPEC) of all complete and separated projection algebras satisfying PROSPEC (see [EPBRDG 87] and [GR 89]).

6. In addition to the specification logics mentioned above, there are several other examples including different kinds of axioms, like universal Horn or full first order axioms, order-sorted signatures and constraints on the syntactical level, and on the semantical level different kinds of algebras and structures, like partial or continuous algebras or models of first-order logic. The first-order specification logic FOSL, for example, has first order signatures and axioms on the syntactical and corresponding models on the semantical level.

2.3 DEFINITION (Free Constructions and Persistency)

1. A specification logic SL <u>has free constructions</u> iff for every specification morphism f:ASPEC1 → ASPEC2 in **ASPEC** there is a functor F_f:**Catmod(ASPEC1)** → **Catmod(ASPEC2)**, called <u>free construction of</u> f, which is left adjoint to V_f.

2. F_f (and, in general, any functor F:**Catmod(ASPEC1)** → **Catmod(ASPEC2)**) is said to be <u>strongly persistent</u> if $V_f \circ F_f = ID$. Given a strongly persistent free functor F_f it can be shown that each identity $id_A:A \to A = V_f(F_f(A))$ has the universal property (see [EBCO 91]). We therefore assume $u(A) = id_A$ for all A whenever F_f is strongly persistent.

3. A specification morphism f is called <u>strongly liberal</u> if there is a strongly persistent free functor F_f left adjoint to V_f.

Remark

Free constructions have been used at the model level to give semantics to parameterized specifications. The equational specification logic EQSL, CEQSL, the behavioral equation specification logic BEQSL and the projection specification logic PROSL have free constructions (see [EM 85], [NO 88] and [GR 89]). In contrast to that the specification logics
EQSLC, CEQSLC and BEQSLC with constraints do not have free constructions in general, although specific specification morphisms are strongly liberal.

2.4 DEFINITION (Pushouts)

A specification logic SL = (ASPEC, Catmod) <u>has pushouts</u> if the category **ASPEC** has pushouts.

Remark

Pushouts are the operations, at the specification level, used to combine specifications. Essentially, if we want to put together two specifications ASPEC1 and ASPEC2 having a common subspecification ASPEC0, the pushout, ASPEC3, of ASPEC1 and ASPEC2 with respect to ASPEC0 would provide the right combination. Almost all specification logics of practical interest have pushouts (see [EM 85] for more detail).

2.5 DEFINITION (Amalgamation)

1. Given a specification logic SL = (ASPEC, Catmod), a pushout diagram (1) in ASPEC

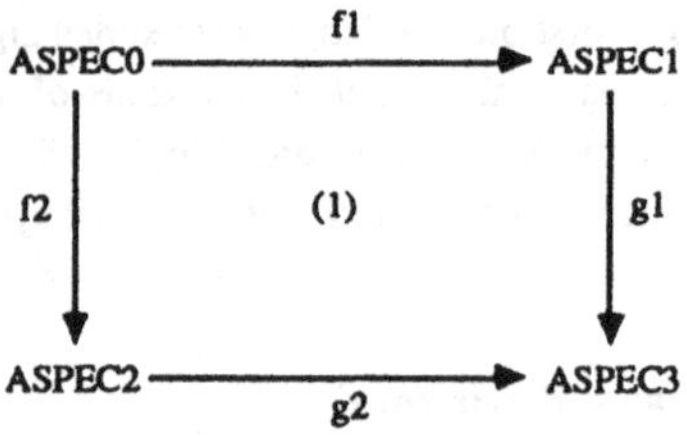

and objects $Ai \in$ **Catmod(ASPECi)** for i = 0, 1, 2 with

$$V_{f1}(A1) = A0 = V_{f2}(A2)$$

then an object $A3 \in$ **Catmod(ASPEC3)** is called <u>amalgamation</u> of A1 and A2 via A0, written

$$A3 = A1 +_{A0} A2,$$

if the properties 1.1 - 1.3 below are satisfied.

1.1 (<u>Projection</u>) $V_{g1}(A3) = A1$ and $V_{g2}(A3) = A2$

1.2 (<u>Uniqueness</u>) A2 is unique w.r.t. decomposition, i.e. for all objects $A3' \in$ **Catmod(ASPEC3)** with $V_{g1}(A3') = A1$ and $V_{g2}(A3') = A2$ we have $A3' = A3$

1.3 (<u>Universal Property</u>) For all morphisms $hi{:}Ai \rightarrow Ai'$ (i = 0, 1, 2) in **Catmod(ASPECi)** with

$$V_{f1}(h1) = h0 = V_{f2}(h2)$$

and all objects $A3' \in$ **Catmod(ASPEC3)** with $V_{g1}(A3') = A1'$ and $V_{g2}(A3') = A2'$ there is a unique morphism $h3{:}A3 \rightarrow A3'$ such that $V_{g1}(h3) = h1$ and $V_{g2}(h3) = h2$

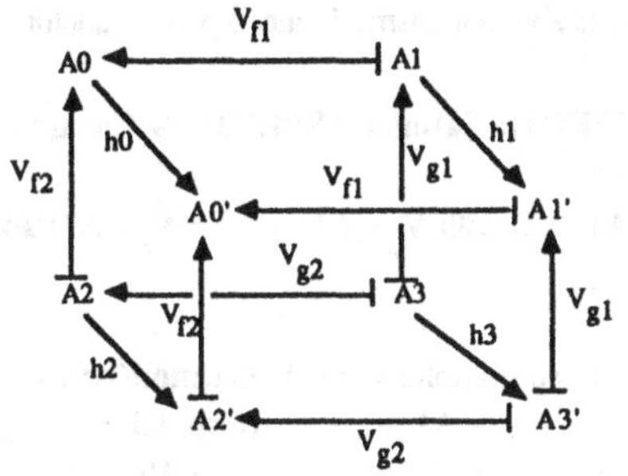

2. A specification logic SL has amalgamation if for every pushout (1) in **ASPEC** and all objects A0, A1, A2 with $V_{f1}(A1) = A0 = V_{f2}(A2)$ as above there is an amalgamation $A3 = A1 +_{A0} A2$ of A1 and A2 via A0.

Remarks

1. Amalgamation allows to define the semantics of a combined specification purely on the semantic level as the class of all possible amalgamations of the specifications which are combined. If amalgamations do exist, however, this class is the same as **Catmod(ASPEC3)**. The specification logics EQSL, CEQSL and PROSL have amalgamation but the behavioral equational specification logic, for example, has not. In particular, in the latter case, not all but at least pushouts satisfying the "observation preserving property" [ONE 88] have associated amalgamation. For pushouts not satisfying this property there are examples of local amalgamations which are not global, i.e. A3 is amalgamation of A1 and A2 via A0 but there may be no amalgamation A3' of A1' and A2' via A0' in 1.3.

2. The uniqueness property 1.2 is independent of the projection property 1.1 and the universal property 1.3. Consider the following specification logic SL = (**ASPEC**, Catmod) where **ASPEC** is the category freely generated by the graph of diagram (1) in 2.5.1 with additional factorization by commutativity of (1). This implies that diagram (1) becomes a pushout in **ASPEC**. Further let **Catmod(ASPECi) = 1** (with object 1 and morphism id_1) for i = 0, 1, 2 and **Catmod(ASPEC3)** the category with two distinct objects A3 and A3' and morphisms id_{A3}, $id_{A3'}$ and a3:A3 → A3' (no isomorphism) and V_{f1}, V_{f2}, V_{g1}, V_{g2} the unique functors with target **1**. Then $A3 = 1 +_1 1$ is a weak amalgamation satisfying the projection and the universal property 1.1 resp. 1.3, but not the uniqueness property 1.2, because $V_{g1}(A3') = 1 = V_{g1}(A3)$ and $V_{g2}(A3') = 1 = V_{g2}(A3)$ does not imply A3' = A3. They are even non isomorphic.

2.6 FACT (Properties of Amalgamation)

Given a specification logic SL with amalgamation for a pushout diagram (1) in 2.5. Then we have:

1. (Amalgamation of Morphisms) For all morphisms hi in **Catmod(ASPECi)** (i = 0, 1, 2) with $V_{f1}(h1) = h0 = V_{f2}(h2)$ there is a unique h3 ∈ **Catmod(ASPEC3)** with $V_{g1}(h3) = h1$ and $V_{g2}(h3) = h2$, called amalgamation $h3 = h1 +_{h0} h2$ of h1 and h2 via h0.

2. (Partial Functor) Amalgamation of objects and morphisms defines a partial functor

$$+: \mathbf{Catmod(ASPEC0)} \times \mathbf{Catmod(ASPEC1)} \times \mathbf{Catmod(ASPEC2)} \rightarrow \mathbf{Catmod(ASPEC3)}$$

which is defined for all objects (A0, A1, A2) with $V_{g1}(A1) = A0 = V_{g2}(A2)$ and similar for morphisms.

3. (Decomposition) For each object A3 (resp. morphism h3) in **Catmod(ASPEC3)** there is a unique representation as amalgamation $A3 = A1 +_{A0} A2$ (resp. $h3 = h1 +_{h0} h2$). The decomposition is given by $A1 = V_{g1}(A3)$, $A2 = V_{g2}(A3)$ and $A0 = V_{f1}(A1) = V_{f2}(A2)$ and similar for morphisms. This leads to the following representation of categories

$$\mathbf{Catmod(ASPEC3)} = \mathbf{Catmod(ASPEC1)} +_{\mathbf{Catmod(ASPEC0)}} \mathbf{Catmod(ASPEC2)}$$

where the right hand side is the category of amalgamated objects and morphisms.

4. (Pullback) The following diagram (2) is a pullback in **CATCAT**

$$\begin{array}{ccc}
\mathbf{Catmod(ASPEC0)} & \xleftarrow{V_{f1}} & \mathbf{Catmod(ASPEC1)} \\
{\scriptstyle V_{f2}}\uparrow & (2) & \uparrow{\scriptstyle V_{g1}} \\
\mathbf{Catmod(ASPEC2)} & \xleftarrow[V_{g2}]{} & \mathbf{Catmod(ASPEC3)}
\end{array}$$

Vice versa the pullback property of (2) implies that the specification logic SL has amalgamation for the pushout diagram (1).

Remarks

1. Amalgamation of morphisms is a stronger version of the universal property 1.3 of 2.5. The universal property means that for each possible choice of A3' there is unique $h3{:}A3 \rightarrow A3'$ s.t. $V_{g1}(h3) = h1$ and $V_{g2}(h3) = h2$. Amalgamation of morphisms, however, means that there is a unique h3 s.t. $V_{g1}(h3) = h1$ and $V_{g2}(h3) = h2$ and hence also a unique A3'.
2. The pushout property of amalgamation in the category of generalized morphisms will be formulated in section 3.
3. The pullback property (2) also implies the amalgamation of functors as stated in [EM 85].
4. The proof of fact 2.6 is given in [EBO 91]. It follows mainly the ideas of the corresponding proofs for algebras in [EM 85].

2.7 DEFINITION (Extension)

1. Given a specification logic SL = (ASPEC, Catmod), a pushout (1) in ASPEC as in 2.5.1 and a strongly persistent functor

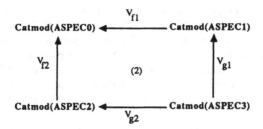

F:Catmod(ASPEC0) → Catmod(ASPEC1)

then a strongly persistent functor

F^*:Catmod(ASPEC2) → Catmod(ASPEC3)

is called extension of F via f2 if the following diagram (2) commutes:

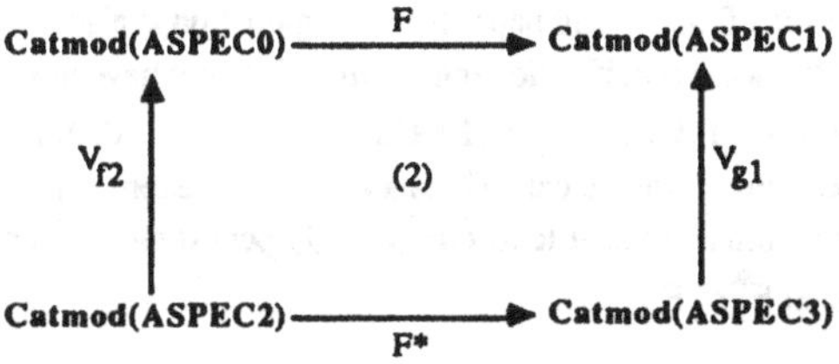

2. The extension F^* of F via f2 is called unique extension if any other extension of F via f2 is equal to F^*, in this case we write

   F^* = Extension (F, f2)

3. The extension F^* of F via f2 is called free extension if $F = F_{f1}$ and $F^* = F_{g2}$ are free functors w.r.t. f1 and g2 respectively.

4. The specification logic SL has extensions (resp. unique extensions) if for every pushout (1) in ASPEC and every strongly persistent functor F there is an extension (resp. unique extension) F^* of F. Similarly, the specification logic SL has free extensions if for every pushout (1) in ASPEC and every strongly persistent free functor F there is a free extension F^* of F.

Remarks

1. Extension is often needed if we want to have correctness and compositionality of the semantics of certain specification building operations. The equational and the conditional specification logic have unique extensions and free extensions (see [EM 85]). This is also true for the behavioural equational specification logic under the same conditions under which it has amalgamations, while for the view specification logic only free extension has been shown (see [ONE 89]). In most examples it is easier to verify amalgamations than extensions and the following result shows that amalgamations are sufficient to have unique and free extensions.
2. If SL has unique extensions and free extensions then also free extensions are unique.
3. The specification logic SL of remark 2 in 2.5 has extensions and free extensions but not unique extensions: The functors $F1^*, F2^*: 1 \to 2$ with $F1^*(1) = 1$ $F2^*(1) = 2$ are both strongly persistent extensions of the strongly persistent free functor $F: 1 \to 2$ but not equal. Moreover, $F1^*$ is free extension of F.

2.8 THEOREM (Extension by Amalgamation)

If a specification logic SL has amalgamations then SL has unique extensions and also free extensions.

Remark

Similar to [EM 85] the extended functor F^* is defined by $F^*(A2) = A2 +_{A0} F(A0)$ where $A0 = V_{f2}(A2)$ and also the proof of [EM 85] can be generalized.
It was pointed out to us by one referee of the present paper that amalgamation is also not necessary for unique extensions. In fact he constructed a specification logic which does not have amalgamation and also no strongly persistent functor F:**Catmod(ASPEC0)** → **Catmod(ASPEC1)**. This specification logic trivially has extensions, unique extensions and free extensions. It remains open to find a non trivial counterexample where there is at least one strongly persistent functor F but neither amalgamation nor a unique extension F^* of F.

3. CATEGORY OF GENERALIZED MORPHISMS

In this section we introduce the notion of generalized morphisms within the framework of a specification logic SL and discuss the connection with amalgamations in SL. This generalizes the notion of generalized homomorphisms introduced by Higgins in [Hig 64] as a concept for homomorphisms between algebras of different signatures (see also [Ru 79], [GB 84], [EM 85], [Ru 90]). On the other hand, considering the specification logic SL as an indexed category, the construction of generalized morphisms defining a category GMSL of generalized morphisms over SL corresponds to the so-called "Grothendieck construction" (see [Gro 63]) or "flattening of indexed categories" (see [BGT 89]).
In this section we will show that amalgamation is a special pushout in **GMSL**. Moreover, we construct general pushouts in **GMSL** using a generalization of Higgins Construction for the factorization of generalized morphisms and discuss the construction in the equational specification logic EQSL.

3.1 DEFINITION (Generalized Morphisms and Category GMSL)

Given a specification logic SL = (ASPEC, Catmod) and objects Ai ∈ **Catmod(ASPECi)** for i = 1,2 a generalized morphism gm:A1 → A2 is a pair gm = (f, h) with

f:ASPEC1 → ASPEC2 in ASPEC, and
h:A1 → V_f(A2)in **Catmod(ASPEC1)**

where V_f = Catmod(f):**Catmod(ASPEC2)** → **Catmod(ASPEC1)** is the forgetful functor (see remarks of 2.1).
The composition of generalized morphisms gm1 = (f1, h1):A1 → A2 and gm2 = (f2, h2):A2 → A3 is defined by

gm2 ∘ gm1 = (f2 ∘ f1, V_{f1}(h2) ∘ h1):A1 → A3

The category **GMSL** of generalized morphisms over SL has as object class the union of all object classes of **Catmod(ASPEC)** ranging over all objects ASPEC in **ASPEC** and as morphisms the generalized morphisms.

3.2 EXAMPLES (Generalized Morphisms)

1. Given the equational specification logic EQSL then generalized morphisms are generalized homomorphisms gm = (f, h):A1 → A2 as mentioned in [EM 85]: This means that Ai is a SPECi-algebra for i = 1, 2, f:SPEC1 → SPEC2 a specification morphism and h:A1 → V_f(A2) is a SPEC1-homomorphism where V_f(A2) is the SPEC1-reduct of A2.
2. Of course, we can also replace EQSL by the corresponding algebraic signature specification logic SIGSL. Then generalized morphisms in SIGSL are pairs of signature morphisms f and homomorphisms h:A1 → V_f(A2).
3. Operator schemes $\Sigma = (I, \alpha)$ in the sense of Higgins can be considered as a scheme for the construction of signatures (see [Hig 64]), where each $\omega \in \Omega$ leads to a family $(\omega\, j)_{j \in J}$ of operation symbols ω_j:$s1_j...sn_j$ → sj. Homomorphisms associated with a change of schemes in [Hig 64], also called general homomorphisms, are generalized morphisms over a suitable specification logic ΩSL, where abstract specifications are operator schemes Σ and Catmod(Σ) is the category of Σ-algebras and Σ-homomorphisms in the sense of [Hig 64].
4. A specification basis B = (I, S, Σ) in the sense of Rus (see [Ru 79], [Ru 90]) can be considered as a special case of Higgins' operator schemes (see example 3 above). Generalized homomorphisms in the sense of Rus are generalized morphisms over a suitable specification logic RSL, where an abstract specification is a specification basis B = (I, S, Σ) and Catmod(B) is the category of Σ-algebras and Σ-homomorphisms in the sense of [Ru 90].
5. For each institution INST we can construct the corresponding specification logic SL(INST) (see 2.2) such that generalized morphisms in SL(INST) correspond to those in [GB 84].
6. Further examples of flattening of indexed categories, and hence of generalized morphisms, are given in [BGT 89].

3.3 DEFINITION (Special Morphisms and Canonical Factorization)

A generalized morphism (f, h):A1 → A2 in GMSL is called standard if f is an identity in ASPEC and model-identical if h is an identity such that A1 = V_f(A2).A factorization of a generalized morphism (f, h):A1 → A2 into a generalized morphism (f, u) and a standard morphism (id, h^*), i.e. (f, h) = (id, h^*) ∘ (f, u), is called canonical if for each other factorization (f, h) = (id, h2) ∘ (f, h1) into a generalized and a standard morphism there is a unique standard morphism (id, h') such that the following diagram commutes

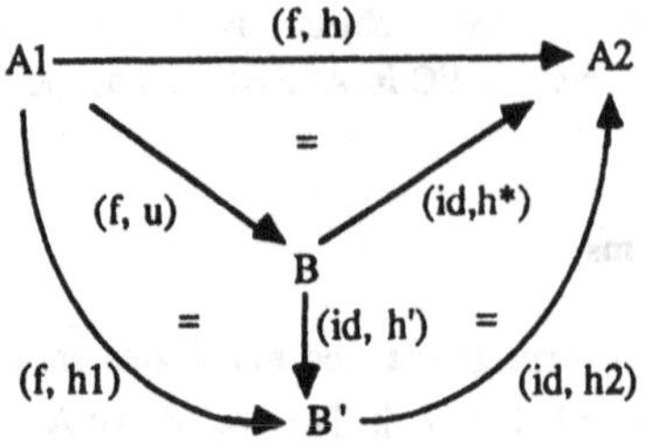

Remark

Canonical factorizations are unique up to isomorphism.

3.4 LEMMA (Canonical Factorization)

Given a specification logic SL with free constructions then each generalized morphism $(f, h):A1 \to A2$ in GMSL has a canonical factorization

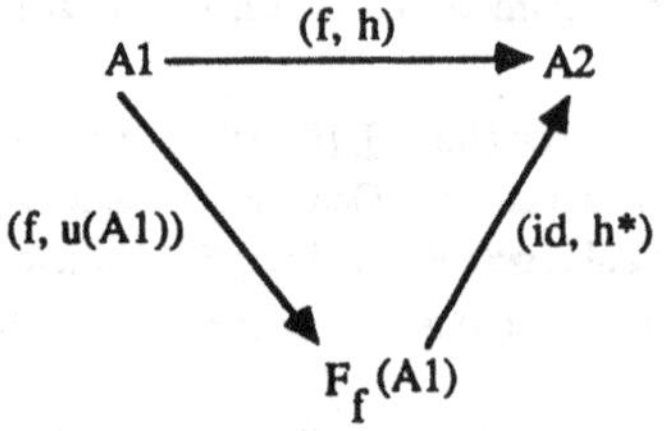

where $u(A1):A1 \to V_f \circ F_f(A1)$ is the universal morphism for A1 and the free functor F_f and $h^*:F_f(A1) \to A2$ is the morphism induced by h.

Remark

This canonical factorization is a generalization of Higgins construction in [Hig 64] resp. [Ru 90]. It follows immediately from the universal properties of u(A1).

3.5 THEOREM (Characterization of Amalgamation via Pushouts)

Given a specification logic SL, a pushout (1) in **ASPEC** as in 2.5 and objects $A_i \in$ Catmod(ASPECi) for i = 0, 1, 2, 3 then the following statements 1 and 2 are equivalent:

1. A3 is the amalgamation of A1 and A2 via A0 i.e. $A3 = A1 +_{A0} A2$.

2. The following diagram (2) of model identical morphisms is a pushout in the category GMSL and A3 satisfies the uniqueness property 1.2 of 2.5

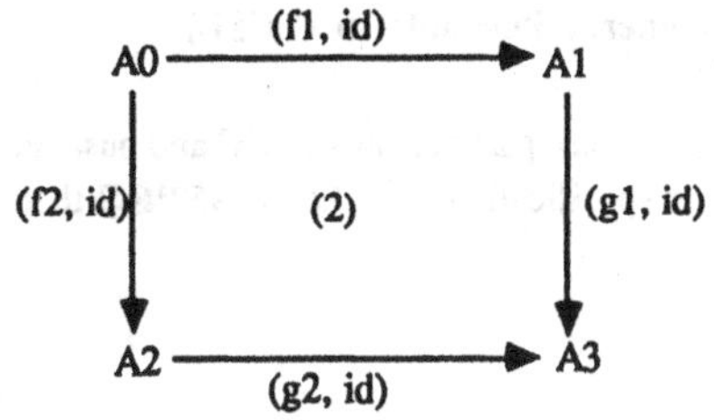

Remarks and Counterexamples

1. Amalgamation in SL is not equivalent to pushouts of model identical morphisms in GMSL, because the example in remark 2 of 2.5 is such a pushout in GMSL but only a weak amalgamation in SL. As shown already the uniqueness property for amalgamation is not satisfied although A3 as pushout object in GMSL is unique up to isomorphism.
2. In diagram (2) the pushout of model identical morphisms (f1, id) and (f2, id) are model identical morphisms (g1, id) and (g2, id). But the following counterexample shows that in general model identical (resp. model isomorphic) morphisms are not preserved under pushouts in GMSL, even if SL has free constructions, pushouts in ASPEC and pushouts in all model categories Catmod(ASPECi) for i = 0, 1, 2, 3:
Consider SL = (ASPEC, Catmod) where ASPEC is generated by diagram (1) in 2.5 which becomes a pushout in ASPEC. Further let Catmod(ASPECi) be the category **1** for i = 0, 3 and the category **2** (with objects 1, 2 and a nonisomorphic morphism a:1 → 2) for i = 1, 2. The forgetful functors for f1, f2, g1 and g2 are defined by $V_{f1}(2) = V_{f2}(2) = 1$ and $V_{g1}(1) = V_{g2}(1) = 2$. Then the following diagram (2) is a pushout in GMSL where (f1, id), (f2, id) are model identical and hence also model isomorphic, but (g1, a), (g2, a) are neither model identical nor model isomorphic because a:1 → 2 is no isomorphism in **2**.

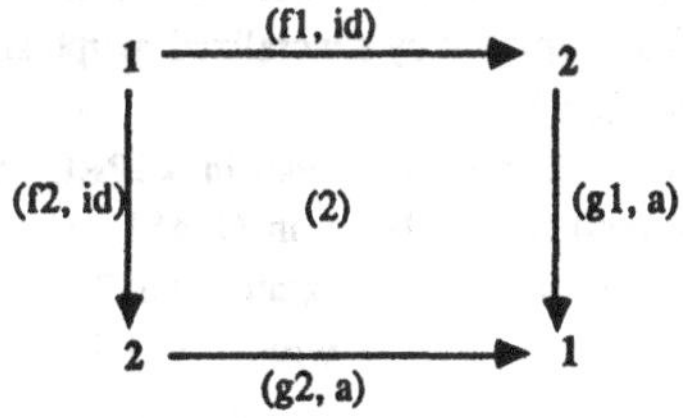

In fact, diagram (2) is a pushout in GMSL because it commutes and for any A4 ∈ Catmod(ASPEC4) and (g1', k1):1 → A4, (g2', k2):1 → A4 we have ASPEC4 = ASPEC3, g1' = g1, g2' = g2, and A4 = 1 s.t. (id, id):1 → A4 is the unique pushout morphism. Of course, A3 = 1 is no amalgamation of A1 = 1 and A2 = 1 in this case because $V_{gi}(1) = 2 \neq 1$ for i = 1, 2.
3. The proof of 3.5 given in [EBO 91] shows explicitly the universal pushout properties from the amalgamation properties and vice versa.

3.6 THEOREM (Construction of General Pushouts in GMSL)

Given a specification logic SL with free constructions, pushouts in **ASPEC** and pushouts in all model categories **Catmod(ASPEC)** for all abstract specifications ASPEC in **ASPEC** then the category **GMSL** has pushouts.

Construction

Given generalized morphisms (f1, h1):A0 → A1 and (f2, h2):A0 → A2 we construct the canonical factorization (see 3.4) of these morphisms leading to the following pushout diagrams (2.0), (2.1) and (2.2) in **GMSL** and (2.3) in **Catmod(ASPEC3)** which is also a pushout in **GMSL**. The morphisms g1 and g2 are given by the pushout (1) of f1 and f2 in **ASPEC** (see 2.5) and f3 is defined by f3 = g1 ∘ f1 = g2 ∘ f2

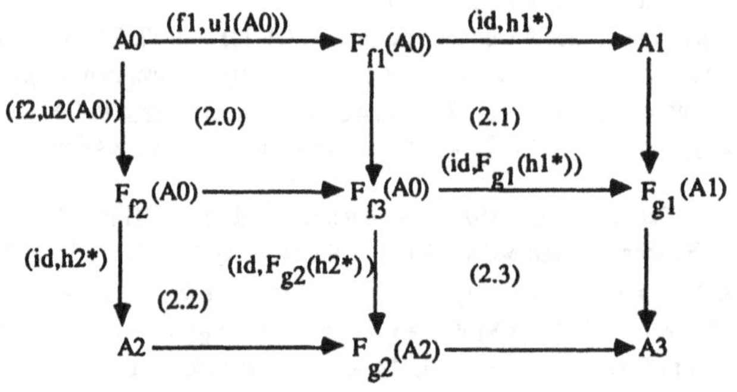

Remarks

1. The pushout object A3 can be interpreted as a generalized amalgamation of A1 and A2 via A0 where the model identities $V_{f1}(A1) = A0 = V_{f2}$ (see 2.5.1) are replaced by generalized morphisms (f1, h1) and (f2, h2) from A0 to A1 and A2 respectively (see section 4).
2. The first component of a pushout in **GMSL** is not necessarily a pushout in **ASPEC**. In fact, the following specification logic SL = (ASPEC, Catmod) has pushouts in **GMSL** where the first component is not a pushout in **ASPEC**: Let **ASPEC** be generated by diagram (1) in 2.5 together with two morphisms k1:ASPEC1 → ASPEC4 and k2:ASPEC2 → ASPEC4 with k1 ∘ f1 = k2 ∘ f2. Since there is no morphism k:ASPEC3 → ASPEC4 in **ASPEC** diagram (1) is not a pushout in **ASPEC**. Now let **Catmod(ASPECi)** = **1** for i = 0, 1, 2, 3 and **Catmod(ASPEC4)** = Ø then the following diagram (5) is a pushout in **GMSL**

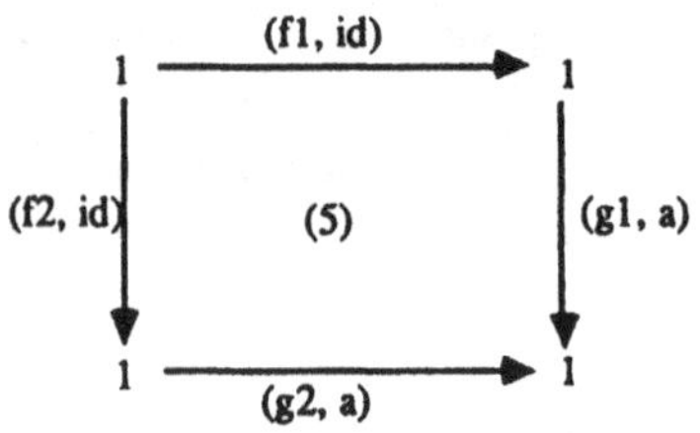

and the ASPEC3-object 1 is amalgamation $1 = 1 +_1 1$. Note, that the counterexample can be extended to the case where Catmod(ASPEC4) = $1 \neq \emptyset$ and Catmod(ASPECi) for i = 1, 2 is discrete with two objects.
3. This result is a special case of a corresponding co-completeness result for flattened indexed categories in [BGT 91]. An explicit proof for our construction is given in [EBO 91].

3.7 EXAMPLE (Pushouts in GMEQSL and Coproducts in Alg(SPEC))

The specification logic EQSL satisfies the assumptions of theorem 3.6 such that pushouts in GMEQSL exist according to the construction in 3.6. In fact, the pushout A3 in GMEQSL is the pushout of $F_{g1}(A1)$ and $F_{g2}(A2)$ via $F_{g3}(A0)$ in the category of ASPEC-algebras. Due to theorem 3.5 this pushout A3 is equal to the amalgamation $A1 +_{A0} A2$ in the special case $h1 = id{:}A0 \to V_{f1}(A1)$ and $h2 = id{:}A0 \to V_{f2}(A2)$. In general, the pushout of ASPEC3-algebras is a quotient of the coproduct of $F_{g1}(A1)$ and $F_{g2}(A2)$. The coproduct A + B of two SPEC-algebras A and B for SPEC = (S, OP, E) can be constructed (in analogy to the A-quotient term algebra in [EM 85]) in the following five steps:

1. $Const(A + B) = \{a{:} \to s \mid a \in A_s \cup B_s, s \in S\}$
2. $Eqns(A + B) = \{(\emptyset, t1, t2) \mid (t1, t2 \in T_{OP(A)}$ and $eval_A(t1) = eval_A(t2))$ or
   $(t1, t2 \in T_{OP(B)}$ and $eval_B(t1) = eval_B(t2))\}$
3. SPEC(A + B) = SPEC + ($\emptyset$, Const(A + B), Eqns (A + B))
4. $T_{SPEC(A+B)}$ = initial SPEC(A + B)-algebra
5. A + B = SPEC-reduct of $T_{SPEC(A+B)}$

In order to show that A + B is a coproduct of A and B it is easy to verify $i_A{:}A \to A + B$ and $i_B{:}B \to A + B$ defined by $i_A(a) = [a]$ and $i_B(b) = [b]$ are SPEC-homomorphisms and for given SPEC-homomorphisms $f{:}A \to C$ and $g{:}B \to C$ we obtain a SPEC(A + B)-algebra

$$C^* = (C, (f(a))_{a \in A}, (g(b))_{b \in B}$$

It remains open to study special cases where the pushout of SPEC-algebras has a simple representation similar to the amalgamation $A3 = A1 +_{A0} A2$ of algebras in the special case mentioned above.

4. GENERALIZED AMALGAMATION AND EXTENSION

In this section we generalize the concepts of amalgamation and extension. In the case of amalgamation we relax the assumptions $V_{f1}(A1) = A0 = V_{f2}(A2)$ by the existence of morphisms $h1{:}A0 \to V_{f1}(A1)$ and $h2{:}A0 \to V_{f2}(A2)$ which are generalized morphisms $(f1, h1){:}A0 \to A1$ and $(f2, h2){:}A0 \to A1$ instead of model identical morphisms where $h1 = id_{A0} = h2$. In the case of extension we relax strong persistency of functors by the existence of a natural transformation $u{:}ID \to V_{f1} \circ F$. For the new concepts, called generalized amalgamation and generalized extension, we start to show properties similar to those of the previous section. But there are still a number of open problems which remain to be studied. This applies especially to the interesting special case of iso-amalgamation and iso-extension, where h1, h2 and u are isomorphisms, which is only sketched in this paper.

4.1 DEFINITION (Generalized Amalgamation)

1. Given a specification logic SL = (ASPEC, Catmod), a pushout diagram (1) in ASPEC

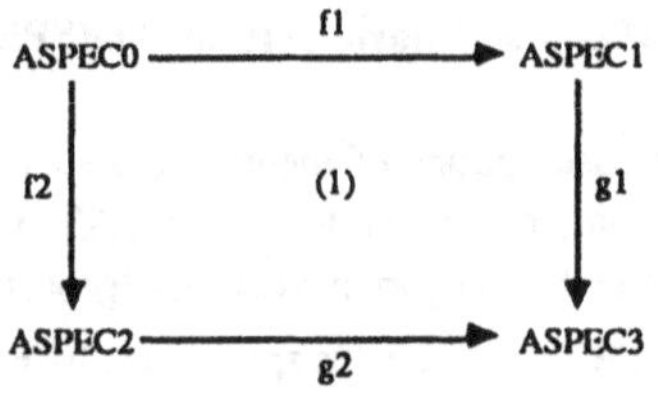

and objects Ai ∈ **Catmod(ASPECi)** for i = 0, 1, 2 together with morphisms

$h1{:}A0 \to V_{f1}(A1)$ and $h2{:}A0 \to V_{f2}(A2)$

in **Catmod(ASPEC0)** then an object A3 ∈ **Catmod(ASPEC3)** together with morphisms

$k1{:}A1 \to V_{g1}(A3)$ and $k2{:}A2 \to V_{g2}(A3)$

is called <u>generalized amalgamation</u> of A1 and A2 via A0, h1 and h2, written

$A3 = A1 +_{A0(h1,\,h2)} A2,$

if the properties 1.1 and 1.2 below are satisfied:

1.1 <u>(Commutativity)</u> $V_{f1}(k1) \circ h1 = V_{f2}(k2) \circ h2$ (back diagram)

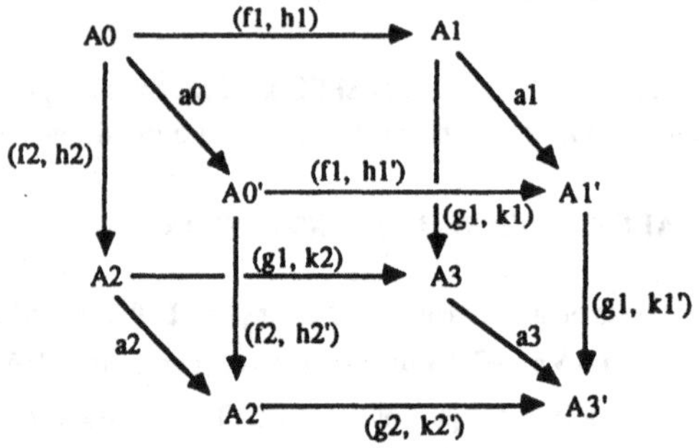

1.2 <u>(Universal Property)</u> For all morphisms ai:Ai → Ai' (i = 0, 1, 2) in **Catmod(ASPECi)** and all morphisms

$h1'{:}A0' \to V_{f1}(A1')$ and $h2'{:}A0' \to V_{f2}(A2')$

satisfying commutativity of top and left diagram, i.e.

$$h1' \circ a0 = V_{f1}(a1) \circ h1 \text{ and } h2' \circ a0 = V_{f2}(a2) \circ h2,$$

and all objects $A3' \in$ **Catmod(ASPEC3)** with morphisms

$$k1':A1' \to V_{g1}(A3') \text{ and } k2':A2' \to V_{g2}(A3')$$

satisfying commutativity of the front diagram, i.e.

$$V_{f1}(k1') \circ h1' = V_{f2}(k2') \circ h2',$$

there is a unique morphism $a3:A3 \to A3'$ such that we have commutativity of the bottom and right diagrams, i.e.

$$k1' \circ a1 = V_{g1}(a3) \circ k1 \text{ and } k2' \circ a2 = V_{g2}(a3) \circ k2.$$

2. A specification logic has generalized amalgamation if for every pushout (1) in **ASPEC** and all objects A0, A1, A2 with morphisms $h1:A0 \to V_{f1}(A1)$ and $h2:A0 \to V_{f2}(A2)$ there is a generalized amalgamation $A3 = A1 +_{A0(h1,\, h2)} A2$ of A1 and A2 via A0, h1 and h2.

3. If all (horizontal and vertical model) morphisms h1, h2, h1', h2' in **Catmod(ASPEC0)** and k1, k1' in **Catmod(ASPEC1)** are isomorphisms then generalized amalgamation is called iso-amalgamation, i.e. amalgamation up to isomorphism.

Remarks and Open Problems

1. The special case of generalized amalgamation where all the morphisms h1, h2, h1', h2', k1, k1', k2, and k2' are identities is weak amalgamation, i.e. amalgamation without uniqueness property 1.2 of 2.5: The assumption $V_{f1}(A1) = A0 = V_{f2}(A2)$ (see 2.5.1) and the projection property $V_{g1}(A3) = A1$ and $V_{g2}(A3) = A2$ (see 1.1 of 2.5) are satisfied if h1, h2 and k1, k2 are identities respectively.
2. It is an open problem to generalize the uniqueness property 1.2 of 2.5 in a suitable way. In the present version generalized amalgamation is equivalent to the pushout property in GMSL and hence unique only up to isomorphism (see 4.2).

4.2 THEOREM (Properties of Generalized Amalgamation)

Given a specification logic SL with generalized amalgamation for pushout diagram (1) in 4.1. Then we have:

1. (Uniqueness up to Isomorphism): Given A0, A1, A2, h1 and h2 then the generalized amalgamation A3 of A1 and A2 via A0, h1 and h2 is unique up to isomorphisms compatible with the corresponding morphisms $k1:A1 \to V_{g1}(A3)$ and $k2:A2 \to V_{g2}(A3)$.

2. (Amalgamation of Morphisms): Let A3 and A3' be generalized amalgamations in the back and the front side of the cube in 4.1.1. Then for all morphisms ai in **Catmod(ASPECi)** (i = 0, 1, 2) s.t. the top and the left side of the cube commutes there is a unique a3:A3 → A3' in **Catmod(ASPEC3)** s.t. the right and the bottom side commutes. In this case a3 is called generalized amalgamation of a1 and a2 via a0, h1, h2, h1', h2'.

3. (Characterization as Pushout in GMSL): Given A0, A1, A2, h1 and h2 as in 4.1.1 then an object A3 together with morphisms k1:A1 → V_{g1}(A3) and k2:A2 → V_{g2}(A3) is generalized amalgamation of A1 and A2 via A0, h1, h2 if and only if A3 together with (g1, k1):A1 → A3 and (g2, k2):A2 → A3 is pushout in GMSL of (f1, h1):A0 → A1 and (f2, h2):A0 → A2.

Remarks and Open Problems

1. Similar to 2.6.2 for the case of amalgamation it can be shown that also generalized amalgamation defines a partial functor. In addition to arguments A0, A1, A2, however, we also have to consider h1 and h2 as arguments. In fact, since generalized amalgamation is equivalent to pushouts in GMSL, the well-known fact that pushouts define a functor on the corresponding diagram categories implies that also generalized amalgamation becomes a (partial) functor.
2. It is an open problem to generalize the decomposition property of amalgamation (see 2.6.3) to generalized amalgamation. Of course, this is closely related to the open problem to generalize uniqueness (see remark 2 in 4.1).
3. In contrast to amalgamation which is equivalent to the pullback property 2.6.4 but not to pushouts in GMSL (see remark 1 in 3.5) generalized amalgamation is equivalent to general pushouts in GMSL (see property 3 above).
4. Existence of generalized amalgamation is a corollary of the characterization as pushouts in GMSL and the existence of pushouts in GMSL (see theorem 3.6).
5. It is an open question under which conditions amalgamation in SL implies generalized amalgamation or vice versa. We only know that amalgamation implies iso-amalgamation if SL "creates isomorphisms for specification forks" in the following sense: Given f1:ASPEC0 → ASPEC1, f2:ASPEC0 → ASPEC2 and objects A1, A2 with V_{f1}(A1) ≅ V_{f2}(A2) there are objects A1', A2' with V_{f1}(A1') = V_{f2}(A2') and A1 ≅ A1', A2 ≅ A2'.
We are almost sure that the equational specification logic EQSL creates isomorphisms for specification forks s.t. EQSL has iso-amalgamations. If we have the property "SL creates isomorphisms" (i.e. for f:ASPEC0 → ASPEC1 and objects A0, A1 with V_{f1}(A1) ≅ A0 there is an object A1' ≅ A1 with V_f(A1') = A0) we can also show that amalgamation implies iso-amalgamation, but EQSL creates isomorphisms only for injective specification morphisms. Note that for non-injective specification morphisms in EQSL there are persistent functors which do not have equivalent strongly persistent functors (see [EM 85]).

4.3 DEFINITION (Generalized Extension)

1. Given a specification logic SL = (ASPEC, Catmod), a pushout (1) in ASPEC as in 4.1.1 and a functor

$$F:\mathbf{Catmod(ASPEC0)} \to \mathbf{Catmod(ASPEC1)}$$

together with a natural transformation

$$u:Id0 \to V_{f1} \bullet F$$

then a functor

$$F^*:\textbf{Catmod(ASPEC2)} \to \textbf{Catmod(ASPEC3)}$$

together with a natural transformation

$$u^*:Id1 \to V_{g2} \bullet F^*$$

where Idi is the identity on **Catmod(ASPECi)** for i = 0, 2 is called <u>generalized</u> extension of (F, u) via f2, if there is a natural transformation

(1a) $$v:F \bullet V_{f2} \to V_{g2} \bullet F^*$$

s.t. the following diagram (1b) of natural transformations commutes (see remark 1) where f3 = g1 • f1 = g2 • f2:

(1b)Thus the notion of compatibility is extended from pairs F, F* (in the ordinary case) to pairs (F, u), (F*, u*) (in the general case).

2.   A generalized extension (F*, u*) of (F, u) via f2 is called <u>strong generalized extension</u> if we have commutativity of (2a) and condition (2b):

(2a)

$$\begin{array}{ccc} \textbf{Catmod(ASPEC0)} & \xrightarrow{\ F\ } & \textbf{Catmod(ASPEC1)} \\ V_{f2} \uparrow & & \uparrow V_{g1} \\ \textbf{Catmod(ASPEC2)} & \xrightarrow{\ F^*\ } & \textbf{Catmod(ASPEC3)} \end{array}$$

(2b) $$V_{f2} \bullet u^* = u \bullet V_{f2}$$

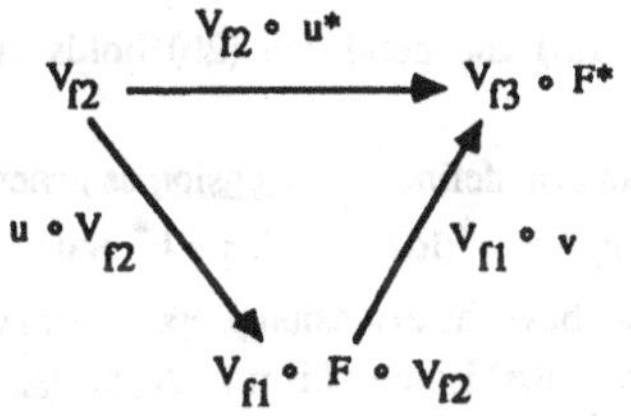

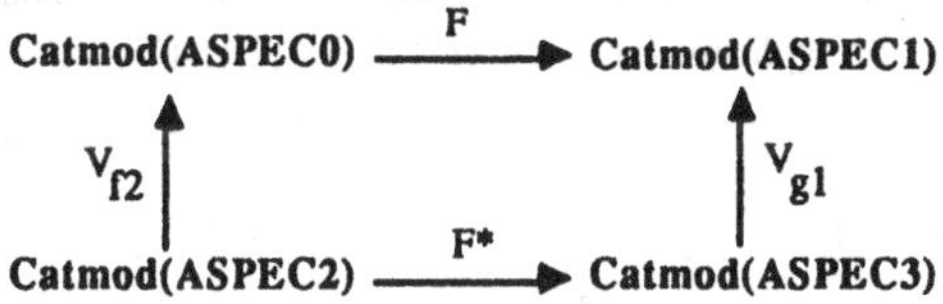

3. The (strong) generalized extension (F^*, u^*) of (F, u) via f2 is called (strong) free generalized extension if $F = F_{f1}$ and $F^* = F_{g2}$ are free functors w.r.t. f1 and g2 and universal transformations u and u^* respectively.

4. The specification logic SL has (strong) generalized extensions if for every pushout (1) in ASPEC and every pair (F, u) as above there is a (strong) generalized extension (F^*, u^*) of (F, u). Similarly, the specification logic SL has (strong) free generalized extensions if for every pushout (1) in ASPEC and every pair (F, u) as above there is a (strong) free generalized extension (F^*, u^*) of (F, u).

Remarks

1. In our notion of generalized extension we do not require the functors F and F* to be strongly persistent as in the case of extension (see 2.7). In fact, the identities $Id0 = V_{f1} \circ F$ and $Id1 = V_{g2} \circ F^*$ implicit in the notion of strong persistency are generalized to natural transformations $u{:}Id0 \to V_{f1} \circ F$ and $u^*{:}Id1 \to V_{g2} \circ F^*$. Moreover, the equality $F \circ V_{f2} = V_{g2} \circ F^*$ (see commutativity of diagram 2 in 2.7.1) is generalized to the existence of a natural transformation $v{:}F \circ V_{f2} \to V_{g2} \circ F^*$.
2. Strong generalized extension is a special case of generalized extension where the natural transformation $v{:}F \circ Vf2 \to Vg2 \circ F^*$ is the identity. In this case conditions (1a) and (1b) imply (2a) and (2b) respectively. In the case of generalized extension diagram (2a) commutes up to the natural transformation $v{:}F \circ Vf2 \to Vg2 \circ F^*$ (see (1a)) and condition (2b) holds up to the natural transformation $V_{f1} \circ v{:}V_{f1} \circ F \circ V_{f2} \to V_{f3} \circ F^*$.
3. Similar to iso-amalgamation (see 4.1.3) we can also define iso-extension as generalized extension where all the natural transformations $u{:}Id0 \xrightarrow{\sim} V_{f1} \circ F$, $u^*{:}Id2 \xrightarrow{\sim} V_{g2} \circ F^*$ and $v{:}F \circ V_{f2} \xrightarrow{\sim} V_{g1} \circ F^*$ are natural isomorphisms. This means that we have the extension property for persistent functors F and F^* where commutativity in (2a) holds up to natural isomorphism v. A free iso-extension would be an iso-extension for free functors $F = F_{f1}$ and $F^* = F_{g2}$.

4.4 THEOREM (Generalized Extension by Generalized Amalgamation)

1. If a specification logic SL has generalized amalgamation then SL has generalized extensions and generalized free extensions.

2. If the category GMSL associated with a specification logic SL (see 3.1) has pushouts which are closed under model identical morphisms (i.e. for each pair ((f1, h1), (f2, id)) we have a pushout of the form

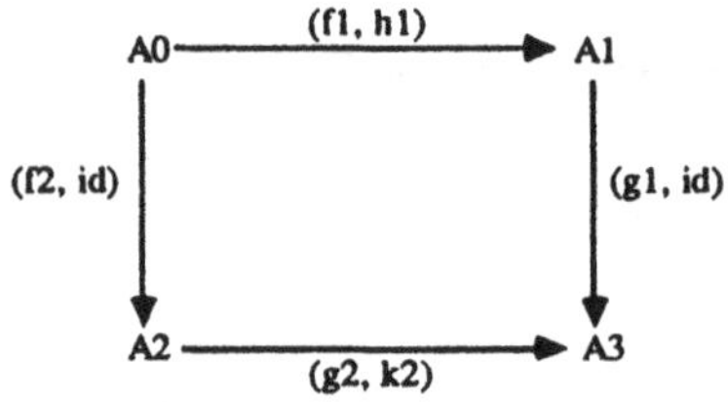

then SL has strong generalized extensions and strong generalized free extensions.

3. If SL has iso-amalgamations then SL has iso-extensions and free iso-extensions.

Remarks and Open Problems

1. Under the assumptions of theorem 3.6 (construction of generalized pushouts in GMSL) we have generalized amalgamation by 8.6.3 and hence generalized extensions and generalized free extensions by part 1 of this theorem.
2. It is an open problem to characterize pushouts which are closed under model identical morphisms. Even in the equational specification logic EQSL there are examples of non-persistent free functors $F = F_{f1}$ and $F^* = F_{g2}$ where diagram (2a) of 4.3 does not commute up to isomorphism (see 8.16 in [EM 85]).
3. In remark 5 of 4.2 we have discussed the existence of iso-amalgamations for a specification logic SL, especially that of EQSL. This implies iso-extensions and free iso-extensions for EQSL, i.e. the extension lemma in [EM 85] for persistent instead of strongly persistent functors.

5. CONCLUSION

In this paper we have started a new theory for the concepts of amalgamation and extension. In section 2 we have formulated these important concepts in the framework of a specification logic while the original versions in [EKTWW 81], [BP 85] and [EM 85] were given for algebras based on equational algebraic specifications only. A new aspect is the point that we have formulated these concepts as local and global properties which allows to speak of amalgamation in specifications although the specification logic does not have amalgamation in general. In any case considered so far amalgamation and extension are based on a strong persistency property: In the case of amalgamation of objects A1 and A2 via A0 we have to require that the reducts of A1 and A2 are equal to A0 and in the case of extension that the corresponding functor F is strongly persistent.
The strong persistency property is required in [EM 85] and [EM 90] in order to obtain correctness and compositionality results for parameterized specifications and module specifications in the equational specification logic EQSL. In fact, the structural theory of [EM 85, 90] can be generalized to an arbitrary specification logic SL with pushouts, free constructions, amalgamation and / or extension (see [Ehr 89] and [EG 91]). This shows the great importance of amalgamation and extension within the theory of algebraic specifications and their applications to software development.
From the practical point of view, however, the assumptions concerning strong persistency are sometimes too strong, because in several cases of software system specifications the strong persistency condition is violated. It is still not too bad if we have persistency up to isomorphism: In these cases we can use iso-amalgamation and iso-extension, which allows to obtain similar structural results up to isomorphism. But it is much worse if completeness or consistency are essentially violated. Such problems occur frequently in connection with error- and exception handling or fully abstract semantics. In these cases the usual theory of parameterized and module specification breaks down because of lack of persistency.
This is the main motivation to investigate new concepts of amalgamation and extension which are not based on strong persistency. In fact, the concepts of generalized amalgamation and generalized extension introduced in section 4 do not require any kind of persistency, but only the existence of

suitable morphisms. Injectivity of these morphisms corresponds to consistency and surjectivity to completeness, but none of these is required in the general theory. Nevertheless it is possible to prove some essential results, like "Properties of Generalized Amalgamation" in 4.2 and "Generalized Extension by Generalized Amalgamation" in 4.4 which are the counterparts of corresponding results "Properties of Amalgamation" in 2.6 and "Extension by Amalgamation" in 2.8 which are based on strong persistency. These are promising steps towards a structural theory of nonpersistent parameterized and / or module specifications. However, it remains open in this paper to develop such a theory. In fact, we have started to work on such a theory already for the special case of nonpersistent specifications which are at least consistent, i.e. the universal morphisms of the free constructions are injective. Unfortunately consistent morphisms are usually not closed under pushouts such that pushouts with a specific "consistency preserving property" similar to the "observation preserving property" in [ONE 89] for behavioural specifications might be useful to consider.

Another alternative would be to consider conservative extensions in the sense of [DGS 91/92] which are closed under pushouts if the specification logic has amalgamation. It is certainly worthwhile to study in more detail the connections between the theory in [DGS 91/92], based on institutions, with our theory of amalgamation and extension based on specification logics in more detail. In fact, our new concepts in [EBO 91], the technical basis for this paper, and the concepts in the technical report [DGS 91] were developed independently of each other at the same time. Although on one hand there is a considerable overlap of both theories there are, on the other hand, concepts and results in each of these theories which have not been considered in the other one up to now.

The category **GMSL** of generalized morphisms over a specification logic SL studied in section 3 constitutes the link between amalgamation and extension based on strong persistency in section 2 and the corresponding generalized concepts in section 4. The key idea is that amalgamation in both cases corresponds to pushouts in **GMSL**. One main result in section 3 is that amalgamation in SL is a special pushout in **GMSL** (see theorem 3.5). This was the main motivation to define generalized amalgamation in such a way that it becomes equivalent to general pushouts in **GMSL** (see 4.2.3.). There is, however, still a conceptual difference: Amalgamation in SL is a pushout of model identical morphisms in **GMSL** and satisfies in addition a uniqueness property (see 1.2 of 2.5) which is independent of the pushout properties (see remark 1 in 3.5). Up to now we have not been able to find a counterpart for this uniqueness property in the case of generalized amalgamation. Moreover, it is still an open problem to characterize pushouts which are closed under model identical morphisms. This is most interesting because it implies strong generalized extensions and strong generalized free extensions (see 4.4.2). The other main result of section 3 is the construction of general pushouts in **GMSL** (see theorem 3.6) which implies the existence of generalized amalgamation (see 4.2) and hence also the existence of generalized extension (see 4.4) under the assumption that SL has free constructions and pushouts in **ASPEC** as well as in the corresponding model categories (see 3.6).

We have mentioned already that this result concerning the existence of general pushouts in **GMSL** is a special case of a corresponding co-completeness result for flattened indexed categories in [BGT 89]. However, our construction in terms of four specific pushouts in **GMSL** seems to be of specific interest because it corresponds to the canonical factorization of generalized morphisms (see 3.4) which is a generalization of Higgins construction in [Hig 64].

This shows that general results for indexed and fibred categories, which have been studied in Category Theory for more than a quarter of a century (see [Gro 63]), turn out to be important for Computer Science. This was observed already in [BGT 89] for the semantics of computations in general. An important additional insight, however, is that the equivalence of the concepts of indexed categories on one hand and specification logics on the other hand allows to apply the theory of indexed categories

also to the theory of institutions in the sense of [GB 84], [ST 84] and [DGS 91], because institutions can be considered as a special case of specification logics (see 2.2).
We prefer the framework of specifications logics to that of institutions as far as general structural properties of specifications and corresponding models are concerned. But we are aware that for other investigations within the theory of specifications, especially for theorem proving problems, it is also important to consider explicitly a satisfaction relation between axioms and models, as in institutions, or a consequence relation, as in π-institutions, or both together as in Meseguer's approach to general logics in [Mes 89].

6. REFERENCES

[Bal 90] Baldamus, M.: Constraints and their Normal Forms in the Framework of Specification Logics (in German), Studienarbeit, TU Berlin (1990)

[Ben 85] Benabou, J.: Fibred categories and the foundations of naive category theory. Journal of Symbolic Logic 50 (1985), 10-37

[BGT 89] Burstall, R.M.; Goguen, J.A.; Tarlecki, A.: Some Fundamental Algebraic Tools for the Semantics of Computation, Part 3: Indexed Categories. Technical Report LFCS Report Series No. ECS-LFCS-89-90, University of Edinburgh, 1989

[BP 85] Blum, E.K.; Parisi-Presicce, F.: The semantics of shared submodules specifications. Proc. TAPSOFT vol 1, 1985, Springer LNCS 185, 359-373

[DGS 91] Diaconescu, R.; Goguen, J.A.; Stefaneas, P.: Logical support for modularization, this volume.

[DGS 92] Diaconescu, R.; Goguen, J.A.; Stefaneas, P.: Logical support for modularization, Techn. Report, Oxford University, August 1991

[EBCO 91] Ehrig, H.; Baldamus, M.; Cornelius, F.; Orejas, F.: Theory of Algebraic Module Specifications including Behavioural Semantics, Constraints and Aspects of Generalized Morphisms (invited paper), Proc. AMAST'91, Iowa City, 1991

[EBCO 92] Ehrig, H.; Baldamus, M.; Cornelius, F.; Orejas, F.: Theory of Algebraic Module Specifications including Behavioural Semantics and Constraints. Final version of Proc. AMAST'91, to appear as a Springer LNCS, 1992

[EBO 91] Ehrig, H.; Baldamus, M.; Orejas, F.: New Concepts for Amalgamation and Extension in the Framework of Specification Logics, Technical Report No. 91/05, TU Berlin 1991

[EG 91] Ehrig, H.; Große-Rhode, M.: Structural Theory of Algebraic Specifications in a Specification Logics, Part 1: Functorial Parameterized Specifications, in preparation

[Ehr 89] Ehrig, H.: Algebraic Specification of Modules and Modular Software Systems within the Framework of Specification Logics, Technical Report 89/17, TU Berlin (1989)

[EKTWW 81] Ehrig, H.; Kreowski, H.-J.; Thatcher, J.W.; Wagner, E.G.; Wright, J.B.: Parameter Passing in Algebraic Specification Languages, Proc. Workshop on Program Specification, Springer LNCS 134 (1981), 322-369, also appeared in TCS (1984)

[EM 85] Ehrig, H.; Mahr, B.: Fundamentals of Algebraic Specification 1. Equations and Initial Semantics. EATCS Monographs on Theoretical Computer Science, Vol. 6, Springer (1985)

[EM 90] Ehrig, H.; Mahr, B.: Fundamentals of Algebraic Specification 2. Module Specifications and Constraints. EATCS Monographs on Theoretical Computer Science, Springer (1990)

[EPO 89] Ehrig, H.; Pepper, P.; Orejas, F.: On Recent Trends in Algebraic Specification, Proc. ICALP'89, Springer LNCS 372 (1989), pp. 263-288

[GB 84] Goguen, J.A.; Burstall, R.M.: Introducing institutions. Proc. Logics of Programming

Workshop, Carnegie-Mellon. LNCS 164, Springer (1984), 221-256

[GR 89] Große-Rhode, M.: Parameterized Data Type and Process Specifications using Projection Algebras, in: Categorical Methods in Computer Science - with Aspects from Topology, (H. Ehrig, H. Herrlich, H.-J. Kreowski, G. Preuß, eds.), Springer LNCS 393 (1989)

[Gra 65] Gray, J.W.: Fibred and cofibred categories. In S. Eilenberg, D.K. Harrison, S. MacLane, H. Röhrl (eds.), Proc. Conf. on Categorical Algebra, Springer-Verlag, 1966, 21-83

[Gro 63] Grothendieck, A.: Catégories fibrées et descente. In Revetements étales et groupe fondamental, Séminaire de Géométrie Algébraique du Bois-Marie 1960/61, Exposé VI, Institut des Hautes Études Scientifiques, Paris, 1963; reprinted in Lect. Not. in Math. 224, Springer-Verlag, 1971, 145-194

[GTW 76/78] Goguen, J.A.; Thatcher, J.W.; Wagner, E.G.: An initial algebra approach to the specification, correctness and implementation of abstract data types. IBM Research Report RC 6487, 1976. Also: Current Trends in Programming Methodology IV: Data Structuring (R. Yeh, ed.), Prentice Hall (1978), 80-144

[Hig 64] Higgin, P.J.: Algebras with a Scheme of Operators, Mathematische Nachrichten 27 [1963/64], pp 115-132

[JP 78] Johnstone, P.T., Paré, R.: Indexed categories and their applications. Lect. Not. in Math. 661, Springer-Verlag, 1978

[Ma 89] Mahr, B.: Empty Carriers: The Categorical Burden on Logic; in: Categorical Methods in Computer Science - with Aspects from Topology, (H. Ehrig, H. Herrlich, H.-J. Kreowski, G. Preuß, eds.), Springer LNCS 393 (1989)

[Mes 89] Meseguer, J.: General Logics, Logic Colloquium'87 (eds. Ebbinghaus et. al.), North-Holland, 1989

[NO 88] Nivela, P.; Orejas, F.: Behavioral semantics for algebraic specification languages, Proc. ADT-Workshop Gullane, 1987, Springer LNCS 332 (1988), 184-207

[ONE 89] Orejas, F.; Nivela, P.; Ehrig, H.: Semantical Constructions for Categories of Behavioral Specifications, in: Computer Science - with Aspects from Topology, (H. Ehrig, H. Herrlich, H.-J. Kreowski, G. Preuß, eds.), Springer LNCS 393 (1989)

[Ru 79] Rus, T.: Data Structures and Operating Systems. John Wiley & Sons (1979)

[Ru 90] Rus, T.: Steps towards Algebraic Construction of Compilers. Technical Report, University of Iowa (1990)

[ST 84] Sannella, D.T.; Tarlecki, A.: Building specifications in an arbitrary institution. Proc. of the Int. Symp. on Semantics of Data Types, LNCS 173, Springer (1984), 337-356. Full version: Information and Computation 76 (1988), 165-210

[TWW 78/82] Thatcher, J.W.; Wagner, E.G.; Wright, J.B.: Data type specification: parameterization and the power of specification techniques. 10th Symp. Theory of Computing (1978), 119-132. Trans. Prog. Languages and Systems 4 (1982), 711-732

Nonequivalence of Categories for Equational Algebraic Specifications

H. Ehrig

Fachbereich Informatik, Technische Universität Berlin
D-1000 Berlin Germany

F. Parisi-Presicce

Dipartimento di Matematica Pura ed Applicata, University of L'Aquila
I-67010 Coppito (AQ) Italy

Abstract Four different alternatives for the definition of standard equational algebraic specifications and the corresponding specification morphisms are studied and compared. Although intuitively the definitions may appear equivalent, they lead to three different equivalence classes of categories. It is shown, in fact, that the construction of pushouts and pullbacks is significantly different in these three cases. Although the corresponding specification logics are all semantical equivalent in a weak sense, three of them are semantical inconsistent with respect to pullback constructions. The nonequivalence of the equational categories has also significant implications for the corresponding high-level-replacement (HLR) system.

0 Introduction

Algebraic methods for the specification of abstract data types and of software systems in general are almost 20 years old [13, 9]. One of the main reasons which led to the introduction and the development of these methods is the (relative) straigthforward way of representing the properties of the functions being defined using equations between terms. In addition to providing unambigous semantics (in the absence of errors), the use of pairs of terms can be easily related to fundamental mechanisms in standard programming languages, such as the assignment in the imperative paradigm, or the symbolic evaluation in the functional one. Many authors have analyzed equational algebraic specifications [9, 12, 2] but not enough emphasis (with some exceptions) has been placed on the form of these universally quantified equations : for many of the properties of interest, the differences appeared negligible. To a practically unanimous consent on the definition of signature morphism f_Σ : SIG1 → SIG2, corresponds a variety of ways in which these morphisms are extended to SPEC1 → SPEC2 to include the way the equations in the two specifications are related. They range from requiring the inclusion in E2 of the translated equations f#(E1) of SPEC1, to allowing the translation f#(E1) to be derivable (in the standard equational logic) from the equations in E2. In all these cases, the correspondence between equations is extensional : if f#(e1) and f#(e2) consist of the same pair of terms, they are considered the same equation, without any trace of their origin.
In this paper, we have analyzed a category of equational algebraic specifications where the equations are labelled and specification morphisms are defined also on labels, allowing the differentiation of two equations with the same meaning (i.e., consisting fo the same pair of terms). The different morphisms lead to significantly different categories: these are related by pairs of adjoint functors which do not preserve pushouts and pullbacks in general. Such categorical constructions arise naturally as mechanisms to build specifications and to model parametrization and parameter passing.
Our investigation has also been motivated by the recent generalization of the algebraic approach

to graph grammars based on a double pushout construction to High Level Replacement System. [4]. The HLR systems can be seen as categorical rewriting systems in which a rewrite rule is represented by a pair $L \leftarrow K \rightarrow R$ of distinguished morphisms and a rewrite step from G to H by a double pushout

$$\begin{array}{ccccc} L & \longleftarrow & K & \longrightarrow & R \\ \downarrow & & \downarrow & & \downarrow \\ G & \longleftarrow & C & \longrightarrow & H \end{array}$$

In such replacement systems, desirable properties such as the Church-Rosser Theorem, the Parallelism Theorem and the Concurrency Theorem are guaranteed by general characteristics grouped together under the name of HLR1 (for C-R and Parallelism Theorems) and HLR2 (for Concurrency Theorem) in [4] . It turns out [8] that only the category of equational algebraic specifications with labelled equations and injective distinguished morphisms satisfies the HLR2 (and hence the HLR1) properties. The use of labelled equations is also desirable for methodological reasons, because they provide a stricter control over the process of documenting the final specified system and over the inevitable subsequent modifications of the specification, by allowing to retrace the source of properties (in this case equations) in a composite system.
In the next section, we define the different categories and show how they are related by pairs of adjoint functors which reduce them to three equivalence classes. In section 2 we show how pushouts and pullbacks are constructed in the different categories, as well as characterize mono, epi- , and isomorphisms, initial and final objects. In section 3 we exhibit specific properties (arising from HLR constructions) which differentiate among the three categories. Some remarks and open problems close the paper.
The proofs are (at most) sketched and can be found in details in [8].

1 Categories of Equational Algebraic Specifications

The following four different alternatives for categories of standard equational algebraic specifications have been introduced in the literature. In the first three types, an equational algebraic specification SPEC = (S, OP, E) consists of a set S of sorts, OP of operation symbols and E of equations as defined in [6]:

Type 1: The specification morphisms f:SPEC $\rightarrow$ SPEC' are pairs $f = (f_S{:}S \rightarrow S', f_{OP}{:}OP \rightarrow OP')$ such that the translated equations f#(E) are contained in cl(E') where cl(E') is the closure of E' under derivability ([6, 11]). The category consisting of these morphisms on specifications (S, OP, E) is denoted by **DER**.

Type 2: As above, but with the condition f#(E) $\subseteq$ E' (see [4, 11, 7]). This subcategory is denoted by **INCL**.

Type 3: The category consisting of the morphisms of Type 2 restricted to specifications SPEC = (S, OP, E) where E is already closed under derivability (theories in the sense of Burstall and Goguen [1]), is denoted by **CLOS**.

Type 4: Specifications SPEC = (S, OP, E) where the set of equations is labelled, (different labels e may correspond to the same triple (X, t1, t2) representing the equation e:t1 = t2), and specification morphisms are triples $f = (f_S{:}S \rightarrow S', f_{OP}{:}OP \rightarrow OP', f_E{:}E \rightarrow E')$ with the usual compatibility properties for f_S and f_{OP} and for (e:t1 = t2) $\in$ E we have (f_E(e):f#(t1) = f#(t2)) $\in$ E' [8]. This category is denoted by **LAB**.

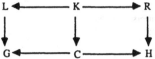

The definition of morphism most used in the literature is the first one, where f#(E) has to be derivable from E' in some fixed framework of derivability, usually equational reasoning. In our discussion, there is no need to specify the type of inference used, since it is immaterial for the results, as ling as it satisfies some obvious properties such as closure under substitution and preservation under signature morphism..

1.1 Theorem (Adjointness between Categories of Algebraic Specifications)
The categories **DER, INCL, LAB** e **CLOS** of equational algebraic specifications are related by the following pairs of adjoint functors:

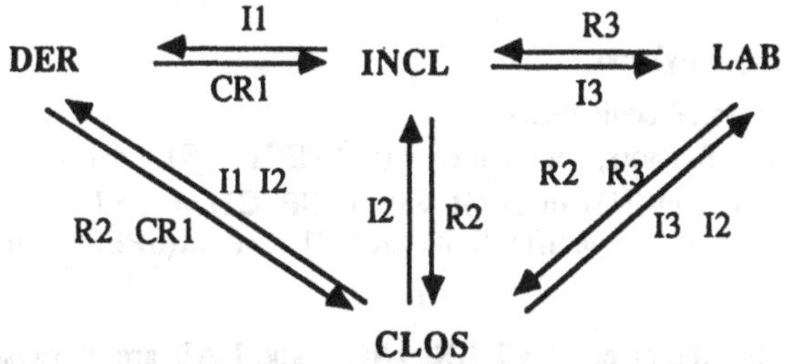

where I1 and I2 are the inclusion functors, I3 associates a distinct label to each equation, R3 forgets the labels, CR1 and R2 both associate to each specification (S, OP, E) the corresponding closed version (S, OP, cl(E)). Furthermore

I1 is left adjoint to CR 1	(coreflector of I1)
I2 is right adjoint to R2	(reflector of I2)
I3 is right adjoint to R3	(reflector of I3)
I3 • I2 is right adjoint to R2 • R3	(reflector of I3 • I2)

I1 • I2 and R2 • CR1 define an equivalence between the categories **DER** and **CLOS**

ProofSketch
Since "F left adjoint to G" is equivalent to "G right adjoint to F" and adjoint functors are closed under composition it suffices to show the following 4 properties, where we make use of the Yoneda Lemma to reduce the proofs to the existence of universal arrows:

1. CR1 right adjoint to I1:

Given SPEC1 ∈ **DER** and SPEC2 ∈ **INCL** and f1: I1(SPEC2) → SPEC1 in **DER**, with couniversal morphism c: I1•CR1(SPEC1) → SPEC1 in **DER** defined by $c_S = id_{S1}$ and $c_{OP} = id_{OP1}$ and CR1(SPEC1) = (S1,OP1,cl(E1)), the unique morphism f2: SPEC2 → CR1(SPEC1) in **INCL**, i.e. f2#(E2) ⊆ cl(E1), such that c • I1(f2) = f1 can easily be defined by taking $f2_S = f1_S$ and $f2_{OP} = f1_{OP}$ since c#cl(E1) ⊆ cl(E1)

2. R2 left adjoint to I2:

Given SPEC1 ∈ **CLOS** and SPEC2 ∈ **INCL** and f2 : SPEC2 → I2(SPEC1) in **INCL**, with universal morphism u : SPEC2 → I2•R2(SPEC2) in **INCL** defined by identities in each component and R2(SPEC2) = (S2, OP2, cl(E2)), the unique f1: R2(SPEC2) → SPEC1 in **CLOS**, i.e. f1#(cl(E2)) ⊆ E1, such that I2(f1) • u = f2 can be given by $f1_S = f2_S$ and $f1_{OP} = f2_{OP}$ because E1 is closed by the assumption on SPEC1 ∈ **CLOS**.

3. R3 left adjoint to I3:

Let the universal morphism u : SPEC3 → I3•R3(SPEC3) in **LAB** be defined by $u_S = id_{S3}$, $u_{OP} = id_{OP3}$, and for e3 ∈ E3, $u_E(e3) = e3_0$ where $e3_0$ is the unique label of the equation whose terms are those of e3, and let R3(SPEC3) = (S3, OP3, $E3_0$) with $E3_0$ the set of equations e3 ∈ E3 without label. Given SPEC2 ∈ **INCL**, SPEC3 ∈ **LAB** and f3 : SPEC3 → I3(SPEC2) in **LAB**, i.e. $f3_E(E3)$ ⊆ E2, there is a unique f2:R3(SPEC3) → SPEC2 in **INCL**, (i.e. $f2\#(E3) \subseteq E2$), such that $I3(f2) \bullet u = f3$ given by $f2_S = f3_S$, $f2_{OP} = f3_{OP}$. For such f2, we have $f2\#(E3) \subseteq E2$ since $f3_E(E3) \subseteq E2$ while $f2_E(u_E(e3)) = f3_E(e3)$ for $e3 \in E3$ follows from the fact that $f3_E(e3)$ has a unique label in I3(SPEC2) and $f2_E$ maps unique labels of equations in I3(R3(SPEC3)) to the corresponding unique labels of equations in I3(SPEC2).

4. Equivalence of **DER** and **CLOS**:

We have:

(a) $R2 \bullet CR1 \bullet I1 \bullet I2 = ID_{CLOS}$ (equality) and

(b) $I1 \bullet I2 \bullet R2 \bullet CR1 \cong ID_{DER}$ (functorial equivalence)

using the definitions of the component functors, where in case (b) SPEC1 = (S1, OP1, E1) is isomorphic to cl(SPEC1) = (S1, OP1, cl(E1)) in **DER** with cl(SPEC1) = I1• I2• R2• CR1(SPEC1). Note, that in **INCL** the specifications SPEC1 and cl(SPEC1) are nonisomorphic.

In the next section we will show that the categories **DER**, **INCL**, and **LAB** are pairwise nonequivalent.

2 Categorical Constructions in Equational Algebraic Specifications

In the following we will give constructions and characterizations of mono-, epi-, and isomorphisms as well as pushouts, pullbacks, initial and final objects in the categories **DER**, **INCL**, and **LAB** of equational algebraic specifications in section 1.

General Assumption We assume without loss of generality to have a fixed countable infinite set V_{fix} of variables such that for each signature (S, OP) we only use variables of the form $V = V_{fix} \times \{S\}$ with $V_s = V_{fix} \times \{s\}$; we can also consider V to be a family $V = (V_s)_{s \in S}$ of disjoint variables. For each equation e = (X, t1, t2) in **DER** and **INCL** or e:(X, t1, t2) in **LAB** we assume $X \subseteq V$, i.e. $X_s \subseteq V_s$ for all $s \in S$.

2.1 Theorem (Categorical Properties of LAB)

1. Characterization of Mono-, Epi-, and Isomorphisms

A morphism f:SPEC → SPEC' in **LAB** is a monomorphism (resp. epi-, iso-) if and only if each component of $f = (f_S, f_{OP}, f_E)$ is injective (resp. surjective, bijective).

2. PO-Construction and Characterization

Pushouts can be constructed separately in each component and a diagram (1) in **LAB**

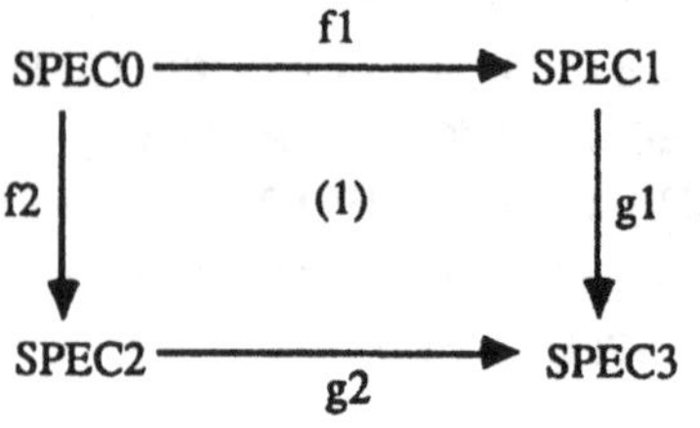

is a pushout in **LAB** if and only if each component of diagram (1) is a pushout in Sets.

3. Mono-PB-Construction and Characterization

Pullbacks in **LAB** can be constructed separately in each component if at least one morphism (g1 or g2) is a monomorphism. A diagram (1) in **LAB** as above with at least one monomorphism is a pullback in **LAB** if and only if each component of diagram (1) is a pullback in **Sets**.

4. General Pullbacks

The category **LAB** has pullbacks which are constructed as pullbacks in **Sets** for the S-, and OP-component, but in general the E-component is only a weak pullback in **Sets**, i.e. for each $e1 \in E1$ and $e2 \in E2$ with $g1\#(e1) = g2\#(e2)$ there is at least one (not necessarily exactly one) $e0 \in E0$ with $f1\#(e0) = e1$ and $f2\#(e0) = e2$.

5. Initial and Final Objects

$SPEC\varnothing = (\varnothing, \varnothing, \varnothing)$ is an initial object and $SPEC1 = (\{s\}, \{op_n{:}s^n \to s \mid n \in \mathbb{N}\}, E1)$ is a final object in **LAB**, where E1 is the set of all equations over the signature of SPEC1, using only variables of the set $V = V_{fix} \times \{s\}$.

Remark Note, that the final object SPEC1 does not consist of final objects in each component.

Proof (Categorical Properties of LAB)

1. Obviously $f = (f_S, f_{OP}, f_E) : SPEC \to SPEC'$ is a monomorphism (resp. epi- or isomorphism) if each component is injective (resp. surjective or bijective). Conversely, we have to show that f is not a monomorphism if f_S, f_{OP}, or f_E is not injective (and similarly for the other cases). *Monomorphism* : if $f_S(s1) = f_S(s2)$ for $s1 \neq s2$ in S then for $SPEC0 = (\{s1\}, \varnothing, \varnothing)$ we have $f1, f2 : SPEC0 \to SPEC$ with $f1_S(s1) = s1$ and $f2_S(s1) = s2$ and $f \bullet f1 = f \bullet f2$. From $f1 \neq f2$ we conclude that f is not a monomorphism. *Epimorphism* : if we have $s' \notin f_S(S)$ then construct $SPEC'' = (S' \cup \{s''\}, OP' \cup OP'', E' \cup E'')$ where OP" (resp. E") is a copy of OP' (resp. E') and each occurrence of s' (resp. of s' or N' using s') is replaced by s" (resp. s" or N"). Now define $f1, f2 : SPEC' \to SPEC''$ by letting f1 be the inclusion and f2 equal to f1 except of the fact that s' is mapped to s" and similar $N' \in OP'$ and $e' \in E'$ to the corresponding $N'' \in OP''$ and $e'' \in E''$. We have $f1 \bullet f = f2 \bullet f$, because f1 and f2 are equal on the image of f, but $f1 \neq f2$. This implies that f is not an epimorphism. Similarly for f_{OP} and f_E. *Isomorphism* : follows from above since in this case isomorphism is equivalent to mono + epi.

2. In order to give a characterization of pushouts and pullbacks we need to have a more explicit description of a specification $SPEC = (S, OP, E)$ in **LAB**. In fact, we consider S, OP and E to be arbitrary sets together with following functions:

$dom{:}OP \to S^*$	(domain of operation symbols)
$ran{:}OP \to S$	(range of operation symbols)
$sor{:}E \to S$	(sort of an equation)
$var{:}E \to \mathcal{P}(V)$	(variables of an equation)
$L{:}E \to T_{OP}(V)$	(left hand side of an equation)
$R{:}E \to T_{OP}(V)$	(right hand side of an equation)

where $V = (V_s)_{s \in S}$ with $V_s = V_{fix} \times \{s\}$. Moreover we have

Compatibility Condition for Specifications

For each $e \in E$ with $sor(e) = s$ and $var(e) = X$ we have $L(e), R(e) \in T_{OP}(X)_s$

Compatibility Condition for Specification Morphisms

For each $f = (f_S, f_{OP}, f_E){:}SPEC \to SPEC'$,the following are commutative diagrams (where $f_V((v, s)) = (v, f_S(s))$ and f# is the extension of (f_S, f_{OP}, f_V) to terms)

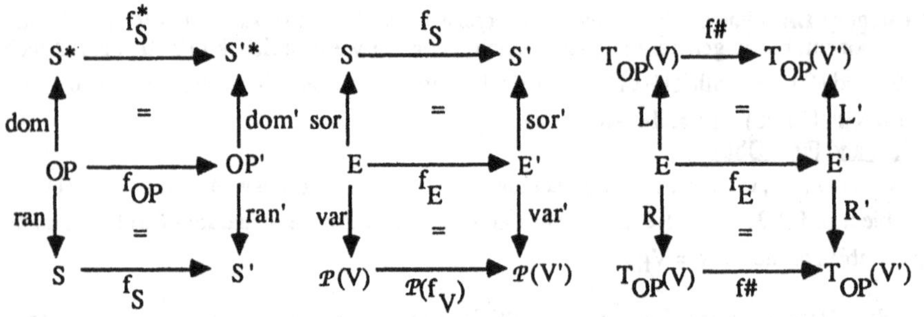

It can be shown that pushouts can be constructed separately in each component S, OP, and E respectively leading to unique functions dom, ran, sor, var, L, and R such that all the compatibility conditions are satisfied. As a consequence the corresponding construction becomes a pushout in the category **LAB** and vice versa each pushout in **LAB** is a pushout in **Sets** for each component using the fact that pushouts are unique up to isomorphisms and isomorphisms in **LAB** are isomorphisms in **Sets** in each component.

3. Given gi : SPECi → SPEC3 for i = 1, 2 in **LAB** where g1 or g2 is a monomorphism, i.e. injective in each component, we can construct SPEC0 together with fi : SPEC0 → SPECi for i = 1, 2 as pullback of (g1, g2) in **LAB** by taking S0 and OP0 as pullbacks in **Sets** leading to unique functions r0: OP0 → S0 and d0: OP0 → S0* with the appropriate commutativity properties (because the free monoid functor C* preserves pullbacks). Hence we have signature morphisms fi: (S0, OP0) → (Si, OPi) for i = 1, 2. Then we construct E0 as pullback in **Sets** leading to s0 by PB-property of S0. From the definition of Vi as $V_i = V_{fix} \times Si$ for i = 0, 1, 2, 3 and the fact that $V_{fix} \times$ - preserves pullbacks we conclude that we have the following pullback (1) in **Sets**:

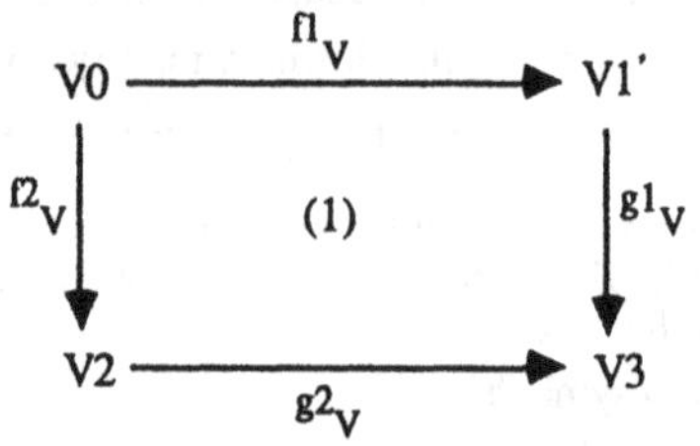

By structural induction we can conclude that also the following diagram (2) is a pullback in **Sets** using the fact that the S- and OP-components are already pullbacks in **Sets**

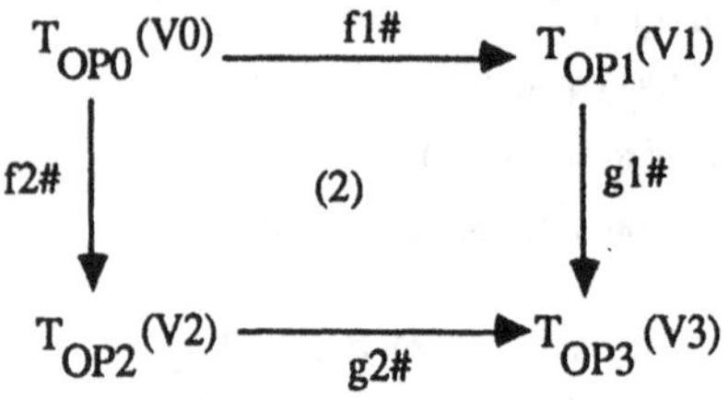

Note that the pullback properties of (1) and (2) are valid without the assumption that one of the morphisms f1, f2, g1, and g2 is a monomorphism.

Summarizing we can show the existence and compatibility of SPEC0 = (S0, OP0, E0) ∈ **LAB** with **LAB**-morphisms fi:SPEC0 → SPECi for i = 1, 2 s.t. g1 • f1 = g2 • f2 and S0, OP0, E0, $S0^*$, $T_{OP0}(V0)$ and $\mathcal{P}(V0)$ are pullbacks in **Sets**. This implies immediately that SPEC0 with (f1, f2) is the pullback of (g1, g2) in **LAB**.

4. We illustrate with an example how general pullbacks are constructed. The following diagram (1) is a pullback in **LAB**:

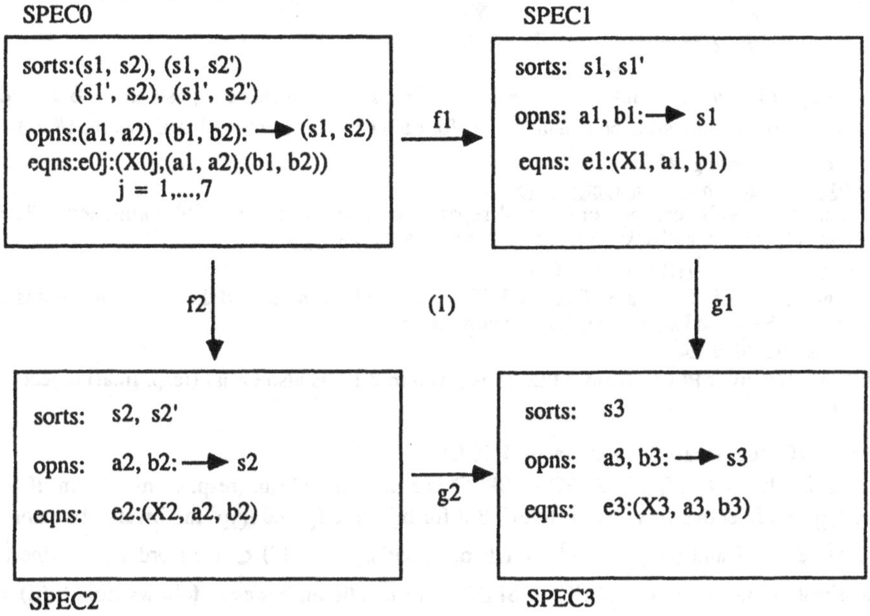

where $Xi = \{(v, si), (v, si')\}$ for i = 1, 2 and $X3 = \{(v, s3)\}$
and $gi_S(si) = gi_S(si') = s3$, $gi_{OP}(ai) = a3$, $gi_{OP}(bi) = b3$ for i = 1, 2
and $X0_1 = \{(v, (s1, s2)), (v, (s1, s2')) (v, (s1', s2)), (v, (s1', s2'))\}$
$X0_2,\ldots,X0_5$ consisting of 3 variables of $X0_1$ each
$X0_6 = \{(v, (s1, s2)), (v, (s1', s2'))\}$
$X0_7 = \{(v, (s1, s2')), (v, (s1', s2))\}$

Note that we have 7 different equations in E0 although the pullback of $(g1_E, g2_E)$ consists of one equation only. The maximal X0 is $X0_1$ which was used to show the weak pullback property in the E-component.

5. It is direct to show that SPEC∅ is the initial and SPEC1 the final object in **LAB**.

2.2 Theorem (Categorical Properties of INCL)

<u>1. Characterization of Mono-, Epi-, and Isomorphisms</u>

A morphism f : SPEC → SPEC' in **INCL** is a monomorphism (resp. epimorphism) if and only if each component of $f = (f_S, f_{OP})$ is injective (resp. surjective). The morphism f is an isomorphism if and only if f_S and f_{OP} are bijective and f#(E) = E'. Equivalently, f is an isomorphism if and only if f_S and f_{OP} are bijective and f is strict in **INCL**, i.e. $f\#^{-1}(E') \subseteq E$.

<u>2. PO-Construction and Characterization</u>

Pushouts in **INCL** can be constructed separately in the S- and the OP-component and the equations E3 of the pushout object SPEC3 in diagram (1) are given by g1#(E1) ∪ g2#(E2). This means that a diagram (1) in **INCL**

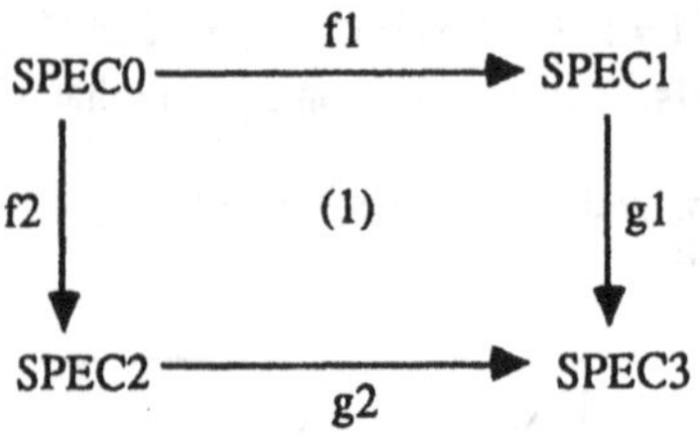

is a pushout in **INCL** if and only if the S- and the OP-components are pushouts in **Sets** and (g1, g2) is jointly surjective on equations, i.e. for each $e3 \in E3$ there is $e1 \in E1$ with $g1\#(e1) = e3$ or $e2 \in E2$ with $g2\#(e2) = e3$.

<u>3. PB-Construction and Characterization</u>

Pullbacks in **INCL** can be constructed separately in the S- and the OP-component. The equations E0 of the pullback object SPEC0 in diagram (1) are given by

$$E0 = f1\#^{-1}(E1) \cap f2\#^{-1}(E2).$$

A diagram (1) in **INCL** is a pullback in **INCL** if and only if the S- and the OP-component is a pullback in **Sets** and E0 satisfies the equation above.

<u>4. Initial and Final Objects</u>

The specification SPEC∅ (resp. SPEC1) as given in 2.1.5 is also initial (resp. final) object in **INCL**.

Proof (Categorical Properties of INCL)

1. Obviously $f = (f_S, f_{OP}) : SPEC \to SPEC'$ is a monomorphism (resp. epimorphism) if f_S and f_{OP} are injective (resp. surjective). But for bijective f_S and f_{OP}, the inverse functions $(f_S)^{-1}: S' \to S$ and $(f_{OP})^{-1}: OP' \to OP$ must satisfy $f^{-1}\#(E') \subseteq E$ in order to define a specification morphism $f^{-1}: SPEC' \to SPEC$. This condition, however, follows from $f\#(E) = E'$. Moreover for bijective f_S and f_{OP} the conditions $f\#(E) = E'$ and $f\#\text{-}1(E') \subseteq E$ are equivalent.

2. The construction of the signature part of pushouts in **INCL** is the same as in 2.1.2 for **LAB**. It can also be shown that (g1, g2) with SPEC3 and $E3 = g1\#(E1) \cup g2\#(E2)$ is a pushout in **INCL**.

3. The construction of the signature part of pullbacks in **INCL** is the same as in the proof of 2.1.4 for **LAB**. To show that (f1, f2) with SPEC0 and $E0 = f1\#^{-1}(E1) \cap f2\#^{-1}(E2)$ is a pullback in **INCL**, let $hi : SPEC \to SPECi$ for $i = 1, 2$ with $g1 \bullet h1 = g2 \bullet h2$. Then there is a unique signature morphism $h : SPEC \to SPEC0$ with $fi \bullet h = hi$ for $i = 1, 2$. To show that h is a **INCL**-morphism, i.e. $h\#(E) \subseteq E0$, let $e \in E$; then $h1\#(e) \in E1$ and $h2\#(e) \in E2$, and this implies that $fi\#(h\#(e)) \in Ei$ and hence $h\#(e) \in fi\#^{-1}(Ei)$ for $i = 1,2$. But this means $h\#(e) \in E0$. Given any other pullback SPEC with (h1, h2) of (g1, g2) we have an isomorphism $h : SPEC \to SPEC0$ with $fi \bullet h = hi$ for $i = 1, 2$. Then $E0 = f1\#^{-1}(E1) \cap f2\#^{-1}(E2)$ implies

$h\#^{-1}(E0) = h\#^{-1}\, f1\#^{-1}(E1) \cap h\#^{-1}\, f2\#^{-1}(E2)$ which is equivalent to

$$E = h1\#^{-1}(E1) \cap h2\#^{-1}(E2).$$

4. Obvious.

2.3 Theorem (Categorical Properties of DER)

<u>1. Characterization of Mono-, Epi-, and Isomorphisms</u>

A morphism $f : SPEC \to SPEC'$ in **DER** is a monomorphism (resp. epimorphism) if and only if each component of $f = (f_S, f_{OP})$ is injective (resp. surjective). The morphism f is an isomorphism if and only if f_S and f_{OP} are bijective and $cl(f\#(E)) = cl(E')$. Equivalently, f is an isomorphism if and only if f_S and f_{OP} are bijective and f is strict in **DER**, i.e. $f\#^{-1}(E') \subseteq cl(E)$.

2. PO-Construction and Characterization

Pushouts in **DER** can be constructed separately in the S- and OP-component and the equations E3 of the pushout object SPEC3 in diagram (1) are given by $g1\#(E1) \cup g2\#(E2)$.

This means that a diagram (1) in **DER**

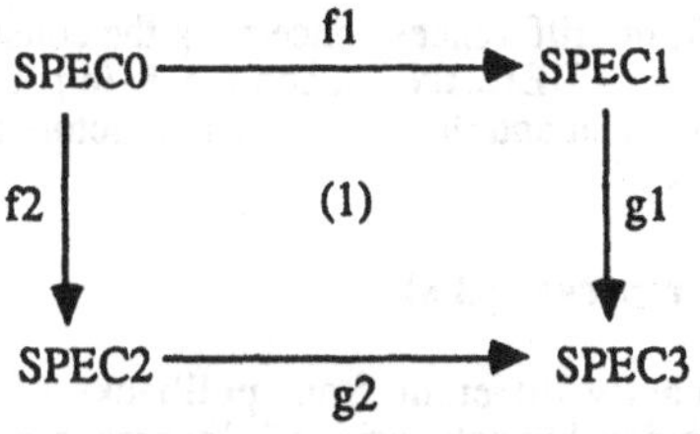

is a pushout in **DER** if and only if the S- and the OP-components are pushouts in **Sets** and (g1, g2) is jointly closure surjective on equations, i.e. for each $e3 \in E3$ we have

$$e3 \in cl(g1\#(E1) \cup g2\#(E2))$$

3. PB-Construction and Characterization

Pullbacks in **DER** can be constructed separately in the S- and the OP-component. The equations E0 of the pullback object SPEC0 in diagram (1) are given by

$$E0 = f1\#^{-1}cl(E1) \cap f2\#^{-1}cl(E2).$$

A diagram (1) in **DER** is a pullback in **Sets** and we have

$$cl(E0) = f1\#^{-1}cl(E1) \cap f2\#^{-1}cl(E2).$$

4. Initial and Final Objects

The specifications SPEC∅ (resp. SPEC1) as given in 2.1.5 is also initial (resp. final) in **DER**.

Proof (Categorical Properties of DER)

1. For the characterization of mono- and epimorphisms we can take the proof of 2.2.1. A morphism $f{:}SPEC \rightarrow SPEC'$ is an isomorphism in **DER** if and only if f_S and f_{OP} are bijective and f^{-1} is a **DER**-morphisms, i.e. $f\#^{-1}(E') \subseteq cl(E)$. But this condition implies for bijective f_S and f_{OP} that $f\#\, f\#^{-1}(E') \subseteq f\#(cl(E))$ and hence $E' \subseteq f\#(cl(E))$ and $(cl(E')) \subseteq cl(f\#(E))$ while $f\#(E) \subseteq cl(E')$ implies $cl(f\#(E)) \subseteq cl(E')$ and hence $cl(E') = cl(f\#(E))$.
Vice versa $cl(E') = cl(f\#(E))$ implies

$$f\#^{-1}(E') \subseteq f\#^{-1}cl(E') = f\#^{-1}(cl(f\#(E))) \subseteq cl(f\#^{-1}(f\#(E))) = cl(E).$$

2. The construction of the signature part of pushouts in **DER** is the same as in the proof of 2.1.2 for **LAB**. To show that (g1, g2) with SPEC3 and $E3 = g1\#(E1) \cup g2\#(E2)$ is a pushout in **DER**, we can use the same proof as in 2.2.2 replacing E by cl(E), because we only have to show $h\#(E3) \subseteq cl(E)$ and we only know $hi\#(Ei) \subseteq cl(E)$ for $i = 1, 2$.
The characterization of the pushout concerning the S- and the OP-component follows from the fact that pushouts are closed under isomorphisms and **DER**-isomorphisms are bijective in the S- and OP-component.

3. The construction of the signature part of pullbacks in **DER** is the same as in the proof of 2.2.3 for **LAB** and so all we need is to show that (f1, f2) with SPEC0 and $E0 = f1\#^{-1}(cl(E1)) \cap f2\#^{-1}(cl(E2))$ is a pullback in **DER**. Given $hi : SPEC \rightarrow SPECi$ for $i = 1, 2$ with $g1 \bullet h1 = g2 \bullet h2$ we have a unique signature morphism $h : SPEC \rightarrow SPEC0$ with $fi \bullet h = hi$ for $i = 1, 2$. To prove that $h\#(E) \subseteq cl(E0)$, i.e. that h is a **DER**-morphism, let $e \in E$: then $h1\#(e) \in cl(E1)$

and h2#(e) ∈ cl(E2). This implies that fi#(h#(e)) ∈ cl(Ei) and hence that h#(e) ∈ $fi\#^{-1}$(cl(Ei)) for i = 1, 2. But this means h#(e) ∈ E0 ⊆ cl(E0).

4. Obvious.

3 Nonequivalence of Equational Categories

In this section we give a list of the most significant differences concerning the construction of pushouts and pullbacks in the equational categories **DER, INCL,** and **LAB.** In particular, we show that these categories are pairwise nonequivalent and that the specific functors introduced in 1.1 do not preserve pushouts and/or pullbacks.

3.1 Fact (I1:INCL → DER does not preserve PB's)

Proof Pullbacks in **INCL** can be significantly different from pullbacks of the same morphisms in **DER**, i.e. they may have nonisomorphic categories of algebras, e.g. for SIG = ({s}, {a, b, c: → s}) diagram (1) is pullback in **DER** and diagram (2) is pullback in **INCL**:

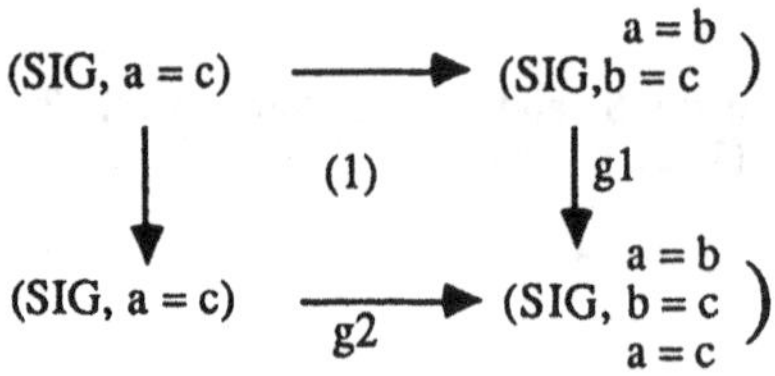

PB in **DER**

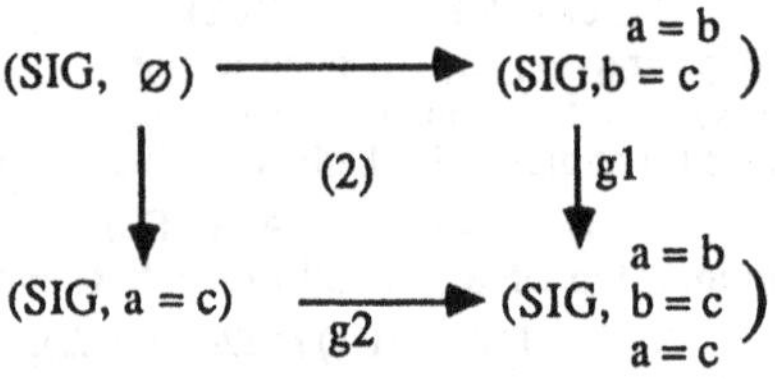

PB in **INCL**

3.2 Fact (I2:CLOS → INCL does not preserve P0's)

Proof Although the pushouts may not be isomorphic in **INCL** they define the same or isomorphic categories of algebras using the same signature SIG as above we have the following pushouts (1') in **CLOS** and (2') in **INCL**:

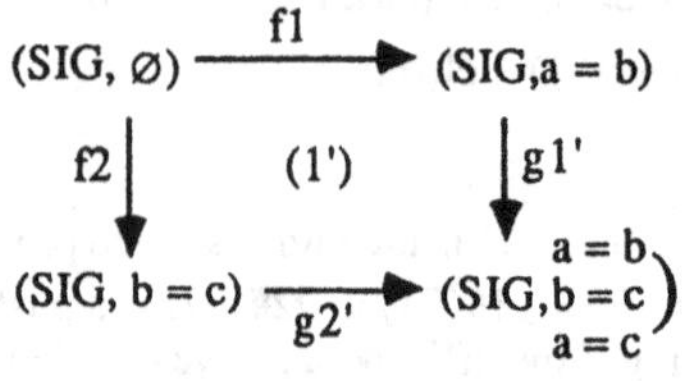

PO in **CLOS**

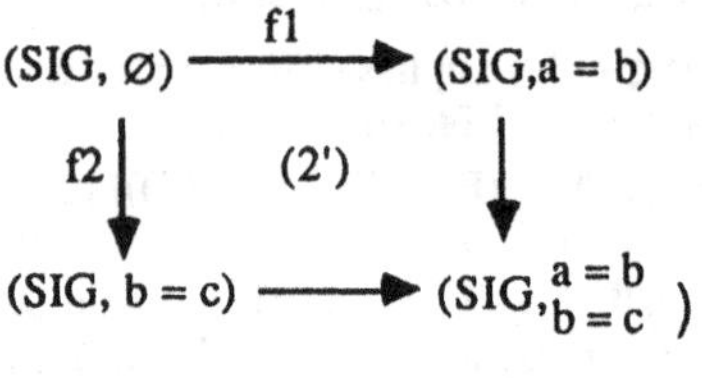

PO in **INCL**

3.3 Fact (R3:LAB → INCL does not preserve PB's)

Proof The pullbacks (2) and (3) in **INCL** and **LAB** of the corresponding morphisms with same semantics can have nonisomorphic semantics:

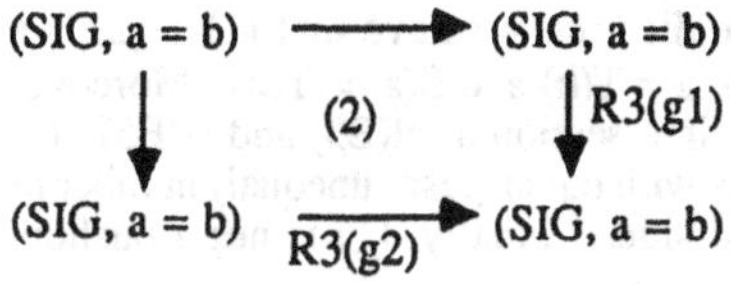

$$\begin{array}{ccc}
(\text{SIG}, a = b) & \longrightarrow & (\text{SIG}, a = b) \\
\Big\downarrow \quad (2) & & \Big\downarrow R3(g1) \\
(\text{SIG}, a = b) & \xrightarrow[R3(g2)]{} & (\text{SIG}, a = b)
\end{array}$$

PB in **INCL**

$$\begin{array}{ccc}
(\text{SIG}, \varnothing) & \longrightarrow & (\text{SIG}, e1{:}a = b) \\
\Big\downarrow \quad (3) & & \Big\downarrow g1 \\
(\text{SIG}, e2{:}a{=}b) & \xrightarrow[g2]{} & (\text{SIG}, \begin{array}{l} e1{:}a = b \\ e2{:}a = b \end{array})
\end{array}$$

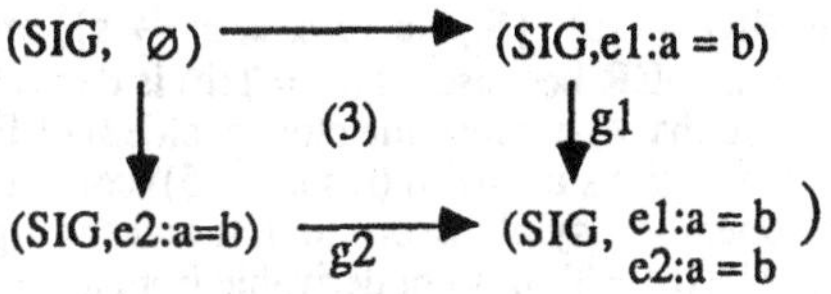

PB in **LAB**

3.4 Fact (DER and INCL do not satisfy component PO-property)

Proof The following diagram with SIG as in 3.1 is a pushout of monomorphisms in **DER** and **INCL**, but the E-component is not a pushout in **Sets**

$$\begin{array}{ccc}
(\text{SIG}, \varnothing) & \xrightarrow{f1} & (\text{SIG}, a = b) \\
f2\Big\downarrow & & \Big\downarrow g1 \\
(\text{SIG}, a{=}b) & \xrightarrow{g2} & (\text{SIG}, a = b)
\end{array}$$

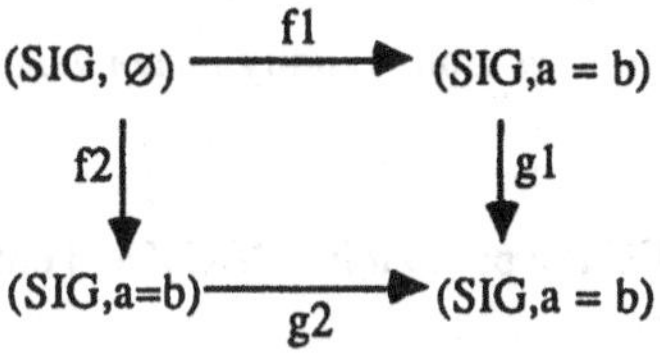

3.5 Fact (Validity of PO-PB-Mono Decomposition Property)

The categories **INCL** and **LAB** satisfy, while the category **DER** does not, the PO-PB-Mono Decomposition Property, i.e., for all diagrams (1) and (2) in **CAT** of the following form

$$\begin{array}{ccccc}
S1 & \xrightarrow{f1} & S2 & \xrightarrow{f2} & S3 \\
h1\Big\downarrow \quad (1) & & h2\Big\downarrow \quad (2) & & \Big\downarrow h3 \\
S4 & \xrightarrow{g1} & S5 & \xrightarrow{g2} & S6
\end{array}$$

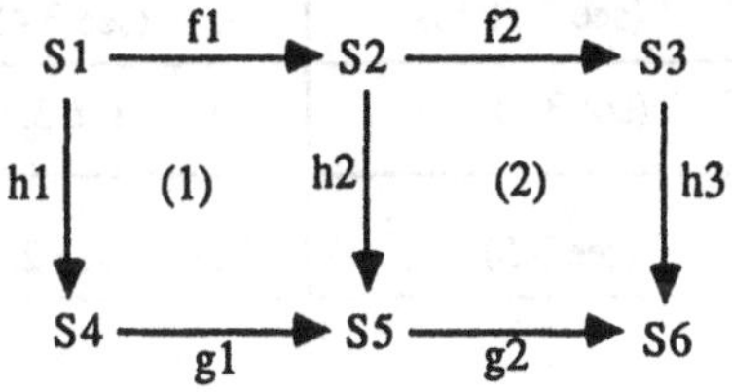

we have that
if (1) + (2) is a pushout, (2) a pullback, h1, h2, h3, f2 and g2 are monomorphisms
then also (1) is a pushout.

Proof

As shown in [4] this property is satisfied by the category **Sets** and hence also by **LAB** using the PO- and PB-characterizations in 2.2.2 and 2.2.3. The property is also satisfied by **INCL** but not by **DER** as shown by the following counter example:

$$\begin{array}{ccccc}
E1 & & E2 & & E3 \\
(\text{SIG}, \varnothing) & \longrightarrow & (\text{SIG}, \varnothing) & \longrightarrow & (\text{SIG}, S(a) = T(b)) \\
\Big\downarrow & (1) & \Big\downarrow & (2) & \Big\downarrow \\
(\text{SIG}, a = T(b)) & \longrightarrow & (\text{SIG}, \begin{array}{c} a = T(b) \\ ST(b) = T(b) \end{array}) & \longrightarrow & \text{SIG}, \begin{array}{l} S(a) = T(b) \\ a = T(b) \\ ST(b) = T(b) \end{array}) \\
E4 & & E5 & & E6
\end{array}$$

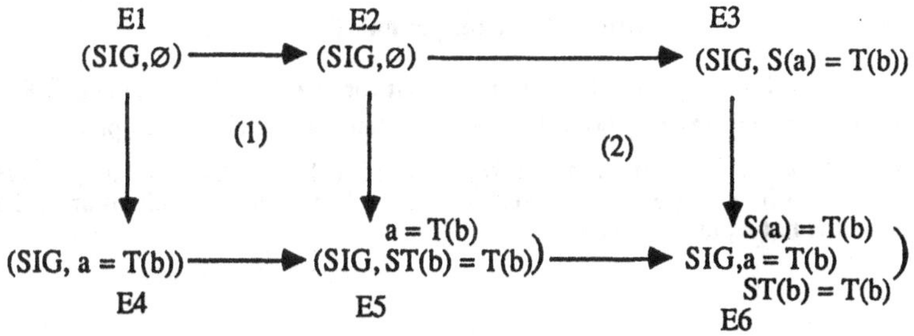

where SIG = ({s}, {S, T:s → s; a, b: → s}) and in the diagram we have that (1) + (2) is a pushout in **DER** because ST(b) = T(b) is derivable from a = T(b) and S(a) = T(b). Moreover (2) is a pullback, because the closure cl(E2) of E2 is the intersection of cl(E3) and cl(E5). (In fact, all equations in cl(E3) (resp. cl(E5)) consist of terms with equal (resp. unequal) number of unary operation symbols on the left and the right hand side.) Finally, (1) is not a pushout because ST(b) = T(b) is not derivable from a = T(b).
Note, that the counter example does not work replacing "ST(b) = T(b)" by the derived equation "S(a) = a" from a = T(b) and S(a) = T(b).

3.6 Theorem (Nonequivalence of Equational Categories)

The categories **DER**, **INCL** and **LAB** are pairwise nonequivalent.

Proof
The nonequivalence of **DER**, **INCL**, and **LAB** follows from validity or nonvalidity of the following categorical properties:
(a) Pushouts of monomorphisms are pullbacks.
(b) PO-PB-Mono Decomposition Property.
(c) Component PO-Property, i.e. a diagram in **SPEC** is a pushout in **SPEC** if and only if each component (S, OP, and E) is a pushout in **Sets**.

	(a) Mono PO's are PB's	(b) PO-PB-Mono-Decomp.	(c) Component PO
DER	NO (see 3.4)	NO (see 3.5)	NO (see 3.4)
INCL	NO (see 3.4)	YES (see 3.5)	NO (see 3.4)
LAB	YES	YES (see 3.5)	YES (see 2.2.2)

3.7 Definitions (M-Morphisms)

For the categories **DER** and **INCL** define the two different classes M of morphisms
M_{inj} = class of all injective specification morphisms, i.e. f_S and f_{OP} injective for f = (f_S, f_{OP}), which are exactly the monomorphisms in **DER** and. **INCL**.
M_{str} = class of all injective and strict specification morphisms, where strictness in **INCL** means $f\#^{-1}(E') \subseteq E$ for f:(S, OP, E) → (S', OP', E') and $f\#^{-1}(E')$ is the set of all equations e over (S, OP) s.t. $f\#(e) \in E'$. In **DER** we require $f\#^{-1}(E') \subseteq cl(E)$.

3.8 Remark (Counterexample for Component PO Property)

In [4] it is claimed in the proof of theorem 7.7 that for (**STRUCT**, M_{str}) and (**INCL**, M_{str}) the component PO-PB-property holds for squares where the horizontal morphisms are in M_{str}, which would simplify the proof of HLR2(3) and HLR2*(4) - (7). Unfortunately this is not true as shown in the following pushout in **INCL** where the horizontal morphisms are strict, but the E-component is not a pushout in **Sets**:

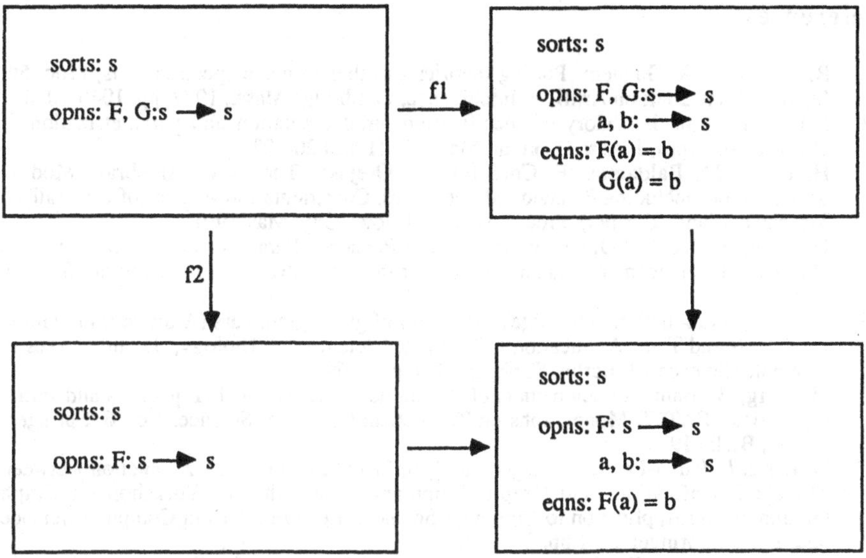

3.9 Fact (Strict Injective Morphisms in DER and INCL)

1. Strict injective morphisms are closed under pushouts and pullbacks in **INCL.**
2. Each pushout of (f1, f2) with f1 strict injective is also a pullback in **DER** and **INCL.**
3. Uniqueness (up to isomorphism) of pushout complements for g1 • f1 with f1 strict injective in **INCL.**

Concluding Remarks

We have illustrated in this paper how apparently equivalent formulations of equational algebraic specifications lead to categories with significantly different properties. These distinct properties depend on different formalizations of the extensions to the equational part of signature morphisms : from the weakest form, in which the translated equations need only be derivable, to the strongest form in which equations are labelled and can be distinguished by such labels, even when signature morphisms may identify the corresponding terms. Elsewhere [8] we have extended this analysis to the properties which define HLR1- and HLR2-categories [4] and shown that only **LAB** , with the set of distinguished morphisms Minj, satisfies the properties which guarantee the Church-Rosser, Parallelism and Concurrency Theorems. For the other categories, it is not known whether there is a class of distinguished morphisms M with which **DER** or **INCL** forms an HLR1 or an HLR2 category. The discussion presented here should also be extended to algebraic specifications which allow conditional equations.

Acknowledgement This research was conducted in part during a visit of H. Ehrig at University of L'Aquila in July 1991 supported by the Gruppo Nazionale di Informatica Matematica of the Consiglio Nazionale delle Ricerche of Italy

References

1. R. Burstall, J.A. Goguen: Putting theories together to make specifications, Proc. 5th Internat. Joint Conf. on Artificial Intelligence, Cambridge Mass., 1977, pp. 1045-1058
2. H.D.Ehrich: On the theory of specification, implementation and parametrization of abstract data types, J. Assoc.Comput.Mach. 29 (1982) 206-227
3. H. Ehrig, M. Baldamus, F. Cornelius, F. Orejas: Theory of Algebraic Module Specifications including Behavioural Semantics, Constraints and Aspects of Generalized Morphisms (invited paper), Proc. AMAST'91, Iowa City, May 1991
4. H. Ehrig, A. Habel, H.-J. Kreowski, F. Parisi-Presicce: Parallelism and Concurrency in High-Level-Replacement Systems, to appear in Math. Structures in Computer Science 1991
5. H. Ehrig: Introduction to the algebraic theory of graph grammars (A Survey) in: Graph Grammars and Their Application to Computer Science and Biology, Lecture Notes in Computer Science 73. Berlin: Springer 1979, pp. 1-69
6. H. Ehrig, B. Mahr: Fundamentals of Algebraic Specification 1. Equations and Initial Semantics. EATCS Monographs on Theoretical Computer Science, Vol. 6, Springer-Verlag, Berlin 1985
7. H. Ehrig, F. Parisi-Presicce: Algebraic Specification Grammars: A Junction Between Module Specifications and Graph Grammars, Proc. 4th Int. Workshop on Graph Grammars and Application to Computer Science, Lecture Notes in Computer Science 532. Berlin: Springer 1991,pp. 292-310
8. H. Ehrig, F. Parisi-Presicce: Nonequivalence of Categories for Equational Algebraic Specifications in view of High Level Replacement Systems, TUB Technical Report 91/16, Technische Universitat Berlin Sept 1991
9. J.V. Guttag, J. J. Horning: The algebraic specification of abstract data types, Acta Informatica 10 (1978) 27-52
10. F. Parisi-Presicce: A Rule-Based Approach to Modular System Design, Proc. 12th Int. Conf. Soft. Eng., Computer Science Press 1990,pp. 202-211
11. F. Parisi-Presicce: Foundations of Rule-Based Design of Modular Systems, Theoret. Comp. Sc. 83, 131-155 (1991)
12. J.W. Thatcher, E.G. Wagner, J.B. Wright, Data type specification : parametrization and the power of specification techniques, Proc. 10th Symp. Theory of Comput. (1978) 119-132 and Trans. Progr. Lang. and Syst. 4 (1982) 711-732
13. S. N. Zilles, Algebraic specification of data types, Project MAC Prograss Report 11, MIT 1974, 28-52

Process Semantics of Temporal Logic Specification

J.L.Fiadeiro, J.F.Costa, A.Sernadas

INESC & Dept. Matemática - IST
Apartado 10105, 1017 Lisboa Codex, PORTUGAL
{llf,fgc,acs}@inesc.pt

T.S.E.Maibaum

Dept. Computing - Imperial College of Science, Technology and Medicine
180 Queen's Gate, London SW7 2BZ, UK
tsem@doc.ic.ac.uk

Abstract. A process semantics for temporal logic specification is provided by relating a category of temporal theories and interpretations between theories where specification configuration and interconnection is achieved via colimits of diagrams, and a category of algebraic models of processes where parallel composition is explained in terms of limits of diagrams. This semantics is proved to be exact in the sense that given a diagram in the categories of theories and a model of it as a diagram in the category of processes, the limit of the process diagram is a model of the colimit of the theory diagram. In fact, any denotation of a system of interconnected specifications corresponds to a configuration of their denotations as a system of interconnected processes.

1 Introduction

In this paper we bring together two lines of research that we have been pursuing to provide formal foundations for object-oriented system development. On the one hand, the realisation that an object is, basically, a process endowed with trace-dependent attributes, led research on algebraic models for objects [eg Sernadas et al 90, Sernadas and Ehrich 91] to capitalise on previous work on process models, mainly [Jonsson 85, Winskel 84]. On the other hand, the great success of formal accounts of change and behaviour based on temporal, dynamic and deontic logics, namely for reasoning about the reactive aspects of systems, led research on logics for object specification and verification [eg Fiadeiro and Maibaum 91a,b] to concentrate on modal logics, and temporal logic in particular following the trend initiated in [Pnueli 77].

We could say that the essence of object-orientation is to identify a system with a *community* of interacting objects. Hence, in both cases, the main tasks involved were to provide (1) a formal notion of object (either algebraic or logical) and (2) a model of object interconnection. Naturally, both semantic domains should match in the sense that, having defined a denotation function from specifications (theories) to algebraic models, given a specification of a complex object as a system of interconnected theories (corresponding to the specification of its components), any configuration of their denotations as a system of interconnected models that agrees with the specified interconnections should provide a model of the complex object.

In the formalisation of each semantic domain (logical and algebraic) we followed the categorial "dogma" that "given a category of widgets, the operation of putting a system of widgets together to form some super-widget corresponds to taking the colimit of the diagram of widgets that shows how to interconnect them" [Goguen 89]. From the specification point of view, this means that objects are specified via (temporal) theories (or theory presentations), and communities of objects are specified via diagrams in the category of theories and interpretations between theories (theory morphisms). On the one hand, this means that the behaviour of an individual object is not defined through a process term of some process language describing its possible computations, but by specifying the constraints (safety and liveness) that the object is required to satisfy. On the other hand, this approach favours the specification of communities of objects by stating how they are interconnected (through a diagram), i.e. how they interfere, rather than prescribing their relative behaviour with the usual program composition primitives such as sequencing, choice, etc. Being more "declarative", this approach is more adequate for supporting the earlier phases of system development during which specifications are required to evolve as new requirements are added, new components are integrated, or existing ones are refined or revised. However, it was not obvious that such specification modules could be given a direct counterpart in terms of the modules out of which the behaviour of a system can be decomposed, a nice algebraic characterisation of which is provided, for instance, by the theory of processes.

The same categorial principle can be applied to such "algebraic models" of systems as well. In fact, this principle first appeared in the context of General Systems Theory [Goguen and Ginali 78], and has been recently reawakened [eg Goguen 91] in an attempt to provide semantic foundations for concurrent interacting objects, namely using sheaf-theory. Other applications of the same principle have been tested, namely for more traditional trace-based process models [eg Costa and Sernadas 91]. A general framework is even now available that unifies various semantic models of objects [Ehrich *et al* 90]. The advantage of these categorial approaches is that they concentrate on the formalisation of what processes are and of the way they can be interconnected in diagrams as a means of specifying more complex processes, without resorting to any specific process language/algebra.

Having both semantic domains (logical and algebraic) structured in categorial terms, the requirement that the models of a composite theory be compositions of models of its components can be analysed in terms of the properties of the functor that sends specifications to the categories of their process models and the properties of these categories. In fact, in the theory of institutions [Goguen and Burstall 84], this property (or a similar one) has been discussed under the name of *(semi-)exactness* [Diaconescu et al 91, Meseguer 89, Sannella and Tarlecki 85].

This is, in fact, the framework that we wish to present in this paper. For simplicity, we have chosen a propositional temporal logic and a trace-based process model. These may provide rather naïve semantic domains when compared to the more sophisticated logics and process models that have been developed more recently, but they allow us to concentrate on the envisaged categorial relationship between temporal specifications and processes. It is expected that the same principles will apply to other logics and process models.

In section 2, we define the very simple process model that we have adopted, and relate it to the semantic models that have been used in some temporal logics [eg Barringer 87]. Basically, we define a category of processes and process morphisms, and explain how parallel composition can be achieved via limits of diagrams. In section 3, we define the propositional temporal logic that we use for process specification and define, for each specification, the category of processes that satisfy it. We then show that this category has a terminal object and that every model of a specification is characterised by its relationship with the terminal model. Finally, in section 4, we define specification morphisms, show that the denotation functor preserves finite colimits, and that the chosen process semantics is exact, ie that the models of a combination of specifications consist of the combinations of models of the specifications. Although we do not obtain an institution in the strict sense [Goguen and Burstall 84], we do follow the institutional way of defining a logic throughout the paper.

2 A categorial process model

In this section we present the categorial model of processes over which we shall interpret temporal specifications. This process model is adapted from [Costa and Sernadas 91]. The main difference with respect to [ibidem] is that whereas the process model developed therein follows a local view on processes, the one we shall use herein assumes a global point of view in the sense that we shall be concerned with the behaviour of processes in all possible environments and not in isolation.

Let us start by recalling the *category of pointed sets* which we shall denote by $Set_\perp$. It has as objects nonempty sets with points, ie, pairs consisting of a set together with a designated element. Morphisms in $Set_\perp$ are functions that preserve the designated points. In particular we have that $(\{\perp\},\perp)$ is a zero object of $Set_\perp$ (both initial and terminal), and $<X\times Y,<\perp_X,\perp_Y>>$ is the categorial product of $<X,\perp_X>$ and $<Y,\perp_Y>$ with the usual projections, since they preserve points. We can extend the existence of products to the existence of all finite limits and so $Set_\perp$ is finitely complete.

Definition 2.1. A *process* $P=<E,\Lambda>$ is a pair consisting of a finite pointed set E and a subset Λ of E^{ω} (each $\lambda \in \Lambda$ is an infinite sequence $\lambda:\omega \rightarrow E$ of elements of E). ◇

The elements of E are called *events* and the elements of Λ *life cycles*. Given a process $P=<E,\Lambda>$ we refer to $E \backslash \{\bot\}$ as $\alpha(P)$ — the *alphabet* of P — and we refer to Λ as $\tau(P)$ — the *life cycles* of P. Several remarks concerning this definition seem to be in order:

• As in [Barringer 87], we are dealing with *open* semantic structures in the sense that we are considering a process as embedded in a wider environment. This open semantics justifies the adoption of an infinite temporal domain: even if the process has a finite life-time, we may assume that the environment will always be able to progress. Steps that are performed by the environment correspond to the occurrence of the designated event $\bot_E$ in a life cycle. When projected to the proper events of the process, a life cycle gives the local behaviour of the process.

• No equivalent of the traditional prefix-closure condition of process semantics is assumed: if a (finite) trace u is the projection of a life-cycle of L to the proper events of the process then, after u, there is no commitment for the process to perform any other event. That is, we work only with *quiescent traces* in the sense of [Misra 84]. In the traditional temporal specification jargon [Manna and Pnueli 81], this means that we are interested in processes that satisfy the liveness requirements that may be specified. Whereas safety properties ("nothing bad will ever happen") are compatible with prefix-closure (the prefix of a "safe" trace is still safe), liveness requirements ("something good will eventually happen") are not.

Definition 2.2. Let h be a morphism (function) from a pointed set A to a pointed set B. The extension of $h:A \rightarrow B$ to A^{ω} is the function $h^{\omega}:A^{\omega} \rightarrow B^{\omega}$ defined by $h^{\omega}(\lambda)=\lambda;h$. (That is, we apply h pointwise to the elements of the sequence.) ◇

Definition 2.3. A *process morphism* $h:<E_1,\Lambda_1> \rightarrow <E_2,\Lambda_2>$ is given by a morphism $h_E:E_1 \rightarrow E_2$ such that $h_E^{\omega}(\Lambda_1) \subseteq \Lambda_2$ (*life cycle inheritance condition*). ◇

Proposition 2.4. Processes and process morphisms constitute a category Proc. ◇

A morphism $h:<E_1,\Lambda_1> \rightarrow <E_2,\Lambda_2>$ can be seen as a way of embedding the process $P_2=<E_2,\Lambda_2>$ within P_1, recognising P_2 a "part-of" P_1. On the one hand, because the alphabet morphism is strict ($\bot$ mapped onto $\bot$), we are saying that events in the environment of P_1 are also in the environment of P_2. On the other hand, because any proper event of P_1 may be mapped onto $\bot$, we are saying that P_1 identifies part of the environment of P_2. The life cycle inheritance condition requires that the behaviour of P_1 be compatible with P_2 ie that life cycles of the whole be mapped to life cycles of the part. This condition also captures the fact that, when viewed from the point of view of a process in which it is embedded, some of the life cycles of a given process may be lost (when viewed from the point of view of the society in which it is embedded, each individual will show a more restricted behaviour).

We are now going to show how process composition can be explained in categorial terms. Consider two processes P and Q and assume that they share no events. Intuitively, the alphabet of their parallel composition P||Q should correspond to the set-theoretic disjoint union of the two alphabets and the Set categorial product of these alphabets, ie

$$\alpha(P) + \alpha(P)\times\alpha(Q) + \alpha(Q)$$

The elements of $\alpha(P)\times\alpha(Q)$ are unordered pairs of elements of $\alpha(P)$ and $\alpha(Q)$. Such pairs stand for concurrent executions of P and Q in a distributed computation. That is, the process P||Q would be able, at each instant, to be involved either in an event of P (while Q remains idle), or in an event of Q (P remaining idle), or in both an event of P and an event of Q. It is easy to see that the product of pointed sets provides us exactly with this construction: the first case corresponds to pairs $a|\bot$ with $a\in\alpha(P)$ (which we identify with a), the second case to pairs $\bot|b$ with $b\in\alpha(Q)$, and the third case to pairs $a|b$ with $a\in\alpha(P)$ and $b\in\alpha(Q)$. Notice that we also obtain two alphabet morphisms π_P and π_Q from, respectively, $E_P\times E_Q$ to E_P and $E_P\times E_Q$ to E_Q defined by $\pi_P(a|b)=a$, $\pi_Q(a|b)=b$.

Having discussed the construction of the alphabet of P||Q, let us now discuss the construction of its life cycles. It is easy to prove that the product in Proc gives us

$$\tau(P||Q)=\{\lambda\in\alpha(P||Q)^{\omega} \mid \pi_P^{\omega}(\lambda)\in\tau(P), \pi_Q^{\omega}(\lambda)\in\tau(Q)\}$$

That is, the life cycles of the product of two processes contains all infinite sequences of events that, once projected into the component alphabets, give life cycles of the component processes. The parallel composition P||Q of two processes having disjoint alphabets allows P and Q to proceed independently and, additionally, if P can perform an event a and Q can perform an event b then P||Q can perform the joint event a|b.

This kind of parallel composition in conjunction with action manipulation (using equalizers) can be used to express synchronism whenever we want it. Indeed, parallel composition with sharing can be achieved by constraining concurrency. Categorially we fulfil such constraints by means of a pullback construction. As we did for products, we shall explain first how pullbacks work for alphabets. Given a diagram of pointed sets $E_1 \xrightarrow{f} E \xleftarrow{g} E_2$, its limit is obtained from the product $E_1\times E_2$ by keeping only the events that, after being projected to E_1 and E_2, are mapped through f and g to the same element of E. As an example take, for instance $E_1=\{\bot,a,c,d\}$, $E_2=\{\bot,b,e,k\}$, and $E=\{\bot,x,y\}$ together with the functions $f=\{\bot\to\bot, a\to\bot, c\to x, d\to y\}$ and $g=\{\bot\to\bot, b\to\bot, e\to x, k\to y\}$.

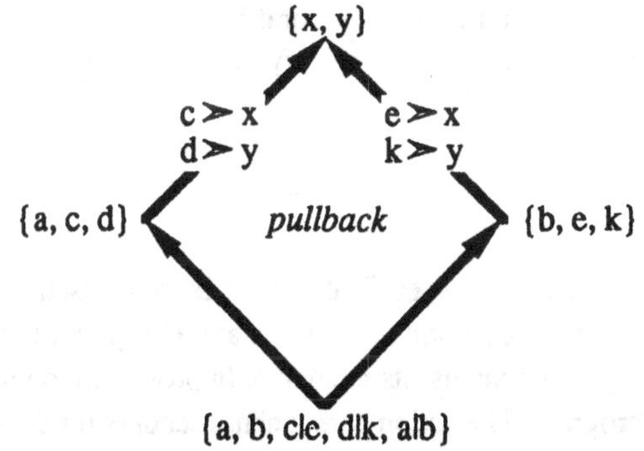

We can see f and g as defining synchronisation pairs c|e and d|k. As we explained above, the product $E_1 \times E_2$ is given by $E_1 \times E_2 = \{\bot, a, c, d, b, e, k, a|b, a|e, a|k, c|b, c|e, c|k, d|b, d|e, d|k\}$. The only events that, after being projected, are mapped through f and g to the same element of E are $\{\bot, a, b, a|b, c|e, d|k\}$.

That is, the alphabet of the process that is the parallel composition of the two given ones synchronising at the given events will contain all the events of the disjoint parallel composition except the ones that are mapped to one of the events of a synchronisation pair but not to the other. Hence, in the case above, we ruled out, for instance, a|e because it contained one of the events of the synchronisation pair c|e but not the other.

The construction of the set of life cycles for the vertex of a pullback diagram in Proc is as for products (see [Costa and Sernadas 91] for more details). The pullback of the alphabets returns two alphabet morphisms $\pi_{P_1}: E_{P_1} \times_p E_{P_2} \to E_{P_1}$ and $\pi_{P_2}: E_{P_1} \times_p E_{P_2} \to E_{P_2}$, and we shall obtain all life cycles that are projected into life cycles of the component processes:

$$\tau(P_1 \|_p P_2) = \{\lambda \in (E_{P_1} \times_p E_{P_2})^{\omega} \mid \pi_{P_1}{}^{\omega}(\lambda) \in \tau(P_1), \pi_{P_2}{}^{\omega}(\lambda) \in \tau(P_2)\}$$

The most general construction for expressing the joint behaviour of a collection of processes is to take the limit of the diagram that displays these processes together with the morphisms that say how they are to synchronise with each other. It is well known that a category has all finite limits (is finitely complete) iff it has a terminal object and pullbacks. We have already hinted at the fact that Proc has pullbacks, and it is also easy to prove that the process $(\{\bot\}, \{\bot^{\omega}\})$ is terminal in Proc. Hence,

Proposition 2.5. Proc is finitely complete. ◇

3 Temporal Specifications

Many temporal logics have been adopted for specifying the reactive aspects of systems since the original proposal by A.Pnueli in 1977 [Pnueli 77]. The logic we adopt herein is very similar to the one presented in [Fiadeiro and Maibaum 91b]. It is also fairly close to the other temporal logics that have been adopted in this field, namely [Barringer 87].

As already motivated in the introduction, our aim is to identify the specification of an object with a theory presentation in that temporal logic, ie with a pair $<\theta, \Phi>$ where θ is a signature and Φ is the set of axioms that specify the behaviour required for the object.

3.1 Language

A temporal signature for an object specification will be comprised of two parts: the state component and the action component. The state component corresponds to the information that the object maintains (its memory). In programming terms, it corresponds to the variables of a program. The action component accounts for the transformations that the object can perform on its state component or for communication with other objects.

Definition 3.1.1. A *temporal signature* θ is a pair $<\zeta,\xi>$ of two disjoint and finite sets. ◇

Elements of ζ are called *state symbols* and elements of ξ are called *action symbols.*

A first-order extension of this logic has been developed in [Fiadeiro and Maibaum 91b] allowing us to work with more complex data structures (such as arrays) and parameterised actions. In the propositional fragment in which we shall work herein, both state and action symbols provide atomic propositions in the language associated with a temporal signature.

Definition 3.1.2. The set of *temporal propositions* (*propositions* for short) PROP(θ) for a signature θ is inductively defined as follows: (a) every state and action symbol is a temporal proposition, (b) BEG is a temporal proposition (denoting the beginning of time), (c) if ϕ is a temporal proposition so are $(\neg\phi)$, $(\mathbf{X}\phi)$ and $(\mathbf{F}\phi)$, and (d) if ϕ_1 and ϕ_2 are temporal propositions so are $(\phi_1 \rightarrow \phi_2)$, $(\phi_1 \wedge \phi_2)$. ◇

The temporal operators are **X** (next) and **F** (sometime in the future).

Definition 3.1.3. A temporal *specification* is a pair $<\theta,\Phi>$ where θ is a signature and Φ is a (finite) set of θ-propositions (the axioms of the specification). ◇

The axioms of a specification assert properties that hold throughout the life of the object. A simple specification is that of a philosopher (as in Dijkstra's dining philosophers):

PHIL
state symbols: eating, l.holding, r.holding
action symbols: l.fork↑, r.fork↑, l.fork↓, r.fork↓, eat

Intuitively, *eating* indicates whether the philosopher is eating or thinking, and l.holding (r.holding) indicate, respectively, whether the philosopher is holding his left (right) fork. The action symbols account for the philosopher picking up and putting down the forks (left and right), and starting to eat.

A specification usually consists of several kinds of axioms, such as initialisation conditions:

ax_1 BEG $\rightarrow \neg$l.holding $\wedge \neg$r.holding $\wedge \neg$eating

specifications of the effects of the actions on the state component:

ax_2 l.fork↑ $\rightarrow$ **X**l.holding

ax_3 l.fork↓ $\rightarrow$ **X**$\neg$l.holding

ax_4 r.fork↑ $\rightarrow$ **X**r.holding

ax_5 r.fork↓ $\rightarrow$ **X**$\neg$r.holding

ax_6 eat $\rightarrow$ **X**eating

ax_7 l.fork↓ $\vee$ r.fork↓$\rightarrow$ **X**$\neg$eating

the conditions under which the actions are permitted to occur:

ax_8 $l.fork\uparrow \rightarrow \neg l.holding$

ax_9 $l.fork\downarrow \rightarrow l.holding$

ax_{10} $r.fork\uparrow \rightarrow \neg r.holding$

ax_{11} $r.fork\downarrow \rightarrow r.holding$

ax_{12} $eat \rightarrow \neg eating \wedge l.holding \wedge r.holding$

and the conditions under which the actions are required to occur:

ax_{13} $\neg eating \rightarrow F eat$

See [Fiadeiro and Maibaum 91b] for a more detailed account of the use of this logic for object specification and verification.

3.2 Process Models

A semantic model for a temporal signature is defined as usual for propositional temporal logics:

Definition 3.2.1. A *θ-model* for a signature $\theta=<\zeta,\xi>$ is a pair $Q=<S,A>$ where S (A) consists of a triple $<W_S,T_S,V_S>$ ($<W_A,T_A,V_A>$) where W_S (W_A) is a set, $T_S:\omega\rightarrow W_S$ ($T_A:\omega\rightarrow W_A$) and $V_S: \zeta \rightarrow 2^{W_S}$ ($V_A:\xi\rightarrow 2^{W_A}$). ◇

Each of the triples <W,T,V> provides a model for the respective fragment of the language (state and action) [Goldblatt 87]: W provides the set of possible worlds, T is an infinite sequence of worlds, and V gives for each symbol the set of worlds in which it holds. Given such a model, we shall interpret the formulae of the language of a signature as follows:

Definition 3.2.2. We define what it means for a proposition ϕ to be true in a model <S,A> at time i, which we write $<S,A>\models^i \phi$, by

- if $\phi\in\zeta$, $<S,A> \models^i \phi$ iff $T_S(i)\in V_S(\phi)$
- if $\phi\in\xi$, $<S,A> \models^i \phi$ iff $T_A(i)\in V_A(\phi)$
- $<S,A> \models^i$ BEG iff $i=0$;
- $<S,A> \models^i (\neg\phi)$ iff it is not the case that $<S,A> \models^i \phi$
- $<S,A> \models^i (X\phi)$ iff $<S,A> \models^{i+1} \phi$
- $<S,A> \models^i (F\phi)$ iff, for some $j>i$, $<S,A> \models^j \phi$
- $<S,A> \models^i (\phi_1 \rightarrow \phi_2)$ iff $<S,A> \models^i \phi_1$ implies $<S,A> \models^i \phi_2$
- $<S,A> \models^i (\phi_1 \wedge \phi_2)$ iff $<S,A> \models^i \phi_1$ and $<S,A> \models^i \phi_2$

The proposition ϕ is said to be *true* in <S,A>, written $<S,A>\models\phi$, iff $<S,A>\models^i\phi$ at every instant i. We also write $<S,A>\models\Phi$ for a collection of propositions Φ meaning that each proposition of Φ is true in <S,A>. Finally, for every set Φ of θ-propositions and every θ-proposition ϕ, ϕ is a consequence of Φ ($\Phi\models_\theta\phi$) iff ϕ is true in every model that makes all the propositions in Φ true. ◇

These Kripke structures are very close to the notion of process defined in the previous section, W_A corresponding to the alphabet of the process and T_A to one of its life cycles. The function V_A relates actions and events: it gives for each action the set of the events during which it occurs. This relationship motivates the notion of process model:

Definition 3.2.3. Given a temporal signature $\theta=<\zeta,\xi>$, a θ-process model is a pair <P,V> where P is a process <E,Λ> and V is a function $\xi\rightarrow 2^{\alpha(P)}$. For each $\lambda\in\Lambda$, <E,λ,V> provides a Kripke structure for the action component (ξ) of the signature. A morphism $h:<<E,\Lambda>,V>\rightarrow<<E',\Lambda'>,V'>$ is a morphism of pointed sets E→E' such that (1) $\lambda;h\in\Lambda'$ for every $\lambda\in\Lambda$ and (2) $V=V';h^{-1}$. That is, h is a process morphism (in the sense of 2.3) satisfying condition (2). This condition is required for having a p-morphism of Kripke structures (see [Goldblatt 87] and [Fiadeiro *et al* 91]). We denote by Mod(θ) the category of θ-process models. ◇

Definition 3.2.4. We say that a θ-process model <<E,Λ>,V> is a model of the specification <θ,Φ> iff, for every $\lambda\in\Lambda$, there is a model S_λ of the state component such that $<S_\lambda,<E,\lambda,V>>\models\Phi$. We denote by Mod(<θ,Φ>) the full subcategory of Mod(θ) whose objects are the process models of <θ,Φ>. ◇

That is, a process together with a way of interpreting the action symbols over the events is a model of a specification iff for every life cycle of the process there is an interpretation for the state symbols that together with the life cycle constitutes a model of the specification. We are now going to study the structure of Mod(<θ,Φ>) more carefully.

Definition 3.2.5. Given a specification <θ,Φ> where $\theta=<\zeta,\xi>$, let $[\![<\theta,\Phi>]\!]$ be the process defined as follows: (a) the set of its possible events $[\![<\theta,\Phi>]\!]_E$ is 2^ξ, and (b) the set of its life cycles is $[\![<\theta,\Phi>]\!]_\Lambda=\{\lambda:\omega\rightarrow 2^\xi \mid <S_\lambda,\lambda^\xi>\models\Phi \text{ for some } S_\lambda\}$ where $\lambda^\xi=<2^\xi,\lambda,V^\xi>$ and $V^\xi(a)=\{D\in 2^\xi \mid a\in D\}$. ◇

It is easy to see that we do obtain a process in the sense of 2.1.1 because each element of $[\![<\theta,\Phi>]\!]_\Lambda$ (life cycle) is of the form $\omega\rightarrow 2^\xi$, the power set 2^ξ being considered as a pointed set (the empty set Ø being the designated element, ie corresponding to an anonymous event of the environment – an event during which none of the actions of the object executes). An event of this alphabet corresponds to a collection of simultaneous occurrences of actions (ie a synchronisation set). The process also consists of all possible life-cycles that satisfy the specification.

Proposition 3.2.6. $<[\![<\theta,\Phi>]\!],V^\xi>$ is a terminal object of Mod(<θ,Φ>). ◇

That is, $[\![<\theta,\Phi>]\!]$ is the "strictest" process that satisfies the specification <θ,Φ>. (Recall that a process morphism is an embedding of the target in the source.) The only proper events of this process are those that are generated from the actions (synchronisation sets), and the set of its life cycles is the largest that is allowed by the specification. This semantics has the flavour of initiality of equational specifications of abstract data types in the sense that we have no "junk" (none of the events of the environment is identified), and no "confusion" (all the synchronisation sets are in the alphabet). However, we have more than what is usual in abstract data type specifications. Indeed, it is possible to prove:

Proposition 3.2.7. Given a specification <θ,Φ>, <P,V> one of its models and a morphism $h:<P',V'>\rightarrow<P,V>$ of θ-process models, <P',V'> is also a model of <θ,Φ>◇

Theorem 3.2.8. Mod(<θ,Φ>) is isomorphic to (Proc↓⟦<θ,Φ>⟧), the comma-category of processes over ⟦<θ,Φ>⟧. ◇

This isomorphism identifies <P,V> as a <θ,Φ>-model with V^{op}:P→ ⟦<θ,Φ>⟧, the unique morphism into the terminal model – defined by $V^{op}(x)=\{y \mid x\in V(y)\}$, and any process morphism h:P→ ⟦<θ,Φ>⟧ with the <θ,Φ>-model <P,$V^{\xi};h^{-1}$>.

As an example, the alphabet of the terminal process defined by our specification of a philosopher consists of every possible subset of {l.fork↑,r.fork↑,r.fork↓,l.fork↓,eat}. Naturally, the way we specified philosophers will rule out some of these events (ie subsets of the action signature) from any life cycle. For instance, although {l.fork↑,l.fork↓} will belong to the alphabet of the philosopher process, it will not belong to any of its life cycles. Indeed, from axioms ax_{11} and ax_{12} it is easy to derive the proposition ¬(l.fork↑ ∧ l.fork↓) as a theorem of the specification, meaning that the two actions may never occur simultaneously. However, some concurrency between other actions is permitted as shown in the following initial segment of a model that validates the specification of philosophers:

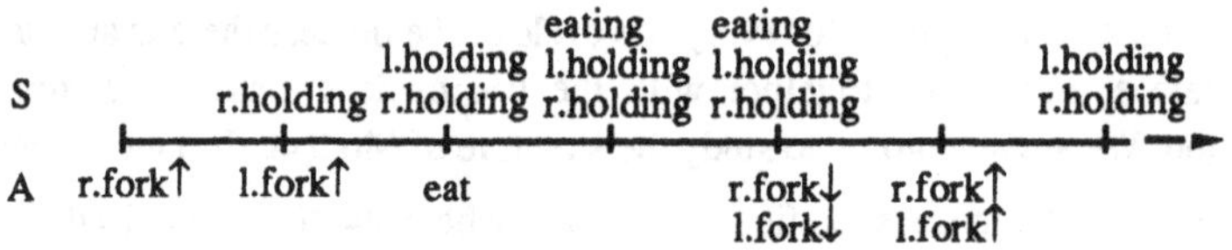

4 Categories of Temporal Specifications

It is easy to see that the same process may be a model of different specifications. In particular, because we do not take into account the state component of the specification, we may have the same process being a model of specifications having completely different state components. Indeed, because we are taking the state component as being just a means of specifying the process, it is intuitive to have a notion of isomorphism that abstracts from a specification its process component. That is, although a specification may involve a state component, this information should be considered to be internal to the process, as a *scafolding* (to use an expression of J.Goguen's) that helped us in defining the desired behaviour but that we wish to *hide* once the specification is completed.

Hiding means preventing interconnections between processes to be established based on the state component of their specifications. Indeed, as motivated in the introduction, our object-oriented discipline of specification is based on the fact that objects keep their state component private. Following the categorial approach that we are adopting, such interconnections are established via morphisms. Hence, hiding the state component of a specification is achieved by defining the category of specifications in a way that prevents the state component from being used as a means of interconnecting processes. This category is defined below.

4.1 Morphisms of Temporal Signatures

Definition 4.1.1. A p-morphism between signatures $<\zeta_1,\xi_1>$ and $<\zeta_2,\xi_2>$ consists of a function $\sigma:\xi_1\to\xi_2$. ◇

That is, when relating two signatures we are only interested in relating their action (process) component; the state component is irrelevant (hidden). That is the reason for the prefix p.

Proposition 4.1.2. Temporal signatures and signature p-morphisms constitute a category p–Sign. This category is finitely cocomplete and has $<\zeta,\emptyset>$ for any ζ as initial objects. ◇

Naturally, sometimes it will be possible to relate the state components of two signatures as well:

Definition 4.1.3. A signature o–morphism σ from $<\zeta_1,\xi_1>$ to $<\zeta_2,\xi_2>$ consists of a pair $<\sigma_\zeta:\zeta_1\to\zeta_2,\sigma_\xi:\xi_1\to\xi_2>$ of functions. ◇

In this case, the prefix o– indicates that it is the whole object (state and process) that we are taking into account. Such morphisms arise in object-oriented specification, for instance, in the semantics of inheritance. Another reason to introduce them here is that they are easier to work with when it comes to relating specifications.

As an example of a signature o-morphism consider, for instance, the following specification:

VIEW
state symbols
  busy
action symbols
  up, down
axioms
  ax_1 BEG→¬busy
  ax_2 up→Xbusy
  ax_3 down→X¬busy
  ax_4 up→¬busy
  ax_5 down→busy

This theory presentation specifies the behaviour of an object that, alternatively, may go up or down. In fact, we shall prove that it specifies a view of the behaviour of a philosopher that corresponds to his use of a fork. It is easy to establish several signature o-morphisms between VIEW and PHIL. We shall be particularly interested in two of them:

left:VIEW→PHIL	right:VIEW→PHIL
state symbols	*state symbols*
busy ↦ l.holding	busy ↦ r.holding
action symbols	*action symbols*
up ↦ l.fork↑	up ↦ r.fork↑
down ↦ l.fork↓	down ↦ r.fork↓

These morphisms "place" the fork being used at the left or at the right hand side of a philosopher.

4.2 Morphisms of Process Specifications

Proposition 4.2.1. Each p-morphism σ from θ_1 to θ_2 defines a functor $Mod(\sigma):Mod(\theta_2) \rightarrow Mod(\theta_1)$ as follows: $Mod(\sigma)(<P,V>)=<P,\sigma;V>$, and is the identity on morphisms. ◇

Notice that we define in this way a functor Mod: p–Sign→Cat^{op} giving a model functor (indexed category) as in institutions [Goguen and Burstall 84].

Definition 4.2.2. Consider now two temporal specifications $<\theta_1,\Phi_1>$ and $<\theta_2,\Phi_2>$ and a signature p-morphism σ from θ_1 to θ_2. We say that σ is a p-interpretation (or a p-morphism of specifications) between $<\theta_1,\Phi_1>$ and $<\theta_2,\Phi_2>$ iff $Mod(\sigma)$ is also a functor $Mod(<\theta_2,\Phi_2>) \rightarrow Mod(<\theta_1,\Phi_1>)$, ie iff for every process model $<P,V>$ of $<\theta_2,\Phi_2>$, $Mod(\sigma)(<P,V>)$ is a model of $<\theta_1,\Phi_1>$. ◇

This corresponds to the "usual" model-theoretic definition of specification morphism. Thanks to 3.2.8 we can prove the following characterisation of p-interpretations:

Proposition 4.2.3. A signature p-morphism σ from θ_1 to θ_2 is a p-interpretation between $<\theta_1,\Phi_1>$ and $<\theta_2,\Phi_2>$ iff σ^{-1} is a morphism between $[\![<\theta_2,\Phi_2>]\!]$ and $[\![<\theta_1,\Phi_1>]\!]$, ie iff $(\sigma^{-1})^{\omega}([\![<\theta_2,\Phi_2>]\!]_\Lambda) \subseteq [\![<\theta_1,\Phi_1>]\!]_\Lambda$. ◇

It is trivial to prove:

Proposition 4.2.4. Specifications and their p-morphisms constitute a category p-Spec. We have also defined a functor $[\![\_]\!]$: p–Spec→$Proc^{op}$. ◇

We shall study the properties of this functor below. We should mention that we do not have an institution because the satisfaction condition does not hold. It does hold however if we work with o-morphisms (see [Fiadeiro *et al* 91]). With the corresponding notion of o-interpretation it is possible to prove that both signature morphisms left and right defined above are specification morphisms. This means that we have defined two possible views of the behaviour of a philosopher: those that correspond to the philosopher using his left or right fork. See [Fiadeiro and Maibaum 91b] for more details on the use of this kind of interpretations for concurrent system specification, namely for object interfacing and interconnection.

4.3 Cocompleteness of p-Spec and Exactness of Proc-semantics

In order to be able to compose specifications, the category p–Spec must be finitely cocomplete, ie for each finite diagram depicting the specifications of the components and their interconnections (p-interpretations) we must be able to compute its colimit (the specification of the complex process together with the morphisms that say how the components fit into it). Moreover, we want the operation of composing the denoted processes by taking limits that we studied in section 2 to "agree" with this operation of specification composition, meaning that Proc provides an exact semantics of p–Spec. That is, we want the models of colimits in specification diagrams to consist of limits of models of its components. The rest of section will be devoted to proving that p–Spec is finitely cocomplete and that the proposed process semantics is, indeed, exact.

For this purpose, we shall prove a stronger result, viz that ⟦_⟧ is finitely cocontinuous, ie it maps colimits of specification diagrams to limits of the corresponding diagram of terminal process models. Using a well known result of category theory, this can be achieved by analysing pushouts and initial specifications.

Because the functor 2^{-1}:Set→Set^{op} that maps sets to their power sets and functions to their inverses preserves colimits, ⟦_⟧ sends colimits of signatures to limits of alphabets. Given a diagram

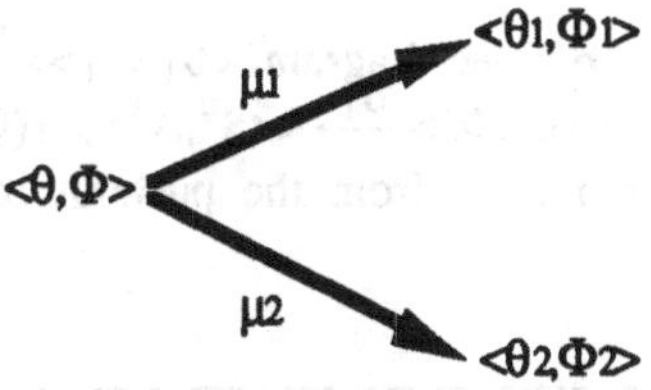

in p–Spec, we can push it out in p–Sign:

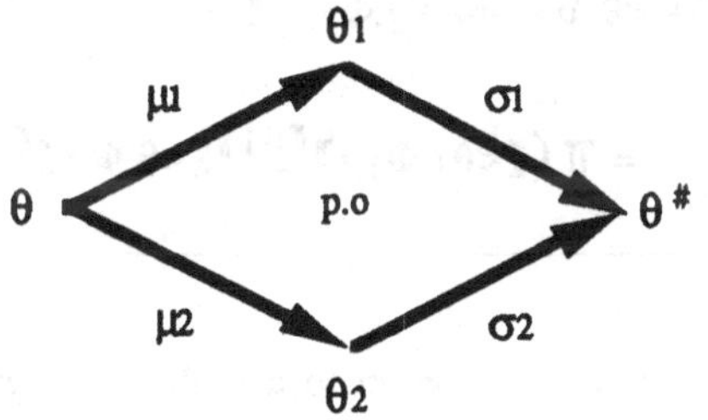

Through the functor ⟦_⟧ we can also obtain a diagram in Proc for which, as proved in section 2, we can compute a pullback:

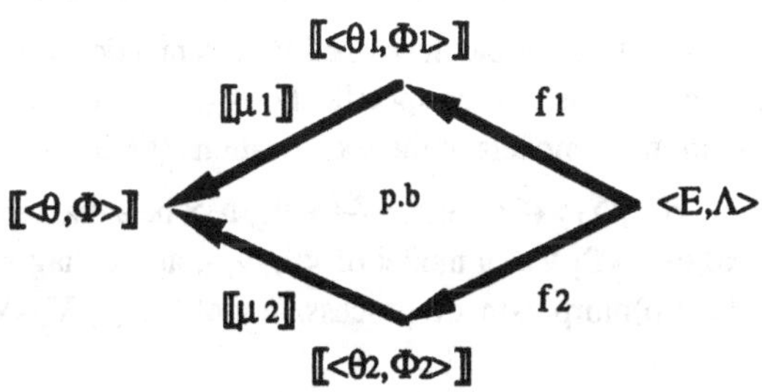

The above mentioned colimit preservation property for p–Sign assures that the resulting process can be taken over an alphabet generated from the vertex $\theta^{\#}$ of the pushout of the p-Sign diagram, ie we can take $E=2A^{\#}$ and $f_i=\sigma_i^{-1}$. If we can prove that this process is the denotation of some specification $<\theta^{\#},\Phi^{\#}>$ then it is easy to prove that we have a pushout diagram in p–Spec as well.

First of all, we are going to define the vertex signature $\theta^{\#}=<\zeta^{\#},\xi^{\#}>$. We know already that we can take an arbitrary state component. We shall take $\zeta^{\#}=\zeta_1+\zeta_2$ in order to obtain signature o-morphisms, which can be proved to be o-interpretations. The action component is given by the amalgamated sum of the action component of the signatures involved, ie $\xi^{\#} = \xi_1+_{\xi}\xi_2$.

As proved in section 2, we have $\Lambda=\{A:\omega\rightarrow 2A^{\#} \mid A|_{\sigma_i}\in [\![<\theta_i,\Phi_i>]\!]_\Lambda\}$. It is easy to prove:

Lemma 4.3.1. $\Lambda=[\![<<S^{\#},A^{\#}>,\sigma_1(\Phi_1)\cup\sigma_2(\Phi_2)>]\!]_\Lambda$. ◇

Hence,

Proposition 4.3.2. Given a p–Spec-diagram $<\theta_1,\Phi_1>\xleftarrow{\mu 1}<\theta,\Phi>\xrightarrow{\mu 2}<\theta_2,\Phi_2>$, its pushout exists and is given by $<\theta_1,\Phi_1>\xrightarrow{\sigma 1}<<S^{\#},A^{\#}>,\sigma_1(\Phi_1)\cup\sigma_2(\Phi_2)>\xleftarrow{\sigma 2}<\theta_2,\Phi_2>$ where $\theta_1\xrightarrow{\sigma 1}<\zeta^{\#},\xi^{\#}>\xleftarrow{\sigma 2}\theta_2$ results from the pushout in p–Sign with $\zeta^{\#}=\zeta_1+\zeta_2$. Moreover,

$$[\![\amalg(<\theta_1,\Phi_1>\xleftarrow{\mu 1}<\theta,\Phi>\xrightarrow{\mu 2}<\theta_2,\Phi_2>)]\!] =$$

$$= \Pi\,([\![<\theta_1,\Phi_1>]\!]\xrightarrow{[\![\mu 1]\!]}[\![<\theta,\Phi>]\!]\xleftarrow{[\![\mu 2]\!]}[\![<\theta_2,\Phi_2>]\!]).$$

That is, $[\![\_]\!]$ sends the pushout diagram to a pullback diagram in the category of processes. On the other hand we can prove

Proposition 4.3.3. Specifications of the form $<<\zeta,\emptyset>,\emptyset>$ are initial in p–Spec and are mapped to the terminal process $<\{\emptyset\},\{\emptyset\}^{\omega}>$, ie $[\![<<\zeta,\emptyset>,\emptyset>]\!]=<\{\emptyset\},\{\emptyset\}^{\omega}>$. ◇

Theorem 4.3.4. p–Spec is finitely co-complete and $[\![\_]\!]$ preserves colimits of finite specification diagrams ($[\![\_]\!]$ sends colimits of specifications to limits of processes). ◇

We can now prove the exactness of the developed Proc-semantics. Intuitively, we want to prove that models of a composition of specifications (a colimit of a p–Spec diagram) correspond to compositions of models of the specifications (limits of Proc diagrams).

Theorem 4.3.5. Let $<\theta_1,\Phi_1>\xleftarrow{\mu 1}<\theta,\Phi>\xrightarrow{\mu 2}<\theta_2,\Phi_2>$ be a diagram of specifications, $<P,V>$ a model of $<\theta,\Phi>$, $<P_i,V_i>$ a model of $<\theta_i,\Phi_i>$, and a diagram $P_1\xrightarrow{h1}P\xleftarrow{h2}P_2$ such that h_i is a (hetero)morphism of process models ie $\mu_i;V_i=V;h_i^{-1}$. Then, any pullback

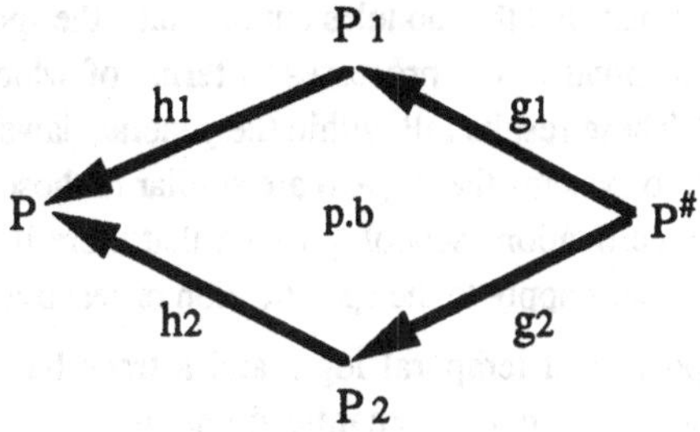

in Proc provides a model for the pushout

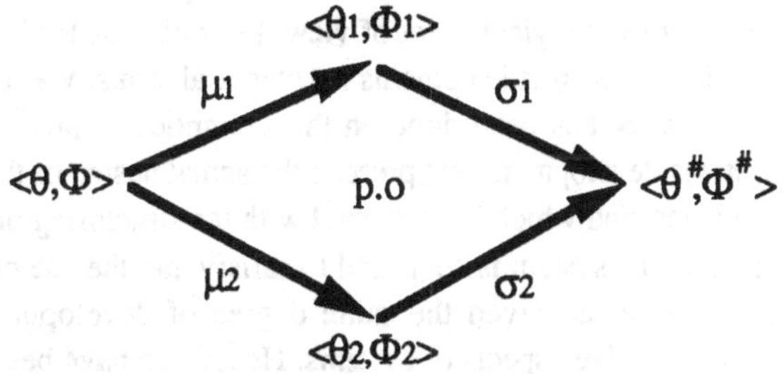

in p–Spec. That is, there is a unique $V^{\#}$ such that $<P^{\#},V^{\#}>$ is a model of $<\theta^{\#},\Phi^{\#}>$ and g_i are heteromorphisms, ie $\sigma_i;V^{\#}=V_i;g_i^{-1}$. ◇

Because the terminal process (in Proc) is a model of the initial specification, we can generalise this property to finite colimits. That is, every combination of models of given specifications is a model of the combined specification. On the other hand, through the reduct functors, every model of the combined specification is a model of its components. Hence, all the models of a complex specification are obtained via combination of models of its components.

5 Concluding Remarks and Further Work

In this paper, we have studied the relationship between two semantic domains for reactive systems specification. On the one hand, we defined a category p-Spec of temporal theories in which components are specified via the temporal properties (safety and liveness) that they are required to satisfy and complex systems are specified via diagrams that show how their components are interconnected. On the other hand, we defined a category Proc of algebraic models of processes where process composition is explained in terms of limits of diagrams. By saying how a process satisfies a specification we were able to prove that the proposed Proc-semantics is exact: the models of a colimit of specifications consist of all limits of models of the component specifications. That is to say, the two semantic domains "agree" in the sense that the modules out of which the specification of a complex system is built do correspond to the processes in terms of which the behaviour of the system is decomposed. These results fall within the general "laws" set up by J.Goguen in his categorial approach to systems theory, and are similar to those that have been pursued within the "algebraic specification" school, proving that there is a natural way in which these categorial constructions apply to the specification of reactive systems.

For simplicity, a propositional temporal logic and a trace-based process model were chosen. These provide rather naïve semantic domains when compared to the more sophisticated logics and process models that have been developed more recently, but they allowed us to concentrate on the envisaged relationship between temporal specifications and processes. Work is now underway towards extending this relationship to other models.

Indeed, we would like the results that we presented in this paper not to be assessed strictly either from the process or the logical point of view, but rather as further evidence of the advantage of structuring our semantic domains in categorial terms. We feel that although a significant amount of work has been done on the semantics of process languages, the earlier stages of systems development that precede the actual design of the system in terms of one of these languages, and which is concerned with the structuring of the specification of the requirements that the system is supposed to satisfy and the use of that structure to guide design, have not yet achieved the same degree of development in relation to concurrency and other reactive aspects of systems. Hence, we have been putting forward ideas extending techniques that have been developed for Abstract Data Type specification, and incorporating results that have been produced within the area of concurrency. For instance, a promising line of research is to extend the work of Olderog [Olderog 91] on transforming specifications to process terms into this setting, capitalising on the acquired ability to structure specifications as diagrams.

Research is also going on towards proof-theoretic characterisation of p-interpretations. The idea is that this characterisation be based on the theorems of the specification that belong to the action fragment of the language ie, intuitively, we would like to have an isomorphism between $\langle\langle S,A\rangle,\Phi\rangle$ and $\langle\langle \emptyset,A\rangle,\Phi^A\rangle$ where Φ^A is the set of theorems of Φ that do not mention state symbols. Preliminary work in this direction suggests that this characterisation may depend on the Craig Interpolation Property. As a corollary, we would obtain an adjunction between p-Spec and $Proc^{op}$ which would provide us with a categorical logic for processes in the sense of [Meseguer 87].

Acknowledgements

We thank our colleagues H.-D.Ehrich and U.Lipeck for many useful discussions on this topic. Our special thanks to Andrzej Tarlecki for having asked the right questions at the right time. This work was partially supported by the JNICT Project PMCT/C/TIT/178/90 (FAC3) and by the Esprit Basic Research Action 3023 (IS-CORE). The work of J.L.Fiadeiro was supported by a grant of the CEC while on leave at Imperial College.

References

[Barringer 87]
H.Barringer, "The Use of Temporal Logic in the Compositional Specification of Concurrent Systems", in A.Galton (ed) *Temporal Logics and their Applications*, Academic Press 1987

[Costa and Sernadas 91]
J.-F.Costa and A.Sernadas, "Process Models within a Categorial Framework", Research Report, INESC 1990

[Diaconescu et al 91]
R.Diaconescu, J.Goguen and P.Stefaneas, *Logical Support for Modularisation*, Research Report, PRG Oxford University 1991

[Ehrich et al 90]
H.-D.Ehrich, J.Goguen and A.Sernadas, "A Categorial Theory of Objects as Observed Processes", in J.deBakker, W.deRoever and G.Rozenberg (eds) *Foundations of Object-Oriented Languages*, LNCS 489, Springer Verlag 1991, 203-228

[Fiadeiro and Maibaum 91a]
J.Fiadeiro and T.Maibaum, "Describing, Structuring, and Implementing Objects", in J.deBakker, W.deRoever and G.Rozenberg (eds) *Foundations of Object-Oriented Languages*, LNCS 489, Springer Verlag 1991, 274-310

[Fiadeiro and Maibaum 91b]
J.Fiadeiro and T.Maibaum, "Temporal Theories as Modularisation Units for Concurrent System Specification", to appear in *Formal Aspects of Computing*

[Fiadeiro et al 91]
J.Fiadeiro, J.-F.Costa, A.Sernadas and T.Maibaum, *Process Semantics of Temporal Logic Specification – extended version*, INESC Research Report 1991

[Goguen 89]
J.Goguen, *A Categorical Manifesto*, Technical Report PRG-72, Programming Research Group, University of Oxford, March 1989

[Goguen 91]
J.Goguen, "Sheaf Semantics of Concurrent Interacting Objects", to appear in *Mathematical Structures in Computer Science*

[Goguen and Burstall 84]
J.Goguen and R.Burstall, "Introducing Institutions", in E.Clarke and D.Kozen (eds) *Logics of Programming Workshop*, LNCS 164, Springer-Verlag 1984, 221-256

[Goguen and Ginali 78]
J.Goguen and S.Ginali, "A Categorical Approach to General Systems Theory", in G.Klir (ed) *Applied General Systems Research*, Plenum 1978, 257-270

[Goguen and Meseguer 82]
J.Goguen and J.Meseguer, "Universal Realisation, Persistence Interconnection and Implementation of Abstract Modules", in M.Nielsen and E.Schmidt (eds) *Proc. 9th International Conference on Automata, Languages and Programming*, LNCS 140, Springer Verlag 1982, 265-281

[Goldblatt 87]
R.Goldblatt, *Logics of Time and Computation*, Centre for the Study of Language and Information 1987

[Jonsson 85]
B.Jonsson, "A Model and Proof System for Asynchronous Networks", in *Proceedings of the 4th Annual ACM Symposium on Principles on Distributed Computing*, Minaki, Canada, 1985

[Manna and Pnueli 81]
Z.Manna and A.Pnueli, "Verification of Concurrent Programs: The Temporal Framework", in R.Boyer and J.Moore (eds) *The Correctness Problem in Computer Science*, Academic Press 1981, 215-273

[Meseguer 89]
J.Meseguer, "General Logics", in H.-D.Ebbinghaus et al (eds) *Logic Colloquium 87*, North-Holland 1989

[Misra 84]
J.Misra, "Reasoning about Networks of Communicating Processes", in INRIA Advanced Nato Study Institute on Logics and Models for Verification and Specification of Concurrent Systems, Nice, France, Reidel 1984

[Olderog 91]
E.-R.Olderog, *Nets Terms and Formulas*, Cambridge Tracts in Theoretical Computer Science 23, Cambridge University Press 1991

[Pnueli 77]
A.Pnueli, "The Temporal Logic of Programs", in *Proc 18th Annual Symposium on Foundations of Computer Science*, IEEE 1977, 45-57

[Sannella and Tarlecki 85]
D.Sannella and A.Tarlecki, "Building Specifications in an Arbitrary Institution", in *Proc. Int. Sym on the Semantics of Data Types*, LNCS 173, Springer Verlag 1985. Extended version in *Information and Control* 76, 1988, 165-210

[Sernadas and Ehrich 91]
A.Sernadas and H.-D.Ehrich, "What is an Object, After All", in R.Meersman, W.Kent and S.Khosla (eds), *Object-oriented Databases: Analysis, Design and Construction*, North-Holland 1991, 39-69

[Sernadas et al 90]
A.Sernadas, H.-D.Ehrich and J.-F.Costa, "From Processes to Objects", *The INESC Journal of Research and Development* 1(1) 1990, 7-27

[Winskel 84]
G.Winskel, "Synchronisation Trees", *Theoretical Computer Science* 34, 1984

The Object-Based Specification Language Π: Concepts, Syntax, and Semantics *

Peter Gabriel

Fraunhofer Gesellschaft, Institute of Software and System Technology, Kurstr. 33,
O-1086 Berlin, Germany

Abstract. The object-based specification language Π aims at the description of modular, concurrent, and distributed software systems. A Π-specification comprises algebraic specifications, imperative programs, and path expressions. This paper presents new results on the formal semantics for some parts of the language. We introduce the semantics of the algebraic specification and the imperative program parts as well as a computational model. Since these definitions caused slightly modifications of the concepts and the syntax of the language itself, we will give a short survey on Π first.

1 Introduction

Π is an object based specification language devoted to the description of modular, concurrent, and distributed software systems. Like ACT TWO (see [Fey88]), it is a descendant of the concept of algebraic module specifications (see [EM90]). Beyond the algebraic part, a Π-specification contains descriptions of algorithms by imperative programs and of scheduling schemes by path expressions. The language was developed at the University of Dortmund within the ESPRIT I project PEACOCK and is now subsidized by the Eureka Software Factory (ESF) project. A detailed presentation is given in [GDS89]. [CFGG91] may serve as a first introduction. The present version 2.0 is defined in [CS90]. As a real-life example a syntax directed editor for a subpart of Π was specified in Π itself and implemented according to the specification (see [WISDOM91]).

The definition of the formal semantics of Π was done in co-operation with the Technical University of Berlin. The language is now equipped with a semantics for its algebraic specifications and its imperative programs. Moreover, we define a computational model which is is totally determined by the the algebraic parts of Π. By this model we view at the system as an abstract machine which contains some kind of state and reacts upon input with output or state modification. All semantics definitions were done within the framework of algebraic module specifications (see [EM90]).

Π may be used in different ways. First, it allows to specify a system before its implementation. This covers the more traditional waterfall model of software engineering which cuts a clear line between specification and implementation. Π supports the rapid prototyping approach: Its algorithmic and scheduling parts may be used

* This work has been funded by the BMFT (EUREKA Software Factory, Grant No. ITS 8802).

as a first approximation to a more efficient program. Secondly, we can specify an already existing implementation. This enables us to look at the existing system in a more abstract manner and to reuse it within another context. Finally, Π may support integration of components in distributed open systems. ESF, which deals besides other things with such systems (see [ESF89]), takes the line that components in an open system should be described by means of a component discription language (CDL). The kernel operating system views all components just by their CDL description. Therefore, the internal structure of a software component is hidden to the outside. Π is proposed as a candidate for a CDL within ESF.

This paper is organized as follows. Sect.2 states the Π–concepts of objects, object classes, communication between objects, and configurations of objects. The third section introduces briefly the syntax of Π. Sect.4 presents small examples of object class and configuration specifications. Sect.5 gives an overview on the semantics of the algebraic parts of a Π–specification. Based on this, we present the computational model for Π in Sect.6. The meaning of the imperative programs is defined in the seventh section. The last section summarizes the main points of this paper and takes a look at the future development of Π.

2 Basic Concepts of Π

Π views a software system as a configuration, i.e. a collection of interacting objects. This section introduces the Π–notions of objects, communication between objects, and configurations. The advantages of object based methods in software engineering in order to achieve a *modular* structure are well known (see e.g. [Mey88]) and need no repetition here. According to the taxonomy of Peter Wegener ([Weg90]) *full concurrency* means the existence of several active threads at the same time. Moreover, he characterizes *strongly distributed* systems as those in which modules do not know the names of other modules, but the names of their own communication ports only. This section shows that both conditions are satisfied by Π. Concurrent threads correspond to concurrent object operation calls (see next subsection). Communication via given communication ports is equivalent to the communication by shared objects (see subsection 2.4).

In contrast to other object-oriented languages, say Eiffel (see [Mey88]) or Smalltalk (see [GR83]), inheritance between object classes does not exist. So we prefer to speak of an *object–based*, rather than an object–oriented, design (for the terminology we refer to [Weg90]). The excessive use of inheritance in object-oriented languages may cause some trouble, if the definition of an object class is spread over a great number of superclasses: Redefinition of a superclass must be checked with respect to all subclasses inheriting features from it. Moreover, the complete definition of a subclass is not given in one place, but is distributed over the whole program or specification. For this reason we do not use inheritance in Π.

2.1 Objects and Object Classes

According to Π, the smallest active entities of a software system are *objects*. They are characterized as follows. An object may have an *object name*, serving as the address of the object. Viewed from outside an object has an ***(internal) state***. The state is an element of a certain abstract data type of sort s, which is specified by an algebraic specification $SPEC = (S, OP, E)$. Clearly, $s \in S$ must hold true. ***Object classes*** are collections of objects possessing states of the same sort s. All objects of an object class offer the same set of ***object operations*** to the outside.

The state of an object is accessible and modifiable only by these object operations. The object may receive operation calls sent to it by its name from outside, i.e. the user or other objects, and react upon them. Π distinguishes two classes of object operations:

Modifiers: The receiving object alters it's internal state according to the operation call. No answer is replied to the sender. Each modifying operation m is part of the algebraic specification and has the type $s \ldots . \rightarrow s$. If we regard $\mathsf{m}(\mathsf{x}_1, \ldots, \mathsf{x}_n)$ as an operation call, then the first argument x_1 is the object that will execute m and change its internal state.

Functions: The adressed object sends back an answer to the caller depending on it's internal state, which remains unchanged. The answer is an object itself. Function operations are represented by $SPEC$–operations with arity $s \ldots \rightarrow s'$. If we consider $\mathsf{f}(\mathsf{x}_1, \ldots, \mathsf{x}_n)$ as an operation call, then the first argument x_1 will execute this call with respect to its internal state.

In order to create objects we need a third class of operations:

Generators: These operation calls are not sent to an object but to the object class which returns a new object. Generators look like $\mathbf{g} : \ldots \rightarrow \mathsf{s}$ which allows even for constant generators.

Therefore, an object class is characterized by a sort name s, and the three sets of operations: modifiers, functions, and generators.

The scheduling of incoming modifier and function operation calls is done ***autonomously*** by each object. Concurrent processing of requested calls, even of object modifying operations, is allowed, if certain consistency criteria hold true. The answering of generator operations is done by the object class. Since each generator call yields a new object, such calls may be executed concurently.

2.2 Global and Local Object Classes

Objects of a ***global object class*** are able to generate new instances of certain ***local object classes***, i.e. to create an object by declaring a new object name. We call the generating object ***global*** and the generated ***local***. Local objects are needed as some kind of local variables in the imperative parts of a Π–specification. Note that the terms ***global*** and ***local*** are relative: A global object class may have several local object classes and may also be local with respect to other object classes.

2.3 Complex and Subclasses

The internal state of a ***complex object*** is an aggregation of the internal states of its ***sub(ordinate) objects***. The execution of a modifying operation call by a complex object results in changes of the states of the sub–objects. Whenever a complex object is generated by declaring a new object name, the corresponding subobjects are automatically created, too. They have no names of their own, but can be *referred* to only by the name of the complex object. Therefore, if the name of some complex object is known, so are the references to its sub–objects. A reference is weaker than a name: the operations of an object can be called by the object name, not by a reference. We will name non–complex objects as ***basic objects***.

Like the relationship of local and global objects, the aggregation of sub–objects to a complex object is a property of object classes: All objects of a class have the same *(sub–)object class structure*, i.e. they are either complex objects built from other objects of the sub-classes or they are basic objects.

2.4 Communication between Objects

Π is based mainly on *communication via shared objects*. In general, there are two ways for objects to interact:

Global and Local Objects: Recall that objects are able to generate local objects. Since a global object knows the name of its local objects, it is capable of directing calls to them. A global object is not able to offer the name of one of its local objects to other local or global objects. Therefore, the relation is a private one between global and local objects. No other object can demand for operations from the local object, since it does not know the local object name.

Shared Objects: Objects may have more than one name and/or reference to it. In this case the object is *shared*. A shared object is known to different objects by different names or references, but all state changes forced by either side are executed with respect to the internal state of the shared object. Shared sub–objects are the only way of communication between two or more objects, where none object is local or sub–object of the others. According to the taxonomy of [Weg90] shared objects serve as communication ports.

Communication by shared objects implies side effects. A main effort is done in *Π* to get rid of unwanted side effects. This is achieved by different means, some of them already mentioned before:

- Operation calls are directed to objects by their names, therefore no broadcasting is possible. Names of variable objects must not be sent as arguments to other objects. Calls can not be addressed to references.
- Parameter passing and returning of results are done by a *call-by-value* mechanism. In terms of programming languages like Eiffel, passing of parameters or results is performed by a *deep copy*.
- Communication is *synchronous*, i.e. the sender of an operation call waits for termination of the call.

Therefore, side effects can be caused by an explicitly announced sharing only. Unwanted, implicit side effects by mistake are not possible.

2.5 Object Configurations

As said above, an *object configuration* is a collection of objects. A subset of this collection serves as a *configuration export*. From outside, operation calls may be directed to the export objects, or some other configuration–altering actions, say sharing of two objects, can be requested. Each object may be seen as a trivial configuration with just one export object. Thus, configurations are generalizations of objects. The combination of different configurations leads to a new configuration. Different sub–configurations can only communicate via shared objects.

According to the philosophy of Π, a software system is a configuration. It comes into life when objects of export object classes (see next section) are created by the outside. Assignments and operation calls may be directed to these objects and will perhaps alter their internal states. New objects may be generated or references can be shared. Therefore, in general a configuration is a dynamic entity: It may change its structure and its behavior. We may say, a Π–specification enlists the possible evolutions of a software system.

3 Syntax

A Π–specification contains algebraic specifications, imperative programs, and path expressions. We will not even try to present the concrete syntax (which is given in [CS90]) or context conditions in detail, but restrict ourselves to the very essentials. A small example given in the next section may help to understand how a specification looks like. Most interesting is the actualization concept of Π which resembles rather module connection concepts of programming languages like Modula 2 or Ada (see [ML87]) than connection concepts of specification languages (see e.g. [EM90] or [Wir90]).

Π knows two kinds of syntactical building blocks: *object class specifications* and *configuration specifications*. Both of them are equipped with finite sets of object classes serving as import interface as well as with object classes forming the export interface. The notion of *component specifications* comprises both object class and configuration specifications.

3.1 Object class specifications

Each object class is specified by an *CEM specification* where CEM is an acronym for 'concurrently executable module'. A CEM consists of a component name and three *views*, each of them describing a different aspect of the object class. The *type view* gives an algebraic specification of the underlying abstract data type. The *imperative view* states programs for the object operations. The *concurrency view* describes the scheduling of object operation calls received by the objects of this class.

Orthogonally to the views, each CEM specification breaks down into three *sections*: The *export section* specifies the object class offered to the outside. The *import section* lists the object classes which are needed, either as local or sub–classes, to provide the export. Finally, the *body section* states how the import is used to gain the export. Let us go into more detail:

Clearly the type view corresponds to a module specification without parameter (see [EM90]). The algebraic specifications of the export and the import are sub-specifications of the body specification. The body operations are classified either as *constructor* or *enrichment operations.*

The export section of the imperative view states the exported object class. The import section names the imported object classes. The body section contains imperative programs for all enrichment operations of the type view body. A program consists of a program head, a declaration part for local objects, a statement part, and a final return expression. Statements may be assignments, modifying operation calls of imported object classes or the object class which is going to be defined, and the usual if then else and while do. Statements may be composed sequentially by ; or concurrent by ||. The final return expressions defines the value which is returned (in case of functions or generators) or becomes the new internal state of the executing object (in case of modifiers).

The concurrency view specifies scheduling schemes for object classes by *path expressions with predicates.* Path expressions were first introduced by [CH74]. Path expressions with predicates go back to [Hab75]. The connection of path expressions and modular systems is described by [See87]. Basic paths with respect to an object class are all modifiers and function operations and the path constant assign (for assignment). Consider two path expressions a and b. *Sequential composition* a · b means 'an object of this class must first execute an operation call a(...) and then an operation call b(...)'. *Alternative composition* a + b stands for 'execute either a or b but not both of them'. *Repetition* a* is 'repeat a n times with $n \geq 0$'. *Parallel composition* a || b has the meaning 'execute a and b in parallel'. Let p be a predicate. The *path expressions with predicate* <p>:a says, 'execute a if p holds true'. Following the export path expressions ensures that neither the object state nor the results of functions become inconsistent or undefined. The import path expressions specify which scheduling schemes are needed to provide the export path expressions. The body path expression states the allowed execution traces for the body operations.

3.2 Configuration specifications

Going beyond the module connection concepts of programming languages, the import section of component specifications is *formal.* Assume for instance the component specifications N and N'. Suppose, we like to actualize an import object class of the component N where its object class is given by the abstract data type sort s with the sets of modifiers, functions, and generators M, F, and G. This class is actualized by the export object class of the component N' which is defined by the sort s' and the modifiers, functions, and generators M', F', and G'. The sort and operation names of both of the classes may be different. Moreover, the export class may offer more operations or 'more concurrency' than actually needed by the import. We just map by an *object class morphism* s to s', operations from M to those of M', and so on. We write this morphism as t : N → N'. In general t need not to be a specification morphism (see example below), contrary to almost all other concepts of module or specification connections, but similiar to the connection of modules within programming languages.

A configuration specification consists of a component name, a *declaration* and a *connection* part, and an *export*. The declaration part allows to declare new components by renaming class or operation names of already existing components. The connection part is a set of object class morphism between given or new declared components. A set of component names forms the export. The configuration provides all export object classes of the export components to the outside. The import is given by all yet not actualized import interfaces of components involved in the configuration.

4 Example: Boolean Values, Natural Numbers, and Lists

In this section we specify a configuration List[Nat] of a class of list–of–natural–numbers objects which provides a sorting operation in ascending order. We start with the type, imperative, and concurrency view of a CEM specification List of list objects with open import classes **data** and **bool**. Then a configuration specification of list–of–nat objects, which has no more open import classes, is given.

Comments in the specifications start with --.

4.1 Type View

The syntax of the type view is more or less borrowed from ACT TWO (see [Fey88]). The type view of the CEM List imports boolean values specified by the algebraic specification Bool and data items given by Data. Data includes an operation < : **data data** → **bool** and is therefore an extension of Bool. We omitt the presentation of Data and Bool and give just the type view import of List:

List_import = Data

The export is defined as

List_export = Data +
sorts list
opns

nil	:		→	list
cons	:	list data	→	list
nil?	:	list	→	bool
head	:	list	→	data
tail	:	list	→	list
concat	:	list list	→	list
sort	:	list	→	list

The type view body specifies sort as bubble sort. It contains the hidden operations **bubble**, ls, and **gte**. The latter are needed in the body section of the imperative view. **bubble**(L,D) places D in the list L before the first element greater than D. ls(L,D) keeps just elements in L less than D. Contrary, **gte**(L,D) eliminates all list elements less than D.

```
list_body = list_export +
   - all new operations are enrichments
   opns
      ls     : list data → list
      gte    : list data → list
      bubble : list data → list
   eqns
                      ls(nil, D) = nil
         ls(cons(L, D1), D2)) = if D1 < D2 then cons(ls(L, D2), D1))
                                else ls(L, D2)
                     gte(nil, D) = nil
        gte(cons(L, D1), D2)) = if not(D1 < D2) then cons(gte(L, D2), D1)
                                else gte(L, D2)
                  bubble(nil, D) = cons(nil, D)
      bubble(cons(L, D1), D2) = if D2 < D1 then cons(bubble(L, D2), D1)
                                else cons(cons(L, D1), D2)
                       sort(nil) = nil
             sort(cons(L, D)) = bubble(sort(L), D)
                             - and the usual equations for cons, head, ...
```

4.2 Imperative View

The export section of the imperative view is defined as

(list, { sort }, {cons, head, tail, ls, gte }, { nil }). The import section is given by the object classes (**data, ∅, { < }, ∅**) and (**bool, ∅, {not, and, or }, { true, false }**).

The body section specifies programs for ls, **gte**, **bubble**, and sort. Let us just consider sort which is described as a quick sort algorithm.

```
sort(L)
   declare
      A : list                 - declaration of local objects
      B : list                 - of class "list" and
      D : nat                  - "data"
   end declare
   if not nil?(L) then
      D := head(L);            - D is first element of L
      cobegin                  - begin of concurrent statements
         A := ls(L, D);        - A becomes list of all elements < D
         sort(A)               - sorting of A
      ||                       - parallel to
         B := gte(tail(L), D); - B becomes list of all elements ≥ D
         sort(B)               - sorting of B
      coend ;                  - end of concurrent statements
      L := concat (A, cons(B, N))
   else
      skip;
   return(L)
```

What happens according to the imperative view, if an object L receives an operation call sort? It creates local objects A and B, assigns values to both of them, and sends operation calls sort to both of them. Afterwards, A and B generate local objects themselves and deliver assignments and operation calls to them. This is recursively done until the local objects are empty lists. Finally, after computing the sorted version of its own internal state, the object L changes actually its internal state to this sorted list. This is indicated by the return statement which ends the computation of the operation call.

4.3 Concurrency View

The export section of the concurrency view is defined by

assign · (assign + sort + (cons* || <not empty> : head* || <not empty> : tail*))*

Its interpretation runs like this: First of all a value must be assigned to the list object. After this, assignments or sorting or any combination of function calls may be done. head and tail are executable only if the list is not empty. The import path expressions for data and bool are empty, which — by default — means that any order of execution is allowed.

4.4 Configuration Specifications

Assume, that the component specifications Nat of natural numbers and Bool of boolean values are given as follows. The import of Nat and Bool are empty. All object operations of all object classes either in import or in export of Nat and Bool are functions. Nat provides a function less : nat nat → bool. Arbitrary sequential or concurrent executions are allways allowed, i.e. all concurrency view sections are empty. Export and body of the type views are the same for both Nat and Bool and all operations are constructors. The configuration

```
config List[Nat]
  export List
  connection
    List is actualized by Bool using
      bool  for bool              - sort actualization
      true  for true              - actualization of operations
            :
    List is actualized by Nat using
      nat   for data              - sort actualization
      less  for <                 - actualization of operation
```

creates a configuration List[Nat] of lists of natural numbers. List[Nat] has no open import. Note that List is actualized twice: The object class data is actualized by the class nat of the component Nat and bool is connected to bool from the component Bool. Nevertheless, the Semantics of List remains unchanged. Its actualization is just done locally. After creating List[Nat], List is a CEM specification with the open import object classes nat and bool.

5 Type View Semantics

This section gives an overview on type view semantics and states the main result on induced internal correctness of type view specifications. The main idea of the type view semantics is to translate the Π–object morphism to module operations as given by [EM90]. Full details are presented in [Ada92].

5.1 Semantic Domain and Semantic Function

Type view semantics of a component specification is defined as an update of a library. Libraries are mappings from component names to module specifications. For each library a syntactically correct definition of a component specification causes a new entry in it. Let MOD be the set of all module specifications, $COMP$ the set of all component specifications and $NAME$ the set of all component specification names. LIB is the set of all partial *library functions* $l : NAME \circ\!\!\rightarrow MOD$. The *semantic domain* is the set of all function mapping libraries to libraries: $(LIB \rightarrow LIB)$. The *semantic function* is of type

$$[\![]\!] : COMP \rightarrow LIB \rightarrow LIB$$

As said before, a component specification is either a CEM specification or a configuration specification. We will consider both cases seperately.

Assume a CEM specification $(N, (TV, IV, CV))$, where $N \in NAME$ and TV, IV, and CV are type, imperative, and concurrency view, respectively. Let $M \in NAME$ and $l \in LIB$. Semantics of the CEM specification is defined as

$$[\![(N,(TV,IV,CV))]\!](l)(M) = \begin{cases} TV & \text{, if } \; N = M \\ l(M) & \text{, otherwise} \end{cases}$$

The transformation of a configuration specification to a module specification proceeds as follows. The module is built from the module specifications which are given as the type view semantics of the subcomponents. The modules of the subcomponents of the configuration are actualized bottom up according to the actualization relationship. This is done for each component by building the union of the modules of the actualized components to whom the import section is connected, building the union of the corresponding object class morphism and using the result to carry out the (partial) composition. This step is iterated until the export components are actualized. Finally, we union all actualized export components. The result is stored in the library.

Assume a configuration specification[2] $(N, (E, C))$ with name $N \in NAME$, a finite set of export component names $E \in \mathcal{P}_{\text{fin}}(NAME)$, and a finite set of object class morphism C. Let $CONN$ be the set of all finite sets of object morphisms. We use the following auxiliary functions

$$\begin{aligned} \text{make\_module} &: \mathcal{P}_{\text{fin}}(NAME) \times CONN \times LIB \rightarrow MOD \\ \text{actualize} &: \mathcal{P}_{\text{fin}}(NAME) \times CONN \times LIB \rightarrow LIB \\ \text{union} &: \mathcal{P}_{\text{fin}}(NAME) \times LIB \rightarrow MOD \end{aligned}$$

[2] For sake of brevity we drop the declaration part.

Let $M \in NAME$ and $l \in LIB$. The semantics of the configuration specification is given by

$$[\![(N,(E,C))]\!](l)(M) = \begin{cases} \text{make\_module}(E,C,l), & \text{if } N = M \\ l(M) & \text{, otherwise} \end{cases}$$

$$\text{make\_module}(E,C,l) = \text{union}(E, \text{actualize}(E,C,l))$$

$$\text{actualize}(E,C,l)(N) = \begin{cases} l(N) & \text{, if } N \notin E \vee N \notin C \\ l(N) \circ_h MOD' & \text{, otherwise} \end{cases}$$

$$\text{union}(E,l) = \bigcup\{l(N) | N \in E\}$$

Consider the third equation. $N \notin C$ stands for 'N is not actualized by any object class morphism in C'. h is the syntactic union of all object class morphisms in C that actualize N, i.e. $h = \bigcup\{h_i : N \to N_i \in C\}$. Context conditions must make sure, that this union is indeed a specification morphism. MOD' is the union of all semantics, i.e. modules of components that are used to actualize N:

$$MOD' = \text{make\_module}(\{N_i | h_i : N \to N_i \in C\}, C, l)$$

5.2 Correctness and Induced Correctness

A component specification named N is *internally correct with respect to a library* l, if the module specification $l(N)$ is internally correct[3]. Let N be a configuration specification built from the components N_1 to N_m. It is shown in [Ada92] that internal correctness of N_1 to N_m with respect to l induces the correctness of N with respect to l. This fact enables us to proof the internal correctness of a configuration by the more easier task of considering the internal correctness of its subparts.

6 The Computational Model

Given a Π-specification we are mostly interested in how a system should behave according to the specification. So, let N be a component name and l a library. Assume that all imports of N are satisfied, i.e. the module specification $l(N)$ has an empty import. For sake of simplicity let body and export section of $l(N)$ be the same algebraic specification $SPEC = (S, OP, E)$. Functorial semantics of the module $l(N)$ is just the initial model in the category of all $SPEC$-algebras. In [Gab92] we specify a *computational model* for this situation within the framework of module specifications. The model describes the behaviour of a software system specified by N. It views the system as an abstract machine which contains some kind of state and reacts upon input with output or state modification.

We need an appropriate model for the sequential and parallel composition of state changing operations. The approach of *process algebra* (see [BW90]) offers an algebraic method for that. Actually we used *projection specifications* (see [EPBRDG90]) which may be seen as an extension of the process algebra approach and allows for the

[3] Internal correctness means the persistency of the free functor from import to body algebras (see [EM90]).

description of infinite processes. Moreover, projection specifications fit well into the frame of module specifications (see [Dim89]). So, the abstract computational model of Π is specified by a projection module specification. The specification is done in four steps. We start with the specification of states, add basic, state-modifying operations, and close with actions and processes. We will not present the specification in full detail, but explain the specification of the computational model almost informally.

6.1 States

For all $s \in S$ let var_s, obj_s, and data_s be sort symbols of of *object names*, *objects*, and *data items*. An S–sorted family of *environment functions* $\varepsilon = (\varepsilon_s : \mathsf{var}_s \to \mathsf{obj}_s)_{s \in S}$ maps object names to objects. $\sigma = (\sigma_s : \mathsf{obj}_s \to \mathsf{data}_s)_{s \in S}$ is an S–sorted family of *store functions* from objects to data items. A *state* of the abstract machine is represented by a pair (ε, σ). The elements of ε and σ are defined for finite subsets of their domains, i.e. they are finite sets of pairs. This allows us to specify states as members of a sort state. Defining states this way enables us to handle shared objects in an easy way (see [Gor79]).

6.2 Basic Operations

Basic operations on the abstract machine transform states into states. For a given state c we have the basic operations declaration of new object names (x : s)c, assignments of expressions to object names (x := e)c, sharing of references (share(r,q))c, and operation calls. The specification of basic operations contains for instance for all $s \in S$ the operation declarations

$(\_ : \mathsf{s})\_ \quad : \quad \mathsf{var}_s, \mathsf{state} \to \mathsf{state}$

$(\_ := \_)\_ : \mathsf{var}_s, \mathsf{expression}_s, \mathsf{state} \to \mathsf{state}$

For each sort $s \in S$ the sort $\mathsf{expression}_s$ is built from combinations of object names on the one hand, and generator and function calls one the other. The basic operation (x := e)c denotes a new state which is almost equal to the state c, but where the internal state of the object x becomes eval(c,e). eval(c,e) evaluates the expression with respect to the state c. It treats the expression e as an $SPEC$–term over object names where the assignments of values, i.e. ground terms of over $SPEC$, are given by c. Like assigments, modifier change the state. Function and generator calls (op(e_2, …, e_n))c return values with respect to a state c. Because of this definition, operation calls behave exactly like the corresponding operations of the underlying algebraic specification. Semantics of operation calls is not defined in an operational but an algebraic manner.

6.3 Actions

Again, we do not present the specification of actions which is an extension of the specification of basic operations, but explain it almost informally. First, we introduce *actions* serving as the atomic parts of processes. x:s, share(r,q), x := e, and op(e_1, …, e_n), are the equivalent actions to the basic operations declaration, sharing, assignment, and the operation calls. action is the sort of actions. Corresponding to the above given specification fragement, the specification of actions contains for all $s \in S$ the operation declarations

$\_ : s \quad : \quad \text{var}_s \rightarrow \text{action}$

$\_ := \_ : \text{var}_s\ \text{expression}_s \rightarrow \text{action}$

Moreover, the specification of processes contains the following operations. $\delta :\rightarrow$ action is the ***deadlock action*** that stops the whole system and $\varepsilon :\rightarrow$ action the ***empty action*** doing nothing. | : action action → action is called ***communication function.*** It's interpretation runs like this: a|b indicates that the action a and b try to access the state simultaneously. The ***write action*** ↑: expression_s → action describes the communication, i.e. the print–out of values, to the outside world.

The ***action function*** act : state action → action specifies, in which way an action is performed with respect to a state. The ***effect function*** eff : state action → state describes which new state results as effect of the action. Take for instance the assignment L := nil by which the internal state of the list object L becomes the empty list. Let c be a state in which the variable object name L is not declared. With respect to c the assigment can not be executed: act(c,L := nil) = δ. Assume another state c' containing a declared L. Now, the assignment can be done: act(c',L := nil) = L := nil. The effect of the modifying operation on the configuration depends on the state, too. eff(s,L := nil) = c, since nothing happens; but eff(c',L := nil) = c", where the state c" is the same as c' except L which internal state is now nil.

The formal specification of action and effect function with respect to the assigment looks like this

$$\text{act}(c,x := e) = \begin{cases} x{:=}\ e & \text{, if x is already declared in c} \\ \delta & \text{, otherwise} \end{cases}$$

$$\text{eff}(c,x{:=}\ e) = (x := e)c$$

The last equations connects the action 'assignment' to the basic operation 'assignment' on states. In the same way all other basic operations are reflected by their corresponding actions.

6.4 Processes

Finally, we come to processes which are collected in the sort process. The operations and their — here not given — equations specify the ***basic process algebra*** including parallelism as ***merge with communication*** (see [BW90]). Each action is an atomic process. The ***sequencial composition*** p · q denotes a process first executing p and afterwards q. ***Alternative composition*** p + q means, execute either p or q but not both of them. ***Parallel composition*** p || q stands for the arbitrary interleaving of the actions of p and q, or communication between them (i.e. access to the store at the same time).

We should like to express how a process is actually executed with respect to a certain state. The idea of the ***state operator*** based on the action and the effect functions (see above) was originated by [BB88]. Λ : state process → process states which actions are performed by a process with respect to state. So, the state operator may be viewed as the extension of the action function to processes. The equations for the state operator are as follows.

$$\Lambda(\mathsf{c},\mathsf{a}) = \mathsf{act}(\mathsf{c},\mathsf{a})$$
$$\Lambda(\mathsf{c},\mathsf{a} \cdot \mathsf{p}) = \mathsf{act}\ (\mathsf{c},\mathsf{a}) \cdot \Lambda(\mathsf{eff}(\mathsf{c},\mathsf{a}),\mathsf{p})$$
$$\Lambda(\mathsf{c},\mathsf{p} + \mathsf{q}) = \Lambda(\mathsf{c},\mathsf{p}) + \Lambda(\mathsf{c},\mathsf{q})$$

7 Semantics of the Imperative View

We have seen that the computational model is totally determined by the type view. The imperative view semantics enables us to compare a algebraic specification and a program with respect to an operation and to mark programs as 'correct' with respect to the type view. Defining program semantics by a process algebra approach follows an idea of [BB88]. A semantics definition in this way for a non–toy language was presented by [Vaa90] for the concurrent and object oriented programming language POOL-T. Full details of our semantics are given in [Gab92].

7.1 Syntactic Domain

A program for object operations consists of a program head, a declaration list, a statement, and a final return expression (see section 3). The *syntactic domains* are given by program for programs with typical elements $\{p, \ldots\}$, head for program heads with typical elements $\{h \ldots\}$, declare for declaration lists with typical elements $\{d, \ldots\}$, statement for statements with typical elements $\{s, \ldots\}$, return for return statements with typical elements $\{r \ldots\}$, expression for expressions with typical elements $\{e, \ldots\}$, and finally bool for boolean expressions with typical elements $\{b, \ldots\}$. The syntactic equations are

$$
\begin{aligned}
p &::= h\ d\ s\ r \\
h &::= \mathsf{op}(\mathsf{x}_1, \ldots, \mathsf{x}_n) \\
d &::= \lambda | \\
&\quad\ \mathsf{x} : \mathsf{s}\ ;\ d \\
s &::= s_1\ ;\ s_2 | \\
&\quad\ s_1 \parallel s_2 | \\
&\quad\ x := e | \\
&\quad\ \mathsf{if}\ b\ \mathsf{then}\ s_1\ \mathsf{else}\ s_2 | \\
&\quad\ \mathsf{while}\ b\ \mathsf{do}\ s_1\ \mathsf{od} | \\
&\quad\ \mathsf{m}(\mathsf{x}, \mathsf{e}_2, \ldots, \mathsf{e}_n) | \\
&\quad\ \mathsf{skip} \\
r &::= \mathsf{return}(e) \\
e &::= \ldots \\
b &::= \ldots
\end{aligned}
$$

7.2 Semantic Functions

Since we do not define new semantic domains, we just have to specify the semantic functions

$$
\begin{array}{rcrcl}
[\![]\!] & : & \text{program} & \rightarrow & \text{process} \\
[\![]\!] & : & \text{declare} & \rightarrow & \text{process} \\
[\![]\!] & : & \text{statement} & \rightarrow & \text{process} \\
[\![]\!] & : & \text{bool} & \rightarrow & \text{process}
\end{array}
$$

by the equations

$$
\begin{aligned}
[\![< h, d, s, r >]\!] &= [\![d]\!] \cdot [\![s]\!] \cdot [\![r]\!] \\
[\![d_1 \; ; \; d_2]\!] &= [\![d_1]\!] \cdot [\![d_2]\!] \\
[\![x\text{: s}]\!] &= x : s \\
[\![s_1 \; ; \; s_2]\!] &= [\![s_1]\!] \cdot [\![s_2]\!] \\
[\![s_1 \parallel s_2]\!] &= [\![s_1]\!] |\!|\!| [\![s_2]\!] \\
[\![\text{if } b \text{ then } s_1 \text{ else } s_2 \text{ fi}]\!] &= [\![b]\!] \cdot [\![s_1]\!] + [\![\neg b]\!] \cdot [\![s_2]\!] \\
[\![\text{while } b \text{ do } s \text{ od}]\!] &= [\![b]\!] \cdot [\![s \; ; \text{ while } b \text{ do } s \text{ od}]\!] + [\![\neg b]\!] \\
[\![x := e]\!] &= x := e \\
[\![\text{m}(x, e_2, \ldots, e_n)]\!] &= \text{m}(x, e_2, \ldots e_n) \\
[\![\text{skip}]\!] &= \epsilon \\
[\![\text{return}(e)]\!] &= \uparrow (e) \\
[\![b]\!] &= \beta(b)
\end{aligned}
$$

The *choice operation* β is defined by

$$
\text{act(s,}\beta\text{(b))} = \begin{cases} \epsilon \text{ , if eval(s,b) = true} \\ \delta \text{ , otherwise} \end{cases}
$$

$$
\text{eff(s,}\beta\text{(b))} = \text{s}
$$

7.3 Correctness of Imperative Programs

Finally, we have to deal with the question: what is a correct program with respect to the type view specification? Assume pr to be a program with the head op(x_1, ..., x_n) and let it contain a while–construct while b do s od . The process semantics of *pr* is an infinite[4] action tree:

$$
[\![\text{pr}]\!] = \ldots [\![b]\!][\![s]\!] \Big([\![b]\!][\![s]\!] \ldots + [\![\neg b]\!] \Big) + [\![\neg b]\!] \ldots
$$

Alternatives describe *external non-determinism*, i.e choices depending on the actual state like the splittingl of if b `then` s_1 else s_2 `fi` into $[\![b]\!][\![s_1]\!] + [\![\neg b]\!][\![s_2]\!]$, or *internal non-determinism*, which stands for different sequentializations of parallel processes, say $[\![s_1 \| s_2]\!] = p_1 + \ldots p_n$.

[4] This is the crucial point where projections become important. The usual initial quotient term algebra doesn't contain infinite terms. Informally, projection specifications introduce such infinite terms (see [EPBRDG90]).

Application of the state operator eliminates all external non–determinism. Now, alternatives are representing internal non–determinism only. Consider the process which is actually executed by pr with respect to a some state c: Λ(c, ⟦ pr ⟧). Each path of the resulting action tree corresponds to one possible sequence of actions. Following the program syntax each finite path ends with an output action. As usual, we consider two correctness properties of programs: termination and partial correctness of pr with respect to a state c. pr is *partial correct with respect to* c, if all finite pathes in the action tree Λ(c,pr), end with the 'correct' output action ↑ eval(c, op(x_1, ..., x_n). pr *terminates* with respect to *c*, if Λ(c, ⟦ pr ⟧) contains just finite pathes. *Correctness* is partial correctness and termination for all states.

8 Summary and Outlook

In this paper we have presented the formal semantics for parts of the specification language Π. First, we introduced the type view semantics of Π by translating the Π–object class morphism to module operations in the sense of [EM90]. Based on this, we specified in the framework of projection module specifications a computational model that looks at the specified software system as an abstract machine. The model was completely determined by the type view. Hereafter, we defined the semantics of the imperative view. A simple notion of correctness connects both imperative and type view. It remains to integrate the concurrency view into this framework.

Starting from the existing editor (see [WISDOM91]) a small Π–environement containing editor, compiler, and object management system is going to be built at the Fraunhofer Institute for Software and System Technology in Berlin. The compiler will transform both imperative and concurrency view to C. Clearly, there is still a number of open questions, say the efficient handling of the call–by–value semantics or the extraction of a fair scheduling algorithm from the concurrency view. Such a Π–environement may serve in the ESF subproject Kernel/2 (which takes place at the Fraunhofer Institute in Berlin, too) as a component description language as well as a wide–spectrum language combining specification and programming aspects of software systems.

Last but not least, on the long term Π is open to include other views, for instance a distribution view stating on which processor objects are placed or a performance view specifying non–functional aspects like time constraints.

References

[Ada92] Helmut Adametz: Semantics of the Type View and the Type Configuration of the Π-Language. To appear as: Technical Report, Fraunhofer Institute of Software and System Technology, Berlin, 1992

[BB88] Jos C. M. Baeten and J. A. Bergstra: Global Renaming Operators in Concrete Process Algebra. Informations and Computing 78 (1988), 205-245

[BW90] Jos C.M. Baeten and W.P. Weijland: Process Algebra. Cambridge Tracts in Theoretical Computer Science 18, 1990

[CH74] R. H. Campbell and A. N. Haberman: The Specification of Process Synchronization by Path Expressions. In: E. Gelenbe and C. Kaiser (ed.): Operating Systems. Lecture Notes in Computer Science, 89-102, Springer 1974

[CS90] Joachim Cramer and Harald Schumann: Syntax Description of the Π-Language with Examples (Version 2.0). University of Dortmund, Department of Computer Science, Software Technology, Report No. 49, July 1990

[CFGG91] Joachim Cramer, Werner Fey, Michael Goedicke and Martin Grosse-Rhode: Towards a Formally Based Component Description Language — a Foundation for Reuse. Structured Programming 12 (1991), 91-110

[Dim89] Cristian Dimitrovici: Projection Module Specifications and Their Basic Interconnections. Technical University of Berlin, Report No. 1989/5, 1989

[ESF89] The Technical Design Group of the ESF–Project: The ESF Technical Reference Guide, Version 1.1. ESF, Berlin, June 1989

[EM90] Hartmut Ehrig and Bernd Mahr: Fundamentals of Algebraic Specifications 2: Modules and Constraints. EACTS Monographs on Theoretical Computer Science 21, Springer 1990

[EPBRDG90] Hartmut Ehrig, Francesco Parisi–Presicce, Paul Boehm, Catharina Rieckhoff, Cristian Dimitrovici, and Martin Grosse-Rhode: Combining Data Type and Recursive Process Specifications using Projection Algebras. Theoretical Computer Science 71 (1990), 347-380

[Fey88] Werner Fey: Pragmatics, Concepts, Syntax, Semantics, and Correctness Notions of ACT TWO: An Algebraic Module Specification and Interconnection Language, Technical University of Berlin, Report No. 88-26, 1988

[Gab92] Peter Gabriel: Specification of a Computational Model for Π. To appear as: Technical Report, Fraunhofer Institute of Software and System Technology, Berlin, 1992

[GDS89] Michael Goedicke, Wolfgang Ditt, and Herbert Schippers: The Π- Language Reference Manual. University of Dortmund, Department of Computer Science, Report No. 295/1989, 1989

[Gor79] Michael J. C. Gordon: The Denotational Description of Programming Languages. Springer 1979

[GR83] Adele Goldberg and David Robson: Smalltalk-80: The Language and it's Implementation. Addison–Wesley 1983

[Hab75] A. N. Haberman: Path Expressions. Carnegie–Mellon University, Technical Report, June 1975

[Mey88] Bertrand Meyer: Object Oriented Software Construction. Prentice Hall International Series in Computer Science, 1988

[ML87] M. Marcotty and H. Ledgard: The World of Programming Languages. Springer 1987

[See87] Silke Seehusen: Determination of Concurrency Properties in Modular Systems With Path Expressions (in German). Thesis, University of Dortmund, 1987

[Vaa90] Frits W. Vaandrager: Process Semantics of POOL. In: Jos C. M. Baeten (ed.): Applications of Process Algebra. Cambridge Tracts in Theoretical Computer Science 17, 1990

[Weg90] Peter Wegener: Concepts and Paradigms of Object–Oriented Programming. ACM OOPS Messenger, 1,1 (1990)

[Wir90] Martin Wirsing: Algebraic Specifications. In: J. van Leeuwen (ed.): Handbook of Theoretical Computer Science, Vol. B, Formal Models and Semantics. 657-788, Elsevier 1990

[WISDOM91] Final Report of the Project–Group WISDOM (in German). University of Dortmund, Department of Computer Science, Software Technology, June 1991

Specifications with Observable Formulae and Observational Satisfaction Relation

Teodor Knapik

LIENS CNRS URA 1327
45 Rue d'Ulm
F – 75230 PARIS Cedex 05 France

e-mail: knapik@dmi.ens.fr or knapik@frulm63.bitnet

1 Introduction

Within an observational approach the loose semantics of a specification may either be defined as a class of algebras **observationally equivalent to models** satisfying the specification in the usual sense or as a class of algebras **observationally satisfying** the specification. The former way has already been deeply explored in [13] while in the latter one, the following problems remains open:

1. How to define an observational satisfaction relation w.r.t. more sophisticated observation techniques than sort observation ?
2. How to generalize the observational satisfaction relation of equational axioms of [10], positive conditional axioms of [14], [8] or [11], first order axioms without existential quantifier nor predicate symbols of [1] or [3] to the full (Many Sorted) First Order Logic with Equality ?
3. Is it possible to provide an observational institution[1] in such a general framework ?

All these questions are investigated in the present paper. For the first one the answer was partially given in [14] and [1] where observable signatures are considered[2] and in [3] where observable terms (possibly with variables) are considered. In the present paper, observable (first order) formulae are considered. More precisely, a set of formulae represents available experiments. An experiment consists of checking the validity of a formula in an algebra for a given assignment of variables. Thus each value is involved only in some experiments. We assume that only the results of such experiments provide an information on what an algebra resembles. It is then impossible to distinguish some values from the others. This is represented by an

[1] See [7] for more details about institutions.
[2] In fact these approaches combine signature and sort observations.

indistinguishability relation defined according to the following **Indistinguishability Assumption**:

> *Two values are indistinguishable with respect to some experiments when it is impossible to see if they are different using the results of these experiments.*

We show that our indistinguishability relation is neither a congruence nor an equivalence relation. We do not think that this is unfortunate. This fact seems rather necessary in order to model the real situations in a better way, for instance the following ones:

1. A specification of sets of natural numbers may be additionally equipped with an operation *choose* which takes a set as argument and returns an element of the set. Sequences over $\mathbb{N}$ should clearly be considered as a correct realization of this specification, *choose* being for instance an operation which returns the head of a sequence. Then the sequences mn and nm are indistinguishable since they represent the same set $\{m, n\}$. But when $n \neq m$ we want the results of $choose(nm)$ and $choose(mn)$ (i.e. n and m) to be distinguishable.
2. Given a specification of something like a metric space, we may want to consider as indistinguishable two elements which are very close, (let us say a and b indistinguishable iff $||a - b|| \leq \varepsilon$, for some fixed ε). Such a relation is clearly non transitive.

Another surprising fact is that the indistinguishability relation is not compatible with the predicates as illustrated by the following example:

spec : OPT-SET
  use : CONST
sort : set
generated by :
  $\emptyset$: $\rightarrow$ set
  add: Const set $\rightarrow$ set
predicates :
  $\_ \in \_$: Const set
axioms :
  $\mathsf{optional(e)} \Rightarrow \mathsf{add(e,s) = s}$
  $\neg(\mathsf{e} \in \emptyset)$
  $\neg\mathsf{optional(e)} \Rightarrow$
   $(\mathsf{e} \in \mathsf{add(e',s)} \Leftrightarrow \mathsf{e = e'} \vee \mathsf{e} \in \mathsf{s})$
observations :
  $\mathsf{optional(e)} \vee \mathsf{e} \in \mathsf{s}$

spec : CONST
sort : Const
generated by :
  $a_1, \ldots, a_n$: $\rightarrow$ Const
  $b_1, \ldots, b_m$: $\rightarrow$ Const
predicates :
  optional : Const
  particular : Const
axioms :
  $\mathsf{optional}(a_1), \ldots, \mathsf{optional}(a_n)$
  $\neg\mathsf{optional}(b_1), \ldots, \neg\mathsf{optional}(b_m)$
  "*Some axioms about* particular"
observations :
  x=y

Figure 1.1: Specification OPT-SET

Example 1.1 *Figure* 1.1 *is an attempt to specify a data type (sort* **set***) whose elements are sets of some constants (sort* Const*). Some of these constants should be considered as optional in the sense that if* optional(c) *holds then* $add(c, \{c_1, \ldots, c_n\})$ *does not necessarily returns* $\{c, c_1, \ldots, c_n\}$*; it may also return* $\{c_1, \ldots, c_n\}$*. We may then consider a realization by the sets with the usual membership but unusual* **add***: non optional constants are always added while the optional ones are added only if some other properties are satisfied (e.g.* particular(c)*). We will show later that in this realization two sets are indistinguishable if they have the same non optional elements. Consequently, the indistinguishability relation is not compatible with "*$\in$*" since, for instance,* $\emptyset$ *and any singleton set* $\{e\}$ *with an optional* e *are indistinguishable, whereas the realization under consideration satisfies* $e \in \{e\}$ *but not* $e \in \emptyset$.

In contrast to the non transitivity and the non compatibility with operations or with predicate symbols, another property causes a serious problem for the indistinguishability relation. In general, the indistinguishability relation is not "transported" through the forgetful functor. This, in part, provides an answer for the third question mentioned at the beginning of the introduction: an institution may be established under some restrictions on the category of signatures. Our institution for observational specifications requires signature morphisms to be injective. However **without such a restriction** our formalism is still a "semi-institution" (only the if part of the Satisfaction Condition holds). This is probably our main contribution since with all the definitions of observational satisfaction relation preceding [3], such a result requires at least the restriction to positive conditional axioms with observable preconditions. In our approach such a restriction is not necessary anymore, due to the following idea. We define observational algebras as usual algebras equipped with an additional equivalence relation called **observational equality** which is used as a non standard interpretation of equality. Moreover, we require an observational equality to be included in the indistinguishability relation. (Thus, in our example of metric-like space, observational equality provides a tiling of space such that the longest distance between two points in a same tile is less than ε.) Unlike the indistinguishability relation, an observational equality is of course "transported" by the forgetful functor.

It is important to notice that, similarly to the indistinguishability relation, an observational equality is not necessarily a congruence. This choice allows more realistic realizations of observational specifications and may be motivated by examples such as sets with **choose** or similar to 1.1. Consequently with our observational semantics, if in a specification one writes the axiom a = b together with f(a) $\neq$ f(b), such a specification may have a model. This points out that approaches with an observational satisfaction relation may have the advantage to be fully observational over the approaches based on the observational equivalence of algebras, where unfortunately some observational features are directly based on the usual ones. In particular, in these approaches observational consistency always coincide with the usual one whereas in ours, a specification being inconsistent (in the usual sense) may still have observational models. (An example of such specifications may be found in [3] or [2].)

In this paper some proofs have been presented in a reduced form. Complete proofs may be found in [2].

2 Algebraic and Logic Preliminaries

We assume that the reader is familiar with algebraic specifications (see e.g. [6] or [9]). A **signature Σ** consists of a finite set S of **sorts** and a finite set of **operation** and **predicate** names with **arities**, ambiguously denoted by **Σ**. We assume that each signature Σ is provided with an S-sorted set of variables X such that X_s is countable for each s ∈ S. We use the following conventions. Given a signature Σ (resp. Σ′), S (resp. S′) denotes the sorts of Σ (resp. Σ′) and X (resp. X′) denotes the variables of Σ (resp. Σ′). A **signature morphism** $\sigma : \Sigma \to \Sigma'$ maps each sort of S to a sort of S′, each operation $(f : s_1 \ldots s_n \to s) \in \Sigma$ to an operation $\sigma(f)$ of Σ′ with the arity $\sigma(s_1) \ldots \sigma(s_n) \to \sigma(s)$, each predicate $(q : s_1 \ldots s_n) \in \Sigma$ to a predicate $\sigma(q)$ of Σ′ with the arity $\sigma(s_1) \ldots \sigma(s_n)$ and each variable of X_s to a variable of $X'_{\sigma(s)}$. Moreover, we assume that a signature morphism is always injective on variables[1].

Remark 2.1 *Our approach to variables is slightly different than the one of* [7] *(page* 36, *Definition* 55 *of* [7]*) where the authors consider an S-sorted set of variables as a map* $X : \mathcal{X} \to S$ *from a fixed set* $\mathcal{X}$ *of variable symbols to sorts. In presence of* $\sigma : \Sigma \to \Sigma'$*, variables used for Σ′-formulae are defined in* [7] *as* $X' = X;\sigma$. *In other words, the authors of* [7] *assume that signature morphisms are always bijective on variables. Consequently, in their approach, there are no variables of sorts* $S' \setminus \sigma(S)$. *This seems to us a bit restrictive.*

Since we deal with predicate symbols, our Σ-algebras are usual **(total)** Σ-algebras equipped additionally with relations $q^A \subseteq A_{s_1} \times \ldots \times A_{s_n}$ for each predicate symbol $(q : s_1 \ldots s_n) \in \Sigma$. Consequently, a **Σ-morphism** in our sense is any usual Σ-morphism $\mu : A \to B$ which additionally satisfies the following condition:

$$\forall\, a_1 \in A_{s_1}, \ldots, a_n \in A_{s_n} \;\; \langle a_1, \ldots, a_n \rangle \in q^A \;\Rightarrow\; \langle \mu(a_1), \ldots, \mu(a_n) \rangle \in q^B$$

The **category of Σ-algebras** is denoted by **Alg[Σ]**. Given a signature morphism $\sigma : \Sigma \to \Sigma'$ the **σ-reduct** of a Σ′-algebra A', written $A'|_\sigma$ is defined in the usual way (with $q^{A'|_\sigma} = \sigma(q)^{A'}$ for each predicate symbol q ∈ Σ) and extending it on Σ′-morphisms we obtain the **forgetful functor** $\_|_\sigma : \mathrm{Alg}[\Sigma'] \to \mathrm{Alg}[\Sigma]$.

Given an S-sorted set E, we denote by $\mathbf{T_\Sigma(E)}$ the free Σ-algebra over E. For instance $\mathbf{T_\Sigma}$ (resp. $\mathbf{T_\Sigma(X)}$) denotes the **Σ-algebra of ground terms** (resp. **terms with variables**), $\mathbf{T_\Sigma}(A)$ (resp. $\mathbf{T_\Sigma}(A \cup X)$) denotes the **Σ-algebra of ground terms** (resp. **terms with variables**) **over the carriers of a Σ-algebra** A. Notice that if A is a free algebra then we have necessarily $q^A = \emptyset$ for any predicate symbol q.

A **valuation** is a morphism $\nu : X \to A$ which maps each $x \in X_s$ to a value $x\nu \in A_s$. The set of all valuations from X to A is written **Val[X,A]**. A **partial valuation** is a valuation preceded by an inclusion $X_0 \subseteq X$. From the freeness of $T_\Sigma(X)$ any

[1] Without this assumption, which in a stronger form appears in [7], it would be impossible to establish that $A' \models \sigma(x = y)$ iff $A'|_\sigma \models x = y$, for instance with $\sigma(x = y) = (x' = x')$.

valuation (resp. partial valuation) ν followed by the inclusion $A \subseteq \mathrm{T}_\Sigma(A)$ (resp. $A \subseteq \mathrm{T}_\Sigma(A \cup \mathrm{X})$) extends to a unique morphism (written ambiguously ν) from $\mathrm{T}_\Sigma(\mathrm{X})$ to $\mathrm{T}_\Sigma(A)$ (resp. $\mathrm{T}_\Sigma(A \cup \mathrm{X})$) which maps each term $\mathrm{t} \in (\mathrm{T}_\Sigma(\mathrm{X}))_s$ to a **valued term** $\mathrm{t}\nu \in (\mathrm{T}_\Sigma(A))_s$ (resp. **partially valued term** $\mathrm{t}\nu \in (\mathrm{T}_\Sigma(A \cup \mathrm{X}))_s$). The **evaluation morphism** from $\mathrm{T}_\Sigma(A)$ to A is defined as the unique Σ-morphism which maps each element of $(\mathrm{T}_\Sigma(A))_s \cap A_s$ to itself. This morphism maps a valued term τ to its **evaluation result** written $\overline{\tau}$.

From $\mathrm{T}_\Sigma(\mathrm{X})$, predicate symbols (including equality), connectives ($\neg, \wedge, \vee, \Rightarrow$, etc.) and quantifiers ($\forall, \exists$), we construct the **set $\mathbf{Wff}_\Sigma(\mathrm{X})$ of well formed Σ-formulae**. Given $\varphi \in \mathrm{Wff}_\Sigma(\mathrm{X})$ among the variables of φ (written **Var**$[\varphi]$) we distinguish between **free** and **bound variables**, both being defined in the usual way. We assume that there are no clashes between them in a formula (otherwise variables are properly renamed). A valuation $\nu : \mathrm{X} \rightarrow A$ may also be applied to a formula φ. We then define valued formulae (resp. partially valued formulae) as follows

$$\begin{array}{rrcl} & \mathrm{Wff}_\Sigma(A) & = & \{\varphi\nu \mid \varphi \in \mathrm{Wff}_\Sigma(\mathrm{X}),\ \nu \in \mathrm{Val}[\mathrm{X}, A]\} \\ (\text{resp.} & \mathrm{Wff}_\Sigma(A \cup \mathrm{X}) & = & \{\varphi\nu \mid \varphi \in \mathrm{Wff}_\Sigma(\mathrm{X}),\ \nu \in \mathrm{Val}[\mathrm{X}, A],\ \nu \text{ is partial}\}) \end{array}$$

Satisfaction relation between Σ-algebras and Σ-formulae is the usual one of (Many Sorted) First Order Logic with Equality. We may also write $A \models \vartheta$ for $\vartheta \in \mathrm{Wff}_\Sigma(A)$ and $A \in \mathrm{Alg}[\Sigma]$, that is we extend the usual notion of satisfaction relation on valued formulae in the following way: elements of A appearing in ϑ are considered as constants interpreted by themselves. The extension of a signature morphism $\sigma : \Sigma \rightarrow \Sigma'$ on formulae is ambiguously denoted by $\boldsymbol{\sigma}$. Given a Σ'-algebra A' we also use σ to denote the extension of a signature morphism on valued formulae, namely $\sigma : \mathrm{T}_\Sigma(A'|_\sigma) \rightarrow \mathrm{T}_{\Sigma'}(A')$.

Definition 2.2 *Given a signature morphism $\sigma : \Sigma \rightarrow \Sigma'$ and a Σ'-algebra A', we define a **σ-reduct of a valuation** $\nu' : \mathrm{X}' \rightarrow A'$ as a valuation $\nu'|_\sigma : \mathrm{X} \rightarrow A'|_\sigma$ satisfying:*

$$\forall\, \mathrm{x} \in \mathrm{X} \quad \sigma(\mathrm{x})\nu' = \mathrm{x}\nu'|_\sigma$$

Moreover given $\nu : \mathrm{X} \rightarrow A'|_\sigma$ we denote by $\boldsymbol{\sigma}(\boldsymbol{\nu})$ the class of all valuations $\nu' : \mathrm{X}' \rightarrow A'$ such that $\nu'|_\sigma = \nu$.

Remark 2.3 *Since our approach to variables is slightly different than the one of [7] (see Remark 2.1) we do not have a one to one map between $\mathrm{Val}[\mathrm{X}, A'|_\sigma]$ and $\mathrm{Val}[\mathrm{X}', A']$. In order to reuse the results of [7] about Satisfaction Condition in various institutions we translate our approach to variables in the Goguen's and Burstall's one as follows: we consider the quotient of $\mathrm{Val}[\mathrm{X}', A']$ by the equivalence relation determined by $\nu'|_\sigma = \mu'|_\sigma$. Consequently there is a one to one map between $\mathrm{Val}[\mathrm{X}, A'|_\sigma]$ and this quotient. Thus any "logical system" which is an institution in a [7]-like approach to variables is also an institution in our approach to variables due to the following lemma:*

Lemma 2.4 *Let φ be a Σ-formula with $\mathrm{Var}[\varphi] = \mathrm{X}_0$ and A be a Σ-algebra. Two valuations which differ on $\mathrm{X} \setminus \mathrm{X}_0$ have the same effect on the truth of φ. In particular* *for a signature morphism* $\sigma : \Sigma \to \Sigma'$ *and a* Σ'*-algebra* A', *any valuations* $\nu', \mu' \in \mathrm{Val}[X', A']$ *such that* $\mu'|_\sigma = \nu'|_\sigma$ *are both solutions (that is valuations which make the formula true) of the same formulae of* $\sigma(\mathrm{Wff}_\Sigma(X))$. *In other words for any* $\nu : X \to A'|_\sigma$ *and any* $\varphi \in \mathrm{Wff}_\Sigma(X)$ *we have that either all elements of the class* $\sigma(\nu)$ *are solutions of* $\sigma(\varphi)$ *or none of them are.* □

Also the following result may be deduced from Goguen's and Burstall's proof of Satisfaction Condition for (Many-Sorted) Equational Logic:

Fact 2.5 *Let* $\sigma : \Sigma \to \Sigma'$ *be a signature morphism and* A' *be a* Σ'*-algebra. For any valued term* $\tau \in T_\Sigma(A'|_\sigma)$ *we have* $\overline{\sigma(\tau)} = \overline{\tau}$. □

3 Indistinguishable Elements

As mentioned in the introduction we need to define an indistinguishability relation on the carriers of an algebra in order to loosen the satisfaction relation. Usually this is done using the concept of observable contexts. Since we observe formulae, we consider **contextual formulae** instead of contexts. The definition of contextual formula requires some additional notations. We assume that a formula φ can be represented by a tree. A **term position** p in φ is a sequence of integers which describe the path from the topmost position of φ to the considered term in φ written $\varphi|_\mathrm{p}$. The replacement of $\varphi|_\mathrm{p}$ by a term t in φ is written $\varphi[\mathrm{t}]_\mathrm{p}$.

Definition 3.1 *Given sorts* $\mathrm{S} = \{\mathrm{s}_1, \ldots, \mathrm{s}_n\}$ *the* **set of contextual variables** *is the (S-indexed) set* $\diamondsuit = \{\diamond_{\mathrm{s}_1}, \ldots \diamond_{\mathrm{s}_n}\}$ *with* $\{\diamond_{\mathrm{s}_i}\}$ *being called the* **contextual variable of sort** s_i. *A* **contextual formula** *over a* Σ*-algebra* A *is a partially valued formula* ϑ *with only one variable being both contextual and free. Consequently, the set of all contextual formulae over* A, *written* $\mathbf{Cf}_\Sigma(\boldsymbol{A})$ *is defined as follows:*

$$\mathrm{Cf}_\Sigma(A) = \bigcup_{s \in S} \mathrm{Wff}_\Sigma(A \cup \{\diamond_s\})$$

The application of $\xi \in \mathrm{Wff}_\Sigma(A \cup \{\diamond_s\})$ *on* $a \in A_s$ *is written* $\boldsymbol{\xi}[\boldsymbol{a}]$.

Our meta-concept of observation is that for each element a of an algebra, there is a set of experiments in which a may be involved. We call such a set **observers of** $\boldsymbol{a}$. Here, an observer of a is some contextual formulae ξ and the corresponding experiment is the truth of $\xi[a]$. In order to define what the observers of a are, we first need two auxiliary definitions:

Definition 3.2 *Let* A *be a* Σ*-algebra. We define the* **partial evaluation relation**, *written* $\underset{\mathbf{pEv}}{\to}$, *on* $\mathrm{Wff}_\Sigma(A)$ *as follows. We say that a formula* $\vartheta_2 \in \mathrm{Wff}_\Sigma(A)$ *is the result of the partial evaluation of* $\vartheta_1 \in \mathrm{Wff}_\Sigma(A)$, *written* $\vartheta_1 \underset{\mathbf{pEv}}{\to} \vartheta_2$, *if there is a term position* p *in* ϑ_1 *satisfying* $\mathrm{Var}[\vartheta_1|_\mathrm{p}] = \emptyset$ *and such that* $\vartheta_1[\overline{\vartheta_1|_\mathrm{p}}]_\mathrm{p} = \vartheta_2$.

The requirement $\mathrm{Var}[\vartheta_1|_\mathrm{p}] = \emptyset$ may seem strange. This is necessary, since given $\varphi \in \mathrm{Wff}_\Sigma(X)$ only the free variables of φ can be mapped to A. Consequently we assume that when applied to φ, a valuation ν is implicitly preceded by the inclusion "free variables of φ" $\subseteq$ X. For instance if ν which maps x to a and y to b is applied on a formula $\exists$ y x $\leq$ y we obtain $\exists$ y $a \leq$ y and not $\exists$ b $a \leq b$. Thus given a valued formula ϑ, in general we do not have $\mathrm{Var}[\vartheta] = \emptyset$.

Definition 3.3 *Let $\Phi \subseteq \mathrm{Wff}_\Sigma(\mathrm{X})$ be a set of formulae and A be a Σ-algebra. The* **closure by partial evaluations of Φ in A**, *written $\widetilde{\Phi}^A$, is defined as follows:*

$$\widetilde{\Phi}^A = \{\vartheta \in \mathrm{Wff}_\Sigma(A) \mid \exists\, \varphi \in \Phi\ \exists\, \nu : \mathrm{X} \to A \quad \varphi\nu \xrightarrow[\mathbf{pEv}]{*} \vartheta\}$$

where $\xrightarrow[\mathbf{pEv}]{*}$ *denotes the reflexive-transitive closure of* $\xrightarrow[\mathrm{pEv}]{}$.

Now if Φ is a set of observable formulae, $\widetilde{\Phi}^A$ provides an information about experiments in which a may by involved:

Definition 3.4 *Let $\Phi \subseteq \mathrm{Wff}_\Sigma(\mathrm{X})$ be a set of formulae which we call* **observable formulae** *and a be an element of a Σ-algebra A. We say that a contextual formula $\xi \in \mathrm{Cf}_\Sigma(A)$ is a* **Φ-observer of a** *(an observer of a, in short) if $\xi[a] \in \widetilde{\Phi}^A$. The set of Φ-observers of a is written* $\mathbf{obs}_{\Phi}(a)$.

Once we know which experiments can be made on a value a, we want to know how to compare their results with the ones made on another value b. We claim that only common observers of a and b (called comparators) may be used for this purpose:

Definition 3.5 *A* **Φ-comparator** *(comparator, in short) of elements a and b of a given carrier of a Σ-algebra, is any Φ-observer of a and b. The set of all comparators of both a and b is denoted by* $\mathbf{cmp}_{\Phi}(a,b)$. *We say that a Φ-comparator ξ* **distinguishes** *a and b iff $A \not\models \xi[a] \Leftrightarrow \xi[b]$.*

We can now state the following definition of indistinguishability:

Definition 3.6 *We say that two elements a and b of a given carrier of a Σ-algebra are* **indistinguishable** *w.r.t. a set of formulae $\Phi \in \mathrm{Wff}_\Sigma(\mathrm{X})$ (or* **Φ-indistinguishable***) written $a \sim_{\Phi} b$, if there is no Φ-comparator which distinguishes them.*

We illustrate these concepts by the following example:

Example 3.7 *Consider an algebra L of sets over the signature of* OPT-SET *(see Figure 1.1) with the usual membership test and with the following* add:

$$add^L(c,\{c_1,\ldots,c_n\}) = \begin{cases} \{c,c_1,\ldots,c_n\} & \text{if } c \in particular^L \text{ or } c \notin optional^L \\ \{c_1,\ldots,c_n\} & \text{otherwise} \end{cases}$$

that is any non optional constant is always added to a set and optional ones are added only if they are particular. The set of observable formulae Opt *of this specification is* {optional(x) $\vee$ x $\in$ s}. *Applying the definition we obtain*

$$\widetilde{\mathsf{Opt}}^L = \{\mathsf{optional}(c) \ \vee\ c \in l \mid c \in L_{\mathsf{Const}}, l \in L_{\mathsf{Set}}\}$$

Consequently any $l \in L_{\mathsf{Set}}$ has the same observers $\{\mathsf{optional}(c) \vee c \in \diamond \mid c \in L_{\mathsf{Const}}\}$. *Such an observer may only distinguish two sets which differ on non optional elements.*

As mentioned in Introduction, we would like to present an institution for observational specifications. Since our observational satisfaction relation (which will be defined further) strongly depends on observers we must first study their properties w.r.t. the forgetful functor and the translation of observable formulae. In this way, we shall provide tools which will be useful to show that the Satisfaction Condition holds in our formalism. Below we give the first important theorem. It is a good occasion to establish some interesting lemmas about partial evaluation.

Theorem 3.8 *Let $\sigma : \Sigma \rightarrow \Sigma'$ be a signature morphism, $\Phi \subseteq \mathrm{Wff}_\Sigma(X)$ and $\Phi' \subseteq \mathrm{Wff}_{\Sigma'}(X')$ be sets of formulae such that $\sigma(\Phi) \subseteq \Phi'$ and A' be a Σ'-algebra. For any element $a \in A'_{|\sigma}$ and any contextual formula $\xi \in \mathrm{Cf}_{\Sigma(A'_{|\sigma})}$ we have*

$$\xi \in \mathrm{obs}_\Phi(a) \quad \Rightarrow \quad \sigma(\xi) \in \mathrm{obs}_{\Phi'}(a)$$

We need the following lemmas for the proof:

Lemma 3.9 *Let $\sigma : \Sigma \rightarrow \Sigma'$ be a signature morphism, and A' be a Σ'-algebra. For any $\vartheta_1, \vartheta_2 \in \mathrm{Wff}_\Sigma(A'_{|\sigma})$ we have:*

$$\vartheta_1 \overset{*}{\underset{\mathbf{pEv}}{\rightarrow}} \vartheta_2 \quad \Rightarrow \quad \sigma(\vartheta_1) \overset{*}{\underset{\mathbf{pEv}}{\rightarrow}} \sigma(\vartheta_2)$$

Proof *Follows directly from Definition 3.2 and Fact 2.5.* □

Lemma 3.10 *Let $\sigma : \Sigma \rightarrow \Sigma'$ be a signature morphism, $\Phi \subseteq \mathrm{Wff}_\Sigma(X)$ and $\Phi' \subseteq \mathrm{Wff}_{\Sigma'}(X')$ be sets of formulae such that $\sigma(\Phi) \subseteq \Phi'$ and A' be a Σ'-algebra. For any $\vartheta \in \mathrm{Wff}_\Sigma(A'_{|\sigma})$ we have:*

$$\vartheta \in \widetilde{\Phi}^{A'_{|\sigma}} \quad \Rightarrow \quad \sigma(\vartheta) \in \widetilde{\Phi'}^{A'}$$

Proof *Assume $\vartheta \in \widetilde{\Phi}^{A'_{|\sigma}}$. By Definition 3.3 we have $\exists\, \varphi \in \Phi\ \exists\, \nu : X \rightarrow A'_{|\sigma}\ \ \varphi\nu \overset{*}{\underset{\mathbf{pEv}}{\rightarrow}} \vartheta$. By Lemma 3.9 we obtain*

$$\exists\, \varphi \in \Phi\ \exists\, \nu : X \rightarrow A'_{|\sigma} \quad \sigma(\varphi\nu) \overset{*}{\underset{\mathbf{pEv}}{\rightarrow}} \sigma(\vartheta) \qquad \text{(i)}$$

It is obvious from Definition 2.2 that for any $\nu' \in \sigma(\nu)$ we have $\sigma(\varphi\nu) = \sigma(\varphi)\nu'$. Let $\varphi' = \sigma(\varphi)$ then from (i), we deduce: $\exists\, \varphi' \in \Phi'\ \exists\, \nu' : X \rightarrow A'\ \ \varphi'\nu' \overset{*}{\underset{\mathbf{pEv}}{\rightarrow}} \sigma(\vartheta)$. By Definition 3.3 this yields $\sigma(\vartheta) \in \widetilde{\Phi'}^{A'}$. □

Proof of Theorem 3.8 *Let $\sigma : \Sigma \rightarrow \Sigma'$ be a signature morphism, $\Phi \subseteq \mathrm{Wff}_\Sigma(X)$ and $\Phi' \subseteq \mathrm{Wff}_{\Sigma'}(X')$ be sets of formulae such that $\sigma(\Phi) \subseteq \Phi'$ and A' a be Σ'-algebra. Let $a \in A'_{|\sigma}$ and assume $\xi \in \mathrm{obs}_\Phi(a)$. By Definition 3.4 we have $\xi[a] \in \widetilde{\Phi}^{A'_{|\sigma}}$, hence by Lemma 3.10 we deduce $\sigma(\xi[a]) \in \widetilde{\Phi'}^{A'}$. By Definition 3.4 this yields $\sigma(\xi) \in \mathrm{obs}_{\Phi'}(a)$.* □

Note that the converse of the above theorem does not hold even if $\sigma(\Phi) = \Phi'$:

Example 3.11 *Consider the signatures $\Sigma = \{\mathrm{q_1}, \mathrm{q_2} : \mathrm{s}\}$ and $\Sigma' = \{\mathrm{q'} : \mathrm{s'}\}$. Let $\Phi = \{\mathrm{q_1}(\mathrm{x})\}$. Consider $\sigma : \Sigma \rightarrow \Sigma'$ such that $\sigma(\mathrm{s}) = \mathrm{s'}$ and $\sigma(\mathrm{q_1}) = \sigma(\mathrm{q_2}) = \mathrm{q'}$. It is clear that for any Σ'-algebra A', $\mathrm{q_2}(\diamond)$ is not a Φ-observer of any element $a \in A'_{|\sigma}$, whereas $\sigma(\mathrm{q_2}(\diamond)) = \mathrm{q'}(\diamond)$ and $\mathrm{q'}(\diamond) \in \mathrm{obs}_{\sigma(\Phi)}(a)$.*

However, for injective signature morphisms the converse of Theorem 3.8 holds:

Theorem 3.12 *Let $\sigma : \Sigma \to \Sigma'$ be an injective signature morphism, $\Phi \subseteq \mathrm{Wff}_\Sigma(\mathrm{X})$ be a set of formulae and A' be a Σ'-algebra. For any $a \in A'_{|_\sigma}$ and any $\xi \in \mathrm{Cf}_\Sigma(A'_{|_\sigma})$ we have:*

$$\xi \in \mathrm{obs}_\Phi(a) \quad \Leftrightarrow \quad \sigma(\xi) \in \mathrm{obs}_{\sigma(\Phi)}(a)$$

Proof sketch *Since σ is injective, the implications in lemmas 3.9, 3.10 become equivalences when $\Phi' = \sigma(\Phi)$. Consequently, we obtain the proof we are looking for, by replacing the implications in the proof of 3.8 by equivalences.* □

The former example shows the real source of problems in our approach. More generally a signature morphism $\sigma : \Sigma \to \Sigma'$ may map two (or more) different sorts $\mathrm{s}_1, \mathrm{s}_2 \in \mathrm{S}$ to the same sort $\mathrm{s}' \in \mathrm{S}'$. By definition of σ-reduct we then have $(A'_{|_\sigma})_{\mathrm{s}_1} = (A'_{|_\sigma})_{\mathrm{s}_2} = A_{\mathrm{s}'}$ but the indistinguishability relations may be different on these three carrier sets even if $\sigma(\Phi) = \Phi'$. Consequently, given $\sim_\Phi$ on an algebra $A'_{|_\sigma}$, we often need to mention the carrier we are working on. This makes the statements of some theorems and their proofs unusually complicated.

4 Properties of the Indistinguishability Relation

The definition 3.6 expresses a situation in which two elements of a Σ-algebra are indistinguishable. Indeed, it defines an S-sorted relation $\sim_\Phi = (\sim_\Phi)_{\mathrm{s}\in\mathrm{S}}$ on an algebra, called the **indistinguishability relation**. Since this relation is the next step toward a complete description of our institution for observational specifications, we must study its properties w.r.t. the forgetful functor and the translation of observable formulae. This will be subsequently necessary for establishing the Satisfaction Condition (see [7]). The following proposition is devoted to this purpose and next we study other interesting properties of the indistinguishability relation.

Proposition 4.1 *Let $\sigma : \Sigma \to \Sigma'$ be a signature morphism, let $\Phi \subseteq \mathrm{Wff}_\Sigma(\mathrm{X})$ and $\Phi' \subseteq \mathrm{Wff}_{\Sigma'}(\mathrm{X}')$ be sets of formulae such that $\sigma(\Phi) \subseteq \Phi'$ and A' be a Σ'-algebra. For any $\mathrm{s}' \in \sigma(\mathrm{S})$, for all $\mathrm{a}, \mathrm{b} \in A'_{\mathrm{s}'}$ we have that if $a \sim_{\Phi'} b$ then for any $\mathrm{s} \in \sigma^{-1}(\mathrm{s}')$, a and b are Φ-indistinguishable in $(A'_{|_\sigma})_\mathrm{s}$.*

We need the following lemma for the proof:

Lemma 4.2 *Let $\sigma : \Sigma \to \Sigma'$ be a signature morphism and A' be a Σ'-algebra. For any valued formula $\vartheta \in \mathrm{Wff}_\Sigma(A'_{|_\sigma})$ we have $A'_{|_\sigma} \models \vartheta$ iff $A' \models \sigma(\vartheta)$.*

Proof sketch *This lemma is a slightly modified version of the Satisfaction Condition (see [7]) for (Many Sorted) First Order Logic with Equality and is proved similarly.* □

Proof of Proposition 4.1 *Assume by contradiction that there exists $\mathrm{s} \in \mathrm{S}$ and $a, b \in A'_{\sigma(s)}$ such that $a \sim_{\Phi'} b$ and $a \not\sim_\Phi b$ in $(A'_{|_\sigma})_s$. By Definition 3.5 there exists $\xi \in \mathrm{cmp}_\Phi(a, b)$ such that $A'_{|_\sigma} \not\models \xi[a] \Leftrightarrow \xi[b]$. Hence from Lemma 4.2 we have:*

$$A' \not\models \sigma(\xi)[a] \Leftrightarrow \sigma(\xi)[b] \tag{i}$$

But according to Theorem 3.8, $\sigma(\xi)$ is a Φ'-observer for both a and b. Thus according to (i), $\sigma(\xi)$ distinguishes a and b. This is in contradiction with the assumption $a \sim_{\Phi'} b$. □

As mentioned at the end of the previous section the converse of this proposition does not hold even if $\sigma(\Phi) = \Phi'$. But once again this converse holds for injective signature morphisms.

The following fact is obvious from the definition of the indistinguishability relation.

Fact 4.3 *The indistinguishability relation is reflexive and symmetric.* □

The next fact fully agrees with our claims:

Fact 4.4 *The indistinguishability relation is neither compatible with operations nor with predicates.*

Proof sketch *It is enough to consider the examples given in Introduction.* □

We have already announced the following fact which is a consequence of our Indistinguishability Assumption together with general form observations we use:

Fact 4.5 *The indistinguishability relation is not transitive in general.*

Proof *Consider* $\Sigma = \{\mathsf{a}, \mathsf{b}, \mathsf{c} :\rightarrow \mathsf{Trans}; \mathsf{q} : \mathsf{Trans}\}$, $\Phi = \{\mathsf{q}(\mathsf{a}), \mathsf{q}(\mathsf{c})\}$ *and a* Σ*-algebra* A *such that* $q^A = \{a^A\}$. *In this algebra we have* $\mathsf{obs}_\Phi(a^A) = \mathsf{obs}_\Phi(c^A) = \{\mathsf{q}(\diamond)\}$ *and* $\mathsf{obs}_\Phi(b^A) = \emptyset$. *Since* a^A *and* b^A *(resp.* b^A *and* c^A*) have no comparator they are indistinguishable. On the other hand,* a^A *and* c^A *are distinguished by* $\mathsf{q}(\diamond)$. *Consequently, in this example the indistinguishability relation is not transitive.* □

More generally, the above result has the following explanation: since we did not impose any restriction on the set of observable formulae, nothing ensures that all the elements of a given data type can be observed in the same way. On the contrary, when all the elements of a carrier set have the same observers, the indistinguishability relation is transitive on this carrier set. This may be illustrated as follows:

Example 4.6 *The indistinguishability relation from Example* 3.7 *is transitive.*

One may think that Fact 4.5 is quite unfortunate and claim that two elements should be indistinguishable if they are in the sense of Definition 3.6 and if additionally they have the same observers. But in our opinion such definition would not be adequate, due to the reason detailed in the following example:

Example 4.7 *Consider a signature* Σ *and assume that we need to provide a set* Φ *of observable formulae which induces on any* Σ*-algebra* A *the following indistinguishability relation*

$$\forall\, a, b \in A \quad a \sim_\Phi b \ \text{ iff } \ \nexists\, \mathsf{t} \in \mathrm{T}_\Sigma \ \ \bar{\mathsf{t}} = a$$

With Definition 3.6 *we obtain this relation by taking* $\Phi = \{\mathsf{l} = \mathsf{r} \mid \mathsf{l}, \mathsf{r} \in (\mathrm{T}_\Sigma)_\mathsf{s}, \mathsf{s} \in \mathrm{S}\}$. *Now if we add to this definition the additional requirement mentioned above, we do not obtain the desired indistinguishability relation whatever* Φ *we consider.*

This example points out that the discussed modification of the Definition 3.6 would decrease the expressive power of our approach. Consequently we are not enthusiastic about such a modification. Moreover, as we will see in the sequel (Definition 6.4), Fact 4.5 raises no particular problem.

5 Observational Algebras

As mentioned in the introduction, in this paper, an observational equality does not necessarily coincide with the indistinguishability relation. This choice was dictated by the fact that the indistinguishability relation is not "transported" by the forgetful functor (the converse of Proposition 4.1 does not hold even if $\Phi' = \sigma(\Phi)$) whereas an observational equality should be "transported" through the forgetful functor as the usual equality does. For this reason we introduce in this section a flexible concept of observational algebras.

Definition 5.1 *Given a signature Σ, an* **observational Σ-algebra** *is a pair $\langle A, \cong\rangle$ where A is a Σ-algebra and $\cong$ is an S-sorted equivalence relation on A, called* **observational equality on A**. *We denote the class of all observational Σ-algebras by* **OAlg[Σ]**.

According to the above definition we consider the equality symbol "=" as a particular predicate symbol. This symbol is explicitly interpreted in an algebra by a particular relation, namely an observational equality.

Example 5.2 *Let L and $\sim_{\mathrm{Opt}}$ be respectively the algebra and the indistinguishability relation described in Example 3.7. Since $\sim_{\mathrm{Opt}}$ is an equivalence relation (c.f. 4.6), the pair $\langle L, \sim_{\mathrm{Opt}}\rangle$ is an observational algebra.*

Definition 5.3 *An* **observational Σ-morphism** *$\mu : \langle A, \cong^A\rangle \to \langle B, \cong^B\rangle$ is any Σ-morphism from A to B which preserves observational equalities i.e:*

$$\forall a, b \in A_s \quad a \cong^A b \Rightarrow \mu(a) \cong^B \mu(b)$$

It is obvious that OAlg[Σ] equipped with the observational Σ-morphisms forms a category.

Definition 5.4 *Let $\sigma : \Sigma \to \Sigma'$ be a signature morphism. The* **σ-reduct** *of an observational Σ'-algebra $\langle A', \cong'\rangle$ is the observational Σ-algebra*

$$\langle A', \cong'\rangle_{|_\sigma} = \langle A'_{|_\sigma}, \cong'_{|_\sigma}\rangle$$

where $A'_{|_\sigma}$ is the usual σ-reduct of the Σ'-algebra A' and $(\cong'_{|_\sigma})_s = (\cong')_{\sigma(s)}$.

The mapping $\_{|_\sigma}$ extends to observational morphisms as in the usual framework. Consequently, it defines the **forgetful functor** from OAlg[Σ'] to OAlg[Σ] associated to σ. Thus OAlg is a functor from the category of signatures Sig to the dual of the category of all categories $\mathrm{Cat}^{\mathrm{op}}$. OAlg maps an object Σ of Sig to the category of the observational Σ-algebras and a signature morphism σ to the corresponding forgetful functor $\_{|_\sigma}$. This provides components upon which an institution can be built.

6 Validity of Observational Formulae

Before introducing observational formulae and defining their validity in observational algebras we give some additional definitions and results.

Definition 6.1 *A solution of an equation* $l = r$ *(resp. atomic formula* $q(t_1, \ldots, t_n)$*) in an observational* Σ*-algebra* $\langle A, \cong \rangle$ *is a valuation* $\nu : X \to A$ *such that* $\overline{l\nu} \cong \overline{r\nu}$ *(resp.* $\langle \overline{t_1\nu}, \ldots, \overline{t_n\nu} \rangle \in q^A$*). The set of solutions of a formula* φ*, written* $[\varphi]_{\langle A, \cong \rangle}$*, is defined recursively as follows:*

- *if* $\varphi = \neg\psi$ *then* $[\varphi]_{\langle A,\cong\rangle} = \mathrm{Val}[X, A] \setminus [\psi]_{\langle A,\cong\rangle}$
- *if* $\varphi = \psi \wedge \psi'$ *then* $[\varphi]_{\langle A,\cong\rangle} = [\psi]_{\langle A,\cong\rangle} \cap [\psi']_{\langle A,\cong\rangle}$
- *if* $\varphi = \forall x \psi$ *then* $[\varphi]_{\langle A,\cong\rangle} =$
  $= \{\nu \in \mathrm{Val}[X, A] \mid \forall \mu \in \mathrm{Val}[X, A] \ (\forall y \in X \setminus \{x\} \ y\mu = y\nu) \Rightarrow \mu \in [\psi]_{\langle A,\cong\rangle}\}$

where ψ, ψ' *are* Σ*-formulae.*

Since all the connectives of the classical logic as well as the existential quantifier can be expressed by means of $\neg$, $\wedge$ and $\forall$, the solutions of an arbitrary first order logic Σ-formula are well defined by the above definition.

Before putting our formalism into an institutional framework we need to investigate the solutions across the forgetful functor and the translation of formulae. This is done in the following theorem:

Theorem 6.2 *Let* $\sigma : \Sigma \to \Sigma'$ *be a signature morphism and* $\langle A', \cong' \rangle$ *be an observational* Σ'*-algebra. For any* Σ*-formula* φ *we have:*

$$\nu \in [\varphi]_{\langle A', \cong' \rangle_{|\sigma}} \quad \text{iff} \quad \sigma(\nu) \subseteq ([\sigma(\varphi)]_{\langle A', \cong' \rangle})_{|\sigma} \qquad \text{(i)}$$

Proof sketch *The proof is based on the fact that (Many-Sorted) First Order Logic is an institution. The Goguen's and Burstall's proof of this fact establishes a one to one map between* $\mathrm{Val}[X, A'_{|\sigma}]$ *and* $\mathrm{Val}[X', A']$ *which is shown to be solution preserving w.r.t. formula translation, that is* (i) *holds (replacing* $\subseteq$ *by* $\in$*) in the usual framework of (Many-Sorted) First Order Logic. According to Remark* 2.3 *which is justified by Lemma* 2.4, (i) *also holds for (Many-Sorted) First Order Logic with our approach to variables. Our "logical system" is not exactly (Many-Sorted) First Order Logic but may be mapped into this in the following way:*

- *We consider the equality symbol as an S-indexed family of ordinary predicate symbols* $=_s$.
- *Since in our approach* $(=_s)_{s \in S}$ *are interpreted by equivalence relations we consider an S-indexed set of axioms* $\mathcal{E} = \{x =_s x, \ x =_s y \Rightarrow y =_s x, \ x =_s y \wedge y =_s z \Rightarrow x =_s z\}$.

Since (i) *holds in the usual framework of (Many-Sorted) First Order Logic, it also holds for a particular class of first order* Σ*-formulae of the form* $\psi \wedge \mathcal{E}$*. Consequently, in the axiomatic theory* $\mathcal{E}$ *underlying our "logical system"* (i) *holds for any first order* Σ*-formula* φ. □

An elementary and complete proof of this theorem may be found in [2].

Definition 6.3 *An* **observational Σ-formula** *is a pair* $\langle \theta, \Phi \rangle$ *where* $\theta \in \mathrm{Wff}_\Sigma(X)$ *is a* Σ*-formula and* $\Phi \subseteq \mathrm{Wff}_\Sigma(X)$ *is a set of formulae. We note* **OWff[Σ]** *the set of all observational* Σ*-formulae.*

Notice that observational formulae are only atomic ones. We have neither "observational connectives" nor "observational quantifiers". It may be interesting to investigate the possibility of including such features to our approach.

As in the usual framework, OWff is extended to a functor from the category of signatures Sig to Set (the category of sets). This functor maps an objet Σ of Sig to the set of all observational Σ-formulae. An arrow σ of $\mathrm{Sig}(\Sigma, \Sigma')$ is mapped by OWff to the corresponding translation of observational formula: $\mathrm{OWff}[\sigma](\langle\theta, \Phi\rangle) = \langle\sigma(\varphi), \sigma(\Phi)\rangle$. (We write shortly σ instead of $\mathrm{OWff}[\sigma]$.)

We have already all the elements necessary to define an observational satisfaction relation:

Definition 6.4 *We say that an observational Σ-algebra $\langle A, \cong\rangle$* **satisfies** *an observational formula $\langle\psi, \Phi\rangle$, written* $\langle \boldsymbol{A}, \cong\rangle \models \langle\boldsymbol{\psi}, \boldsymbol{\Phi}\rangle$, *iff:*

$$[\psi]_{\langle A,\cong\rangle} = \mathrm{Val}[\mathrm{X}, A] \qquad \text{(i)}$$

$$\cong \; \subseteq \; \sim_\Phi \qquad \text{(ii)}$$

Notice that in the above we have defined a family of relations $\{\models_\Sigma\}_{\Sigma:\mathrm{Sig}}$ with

$$\models_\Sigma \; \subseteq \; \mathrm{OAlg}[\Sigma] \times \mathrm{OWff}[\Sigma]$$

We examine now how our satisfaction relation behaves w.r.t. the variance of observational formulae (translation) and the covariance of algebras (σ-reduct). We start by the first requirement of Definition 6.4:

Proposition 6.5 *Let $\sigma : \Sigma \to \Sigma'$ be a signature morphism. For any set of formulae $\Phi \subseteq \mathrm{Wff}_\Sigma(\mathrm{X})$, any observational Σ'-algebra $\langle A', \cong'\rangle$ and any Σ-formula φ we have:*

$$[\sigma(\varphi)]_{\langle A',\cong'\rangle} = \mathrm{Val}[\mathrm{X}', A'] \quad \textit{iff} \quad [\varphi]_{\langle A',\cong'\rangle|_\sigma} = \mathrm{Val}[\mathrm{X}, A'|_\sigma]$$

Proof *We have* $[\sigma(\varphi)]_{\langle A',\cong'\rangle} = \mathrm{Val}[\mathrm{X}', A']$ *which is equivalent to* $([\sigma(\varphi)]_{\langle A',\cong'\rangle})|_\sigma = (\mathrm{Val}[\mathrm{X}', A'])|_\sigma$*, which by Theorem 6.2 is equivalent to:*

$$[\varphi]_{\langle A',\cong'\rangle|_\sigma} = (\mathrm{Val}[\mathrm{X}', A'])|_\sigma \qquad \text{(i)}$$

Since $-|_\sigma$ is surjective on valuations we have $(\mathrm{Val}[\mathrm{X}', A'])|_\sigma = \mathrm{Val}[\mathrm{X}, A'|_\sigma]$. *Thus, the formula* (i) *is equivalent to* $[\varphi]_{\langle A',\cong'\rangle|_\sigma} = \mathrm{Val}[\mathrm{X}, A'|_\sigma]$. □

The next step is to study the second condition of Definition 6.4 w.r.t. formula translation and the forgetful functor.

Proposition 6.6 *Let $\sigma : \Sigma \to \Sigma'$ be a signature morphism. For all sets of formulae $\Phi \subseteq \mathrm{Wff}_\Sigma(\mathrm{X})$, $\Phi' \subseteq \mathrm{Wff}_{\Sigma'}(\mathrm{X}')$ such that $\sigma(\Phi) \subseteq \Phi'$ and for any observational Σ'-algebra $\langle A', \cong'\rangle$ we have:*

$$\cong' \subseteq \sim_{\Phi'} \;\Rightarrow\; \cong'|_\sigma \subseteq \sim_\Phi$$

where $\sim_{\Phi'}$ and $\sim_\Phi$ are the indistinguishability relations on A' and $A'|_\sigma$ respectively.

Proof *Assume that* $\forall\, a, b \in A' \;\; a \cong' b \;\Rightarrow\; a \sim_{\Phi'} b$. *Applying Definition 5.4 we obtain* $\forall\, a, b \in A'|_\sigma \;\; a \cong'|_\sigma b \;\Rightarrow\; a \sim_{\Phi'} b$. *But from Proposition 4.1 it follows that* $a \sim_{\Phi'} b \Rightarrow a \sim_\Phi b$. *Consequently* $\cong'|_\sigma \subseteq \sim_\Phi$. □

The next step would be to prove the converse of the above proposition when restricted to $\Phi' = \sigma(\Phi)$. Unfortunately this is not true in general. The following example illustrates this fact:

Example 6.7 *Consider* $\Sigma = \{\mathrm{a}, \mathrm{b} :\to \mathrm{s};\ \mathrm{p}, \mathrm{q} : \mathrm{s}\}$ *and* $\Sigma' = \{\mathrm{c}, \mathrm{d} :\to \mathrm{s};\ \mathrm{r} : \mathrm{s}\}$. *Let* $\Phi = \{\mathrm{p}(\mathrm{a}), \mathrm{q}(\mathrm{b})\}$. *Notice that in any* Σ*-algebra* A *we have*

$$a^A \sim_\Phi b^A \tag{i}$$

because a^A *and* b^A *have no comparator. Consider* $\sigma : \Sigma \to \Sigma'$ *defined by:* $\sigma(\mathrm{s}) = \mathrm{s}$, $\sigma(\mathrm{a}) = \mathrm{c}$, $\sigma(\mathrm{b}) = \mathrm{d}$, $\sigma(\mathrm{p}) = \sigma(\mathrm{q}) = \mathrm{r}$. *Notice that in any* Σ'*-algebra* A' *we have*

$$\mathrm{cmp}_{\sigma(\Phi)}(c^{A'}, d^{A'}) = \{\mathrm{r}(\diamond)\} \tag{ii}$$

since $\sigma(\Phi) = \{\mathrm{r}(\mathrm{c}), \mathrm{r}(\mathrm{d})\}$. *Consider then a reachable observational* Σ'*-algebra* $\langle A', \cong' \rangle$ *such that*

$$A' \not\models r^{A'}(c^{A'}) \Leftrightarrow r^{A'}(d^{A'}) \tag{iii}$$

$$c^{A'} \cong' d^{A'} \tag{iv}$$

Notice that $\cong'|_\sigma = \{(a^{A|_\sigma}, b^{A|_\sigma})\}$. *Therefore, according to* (i) *we have* $\cong'|_\sigma \subseteq \sim_\Phi$ *but* $\cong' \not\subseteq \sim_{\sigma(\Phi)}$ *since from* (ii) *and* (iii) *we have* $c^{A'} \not\sim_{\sigma(\Phi)} d^{A'}$ *while* (iv) *holds.*

From this negative result we may conclude that, in order to define institutions within our approach, we will be constrained to restrict somehow our formalism. This will be the subject of Section 9.

7 Observational Specifications

This section is devoted to some general notions about observational specifications.

Definition 7.1 *An* **observational specification** OSP *is a triplet* $\langle \Sigma, \Theta, \Phi \rangle$, *where* Σ *is the signature of* OSP, Θ *the (finite) set of its axioms and* Φ *is a set of formulae,* $\Phi \subseteq \mathrm{Wff}_\Sigma(\mathrm{X})$, *called* **observations** *of* OSP.

The models are defined as in the usual approach except that we use the observational satisfaction instead of the usual one:

Definition 7.2 *Let* $\mathrm{OSP} = \langle \Sigma, \{\theta_1, \ldots, \theta_n\}, \Phi \rangle$ *be an observational specification. We say that an observational* Σ*-algebra* $\langle A, \cong \rangle$ *is a* **model** *of* OSP *iff:*

$$\langle A, \cong \rangle \models\!\!\!\!\!\!\!\!\;\;\! \mathrel{\text{\textcent}} \langle \theta_1 \wedge \ldots \wedge \theta_n, \Phi \rangle$$

We note **OAlg[OSP]** *the class of all observational models of* OSP.

OAlg[OSP] with observational Σ-morphisms is a full subcategory of OAlg[Σ].

Fact 7.3 *The observational algebra* $\langle L, \sim_{\mathrm{Opt}} \rangle$, *described in Example* 5.2, *is a model of the observational specification* OPT-SET.

Proof *Since the observational equality on* $\langle L, \sim_{\mathrm{Opt}} \rangle$ *is just the indistinguishability relation, we only need to prove that for any axiom* θ *of* OPT-SET *we have*

$$[\theta]_L = \mathrm{Val}[\mathrm{X}, L] \tag{i}$$

• *For the first axiom the requirement* (i) *is satisfied because for any set* $\{c_1, \ldots, c_n\} \in L_{\mathsf{Set}}$ *and any optional constant* c *the result of* $add^L(c, \{c_1, \ldots, c_n\})$ *is either* $\{c, c_1, \ldots, c_n\}$ *or* $\{c_1, \ldots, c_n\}$ *(depending on whether* c *is particular or not) and we know (see* 3.7*) that* $\{c, c_1, \ldots, c_n\}$ *and* $\{c_1, \ldots, c_n\}$ *are in the same equivalence class of the observational equality* $\sim_{\mathsf{Opt}}$.

• *Since* $\in^L$ *is the usual membership, it is clear that the requirement* (i) *is also satisfied by the second and the third axiom.* □

The next result points out that our observational specifications generalize the usual approach. On one hand an algebra A can be viewed as the observational algebra $\langle A, =\rangle$. On the other hand, an algebraic specification $\langle\Sigma, \Theta\rangle$ can be considered as an observational one in the straightforward way:

Proposition 7.4 *Let* $\langle\Sigma, \Theta\rangle$ *be an algebraic specification. Each model of* $\langle\Sigma, \Theta, \Phi\rangle$ *with* $\Phi = \{\mathrm{x_s = y_s} \mid \mathrm{s} \in \mathrm{S}\}$ *is of the form* $\langle A, =\rangle$ *with* $A \in \mathrm{Alg}[\langle\Sigma, \Theta\rangle]$.

Proof *Note first that* $\sim_\Phi$ *is the identity relation on any* Σ*-algebra. This is obvious since all* $a, b \in A_s$, $a \neq b$, *are distinguished by e.g.* $(\diamond = a) \in \mathrm{cmp}_\Phi(a, b)$. *According to Definition* 6.4 *for any* $\langle A, \cong\rangle \in \mathrm{OAlg}[\langle\Sigma, \Theta, \Phi\rangle]$ *we should have* $\cong\, \subseteq\, \sim_\Phi$. *Thus* $\cong$ *is just the usual equality. From the requirement* $[\Theta]_{\langle A,=\rangle} = \mathrm{Val}[\mathrm{X}, A]$ *we deduce that* $A \in \mathrm{Alg}[\langle\Sigma, \Theta\rangle]$. *Conversely, it is clear that for any* $B \in \mathrm{Alg}[\langle\Sigma, \Theta\rangle]$ *we have* $\langle B, =\rangle \in \mathrm{OAlg}[\langle\Sigma, \Theta, \Phi\rangle]$. □

Up to now, we have not been studying modularity issues. We have only defined the semantics of "flat" specifications. In fact, as in [1], our semantics extends to an observational **stratified loose semantics** [4] without additional assumptions. For instance, the next theorem shows that our approach fulfills the requirement of "reusing by restriction" of [4].

Theorem 7.5 *Let* $\sigma : \Sigma \rightarrow \Sigma'$ *be a signature morphism. For all observational specifications* $\mathrm{OSP} = \langle\Sigma, \Theta, \Phi\rangle$ *and* $\mathrm{OSP}' = \langle\Sigma', \Theta', \Phi'\rangle$ *such that* $\sigma(\Theta) \subseteq \Theta'$ *and* $\sigma(\Phi) \subseteq \Phi'$ *we have:*

$$\mathrm{OAlg}[\mathrm{OSP}']_{|_\sigma} \subseteq \mathrm{OAlg}[\mathrm{OSP}]$$

Proof *From definitions* 7.2 *and* 6.4 *it is enough to prove:*

$$\forall\, \langle A', \cong'\rangle \in \mathrm{OAlg}[\Sigma'] \quad [\Theta']_{\langle A', \cong'\rangle} = \mathrm{Val}[\mathrm{X}', A'] \;\Rightarrow\; [\Theta]_{\langle A', \cong'\rangle_{|_\sigma}} = \mathrm{Val}[\mathrm{X}, A'_{|_\sigma}] \qquad \text{(i)}$$

$$\forall\, \langle A', \cong'\rangle \in \mathrm{OAlg}[\Sigma'] \quad \cong'\, \subseteq\, \sim_{\Phi'} \;\Rightarrow\; \cong'_{|_\sigma}\, \subseteq\, \sim_\Phi \qquad \text{(ii)}$$

• **Proof of (i)** *Let* $\langle A', \cong'\rangle \in \mathrm{OAlg}[\Sigma']$ *such that* $[\Theta']_{\langle A', \cong'\rangle} = \mathrm{Val}[\mathrm{X}', A']$. *Since* $\sigma(\Theta)$ *is included in* Θ', *by definition of solution of a conjunction of formulae (c.f.* 6.1*) we have* $\sigma(\Theta)_{\langle A', \cong'\rangle} \supseteq \Theta'_{\langle A', \cong'\rangle}$. *Hence* $[\sigma(\Theta)]_{\langle A', \cong'\rangle} = \mathrm{Val}[\mathrm{X}', A']$ *which according to Proposition* 6.5 *implies that* $[\Theta]_{\langle A', \cong'\rangle_{|_\sigma}} = \mathrm{Val}[\mathrm{X}, A'_{|_\sigma}]$.

• **Proof of (ii)** *follows directly from Proposition* 6.6. □

This result corresponds to a very fundamental property which holds in most non observational frameworks. With all the definitions of observational satisfaction relation preceding [3], such a result holds only for equational axioms or positive-conditional axioms with observable preconditions which is a rather strong restriction. It may be then surprising that in our approach the former theorem holds without restrictions even if the axioms are arbitrary first order formulae. The reason is that our observational equality is not fixed by observations, even though the indistinguishability relation is fixed. Unlike [1], [14], [8], [10] and [11], our observational equality does not coincide with the indistinguishability relation. This choice was dictated by the fact that the indistinguishability relation is "disconnected" from the forgetful functor. On the contrary, our observational equality, similarly to the usual equality, is always "transported" through the forgetful functor. In short, the main difference of our approach with the above-mentioned works is that our satisfaction relation is based on an observational equality which does not coincide with the indistinguishability relation. This situation (in part) guarantees such a general result as Theorem 7.5.

We may also consider a particular case of this theorem with $\Theta' = \sigma(\Theta)$. This points out that observations act on the semantics of a specification in a similar way as the axioms do: by adding observations we diminish the class of the observational models. This is yet another reason for introducing observational formulae, especially in context of the next section. We argue that in any approach with an observational satisfaction relation, the Satisfaction Condition may hold only if the translation of observations is considered at the same level as the translation of axioms.

8 Relationship with Behavioural Equivalence

In this section we investigate deeper the relationship of our approach with behavioural equivalence of algebras.

Several papers dealing with an observational satisfaction relation provide also a definition of a **behavioural equivalence** $\equiv_{\mathrm{Obs}}$ of algebras which aims at reflecting the situation when algebras behave in the same way w.r.t. some observations Obs. One may then define the class of **behaviours** of a specification SP, written $\mathrm{Beh}_{\mathrm{Obs}}[\mathrm{SP}]$ as the closure of the usual class of the models of SP by the equivalence $\equiv_{\mathrm{Obs}}$:

$$\mathrm{Beh}_{\mathrm{Obs}}[\mathrm{SP}] \quad = \quad \{A \in \mathrm{Alg}[\Sigma] \mid \exists\ \mathrm{B} \in \mathrm{Alg}[\mathrm{SP}],\ \mathrm{A} \equiv_{\mathrm{Obs}} \mathrm{B}\} \qquad \text{(8–i)}$$

In such a framework it is interesting to establish that the class of the behaviours of $\mathrm{SP} = \langle \Sigma, \Theta \rangle$ coincides with the class of observational models of SP:

$$\mathrm{Beh}_{\mathrm{Obs}}[\langle \Sigma, \Theta \rangle] = \mathrm{OAlg}[\langle \Sigma, \Theta, \mathrm{Obs} \rangle]$$

This result cannot hold in our approach since, according to (8–i), for an inconsistent specification SP ($\mathrm{Alg}[\mathrm{SP}] = \emptyset$) we have always $\mathrm{Beh}_{\mathrm{Obs}}[\mathrm{SP}] = \emptyset$, whereas the class of the observational models of SP may be not empty. This is due to the fact that our observational satisfaction relation is based on an observational equality which is not necessarily a congruence. But this phenomenon disappears when we restrict to observational equalities being congruences. It is then interesting to investigate the relationship between behavioural equivalence on algebras and our approach in this restricted framework.

> We assume for the scope of this section that **observational equalities are congruences**. Consequently, in this section an element of $\mathrm{OAlg}[\Sigma]$ is any pair $\langle A, \cong \rangle$ such that A is a Σ-algebra and $\cong$ is a congruence.

Under this assumption it is always possible to consider the quotient $A_{/\cong}$. This allows to provide an adequate to our approach definition of behavioural equivalence of observational algebras w.r.t. a set of formulae.

Definition 8.1 *We say that two observational Σ-algebras $\langle A, \cong^A\rangle$ and $\langle B, \cong^B\rangle$ are behaviourally equivalent w.r.t. a set of Σ-fromulae Φ, written $\langle A, \cong^A\rangle \equiv_\Phi \langle B, \cong^B\rangle$, iff*

$$\cong^A \subseteq \sim_\Phi^A \;\Leftrightarrow\; \cong^B \subseteq \sim_\Phi^B \qquad \text{(i)}$$

$$A_{/\cong^A} \;=\; B_{/\cong^B} \qquad \text{(ii)}$$

where $\sim_\Phi^A$ and $\sim_\Phi^B$ are the indistinguishability relations on A and B respectively.

The formula (8–i) which defines the class of behaviours is adapted to observational algebras:

Definition 8.2 *Given an observational specification $\langle\Sigma, \Theta, \Phi\rangle$, the class of its behaviours, written* $\mathbf{Beh}_\Phi[\langle\Sigma,\Theta\rangle]$, *is defined as follows*

$$\text{Beh}_\Phi[\langle\Sigma,\Theta\rangle] \;=\; \{\langle A, \cong\rangle \in \text{OAlg}[\Sigma] \mid \exists\, B \in \text{Alg}[\langle\Sigma,\Theta\rangle],\ \langle A, \cong\rangle \equiv_\Phi \langle \text{B}, =\rangle\}$$

The result we are interested in may be stated as follows:

Theorem 8.3 *For any observational specification $\langle\Sigma, \Theta, \Phi\rangle$ we have*

$$\text{Beh}_\Phi[\langle\Sigma,\Theta\rangle] = \text{OAlg}[\langle\Sigma,\Theta,\Phi\rangle]$$

We need an auxiliary definition as well as some lemmas for the proof.

Lemma 8.4 *For any specification $\langle\Sigma, \Theta, \Phi\rangle$ and any observational Σ-algebra $\langle A, \cong\rangle$ we have $\langle A, \cong\rangle \in \text{Beh}_\Phi[\langle\Sigma,\Theta\rangle]$ iff $A_{/\cong} \models \Theta$ and $\cong \subseteq \sim_\Phi^A$.*

Proof *Let $\langle A, \cong\rangle \in \text{Beh}_\Phi[\langle\Sigma,\Theta\rangle]$. By Definition 8.2 this is equivalent to*

$$\exists\, B \in \text{Alg}[\langle\Sigma,\Theta\rangle]\ \ \langle A, \cong\rangle \equiv_\Phi \langle B, =\rangle$$

Since $= \subseteq \sim_\Phi^B$ by Definition 8.1 this is equivalent to

$$\exists\, B \in \text{Alg}[\Sigma]\ \ A_{/\cong} = B,\ \ B \models \Theta \ \text{ and } \ \cong \subseteq \sim_\Phi^A$$

which is equivalent to $A_{/\cong} \models \Theta$ and $\cong \subseteq \sim_\Phi^A$. □

Definition 8.5 *Let $\cong$ be a congruence on a Σ-algebra A and let $\nu : \text{X} \to A$ be a valuation. Then $\nu_{/\cong} : \text{X} \to A_{/\cong}$ is defined as a valuation such that if $\text{x}\nu = a$ then $\text{x}\nu_{/\cong} = [a]_\cong$ where $[a]_\cong$ is the equivalence class of a w.r.t. $\cong$.*

Lemma 8.6 *Let $\cong$ be a congruence on a Σ-algebra A and let $\nu : \text{X} \to A$ and $\mu : \text{X} \to A_{/\cong}$ be valuations such that $\mu = \nu_{/\cong}$. For any $\varphi \in \text{Wff}_\Sigma(\text{X})$ we have*

$$\nu \in [\varphi]_{\langle A,\cong\rangle} \ \text{ iff } \ \mu \in [\varphi]_{\langle A_{/\cong},\, =\rangle}$$

Proof *Obvious from the fact that if $\nu_{1/\cong} = \nu_{2/\cong}$ then $\nu_1 \in [\varphi]_{\langle A,\cong\rangle} \Leftrightarrow \nu_2 \in [\varphi]_{\langle A,\cong\rangle}$ for any formula φ.* □

Lemma 8.7 *Let $\cong$ be a congruence on a Σ-algebra A. For any $\varphi \in \text{Wff}_\Sigma(\text{X})$ we have*

$$[\varphi]_{\langle A,\cong\rangle} = \text{Val}[\text{X}, A] \ \text{ iff } \ [\varphi]_{\langle A_{/\cong},\, =\rangle} = \text{Val}[\text{X}, A_{/\cong}]$$

Proof *Obvious from the previous lemma.* □

Proof of Theorem 8.3 *Let $\langle A, \cong\rangle \in \mathrm{Beh}_\Phi[\langle\Sigma,\Theta\rangle]$. By Lemma 8.4 this is equivalent to*

$$[\Theta]_{\langle A_{/\cong}, =\rangle} = \mathrm{Val}[X, A_{/\cong}] \text{ and } \cong \subseteq \sim_\Phi^A$$

which by Lemma 8.7 and Definition 7.2 is equivalent to $\langle A, \cong\rangle \in \mathrm{OAlg}[\langle\Sigma,\Theta,\Phi\rangle]$. □

Theorem 8.3 shows that, when observational equalities are restricted to congruences, the class of such observational models may be characterized as the closure of the usual class of the models by an appropriate behavioural equivalence.

9 Towards an Institution of Observational Specifications

In this section, based on the formalism we have developed so far, we propose an institution for observational specifications. As mentioned in Section 6, this task requires to introduce some restrictions in our general formalism.

According to the definition of [7] the quadruple $\langle \mathrm{Sig}, \mathrm{OWff}, \mathrm{OAlg}, \models\rangle$ could be an institution provided that it would fulfill the Satisfaction Condition which in our formalism is expressed by the following property:

Property 9.1 *For any $\sigma : \Sigma \to \Sigma'$, any observational Σ-formula $\langle\theta,\Phi\rangle$ and any observational Σ'-algebra we have:*

$$\langle A', \cong'\rangle \models \sigma(\langle\theta,\Phi\rangle) \quad \text{iff} \quad \langle A', \cong'\rangle_{|\sigma} \models \langle\theta,\Phi\rangle$$

To show that this property holds, by definition 6.4, it is enough to prove that for any observational Σ'-algebra the following conditions hold:

$$[\sigma(\varphi)]_{\langle A', \cong'\rangle} = \mathrm{Val}[X', A'] \;\Leftrightarrow\; [\varphi]_{\langle A', \cong'\rangle_{|\sigma}} = \mathrm{Val}[X, A'_{|\sigma}] \qquad \text{(i)}$$

and

$$\cong' \subseteq \sim_{\sigma(\Phi)} \;\Leftrightarrow\; \cong'_{|\sigma} \subseteq \sim_\Phi \qquad \text{(ii)}$$

The first requirement is guaranteed by 6.5. From Proposition 6.6 we have the if part of the second requirement. Unfortunately, we know from Example 6.7 that its converse part does not hold without additional assumptions. The following is the necessary and sufficient condition of the converse part of (ii).

Property 9.2 *Let $\sigma : \Sigma \to \Sigma'$ be a signature morphism and $\Phi \subseteq \mathrm{Wff}_\Sigma(X)$ be a set of formulae. For any Σ'-algebra A', any $s' \in \sigma(S)$ and all $a, b \in A'_{s'}$, $\sigma(\Phi)$-distinguishable, there exist $s \in \sigma^{-1}(s')$ such that a and b are Φ-distinguishable when considered as elements of $(A'_{|\sigma})_s$.*

Proposition 9.3 *Let $\sigma : \Sigma \to \Sigma'$ be a signature morphism. The property 9.2 holds for a set Φ of Σ-formulae if and only if*

$$\cong'_{|\sigma} \subseteq \sim_\Phi \;\Rightarrow\; \cong' \subseteq \sim_{\sigma(\Phi)}$$

holds on all $\langle A', \cong'\rangle \in \mathrm{OAlg}[\Sigma']$.

Proof

• $\Rightarrow$
Let $\langle A', \cong' \rangle \in \mathrm{OAlg}[\Sigma']$. *Assume that*

$$\forall\, a, b \in A'_{|_\sigma} \quad a \cong'_{|_\sigma} b \;\Rightarrow\; a \sim_\Phi b \tag{i}$$

By contradiction assume that there exist $a_0, b_0 \in A'_{\sigma(s)}$ *such that* $a_0 \not\sim_{\sigma(\Phi)} b_0$ *and*

$$a_0 \cong' b_0 \tag{ii}$$

Using Property 9.2, *we find that there exist* $s_0 \in \sigma^{-1}(\sigma(s))$ *such that* $a_0 \not\sim_\Phi b_0$ *in* $(A'_{|_\sigma})_{s_0}$. *But according to* (ii) *we conclude that* $a_0 \cong'_{|_\sigma} b_0$. *Therefore* $a_0 \cong'_{|_\sigma} b_0 \quad\not\Rightarrow\quad a_0 \sim_\Phi b_0$ *which is a contradiction to the assumption* (i).

• $\Leftarrow$ (We use the contrapositive method for the proof.)
Let $\sigma : \Sigma \to \Sigma$ *and* $\Phi \subseteq \mathrm{Wff}_\Sigma(X)$ *for which the property* 9.2 *does not hold. Consequently, there is a* Σ'*-algebra* A' *with elements* $a, b \in A'_{\sigma(s_0)}$ *(for some* $s_0 \in S$*)* $\sigma(\Phi)$*-distinguishable, such that for any* $s \in S$ *satisfying* $\sigma(s) = \sigma(s_0)$, a *and* b *are* Φ*-indisintguishable in* $(A'_{|_\sigma})_s$. *Let* A' *be provided with* $\cong'$ *so that* $c \cong' d \Rightarrow c \sim_{\sigma(\Phi)} d$ *for all* $c, d \in A'$ *except for* a, b *where* $a \cong' b$ *and as assumed* $a \not\sim_{\sigma(\Phi)} b$. *It is clear from the proof of* 6.6 *that for all of these* c, d *we have also:*

$$c \cong'_{|_\sigma} d \Rightarrow c \sim_\Phi d$$

It follows from the above formula that $\cong'_{|_\sigma} \subseteq \sim_\Phi$, *since by Definition* 5.4 *we have* $a \cong'_{|_\sigma} b$ *and we assumed that* $a \sim_\Phi b$. *Now* $\cong' \not\subseteq \sim_{\sigma(\Phi)}$ *because* $a \cong' b$ *and we have assumed that* $a \not\sim_{\sigma(\Phi)} b$. □

We can conclude from the above that in our approach, the Satisfaction Condition does not hold in general. Only the if part of Property 9.1 holds. Consequently, according to [12], our approach defines a reduction-preserving pre-institution. The converse part of 9.1 holds only for the signature morphisms and the observations which preserve 9.2. Therefore our approach is another motivation for more liberal formalizations than institutions of the notion of "logical system" such as e.g. specification logic [5] or pre-institutions [12].

Since the Satisfaction Condition holds only for some signature morphisms, in order to define an institution in our framework, one could ignore the problematic arrows of Sig and consider as a category of signatures a category which has the same objects as Sig but less arrows. Then the question is which signature morphisms we should eliminate in order to obtain an institution. It is easy to see that examples similar to 6.7 can be constructed, as soon as we have an non injective signature morphism. We conclude that an observational institution can be provided within our formalism under the restriction of the arrows of Sig to injective morphisms only.

Proposition 9.4 *Consider the quadruple* OAlgSpec = ⟨ISig, OWff, OAlg, $\models$⟩ *where ISig is the category whose objects are the usual signatures and whose arrows are the injective signature morphisms. Then* OAlgSpec *is an institution.*

Proof *It is sufficient to prove that Property* 9.2 *holds for injective signature morphisms.*

Let $\sigma : \Sigma \to \Sigma'$ *be an injective signature morphism, let* $\Phi \subseteq \mathrm{Wff}_\Sigma(X)$ *be a set of formulae,* A' *a* Σ'*-algebra and let* $a, b \in A'_{\sigma(s)}$ $\sigma(\Phi)$*-distinguishable. Let* $\xi' \in \mathrm{cmp}_{\sigma(\Phi)}(a, b)$ *be a comparator which distinguishes* a *from* b. *Since* σ *is injective, there is a unique* $\xi \in \mathrm{Cf}_\Sigma(A'_{|_\sigma})$ *such that* $\sigma(\xi) = \xi'$. *According to Theorem* 3.12, ξ *is an observer of* a *and* b. *So* $\xi \in \mathrm{cmp}_\Phi(a, b)$. *Since* $A' \not\models \xi'[a] \Leftrightarrow \xi'[b]$, *from Lemma* 4.2 *we deduce that* $A'_{|_\sigma} \not\models \xi[a] \Leftrightarrow \xi[b]$. *Therefore, by Definition* 3.5 *we have* $a \not\sim_\Phi b$. □

A drawback of our approach is the necessity to restrict the category of signatures to ISig, in order to have an institution. However, except for some particular examples of parameter-passing morphisms, non injective signature morphisms seem to be not very useful. In spite of this restriction, OAlgSpec may be used for modular specifications with no parameterized modules. (Observational semantics of parameterized specifications is one of our current research topics.)

10 Conclusions

We have presented an observational semantics of algebraic specifications supporting full first order axioms and full first order formulae as observations. This has been achieved by defining an observational satisfaction relation whose cornerstone is the use of a non standard interpretation of equality. We have shown that our formalism is a reduction-preserving pre-institution and may, under some restrictions, even provide an institution.

This work may continue along different lines. Since our observational formulae are in some sense only atomic ones, one may want to define some observational connectives or quantifiers together with their semantics. This may lead to an "Observational Model Theory". A much more problematic, still missing contribution, would be the corresponding "Observational Proof Theory". However, the results of this research area are crucial for most applications of observational specifications in software engineering.

Acknowledgments I gratefully acknowledge Gilles Bernot, Michel Bidoit and Fernando Orejas for their extensive comments and numerous fruitful discussions. I also wish to thank particularly Regina Yillah for the careful proof reading of this paper. This work is partially supported by ESPRIT Working Group COMPASS and CNRS GDR de Programmation.

References

[1] G. Bernot and M. Bidoit. Proving the correctness of algebraically specified software: Modularity and observability issues. In *Proceedings of Second International Conference on Algebraic Methodology and Software Technology*, pages 139–161, Iowa City, May 1991.

[2] G. Bernot, M. Bidoit, and T. Knapik. Observational approaches and indistinguishability assumption. Technical Report LIENS–92–3, Laboratoire d'Informatique de l'Ecole Normale Supérieure, 1992.

[3] G. Bernot, M. Bidoit, and T. Knapik. Towards an adequate notion of observation. In B. Krieg-Brückner, editor, *European Syposium on Programming*, LNCS 582, pages 39–55, Rennes, Feb. 1992.

[4] M. Bidoit. The stratified loose approach: A generalization of initial and loose semantics. In D. Sannella and A. Tarlecki, editors, *Recent Trends in Data Type Specification*, LNCS 332, pages 1–22, Gullane, Sept. 1987. Selected papers from 5th Workshop on Specification of Abstract Data Types.

[5] H. Ehrig, M. Baldamus, and F. Orejas. New concepts for amalgamation and extension in the framework of specification logics. Technical Report 91/05, Technische Universität Berlin, May 1991.

[6] H. Ehrig and B. Mahr. *Fundamentals of Algebraic Specifications*, volume 6 of *EATCS Monographs on Theoretical Computer Science*. Springer-Verlag, 1985.

[7] J. Goguen and R. Burstall. Institutions: Abstract model theory for specification and programming. Technical Report ECS–LFCS–90–106, Department of Computer Science, University of Edinburgh, Jan. 1990.

[8] J. A. Goguen and J. Meseguer. Persistent interconnection and implementation of abstract modules. In M. Nielsen and E. M. Schmidt, editors, *ICALP*, LNCS 140, pages 256–281, Aarhus, May 1982.

[9] J. A. Goguen, J. W. Thatcher, and E. G. Wagner. An initial approach to the specification, correctness and implementation of abstract data types. In R. T. Yeh, editor, *Data Structuring*, volume 4 of *Current Trends in Programming Methodology*, pages 80–149. Prentice Hall, 1978.

[10] P. Nivela and F. Orejas. Initial behaviour semantics for algebraic specification. In D. Sannella and A. Tarlecki, editors, *Recent Trends in Data Type Specification*, LNCS 332, pages 184–207, Gullane, Sept. 1987. Selected papers from 5th Workshop on Specification of Abstract Data Types.

[11] H. Reichel. Behavioural validity of conditional equations in abstract data types. In *Contributions to General Algebra 3*, pages 301–324, 1984. Proceedings of the Vienna Conference.

[12] A. Salibra and G. Scollo. A soft stairway to institutions. In this volume.

[13] D. Sannella and A. Tarlecki. On observational equivalence and algebraic specification. *J. Comput. Syst. Sci.*, (34):150–178, 1987.

[14] N. W. P. van Diepen. Implementation of modular algebraic specifications. In H. Ganzinger, editor, *European Syposium on Programming*, LNCS 300, pages 64–78, Nancy, Mar. 1988.

Event Logic for Specifying Abstract Dynamic Data Types*

Gianna Reggio

Dipartimento di Informatica e Scienze dell'Informazione
Università di Genova - Italy

Introduction

Abstract and concrete dynamic data types, have been introduced by the author and others in several previous papers (e.g., [2, 3, 6, 10]).

A concrete dynamic data type (dynamic algebra) is just a many-sorted algebra with predicates such that for some of the sorts (sorts of dynamic elements, or dynamic sorts) there is a special predicate defining a labelled transition relation; thus the dynamic elements are modelled by means of labelled transition systems. An abstract dynamic data type (addt) is an isomorphism class of dynamic algebras.

To obtain specifications for addt's in some papers (e.g., [2, 3]) we have used first-order logic; however such logic is not suitable for expressing all interesting abstract properties of dynamic elements. Extensions of first-order logic, particularly suitable to such purpose, have been proposed in other papers; in [6] by adding branching-time temporal logic combinators for expressing abstract properties on the activity of dynamic elements and in [10, 4] by adding special combinators for expressing abstract properties on the concurrent/distributed structure of the dynamic elements (e.g. no multilevel parallelism).

In this paper we present an "event logic" for specifying addt's; the name "event" comes from "event structures" (see, e.g., [13]). Event structures are a nice formalism for abstractly modelling dynamic elements, which allows to express properties such as causality and true concurrency; but they lack well-developed techniques for structuring detailed descriptions of complex systems. Event logic is an attempt at building up an integrated specification framework for:

- expressing abstract properties of dynamic elements by giving some "relationships" between events;
- modelling dynamic elements in a simple and intuitive way as labelled transition systems.

The basic idea is that, given a labelled transition system, an "event" is just a set of partial execution paths (those corresponding to occurrences of that event). Thus, for example, a causality relationship e' **causes** e'' holds on a labelled transition system L iff for all execution paths σ of L, if $\sigma = \sigma_1\sigma'\sigma_2$, where σ' is a partial path

* This work has been supported by "Progetto Finalizzato Sistemi Informatici e Calcolo Parallelo" of C.N.R. (Italy), COMPASS-Esprit-BRA-W.G. n 3264 and by a grant ENEL/CRA (Milano Italy).

corresponding to an occurrence of e', then $\sigma_2 = \sigma_3\sigma''\sigma_4$, where σ'' is a partial path corresponding to an occurrence of e''.

As a consequence, we have that in this framework events are not considered instantaneous and so we can also express finer relationships between them, as:

- there is no instant at which e' and e'' occur simultaneously,
- e is the sequential composition of e' and e'',
- each occurrence of e' includes an occurrence of e'' (i.e., e'' starts either together or after e' and terminates either before or together e').

It is important to note that the use of non-instantaneous events for specifying labelled transition systems allows us to give very abstract specifications without fixing the atomic grain of the activity of the dynamic elements.

Moreover, in this algebraic framework events are not just a set of names; they are instead elements of particular sorts of a dynamic data type (one sort of events for each sort of dynamic elements) and so it is possible to define operations and predicates having arguments and/or results of event sort. As a consequence:

- we have events of different sort and thus we can relate, for example, the events of compound dynamic elements with the events of their dynamic subcomponents;
- complex events may be described by composing several simpler events, and that helps in writing modular and readable specifications.

Event logic includes as a sublanguage the temporal logic of [6] (the only difference is that here we consider also the past); in some sense the formalism of [6] considers only "instantaneous" events (i.e., events whose occurrences are just paths consisting either of one state or of one transition); while here we still use the same temporal combinators for expressing temporal relationships between non-instantaneous events.

In the literature there are other attempts to combine events and logic (see, e.g., [8]); the main difference with our work is that they use logic to specify classical event structures; while here we consider as models labelled transition systems equipped with non-instantaneous events.

However there are still some points about our event logic, which are worth to be further investigated.

First of all we need a rigorous definition of a kind of ***non-classical event structures***, different from those of [13], where events are non-instantaneous and the relationships between events are not simply causality and conflict. Then, we are interested to study the relationships between non-classical and classical event structures. For example, can the first be "simulated" by the latter ?

Moreover it seems that we can associate with each labelled transition system equipped with non-instantaneous events a non-classical event structure and so a specification given using our event logic may have models at two different levels:

- a kind of non-classical event structures;
- labelled transition systems equipped with non-instantaneous events.

Then, we can define an "implementation relationship" between a non-classical event structure and a labelled transition system equipped with non-instantaneous events s.t. given an event logic specification SP:

for all event structures ES, if ES is a model of SP and it is implemented by L, then L is a model of SP;
for all labelled transition systems L, if L is a model of SP, there exists an event structure ES which is a model of SP and is implemented by L.

In this paper we present the event logic; in Sect. 1 we shortly introduce concrete and abstract dynamic data types and show how to integrate the notion of non-instantaneous event; the logic is formally defined in Sect. 2; finally in Sect. 3 we report some simple illustrative examples. It is worth noticing that the resulting specification formalism is an institution (see [5]). For lack of room we cannot report neither the proof that the event logic is an institution, nor a sound deductive system nor more interesting examples of specifications; these parts are reported in the full paper [11].

1 Abstract Dynamic Data Types and their Specification

1.1 Dynamic Algebras and Specifications

First we briefly report the essential definitions about concrete and abstract dynamic data types and their specification (see, e.g., [3, 6]); and then show how events may be introduced in this framework.

Dynamic Algebras. A dynamic algebra (concrete dynamic data type) is just a many-sorted algebra with predicates (see [7]) such that for some of the sorts (sorts of dynamic elements, or dynamic sorts) there is a special predicate defining a labelled transition relation; thus the dynamic elements are modelled by means of labelled transition systems.

Definition 1.

- A *dynamic signature* $D\Sigma$ is a couple (Σ, DS) where:
  - $\Sigma = (S, OP, PR)$ is a predicate signature,
  - $DS \subseteq S$ (the elements in DS are the *dynamic sorts*),
  - for all $ds \in DS$ there exists a sort $lab(ds) \in S - DS$ (labels of the transitions of the elements of sort ds) and a predicate $\_ \xrightarrow{\_} \_ : ds \times lab(ds) \times ds \in PR$ (the transition relation of the dynamic elements of sort ds).
- A *dynamic algebra* on $D\Sigma$ (shortly $D\Sigma$-algebra) is just a Σ-algebra. □

In this paper, for some of the operation and predicate symbols, we use a mixfix notation. For instance, $\rightarrow: ds \times lab(ds) \times ds$ means that we shall write $t \xrightarrow{t'} t''$ instead of $\rightarrow (t, t', t'')$; i.e. terms of appropriate sorts replace underscores.

If DA is a $D\Sigma$-algebra and $ds \in DS$, then the carrier of sort ds, DA_{ds}, the carrier of sort $lab(ds)$, $DA_{lab(ds)}$, and the interpretation of the predicate $\rightarrow$, $\rightarrow^{DA}$, are respectively the states, the labels and the transition relation of a labelled transition system describing the activity of the dynamic elements of sort ds.

Dynamic Specifications. Following a widely accepted idea (see e.g. [14]) a (static) ***abstract data type*** (shortly ***adt***) is an isomorphism class of Σ-algebras (note that [14] considers only term-generated algebras). A *(simple) specification* is a couple $SP = (\Sigma, AX)$, where Σ is a signature and AX a set of first-order formulae on Σ (the *axioms* of SP); the *models* of SP are the Σ-algebras satisfying the axioms in AX.

In the *initial algebra approach* SP defines the adt consisting of the (isomorphism class of the) initial elements, if any, of the class $Mod(SP)$. In the *loose*approach, instead, SP is viewed as a description of the main properties of an adt; thus it represents a class, consisting of all the adt's satisfying the properties expressed by the axioms (more formally: the class of all isomorphism classes included in $Mod(SP)$).

The above definitions can be easily adapted to the dynamic case: an ***abstract dynamic data type*** (shortly ***addt***) is an isomorphism class of dynamic algebras and a *(simple) dynamic specification* is a couple $DSP = (D\Sigma, AX)$. In this case the set of axioms AX must express both usual "static" properties of the data and properties about the activity of the dynamic elements; the problem is, now, to find an appropriate logic for expressing such properties.

In some previous papers (see e.g., [3]) we have used first-order logic; since dynamic signatures include explicitly a predicate corresponding to the transition relation, we can formalize several properties about the activity of the dynamic elements using first-order logic. For example $\not\exists l, s \; . \; t \xrightarrow{l} s \wedge P(s)$ requires that the dynamic element represented by the term t cannot pass into a state s s.t. $P(s)$ holds. However, these are only "local" properties on the activity of the dynamic elements (about the immediate future and past). In general we want to express "global properties" as liveness and safety properties.

Given a dynamic algebra DA and a dynamic sort ds, a global view of the activity of a dynamic element $d \in DA_{ds}$ may be represented by the set of all its *execution paths*, i.e. maximal sequences of labelled transitions of the form:

$$\ldots d_{-2} \xrightarrow{l_{-2}}{}^{DA} d_{-1} \xrightarrow{l_{-1}}{}^{DA} d \xrightarrow{l_0}{}^{DA} d_1 \xrightarrow{l_1}{}^{DA} d_2 \ldots$$

(clearly such sequences may be either bounded or unbounded both at the left and at the right); a sequence as above represents a possible behaviour of d; the partial execution path $\ldots d_{-2} \xrightarrow{l_{-2}}{}^{DA} d_{-1} \xrightarrow{l_{-1}}{}^{DA} d$ represents the past and $d \xrightarrow{l_0}{}^{DA} d_1 \xrightarrow{l_1}{}^{DA} d_2 \ldots$ the future of such behaviour. A graphic representation of the activity of a dynamic element is reported in Fig. 1. Thus a property on the activity of d may be formalized as a property of the execution paths for d.

The temporal logic for specifications of addt's of [6] already allows to do that; however it permits only to express properties about the "points" of the paths (i.e. on the states and on the labels of the paths). For example, the formula $\Delta(t, \Diamond[\lambda s.P(s)])$ requires that each execution path of the dynamic element represented by the term t contains a state s s.t. $P(s)$; while $\nabla(t, \Box{<}\lambda l.Q(l){>})$ requires that the dynamic element represented by the term t has at least one execution path with labels l s.t. $Q(l)$. But in that formalism it is rather hard to require that after receiving in input a value eventually the system will output some other value, when inputting

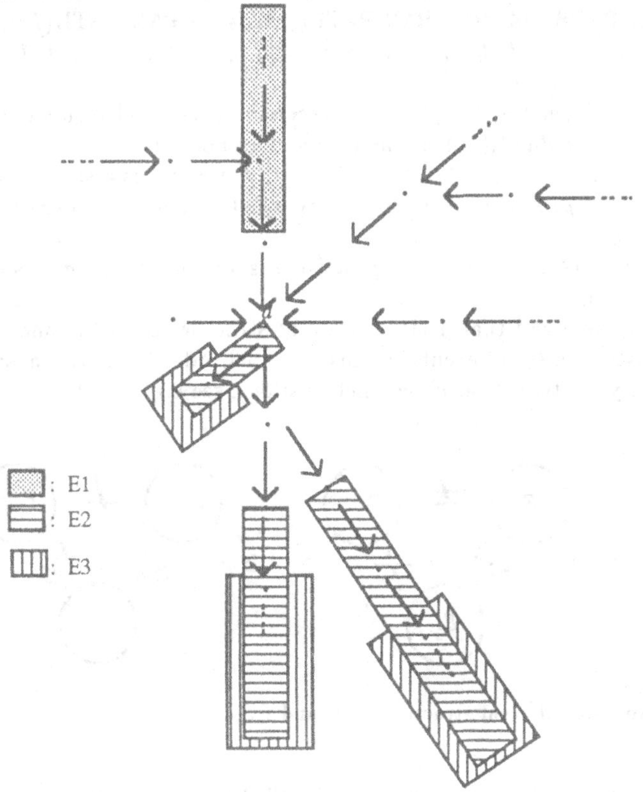

Fig. 1. The activity of a dynamic element d

and outputting a value consists of several transitions (e.g., because each transition corresponds to move one bit).

1.2 Event Algebras

Paths and Events. Given a $D\Sigma$-dynamic algebra DA and a dynamic sort ds of $D\Sigma$, PAR_PATH(DA, ds) denotes the set of the *partial execution paths* for the dynamic elements of sort ds, i.e. it is the set of all sequences having either form either (1), ... or (4) below:

(1)	$\ldots\ d_{-2}\ l_{-2}\ d_{-1}\ l_{-1}\ d_0\ l_0\ d_1\ l_1\ d_2\ l_2\ \ldots$		(unbounded path),
(2)	$d_0\ l_0\ d_1\ l_1\ d_2\ l_2\ \ldots$		(right-unbounded path),
(3)	$\ldots\ d_{-2}\ l_{-2}\ d_{-1}\ l_{-1}\ d_0$		(left-unbounded path),
(4)	$d_0\ l_0\ d_1\ l_1\ d_2\ l_2\ \ldots\ d_n$	$n \geq 0$	(bounded path),

where for all integer i $d_i \in DA_{ds}, l_i \in DA_{lab(ds)}$ and $(d_i, l_i, d_{i+1}) \in \rightarrow^{DA}$.

A (partial) *composition operation* is defined on the elements of PAR_PATH(DA, ds):
$\_ \cdot \_$: PAR_PATH(DA, ds) $\times$ PAR_PATH(DA, ds) $\rightarrow$ PAR_PATH(DA, ds)
$\sigma \cdot \sigma' =_{def}$ if $\sigma = \ldots\ d_n\ l_n\ d_{n+1}$ and $\sigma' = d_{n+1}\ l_{n+1}\ \ldots$ then $\ldots\ d_n\ l_n\ d_{n+1}\ l_{n+1}\ \ldots$ else undefined.

PATH(DA, ds) denotes the set of the *execution paths* for elements of sort ds, i.e.:
$\{\sigma \mid \sigma \in$ PAR_PATH(DA, ds) and there does not exist $\sigma' \in$ PAR_PATH(DA, ds) s.t. $\sigma' \neq \sigma$ and σ is a subpath of $\sigma'\}$
where σ is a *subpath* of σ' iff there exist σ_1, σ_2 s.t. either $\sigma' = \sigma_1 \cdot \sigma \cdot \sigma_2$ or $\sigma' = \sigma_1 \cdot \sigma$ or $\sigma' = \sigma \cdot \sigma_2$.

Given $d \in DA_{ds}$, an *execution path for* d is a triple $<\sigma_p, d, \sigma_f>$ s.t. $\sigma_p \cdot d \cdot \sigma_f \in$ PATH(DA, ds).

In brief, we recall that a classical event structure of instantaneous events (see [13]) consists of a set of events E plus a partial order $\geq$ on E (causality relation) and a binary relation $\neq$ on E (conflict relation); see e.g. Fig. 2.

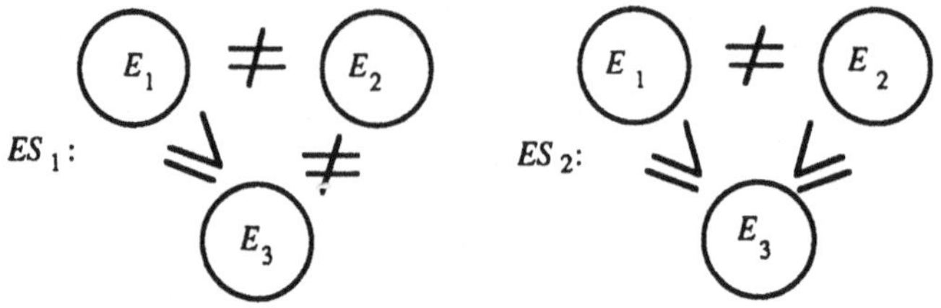

Fig. 2. Two classical event structures ES_1 and ES_2

Now we have to connect events and labelled transition systems; the basic idea is that an event e corresponds to the set of its occurrences i.e. to the set of the partial execution paths corresponding to its occurrences; and that a relation R among e_1, $\ldots, e_n$ corresponds to a relation R' among the occurrences of $e_1, \ldots, e_n$. For example in Fig. 1 we have outlined some partial execution paths corresponding to occurrences of the three events E_1, E_2, E_3; notice that the relationships described by ES_2 are satisfied, while those of ES_1 are not. But, note that here the relationship between E_2 and E_3 is finer than the one formalized by ES_2: E_2 terminates with E_3 (i.e., each occurrence of E_3 terminates with an occurrence of E_2).

Event Signatures and Algebras. Event algebras are particular dynamic algebras where with each dynamic sort a special event sort is associated, whose elements are events, i.e. sets of event occurrences, i.e. sets of partial execution paths.

Definition 2.

- An *event signature* $E\Sigma$ is a dynamic signature (Σ, DS) where for all $ds \in DS$ there exists a sort $event(ds) \in S - DS$.
- An *event algebra* EA on $E\Sigma$ ($E\Sigma$-algebra) is an $E\Sigma$-dynamic algebra s.t. for all $ds \in DS$ $EA_{event(ds)} = \mathcal{P}(\text{PAR\_PATH}(EA, ds))$ [2].

[2] If A is a set, then $\mathcal{P}(A)$ denotes the set of the parts of A.

- Given two $E\Sigma$-algebras EA and EB, an *$E\Sigma$-event morphism* p from EA into EB (written $p: EA \to EB$) is a Σ-morphism of total algebras with predicates s.t. for all $ds \in DS$, $e \in EA_{event(ds)}$ $p(e) \supseteq$
$$\{\ldots\ p(d_{i-1})\ p(l_{i-1})\ p(d_i)\ p(l_i)\ p(d_{i+1})\ p(l_{i+1})\ \ldots \mid \ldots d_{i-1}\ l_{i-1}\ d_i\ l_i\ d_{i+1} l_{i+1}\ \ldots \in e\}.\square$$

For a dynamic sort $ds \in DS$ each element of sort $event(ds)$ represents an event suitable for the dynamic elements of sort ds; such an event consists of the set of all partial execution paths corresponding to its occurrences; every such path will be called an *occurrence* of the event.

Event morphisms are particular morphisms of algebras with predicates; thus they preserve the truth of predicates (see [7]) and so also the activity of the dynamic elements: if $d \xrightarrow{l} d'$ in EA, then $p(d) \xrightarrow{p(l)} p(d')$ in EB. For this reason they also preserve the partial paths, i.e. if an event e has an occurrence σ in EA, then the image of σ by p is a partial path in EB.

Event algebras and morphisms on a signature $E\Sigma$ constitute a category, denoted by $EAlg(E\Sigma)$.

2 Event Logic

2.1 Syntax and Informal Semantics

Here we introduce a minimal set of combinators for the event logic; several other interesting derived combinators are reported in Appendix A.

In the following let $E\Sigma = (\Sigma, DS)$, with $\Sigma = (S, OP, PR)$, be an event signature and $\mathcal{X}$ an infinite set of variable symbols. We recall that a *sort assignment* for $E\Sigma$ is a partial function $X: \mathcal{X} \to S$ and it will be seen as an S-indexed family $\{X_s\}_{s \in S}$, where $X_s = \{x \mid x \in \mathcal{X} \text{ and } X(x) = s\}$.

Definition 3. The *terms*, the *path formulae* and the *event logic formulae* on $E\Sigma$ and a sort assignment X for $E\Sigma$ are defined as follows. We denote respectively by $\{T_{E\Sigma}(X)_s\}_{s \in S}$ (the family of the sets of terms), $\{PF_{E\Sigma}(X)_{ds}\}_{ds \in DS}$ (the family of sets of path formulae) and $EF_{E\Sigma}(X)$ (the set of the event logic formulae). For all $s \in S$, $ds \in DS$

- *terms*

- $X_s \subseteq T_{E\Sigma}(X)_s$
- $Op(t_1, \ldots, t_n) \in T_{E\Sigma}(X)_s$ for all $Op: s_1 \times \ldots \times s_n \to s \in OP$, $t_i \in T_{E\Sigma}(X)_{s_i}$ $i = 1, \ldots, n$
- $e_1 ; e_2 \in T_{E\Sigma}(X)_{event(ds)}$ for all $e_1, e_2 \in T_{E\Sigma}(X)_{event(ds)}$
- e_1 **and** $e_2 \in T_{E\Sigma}(X)_{event(ds)}$ for all $e_1, e_2 \in T_{E\Sigma}(X)_{event(ds)}$
- **not** $e, e^+, e^\omega \in T_{E\Sigma}(X)_{event(ds)}$ for all $e \in T_{E\Sigma}(X)_{event(ds)}$
- $[\lambda x.\phi] \in T_{E\Sigma}(X)_{event(ds)}$ for all $x \in X_{ds}$, $\phi \in EF_{E\Sigma}(X)$
- $<\lambda x.\phi> \in T_{E\Sigma}(X)_{event(ds)}$ for all $x \in X_{lab(ds)}$, $\phi \in EF_{E\Sigma}(X)$

- *path formulae*

- $\triangleright e, e \triangleleft \in PF_{E\Sigma}(X)_{ds}$ for all $e \in T_{E\Sigma}(X)_{event(ds)}$
- π_1 **until** π_2, π_1 **since** $\pi_2 \in PF_{E\Sigma}(X)_{ds}$ for all $\pi_1, \pi_2 \in PF_{E\Sigma}(X)_{ds}$
- $\neg\pi_1, \pi_1 \supset \pi_2, \forall x.\pi_1 \in PF_{E\Sigma}(X)_{ds}$ for all $\pi \in PF_{E\Sigma}(X)_{ds}, x \in X$

- *formulae*

- $Pr(t_1, \ldots, t_n) \in EF_{E\Sigma}(X)$ for all $Pr: s_1 \times \ldots \times s_n \in PR$, $t_i \in T_{E\Sigma}(X)_{s_i}$ $i = 1, \ldots, n$
- $t_1 = t_2 \in EF_{E\Sigma}(X)$ for all $t_1, t_2 \in T_{E\Sigma}(X)_s$
- $\neg\phi_1, \phi_1 \supset \phi_2, \forall x.\phi_1 \in EF_{E\Sigma}(X)$ for all $\phi_1, \phi_2 \in EF_{E\Sigma}(X), x \in X$
- $e_1 \Rightarrow e_2 \in EF_{E\Sigma}(X)$ for all $e_1, e_2 \in T_{E\Sigma}(X)_{event(ds)}$
- $\Delta(t, \pi) \in EF_{E\Sigma}(X)$ for all $t \in T_{E\Sigma}(X)_{ds}, \pi \in PF_{E\Sigma}(X)_{ds}$ □

The semantics of the various combinators is informally described below and defined formally in Def. 4. To do that we need the following definitions on paths. Given $\sigma, \sigma' \in$ PAR_PATH(DA, ds):

- if σ is right-bounded, $Last(\sigma)$ denotes the *last element* of σ; analogously if σ is left-bounded, $First(\sigma)$ denotes the *first element* of σ;
- σ is a *prefix* (*postfix*) of σ' iff either $\sigma = \sigma'$ or there exists σ'' s.t. $\sigma' = \sigma \cdot \sigma''$ ($\sigma' = \sigma'' \cdot \sigma$);
- σ is a *proper* prefix (postfix) of σ' iff σ is a prefix (postfix) of σ' and $\sigma \neq \sigma'$;
- if σ' is a prefix (postfix) of σ, then $\sigma - \sigma'$ denotes the path σ'' s.t. $\sigma' \cdot \sigma'' = \sigma$ ($\sigma'' \cdot \sigma' = \sigma$), if it exists. Notice that if σ is left (right) bounded, then $\sigma - \sigma = First(\sigma)$ ($\sigma - \sigma = Last(\sigma)$) since σ is both a prefix and a postfix of itself.

The special operators, which represent events, are described by giving the occurrences of the represented events.

" ; " sequential composition of two events: an occurrence of $e_1; e_2$ is a partial path consisting of the composition of an occurrence of e_1 and of an occurrence of e_2.

"**and**" conjunction of events: an occurrence of e_1 **and** e_2 is a partial path which is an occurrence of e_1 and of e_2.

"**not**" negation of an event: an occurrence of **not** e is a partial path which is not an occurrence of e.

" +" finite repetition of an event: an occurrence of e^+ is a finite (non-null) sequence of occurrences of e.

" ω" infinite repetition of an event: an occurrence of e^ω is a countably infinite sequence of occurrences of e.

"[...]" conditional state event: an occurrence of $[\lambda x.\phi]$ is a partial path consisting of one state satisfying the condition expressed by the formula ϕ.

"<...>" conditional atomic event: an occurrence of $<\lambda x.\phi>$ is a partial path consisting of one transition labelled with a label satisfying ϕ.

Path formulae express properties of the execution paths for some dynamic element; thus, given an execution path for a dynamic element d, say $\delta = <\sigma_p, d, \sigma_f>$, we have that:

"$\triangleright$" occurrence of an event in the future: $\triangleright e$ holds on δ iff there exists σ occurrence of e which is a prefix of σ_f;

"$\triangleleft$" occurrence of an event in the past: $e\triangleleft$ holds on δ iff there exists σ occurrence of e which is a postfix of σ_p;

until is defined analogously to the homonymous temporal logic combinator; π_1 **until** π_2 holds on δ iff there exists σ postfix of σ_f s.t.
- π_2 holds on $<\sigma_p \cdot (\sigma_f - \sigma), First(\sigma), \sigma>$,
- π_1 holds in each point between d and the beginning of σ, i.e. for all proper prefixes σ' of $\sigma_f - \sigma$, π_1 holds on $<\sigma_p \cdot \sigma', Last(\sigma'), \sigma_f - \sigma'>$ (notice that σ' is also a prefix of σ_f so we can consider $\sigma_f - \sigma'$).

The above condition is graphically represented in Fig. 3.

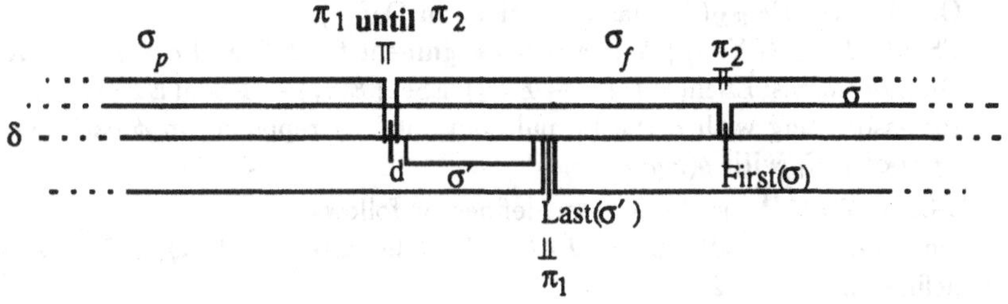

Fig. 3. The until operator

π_1 **since** π_2 is the analogous of **until** for the past.

$\pi_1 \supset \pi_2$ holds on δ iff either π_1 does not hold on δ or π_2 holds on δ; analogously $\neg$ and $\forall$ are defined as the analogous first order combinators.

$\Delta(t, \pi)$ holds iff each execution path for the element represented by the term t satisfies the condition expressed by the path formula π.

$e_1 \Rightarrow e_2$ holds iff each occurrence of e_1 is also an occurrence of e_2.

2.2 The Institution of Event Logic

In this section we state (without proof which is in [11]) that the logical formalism defined in the previous section constitutes an institution (see [5])

$$\mathcal{EV} = (\mathbf{ESig}, \mathrm{ESen}, \mathrm{EMod}, \models)$$

whose components are defined below.

In [5] the concept of institution has been advocated as a rigorous presentation of a logical formalism; being an institution means that a a formalism has an intrinsic coherence and of course various results are at hand for building specifications, specification languages, transferring results from an institution to another (see, e.g. [12, 5, 1, 9]).

In the following $\mathcal{P} = (\mathbf{PSig}, \mathrm{PSen}, \mathrm{PMod}, \models^{P})$ denotes the institution of the total (many-sorted) algebras with predicates and first-order formulae (see [5]).

ESig is the category defined as follows.

- The objects are the event signatures (see Def. 2);
- The morphisms: given $E\Sigma_1 = (\Sigma_1, DS_1)$ and $E\Sigma_2 = (\Sigma_2, DS_2)$, $\rho \in \mathbf{ESig}(E\Sigma_1, E\Sigma_2)$ iff $\rho \in \mathbf{PSig}(\Sigma_1, \Sigma_2)$ and for all $ds \in DS_1$
  - $\rho(ds) \in DS_2$,
  - $\rho(lab(ds)) = lab(\rho(ds))$,
  - $\rho(event(ds)) = event(\rho(ds))$,
  - $\rho(- \xrightarrow{-} -: ds \times lab(ds) \times ds) = - \xrightarrow{-} -: \rho(ds) \times lab(\rho(ds)) \times \rho(ds)$.
- The identities: given $E\Sigma = (\Sigma, DS)$ $I_{E\Sigma} = I_\Sigma$ (identity of Σ in $\mathcal{P}$).
- The morphism composition: given $\rho_1: E\Sigma_1 \rightarrow E\Sigma_2$, $\rho_2: E\Sigma_2 \rightarrow E\Sigma_3$ $\rho_1 \cdot \rho_2 = \rho_1 \cdot_{\mathcal{P}} \rho_2$, where $\cdot_{\mathcal{P}}$ is the morphism composition of **PSig**.

ESen: **ESig** $\rightarrow$ **Set** is the functor defined as follows.

- On objects ($EF_{E\Sigma}(X)$ has been given in Def. 3): $\text{ESen}(E\Sigma) = \{(X, \phi) \mid X$ is a sort assignment for $E\Sigma$ and $\phi \in EF_{E\Sigma}(X)\}$.
- On morphisms: $\text{ESen}(\rho: E\Sigma_1 \rightarrow E\Sigma_2): \text{ESen}(E\Sigma_1) \rightarrow \text{ESen}(E\Sigma_2)$ is the functor associating with ϕ the formula obtained by replacing in ϕ each symbol Sym of $E\Sigma_1$ with $\rho(Sym)$.

EMod: **ESig** $\rightarrow$ $\mathbf{Cat}^{\mathbf{OP}}$ is the functor defined as follows.

- On objects: $\text{EMod}(E\Sigma) = EAlg(E\Sigma)$ (the category $EAlg(E\Sigma)$ has been defined in Sect. 1.2).
- On morphisms: given $\rho: E\Sigma_1 \rightarrow E\Sigma_2$ $\text{EMod}(\rho)$ is the restriction of $\text{PMod}(\rho)$ to $\text{EMod}(E\Sigma_1)$.

Validity relation: it is given in the following definition.

We recall that given an $E\Sigma$-algebra EA, a *valuation of the variables* in X into EA is a family of total functions $V = \{V_s\}_{s \in S}$ s.t. for all $s \in S$ $V_s: X_s \rightarrow EA_s$.

Definition 4. Let EA be an $E\Sigma$-algebra and V a valuation of X into EA; then we define by multiple induction:

- the interpretation of a term t in EA under V ($t^{EA,V}$),
- when a path formula π holds on δ (an execution path for a dynamic element) in EA under V (written $\delta, EA, V \models \pi$),
- when a formula ϕ holds in EA under V (written $EA, V \models \phi$)

in the following way (where we assume that each formula is well-formed).

• *Interpretation of terms*

- $x^{EA,V} = V(x)$
- $Op(t_1, \ldots, t_n)^{EA,V} = Op^{EA}({t_1}^{EA,V}, \ldots, {t_n}^{EA,V})$
- $(e_1; e_2)^{EA,V} = \{\sigma_1 \cdot \sigma_2 \mid \sigma_1 \in {e_1}^{EA,V}, \sigma_2 \in {e_2}^{EA,V}$ and $\sigma_1 \cdot \sigma_2$ is defined$\}$
- $(e_1 \textbf{ and } e_2)^{EA,V} = e_1^{EA,V} \cap e_2^{EA,V}$
- $(\textbf{not}\, e)^{EA,V} = \text{PAR\_PATH}(EA, ds) - e^{EA,V}$
- $(e^+)^{EA,V} =$ $\{\sigma_1 \cdot \ldots \cdot \sigma_n \mid n \geq 1$, for $i = 1, \ldots, n$ $\sigma_i \in e^{EA,V}$ and $\sigma_1 \cdot \ldots \cdot \sigma_n$ is defined$\}$
- $(e^\omega)^{EA,V} = \{\sigma_1 \cdot \ldots \cdot \sigma_n \cdot \ldots \mid$ for $i \geq 1$ $\sigma_i \in e^{EA,V}$ and $\sigma_1 \cdot \ldots \cdot \sigma_n \cdot \ldots$ is defined$\}$
- $[\lambda x.\phi]^{EA,V} = \{d \mid d \in EA_{ds}$ and $EA, V[d/x] \models \phi\}$

- $<\lambda x.\phi>^{EA,V} =$
$$\{d\ l\ d' \mid d, d' \in EA_{ds}, l \in EA_{lab(ds)}, (d, l, d') \in \rightarrow^{EA} \text{ and } EA, V[l/x] \models \phi\}$$

- *Validity of path formulae* In the following we assume $\delta = <\sigma_p, d, \sigma_f>$.

- $\delta, EA, V \models \triangleright e$	iff	there exists $\sigma \in e^{EA,V}$ s.t. σ is a prefix of σ_f
- $\delta, EA, V \models e \triangleleft$	iff	there exists $\sigma \in e^{EA,V}$ s.t. σ is a postfix of σ_p
- $\delta, EA, V \models \pi_1$ **until** π_2	iff	there exists σ postfix of σ_f s.t. ⋆ $<\sigma_p \cdot (\sigma_f - \sigma), First(\sigma), \sigma>, EA, V \models \pi_2$ ⋆ for all proper prefixes σ' of $\sigma_f - \sigma$ $<\sigma_p \cdot \sigma', Last(\sigma'), \sigma_f - \sigma'>, EA, V \models \pi_1$
- $\delta, EA, V \models \pi_1$ **since** π_2	iff	there exists σ prefix of σ_p s.t. ⋆ $<\sigma, Last(\sigma), (\sigma_p - \sigma) \cdot \sigma_f>, EA, V \models \pi_2$ ⋆ for all proper postfixes σ' of $\sigma_p - \sigma$ $<\sigma_p - \sigma', First(\sigma'), \sigma' \cdot \sigma_f>, EA, V \models \pi_1$
- $\delta, EA, V \models \neg\pi$	iff	$\delta, EA, V \not\models \pi$
- $\delta, EA, V \models \pi_1 \supset \pi_2$	iff	either $\delta, EA, V \not\models \pi_1$ or $\delta, EA, V \models \pi_2$
- $\delta, EA, V \models \forall x.\pi$	iff	for all $v \in EA_s$ $\delta, EA, V[v/x] \models \pi$

- *Validity of event logic formulae*

- $EA, V \models Pr(t_1, \ldots, t_n)$	iff	$<t_1{}^{EA,V}, \ldots, t_n{}^{EA,V}> \in Pr^{EA}$
- $EA, V \models t_1 = t_2$	iff	$t_1{}^{EA,V} = t_2{}^{EA,V}$
- $EA, V \models \neg\phi$	iff	$EA, V \not\models \phi$
- $EA, V \models \phi_1 \supset \phi_2$	iff	either $EA, V \not\models \phi_1$ or $EA, V \models \phi_2$
- $EA, V \models \forall x.\phi$	iff	for all $v \in EA_s$ $EA, V[v/x] \models \phi$
- $EA, V \models e_1 \Rightarrow e_2$	iff	$e_1{}^{EA,V} \subseteq e_2{}^{EA,V}$
- $EA, V \models \Delta(t, \pi)$	iff	for all execution paths δ for $t^{EA,V}$ $\delta, EA, V \models \pi$.

$\phi \in EF_{E\Sigma}(X)$ is *valid* in EA ($EA \models \phi$) iff $EA, V \models \phi$ for all valuations V. □

Proposition 5. *$\mathcal{EV}$ is an institution.* □

3 Examples

Here we give two simple examples illustrating the main features of our specification formalism; in [11] more interesting specifications of well-known examples in the field of concurrency are given (e.g., alternating bit protocol, serializable data base).

In this section for keeping the specifications simpler and more readable, we

- use the derived combinators of the event logic given in the appendix A;
- write **sorts** S **dsorts** DS **opns** OP **preds** PR for the event signature (Σ, DS), where Σ is:
$(S \cup DS \cup \{lab(ds), event(ds) \mid ds \in DS\}, OP,$
$PR \cup \{- \xrightarrow{-} -: ds \times lab(ds) \times ds \mid ds \in DS\}),$
i.e. we leave the canonical sorts and predicates implicit;
- use the following well-known constructs for structuring specifications: ... + ... (sum of specifications), **enrich**... **by** ... and ... [.../...] (renaming of either sort or operation or predicate symbols), see e.g., [14].

3.1 Specification of a Sequential Nondeterministic Program with Interactive I/O.

In this paragraph we abstractly specify a nondeterministic sequential program with interactive I/O, i.e. where I/O is realized by dynamically interacting with an external environment (e.g., a terminal).

We operationally model the program by means of a labelled transition system, with labels correspond to input and output actions. Specifying such a program means to require some relationship between the receiving of some input and the returning of some output: precisely some relationship among the "values" which constitute the inputs and the outputs and "temporal"/"causal" relationships among the transitions corresponding to inputting and outputting.

Static Properties. First we abstractly qualify what are the inputs and the outputs of the program by giving two classical (static) specifications. For example, if

spec *INPUT* =
  sorts input
  opns
    $-\&-: input \times input \rightarrow input$
  preds
    Atomic: *input*
  axioms
    $i\&(i'\&i'') = (i\&i')\&i''$

spec *OUTPUT* =*INPUT*[*output*/*input*]

we only require that there are "atomic" inputs (not further specified) and an associative composition operation; analogously for outputs.

Using algebraic specifications we can also describe which are the correct outputs for the various inputs (i.e., what the program calculates).

spec *CORRECTNESS* =
  enrich *INPUT*+ *OUTPUT* **by**
  preds
    Corr: *input* × *output*
  axioms
    ... properties about *Corr* ...

Notice that we use a predicate *Corr* and not an operation from inputs to outputs, since we consider nondeterministic programs.

Dynamic Properties. We consider two kind of events:

- *input events* (the inputting of some value) and
- *output events* (the outputting of some value).

spec *PROG* =
  enrich *CORRECTNESS* **by**

dsorts prog
opns

$Init\colon \rightarrow prog$
$Input\colon input \rightarrow lab(prog)$
$Output\colon output \rightarrow lab(prog)$
$IN\colon input \rightarrow event(prog)$
$OUT\colon output \rightarrow event(prog)$

axioms

$\not\exists p, l.p \xrightarrow{l} Init$

– *Init* is truly the initial state

. . . axioms expressing dynamic properties . . .

Here we do not give just one specification *PROG*, but instead show how to express various sample dynamic properties of the program.

Properties About Events. Recall that events are particular data of our specification, so we can express properties about them "in isolation".

- Input events are finite. $IN(i)$ **is finite**
- Inputting a compound value is the same that inputting the component values.

$$IN(i_1 \& i_2) = IN(i_1); IN(i_2)$$

- The input event of an atomic value consists in performing one transition labelled in a particular way.

$$Atomic(i) \supset IN(i) = <Input(i)>$$

For the output events we can give either similar or different properties.

Relationships Between Events.

- During the activity of the program at most one input event may happen.

$$i \neq i' \supset \Delta(p, \rhd IN(i) \supset \neg \blacklozenge \rhd IN(i')) \qquad \Delta (p, \rhd IN(i) \supset \neg \Diamond IN(i))$$

If at a certain moment the inputting of i starts, then in the future (including now) i' s.t. $i' \neq i$ will never be input and in the future (excluding now) i will never be input.
Notice that the axiom $\Delta(Init, \rhd IN(i) \supset \neg \blacklozenge \rhd IN(i'))$ does not formalize this property; indeed it would prevent any occurrence of the the input events.

- The so called "partial correctness" with respect to the requirement expressed by *Corr*, i.e., whatever output is the result of a correct elaboration of some input (output events are caused by appropriate input events).

$$\Delta(p, \rhd OUT(o) \supset (\exists i.Corr(i, o) \wedge \blacklozenge \mathbf{P} \rhd IN(i)))$$

If at a certain moment the output of o starts, then there exists an appropriate i s.t. the input of i started sometimes in the past.
In Fig. 4 we report a graphical representation of the activity of two programs with occurrences of input and output events satisfying and not the above axiom.

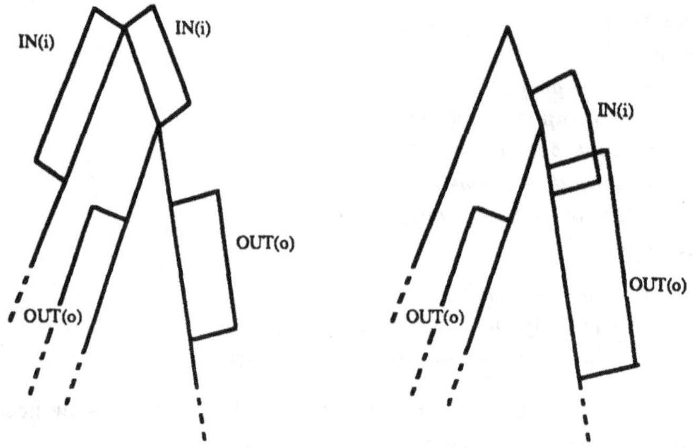

Fig. 4. Programs respecting and not the partial correctness requirement

- The so called "total correctness" with respect to the requirement expressed by *Corr*, i.e. the reception of some input will result in the outputting of a correct output (input events cause appropriate output events).

  $$\Delta(p, \rhd IN(i) \supset (\exists o.Corr(i,o) \wedge \blacklozenge\, OUT(o)))$$

  If at a certain moment the input of i starts, then there exists an appropriate o s.t. the output of o eventually will start. The first case of Fig. 4 does not satisfy the above axiom, while the second does.

Notice that these axioms do not require that the input event ends before the output event; so the specification has models corresponding to programs which terminate by inputting a special value.

- Input and output events are mutually exclusive.

  $$IN(i)\ \texttt{disjoint with}\ OUT(o)$$

  Without this axiom the specification has models where, for example, while part of the output is printed, part of the input is received (e.g., programs which go on receiving one value, processing it and then printing the result) see second case of Fig. 4.

3.2 A buffer

Here we specify an unbounded buffer with the following properties: it

- preserves the order of the received messages;
- is safe (it cannot corrupt any message);
- cannot loose nor duplicate any message (where "cannot loose" is not to be intended that it will deliver each received message, but only that if it delivers a message m, then it has already delivered all messages received before m);

- interacts synchronously with the users (it delivers a message only iff there is a user ready to accept it);
- cannot receive and/or deliver simultaneously several messages.

We have no information about the nature of the messages, thus they are described by the (static) specification:

spec *MESSAGE* = **sorts** *message*

The interesting events, which may happen during the activity of a buffer, are receiving and delivering a message. Since the buffer interacts with the users in a synchronous way, such events correspond to perform transitions labelled by $Rec(m)$ and $Del(m)$ respectively. Notice that in this way we have that receiving and delivering cannot occur simultaneously. For expressing the buffer properties we use the complex events corresponding to receive and deliver in an orderly way a sequence of messages (defined by the operations *REC_LIST* and *DEL_LIST*).

SEQ is the parametric specification of finite sequences with the operations $\Lambda\colon \rightarrow seq(elem)$ (empty sequence) and $-\&-\colon seq(elem) \times elem \rightarrow seq(elem)$ (adding an element at the end of a sequence).

spec *BUFFER* =
  enrich SEQ(*MESSAGE*) **by**
  dsorts *buffer*
  opns
    $Init\colon \rightarrow buffer$
  – the initial state of the buffer
    $Rec, Del\colon message \rightarrow lab(buffer)$
    $NOT\_REC, NOT\_DEL\colon message \rightarrow event(buffer)$
    $REC\_LIST, DEL\_LIST\colon seq(message) \rightarrow event(buffer)$
  – auxiliary event operations
  axioms
    $\nexists c, l.c \xrightarrow{l} Init$
  – *Init* is truly the initial state
    $NOT\_REC = <\nexists m.l = Rec(m)>^{\star}$
    $REC\_LIST(\Lambda) = NOT\_REC$
    $REC\_LIST(sm\&m) = REC\_LIST(sm); NOT\_REC; < Rec(m) >$
    $NOT\_DEL = <\nexists m.l = Del(m) >^{\star}$
    $DEL\_LIST(\Lambda) = NOT\_DEL$
    $DEL\_LIST(sm\&m) = DEL\_LIST(sm); NOT\_DEL; < Del(m) >$
  – definition of the auxiliary event operations
    $[Init]; DEL\_LIST(sm) \Rightarrow [Init]; REC\_LIST(sm); \texttt{all}$
  – a partial path starting from *Init* corresponding to deliver a sequence of messages always has a prefix corresponding to receive the same sequence of values this axiom correspond to require all the buffer properties (ordered, safety, no lost messages, no duplications)
    $\Delta(c, \blacklozenge \rhd [\exists x'.x \xrightarrow{Rec(m)} x'])$
  – responsiveness (the buffer cannot refuse forever to receive a message)

Notice that the last axiom requires that eventually the buffer will have the capability of receiving the message m and that is strongly different from $\Delta(c, \blacklozenge \triangleright\!<\!Rec(m)\!>)$ requiring that eventually the buffer will receive the message m.

4 Conclusions

By looking at the examples of Sect. 3 we can see some of the advantages of the use of event logic with respect to first-order/temporal logic.

In this framework we can specify dynamic elements modelled as labelled transition systems without fixing the atomicity grain of the system transitions. In the example of Sect. 3.1 we do not fix the atomicity grain of the transitions of the system representing the program. Thus we can have a specification *PROG* having models where non-internal transitions correspond to inputting/outputting respectively files, atomic values and bits. However by the same formalism we can give also "less abstract" specifications, by qualifying the system transitions (for example in Sect. 3.2 where receiving and delivering a message is an atomic transition).

Since in our algebraic formalism events are particular data, *we can first describe complex events and then we can express relationships between such events.* For example, in Sect. 3.2, the "being caused and ending before" relation between the two events "delivering a sequence of messages" and "receiving the same sequence" describes the main properties of the buffer. In Sect. 3.1 we can simply express properties as partial/total correctness also in the case of programs performing I/O bit after bit (just add axioms qualifying the events *IN* and *OUT*); while using only instantaneous events (corresponding to perform one transition) such properties are very hard to express.

On the other hand, our event logic considers non-instantaneous events and so there are also some advantages with respect to classical event structures; for example in our framework *we can express relationship between events finer than causality and conflict*. In Sect. 3.1 the causality property between input and output events (total correctness) does not mean that the second event must occur after the first one is terminated. Thus, we can give a specification *PROG* having very reasonable models, where inputs events terminate after the caused output events. Think, for example, of programs which go on receiving a value, processing it and then returning the result, until they receive a special value, signalling the end of the activity.

A Derived Event Operations and Logical Combinators

Whenever x is the only variable occurring free in ϕ, $[\lambda x.\phi]$ is shortened in $[\phi]$; moreover $[x = t]$ is further shortened in $[t]$. Analogous abbreviations are defined for $<\ldots>$.

- Nondeterministic choice between two events: an occurrence of e_1 **or** e_2 is either an occurrence of e_1 or an occurrence of e_2.

$$e_1 \ \mathbf{or}\ e_2 =_{\mathrm{def}} \mathbf{not}((\mathbf{not}\, e_1)\ \mathbf{and}\ (\mathbf{not}\, e_2))$$

- Difference between two events: an occurrence of $e_1 - e_2$ is an occurrence of e_1 which is not an occurrence of e_2.

$$e_1 - e_2 =_{\mathrm{def}} e_1 \textbf{ and not } e_2$$

- The universal instantaneous event: an occurrence of **inst** is a partial path consisting of one state.

$$\texttt{inst} =_{\mathrm{def}} [\,\texttt{true}\,]$$

- Either null or finite repetition of an event: an occurrence of $e^\star$ is a finite or null sequence of occurrences of e.

$$e^\star =_{\mathrm{def}} \texttt{inst or } e^+$$

- The universal atomic event: an occurrence of **step** is a partial path consisting of one transition.

$$\texttt{step} =_{\mathrm{def}} <\texttt{true}>$$

- The finite universal event: an occurrence of **steps** is a finite partial path.

$$\texttt{steps} =_{\mathrm{def}} \texttt{step}^\star$$

- The universal event: an occurrence of **all** is a partial path

$$\texttt{all} =_{\mathrm{def}} \texttt{step}^\omega \texttt{ or step}^\star$$

- Test of (weak) disjunction between two events: e_1 and e_2 are (weakly) disjoint iff there is no transition where both events are occurring (**not all** is the impossible event, i.e. the one without occurrences).

e_1 **disjoint with** $e_2 \Leftrightarrow_{\mathrm{def}}$

$$[((e_1;\texttt{steps}) \textbf{ and } (\texttt{steps};e_2)) - (e_1;\texttt{step}^+;e_2)] \texttt{ or}$$
$$[e_1 \textbf{ and } (\texttt{steps};e_2;\texttt{steps})] \texttt{ or}$$
$$[((e_2;\texttt{steps}) \textbf{ and } (\texttt{steps};e_1)) - (e_2;\texttt{step}^+;e_1)] \texttt{ or}$$
$$[e_2 \textbf{ and } (\texttt{steps};e_1;\texttt{steps})] = \texttt{not all}$$

- Check of finiteness/infiniteness of an event: e **is finite** (e **is infinite**) iff all occurrences of e are finite (infinite).

$$e \texttt{ is finite} =_{\mathrm{def}} e \Rightarrow \texttt{steps} \qquad e \texttt{ is infinite} =_{\mathrm{def}} e \Rightarrow \texttt{step}^\omega$$

Temporal Logic Combinators

- Eventually and always in the future including the present.

$$\blacklozenge\pi =_{\mathrm{def}} \texttt{true until } \pi \qquad \blacksquare\pi =_{\mathrm{def}} \neg\blacklozenge\neg\pi$$

- Sometimes and always in the past including the present.

$$\blacklozenge\mathbf{P}\pi =_{\mathrm{def}} \texttt{true since } \pi \qquad \blacksquare\mathbf{P}\pi =_{\mathrm{def}} \neg\blacklozenge\mathbf{P}\neg\pi$$

- Eventually and always in the future excluding the present.

$$\Diamond\pi =_{\mathrm{def}} \blacklozenge\pi \wedge \neg\pi \qquad \Box\pi =_{\mathrm{def}} \neg\Diamond\neg\pi$$

- Sometimes and always in the past excluding the present.

$$\Diamond\mathbf{P}\pi =_{\mathrm{def}} \blacklozenge\mathbf{P}\pi \wedge \neg\pi \qquad \Box\mathbf{P}\pi =_{\mathrm{def}} \neg\Diamond\mathbf{P}\neg\pi$$

References

1. E. Astesiano and M. Cerioli. Relationships between logical frameworks. In the same volume, 1992.
2. E. Astesiano and G. Reggio. SMoLCS-driven concurrent calculi. In H. Ehrig, R. Kowalski, G. Levi, and U. Montanari, editors, *Proc. TAPSOFT'87, Vol. 1*, number 249 in Lecture Notes in Computer Science, pages 169–201, Berlin, 1987. Springer Verlag.
3. E. Astesiano and G. Reggio. A structural approach to the formal modelization and specification of concurrent systems. Technical Report 0, Formal Methods Group, Dipartimento di Matematica, Università di Genova, Italy, 1991.
4. E. Astesiano and G. Reggio. Entity institutions: Frameworks for dynamic systems. in preparation, 1992.
5. R.M. Burstall and J.A. Goguen. Introducing institutions. In E. Clarke and D. Kozen, editors, *Logics of Programming Workshop*, number 164 in Lecture Notes in Computer Science, pages 221–255, Berlin, 1984. Springer Verlag.
6. G. Costa and G. Reggio. Abstract dynamic data types: a temporal logic approach. In A. Tarlecki, editor, *Proc. MFCS'91*, number 520 in Lecture Notes in Computer Science, pages 103–112, Berlin, 1991. Springer Verlag.
7. J. Gouguen and J. Meseguer. Models and equality for logic programming. In *Proc. TAPSOFT'87, Vol. 2*, number 250 in Lecture Notes in Computer Science, pages 1–22, Berlin, 1987. Springer Verlag.
8. K. Lodaya and P. S. Thiagarajan. A modal logic for a subclass of event structures. In T. Ottmann, editor, *Proceeding of ICALP'87*, number 267 in Lecture Notes in Computer Science, pages 290–303, Berlin, 1987. Springer Verlag.
9. J. Meseguer. General logic. In *Logic Colluqium'87*, Amsterdam, 1989. North-Holland.
10. G. Reggio. Entities: an istitution for dynamic systems. In H. Ehrig, K.P. Jantke, F. Orejas, and H. Reichel, editors, *Recent Trends in Data Type Specification*, number 534 in Lecture Notes in Computer Science, pages 244–265, Berlin, 1991. Springer Verlag.
11. G. Reggio. Event logic for specifying abstract dynamic data types - Extended version. Technical Report 13, Formal Methods Group, Dipartimento di Matematica, Università di Genova, Italy, 1991.
12. D. Sannella and A. Tarlecki. Specifications in an arbitrary institution. *Information and Computation*, 76, 1988.
13. G. Winskel. An introduction to event structures. In J.W. de Bakker, W.-P. de Roever, and G. Rozemberg, editors, *Linear Time, Branching Time and Partial Order in Logics and Models for Concurrency*, number 354 in Lecture Notes in Computer Science, pages 364–397, Berlin, 1989. Springer Verlag.
14. M. Wirsing. Algebraic specifications. In van Leeuwen Jan, editor, *Handbook of Theoret. Comput. Sci.*, volume B, pages 675–788. Elsevier, 1990.

A Soft Stairway to Institutions

Antonino Salibra[1] and Giuseppe Scollo[2*]

[1] University of Pisa, Dip. Informatica
C.so Italia 40, I-56125 Pisa, Italy
[2] University of Twente, Fac. Informatica
P.O. Box 217, NL-7500AE Enschede, The Netherlands

Abstract. The notion of institution is dissected into somewhat weaker notions. We introduce a novel notion of institution morphism, and characterize preservation of institution properties by corresponding properties of such morphisms. Target of this work is the stepwise construction of a general framework for translating logics, and algebraic specifications using logical systems. Earlier translations of order-sorted conditional equational logic and of conditional equational logics for partial algebras into equational type logic are revisited in this light. Model-theoretic results relating to compactness are presented as well.

1 Introduction

In [5] the following question is proposed (among others):

> "Anyone who has worked with extensions of $L_{\omega,\omega}$ knows that some results are entirely "soft" in that they use only very general properties of the logic, properties that carry over to a large number of other logics. Shouldn't such results be part of an axiomatic treatment of logics?"

The meaning of "soft" in the title of this paper is precisely as explained in the question quoted above. Target of our investigation is the notion of institution, which was introduced in [13] as a vehicle for the application of abstract model theory to computer science. The theory of institutions became rapidly popular in computer science, within the algebraic specification community especially, thanks to the neat conceptual support that it offers to modeling of, and reasoning about, a wide variety of specification and programming phenomena. The category-theoretic design of this theory is part of the explanation of that success.

In our case, concrete motivation for the choice of working with institutions was the following, instructive experience. In the elaboration of a few results relating to the expressiveness of equational type logic [18] in comparison to other logics, a number of technical aspects, relating to the translation of the target logic into our framework, show a striking formal commonality over the different translations. These aspects essentially are: representation of models, translation of sentences, structure of completeness proofs. The search for a more general framework, where as much as possible of that commonality could be factored out, is just as natural. For such an

* on temporary leave at: LIENS/DMI, École Normale Supérieure, 45 Rue d'Ulm, F-75230 Paris, France

aim, the category of institutions, rooted as it is in abstract model theory, seems to offer the obvious framework to work with. Two facts, however, concur to indicate that this choice is not entirely obvious.

In the first place, we are interested in general tools for lifting results of work done for one logic to other logics, without having to do the work all over again for each of them. In fact, that is the main reason for the popularity of institutions in computer science. However, from the way in which the expressiveness results in [18] are obtained, we are led to observe that pointwise translation of sentences and models is not always that easy to work with. More generally, we wish to translate presentations (i.e. *sets* of sentences) to presentations, and to associate a *class* of models in the target logic to each model of the source logic. The notion of ***institution morphism*** proposed in [13] deserves generalization, thus.

In the second place, we observed that not every feature of the institution concept had some rôle to play in the trial applications of our interest. The softness of the ***satisfaction condition***, in particular, seems to depend on the scales one is using (more precisely, on the planet where the scales are taken). Although "style has to count for something", in the sense that the temptation toward maximum generality at the expense of intuition should be resisted [5], style and intuition deserve analysis and testing, once in while.

The net result of putting together the two facts that occurred to our observation is thus a strong motivation for a twofold effort towards generality. That is, we wish to dissect the notion of institution into somewhat weaker notions, on the one hand, and to manipulate the resulting weaker structures by means of easier-to-use morphisms, on the other hand. In both directions, of course, we should be able to find the notions considered in [13] as particular cases, when appropriate steps along the specialization 'stairway' are taken. Isolating and characterizing such steps, each independently of the others, meets a principle of orthogonality in the analysis of concepts, appears sensible to intuition, and may yield useful results—for example it might lead one to uncover a wider applicability of known facts.

The sense of, and motivation for (the title of) this paper being now clear, a short outline of the organization of the paper with a summary of results are as follows.

In Sect. 2 we introduce pre-institutions and transformations thereof, and define a few properties that these structures may have, such as satisfaction preservation in pre-institutions, or (full) adequacy and finitarity of pre-institution transformations. The relative expressiveness of pre-institutions is characterized by the existence of suitable transformations. We show how the classical notion of relative expressiveness of logical systems fits in our more general setting.

In Sect. 3 we first show that pre-institutions, with transformations as morphisms, form a category, of which subcategories are obtained by requiring transformation properties—which prove preserved by composition, thus. We also show that preservation of institution properties by transformations is ensured by corresponding properties of those transformations, and that, while every transformation is sound with respect to consequence, adequate transformations are also complete. Invertibility of transformations is then characterized, and sufficient conditions for invertibility are given, which thereby ensure exactly equivalent expressiveness of pre-institutions.

In Sect. 4 a compactness theorem is presented, showing that fully adequate transformations ensure contravariant preservation of compactness, and that consequence-compactness (a stronger property) is so preserved if the transformation is also finitary, modulo logical equivalence.

In Sect. 5 a couple of expressiveness results for equational type logic given in [18] are revisited. We show how easily the completeness of the transformations can be proven in the present framework.

In Sect. 6 we quickly review related work; in particular, we indicate how the notion of institution simulation proposed by [4] is related to our notion of pre-institution transformation.

Conclusions are drawn in Sect. 7, where we also mention a few directions for further work.

2 Basic Notions and Notations

A preliminary word about foundations. In this paper we use the term 'set' in a rather comprehensive meaning, that generally includes proper classes. Whenever a need arises to exclude proper classes, we talk of 'small sets'. SET is thus actually a 'metacategory'[3], according to [15].

Definition 1. A *pre-institution* is a 4-tuple $\mathcal{I} = (\mathsf{Sig}, \mathsf{Sen}, \mathsf{Mod}, \models)$, with:

(i) Sig a category, whose objects are called *signatures*,

(ii) $\mathsf{Sen} : \mathsf{Sig} \to \mathrm{SET}$ a functor, sending each signature Σ to the set $\mathsf{Sen}(\Sigma)$ of Σ-sentences, and each signature morphism $\tau : \Sigma \to \Sigma'$ to the mapping $\mathsf{Sen}(\tau) : \mathsf{Sen}(\Sigma) \to \mathsf{Sen}(\Sigma')$ that translates Σ-sentences to Σ'-sentences,

(iii) $\mathsf{Mod} : \mathsf{Sig}^{op} \to \mathrm{SET}$ a functor, sending each signature Σ to the set $\mathsf{Mod}(\Sigma)$ of Σ-models, and each signature morphism $\tau : \Sigma \to \Sigma'$ to the τ-reduction function $\mathsf{Mod}(\tau) : \mathsf{Mod}(\Sigma') \to \mathsf{Mod}(\Sigma)$,

(iv) $\models : |\mathsf{Sig}| \to ||\mathrm{REL}||$ a function,[4] yielding a binary relation $\models_\Sigma \subseteq \mathsf{Mod}(\Sigma) \times \mathsf{Sen}(\Sigma)$ for each signature Σ, that is the satisfaction relation between Σ-models and Σ-sentences. □

Definition 2. Let $\mathcal{I} = (\mathsf{Sig}, \mathsf{Sen}, \mathsf{Mod}, \models)$ be a pre-institution, $\tau : \Sigma \to \Sigma'$ a signature morphism in Sig, φ a Σ-sentence and M′ a Σ'-model. With henceforth adoption of the abbreviations:

(a) $\tau\varphi$ for $\mathsf{Sen}(\tau)(\varphi)$,

(b) $\mathrm{M}'\tau$ for $\mathsf{Mod}(\tau)(\mathrm{M}')$,

we say that

(i) *reduction preserves satisfaction* in $\mathcal{I}$, or that $\mathcal{I}$ has the *rps* property (or that $\mathcal{I}$ is *rps*, for short), iff $\mathcal{I}$ meets the following requirement:
$\forall \Sigma, \Sigma' \in \mathsf{Sig}, \forall \tau : \Sigma \to \Sigma', \forall \varphi \in \mathsf{Sen}(\Sigma), \forall \mathrm{M}' \in \mathsf{Mod}(\Sigma')$:
(†) $\mathrm{M}' \models_{\Sigma'} \tau\varphi \;\Rightarrow\; \mathrm{M}'\tau \models_\Sigma \varphi$

(ii) *expansion preserves satisfaction* in $\mathcal{I}$, or that $\mathcal{I}$ has the *eps* property (or that $\mathcal{I}$ is *eps*, for short), iff $\mathcal{I}$ meets the following requirement:
$\forall \Sigma, \Sigma' \in \mathsf{Sig}, \forall \tau : \Sigma \to \Sigma', \forall \varphi \in \mathsf{Sen}(\Sigma), \forall \mathrm{M}' \in \mathsf{Mod}(\Sigma')$:
(‡) $\mathrm{M}'\tau \models_\Sigma \varphi \;\Rightarrow\; \mathrm{M}' \models_{\Sigma'} \tau\varphi$

---

[3] resting at some floor of 'palais Grothendieck'

[4] REL is the category of sets with binary relations as morphisms; ||C|| is the set of morphisms of category C.

(iii) $\mathcal{I}$ *preserves satisfaction*, or that $\mathcal{I}$ has the *ps* property (or that $\mathcal{I}$ is *ps*, for short), iff $\mathcal{I}$ is both *rps* and *eps*. □

Remark 3. An *institution* [13] is thus a pre-institution that preserves satisfaction and where model sets and reduction have categorial structure, that is, an institution rather has a functor $\mathsf{Mod}:\mathsf{Sig}^{op}\to\mathrm{CAT}$, sending each signature Σ to the category $\mathsf{Mod}(\Sigma)$ of Σ-models, and each signature morphism $\tau:\Sigma\to\Sigma'$ to the τ-reduction functor $\mathsf{Mod}(\tau):\mathsf{Mod}(\Sigma')\to\mathsf{Mod}(\Sigma)$. □

It seems interesting to investigate which properties of institutions do actually depend on requirements (†) and/or (‡) of Definition 2, and/or on the categorial structure of model sets and reduction, and which do *not*, thus holding for larger classes of pre-institutions as well.

According to the motivation proposed in Sect. 1, we are interested in general tools for lifting results from one pre-institution to another pre-institution. Pointwise translation of sentences and models is not always easy to use for this purpose. For example, to recover and possibly further extend the results obtained in [18] we need, more generally, to translate presentations to presentations, and to associate a *set* of models (in the target pre-institution) to each model of the source pre-institution. A suitable notion of pre-institution morphism will serve to this purpose, for which a few preliminaries are needed.

We recall that the powerset functor $\wp : \mathrm{SET}\to\mathrm{SET}$ sends every set to the collection of its subsets[5], and every function $f : S\to S'$ to the function yielding the f-image of each subset of S. The functor $\wp_+$ is analogously defined, except that the empty set is excluded from the collection $\wp_+(S)$, for all sets S.

In every pre-institution $\mathcal{I} = (\mathsf{Sig}, \mathsf{Sen}, \mathsf{Mod}, \models)$ we thus define the functor $\mathsf{Pre} = \wp\mathrm{o}\mathsf{Sen} : \mathsf{Sig}\to\mathrm{SET}$ that sends each signature Σ to the set $\mathsf{Pre}(\Sigma)$ of Σ-presentations, and each signature morphism $\tau : \Sigma\to\Sigma'$ to the mapping $\mathsf{Pre}(\tau) : \mathsf{Pre}(\Sigma)\to\mathsf{Pre}(\Sigma')$ that translates Σ-presentations to Σ'-presentations. For convenience, we often write $\mathcal{I} = (\mathsf{Sig}, \mathsf{Pre}, \mathsf{Mod}, \models)$ instead of the more customary notation introduced in Definition 1.

Definition 4. A *pre-institution transformation* $\mathcal{T} : \mathcal{I}\to\mathcal{I}'$, where $\mathcal{I} = (\mathsf{Sig},\mathsf{Pre},\mathsf{Mod},\models)$ and $\mathcal{I}' = (\mathsf{Sig}',\mathsf{Pre}',\mathsf{Mod}',\models')$ are pre-institutions, is a 3-tuple $\mathcal{T} = (\mathsf{Si}_\mathcal{T}, \mathsf{Pr}_\mathcal{T}, \mathsf{Mo}_\mathcal{T})$, with:

(i) $\mathsf{Si}_\mathcal{T} : \mathsf{Sig}\to\mathsf{Sig}'$ a functor—we shall henceforth write $\Sigma_\mathcal{T}$ for $\mathsf{Si}_\mathcal{T}(\Sigma)$, and $\tau_\mathcal{T}$ for $\mathsf{Si}_\mathcal{T}(\tau)$,

(ii) $\mathsf{Pr}_\mathcal{T} : \mathsf{Pre}\to\mathsf{Pre}'\mathrm{o}\mathsf{Si}_\mathcal{T}$ a natural transformation, i.e. for each $\Sigma\in\mathsf{Sig}$ a function $\mathsf{Pr}_{\mathcal{T}_\Sigma} : \mathsf{Pre}(\Sigma)\to\mathsf{Pre}'(\Sigma_\mathcal{T})$ sending Σ-presentations to $\Sigma_\mathcal{T}$-presentations, such that for every signature morphism $\tau : \Sigma_1\to\Sigma_2$ in Sig the following diagram commutes,

[5] $\wp$ lives in the elevator of 'palais Grothendieck', thus, lifting its argument up one floor.

$$
\begin{array}{ccc}
\mathsf{Pre}(\Sigma_1) & \xrightarrow{\mathsf{Pr}_{\mathcal{T}_{\Sigma_1}}} & \mathsf{Pre}'(\Sigma_{1\mathcal{T}}) \\
\Big\downarrow {\scriptstyle \mathsf{Pre}(\tau)} & & \Big\downarrow {\scriptstyle \mathsf{Pre}'(\tau_{\mathcal{T}})} \\
\mathsf{Pre}(\Sigma_2) & \xrightarrow{\mathsf{Pr}_{\mathcal{T}_{\Sigma_2}}} & \mathsf{Pre}'(\Sigma_{2\mathcal{T}})
\end{array}
$$

(iii) $\mathsf{Mo}_{\mathcal{T}} : \mathsf{Mod} \rightarrow \wp_{+} \circ \mathsf{Mod}' \circ \mathsf{Si}_{\mathcal{T}}$ a natural transformation, i.e. for each $\Sigma \in \mathsf{Sig}$ a map $\mathsf{Mo}_{\mathcal{T}_\Sigma} : \mathsf{Mod}(\Sigma) \rightarrow \wp_{+}(\mathsf{Mod}'(\Sigma_{\mathcal{T}}))$ assigning a nonempty set $\mathsf{Mo}_{\mathcal{T}_\Sigma}(\mathrm{M})$ of $\Sigma_{\mathcal{T}}$-models to each Σ-model M, such that for every signature morphism $\tau : \Sigma_1 \rightarrow \Sigma_2$ in Sig the following diagram commutes,

$$
\begin{array}{ccc}
\mathsf{Mod}(\Sigma_2) & \xrightarrow{\mathsf{Mo}_{\mathcal{T}_{\Sigma_2}}} & \wp_{+}(\mathsf{Mod}'(\Sigma_{2\mathcal{T}})) \\
\Big\downarrow {\scriptstyle \mathsf{Mod}(\tau)} & & \Big\downarrow {\scriptstyle \wp_{+} \circ \mathsf{Mod}'(\tau_{\mathcal{T}})} \\
\mathsf{Mod}(\Sigma_1) & \xrightarrow{\mathsf{Mo}_{\mathcal{T}_{\Sigma_1}}} & \wp_{+}(\mathsf{Mod}'(\Sigma_{1\mathcal{T}}))
\end{array}
$$

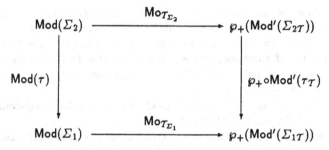

such that the following ***satisfaction invariant*** holds:

$$\forall \Sigma \in \mathsf{Sig},\ \forall \mathrm{E} \in \mathsf{Pre}(\Sigma),\ \forall \mathrm{M} \in \mathsf{Mod}(\Sigma): \quad \mathrm{M} \models \mathrm{E} \ \Leftrightarrow\ \mathrm{M}_{\mathcal{T}} \models' \mathrm{E}_{\mathcal{T}}$$

where satisfaction is extended to presentations and model sets in the usual way, and with henceforth adoption of the following abbreviations:
(a) $\mathrm{E}_{\mathcal{T}}$ for $\mathsf{Pr}_{\mathcal{T}_\Sigma}(\mathrm{E})$,
(b) $\varphi_{\mathcal{T}}$ for $\{\varphi\}_{\mathcal{T}}$, for a one-sentence presentation $\{\varphi\}$,
(c) $\mathrm{M}_{\mathcal{T}}$ for $\mathsf{Mo}_{\mathcal{T}_\Sigma}(\mathrm{M})$,
(d) $\models$ for $\models_\Sigma$ and $\models'$ for $\models'_{\Sigma_{\mathcal{T}}}$ (and even $\models$ for $\models'$, if no ambiguity arises). □

The intuitive reason for the non-emptiness requirement on $\mathsf{Mo}_{\mathcal{T}_\Sigma}(\mathrm{M})$ is that the existence of a pre-institution transformation is intended to entail the 'representability' of every source model by some target model.

The reason for the requirement expressed by the satisfaction invariant is the ***soundness*** of deduction in the image of the transformation with respect to deduction in the source, which fact is apparent from the simple proof of Proposition 16(i).

It may seem strange that presentation transformation is allowed not to respect the set-theoretic structure of presentations, that is, it need not be constructed elementwise. Our design principle, in this case as well as everywhere else in this paper, is that requirements restrict generality, hence there must be sufficient evidence of their necessity to set them a priori rather than introducing them as properties a posteriori. As an instance of the classical "Occam's razor", we have adopted the rule: ***leges non sunt multiplicanda præter necessitatem.***

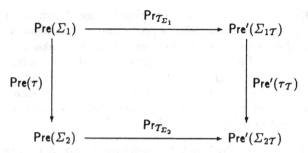

Definition 4(iii) doesn't require $M_{\mathcal{T}}$ to be closed under 'isomorphism'. In fact, no notion of isomorphism between models in a pre-institution is available at all. In some cases, one can replace isomorphism between models by the weaker equivalence that reflects indiscernibility of models by the logical means that is available 'inside the pre-institution', viz. the straightforward generalization of elementary equivalence that is formalized in the first part of the next definition. The second part of the definition formalizes logical equivalence of sentences inside a pre-institution, which fact justifies the overloading of the equivalence symbol.

Definition 5. Let $\mathcal{I} = (\mathsf{Sig},\mathsf{Pre},\mathsf{Mod},\models)$ be a pre-institution, Σ a signature in Sig.
(i) Any two models $M_1, M_2 \in \mathsf{Mod}(\Sigma)$ are $\mathcal{I}$-equivalent, written $M_1 \equiv_{\mathcal{I}} M_2$, iff $\forall E \in \mathsf{Pre}(\Sigma)$: $M_1 \models E \Leftrightarrow M_2 \models E$.
(ii) Any two sentences $\varphi, \psi \in \mathsf{Sen}(\Sigma)$ are $\mathcal{I}$-equivalent, written $\varphi \equiv_{\mathcal{I}} \psi$, iff $\forall M \in \mathsf{Mod}(\Sigma)$: $M \models \varphi \Leftrightarrow M \models \psi$. □

Remark 6. In a pre-institution $\mathcal{I}$, two Σ-sentences are $\mathcal{I}$-equivalent iff no Σ-model distinguishes them. Conversely, two Σ-models are $\mathcal{I}$-equivalent iff no Σ-presentation distinguishes them. The latter notion enables us to introduce a few properties of pre-institution transformations, that we propose without further analysis.
(i) a pre-institution transformation $\mathcal{T} : \mathcal{I} \to \mathcal{I}'$ is insensitive to $\mathcal{I}$-equivalence iff $M_1 \equiv_{\mathcal{I}} M_2 \Rightarrow M_{1\mathcal{T}} = M_{2\mathcal{T}}$,
(ii) a pre-institution transformation $\mathcal{T} : \mathcal{I} \to \mathcal{I}'$ is closed under $\mathcal{I}'$-equivalence iff $(M' \in M_{\mathcal{T}} \wedge M'' \equiv_{\mathcal{I}'} M') \Rightarrow M'' \in M_{\mathcal{T}}$,
(iii) a pre-institution transformation $\mathcal{T} : \mathcal{I} \to \mathcal{I}'$ abstracts from indiscernibility iff it is both insensitive to $\mathcal{I}$-equivalence and closed under $\mathcal{I}'$-equivalence. □

Additional requirements characterize certain classes of pre-institution transformations that will prove useful later.

Definition 7. Let $\mathcal{T} : \mathcal{I} \to \mathcal{I}'$ be a pre-institution transformation, with $\mathcal{I}$, $\mathcal{I}'$ as in Definition 4.
(i) $\mathcal{T}$ is ***adequate*** iff it meets the following requirement:
$\forall \Sigma \in \mathsf{Sig}$, $\forall E \in \mathsf{Pre}(\Sigma)$, $\forall M' \in \mathsf{Mod}'(\Sigma_{\mathcal{T}})$:
(§§) $M' \models' E_{\mathcal{T}} \Rightarrow \exists M \in \mathsf{Mod}(\Sigma)$: $M' \in M_{\mathcal{T}} \wedge M \models E$
(ii) $\mathcal{T}$ is ***fully adequate*** iff it meets the following requirement:
$\forall \Sigma \in \mathsf{Sig}$, $\forall M' \in \mathsf{Mod}'(\Sigma_{\mathcal{T}})$, for all indexed families $\{E_j\}_{j \in J}$ of Σ-presentations:
(§§§) $M' \models' \bigcup_{j \in J}(E_j)_{\mathcal{T}} \Rightarrow \exists M \in \mathsf{Mod}(\Sigma)$: $M' \in M_{\mathcal{T}} \wedge M \models \bigcup_{j \in J} E_j$. □

Although, at a first glance, our definition of adequacy of pre-institution transformations may seem to resemble that of soundness of institution morphisms in [13], such a resemblance is merely formal and has no significance, since model mapping has opposite directions in the two notions.[6] As we shall see in the next Section, adequacy ensures completeness of the transformation with respect to consequence. Full adequacy is just a stronger form of adequacy (clearly, every fully adequate transformation is adequate as well), that proves connected to compactness of pre-institutions, as shown in Sect. 4.

A sufficient criterion for full adequacy is as follows.

[6] The credit for this clarification is given to Andrzej Tarlecki.

Lemma 8. Let $\mathcal{T} : \mathcal{I} \rightarrow \mathcal{I}'$ be a pre-institution transformation, with $\mathcal{I}$, $\mathcal{I}'$ as in Definition 4. If $\mathcal{T}$ is adequate and meets the following condition:
$\forall \Sigma \in \mathsf{Sig}, \forall M_1, M_2 \in \mathsf{Mod}(\Sigma), \forall M' \in \mathsf{Mod}'(\Sigma_\mathcal{T})$: $(M' \in M_{1\mathcal{T}} \wedge M' \in M_{2\mathcal{T}}) \Rightarrow M_{1\mathcal{T}} = M_{2\mathcal{T}}$,
then $\mathcal{T}$ is fully adequate.

Proof. Let $\{E_j\}_{j \in J}$ be a family of Σ-presentations and $M' \models' \bigcup_{j \in J}(E_j)_\mathcal{T}$, thus $\forall j \in J$: $M' \models' (E_j)_\mathcal{T}$. $\mathcal{T}$ is adequate, so for each $j \in J$ $\exists M_j \in \mathsf{Mod}(\Sigma)$: $M_j \models E_j \wedge M' \in (M_j)_\mathcal{T}$. Then $(M_j)_\mathcal{T} \models' (E_j)_\mathcal{T}$ by the satisfaction invariant, and $\forall j,k \in J$ $(M_j)_\mathcal{T} = (M_k)_\mathcal{T}$ by hypothesis, hence $(M_k)_\mathcal{T} \models' (E_j)_\mathcal{T}$, thus $M_k \models E_j$ by the satisfaction invariant. Choose then any $k \in J$; $M_k \models \bigcup_{j \in J} E_j$ and $M' \in (M_k)_\mathcal{T}$ follow at once. □

Our notions of adequacy play a significant rôle in the following definition.

Definition 9. Let $\mathcal{I}$ and $\mathcal{I}'$ be two pre-institutions.

(i) $\mathcal{I}'$ is ***adequately expressive for*** $\mathcal{I}$, written $\mathcal{I} \preceq \mathcal{I}'$, iff there exists an adequate pre-institution transformation $\mathcal{T} : \mathcal{I} \rightarrow \mathcal{I}'$;
(ii) $\mathcal{I}'$ is ***fully expressive for*** $\mathcal{I}$, written $\mathcal{I} \sqsubseteq \mathcal{I}'$, iff there exists a fully adequate pre-institution transformation $\mathcal{T} : \mathcal{I} \rightarrow \mathcal{I}'$. □

Fact 10. $\preceq$ and $\sqsubseteq$ are pre-orders. □

Definition 11. Let $\mathcal{I}$ and $\mathcal{I}'$ be two pre-institutions.

(i) $\mathcal{I}$ and $\mathcal{I}'$ have ***equivalent expressiveness*** iff $\mathcal{I} \preceq \mathcal{I}'$ and $\mathcal{I}' \preceq \mathcal{I}$.
(ii) $\mathcal{I}$ and $\mathcal{I}'$ have ***fully equivalent expressiveness*** iff $\mathcal{I} \sqsubseteq \mathcal{I}'$ and $\mathcal{I}' \sqsubseteq \mathcal{I}$. □

The formal notions of relative expressiveness introduced above generalize the classical notion of relative expressiveness of logical systems in the sense of abstract model theory (see [11]). These have the limitation of being based on first-order models; as a consequence, also the category of (first-order) signatures is fixed for all logical systems. Our notions are more liberal in that only a functor is required between the signature categories, and model-independence is achieved in a most general manner. To clarify this comparison, we show how the classical notion of relative expressiveness between logical systems can be captured by a particular transformation of the corresponding pre-institutions.

Example 12. Let $\mathcal{L}$, $\mathcal{L}'$ be logical systems. According to [11] (p. 194, Definition 1.2), and [10] (p. 27, Definition 1.1.1), $\mathcal{L}'$ is ***at least as strong as*** $\mathcal{L}$, which is written $\mathcal{L} \leq \mathcal{L}'$, iff for every first-order signature Σ, for every Σ-sentence φ in $\mathcal{L}$ there is some Σ-sentence ψ in $\mathcal{L}'$ that has the same models. Let $\mathcal{L}_I$, $\mathcal{L}'_I$ be the pre-institutions that respectively correspond to $\mathcal{L}$, $\mathcal{L}'$, with $\mathsf{Sig} = \mathsf{Sig}'$ the category of first-order signatures having only renamings[7] as morphisms. A transformation $\mathcal{T} : \mathcal{L}_I \rightarrow \mathcal{L}'_I$ which captures the classical notion of relative expressiveness mentioned above is as follows: whenever $\mathcal{L} \leq \mathcal{L}'$, define $\Sigma_\mathcal{T} = \Sigma$, $E_\mathcal{T} = \{\psi \mid \exists \varphi \in E\colon \mathsf{Mod}(\varphi) = \mathsf{Mod}'(\psi)\ \}$, $M_\mathcal{T} = \{M\}$. It is easy to see (using Lemma 8) that $\mathcal{T}$ is a fully adequate transformation. □

[7] that is, bijective arity-preserving maps

3 Basic Facts

The extent to which the properties introduced in Definition 2 for pre-institutions, and in Definition 7 for pre-institution transformations, are (not) relevant is revealed by the following facts.

Proposition 13. Let $\mathcal{T} : \mathcal{I} \to \mathcal{I}'$ be a pre-institution transformation, with $\mathcal{I}$, $\mathcal{I}'$ as in Definition 4, and $\Sigma \in \mathsf{Sig}$.

(i) If $M' \in M_{\mathcal{T}}$ for some M, then $M' \models' \emptyset_{\mathcal{T}}$ (where $\emptyset$ is the empty Σ-presentation).

(ii) Let $R \subseteq \mathsf{Mod}(\Sigma)$ and $\varphi \in \mathsf{Sen}(\Sigma)$. Then $R \models \varphi \Leftrightarrow \bigcup_{M \in R} M_{\mathcal{T}} \models' \varphi_{\mathcal{T}}$.

(iii) Let $M \in \mathsf{Mod}(\Sigma)$ and $E \in \mathsf{Pre}(\Sigma)$. Then $M_{\mathcal{T}} \models' E_{\mathcal{T}} \Leftrightarrow M_{\mathcal{T}} \models' \bigcup_{\varphi \in E} \varphi_{\mathcal{T}}$.

Proof.

(i) and (ii) are immediate consequence of the satisfaction invariant (Definition 4).

(iii) If $M_{\mathcal{T}} \models' E_{\mathcal{T}}$, then $M \models E$ by the satisfaction invariant, that is $M \models \varphi$ for all $\varphi \in E$, which entails $M_{\mathcal{T}} \models' \varphi_{\mathcal{T}}$ again by the satisfaction invariant.
Conversely, if $\forall \varphi \in E\ M_{\mathcal{T}} \models' \varphi_{\mathcal{T}}$, then $\forall \varphi \in E\ M \models \varphi$ by the satisfaction invariant, therefore $M \models E$, whence $M_{\mathcal{T}} \models' E_{\mathcal{T}}$ again by the satisfaction invariant. □

We introduced pre-institution transformations as "morphisms", but we did not fully justify that terminology as yet. The following proposition deals with this kind of details.

Proposition 14. (*pre-institution categories*)

(i) The identity transformation $\mathcal{E}_{\mathcal{I}} : \mathcal{I} \to \mathcal{I}$ (where $\Sigma_{\mathcal{E}_{\mathcal{I}}} = \Sigma$, $E_{\mathcal{E}_{\mathcal{I}}} = E$, $M_{\mathcal{E}_{\mathcal{I}}} = \{M\}$) meets the satisfaction invariant, and is fully adequate.

(ii) If $\mathcal{T} : \mathcal{I} \to \mathcal{I}'$ and $\mathcal{T}' : \mathcal{I}' \to \mathcal{I}''$ are pre-institution transformations, then so is their composition $\mathcal{T}' \circ \mathcal{T} : \mathcal{I} \to \mathcal{I}''$, where:
$\Sigma_{\mathcal{T}' \circ \mathcal{T}} = (\Sigma_{\mathcal{T}})_{\mathcal{T}'}$,
$\tau_{\mathcal{T}' \circ \mathcal{T}} = (\tau_{\mathcal{T}})_{\mathcal{T}'}$,
$E_{\mathcal{T}' \circ \mathcal{T}} = (E_{\mathcal{T}})_{\mathcal{T}'}$,
$M_{\mathcal{T}' \circ \mathcal{T}} = \bigcup_{M' \in M_{\mathcal{T}}} M'_{\mathcal{T}'}$.

(iii) $\mathcal{T}' \circ \mathcal{T}$ is adequate if both $\mathcal{T}$ and $\mathcal{T}'$ are adequate.

(iv) $\mathcal{T}' \circ \mathcal{T}$ is fully adequate if both $\mathcal{T}$ and $\mathcal{T}'$ are fully adequate.

(v) Pre-institutions, together with transformations as morphisms form a category PT, of which a subcategory APT is obtained by taking only adequate transformations as morphisms, of which a subcategory FAPT is obtained by taking only fully adequate transformations as morphisms.

Proof.

(i) Immediate, using Lemma 8.

(ii) We have only to check that $\mathcal{T}' \circ \mathcal{T}$ meets the satisfaction invariant, which easily follows from the definition of $\mathcal{T}' \circ \mathcal{T}$.

(iii) If $M'' \models E_{\mathcal{T}' \circ \mathcal{T}}$ then, since $\mathcal{T}'$ is adequate, there exists $M' \in \mathsf{Mod}(\Sigma_{\mathcal{T}})$ such that $M'' \in M'_{\mathcal{T}'}$ and $M' \models E_{\mathcal{T}}$. This, and the adequacy of $\mathcal{T}$ entail that there exists $M \in \mathsf{Mod}(\Sigma)$ such that $M' \in M_{\mathcal{T}}$ and $M \models E$. Then $M'' \in M'_{\mathcal{T}'}$ and $M' \in M_{\mathcal{T}}$ together imply $M'' \in M_{\mathcal{T}' \circ \mathcal{T}}$, and since $M \models E$, it follows that $\mathcal{T}' \circ \mathcal{T}$ is adequate as well.

(iv) If $M'' \models (E_j)_{\mathcal{T}' \circ \mathcal{T}}$ for all $j \in J$, then the full adequacy of $\mathcal{T}'$ entails the existence of a $M' \in \mathsf{Mod}(\Sigma_{\mathcal{T}})$ such that $M'' \in M'_{\mathcal{T}'}$ and $M' \models (E_j)_{\mathcal{T}}$ for all $j \in J$. The full adequacy of $\mathcal{T}$ then entails that there exists $M \in \mathsf{Mod}(\Sigma)$ such that $M' \in M_{\mathcal{T}}$ and $M \models E_j$ for all $j \in J$. Then $M'' \in M'_{\mathcal{T}'}$ and $M' \in M_{\mathcal{T}}$ together imply $M'' \in \bigcup_{M' \in M_{\mathcal{T}}} M'_{\mathcal{T}'} = M_{\mathcal{T}' \circ \mathcal{T}}$, and since $M \models E_j$ for all $j \in J$, it follows that $\mathcal{T}' \circ \mathcal{T}$ is fully adequate as well.

(v) Validity of the standard categorial laws in PT is easily verified. APT is a subcategory of PT since identities are adequate and composition preserves adequacy. FAPT is a subcategory of APT since identities are fully adequate and composition preserves full adequacy. □

Note that the identity transformation of Proposition 14(i) enjoys none of the properties introduced in Remark 6. Clearly, this is the 'safest' identity, in that coarser identities can always be obtained by appropriate quotients. For example, the coarser identity transformation $\mathcal{A}_I : \mathcal{I} \rightarrow \mathcal{I}$, where $\Sigma_{\mathcal{A}_I} = \Sigma$, $E_{\mathcal{A}_I} = E$, $M_{\mathcal{A}_I} = \{M' | M' \equiv_{\mathcal{I}} M\}$, abstracts from indiscernibility (proof: $\mathcal{A}_I$ is evidently closed under $\mathcal{I}$-equivalence; its insensitivity to $\mathcal{I}$-equivalence follows from extensionality of sets).

The following fact shows that pre-institution transformations enjoy 'contravariant' preservation of the *rps* and *eps* properties. This fact seems to be only the first phenomenon of a wealthy situation; the compactness theorem in the next Section is another such case. Preservation is 'contravariant' in the sense that, if $\mathcal{T} : \mathcal{I} \rightarrow \mathcal{I}'$ is a pre-institution transformation and $\mathcal{I}'$ has the property under consideration, then $\mathcal{I}$ has that property as well.

These results demonstrate the usefulness of our notion of transformation, in that they support interesting proof techniques. For example, if a proof of a certain theorem in a pre-institution $\mathcal{I}$ is sought, and the theorem is known to hold in a pre-institution $\mathcal{I}'$, it will suffice to find a transformation $\mathcal{T} : \mathcal{I} \rightarrow \mathcal{I}'$, since this allows the transfer of the known result back to $\mathcal{I}$.

Another, perhaps more interesting application of these results is concerned with negative results on comparing the expressiveness of pre-institutions, in the sense of Definition 9. The proof technique, which has a 'contrapositive' flavour, simply consists in showing that some of the properties which are contravariantly preserved by (possibly 'suitable') pre-institution transformations is enjoyed by $\mathcal{I}'$ but not by $\mathcal{I}$. In such a case, then, one can infer that no ('suitable') pre-institution transformation $\mathcal{T} : \mathcal{I} \rightarrow \mathcal{I}'$ exists (where 'suitable' means: with some additional property, such as adequacy). An application of this proof method is in Sect. 5.1 below.

Proposition 15. Let $\mathcal{T} : \mathcal{I} \rightarrow \mathcal{I}'$ be a pre-institution transformation, with $\mathcal{I}$, $\mathcal{I}'$ as in Definition 4.

(i) If $\mathcal{I}'$ is *rps*, then $\mathcal{I}$ is *rps*.
(ii) If $\mathcal{I}'$ is *eps*, then $\mathcal{I}$ is *eps*.
(iii) If $\mathcal{I}'$ is *ps*, then $\mathcal{I}$ is *ps*.

Proof. For all signature morphisms $\tau : \Sigma_2 \rightarrow \Sigma_1$ in Sig, $\forall M \in \mathsf{Mod}(\Sigma_2)$, $\forall \varphi \in \mathsf{Sen}(\Sigma_1)$:

(i) If $M \models \tau\varphi$, then $\forall M' \in M_{\mathcal{T}}$: $M' \models' (\tau\varphi)_{\mathcal{T}}$ by the satisfaction invariant, therefore $\forall M' \in M_{\mathcal{T}}$: $M'\tau_{\mathcal{T}} \models' \varphi_{\mathcal{T}}$ by hypothesis and since $(\tau\varphi)_{\mathcal{T}} = \tau_{\mathcal{T}}\varphi_{\mathcal{T}}$ according to the commutativity of the diagram in Definition 4(ii). Moreover, the commutativity of the diagram in Definition 4(iii) entails that $(\mathrm{M}\tau)_{\mathcal{T}} = \{\mathrm{M}'\tau_{\mathcal{T}} | \mathrm{M}' \in \mathrm{M}_{\mathcal{T}}\}$, therefore $(\mathrm{M}\tau)_{\mathcal{T}} \models' \varphi_{\mathcal{T}}$, whence $\mathrm{M}\tau \models \varphi$ by the satisfaction invariant.

(ii) If $\mathrm{M}\tau \models \varphi$, then $(\mathrm{M}\tau)_{\mathcal{T}} \models' \varphi_{\mathcal{T}}$ by the satisfaction invariant, therefore $\forall \mathrm{M}' \in \mathrm{M}_{\mathcal{T}}$: $\mathrm{M}'\tau_{\mathcal{T}} \models' \varphi_{\mathcal{T}}$ since the commutativity of the diagram in Definition 4(iii) entails that $(\mathrm{M}\tau)_{\mathcal{T}} = \{\mathrm{M}'\tau_{\mathcal{T}} | \mathrm{M}' \in \mathrm{M}_{\mathcal{T}}\}$. Then $\forall \mathrm{M}' \in \mathrm{M}_{\mathcal{T}}$: $\mathrm{M}' \models' (\tau\varphi)_{\mathcal{T}}$ holds by hypothesis and since $(\tau\varphi)_{\mathcal{T}} = \tau_{\mathcal{T}}\varphi_{\mathcal{T}}$ according to the commutativity of the diagram in Definition 4(ii), therefore $\mathrm{M} \models \tau\varphi$ by the satisfaction invariant.

(iii) From (i) and (ii), according to Definition 2(iii). □

The reason why (full) adequacy of the transformation is required as a criterion for (full) expressiveness is apparent from the following fact, where $\models$ denotes logical consequence, defined in the usual semantical way.

Proposition 16. Let $\mathcal{T} : \mathcal{I} \rightarrow \mathcal{I}'$ be a pre-institution transformation, with $\mathcal{I}$, $\mathcal{I}'$ as in Definition 4. Then $\forall \varphi \in \mathsf{Sen}(\Sigma)$, $\forall \psi \in \mathsf{Sen}'(\Sigma_{\mathcal{T}})$, $\forall \mathrm{E}, \mathrm{E}_j \in \mathsf{Pre}(\Sigma)$:

(i) $\mathrm{E}_{\mathcal{T}} \models \varphi_{\mathcal{T}} \;\Rightarrow\; \mathrm{E} \models \varphi$.

(ii) $\mathrm{E} \models \varphi \;\Rightarrow\; \mathrm{E}_{\mathcal{T}} \models \varphi_{\mathcal{T}}$ if $\mathcal{T}$ is adequate.

(iii) $\bigcup_{j \in J} (\mathrm{E}_j)_{\mathcal{T}} \models \psi \;\Rightarrow\; (\bigcup_{j \in J} \mathrm{E}_j)_{\mathcal{T}} \models \psi$ if $\mathcal{T}$ is adequate.

(iv) $(\bigcup_{j \in J} \mathrm{E}_j)_{\mathcal{T}} \models \psi \;\Rightarrow\; \bigcup_{j \in J} (\mathrm{E}_j)_{\mathcal{T}} \models \psi$ if $\mathcal{T}$ is fully adequate.

Proof.

(i) Let $\mathrm{M} \in \mathsf{Mod}(\Sigma)$, assume $\mathrm{M} \models \mathrm{E}$. By the satisfaction invariant $\mathrm{M}_{\mathcal{T}} \models \mathrm{E}_{\mathcal{T}}$, therefore $\mathrm{M}_{\mathcal{T}} \models \varphi_{\mathcal{T}}$ by hypothesis, whence $\mathrm{M} \models \varphi$ by the satisfaction invariant.

(ii) Let $\mathrm{M}' \in \mathsf{Mod}'(\Sigma_{\mathcal{T}})$, assume $\mathrm{M}' \models \mathrm{E}_{\mathcal{T}}$. By adequacy of $\mathcal{T}$, there exists $\mathrm{M} \in \mathsf{Mod}(\Sigma)$ such that $\mathrm{M}' \in \mathrm{M}_{\mathcal{T}}$ and $\mathrm{M} \models \mathrm{E}$, hence $\mathrm{M} \models \varphi$ by hypothesis, whence $\mathrm{M}' \models \varphi_{\mathcal{T}}$ by the satisfaction invariant.

(iii) Let $\mathrm{M}' \in \mathsf{Mod}'(\Sigma_{\mathcal{T}})$, assume $\mathrm{M}' \models (\bigcup_{j \in J} \mathrm{E}_j)_{\mathcal{T}}$. Then there exists $\mathrm{M} \in \mathsf{Mod}(\Sigma)$ such that $\mathrm{M}' \in \mathrm{M}_{\mathcal{T}}$ and $\mathrm{M} \models \bigcup_{j \in J} \mathrm{E}_j$, by adequacy of $\mathcal{T}$. Thus $\forall j \in J$: $\mathrm{M} \models \mathrm{E}_j$, hence $\forall j \in J$: $\mathrm{M}_{\mathcal{T}} \models (\mathrm{E}_j)_{\mathcal{T}}$ by the satisfaction invariant, so $\mathrm{M}_{\mathcal{T}} \models \bigcup_{j \in J} (\mathrm{E}_j)_{\mathcal{T}}$, whence $\mathrm{M}_{\mathcal{T}} \models \psi$ by hypothesis. Since $\mathrm{M}' \in \mathrm{M}_{\mathcal{T}}$, $\mathrm{M}' \models \psi$ follows.

(iv) Let $\mathrm{M}' \in \mathsf{Mod}'(\Sigma_{\mathcal{T}})$, assume $\mathrm{M}' \models \bigcup_{j \in J} (\mathrm{E}_j)_{\mathcal{T}}$. Since $\mathcal{T}$ is *fully* adequate, there exists $\mathrm{M} \in \mathsf{Mod}(\Sigma)$ such that $\mathrm{M}' \in \mathrm{M}_{\mathcal{T}}$ and $\mathrm{M} \models \bigcup_{j \in J} \mathrm{E}_j$, hence $\mathrm{M}_{\mathcal{T}} \models (\bigcup_{j \in J} \mathrm{E}_j)_{\mathcal{T}}$ by the satisfaction invariant, whence $\mathrm{M}_{\mathcal{T}} \models \psi$ by hypothesis. Since $\mathrm{M}' \in \mathrm{M}_{\mathcal{T}}$, it follows that $\mathrm{M}' \models \psi$. □

If two pre-institutions enjoy equivalent expressiveness, it is sensible to wonder whether the transformations that establish the equivalence are 'inverse' to each other in some sense. The first such sense which comes to mind is the categorial one, viz. that of pre-institution isomorphism, which requires the composition of the two pre-institution transformations, in either order, to be the identity transformation on the corresponding pre-institution. Clearly, the isomorphism condition is stronger than that required for equivalent expressiveness, and is veritably too strong for practical purposes—based as it is on the smallest identity at all levels: signatures, presentations, models.

The strength introduced by the isomorphism condition can be weakened in various ways, e.g. according to coarser equivalences on presentations or on models. Among such possibilities, we formalize a notion of equivalence that requires the transformation of logical theories to be the identity; more precisely, the presentation obtained by applying such a transformation and then its inverse to any given presentation is required to have exactly the same consequences as the original presentation. As usual, if E is a Σ-presentation, Th(E) denotes the closure of E under consequence, whereas if M is a Σ-model, then Th(M) denotes the largest Σ-presentation that is satisfied by M.

Definition 17. Let $\mathcal{T} : \mathcal{I} \to \mathcal{I}'$ be a pre-institution transformation, with $\mathcal{I}, \mathcal{I}'$ as in Definition 4. $\mathcal{T}$ is *invertible* if there exists a pre-institution transformation $\mathcal{R} : \mathcal{I}' \to \mathcal{I}$ such that $\forall \Sigma \in \mathsf{Sig}$, $\forall E \in \mathsf{Pre}(\Sigma)$: $\mathrm{Th}(E) = \mathrm{Th}((E_{\mathcal{T}})_{\mathcal{R}})$, in which case $\mathcal{R}$ is termed *inverse* of $\mathcal{T}$, and the two pre-institutions $\mathcal{I}, \mathcal{I}'$ have ***exactly equivalent expressiveness.*** □

As a simple illustration, with reference to Example 12, it is easily seen that if $\mathcal{L} \leq \mathcal{L}'$ and $\mathcal{L}' \leq \mathcal{L}$, then the transformation $\mathcal{T} : \mathcal{L}_I \to \mathcal{L}'_I$ is invertible (indeed it has a fully adequate inverse), i.e. $\mathcal{L}_I$ and $\mathcal{L}'_I$ have exactly equivalent expressiveness.

The Galois connection nature of invertible pre-institution transformations is revealed by the following characterization.

Proposition 18. Let $\mathcal{T} : \mathcal{I} \to \mathcal{I}'$ and $\mathcal{R} : \mathcal{I}' \to \mathcal{I}$ be two pre-institution transformations, with $\mathcal{I}, \mathcal{I}'$ as in Definition 4. The following conditions are equivalent:

(a) $\mathcal{R}$ is inverse of $\mathcal{T}$
(b) $\mathcal{T}$ is inverse of $\mathcal{R}$
(c) $\forall \Sigma \in \mathsf{Sig}$, $\forall E \in \mathsf{Pre}(\Sigma)$, $\forall M' \in \mathsf{Mod}(\Sigma_{\mathcal{T}})$: $M' \models' E_{\mathcal{T}} \Leftrightarrow (M')_{\mathcal{R}} \models E$
(d) $\forall \Sigma' \in \mathsf{Sig}'$, $\forall E' \in \mathsf{Pre}'(\Sigma')$, $\forall M \in \mathsf{Mod}(\Sigma'_{\mathcal{R}})$: $M \models E'_{\mathcal{R}} \Leftrightarrow M_{\mathcal{T}} \models' E'$

Proof. It is sufficient to show the two implications (a) $\Rightarrow$ (c), (d) $\Rightarrow$ (a), since the two implications (b) $\Rightarrow$ (d), (c) $\Rightarrow$ (b), respectively follow by symmetry.
(a) $\Rightarrow$ (c):
Let E be a Σ-presentation and M' a $\Sigma_{\mathcal{T}}$-model. Then $M' \models' E_{\mathcal{T}} \Leftrightarrow (M')_{\mathcal{R}} \models (E_{\mathcal{T}})_{\mathcal{R}}$ by the satisfaction invariant, and $(M')_{\mathcal{R}} \models (E_{\mathcal{T}})_{\mathcal{R}} \Leftrightarrow (M')_{\mathcal{R}} \models E$ by hypothesis (a).
(d) $\Rightarrow$ (a):
Let E be a Σ-presentation and M a Σ-model. Then $M \models E \Leftrightarrow M_{\mathcal{T}} \models' E_{\mathcal{T}}$ by the satisfaction invariant, and $M_{\mathcal{T}} \models' E_{\mathcal{T}} \Leftrightarrow M \models (E_{\mathcal{T}})_{\mathcal{R}}$ by hypothesis (d). □

Sufficient conditions for exactly equivalent expressiveness may be of help in the construction of such equivalences. Of the two conditions given below, the second one is stronger, but may turn out to be more useful in practice.

Proposition 19. Let $\mathcal{T} : \mathcal{I} \to \mathcal{I}'$ and $\mathcal{R} : \mathcal{I}' \to \mathcal{I}$ be two pre-institution transformations, with $\mathcal{I}, \mathcal{I}'$ as in Definition 4. The following conditions are sufficient for $\mathcal{R}$ to be inverse of $\mathcal{T}$.
(i) $\forall \Sigma \in \mathsf{Sig}$, $\forall M \in \mathsf{Mod}(\Sigma)$, $\forall E' \in \mathsf{Pre}(\Sigma_{\mathcal{T}})$: $M \in (M_{\mathcal{T}})_{\mathcal{R}} \wedge (M \models E'_{\mathcal{R}} \Rightarrow M_{\mathcal{T}} \models' E')$
(ii) $\forall \Sigma \in \mathsf{Sig}$, $\forall M \in \mathsf{Mod}(\Sigma)$: $M \in (M_{\mathcal{T}})_{\mathcal{R}} \wedge (M_{\mathcal{T}})_{\mathcal{R}} \subseteq \mathsf{Mod}(\mathrm{Th}(M))$
Proof.
(i) Let M be a Σ-model and E a Σ-presentation. If $M \models E$, then $(M_{\mathcal{T}})_{\mathcal{R}} \models (E_{\mathcal{T}})_{\mathcal{R}}$ by the satisfaction invariant, hence $M \models (E_{\mathcal{T}})_{\mathcal{R}}$ by the hypothesis $M \in (M_{\mathcal{T}})_{\mathcal{R}}$. On the other hand, $M \models (E_{\mathcal{T}})_{\mathcal{R}}$ entails $M_{\mathcal{T}} \models' E_{\mathcal{T}}$ by hypothesis, hence $M \models E$ by the satisfaction invariant.

(ii) $(M_{\mathcal{T}})_{\mathcal{R}} \subseteq \mathsf{Mod}(\mathrm{Th}(M))$ entails the implication $M \models E'_{\mathcal{R}} \Rightarrow (M_{\mathcal{T}})_{\mathcal{R}} \models E'_{\mathcal{R}}$, whence the validity of condition (i) under condition (ii) follows from the satisfaction invariant. □

The conditions in the previous proposition also ensure full adequacy of the inverse transformation, as shown by the following.

Proposition 20. If $\mathcal{R} : \mathcal{I}' \rightarrow \mathcal{I}$ is an inverse of $\mathcal{T} : \mathcal{I} \rightarrow \mathcal{I}'$ such that $\forall \Sigma \in \mathsf{Sig}, \forall M \in \mathsf{Mod}(\Sigma)$: $M \in (M_{\mathcal{T}})_{\mathcal{R}}$, then

(i) $\mathcal{R}$ is fully adequate
(ii) $\mathcal{R} \circ \mathcal{T}$ is fully adequate

Proof.

(i) Let $M \models (E'_j)_{\mathcal{R}}$ $\forall j \in J$. Since $M \in (M_{\mathcal{T}})_{\mathcal{R}}$ by hypothesis, $\exists M' \in M_{\mathcal{T}}$: $M \in (M')_{\mathcal{R}}$. Furthermore, $M \models (E'_j)_{\mathcal{R}} \Rightarrow M_{\mathcal{T}} \models' E'_j$ by Proposition 18(d) and (a), therefore $M' \models' E'_j$ for all $j \in J$.
(ii) Let $M \models (E_{j\mathcal{T}})_{\mathcal{R}}$ for all $j \in J$. Then $M_{\mathcal{T}} \models' (E_j)_{\mathcal{T}}$ for all $j \in J$ according to Proposition 18(d) and (a), hence $M \models E_j$ for all $j \in J$ by the satisfaction invariant, and $M \in (M_{\mathcal{T}})_{\mathcal{R}}$ by hypothesis. □

4 Compactness

In this Section we show the relevance of the basic framework outlined so far to the model-theoretic concept of compactness. In particular, we shall show the 'contravariant' (in the sense explained in Sect. 3) preservation of (two notions of) compactness by 'suitable' pre-institution transformations. The pre-institution transformation is to be 'suitable' in the sense that it may have to fulfil certain requirements, such as (full) adequacy, depending on the property under consideration.

Definition 21. (*Compactness*)
Let $\mathcal{I} = (\mathsf{Sig}, \mathsf{Sen}, \mathsf{Mod}, \models)$ be a pre-institution, with $\mathsf{Pre} = \wp \circ \mathsf{Sen} : \mathsf{Sig} \rightarrow \mathrm{SET}$.

(i) $\mathcal{I}$ is *compact* iff $\forall \Sigma \in \mathsf{Sig}, \forall E \in \mathsf{Pre}(\Sigma)$: E is satisfiable $\Leftrightarrow$ E is finitely satisfiable.
(ii) $\mathcal{I}$ is *consequence-compact* iff $\forall \Sigma \in \mathsf{Sig}, \forall E \in \mathsf{Pre}(\Sigma), \forall \varphi \in \mathsf{Sen}(\Sigma)$:
$E \models \varphi \Rightarrow \exists F \subseteq E$: F finite $\wedge$ $F \models \varphi$. □

The two notions of compactness are equivalent for pre-institutions that are closed under negation (see [11], p. 196, Lemma 2.1), where $\mathcal{I}$ is closed under negation whenever $\forall \Sigma \in \mathsf{Sig}, \forall \varphi \in \mathsf{Sen}(\Sigma), \exists \psi \in \mathsf{Sen}(\Sigma), \forall M \in \mathsf{Mod}(\Sigma)$: $M \models \varphi$ iff not $M \models \psi$.

Since finiteness of (sub-)presentations plays an essential rôle in both notions of compactness, one may expect that 'suitable' pre-institution transformations for such notions ought to preserve that finiteness somehow. The basic, most intuitive idea is that every sentence should be transformed into a finite set of sentences. This idea is affected by too much of 'syntax', though, in the following sense.

If one accepts the abstract model-theoretic purpose proposed in [16], that is "to get *away* from the syntactic aspects of logic completely and to study classes of structures more in the spirit of universal algebra" then two softenings of the basic idea are in place. First, 'finiteness' of the transform $\varphi_{\mathcal{T}}$ of any sentence φ should be measured excluding the 'tautological' part of φ_T ('tautological' relatively to T, in a sense made precise below), since model classes are insensitive to tautologies. Second, and more generally in fact, 'finiteness' of sentence transformation should only be 'up to logical equivalence' in the target pre-institution, since logically equivalent sentences specify identical model classes.

The following definition tells, for a given pre-institution transformation, which sentences of the target pre-institution are 'viewed as tautologies' in the source pre-institution; we are thus considering a sort of 'stretching' of the classical notion of tautology along the transformation arrow. The subsequent definition, then, formalizes the two 'soft' forms of the property we are looking for, according to the rationale given above. The second, softer form is just what we need to prove the relevant part of the main theorem, which concludes the present analysis of compactness.

Definition 22. Let $T : \mathcal{I} \rightarrow \mathcal{I}'$ be a pre-institution transformation, with $\mathcal{I}$, $\mathcal{I}'$ as in Definition 4. Then, for every $\Sigma \in \mathsf{Sig}$:
(i) a sentence $\psi \in \mathsf{Sen}(\Sigma_T)$ is a T-tautology iff $\forall \mathrm{M} \in \mathsf{Mod}(\Sigma)$, $\forall \mathrm{M}' \in \mathrm{M}_T$: $\mathrm{M}' \models' \psi$,
(ii) $\mathrm{Taut}_T(\Sigma)$ is the set of T-tautologies in $\mathsf{Sen}(\Sigma_T)$. □

Clearly, every Σ_T-tautology (in the classical sense) is in $\mathrm{Taut}_T(\Sigma)$. This may contain more sentences, however, e.g. if $\emptyset_\Sigma$ is the 'empty' Σ-presentation, then clearly $(\emptyset_\Sigma)_T \subseteq \mathrm{Taut}_T(\Sigma)$, and the sentences in $(\emptyset_\Sigma)_T$ need not be Σ_T-tautologies.

Definition 23. Let $T : \mathcal{I} \rightarrow \mathcal{I}'$ be a pre-institution transformation, with $\mathcal{I}$, $\mathcal{I}'$ as in Definition 4.
(i) T is *finitary* iff $\forall \Sigma \in \mathsf{Sig}$, $\forall \varphi \in \mathrm{Sen}(\Sigma)$: $\varphi_T - \mathrm{Taut}_T(\Sigma)$ finite.
(ii) T is *quasi-finitary* iff $\forall \Sigma \in \mathsf{Sig}$, $\forall \varphi \in \mathrm{Sen}(\Sigma)$: $(\varphi_T - \mathrm{Taut}_T(\Sigma))/\equiv_{\mathcal{I}'}$ finite. □

The difference between finitarity and quasi-finitarity is illustrated by the transformation in Example 12, which is quasi-finitary but not necessarily finitary.

Theorem 24. (*Compactness*) Let $T : \mathcal{I} \rightarrow \mathcal{I}'$ be a fully adequate pre-institution transformation, with $\mathcal{I}$, $\mathcal{I}'$ as in Definition 4.
(i) If $\mathcal{I}'$ is compact, then $\mathcal{I}$ is compact.
(ii) If $\mathcal{I}'$ is consequence-compact and T is quasi-finitary, then $\mathcal{I}$ is consequence-compact.

Proof.
(i) One direction of the compactness condition is trivial. Let then E be finitely satisfiable. If we can show that $\bigcup_{\psi \in E} \psi_T$ is finitely satisfiable as well, then $\bigcup_{\psi \in E} \psi_T$ is satisfiable by the hypothesis of compactness of $\mathcal{I}'$, viz. there is a model M' in $\mathcal{I}'$ such that $\mathrm{M}' \models' \bigcup_{\psi \in E} \psi_T$. Since T is fully adequate, $\mathrm{M}' \in \mathrm{M}_T$ and $\mathrm{M} \models \mathrm{E}$ for some model M in $\mathcal{I}$.
The finite satisfiability of $\bigcup_{\psi \in E} \psi_T$ is shown as follows.
Let G be any finite subset of $\bigcup_{\psi \in E} \psi_T$.
For each $\chi \in \mathrm{G}$ pick a $\psi_\chi \in \mathrm{E}$ such that $\chi \in (\psi_\chi)_T$.
So $\mathrm{F} = \{\psi_\chi \mid \chi \in \mathrm{G}\}$ is a finite subset of E, thus satisfiable by hypothesis.
There exists then a model M in $\mathcal{I}$ such that $\mathrm{M} \models \mathrm{F}$, thus $\forall \chi \in \mathrm{G}$: $\mathrm{M} \models \psi_\chi$, whence $\forall \chi \in \mathrm{G}$: $\mathrm{M}_T \models' (\psi_\chi)_T$ by the satisfaction invariant. Since $\forall \chi \in \mathrm{G}$: $\chi \in (\psi_\chi)_T$, we must conclude that $\mathrm{M}_T \models' \mathrm{G}$, thus $\bigcup_{\psi \in E} \psi_T$ is finitely satisfiable.

(ii) Let E $\models \varphi$ in $\mathcal{I}$, with $\varphi \in \mathsf{Sen}(\Sigma)$ and $E \in \mathsf{Pre}(\Sigma)$ for some $\Sigma \in \mathsf{Sig}$. Then $E_{\mathcal{T}} \models \varphi_{\mathcal{T}}$ by adequacy of $\mathcal{T}$ and Proposition 16(ii), thus $\bigcup_{\psi \in E} \psi_{\mathcal{T}} \models \varphi_{\mathcal{T}}$ by full adequacy of $\mathcal{T}$ and Proposition 16(iv), that is $\bigcup_{\psi \in E} \psi_{\mathcal{T}} \models \xi$ for all $\xi \in \varphi_{\mathcal{T}}$. Consequence-compactness of $\mathcal{I}'$ implies that for each $\xi \in \varphi_{\mathcal{T}}$ there exists a finite $G_\xi \subseteq \bigcup_{\psi \in E} \psi_{\mathcal{T}}$ such that $G_\xi \models \xi$.
Now, for each $\chi \in G_\xi$ pick a $\psi_\chi \in E$ such that $\chi \in (\psi_\chi)_{\mathcal{T}}$.
Let $F_\xi = \{\psi_\chi \mid \chi \in G_\xi\} \subseteq E$. Moreover, let $\widehat{\varphi_{\mathcal{T}}}$ be a set of representatives for the equivalence classes in the quotient $(\varphi_{\mathcal{T}} - \mathrm{Taut}_{\mathcal{T}}(\Sigma))/\equiv_{\mathcal{I}'}$, with $\widehat{\varphi_{\mathcal{T}}}$ consisting of exactly one representative per equivalence class. Define then $F = \bigcup_{\xi \in \widehat{\varphi_{\mathcal{T}}}} F_\xi$.
Clearly $F \subseteq E$.
F is finite since G_ξ finite implies F_ξ finite and $\mathcal{T}$ quasi-finitary implies that $(\varphi_{\mathcal{T}} - \mathrm{Taut}_{\mathcal{T}}(\Sigma))/\equiv_{\mathcal{I}'}$ is finite, hence $\widehat{\varphi_{\mathcal{T}}}$ finite. $G_\xi \models \xi$ and $G_\xi \subseteq \bigcup_{\chi \in G_\xi} (\psi_\chi)_{\mathcal{T}}$ together entail $\bigcup_{\chi \in G_\xi} (\psi_\chi)_{\mathcal{T}} \models \xi$, which, by the definition of F_ξ, is equal to $\bigcup_{\psi \in F_\xi} \psi_{\mathcal{T}} \models \xi$. This, together with the definition of F thus yield $\bigcup_{\psi \in F} \psi_{\mathcal{T}} \models \widehat{\varphi_{\mathcal{T}}}$, therefore $\bigcup_{\psi \in F} \psi_{\mathcal{T}} \models \varphi_{\mathcal{T}} - \mathrm{Taut}_{\mathcal{T}}(\Sigma)$ since consequence in $\mathcal{I}'$ is preserved under $\mathcal{I}'$-equivalence. Now, $\bigcup_{\psi \in F} \psi_{\mathcal{T}} \models \mathrm{Taut}_{\mathcal{T}}(\Sigma)$ if for some $\psi \in F$ $\psi_{\mathcal{T}} \models \mathrm{Taut}_{\mathcal{T}}(\Sigma)$, which easily follows from adequacy of $\mathcal{T}$ and Proposition 16(ii) together with Definition 22. Thus $\bigcup_{\psi \in F} \psi_{\mathcal{T}} \models \varphi_{\mathcal{T}}$, whence $F_{\mathcal{T}} \models \varphi_{\mathcal{T}}$ by adequacy of $\mathcal{T}$ and Proposition 16(iii), and thus finally $F \models \varphi$ by Proposition 16(i). □

5 Application Examples

In [18], among others, translations of order-sorted conditional equational logic [14] and of conditional equational logics for partial algebras [1, 2, 7, 8, 22] into equational type logic [17] were made available, and were shown sound and complete with respect to deduction, as well as with respect to translation of signature declarations by equational type axioms.

In this Section, we slightly extend each of the aforementioned translations, to obtain pre-institution transformations which are easily shown to be fully adequate. The completeness results are then immediate consequence of Proposition 16 (soundness being ensured by the satisfaction invariant).

5.1 Order-Sorted Algebra

We recall the translation defined in [18] for order-sorted conditional equational logic, that consists of the following:

1. If $\Sigma = \langle S, \leq, \Sigma_{op} \rangle$ is an order-sorted signature, its translation $\Sigma_{\mathcal{T}}$ is the unsorted signature that has as 0-ary operators the nullary operators of Σ and the sorts in S, and as k-ary operators the operators of Σ_{op} with k arguments, for k>0.
2. If E is a set of order-sorted Σ-sentences, thus a set of conditional equations over an order-sorted signature Σ as in 1 above and a system of variables V on Σ, let $V_{\mathcal{T}} = |V| \cup Y$, where $|V|$ is the underlying set of variables in V and Y $= \{y, y_1, \ldots, y_n, \ldots\}$ is a countable set of new variables (viz. $|V| \cap Y = \emptyset$). The translation $E_{\mathcal{T}}$ is the smallest set of $\Sigma_{\mathcal{T}}$-sentences of equational type logic that contains:

(a) for each operator ω:$s_1,\ldots,s_n \to s$ in Σ_{op}, the $\Sigma_{\mathcal{T}}$-sentence
$(\omega)_{\mathcal{T}} \stackrel{def}{=} y_1 : s_1, \ldots, y_n : s_n \to \omega(y_1,\ldots,y_n) : s$;

(b) for each sort inclusion $s \leq s'$ in Σ, the $\Sigma_{\mathcal{T}}$-sentence
$(s \leq s')_{\mathcal{T}} \stackrel{def}{=} y : s \to y : s'$;

(c) for each Σ-sentence $\varphi = \forall X.e_1,\ldots,e_n \to e$ in E, the $\Sigma_{\mathcal{T}}$-sentence
$\varphi_{\mathcal{T}} \stackrel{def}{=} x_1 : s_1, \ldots, x_m : s_m, e_1,\ldots,e_n \to e$,
with $x_1,\ldots,x_m$ the variables of φ, thus in X, $s_1,\ldots,s_m$ their respective sorts therein.

3. If M is an order-sorted Σ-algebra, its translation $M_{\mathcal{T}}$ is the closure under isomorphism of the set of $\Sigma_{\mathcal{T}}$:-algebras M′ that meet the following requirements:
carrier: $|M'| \supseteq \bigcup_{s \in S} M_s$
typing: for every $s \in S$, $a :_{M'} s^{M'} \Leftrightarrow a \in M_s$
operations: for every ω:$s_1,\ldots,s_n \to s$ in Σ_{op},
$$\omega^{M'}(a_1,\ldots,a_n) = \omega^{M}(a_1,\ldots,a_n) \text{ if } a_1 :_{M'} s_1^{M'}, \ldots, a_n :_{M'} s_n^{M'}.$$

To obtain a pre-institution transformation from the above translation, one must define the translation of order-sorted signature morphisms, check the naturality of the presentation as well as model transformations, and check the validity of the satisfaction invariant.

The first item in this task is easy: if τ:$\Sigma_1 \to \Sigma_2$ is an order-sorted signature morphism, define $\tau_{\mathcal{T}}\omega = \tau\omega$ for all ω in $\Sigma_{1\mathcal{T}}$. This yields naturality of the presentation transformation, as it is easy to check.

The remaining items preliminarily require the choice of the appropriate notion of model reduction in equational type logic. Order-sorted (as well as many-sorted) reduction may forget not only operations but also carriers; precisely, it forgets those carriers that have no designation in the image of the signature morphism. In [17] we argued, on intuitive grounds, that algebraic ⟨1:0⟩-reduction in equational type logic was an appropriate reflection of this feature. To see this, we first recall a few notions relating to algebraic reduction in equational type logic.

First, relatively to a signature morphism[8] τ:$\Omega \to \Omega'$, the standard reduct of an Ω'-signed type algebra (or Ω':-algebra) $\mathcal{A}'$ is the Ω:-algebra $\mathcal{A}$ that has the same carrier and typing, and operators' interpretation $\omega^{\mathcal{A}} \stackrel{def}{=} (\tau\omega)^{\mathcal{A}'}$ for all $\omega \in \Omega$. Thus, like with universal algebras, no elements are forgotten by standard reduction, but only operations. Then, relatively to a signature morphism τ:$\Omega \to \Omega'$, the ⟨0:0⟩-reduct (actually a subreduct) of an Ω':-algebra is the least Ω-subalgebra of the standard reduct of that type algebra. Finally, relatively to a signature morphism as above, a ⟨1:0⟩-reduct of a type algebra is the least subalgebra of the standard reduct that contains every element that is typed by some element of the ⟨0:0⟩-reduct (which is thus a subalgebra of the ⟨1:0⟩-reduct as well).

Now, the present framework enables us to confirm our aforementioned expectation on formal grounds, since the model transformation as defined above enjoys naturality under ⟨1:0⟩-reduction only.

---

[8] i.e., an arity-preserving map on the operation symbols

In passim, we note that equational type logic with ⟨1:0⟩-reduction is *rps* (see Definition 2), but not *eps*,[9] hence not *ps*, whilst the order-sorted logic of our concern, as well as many-sorted conditional equational logic, do enjoy the *ps* property. Proposition 15 then entails that the transformation above has no inverse; more generally, it entails that a search for a pre-institution transformation in the converse direction to that here exemplified makes sense for equational type logic with standard reduction only.

Validity of the satisfaction invariant is the content of Proposition 3.5 in [18], whose Proposition 3.6 shows adequacy of the transformation above. Finitarity of the transformation is evident. Note that adequacy and full adequacy coincide in this example because of the elementwise definition of the presentation transformation—which may be expected to be the case in many practical situations.

5.2 Partial Algebra

We recall that unsorted partial algebras differ from total ones in that the carrier of a partial algebra need not be closed w.r.t. application of the operations of the algebra. As a matter of notation, $\omega^{\mathcal{A}}\downarrow\langle a_1,\ldots,a_n\rangle$ means that the application of the n-ary operation $\omega^{\mathcal{A}}$ to argument $\langle a_1,\ldots,a_n\rangle\in|\mathcal{A}|^n$ is defined in $\mathcal{A}$. A strictness requirement applies to definedness of terms representing such applications, saying that if the interpretation of a ground term is defined, then so must be the interpretation of every subterm of that term.

We further recall that the conditional equational logics of unsorted partial algebras considered in [18] may have ***weak*** as well as ***strong*** conditional equations as sentences. These respectively follow two variants of the common form $e_1,\ldots,e_n \rightarrow e$, with $e_1,\ldots,e_n$ weak equations in both cases, and e a weak, resp. strong equation. The two variants differ in the conclusion of the conditional, thus. This form can cater for definedness predicates, since D(t) is equivalent to the weak equation $t \stackrel{w}{\equiv} t$, but not for the partial conditional equations considered in [3], which admit strong equations in the premiss; that logic does not always have initial models, hence its faithful translation in equational type logic is not possible.

The translation in [18] of the aforementioned logics into equational type logic consists of the following:

1. If Ω is an unsorted partial algebra signature, its translation $\Omega_{\mathcal{T}}$ is the extension of Ω with the nullary operator $\top$ (assuming $\top \notin \Omega$).
2. If E is an unsorted conditional equational partial algebra presentation, viz. a set of weak or strong conditional equations over an unsorted signature Ω and a set of variables V, let $\Omega_{\mathcal{T}}$ be the signature as in 1 above, and $V_{\mathcal{T}}=V\cup Y$, where $Y = \{y_1,\ldots,y_n,\ldots\}$ is a countable set of new variables (viz. $V\cap Y=\emptyset$). The translation $E_{\mathcal{T}}$ is then the smallest set of $\Omega_{\mathcal{T}}$-sentences of equational type logic that contains:

[9] Failure of the *eps* property in equational type logic with ⟨1:0⟩-reduction is shown by the following counterexample. Consider a two-element type algebra, on a signature consisting of one nullary operator only, and with the typing relation empty. Relatively to the identity signature morphism, the ⟨1:0⟩-reduct coincides with the ⟨0:0⟩-reduct in this case, hence it satisfies the equation $x = x$, which is not valid in the original type algebra.

(a) for each n-ary operator ω in Ω, the following n Ω_T-sentences:
$\omega(y_1,\ldots,y_n) : \mathsf{T} \rightarrow y_1 : \mathsf{T}, \ldots, \omega(y_1,\ldots,y_n) : \mathsf{T} \rightarrow y_n : \mathsf{T}$

(b) for each weak conditional equation $t_1 \overset{w}{\equiv} u_1, \ldots, t_n \overset{w}{\equiv} u_n \rightarrow t \overset{w}{\equiv} u$ the following two Ω_T-sentences:
$t_1 : \mathsf{T}, \ldots, t_n : \mathsf{T}, t_1 \equiv u_1, \ldots, t_n \equiv u_n \rightarrow t : \mathsf{T}$
$t_1 : \mathsf{T}, \ldots, t_n : \mathsf{T}, t_1 \equiv u_1, \ldots, t_n \equiv u_n \rightarrow t \equiv u$

(c) for each strong conditional equation $t_1 \overset{w}{\equiv} u_1, \ldots, t_n \overset{w}{\equiv} u_n \rightarrow t \overset{s}{\equiv} u$ the following two Ω_T-sentences:
$t_1 : \mathsf{T}, \ldots, t_n : \mathsf{T}, t_1 \equiv u_1, \ldots, t_n \equiv u_n , t : \mathsf{T} \rightarrow t \equiv u$
$t_1 : \mathsf{T}, \ldots, t_n : \mathsf{T}, t_1 \equiv u_1, \ldots, t_n \equiv u_n , u : \mathsf{T} \rightarrow t \equiv u$

3. If M is an unsorted partial Ω-algebra, its translation M_T is the closure under isomorphism of the set of Ω_T:-algebras M′ that meet the following requirements:
carrier: $|M'| \supseteq |M|$
typing: $a :_{M'} \mathsf{T}^{M'}$ iff $a \in |M|$
operations: the constant $\mathsf{T}^{M'}$, and for each n-ary operator $\omega \in \Omega$, $\forall a_1,\ldots,a_n \in |M'|$:

$$\text{(i) } (a_1 :_{M'} \mathsf{T}^{M'} \wedge \ldots \wedge a_n :_{M'} \mathsf{T}^{M'} \wedge \omega^M \downarrow \langle a_1,\ldots,a_n\rangle) \Rightarrow \omega^{M'}(a_1,\ldots,a_n) = \omega^M(a_1,\ldots,a_n)$$

$$\text{(ii) } \omega^{M'}(a_1,\ldots,a_n) :_{M'} \mathsf{T}^{M'} \Rightarrow (a_1 :_{M'} \mathsf{T}^{M'} \wedge \ldots \wedge a_n :_{M'} \mathsf{T}^{M'} \wedge \omega^M \downarrow \langle a_1,\ldots,a_n\rangle)$$

To obtain a pre-institution transformation from the above translation, we define the translation of signature morphisms as follows: if $\tau:\Omega_1 \rightarrow \Omega_2$ is an unsorted signature morphism, then $\tau_T \mathsf{T} = \mathsf{T}$ and $\tau_T\omega = \tau\omega$ for all remaining ω in Ω_{1T}. It is easy to check that this yields naturality of the presentation transformation, and naturality of the model transformations as well as validity of the satisfaction invariant, under the standard algebraic reduction in equational type logic (because of the unsortedness of the partial algebras of our concern, here).

Validity of the satisfaction invariant is the content of Proposition 4.6 in [18], whose Proposition 4.7 shows adequacy of the transformation above. Finitarity of the transformation is evident. Adequacy and full adequacy here coincide, again because of the elementwise definition of the presentation transformation.

We conclude by noting that, in this example, the possibility of translating a sentence by a *set* of sentences proves indeed useful; had one to work with pointwise sentence translation, a preliminary lifting to pre-institutions with sentences formed by (finite) sets of sentences would have been necessary, which would have made the translation quite indirect.

6 Related Work

This work shares with [4] the motivation for focussing on the morphisms of institution categories more than on their objects. Clearly, reason for this is the interest that institution-independent specification [24] and general logics [10, 19] naturally find in computer science. It may be source of some surprise, thus, that so far no general agreement has been reached on the most convenient notion of institution morphism. A careful analysis and comparison of several, quite distinct such notions can be found in [4]. To that, we wish to add the following, necessarily quick and preliminary considerations.

In comparison with the notions of institution morphism proposed in [13, 19, 4], our notion is the only one where the three arrows (respectively relating to signatures, sentences, models) are all covariant. Of those three notions, the one which seems closest to ours is that of *basic simulation* [4], which essentially differs from ours in two respects: 1) it sends sentences to sentences, whereas ours sends presentations to presentations, and 2) model transformation is contravariant, but by a surjective, partial natural transformation. The latter could thus be turned into a covariant, total natural transformation, sending models to sets of models, like in our case. Of course, the model sets ought to be disjoint; this condition, arising from well-definedness of the model transformation as defined for basic simulations, closely corresponds to the sufficient condition for full adequacy given in Lemma 8 above—modulo some equivalence of models in the source institution, however.

Although more interested in the morphisms than in the objects, the less restrictive definition of the objects in our framework also contributes to widening the applicability of abstract model-theoretic tools in algebraic specification. Most of the specification frameworks studied so far, fit the institutions scheme, yet not all of them do. Cases where (at least the *eps* half of) the satisfaction condition is known to fail include equational type logic with non-standard reduction (as exemplified in Sect. 5) and, most notably, behavioural semantics [6, 20, 21]. These frameworks fit the pre-institutions scheme, as well as the drastically general scheme proposed in [12]—where hardly anything of the abstract model-theoretic approach underlying the theory of institutions can be recognized, though.

7 Conclusions

We revisit the motivation for the present work in the light of the results obtained in Sects. 3 and 4, and draw a couple of conclusions from the application examples worked out in Sect. 5. We finally mention a few topics of future work.

We motivated our present study by arguing the interest of investigating which properties of institutions do actually depend on the satisfaction condition and/or on the categorial structure on models, and which do not. Now, the results in Sects. 3 and 4 of the present paper offer a first blend of properties which do not depend on either feature of institutions, thus holding for the larger class of pre-institutions.

The blend is further, significantly extended in [23]; there, however, we also obtain a result where a slightly weaker form of the *ps* property is made use of. This is the *renaming* property [10], which is just the *ps* property but limited to signature isomorphisms only. The result which depends on this property is a straightforward generalization of the Hanf theorem to pre-institutions with cardinal numbers. The Hanf theorem, giving 'smallness' conditions that ensure existence of Hanf numbers (and a similar theorem on the existence of Löwenheim numbers) is quite fundamental in abstract model theory, and certainly does make a strong case for the renaming property. This does not invalidate the approach followed in the present paper, however, where we have favoured the analysis of the effect of properties a posteriori to their a priori requirement.

A not dissimilar viewpoint motivates the absence of categorial structure on models in pre-institutions. Morphisms between models 'exist in nature'; no account of them is taken in the notion of pre-institution for the simple reason that they play no rôle in establishing merely logical results like those presented in this paper, as well as those in [23]—and potentially many others, we guess. But model morphisms, and (properties of) their transformations especially, certainly have a rôle to play for investigations of greater mathematical depth, such as algebraic ones. There, the categorially richer structure of institutions is surely well-motivated, in fact necessary. We expect the work on pre-institutions to prove still useful in that wider context, for instance to gain more modularity in the application of the theory of institutions—which fact seems interesting from a 'theory engineering' viewpoint.

So far about theory and its motivations. Concerning applications, two facts seem apparent from the analysis worked out in Sect. 5. On the one hand, the recasting of the translations of our concern into the formal structure of a pre-institution transformation slightly increases the construction work (translation of signature morphisms) and slightly decreases the proof work (completeness with respect to deduction). On the other hand, however, the proof work is made easier somewhat, in that general requirements and facts which ensure soundness and other desirable properties are known in advance. In other words, a proof structure is available in the general framework, that the specific transformation design has to 'fill in' with appropriate details.

Finally, topics for future work that attract our current interest include: the generalization of abstract model theory towards model independence (what could be properly understood as 'soft model theory', where 'soft' applies to 'model' no less than to 'theory'); the investigation of initiality and freeness in this framework (for which [25, 26] offer a solid starting point); the study of whether and how could the present framework be extended to cater for proof calculi [19]; and, last but not least, the investigation of applications, whereby further insight is to be expected.

References

1. Andréka, H., Burmeister, P., Németi, I.: Quasivarieties of Partial Algebras – A Unifying Approach towards a Two-Valued Model Theory for Partial Algebras. Studia Sci. Math. Hungar. **16** (1981) 325–372
2. Andréka, H., Németi, I.: Generalization of Variety and Quasivariety Concepts to Partial Algebras through Category Theory. Dissertationes Mathematicæ (Rozprawy Matematyczne) **204** (Warsaw, 1983)
3. Astesiano E., Cerioli, M.: On the Existence of Initial Models for Partial (Higher-Order) Conditional Specifications, In: Diaz, J., Orejas, F. (Eds.) TAPSOFT'89, LNCS **351** (Springer-Verlag, Berlin, 1989) 74–88
4. Astesiano E., Cerioli, M.: Commuting between Institutions via Simulation. University of Genova, Formal Methods Group, Technical Report n. 2 (1990)
5. Barwise, K. J.: Axioms for Abstract Model Theory. Ann. Math. Logic **7** (1974) 221–265
6. Bernot, G., Bidoit, M.: Proving the Correctness of Algebraically Specified Software: Modularity and Observability Issues. Proc. 2nd Int. Conf. Algebraic Methodology And Software Technology, Iowa City, (Iowa, USA, May 22–25, 1991) 139–161
7. Broy, M., Wirsing, M.: Partial Abstract Types. Acta Informatica, **18**, 3 (1982) 47–64

8. Burmeister, P.: A Model-Theoretic Oriented Approach to Partial Algebras. Mathematical Research, Volume 31, (Akademie-Verlag, Berlin, 1986)
9. Chang, C.C., Keisler, H.J.: Model Theory. Third Edition (North-Holland, Amsterdam, 1990)
10. Ebbinghaus, H.-D.: Extended logics: the general framework. In: Barwise, J., Feferman, S. (Eds.) Model-Theoretic Logics (Springer-Verlag, Berlin, 1985) 25–76
11. Ebbinghaus, H.-D., Flum, J., Thomas, W.: Mathematical Logic. (Springer-Verlag, New York, 1984)
12. Ehrig, H., Baldamus, M., Cornelius, F., Orejas, F.: Theory of Algebraic Module Specification Including Behavioural Semantics, Constraints and Aspects of Generalized Morphisms. Proc. 2nd Int. Conf. Algebraic Methodology And Software Technology, Iowa City, (Iowa, USA, May 22–25, 1991) 101–125
13. Goguen, J.A., Burstall, R.: Introducing Institutions. In: Clarke, E., Kozen, D. (Eds.), Logics of Programs, LNCS **164** (Springer-Verlag, Berlin, 1984) 221–256
14. Goguen, J.A., Meseguer, J.: Order-Sorted Algebra I: Equational Deduction for Multiple Inheritance, Overloading, Exceptions and Partial Operations. Report SRI-CSL-89-10, SRI International, Computer Science Laboratory (Menlo Park, California, July 1989)
15. Mac Lane, S.: Categories for the Working Mathematician. Graduate Texts in Mathematics, Volume 5 (Springer-Verlag, New-York, 1971)
16. Makowski, J.-A.: Compactness, Embeddings an Definability. In: Barwise, J., Feferman, S. (Eds.) Model-Theoretic Logics (Springer-Verlag, Berlin, 1985) 645–716
17. Manca, V., Salibra, A., Scollo, G.: Equational Type Logic. Theoret. Comput. Sci. **77** (1990) 131–159
18. Manca, V., Salibra, A., Scollo, G.: On the Expressiveness of Equational Type Logic. In: Rattray, C.M.I., Clark R.G. (Eds.) The Unified Computation Laboratory, Proc. IMA Conf., Stirling, Scotland, July 3-6, 1990; to appear (Oxford University Press, 1992)
19. Meseguer, J.: General Logics. In: Ebbinghaus, H.-D. et al. (Eds.) Logic Colloquium'87 (North-Holland, Amsterdam, 1989) 275–329
20. Nivela, M.P., Orejas, F.: Initial Behaviour Semantics for Algebraic Specifications. In: Sannella, D.T., Tarlecki, A. (Eds.) Recent Trends in Data Type Specification, LNCS **332** (Springer-Verlag, Berlin, 1988) 184–207
21. Orejas, F., Nivela, M.P., Ehrig, H.: Semantical Constructions for Categories of Behavioural Specifications. In: Ehrig, H., Herrlich, H., Kreowski, H.-J., Preuß, G. (Eds.) Categorical Methods in Computer Science – with Aspects from Topology, LNCS **393** (Springer-Verlag, Berlin, 1989) 220–243
22. Reichel, H.: Initial Computability, Algebraic Specifications, and Partial Algebras. The International Series of Monographs on Computer Science, Volume 2 (Oxford University Press, Oxford, 1987)
23. Salibra, A., Scollo, G.: Compactness and Löwenheim-Skolem Properties in Pre-Institution Categories. Memoranda Informatica 92–27, TIOS 92/12, University of Twente, March 1992; submitted for publication.
24. Sannella, D.T., Tarlecki, A.: Specifications in an Arbitrary Institution. Information and Computation **76** (1988) 165–210
25. Tarlecki, A.: On the Existence of Free Models in Abstract Algebraic Institutions. Theoret. Comput. Sci. **37** (1985) 269–304
26. Tarlecki, A.: Quasi-Varieties in Abstract Algebraic Institutions, J. of Computer and System Sciences **33** (1986) 333–360

Generic Classes in an Object-based Language

Eric G. Wagner

IBM Research Division, T. J. Watson Research Center,
Yorktown Heights, NY 10598, USA

Abstract. This paper investigates the syntax and semantics of specifications of generic classes (parameterized types) in an object-based language, $\mathbf{LD^3}$, developed by the author. the hope is that this specific example will suggest a general approach to generic types involving objects (= data types with internal states). In an earlier paper [5] we presented the syntax for generic classes in $\mathbf{LD^3}$ and showed that the passing of parameters could be treated in terms of pushouts in a manner close to that found in the treatment of algebraic data types but with different categories. This paper summarizes those results and then introduces a treatment of the semantics of generic classes for $\mathbf{LD^3}$. Again, while the categories involved are very different, the results are very reminiscent of those found in algebraic specifications.

1 Introduction

For some years much of my research has centered on applying semantic constructs to the development of an object-based programming language called $\mathbf{LD^3}$ = (Language for Data Directed Design) [3, 4, 6, 5]. In particular, at the 7th workshop on Specification of Abstract Data Types I presented a paper, [5], on the syntax of generic classes in $\mathbf{LD^3}$. In that paper I showed that the manipulation of the syntax can be carried out using pushouts on categories of class-systems in a manner that is very reminiscent of the use of pushouts in the algebraic treatment of generic data types (= parameterized data types) [2, 1]. In this paper I extend that earlier work to include a treatment of the semantics of generic classes. Again I make comparisons with the corresponding work on algebraic data type specification. Here the analogy between the two approaches is not as close: the presence of internal states in objects precludes a truly algebraic model of the semantics. But there is a significant sense in which things "look algebraic" which, when pursued with care, provides guidance and leads to analogous results even though the categories involved are quite different. In particular, I show, in Sect. 9, that there are results analogous to the extension lemma of algebraic specification theory [1] which we review in Sect. 2. Section 3 presents some underlying results on strings-of-strings. Section 4 gives the abstract syntax and semantics of $\mathbf{LD^3}$. Section 5 contains additional, new material on the semantics. Sections 6 and 7 provide the background material from [5] on categories of class-systems and generic class-systems (the $\mathbf{LD^3}$ analogue of parameterized specifications). Section 8 introduces the concept of a pseudo-algebra – a way of dealing with internal states in an algebra-like setting. As noted above, Sect. 9 gives the main new results. Finally, Sect. 10 contains some concluding remarks including a brief discussion of how some of the techniques developed in this paper can be applied to other varieties of programming languages.

2 Review of Algebraic Specification

In order to be able to compare what happens in $\mathbf{LD^3}$ with the "classical" approach to algebraic specifications, we give a short review of some of the basic definitions and results of the algebraic approach.

First of all, data types are specified by presentations.

Definition 1. A *presentation* is a triple $\langle S,\ \Sigma,\ E\rangle$ where S is a set of *sorts*, $\Sigma = \langle \Sigma_{w,s} \mid w \in S^*,\ s \in S\rangle$ is an *S-sorted signature*, and E is a set of equations over Σ. We can then define a category of presentations, **PRES**, with presentations as objects, and, with morphisms $\langle f_S,\ f_\Sigma\rangle : \langle S,\ \Sigma,\ E\rangle \to \langle S',\ \Sigma',\ E'\rangle$ where $f_S : S \to S'$ and $f_\Sigma = \langle (f_\Sigma)_{w,s} : \Sigma_{w,s} \to \Sigma'_{f_S(w),f_S(s)} \mid w \in S^*, s \in S\rangle$ which "preserve the equations".

Proposition 2. **PRES** *has colimits.*

Definition 3. Given a presentation $P = \langle S,\ \Sigma,\ E\rangle$ a *P-algebra* A consists of an S-indexed family of sets $A = \langle A_s \mid s \in S\rangle$ together with, for each $w \in S^*$, $s \in S$, and $\sigma \in \Sigma_{w,s}$, a mapping $\sigma_A : A^w \to A_s$ where, if $w = s_1 \cdots s_n$ then $A^w = A_{s_1} \times \cdots A_{s_n}$.

For any $P = \langle S,\ \Sigma,\ E\rangle$ let $\mathbf{Alg}_{\Sigma,E}$ be the category of all P-algebras together with the P-homomorphisms between them.

Proposition 4. *A presentation morphism* $f = \langle f_S,\ f_\Sigma\rangle : \langle S,\ \Sigma,\ E\rangle \to \langle S',\ \Sigma',\ E'\rangle$ *induces a functor* $f^\flat : \mathbf{Alg}_{\Sigma',E'} \to \mathbf{Alg}_{\Sigma,E}$ *such that, for every algebra* $A \in \mathbf{Alg}_{\Sigma',E'}$,

$$(f^\flat(A))_s = A_{f_S(s)}$$
$$\sigma_{f^\flat(A)} = f_\Sigma(\sigma)_A$$

Definition 5. Let $P = \langle S,\ \Sigma,\ E\rangle$, $P' = \langle S',\ \Sigma',\ E'\rangle$, $A \in \mathbf{Alg}_{\Sigma,E}$, and let $B \in \mathbf{Alg}_{\Sigma',E'}$, then a *generalized homomorphism* $H = \langle f,\ h\rangle : A \to B$ consists of $f : \langle S,\ \Sigma,\ E\rangle \to \langle S',\ \Sigma',\ E'\rangle$ in **PRES**, and $h : A \to f^\flat(B)$ in $\mathbf{Alg}_{\Sigma,E}$.

Proposition 6. *Given* $f : \langle S,\ \Sigma,\ E\rangle \to \langle S',\ \Sigma',\ E'\rangle$ *then* $f^\flat : \mathbf{Alg}_{\Sigma',E'} \to \mathbf{Alg}_{\Sigma,E}$ *has a left adjoint* $f^\sharp : \mathbf{Alg}_{\Sigma,E} \to \mathbf{Alg}_{\Sigma',E'}$.

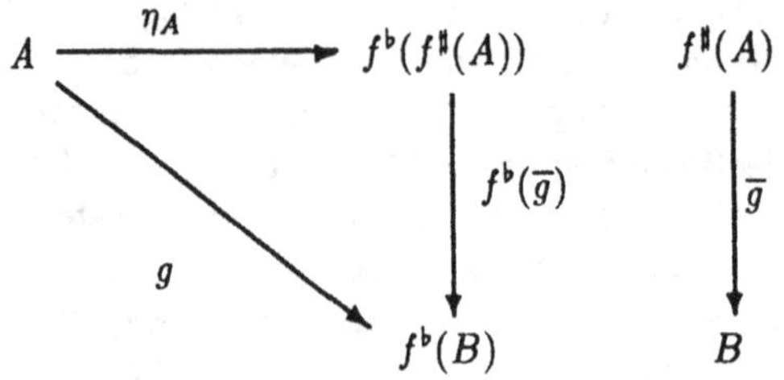

Where $\eta = \langle \eta_A \mid A \in \mathbf{Alg}_{\Sigma,E}\rangle$ *is a natural transformation,* $\eta : \mathbf{1} \dot{\to} f^\flat \bullet f^\sharp$.

We say f is *persistent* if η is a natural isomorphism.

Proposition 7 The extension lemma. *Let P_0, P_1, $P_2 \in$ **PRES**, let $f : P_0 \to P_1$ be persistent, let $g : P_0 \to P_2$ and let $\langle P_3, \overline{f}, \overline{g}\rangle$ be a pushout for $\langle f, g\rangle$. Then $\overline{f}$ is also persistent and $\overrightarrow{g}^{\flat} \bullet \overline{f}^{\sharp} = f^{\sharp} \bullet g^{\flat}$.*

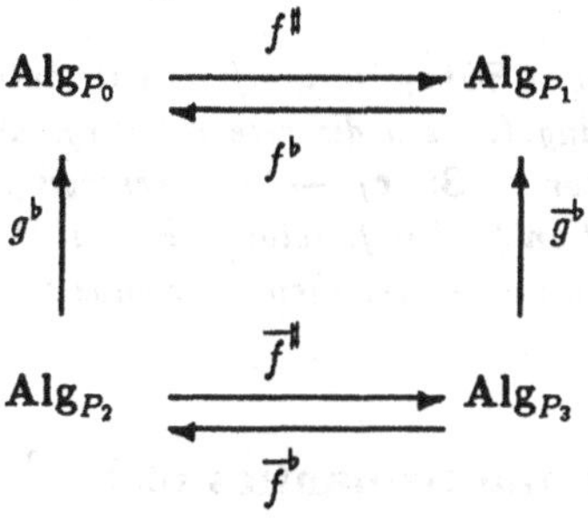

3 Strings and Things

The notion of a string-of-strings over an alphabet K will play an important role in this paper. In this section we give a precise definition of strings-of-strings and show how they form a category.

Let ω denote the set of natural numbers, $\omega = \{0, 1, \cdots\}$. For $n \in \omega$ let $[n]$ denote the set $[n] = \{1, \cdots, n\}$, so $[0] = \emptyset$.

For any set K, a *string of length n over K* is a mapping $s : [n] \to K$. Let K^* denote the *set of all strings over K*. Let $\mathbf{Str}_K$ denote the *category of strings over K* with, as objects, all strings over K, and, as morphisms, $\alpha : u \to v$, where $u : [n] \to K$ and $v : [p] \to K$, all triples $\alpha = \langle u, \overline{\alpha} : [n] \to [p], v\rangle$ where $\overline{\alpha}$ is a mapping from $[n]$ to $[p]$ such that $v \bullet \overline{\alpha} = u$.

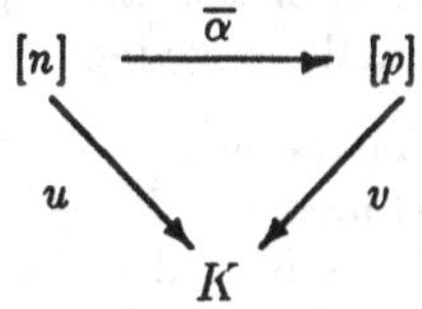

Let $(K^*)^*$ denote the *set of strings-of-strings* over K, i.e., all mappings $u : [n] \to K^*$ for all $n \in \omega$. We will frequently write $(u_1)(u_2)\cdots(u_n)$ for the strings $u : [n] \to K^*$ where $u(i) = u_i \in K^*$, for $i \in [n]$. We often write $(\ )$ for the mapping $[1] \to K^*$ taking 1 to the unique string $\lambda : [0] \to K$ (the empty string on K).

Define $\mathbf{SStr}_K$, *the category of strings-of-strings over K*, to have, as objects, all $u \in (K^*)^*$, and, as morphisms $\alpha : u \to v$ for $u : [n] \to K^*$ and $v : [p] \to K^*$, all triples $\langle u, \langle \alpha_0, \alpha_1, \cdots, \alpha_n\rangle, v\rangle$ where α_0 is a mapping $\alpha_0 : [n] \to [p]$, and for $i = 1, \cdots, n$, $\alpha_i : v_{\alpha_0(i)} \to u_i$ in $\mathbf{Str}_K$.

Proposition 8. *The category $\mathbf{SStr}_K$ has products and coproducts. If $u = (u_1)(u_2)\cdots(u_n)$ and $w = (w_1)(w_2)\cdots(w_p)$ then their product object is*

$$(u_1w_1)(u_1w_2)\cdots(u_1w_p)(u_2w_1)\cdots(u_nw_p)$$

and their coproduct object is

$$(u_1)\cdots(u_n)(w_1)\cdots(w_p)$$

the initial object is $\mathbf{0} : [0] \to K^*$ *and the terminal object is* $\mathbf{1} = (\ ) : [1] \to K^*$, *as above.*

Proposition 9. *The category* $\mathbf{SStr}_K$ *is the free distributive category generated by* K. *So, in particular, viewing* K *as a discrete category, any functor* $F : K \to \mathbf{Set}$ *extends uniquely to a functor* $\widehat{F} : \mathbf{SStr}_K \to \mathbf{Set}$ *preserving products and coproducts. Furthermore, the construction "*$\widehat{\ }$*" is functorial in that if* $F, G : K \to \mathbf{Set}$ *and* η *is a natural transformation,* $\eta : F \to G$, *then* η *extends to a natural transformation* $\widehat{\eta} : \widehat{F} \to \widehat{G}$.

4 Abstract Syntax and Semantics of $\mathbf{LD^3}$

The development of the language $\mathbf{LD^3}$ was guided by the belief that it would be advantageous to develop a programming language as a mathematical entity before making it into user-friendly software entity. This idea is, in turn, coupled with a step-by-step approach in which one first defines a core language and then uses this as the basis for developing additional features. Thus the language presented in this section is the mathematical version of the core of $\mathbf{LD^3}$ and the material on generic types is an example of an additional feature built up using this mathematical foundation. The syntax for $\mathbf{LD^3}$ given below is mathematician-friendly but not programmer-friendly, that is, it lends itself to mathematical treatment (e.g., see Sect. 6), but is hard to read and write. The language has been implemented using both this syntax and an equivalent syntax that is more programmer-friendly but less mathematician-friendly.

The entities corresponding to programs in $\mathbf{LD^3}$ are called *class-systems.* They play the same syntactic role here as presentations play in the algebraic setting. A class-system, Γ, is specified abstractly by giving:

- K a set, called *the set of class names for* Γ.
- Σ a set, called *the set of method names of* Γ.
- $\alpha = \langle \alpha_1, \alpha_2, \alpha_3 \rangle : \Sigma \to K \times K^* \times K$, called the *arity function of* Γ. If $\alpha(\sigma) = \langle k, u, k' \rangle$ where $u = u_1 \cdots u_n \in K^n$ then σ *belongs* to the class k, has n *arguments*, the ith argument being of class u_i, and σ *returns* a value of class k'.
- $\iota : K \to (K^*)^*$ which specifies the *form* of the objects belonging to class k in Γ. The string of strings $(u_1)(u_2)\cdots(u_n)$, $u_i \in K^*$, is interpreted as a sum of products of classes.
- $\tau : \Sigma \to K^*$ which declares the *local variables* to be used for each method of Γ. That is, the ith variable of method σ is declared to be of class $\tau(\sigma)_i$.
- $\xi : \Sigma \to Expr$ which specifies the *body* of each method of Γ. $Expr = \bigcup\langle Expr_{k,\sigma} \mid k \in K,\ \sigma \in \Sigma \rangle$ as defined below.

For each $k \in K$ and $\sigma \in \Sigma$ we will define a set, $Expr_{k,\sigma}$, of *k-σ-expressions.* Intuitively a k-σ-expression is an expression, or block of code, that returns an object of class k and can be used as a subexpression in $\xi(\sigma)$. Write $e : \langle k, \sigma \rangle$ for $e \in Expr_{k,\sigma}$. The set of k-σ-expressions is then given by the set of deductive rules given below. For any specific choice of K, Σ, α, ι, and τ these rules can be reduced to a context-free grammar.

The rules for forming k-σ-expressions are designed to enforce the encapsulation of classes. Inspection of the rules will show that an expression can make use of the "inner structure of objects of class k" (i.e., of $\iota(k)$ and $\tau(k)$) only if σ belongs to class k (i.e., if $\alpha_1(\sigma) = k$.

$$\mathtt{NIL}_k : \langle k, \sigma \rangle \qquad \frac{\alpha(\sigma) = \langle h, u, s \rangle,\ i \in [|u|],\ u_i = k}{\mathtt{P}_{\sigma,i} : \langle k, \sigma \rangle}$$

$$\frac{i \in [|\tau(\sigma)|],\ \tau(\sigma)_i = k}{\mathtt{T}_{\sigma,i} : \langle k, \sigma \rangle} \qquad \frac{e_1 : \langle j, \sigma \rangle,\ e_2 : \langle k, \sigma \rangle}{e_1 ; e_2 : \langle k, \sigma \rangle}$$

$$\frac{e_0 : \langle j, \sigma \rangle,\ e_1 : \langle k, \sigma \rangle,\ e_2 : \langle k, \sigma \rangle}{\mathtt{INST}_j(e_0, e_1, e_2) : \langle k, \sigma \rangle} \qquad \frac{i \in [|\tau(\sigma)|],\ \tau(\sigma)_i = k,\ e_1 : \langle k, \sigma \rangle}{\mathtt{ASSIGN}_{\sigma,i}(e_1) : \langle k, \sigma \rangle}$$

$$\frac{\rho \in \Sigma,\ \alpha(\rho) = \langle t, w, k \rangle,\ (\forall i \in [|w|])(e_i : \langle w_i, \sigma \rangle)}{\mathtt{CALL}_{t,\rho}(e_1, \ldots, e_{|w|}) : \langle k, \sigma \rangle}$$

$$\frac{\alpha(\sigma) = \langle k, u, t \rangle,\ i \in [|\iota(k)|]}{\mathtt{NEW}_{k,i} : \langle k, \sigma \rangle}$$

$$\frac{\alpha(\sigma) = \langle h, u, s \rangle,\ e_0 : \langle h, \sigma \rangle,\ (\forall i \in [|\iota(h)|])(e_i : \langle k, \sigma \rangle)}{\mathtt{CASE}_h(e_0, e_1, \ldots, e_{|\iota(h)|}) : \langle k, \sigma \rangle}$$

$$\frac{\alpha(\sigma) = \langle k, u, s \rangle,\ i \in [|\iota(k)|],\ (\forall j \in [|\iota(k)_i|])(e_j : \langle \iota(k)_{i,j}, \sigma \rangle),\ e_0 : \langle k, \sigma \rangle}{\mathtt{CHANGE}_{k,i}(e_0, e_1, \ldots, e_{|\iota(k)_i|}) : \langle k, \sigma \rangle}$$

$$\frac{\alpha(\sigma) = \langle h, u, s \rangle,\ e_0 : \langle h, \sigma \rangle,\ i \in [|\iota(h)|],\ j \in [|\iota(h)_i|],\ \iota(h)_{i,j} = k}{\mathtt{ACCESS}_{h,i,j}(e_0) : \langle k, \sigma \rangle}$$

Here is a brief, formal semantics for $\mathbf{LD}^3$. In Sect. 5 and 8 we will restate the semantics in a more algebra-like setting.

Definition 10. Let $\Gamma = \langle K, \Sigma, \alpha, \iota, \tau, \xi \rangle$ be a class-system. View K as a discrete category, then a *ι-state*, μ, is a natural transformation, $\mu : I_\mu \dot{\rightarrow} O_\mu^\iota$ where:

$I_\mu : K \rightarrow \mathbf{Set}$ is a functor. Intuitively, $I_\mu(k)$ is the set of instances of objects of class k in the state μ. In this particular semantics, I_μ takes $k \in K$, to a set $I_\mu(k) = \{\langle j, k \rangle \mid j = 1, 2, \cdots, n_k\}$ for some $n_k \geq 0$.

$O_\mu : K \rightarrow \mathbf{Set}$ is a functor taking $k \in K$ to $I_\mu(k) + \mathbf{1}$. For the purposes of this particular semantics we take $O_\mu(k) = I_\mu(k) \cup \{\langle 0, k \rangle\}$. We regard $\langle 0, k \rangle$ as a special object, nil_k, the *nil-object of class k*, and $O_\mu(k)$ is the set of all objects of class k in the state μ.

$O_\mu^\iota : K \rightarrow \mathbf{Set}$ is the functor taking $k \in K$ to $\widehat{O}_\mu(\iota(k))$ ($\widehat{O}_\mu$ as defined in Proposition 9). Intuitively, if $x \in I_\mu(k)$, then $\mu(x) \in \widehat{O}_\mu(\iota(k))$ is the *value* of the object-instance x in the state μ.

Given Γ and $\sigma \in \Sigma$, a *σ-state* consists of a ι-state together with tuples t and p where $t \in \widehat{O}_\mu(\tau(\sigma))$ and $p \in \widehat{O}_\mu(\alpha_2(\sigma))$. Intuitively, t is the tuple of the objects assigned to the local variables of σ, and p is the tuple of the objects that are are current parameters of σ.

Let $\mathbf{ST}_{\iota,\sigma}$ denote the set of all σ-states (we write $\mathbf{ST}_\sigma$ when the ι is clear from context).

Intuitively, the semantics of a k-σ-expression, e, will be a partial function

$$[\![e]\!] : \mathbf{ST}_{\iota,\sigma} \rightharpoonup \mathbf{ST}_{\iota,\sigma} \times (\omega \times \{k\})$$

such that if $\mu \in \mathbf{ST}_{\iota,\sigma}$ and $[\![e]\!](\mu) = \langle \mu', \langle n, k\rangle\rangle$ then $\langle n, k\rangle \in O_{\mu'}(k)$. We say then that e applied to μ *is defined, yields the new state* μ' and *returns the object* $\langle n, k\rangle$. See the next section for a more sophisticated view of $[\![e]\!]$ as a functor.

Definition 11. We give the semantics on a case-by-case basis in terms of the primitive operations.

1. $[\![\mathtt{NIL}_k]\!](\mu) \;=\; \langle \mu,\ \langle 0, k\rangle\rangle$
2. $[\![\mathrm{P}_{\sigma,i}]\!](\mu) \;=\; \langle \mu,\ p_k(\mathrm{P}_{\sigma,i})\rangle$.
3. $[\![\mathrm{T}_{\sigma,i}]\!](\mu) \;=\; \langle \mu,\ t_k(\mathrm{T}_{\sigma,i})\rangle$.
4. $[\![e_1;e_2]\!](\mu)$: If $[\![e_1]\!](\mu) \;=\; \langle \mu', x'\rangle$ then $[\![e_1;e_2]\!](\mu) \;=\; [\![e_2]\!](\mu')$.
5. $[\![\mathtt{ASSIGN}_i(e_1)]\!](\mu)$: If $[\![e_1]\!](\mu) = \langle \mu', x'\rangle$ then $[\![\mathtt{ASSIGN}_i(e_1)]\!](\mu) \;=\; \langle \mu'', x'\rangle$ where μ'' is the same as μ' except that $t''_k(\mathrm{T}_{\sigma,i}) = x'$.
6. $[\![\mathtt{NEW}_{k,i}]\!](\mu)$: If $O_\mu(k) = \{\langle 0, k\rangle, \langle 1, k\rangle, \ldots, \langle n, k\rangle\}$ then

$$[\![\mathtt{NEW}_{k,i}]\!](\mu) \;=\; \langle \mu',\ \langle n+1, k\rangle\rangle$$

   where μ' is the result of adding the object $\langle n+1, k\rangle$ to $O_\mu(k)$, and, where, if $\iota(k) = (u_1)\cdots(u_p)$, with $u_i = u_{i,1}\cdots u_{i,n_i}$, then $\mu'_k(\langle n+1, k\rangle) = \langle\langle 0, u_{i,1}\rangle, \langle 0, u_{i,2}\rangle, \cdots, \langle 0, u_{i,n_i}\rangle\rangle \in$
   $\widehat{O}_\mu(u_i)$.
7. $[\![\mathtt{CASE}(e_0, e_1, \ldots, e_n)]\!](\mu)$: If $[\![e_0]\!](\mu) \;=\; \langle \mu', \langle m, h\rangle\rangle$, and furthermore $\iota(h) = (u_1)\cdots(u_p)$ then

$$[\![\mathtt{CASE}(e_0, e_1, \ldots, e_n)]\!](\mu) = \begin{cases} [\![e_j]\!](\mu') \text{ if } m > 0 \\ \qquad\qquad \text{and } \mu'_h(\langle m, h\rangle) \in \widehat{O}_{\mu'}(u_j) \\ \langle \mu', 0\rangle \quad \text{otherwise.} \end{cases}$$

8. $[\![\mathtt{ACCESS}_{i,j}(e_0)]\!](\mu)$: If $[\![e_0]\!](\mu) = \langle \mu', \langle n, h\rangle\rangle$ and $\iota(h) = (u_1)\cdots(u_p)$ then

$$[\![\mathtt{ACCESS}_{i,j}(e_0)]\!](\mu) \;=\; \begin{cases} \langle \mu', \mu'_h(\langle n, h\rangle)_j\rangle \text{ if } n > 0 \\ \qquad\qquad \text{and } \mu'_h(\langle n, h\rangle) \in \widehat{O}_{\mu'}(u_i) \\ \langle \mu', \langle 0, h\rangle\rangle \quad \text{otherwise.} \end{cases}$$

9. $[\![\mathtt{INST}(e_0, e_1, e_2)]\!](\mu)$: If $[\![e_0]\!](\mu) = \langle \mu',\ \langle n, j\rangle\rangle$ then,

$$[\![\mathtt{INST}(e_0, e_1, e_2)]\!](\mu) \;=\; \begin{cases} [\![e_1]\!](\mu') \text{ if } n > 0 \\ [\![e_2]\!](\mu') \text{ if } n = 0. \end{cases}$$

10. $[\![\mathtt{CALL}_\rho(e_1,\ldots,e_n)]\!](\mu)$: If $[\![e_1]\!](\mu) = \langle \mu_1, x_1 \rangle$ and, for $i = 2,\ldots,n$, $[\![e_i]\!](\mu_{i-1}) = \langle \mu_i, x_i \rangle$, then change the σ-state μ_n into a ρ-state μ' by taking $p_\rho(\mathtt{T}_{\rho,i}) = x_i$ for $i = 1,\ldots,n$, and taking $t_\rho(\mathtt{T}_{\rho,j}) = nil_{\tau(\rho)_j}$ for $j = 1,\ldots,|\ \tau(\rho)\ |$. Then where $[\![\xi(\rho)]\!](\mu') = \langle \mu'', n' \rangle$, let μ''' be the σ-state resulting from changing μ'' by replacing p''_ρ and t''_ρ by $p'''_{\iota,\sigma}$ and $t'''_{\iota,\sigma}$ respectively where, for each i, $p'''_{\iota,\sigma}(\mathtt{P}_{\sigma,i}) = p_{\iota,\sigma}(\mathtt{P}_{\sigma,i})$ and $t'''_{\iota,\sigma}(\mathtt{T}_{\sigma,i}) = t_{\iota,\sigma}(\mathtt{T}_{\sigma,i})$. Then $[\![\mathtt{CALL}_\rho(e_1,\ldots,e_n)]\!](\mu) = \langle \mu''', n' \rangle$.
11. $[\![\mathtt{CHANGE}_{k,i}(e_0,e_1,\ldots,e_n)]\!](\mu)$: Let $\langle \mu_0, \langle n_0, k \rangle\rangle = [\![e_0]\!](\mu)$ and, for $i = 1,\ldots,n$, let $\langle \mu_i, x_i \rangle = [\![e_i]\!](\mu_{i-1})$. Then

$$[\![\mathtt{CHANGE}_{k,i}(e_0,e_1,\ldots,e_n)]\!](\mu) = \begin{cases} \langle \mu_0, \langle 0, k \rangle\rangle & \text{if } n_0 = 0 \\ \langle \mu', \langle n_0, k \rangle\rangle & \text{if } n_0 \neq 0 \end{cases}$$

where μ' is the σ-state that is the same as μ_n except that $\mu'_k(\langle n_0, k \rangle) = \langle x_1,\ldots,x_n \rangle$.

5 More about Semantics

In this section we first show that by making the source and target of $[\![e]\!]$ into categories we can make $[\![e]\!]$ into a partial functor. We then make use of this to show that the semantics of a class system has a number of desireable properties. Precise definitions are given below, but loosely speaking, we claim that:

1. Every $[\![\sigma]\!]$ is object-preserving, i.e., while it may create new objects, and change the value of objects, it never destroys an object.
2. If $J \subseteq K$ such that $\iota(j) \in (J^*)^*$ for all $j \in J$ and $\sigma \in \Sigma$ such that $\alpha_2(\sigma) \in J^*$, and $\alpha_3 \in J$ then the "behavior" of $[\![\sigma]\!]$ can be described using only objects belonging to classes in J. Exploiting this we can reduce the functor $[\![\sigma]\!]$ to a functor on a smaller domain. This kind of reduction will play a key role in the semantics of parameter passing.
3. The function $\xi : \Sigma \to Expr$ which assigns a body to each method name, can be given a semantics in which the assignment to each $\sigma \in \Sigma$ of its meaning $[\![\sigma]\!]$ is a natural transformation arising as a fixpoint of a functor induced by ξ.

We make $\mathbf{ST}_\iota$ into a category in which a morphism $\eta : \mu_1 \to \mu_2$ is given by an injective natural transformation $\eta : I_{\mu_1} \dot{\to} I_{\mu_2}$ such that $\mu_2 \bullet \eta = \overline{\eta}_\iota \bullet \mu_1$. That is, for each $k \in K$, let $\overline{\eta}_k = (\eta_k + 1_1) : O_{\mu_1} \to O_{\mu_2}$ and let $\widehat{\overline{\eta}}$ be the extension of $\overline{\eta}$ given by Proposition 9, then we require that the following diagram

$$\begin{array}{ccc} I_{\mu_1}(k) & \xrightarrow{\eta_k} & I_{\mu_2}(k) \\ \Big\downarrow{\scriptstyle (\mu_1)_k} & & \Big\downarrow{\scriptstyle (\mu_2)_k} \\ O^\iota_{\mu_1}(k) & \xrightarrow{\widehat{\overline{\eta}}_{\iota(k)}} & O^\iota_{\mu_2}(k) \end{array}$$

commutes.

Similarly, we make $\mathbf{ST}_{\iota,\sigma}$ into a category where the morphisms are those morphisms from $\mathbf{ST}_\iota$ that preserve p and t, that is, that $\widehat{\overline{\eta}}_{\tau(\sigma)} \bullet t_1 = t_2$ and $\widehat{\overline{\eta}}_{\alpha_2(\sigma)} \bullet p_1 = p_2$.

For each $v \in (K^*)^*$ define $U^v : \mathbf{ST}_\iota \to \mathbf{Set}$ to be the functor taking state μ to the set $\widehat{O}_\mu(v)$, and taking $\eta : \mu \to \mu'$ to $\widehat{\overline{\eta}}_v$.

From U^v we (use the Grothendieck construction to) define a category $\overline{O}^v_{\iota,K}$ with objects $\langle \mu, e \rangle$ where $e \in U^v(\mu) = \widehat{O}_\mu(v)$ and, as morphisms from $\langle \mu, e \rangle$ to $\langle \mu', e' \rangle$ those morphisms $\eta : \mu \to \mu'$ such that $U^v(\eta)(e) = e'$. We will omit the subscripts on $\overline{O}^v_{\iota,K}$ when they are clear from the context. Define $\Pi : \overline{O}^v \to \mathbf{ST}_\iota$ to be the *projection* taking $\langle \mu, e \rangle$ to μ.

In like manner, define $\overline{\overline{O}}^v$ to be the category with objects of the form $\langle \langle \mu, t, p \rangle, e \rangle$ based on σ-states, and let $\Pi : \overline{\overline{O}}^v \to \mathbf{ST}_\iota$ to be the *projection* taking $\langle \langle \mu, t, p \rangle, e \rangle$ to μ.

Definition 12. Given categories $\mathbf{C}$ and $\mathbf{D}$ a *partial functor* F from $\mathbf{C}$ to $\mathbf{D}$ consists of partial maps $|F| : Obj(\mathbf{C}) \to Obj(\mathbf{D})$ and $F : Mor(\mathbf{C}) \to Mor(\mathbf{D})$ such that

1. For $f : A \to B$ in $\mathbf{C}$, $F(f)$ is defined iff both $|F|(A)$ and $|F|(B)$ are defined.
2. If $g \bullet f$, $F(f)$ and $F(g)$ are defined then $F(g \bullet f)$ is defined and equal to $F(g) \bullet F(f)$.

Then we have the following

Proposition 13. *For each k-σ-expression e, $[\![e]\!] : \mathbf{ST}_{\iota,\sigma} \to \overline{\overline{O}}^{(k)}$ is a partial functor, with the additional property (*the object preservation property*) that if $[\![e]\!](\mu)$ is defined then for every $k \in K$, $I_\mu(k) \subseteq I_{\Pi([\![e]\!](\mu))}(k)$.*

Using the same framework we get:

Proposition 14. *If $\sigma \in \Sigma$ then its semantics define a partial functor $[\![\sigma]\!] : \overline{O}^{\alpha_2(\sigma)} \to \overline{O}^{\alpha_3(\sigma)}$ with the object preservation property.*

The functorality says, among other things, that if we have states μ_1 and μ_2 such that μ_2 extends μ_1 in the sense that for all $k \in K$, $I_{\mu_1}(k) \subseteq I_{\mu_2}(k)$ and $(\mu_2)_k$ restricted to I_{μ_1} equals $(\mu_1)_k$, then the same is true, up-to-isomorphism, for $[\![e]\!](\mu_1)$ and $[\![e]\!](\mu_2)$. That is, speaking informally, adding objects to a state does not essentially change what a given expression will do to it.

The object preservation property, $I_\mu(k) \subseteq I_{\Pi([\![e]\!](\mu))}(k)$, corresponds to the idea that no objects are ever destroyed once they have been created. This property would have to be modified if we changed the semantics to include "garbage collection", but, even then, an analogous condition would hold since no object would be destroyed unless it was "truly garbage".

Definition 15. Let K be a set, let $\iota : K \to (K^*)^*$ be a mapping, and let $J \subseteq K$. Define $\overline{J}$, the *ι-closure of J*, to be the smallest set $\overline{J} \subseteq K$ such that $J \subseteq \overline{J}$ and $\iota(j) \in (J^*)^*$ for all $j \in J$. If $\overline{J} = J$ we say J is *ι-closed.*

The following proposition introduces some useful notation.

Proposition 16. *If $J \subseteq K$, and $\mathbf{j} : J \hookrightarrow K$ and $\mathbf{j}^{**} : (J^*)^* \hookrightarrow (K^*)^*$ are the indicated inclusion mappings then there exists a unique mapping $\overline{\iota} : J \to (J^*)^*$ such that $\iota \bullet \mathbf{j} = \mathbf{j}^{**} \bullet \overline{\iota}$.*

Definition 17. Let Γ, J, $\mathbf{j} : J \hookrightarrow K$, and $\bar{\iota} : J \rightarrow (J^*)^*$ be as above. Then, for each $u \in (J^*)^*$, define

$$R_J^u : \overrightarrow{O}^u_{\iota,K} \rightarrow \overrightarrow{O}^u_{\bar{\iota},J}$$
$$\langle \mu, \langle e_1, \cdots, e_n \rangle \rangle \mapsto \langle \mu', \langle e_1, \cdots, e_n \rangle \rangle$$

where if $\mu : I_\mu \rightarrow O^\iota_\mu$ then $\mu' : I_{\mu'} \rightarrow O^{\bar{\iota}}_{\mu'}$ where $I_{\mu'} = I_\mu \bullet \mathbf{j} : J \rightarrow \mathbf{Set}$ and, for every $j \in J$, $\mu'_j = \mu_j$.

We say that a partial functor $F : \overrightarrow{O}^u_{\iota,K} \rightarrow \overrightarrow{O}^v_{\iota,K}$ is *reducible* if for every ι-closed $J \subseteq K$, such that $u, v \in (J^*)^*$ there exists a unique partial functor $\overline{F}_J : \overrightarrow{O}^u_{\bar{\iota},J} \rightarrow \overrightarrow{O}^v_{\bar{\iota},J}$ such that $R^v_J \bullet F = \overline{F}_J \bullet R^u_J$. We call $\overline{F}_J$ *the reduction of F to J*.

Proposition 18. *If $\Gamma = \langle K, \Sigma, \alpha, \iota, \tau, \xi \rangle$ is a class-system then, for every $\sigma \in \Sigma$, $[\sigma]$ is reducible.*

Definition 19. Given a set K and a mapping $\iota : K \rightarrow (K^*)^*$ define $\mathbf{VAL}_{\iota,K}$ be the category with, as objects, the categories $\overrightarrow{O}^v_{\iota,K}$ where $v \in (K^*)^*$, and, as morphisms from $\overrightarrow{O}^v_{\iota,K}$ to $\overrightarrow{O}^w_{\iota,K}$ all partial functors $F : \overrightarrow{O}^v_{\iota,K} \rightarrow \overrightarrow{O}^w_{\iota,K}$ which are reducible and have the object preservation property.

Definition 20. Given a total class-system $\Gamma = \langle K, \Sigma, \alpha, \iota, \tau, \xi \rangle$ view Σ as a discrete category and, for $i = 2, 3$, let $\overline{\alpha}_i$ be the functor

$$\overline{\alpha}_i : \Sigma \rightarrow \mathbf{VAL}_{\iota,K}$$
$$\sigma \mapsto \widehat{O}^{\alpha_i(\sigma)}_{\iota,K}.$$

(Note we are implicitly coercing elements of K and K^* into $(K^*)^*$ in this definition). Define M_Σ to be the set of all natural transformations $\delta : \overline{\alpha}_2 \dot{\rightarrow} \overline{\alpha}_3$. Let M_Σ be ordered in accordance with the partiality of the partial functors (the δ_σ's).

The intuition is that a δ is a Σ-tuple of functors of the appropriate arities as given by α.

Proposition 21. *In the evident way, $\xi : \Sigma \rightarrow Expr$ induces a monotone function $\ddot{\xi} : M_\Sigma \rightarrow M_\Sigma$ which has a least fixpoint $\xi^\dagger \in M_\Sigma$ such that $\ddot{\xi}(\xi^\dagger) = \xi^\dagger$. Furthermore, for each $\sigma \in \Sigma$, $\xi^\dagger(\sigma) = [\sigma]$.*

6 Categories of Class-Systems

In this section we introduce two categories of class-systems: the category, **TCS**, of total class-systems and the category, **PCS**, of partial class-systems. The category **PCS** will play a role analogous to that of the category **PRES** of presentations in algebraic specifications of parameterized data types. It is necessary to introduce the partiality because class-systems, as defined earlier, completely specify their semantics, so we need partiality in order to be able to introduce "formal parameters".

Definition 22. The category, **TCS** of *total class-systems* has, as object, all class-systems Γ, and, as morphisms, the total class-system morphisms defined as follows: Given $\Gamma_i = \langle K_i, \Sigma_i, \alpha_i, \iota_i, \tau_i, \xi_i \rangle$, $i = 1, 2$, a **total class-system morphism** from Γ_1 to Γ_2 is a quadruple

$$\langle \Gamma_1,\ f_\Sigma : \Sigma_1 \to \Sigma_2,\ f_K : K_1 \to K_2,\ \Gamma_2 \rangle$$

such that, the diagrams

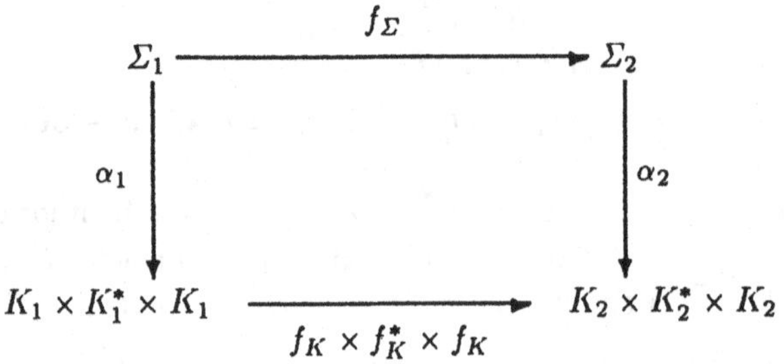

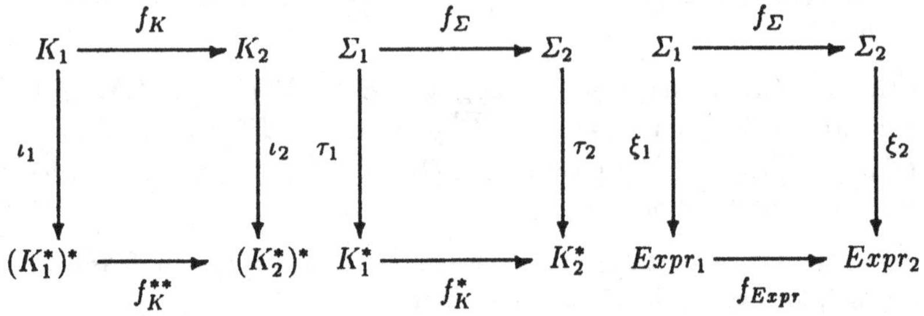

commute, where f^* and f^{**} are the evident extensions of f to strings and strings-of-strings, and f_{Expr} is inductively defined from f_K and f_Σ as follows:

$$\begin{aligned}
&f_{Expr} : Expr_1 \to Expr_2\\
&\mathtt{NIL}_k \mapsto \mathtt{NIL}_{f_K(k)}\\
&\mathtt{P}_{\sigma,i} \mapsto \mathtt{P}_{f_\Sigma(\sigma),i}\\
&\mathtt{T}_{\sigma,i} \mapsto \mathtt{T}_{f_\Sigma(\sigma),i}\\
&\mathtt{INST}_j(e_0, e_1, e_2) \mapsto \mathtt{INST}_{f_K(j)}(f_{Expr}(e_0), f_{Expr}(e_1), f_{Expr}(e_2))\\
&\mathtt{ASSIGN}_{\sigma,i}(e_1) \mapsto \mathtt{ASSIGN}_{f_\Sigma(\sigma),i}(f_{Expr}(e_1))\\
&\mathtt{CALL}_{t,\rho}(e_1, \ldots, e_p) \mapsto \mathtt{CALL}_{f_K(t), f_\Sigma(\rho)}(f_{Expr}(e_1) \ldots f_{Expr}(e_p))\\
&\mathtt{NEW}_{k,i} \mapsto \mathtt{NEW}_{f_K(k),i}\\
&\mathtt{CASE}_h(e_0, e_1, \ldots e_n) \mapsto \mathtt{CASE}_{f_K(h)}(f_{Expr}(e_0), f_{Expr}(e_1), \ldots, f_{Expr}(e_n))\\
&\mathtt{CHANGE}_{k,i}(e_0, e_1, \ldots e_n) \mapsto \mathtt{CHANGE}_{f_K(k),i}(f_{Expr}(e_0), f_{Expr}(e_1), \ldots, f_{Expr}(e_n))\\
&\mathtt{ACCESS}_{h,i,j}(e_0) \mapsto \mathtt{ACCESS}_{f_K(h),i,j}(f_{Expr}(e_0)).
\end{aligned}$$

Definition 23. A *partial class-system* is given by a tuple $\Gamma = \langle K, \Sigma, \alpha,\ \iota,\ \tau,\ \xi \rangle$, where ι, τ and ξ are partial mappings. As discussed in [5], such a partial class-system is well-defined only if, for every $\sigma \in \Sigma$ such that $\xi(\sigma)$ is defined, $\xi(\sigma)$ only employs primitives that are supported by ι and τ. For the purposes of this paper this means that, for every $\sigma \in \Sigma$:

1. $\xi(\sigma)$ is defined iff $\tau(\sigma)$ is defined.
2. if $\alpha(\sigma) = \langle k, u, j \rangle$ and $\xi(\sigma)$ is defined then $\xi(\sigma)$ employs the primitives $\mathtt{NEW}_{k,i}$, $\mathtt{CASE}_k$, $\mathtt{CHANGE}_{k,i}$, or $\mathtt{ACCESS}_{k,i,j}$ only if $\iota(k)$ is defined.

The category, **PCS** of *partial class-systems* has, as objects, all partial class-systems Γ, and, as morphisms, the partial class-system morphisms defined as follows:

A *partial class-system morphism* is one where the diagrams "partial commute", i.e.,

$$\overline{f_K} \bullet \alpha_1 \sqsubseteq \alpha_2 \bullet f_K$$

$$f_K^{**} \bullet \iota_1 \sqsubseteq \iota_2 \bullet f_K$$

$$f_K^{*} \bullet \tau_1 \sqsubseteq \tau_2 \bullet f_\Sigma$$

and

$$f_{Expr} \bullet \xi_1 \sqsubseteq \xi_2 \bullet f_\Sigma,$$

7 Generic Class-Systems

In the context of algebraic specification both a generic type and an instantiation are given as presentation morphisms and the passing of of the parameters is given by a pushout. For generic types and instantiations in $\mathbf{LD}^3$ we have a similar situation using the category, **PCS**, of partial class-systems.

Definition 24. A *generic class-system* is specified by a partial class-system morphism $\gamma : \Gamma_0 \to \Gamma_1$ where

$$\Gamma_0 = \langle K_0,\ \Sigma_0,\ \alpha_0,\ \bot,\ \bot,\ \bot\rangle$$

and

$$\Gamma_1 = \langle K_0 + K_1,\ \Sigma_0 + \Sigma_1,\ [\overline{\gamma_K} \bullet \alpha_0,\ \alpha_1],\ [\bot,\ \iota_1],\ [\bot,\ \tau_1],\ [\bot,\ \xi_1]\rangle$$

where $\gamma_K : K_0 \to (K_0 + K_1)$ and $\gamma_\Sigma : \Sigma_0 \to (\Sigma_0 + \Sigma_1)$ are coproduct injections in **Pfn**, where $\overline{\gamma_K} = \gamma_K \times \gamma_K^* \times \gamma_K$, and where $\bot$ is "the" everywhere undefined function. In all cases, $[f, g]$ denotes the coproduct mediator for f and g.

Definition 25. An *instantiation* of a generic class-system $\gamma : \Gamma_0 \to \Gamma_1$, is a class-system morphism $\theta : \Gamma_0 \to \Gamma_2$ where $\Gamma_2 \in$ **PCS**.

Theorem 26. *Let $\gamma : \Gamma_0, \to \Gamma_1$ be a generic class-system and let $\theta : \Gamma_0 \to \Gamma_2$ be an instantiation for γ. Then $\langle \Gamma_3,\ \theta,\ \gamma\rangle$ has a pushout $\langle \overline{\theta},\ \overline{\gamma}\rangle$ in* **PCS**.

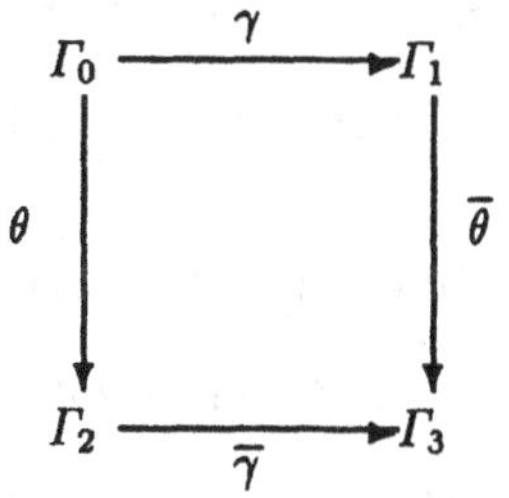

Furthermore, $\Gamma_2 \in$ **TCS** *implies $\Gamma_3 \in$* **TCS**.

While the above looks very similar to the corresponding result for algebraic specifications it is more delicate in that the result depends on the definition of generic type since **PCS** does not have pushouts for arbitrary pairs $\langle f : \Gamma_0 \to \Gamma_1, g : \Gamma_0 \to \Gamma_2\rangle$.

8 Pseudo-algebras

We turn now to the semantics of generic types. The first step is to introduce what we call pseudo-algebras. Pseudo-algebras will play a role analogous to that played by ordinary algebras in algebraic specifications. The principle difference between pseudo-algebras and ordinary algebras is that in a pseudo-algebra the carriers and operations involve states. The groundwork for this was introduced in Sect. 5 where the operation corresponding to a method name $\sigma \in \Sigma$ was defined to be a partial functor $[\![\sigma]\!] : \overline{O}^{\alpha_2(\sigma)} \to \overline{O}^{\alpha_3(\sigma)}$. One problem with this is that $Obj(\overline{O}^{alpha_1(\sigma)}$ is not a small set. The definition of pseudo-algebra solves this problem.

Definition 27. Let K be a set, let $\iota : K \to (K^*)^*$ and let $F \in \mathbf{VAL}_{\iota,K}(\overline{O}^*, \overline{O}^w)$. Let $A = \langle A_k \subseteq Obj(\overline{O}^{(k)}) \mid k \in K\rangle$ be a K-indexed family of sets. Given $v \in (K^*)^*$ with $v = k_1 \cdots k_n$, let A^v denote the set $\{\langle \mu, \langle e_1, \cdots, e_n\rangle\rangle \mid \langle \mu, e_i\rangle \in A_{k_i}\ for\ i = 1, \cdots, n\}$. Then we say that A *is closed under* F if $F(\overline{a}) \in A^w$ for every $\overline{a} \in A^*$ such that $F(\overline{a})$ is defined.

Definition 28. Let $\Gamma = \langle K, \Sigma, \alpha, \iota, \tau, \xi\rangle$ be a total class-system. The *empty state* for Γ is the the unique ι-state ϕ such that $I_\phi(k) = \emptyset$ for all $k \in K$. For any $\sigma \in \Sigma$ the *empty σ-state* is uniquely determined (t and p are "tuples of nils").

Definition 29. Let $\Gamma = \langle K, \Sigma, \alpha, \iota, \tau, \xi\rangle$ be a total class-system. A *Γ-pseudo-algebra*, A, is a K-indexed family of sets, $A = \langle A_k \mid k \in K\rangle$ such that, for each $k \in K$, A_k is a subset of $Obj(\overline{O}^{(k)})$, and

1. $\langle \phi, nil_k\rangle \in A_k$
2. A is closed under $[\![\sigma]\!]$ for every $\sigma \in \Sigma$,

It appears that the closest thing to homomorphisms between Γ-pseudo algebras are inclusions between the carriers, i.e., given two Γ-pseudo-algebras A and B we say $A \leq B$ if $A_k \subseteq B_k$ for all $k \in K$ – this gives us a poset-category structure on the set of Γ-pseudo-algebras.

We now want to extend these ideas to partial class-systems.

Proposition 30. *Given a partial class-system $\Gamma = \langle K, \Sigma, \alpha, \iota, \tau, \xi\rangle$, let $\Sigma = \Sigma_1 + \Sigma_2$ where*

$$\Sigma_1 = \{\sigma \in \Sigma \mid \xi(\sigma)\ is\ defined\}$$

$$\Sigma_2 = \{\sigma \in \Sigma \mid \xi(\sigma)\ is\ not\ defined\}.$$

Then $M_\Sigma = M_{\Sigma_1+\Sigma_2} \cong M_{\Sigma_1} \times M_{\Sigma_2}$, and ξ defines a monotone function $\ddot{\xi} : M_{\Sigma_1} \times M_{\Sigma_2} \to M_{\Sigma_1}$. Furthermore $\ddot{\xi}$ has a least fixpoint $\xi^\dagger : M_{\Sigma_2} \to M_{\Sigma_1}$, where $\xi^\dagger$ is a fixpoint in the sense that $\ddot{\xi} \bullet \langle \xi^\dagger, 1_{M_{\Sigma_2}}\rangle = \xi^\dagger$.

Proposition 31. *Let $\Gamma = \langle K, \Sigma, \alpha, \iota, \tau, \xi\rangle$ be a partial class-system together with*

1. *J, a set.*

2. $\bar{\iota} : (K + J) \to ((K + J)^*)^*$ *extending* ι.
3. $\delta_2 \in M_{\Sigma_2}$.

then there exists a least $\delta_1 \in M_{\Sigma_1}$ *such that* $\ddot{\xi}(\delta_1, \delta_2) = \delta_1$. *(Where* $\Sigma = \Sigma_1 + \Sigma_2$ *as in Proposition 30, and* M_{Σ_1} *and* M_{Σ_2} *are defined using* $\mathbf{VAL}_{\bar{\iota},K+J}$*.)*

Definition 32. Let $\Gamma = \langle K, \Sigma, \alpha, \iota, \tau, \xi \rangle$ be a partial class-system. Let J be a set, and let $\bar{\iota} : (K + J) \to ((K + J)^*)^*$ be a total mapping extending ι and such that $K + J$ is the $\bar{\iota}$-closure of K in $K + J$. Then a $\langle \Gamma, J, \bar{\iota} \rangle$*-pseudo-algebra* is given by the data

1. $\delta = \langle \delta_1, \delta_2 \rangle$ with δ_1 and δ_2 as in the preceeding proposition,
2. $A = \langle A_h \subseteq Obj(\overline{O}^{(h)}) \mid h \in K + J \rangle$ a family of sets closed under δ_σ for every $\sigma \in \Sigma$ and such that $\langle \emptyset, nil_h \rangle \in A_h$ for every $h \in K + J$.

Let $\mathbf{Palg}_{\Gamma,J,\bar{\iota}}$ denote the set of such pseudo-algebras ordered by inclusion on "the carriers" A.

Note that for $\Gamma \in \mathbf{TCS}$ this definition gives the same algebras as does Definition 29 since then K is already ι-closed so $J = \emptyset$ and $\bar{\iota} = \iota$.

9 The Main Results

The following definition and two propositions are the analogues of the algebraic specification constructs given in Propositions 4, 6, and 7.

Definition 33. Let $\gamma = \langle \gamma_K, \gamma_\Sigma \rangle : \Gamma_0 \to \Gamma_1$ where $\Gamma_i = \langle K_i, \Sigma_i, \alpha_i, \iota_i, \tau_i, \xi_i \rangle$ for $i = 0, 1$ and Γ_0 is partial and γ_K is injective. Let J_0 and J_1 be sets with $\mathbf{j} : J_0 \hookrightarrow K_1 + J_1$ and for $i = 0, 1$ let $\bar{\iota}_i : (K_i + J_i) \to ((K_i + J_i)^*)^*$ extend ι_i so that $K_i + J_i$ is the $\bar{\iota}_i$-closure of K_i in $K_i + J_i$, and $\bar{\iota}_1 \bullet (\gamma_K + \mathbf{j}) = (\gamma_K + \mathbf{j})^{**} \bullet \bar{\iota}_0$ (so $\gamma_K(K_0) + J_0$ is the $\bar{\iota}_1$-closure of $\gamma_K(K_0) = K_0$ in $K_1 + J_1$).

Then we define

$$\gamma^\flat : \mathbf{Palg}_{\Gamma_1,J_1,\bar{\iota}_1} \to \mathbf{Palg}_{\Gamma_0,J_0,\bar{\iota}_0}$$

to be such that it takes a $\langle \Gamma_1, J_1, \bar{\iota}_1 \rangle$-pseudo-algebra A, given by data $\langle \delta^1, \langle A_h \mid h \in K_1 + J_1 \rangle \rangle$ to the $\langle \Gamma_0, J_0, \bar{\iota}_0 \rangle$-pseudo-algebra given by data

1. $\delta^0 \in M_{\Sigma_0}$, δ^0_σ is the reduction of $\delta^1(\sigma)$ to $K_0 + J_0$, for all $\sigma \in \Sigma_0$
2. $(\gamma^\flat(A))_h = R^{(h)}_{K_0+J_0}(A_{(h)})$ for all $h \in (K_0 + J_0)$.

Proposition 34. *With the same conditions as in Definition 32 there exists*

$$\gamma^\sharp : \mathbf{Palg}_{\Gamma_0,J_0,\bar{\iota}_0} \to \mathbf{Palg}_{\Gamma_1,J_1,\bar{\iota}_1}$$

such that for every $A \in \mathbf{Palg}_{\Gamma_0,J_0,\bar{\iota}_0}$, *we have*

$A \leq \gamma^\flat(\gamma^\sharp(A))$
If $A \leq \gamma^\flat(B)$ *then* $\gamma^\sharp(A) \leq B$.

Proposition 35. *Let $\gamma : \Gamma_0 \to \Gamma_1$ be a generic class-system, with*

$$\Gamma_0 = \langle K_0,\ \Sigma_0,\ \alpha_0,\ \bot,\ \bot,\ \bot \rangle$$

and

$$\Gamma_1 = \langle K_0 + K_1,\ \Sigma_0 + \Sigma_1,\ [\overline{\gamma_K} \bullet \alpha_0,\ \alpha_1],\ [\bot,\ \iota_1],\ [\bot,\ \tau_1],\ [\bot,\ \xi_1] \rangle$$

where $\gamma_K : K_0 \to (K_0 + K_1)$ and $\gamma_\Sigma : \Sigma_0 \to (\Sigma_0 + \Sigma_1)$ are coproduct injections in **Pfn**, *let $\theta = \langle \theta_K, \theta_\Sigma \rangle : \Gamma_0 \to \Gamma_2$ (be an instantiation) with θ_K injective, and $\Gamma_2 = \langle K_2, \Sigma_2, \alpha_2, \iota_2, \tau_2, \xi_2 \rangle$ and let $\langle \Gamma_3, \overline{\gamma}, \overline{\theta} \rangle$ be a pushout for $\langle \gamma, \theta \rangle$ in* **PCS**, *where $\Gamma_3 = \langle K_3, \Sigma_3, \alpha_3, \iota_3, \tau_3, \xi_3 \rangle$, then $K_3 = K_1 + K_2$ and ι_3 is completely determined by $\iota_1 + \iota_2$.*

Theorem 36. *Let $\gamma : \Gamma_0 \to \Gamma_1$ be a generic class-system, let $\theta = \langle \theta_K, \theta_\Sigma \rangle : \Gamma_0 \to \Gamma_2$ (be an instantiation) with θ_K injective, and let $\langle \Gamma_3, \overline{\gamma}, \overline{\theta} \rangle$ be a pushout for $\langle \gamma, \theta \rangle$ in* **PCS**. *Identify K_0, $\theta_K(K_0)$, and $\gamma_K(K_0)$ (i.e., regard the injections as inclusions). For any set J_2 and $\overline{\iota}_2 : (K_2 + J_2) \to ((K_2 + J_2)^*)^*$ such that $K)2 + J_2$ is the $\overline{\iota}_2$-closure of K_2, take $J_0 \subseteq K_2 + J_2$ to be the $\overline{\iota}_2$-closure of K_0 in $K_2 + J_2$ and define $\overline{\iota}_0$ to be the restriction of $\overline{\iota}_2$ to $K_0 + J_0$, and take $J_1 = J_0$ and $J_3 = J_2$. Then the diagram*

$$\begin{array}{ccc}
\mathbf{Palg}_{\Gamma_0, J_0, \overline{\iota}_0} & \overset{\gamma^\sharp}{\underset{\gamma^\flat}{\rightleftarrows}} & \mathbf{Palg}_{\Gamma_1, J_1, \overline{\iota}_1} \\
\theta^\flat \uparrow & & \uparrow \overline{\theta}^\flat \\
\mathbf{Palg}_{\Gamma_2, J_2, \overline{\iota}_2} & \overset{\overline{\gamma}^\sharp}{\underset{\overline{\gamma}^\flat}{\rightleftarrows}} & \mathbf{Palg}_{\Gamma_3, J_3, \overline{\iota}_3}
\end{array}$$

is such that $\gamma^\flat \bullet \gamma^\sharp = 1_{\mathbf{Palg}_{\Gamma_0, J_0, \overline{\iota}_0}}$, $\overline{\gamma}^\flat \bullet \overline{\gamma}^\sharp = 1_{\mathbf{Palg}_{\Gamma_2, J_2, \overline{\iota}_2}}$, and $\overline{\theta}^\flat \bullet \overline{\gamma}^\sharp = \gamma^\sharp \bullet \theta^\flat$.

The most significant difference between these results and those of Sect. 2 (other than the differences in the categories) is the requirement that θ_K be injective. (Of course we require that γ_K is injective but this is also required in the algebraic specifications as a consequence of persistency.) It remains to be seen if an appropriate $\flat$-construction can be defined for non-injective morphisms in **PCS**.

10 Concluding Remarks

This paper presented a treatment of the syntax and semantics of generic classes in the language $\mathbf{LD}^3$, and showed how the form of the results are quite similar to those found in the algebraic treatment of parameterized data types. This suggests that these common results may hold in a very general setting – more general, probably, than found in the already quite general settings provided by institutions or specification logics. However, I have not investigated this possibility at any length.

Since the results on generic types (or parameterized data types) appear to depend significantly on the concept of encapsulation, these results will probably not extend to languages in which there is no encapsulation, e.g, ordinary imperative languages. However, many of the concepts introduced in this paper can be extended to a wide variety of programming languages, including imperative languages.

For example, the ideas that underlie the abstract syntax we gave for $\mathbf{LD}^3$ can be used to give a syntax for an imperative programming language with labels in such a manner that all, and only, correct programs are specified. The intuitive idea is quite simple: take K to be the set of labels and take $\xi : K \rightarrow Expr$ to be such that it maps each label to "the code between it and the next label".

For another example, the notion of state used in this paper can be generalized to imperative, or other, programming languages based on a set of given types. The idea is as follows: let G be the set of names of the given types , e.g., $G = \{\mathtt{INT}, \mathtt{BOOL}, \mathtt{REAL}\}$, then a state μ is a natural transformation, $\mu : var \dot{\rightarrow} val$ between functors var and val where, viewing G as a discrete category, $var : G \rightarrow \mathbf{Set}$ taking each $g \in G$ to "the set of variables currently declared to be of type g", and $val : G \rightarrow \mathbf{Set}$ taking each $g \in G$ to "the set of things of type g", i.e, BOOL goes to set the $\{true,\ false\}$. Starting from this notion of state we can develop various semantics for procedures akin to what we did above for methods.

These, and other, examples suggests the semantics of a variety of languages can be treated in the semantic framework developed here. However, the results on generic types only extend to languages for which the corresponding pseudo-algebras have special properties that, as noted above, correspond to some form of encapsulation.

References

1. H. Ehrig and B. Mahr. *Fundamentals of Algebraic Specification 1.* Springer-Verlag, Berlin, 1985.
2. J.W. Thatcher, J.B. Wright, and E. G. Wagner. Data type specification: Parameterization and the power of specification techniques. *TOPLAS*, 4:711–732, 1982.
3. Eric G. Wagner. Algebraic aspects of data directed design. In *Proceedings of the First Maghrebin Conference on Artificial Intelligence and Software Engineering.* University of Constantine, Constantine, Algeria, 1989.
4. Eric G Wagner. An algebraically specified language for data directed design. *Theoretical Computer Science*, 77:195–219, 1990.
5. Eric G. Wagner. Generic types in a language for data directed design. In *Recent Trends in Data Type Specification: Proceedings of the 7th Workshop on Specification of Abstract Data Types*, pages 341–361. LNCS 534, Springer Verlag, 1990.
6. Eric G. Wagner. Some mathematical thoughts on languages for data directed design. In *Proceedings of the conference 'the Unified Computation Laboratory' at the University of Stirling, Stirling, Scotland*, 1990. *To appear.*

Lecture Notes in Computer Science

For information about Vols. 1–579
please contact your bookseller or Springer-Verlag

Vol. 580: A. Pirotte, C. Delobel, G. Gottlob (Eds.), Advances in Database Technology – EDBT '92. Proceedings. XII, 551 pages. 1992.

Vol. 581: J.-C. Raoult (Ed.), CAAP '92. Proceedings. VIII, 361 pages. 1992.

Vol. 582: B. Krieg-Brückner (Ed.), ESOP '92. Proceedings. VIII, 491 pages. 1992.

Vol. 583: I. Simon (Ed.), LATIN '92. Proceedings. IX, 545 pages. 1992.

Vol. 584: R. E. Zippel (Ed.), Computer Algebra and Parallelism. Proceedings, 1990. IX, 114 pages. 1992.

Vol. 585: F. Pichler, R. Moreno Díaz (Eds.), Computer Aided System Theory – EUROCAST '91. Proceedings. X, 761 pages. 1992.

Vol. 586: A. Cheese, Parallel Execution of Parlog. IX, 184 pages. 1992.

Vol. 587: R. Dale, E. Hovy, D. Rösner, O. Stock (Eds.), Aspects of Automated Natural Language Generation. Proceedings, 1992. VIII, 311 pages. 1992. (Subseries LNAI).

Vol. 588: G. Sandini (Ed.), Computer Vision – ECCV '92. Proceedings. XV, 909 pages. 1992.

Vol. 589: U. Banerjee, D. Gelernter, A. Nicolau, D. Padua (Eds.), Languages and Compilers for Parallel Computing. Proceedings, 1991. IX, 419 pages. 1992.

Vol. 590: B. Fronhöfer, G. Wrightson (Eds.), Parallelization in Inference Systems. Proceedings, 1990. VIII, 372 pages. 1992. (Subseries LNAI).

Vol. 591: H. P. Zima (Ed.), Parallel Computation. Proceedings, 1991. IX, 451 pages. 1992.

Vol. 592: A. Voronkov (Ed.), Logic Programming. Proceedings, 1991. IX, 514 pages. 1992. (Subseries LNAI).

Vol. 593: P. Loucopoulos (Ed.), Advanced Information Systems Engineering. Proceedings. XI, 650 pages. 1992.

Vol. 594: B. Monien, Th. Ottmann (Eds.), Data Structures and Efficient Algorithms. VIII, 389 pages. 1992.

Vol. 595: M. Levene, The Nested Universal Relation Database Model. X, 177 pages. 1992.

Vol. 596: L.-H. Eriksson, L. Hallnäs, P. Schroeder-Heister (Eds.), Extensions of Logic Programming. Proceedings, 1991. VII, 369 pages. 1992. (Subseries LNAI).

Vol. 597: H. W. Guesgen, J. Hertzberg, A Perspective of Constraint-Based Reasoning. VIII, 123 pages. 1992. (Subseries LNAI).

Vol. 598: S. Brookes, M. Main, A. Melton, M. Mislove, D. Schmidt (Eds.), Mathematical Foundations of Programming Semantics. Proceedings, 1991. VIII, 506 pages. 1992.

Vol. 599: Th. Wetter, K.-D. Althoff, J. Boose, B. R. Gaines, M. Linster, F. Schmalhofer (Eds.), Current Developments in Knowledge Acquisition - EKAW '92. Proceedings. XIII, 444 pages. 1992. (Subseries LNAI).

Vol. 600: J. W. de Bakker, C. Huizing, W. P. de Roever, G. Rozenberg (Eds.), Real-Time: Theory in Practice. Proceedings, 1991. VIII, 723 pages. 1992.

Vol. 601: D. Dolev, Z. Galil, M. Rodeh (Eds.), Theory of Computing and Systems. Proceedings, 1992. VIII, 220 pages. 1992.

Vol. 602: I. Tomek (Ed.), Computer Assisted Learning. Proceedings, 1992. X, 615 pages. 1992.

Vol. 603: J. van Katwijk (Ed.), Ada: Moving Towards 2000. Proceedings, 1992. VIII, 324 pages. 1992.

Vol. 604: F. Belli, F.-J. Radermacher (Eds.), Industrial and Engineering Applications of Artificial Intelligence and Expert Systems. Proceedings, 1992. XV, 702 pages. 1992. (Subseries LNAI).

Vol. 605: D. Etiemble, J.-C. Syre (Eds.), PARLE '92. Parallel Architectures and Languages Europe. Proceedings, 1992. XVII, 984 pages. 1992.

Vol. 606: D. E. Knuth, Axioms and Hulls. IX, 109 pages. 1992.

Vol. 607: D. Kapur (Ed.), Automated Deduction – CADE-11. Proceedings, 1992. XV, 793 pages. 1992. (Subseries LNAI).

Vol. 608: C. Frasson, G. Gauthier, G. I. McCalla (Eds.), Intelligent Tutoring Systems. Proceedings, 1992. XIV, 686 pages. 1992.

Vol. 609: G. Rozenberg (Ed.), Advances in Petri Nets 1992. VIII, 472 pages. 1992.

Vol. 610: F. von Martial, Coordinating Plans of Autonomous Agents. XII, 246 pages. 1992. (Subseries LNAI).

Vol. 611: M. P. Papazoglou, J. Zeleznikow (Eds.), The Next Generation of Information Systems: From Data to Knowledge. VIII, 310 pages. 1992. (Subseries LNAI).

Vol. 612: M. Tokoro, O. Nierstrasz, P. Wegner (Eds.), Object-Based Concurrent Computing. Proceedings, 1991. X, 265 pages. 1992.

Vol. 613: J. P. Myers, Jr., M. J. O'Donnell (Eds.), Constructivity in Computer Science. Proceedings, 1991. X, 247 pages. 1992.

Vol. 614: R. G. Herrtwich (Ed.), Network and Operating System Support for Digital Audio and Video. Proceedings, 1991. XII, 403 pages. 1992.

Vol. 615: O. Lehrmann Madsen (Ed.), ECOOP '92. European Conference on Object Oriented Programming. Proceedings. X, 426 pages. 1992.

Vol. 616: K. Jensen (Ed.), Application and Theory of Petri Nets 1992. Proceedings, 1992. VIII, 398 pages. 1992.

Vol. 617: V. Mařík, O. Štěpánková, R. Trappl (Eds.), Advanced Topics in Artificial Intelligence. Proceedings, 1992. IX, 484 pages. 1992. (Subseries LNAI).

Vol. 618: P. M. D. Gray, R. J. Lucas (Eds.), Advanced Database Systems. Proceedings, 1992. X, 260 pages. 1992.

Vol. 619: D. Pearce, H. Wansing (Eds.), Nonclassical Logics and Information Proceedings. Proceedings, 1990. VII, 171 pages. 1992. (Subseries LNAI).

Vol. 620: A. Nerode, M. Taitslin (Eds.), Logical Foundations of Computer Science – Tver '92. Proceedings. IX, 514 pages. 1992.

Vol. 621: O. Nurmi, E. Ukkonen (Eds.), Algorithm Theory – SWAT '92. Proceedings. VIII, 434 pages. 1992.

Vol. 622: F. Schmalhofer, G. Strube, Th. Wetter (Eds.), Contemporary Knowledge Engineering and Cognition. Proceedings, 1991. XII, 258 pages. 1992. (Subseries LNAI).

Vol. 623: W. Kuich (Ed.), Automata, Languages and Programming. Proceedings, 1992. XII, 721 pages. 1992.

Vol. 624: A. Voronkov (Ed.), Logic Programming and Automated Reasoning. Proceedings, 1992. XIV, 509 pages. 1992. (Subseries LNAI).

Vol. 625: W. Vogler, Modular Construction and Partial Order Semantics of Petri Nets. IX, 252 pages. 1992.

Vol. 626: E. Börger, G. Jäger, H. Kleine Büning, M. M . Richter (Eds.), Computer Science Logic. Proceedings, 1991. VIII, 428 pages. 1992.

Vol. 628: G. Vosselman, Relational Matching. IX, 190 pages. 1992.

Vol. 629: I. M. Havel, V. Koubek (Eds.), Mathematical Foundations of Computer Science 1992. Proceedings. IX, 521 pages. 1992.

Vol. 630: W. R. Cleaveland (Ed.), CONCUR '92. Proceedings. X, 580 pages. 1992.

Vol. 631: M. Bruynooghe, M. Wirsing (Eds.), Programming Language Implementation and Logic Programming. Proceedings, 1992. XI, 492 pages. 1992.

Vol. 632: H. Kirchner, G. Levi (Eds.), Algebraic and Logic Programming. Proceedings, 1992. IX, 457 pages. 1992.

Vol. 633: D. Pearce, G. Wagner (Eds.), Logics in AI. Proceedings. VIII, 410 pages. 1992. (Subseries LNAI).

Vol. 634: L. Bougé, M. Cosnard, Y. Robert, D. Trystram (Eds.), Parallel Processing: CONPAR 92 – VAPP V. Proceedings. XVII, 853 pages. 1992.

Vol. 635: J. C. Derniame (Ed.), Software Process Technology. Proceedings, 1992. VIII, 253 pages. 1992.

Vol. 636: G. Comyn, N. E. Fuchs, M. J. Ratcliffe (Eds.), Logic Programming in Action. Proceedings, 1992. X, 324 pages. 1992. (Subseries LNAI).

Vol. 637: Y. Bekkers, J. Cohen (Eds.), Memory Management. Proceedings, 1992. XI, 525 pages. 1992.

Vol. 639: A. U. Frank, I. Campari, U. Formentini (Eds.), Theories and Methods of Spatio-Temporal Reasoning in Geographic Space. Proceedings, 1992. XI, 431 pages. 1992.

Vol. 640: C. Sledge (Ed.), Software Engineering Education. Proceedings, 1992. X, 451 pages. 1992.

Vol. 641: U. Kastens, P. Pfahler (Eds.), Compiler Construction. Proceedings, 1992. VIII, 320 pages. 1992.

Vol. 642: K. P. Jantke (Ed.), Analogical and Inductive Inference. Proceedings, 1992. VIII, 319 pages. 1992. (Subseries LNAI).

Vol. 643: A. Habel, Hyperedge Replacement: Grammars and Languages. X, 214 pages. 1992.

Vol. 644: A. Apostolico, M. Crochemore, Z. Galil, U. Manber (Eds.), Combinatorial Pattern Matching. Proceedings, 1992. X, 287 pages. 1992.

Vol. 645: G. Pernul, A M. Tjoa (Eds.), Entity-Relationship Approach – ER '92. Proceedings, 1992. XI, 439 pages, 1992.

Vol. 646: J. Biskup, R. Hull (Eds.), Database Theory – ICDT '92. Proceedings, 1992. IX, 449 pages. 1992.

Vol. 647: A. Segall, S. Zaks (Eds.), Distributed Algorithms. X, 380 pages. 1992.

Vol. 648: Y. Deswarte, G. Eizenberg, J.-J. Quisquater (Eds.), Computer Security – ESORICS 92. Proceedings. XI, 451 pages. 1992.

Vol. 649: A. Pettorossi (Ed.), Meta-Programming in Logic. Proceedings, 1992. XII, 535 pages. 1992.

Vol. 650: T. Ibaraki, Y. Inagaki, K. Iwama, T. Nishizeki, M. Yamashita (Eds.), Algorithms and Computation. Proceedings, 1992. XI, 510 pages. 1992.

Vol. 651: R. Koymans, Specifying Message Passing and Time-Critical Systems with Temporal Logic. IX, 164 pages. 1992.

Vol. 652: R. Shyamasundar (Ed.), Foundations of Software Technology and Theoretical Computer Science. Proceedings, 1992. XIII, 405 pages. 1992.

Vol. 653: A. Bensoussan, J.-P. Verjus (Eds.), Future Tendencies in Computer Science, Control and Applied Mathematics. Proceedings, 1992. XV, 371 pages. 1992.

Vol. 654: A. Nakamura, M. Nivat, A. Saoudi, P. S. P. Wang, K. Inoue (Eds.), Prallel Image Analysis. Proceedings, 1992. VIII, 312 pages. 1992.

Vol. 655: M. Bidoit, C. Choppy (Eds.), Recent Trends in Data Type Specification. X, 344 pages. 1993.

Vol. 656: M. Rusinowitch, J. L. Rémy (Eds.), Conditional Term Rewriting Systems. Proceedings, 1992. XI, 501 pages. 1993.